American Government

POWER AND PURPOSE

BRIEF TENTH EDITION

American | Government

POWER AND PURPOSE

THEODORE J. LOWI
CORNELL UNIVERSITY

BENJAMIN GINSBERG
THE JOHNS HOPKINS UNIVERSITY

KENNETH A. SHEPSLE
HARVARD UNIVERSITY

W. W. NORTON & COMPANY
NEW YORK • LONDON

W. W. Norton & Company has been independent since its founding in 1923, when William Warder Norton and Mary D. Herter Norton first published lectures delivered at the People's Institute, the adult education division of New York City's Cooper Union. The firm soon expanded its program beyond the Institute, publishing books by celebrated academics from America and abroad. By mid-century, the two major pillars of Norton's publishing program—trade books and college texts—were firmly established. In the 1950s, the Norton family transferred control of the company to its employees, and today—with a staff of four hundred and a comparable number of trade, college, and professional titles published each year—W. W. Norton & Company stands as the largest and oldest publishing house owned wholly by its employees.

Manufacturing by Quebecor World—Taunton Division
Editor: Ann Shin
Manuscript editor: Abigail Winograd
Project editor: Lory A. Frenkel
Electronic media editor: Dan Jost
Graphic artist: John McAusland
Book design by Anna Palchik
Production manager: Jane Searle
Editorial assistant: Mollie Eisenberg

ISBN 978-0-393-11384-6 (pbk.)

W. W. Norton & Company Inc.
500 Fifth Avenue, New York, N.Y. 10110
www.wwnorton.com

W. W. Norton & Company Ltd.
Castle House, 75/76 Wells Street, London W1T 3QT
1 2 3 4 5 6 7 8 9 0

Contents

PART 2

INSTITUTIONS

5 Congress: The First Branch   117

6 The President   151

7 The Executive Branch   184

11   Political Parties

Preface to the Brief Tenth Edition

This Brief Edition of *American Government: Power and Purpose* is designed specifically for use in courses whose length or format requires a more concise text. We preserved as much as possible of the narrative style and analysis of the larger text. Though this is a brief edition, we have sought to provide a full and detailed discussion of every topic that, in our view, is central to understanding American government and politics. We hope that we have written a book that is physically brief but is not intellectually sketchy.

A good teaching book, like a good novel or play, is written on two levels. One is the level of the narrative, the story line, the characters in action. The second is the level of character development, of the argument of the book or play. We would not be the first to assert that there is much of the theatrical about politics today, but our book may be unusual to the extent that we took that assertion as a guide. We have packed it full of narrative—with characters and facts about the complex situations in which they find themselves. We have determined not to lose sight of the second level, providing a logic and context to link the disparate parts of what we are treating as a single system of government and politics.

Most Americans are somewhat familiar with the politics and government of their own country. No fact about the government is intrinsically difficult to grasp, and in such an open society, facts abound. In the United States, information about the government is readily available that would be suppressed elsewhere. The ubiquity of political information can be a problem when the sheer quantity of facts and news overwhelms us, but it can be turned into a virtue. Common knowledge about the government gives us a vocabulary that is widely shared, and enables us to communicate effectively at the narrative level of the book, avoiding abstract concepts and professional jargon. However, reaching beyond the common knowledge identifies what is, to us, the single most important task of the teacher of political science—confronting the popular ideas and choosing from among them the small number of really significant concepts.

We have tried to provide a framework to help teachers make choices among facts and to help students make some of the choices for themselves. This is good political science, and it is good citizenship, which means more than mere obedience and voting; it means being able to pierce through the information explosion to the core of political reality.

FEATURES OF THE TENTH EDITION

This edition strives to present the material in a way that is straightforward and accessible to students. The design and pedagogical features have been refined and augmented to help students grasp the content and build on what they learn in each chapter.

NEW "Analyzing the Evidence" units in every chapter take a closer look at how political scientists analyze data (both quantitative and qualitative) to understand some political phenomenon discussed in the chapter. These two-page spreads use strong graphics to help students see *how we know what we know* about a specific topic.

"Core of the Analysis" outlines at the start of each chapter preview the main points of the chapter. Within the chapter, **"In Brief"** boxes summarize fundamental material and have proven invaluable to students in preparing for exams, according to reviewers. **Key terms** are now defined in the adjacent margin, as well as in the glossary.

NEW single-column design. Instructors and students alike told us that they preferred to read text in a single-column format, and this new edition answers that request with a new, easier-to-read design. While the actual length of the text has not increased, this has resulted in a slightly higher number of pages.

NEW integrated Online Reader. An "Online Reader" icon in the margin next to a citation in the notes or "Further Readings" section indicates works that are represented in the *Norton American Politics Online Reader*. Recognizing that many instructors assign a brief text to allow room on the syllabus for supplementary readings, W. W. Norton provides free access to the *Norton American Politics Online Reader* with each new copy of the Tenth Edition.

ACKNOWLEDGMENTS

Our students at Cornell, Johns Hopkins, and Harvard have been an essential factor in the writing of this book. They have been our most immediate intellectual community, a hospitable one indeed. Another part of our community, perhaps a large suburb, is the discipline of political science itself. Our debt to the scholarship of our colleagues is scientifically measurable, probably to several decimal points, in the footnotes and Further Readings sections of each chapter. Despite many complaints that the field is too scientific or not scientific enough, political science is alive and well in the United States. It is an aspect of democracy itself, and it has grown and changed in response to the developments in government and politics that we have chronicled in our book.

We are pleased to acknowledge our debt to the many colleagues who had a direct and active role in criticism and preparation of the manuscript. In drafting previous editions, we relied heavily on the thoughtful reviews we received from David Canon, University of Wisconsin; Russell Hanson, Indiana University; William Keech, University of North Carolina; Donald Kettl, University of Wisconsin; Anne Khademian, University of Wisconsin; William McLauchlan, Purdue University; J. Roger Baker, Wittenburg University; James Lennertz, Lafayette College; Allan McBride, Grambling State University; Joseph Peek Jr., Georgia State University; Douglas Costain, University of Colorado; Robert Hoffert, Colorado State University; David Marcum, University of Wyoming; Mark Silverstein, Boston University; and

Norman Thomas, University of Cincinnati. The following reviewers provided feedback that guided our revisions for this tenth edition: Andrew Battista, East Tennessee State University; Timothy Boylan, Winthrop University; Terri Fine, University of Central Florida; Samuel Hoff, Delaware State University; Marilyn Hoskin, University of New Hampshire; Richard Johnson, Oklahoma City University; Mark Joslyn, University of Kansas-Lawrence; Stephanie Slocum-Schaffer, Shepherd University; Katy Stenger, Gustavus Adolphus College; and Robert Watson, Florida Atlantic University.

An important contribution to the Tenth Edition was made by the authors of the new "Analyzing the Evidence" units. Jamie Carson of the University of Georgia authored the "Analyzing the Evidence" spreads for Chapters 5, 6, 7, 8, 10, and 11. Dan Kapust, also of the University of Georgia, authored the spreads in Chapters 1, 2, 3, and 12. John Sides of George Washington University wrote the "Analyzing the Evidence" units for Chapters 9 and 13. We thank the three of them for their excellent contributions to the book. We also are grateful for the talents and hard work of Erin Ackerman, who helped compile the accompanying online reader, and Sean Boutin, who researched data to update the many figures and tables in the text.

Perhaps above all, we wish to thank those who kept the production and all the loose ends of the book coherent and in focus. Ann Shin has been an extremely talented editor, continuing to offer numerous suggestions for each new edition. Mollie Eisenberg helped keep track of the many details. Lory Frenkel has been a superb project editor, following the great tradition of her predecessors. Jane Searle has been an efficient production manager.

We are more than happy, however, to absolve all these contributors from any flaws, errors, and misjudgments that will inevitably be discovered. From that standpoint, a book ought to try to be perfect. But substantively we have not tried to write a flawless book; we have not tried to write a book to please everyone. We have again tried to write an effective book, a book that cannot be taken lightly. Our goal was to restore politics as a subject matter of vigorous and enjoyable discourse, recapturing it from the bondage of the thirty-second sound bite and the thirty-page technical briefing. Every person can be knowledgeable because everything about politics is accessible. One does not have to be a television anchor to profit from political events. One does not have to be a philosopher to argue about the requisites of democracy, a lawyer to dispute constitutional interpretations, an economist to debate a public policy. We would be very proud if our book contributes in a small way to the restoration of the ancient art of political controversy.

Theodore J. Lowi
Benjamin Ginsberg
Kenneth A. Shepsle

Part One
Foundations

Introduction: Making Sense of Government and Politics

HOW DOES AMERICAN GOVERNMENT WORK?

American government and politics are extraordinarily complex. The United States has many levels of government: federal, state, county, city and town—to say nothing of a host of special and regional authorities. Each of these governments operates under its own rules and statutory authority and is related to the others in complex ways. Each level of government, moreover, consists of an array of departments, agencies, offices, and bureaus undertaking a variety of sometimes overlapping tasks. Sometimes this complexity gets in the way of effective governance, as in the case of governmental response to emergencies. America's federal, state, and local public safety agencies seldom share information and frequently use incompatible communications equipment, so they are often not even able to speak to one another. For example, on September 11, 2001, New York City's police and fire departments could not effectively coordinate their actions because their communications systems were not linked.

The complexity of America's government is no accident. Complexity was one element of the founders' grand constitutional design. The framers of the Constitution hoped that an elaborate division of power among institutions and between the states and the federal government would allow a variety of competing groups, forces, interests, and ideas to have a voice in public affairs—while preventing any

● Core of the Analysis

● Government has become a powerful and complex force in the United States.

● Government is necessary to maintain order, to protect property, and to provide public goods.

● American government is based on democratic electoral institutions and popular representative bodies.

single group or coalition from monopolizing power. One set of interests might be active and powerful in some states, other forces would be influential in the national legislature, and still other groups might prevail in the executive branch. The overall pattern would disperse power and opportunity, allowing many groups to achieve at least some of their political goals. In this way, America's political tradition associates complexity with liberty and political opportunity.

But while America's institutional complexity may create many avenues and possibilities for political action, this complexity also places a considerable burden on citizens who might wish to achieve something through political participation, for they may not easily discern where particular policies are actually made, who the influential decision makers are, and what forms of political participation are most likely to be effective. This is one of the paradoxes of political life: In a dictatorship, lines of political authority may be simple, but opportunities to influence the use of power are few; in America, political opportunities are plentiful, but how they should be used is far from obvious. Indeed, precisely because America's institutional and political arrangements are so complex, many Americans are mystified by government. As we shall see in Chapter 9, most Americans have diffiiculty making sense of even the basic features of the Constitution.

If America's government seems complex, its politics can be utterly bewildering. Like the nation's governmental structure, its political processes have numerous components. For most Americans, the focal point of the politics is the electoral process. As we will see in Chapter 10, tens of millions of Americans participate in a host of national, state, and local elections in which they listen to thousands of candidates debate what may seem to be a perplexing array of issues. Candidates fill the air with promises, charges, and countercharges while an army of pundits and journalists, which we will discuss in Chapter 9, adds its own clamor to the din.

Politics, however, does not end on Election Day. Indeed, given the growing tendency of losers to challenge election results in the courts, even elections do not end on Election Day. Long after the voters have spoken, political struggles continue in the Congress, the executive branch, and the courts and embroil political parties, interest groups, and the mass media. In some instances, the participants in political struggles and their goals seem fairly obvious. For example, it is no secret that business and upper-income wage earners strongly support programs of tax reduction; farmers support maintenance of agricultural price supports; labor unions oppose "outsourcing" of production. Each of these forces has created or joined organized groups to advance its cause. We will examine some of these groups in Chapter 12.

In other instances, though, the participants in political struggles and their goals are not so clear. Sometimes corporate groups hide behind environmental causes to surreptitiously promote economic interests. Sometimes groups claiming to want to help the poor and downtrodden seek only to help themselves. And to make matters worse, many of the government's policies are made behind closed doors, away from the light of publicity.

Ordinary citizens can hardly be blamed for failing to understand bureaucratic rule making and other obscure techniques of government. For the most part, these are topics that even experienced journalists fail to fully comprehend. Take, for example, a presidential office called OIRA, the Office of Information and Regulatory Assessment. This office within the White House Office of Management and Budget (OMB) is responsible for the president's regulatory agenda. OIRA has become an important instrument of presidential power but has gone largely unnoticed by the press. Can you recall reading a story about OIRA? Try an online search and see how often the media mention OIRA and its mission. Then keep this in mind as you read Chapters 6 and 7.

MAKING SENSE OF GOVERNMENT AND POLITICS

Can we find order in the apparent chaos of politics? The answer is that we can, and that is precisely the purpose of our text. In this chapter, we shall offer a number of concepts that we hope will clarify why American government works the way it does. **Government** is the term generally used to describe the formal institutions through which a land and its people are ruled. To govern is to rule. Government is composed of institutions and processes that rulers establish to strengthen and perpetuate their power or control over a territory and its inhabitants. A government may be as simple as a tribal council that meets occasionally to advise the chief, or as complex as our own vast establishment with its forms, rules, and bureaucracies.

Forms of Government

Governments vary in their structure, in their size, and in the way they operate. Two questions are of special importance in determining how governments differ from one another. Who governs? How much government control is permitted?

In some nations, a single individual—a monarch or dictator—governs. This is called **autocracy.** Where a small group of landowners, military officers, or wealthy merchants control most of the governing decisions, that government is an **oligarchy.** If many people participate, and if the populace is deemed to have some influence over the leaders' actions, that government is tending toward **democracy.**

Governments also vary considerably in how they govern. In the United States and a small number of other nations, governments are severely limited by law as to what they are permitted to control (substantive limits), as well as how they go about it (procedural limits). Governments that are so limited are called **constitutional**, or liberal, governments. In other nations, including many in Europe, South America, Asia, and Africa, political and social institutions that the government is unable to control—such as an organized church, organized business groups, or organized labor unions—may help keep the government in check, but the law imposes few real limits. Such governments are called **authoritarian.** In a third group of nations, including the Soviet Union under Joseph Stalin, governments not only are free of legal limits but seek to eliminate those organized social groupings or institutions that might challenge or limit their authority. Because these governments typically attempt to dominate every sphere of political, economic, and social life, they are called **totalitarian.**

government Institutions and procedures through which a territory and its people are ruled.

autocracy A form of government in which a single individual—a monarch or dictator—rules.

oligarchy A form of government in which a small group—landowners, military officers, or wealthy merchants—controls most of the governing decisions.

democracy A system of rule that permits citizens to play a significant part in the governmental process, usually through the election of key public officials.

constitutional government A system of rule in which formal and effective limits are placed on the powers of the government.

authoritarian government A system of rule in which the government recognizes no formal limits but may, nevertheless, be restrained by the power of other social institutions.

totalitarian government A system of rule in which the government recognizes no formal limits on its power and seeks to absorb or eliminate other social institutions that might challenge it.

TABLE 1.1 The Means of Coercion

Form	Instances	Level of Government
Arrests	10,047,300	Federal, state, and local (2004)
Prison inmates	1,496,629	Federal and state (2004)
Jail inmates	713,990	County and municipal (2004)
Executions	60	State (2005)

Source: U.S. Bureau of the Census, *Statistical Abstract of the United States: 2006* (Washington, D.C.: U.S. Department of Commerce, 2006).

Foundations of Government

Whatever their makeup, governments historically have included two basic components: a means of coercion, such as an army or police force, and a means of collecting revenue. Some governments, including many in the less developed nations today, have consisted of little more than an army and a tax-collecting agency. Other governments, especially those in the developed nations such as the United States, attempt to provide services as well as to collect taxes in order to secure popular consent for control. For some, power is an end in itself. For most, power is necessary to maintain public order.

The Means of Coercion   Government must have the powers to get people to obey its laws and punish them if they do not. *Coercion* takes many forms, and each year millions of Americans are subject to one form of government coercion or another. One aspect of coercion is conscription, whereby the government requires certain involuntary services of citizens. The best-known example of conscription is military *conscription*, which is called "the draft." Although there has been no draft since 1974, there were drafts during the Civil War, World War I, World War II, the postwar period, and the wars in Korea and Vietnam. With these drafts, the American government compelled millions of men to serve in the armed forces; one-half million of these soldiers made the ultimate contribution by giving their lives in their nation's service. If the need arose, military conscription would probably be reinstituted. Eighteen-year-old men are required to register today, just in case. American citizens can also, by law, be compelled to serve on juries; to appear before legal tribunals when summoned; to file a great variety of official reports, including income tax returns; and to attend school or to send their children to school. Government also has the power to punish those who do not obey its laws (Table 1.1).

The Means of Collecting Revenue   Each year American governments on every level collect enormous sums from their citizens to support their institutions and programs. Taxation has grown steadily over the years. In 2005, the national government alone collected $1.1 trillion in individual income taxes, $307 billion in corporate income taxes, $771 billion in social insurance taxes, $87 billion in excise,

coercion Forcing a person to do something by threats or pressure.

conscription An aspect of coercion whereby the government requires certain involuntary services of citizens, such as compulsory military service, known as "the draft."

estate, and gift taxes, and another $31 billion in customs duties. The grand total amounted to almost 2 trillion dollars, or almost $6,500 from every living soul in the United States. But not everyone benefits equally from programs paid for by their tax dollars. One of the perennial issues in American politics is the distribution of tax burdens versus the distribution of program benefits. Every group would like more of the benefits while passing more of the burdens of taxation onto others.

Why Is Government Necessary?

As we have just seen, control is the basis for government. But what forms of government control are justifiable? To answer this question, we begin by examining the ways in which government makes it possible for people to live together in harmony.

To Maintain Order   Human beings usually do not venture out of their caves (or the modern counterpart) unless there is a reasonable probability that they can return safely. But for people to live together peacefully, law and order are required, the institutionalization of which is called government. From the standpoint of this definition, the primary purpose of government is to maintain order. But order can come about only by controlling a territory and its people. This may sound like a threat to freedom until you ponder the absence of government, or anarchy—the absence of rule. According to Thomas Hobbes (1558–1679), author of *Leviathan*, the first masterpiece of political philosophy in English, anarchy is even worse than the potential tyranny of government because anarchy, or life outside "the state," is characterized by "continual fear, and danger of violent death . . . [where life is] solitary, poor, nasty, brutish and short."[1] Governmental power can be a threat to freedom, yet we need government to maintain order so that we can enjoy our freedom.

To Protect Property   After safety of persons comes security of a person's labor, which we call property, or private property. Protection of property is almost universally recognized as a justifiable function of government. John Locke (1632–1704), the worthy successor to Hobbes, was the first to assert clearly that whatever we have removed from nature and also mixed our labor with is considered our property. But even Locke recognized that although the right to own what we have produced by our own labor is absolute, it means nothing if someone with greater power than ours decides to take it or trespass on it.

So something we call our own is ours only as long as the laws against trespass improve the probability that we can enjoy it, use it, consume it, trade it, or sell it. In reality, then, property can be defined as all the laws against trespass that permit us not only to call something our own but also to make sure that our claim sticks. In other words, property—that is, private property—is virtually meaningless without a government of laws and policies that makes trespass prohibitive.

---

[1]Thomas Hobbes, *Leviathan, or The Matter, Forme, and Power of a Common Wealth, Ecclesiasticall and Civil* (1651; repr., New York: Macmillan, 1947), p. 82.

The Nature and Purpose of Government

One way for political scientists to understand government is to compare how different societies and thinkers have understood government in the past. For example, classical political thinkers such as Plato (429–347 BCE), Aristotle (384–322 BCE), and Cicero (106–43 BCE), differed from modern social contract thinkers in crucial ways.

As Aristotle wrote in *Politics*, "man is by nature a political animal."[1] What he meant is that certain distinctively human attributes can best be achieved within a political association. Many classical political thinkers viewed political associations as natural communities with broad moral purposes, such as fostering unity or promoting virtue through education. The central question of ancient political thought, then, centered on the issue of justice and what kind of state best realized particular human excellences.

By contrast, social contract thinkers such as Thomas Hobbes (1588–1679) and John Locke (1632–1704), approached political association in a very different way. Rather than viewing the state as a natural entity designed to foster virtues or develop particular capacities, social contract theorists saw the state as a human creation designed for more specific purposes. Social contract thinkers typically resorted to the philosophical construct of a state of nature in which human beings lived prior to political associations. In this state of nature, human beings are considered equal and possess certain rights. From this pre-political state of nature, and due to problems associated with it, humans established governments by conscious collective decisions.

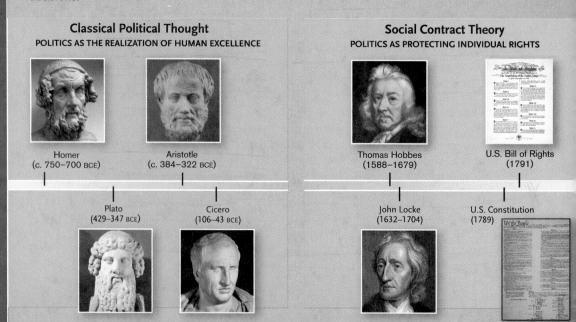

| Classical Political Thought | Social Contract Theory |
| POLITICS AS THE REALIZATION OF HUMAN EXCELLENCE | POLITICS AS PROTECTING INDIVIDUAL RIGHTS |

Homer
(c. 750–700 BCE)

Aristotle
(c. 384–322 BCE)

Thomas Hobbes
(1588–1679)

U.S. Bill of Rights
(1791)

Plato
(429–347 BCE)

Cicero
(106–43 BCE)

John Locke
(1632–1704)

U.S. Constitution
(1789)

Article I

Congress shall make no law respecting an establishment of religion, or prohibiting the free exercise thereof; or abridging the freedom of speech, or of the press; or the right of the people peaceably to assemble, and to petition the Government for a redress of grievances.

Building on the ideas of social contract thinkers, the American founders saw government as having two broad purposes: protecting individual rights and providing avenues for citizens to affect governance. These purposes are evident in the Bill of Rights. For example, the free exercise clause can be seen as an example of *freedom from* government, whereas the right to petition the government for redress of grievances can be seen as *freedom to affect* government.

The social contract understanding of the nature and origins of political association yields two important consequences: (1) because humans are by nature free, legitimate authority derives from those who create governments; and (2) restrictions on human freedom must be (at least in principle) consensual. Such a conception of government, then, views the protection of individuals and their rights—both freedom from government and freedom to affect government—as the paramount concern of government. We will see in subsequent chapters that the protection of individual rights was a key concern for the founders of the United States and affected how they designed the framework for American government.

---

[1]Aristotle. *Politics*. Translated by C.D.C. Reeve. (Indianapolis: Hackett, 1998), p. 4.

To Provide Public Goods David Hume (1711–76), another worthy successor to Hobbes, observed that although two neighbors may agree voluntarily to cooperate in draining a swampy meadow, the more neighbors there are, the more difficult it will be to cooperate to get the task done. A few neighbors might clear the swamp because they understand the benefits each of them will receive. But as you expand the number of neighbors who benefit from clearing the swamp, many neighbors will realize that all of them can get the same benefit if only a few clear the swamp and the rest do nothing. A *public* (or collective) *good* is, therfore, a benefit that neighbors or members of a group cannot be kept from enjoying once any individual or a small minority of members have provided the benefit for themselves—the clearing of the swamp, for example, or national defense, for another. National defense is one of the most important public goods—especially when the nation is threatened by war or terrorism. Without government's coercive powers through a policy (backed by taxation) to build a bridge, produce an army, or provide a swamp-free meadow, "legal tender," or uniform standards of weights and measures, there is no incentive—in fact, very often there is a disincentive—for even the richest, most concerned members to provide the benefit.[2]

Influencing the Government: Politics

In its broadest sense, the term politics refers to conflicts over the character, membership, and policies of any organizations to which people belong. As Harold Lasswell, a famous political scientist, once put it, politics is the struggle over "who gets what, when, how."[3] Although politics is a phenomenon that can be found in any organization, our concern in this book is more narrow. Here, *politics* will refer only to conflicts and struggles over the leadership, structure, and policies of governments. The goal of politics, as we define it, is to have a share or a say in the composition of the government's leadership, how the government is organized, and what its policies are going to be. Having such a share is called *power* or influence. Most people are eager to have some "say" in matters affecting them; witness the willingness of so many individuals over the past two centuries to risk their lives for voting rights and representation. In recent years, of course, Americans have become more skeptical about their actual "say" in government, and many do not bother to vote. This increased skepticism, however, does not mean that Americans no longer want to have a share in the governmental process. Rising levels of skepticism mean, rather, that many Americans doubt the capacity of the political system to provide them with influence.

As we shall see throughout the book, not only does politics influence government, but the character and actions of government also influence a nation's politics. The rules and procedures established by political institutions influence what forms

public good A good that (1) may be enjoyed by anyone if it is provided and (2) may not be denied to anyone once it has been provided.

politics The conflicts and struggles over the leadership, structure, and policies of government.

power Influence over a government's leadership, organization, or policies.

[2] The most instructive treatment of the phenomenon of public goods and the free rider is Mancur Olson Jr., *The Logic of Collective Action: Public Goods and the Theory of Groups* (1965; repr., Cambridge, Mass.: Harvard University Press, 1971), pp. 33–43, esp. n. 53.

[3] Harold Lasswell, *Politics: Who Gets What, When, How* (New York: Meridian Books, 1958).

> **In Brief ✦ Scope and Limits of Power in Constitutional, Authoritarian, and Totalitarian Governments**
>
> **Constitutional Governments**
> *Scope:* power prescribed by a constitution.
> *Limits:* society can challenge government when it oversteps constitutional boundaries.
> *Examples:* United States, France, Canada.
>
> **Authoritarian Governments**
> *Scope:* answer only to a small number of powerful groups.
> *Limits:* recognize no obligations to limit actions, whether or not such obligations exist.
> *Examples:* Spain from the 1930s to the 1970s (under General Francisco Franco) and Portugal from the 1930s to the 1970s (under Prime Minister Antonio Salazar).
>
> **Totalitarian Governments**
> *Scope:* government encompasses all important social institutions.
> *Limits:* rivals for power are not tolerated.
> *Examples:* Germany's Third Reich in the 1930s and 1940s (under Adolf Hitler) and the Soviet Union from the 1930s through the 1950s (under Joseph Stalin).

political activity may take. We define ***institutions*** as the rules and procedures that guide political behavior. The institutions of a constitutional government like the United States are designed to gain popular consent by opening channels for political expression.

FROM COERCION TO CONSENT

Americans have the good fortune to live in a constitutional democracy, with legal limits on what government can do and how it does it. Such democracies were unheard of before the modern era. Prior to the eighteenth and nineteenth centuries, governments seldom sought—and rarely received—the support of their ordinary subjects. But beginning in the seventeenth century, in a handful of Western nations, two important changes began to take place in the character and conduct of government. First, governments began to acknowledge formal limits on their power. Second, a small number of governments began to provide the ordinary citizen with a formal voice in public affairs through the vote.

Limiting Government   The key force behind the imposition of limits on government power was a new social class, the "bourgeoisie." Bourgeois is French for freeman of the city, or bourg. Being part of the bourgeoisie later became associated with being "middle class" and with being in commerce or industry. In order to gain a share of control of government—to join the kings, monarchs, and gentry who had dominated governments for centuries—the bourgeoisie sought to change existing institutions—especially parliaments—into instruments of real political participation. Parliaments had existed for hundreds of years, controlling from the top and

institutions The rules and procedures that guide political behavior.

In Brief ✦ The Expansion of Democratic Politics

Causes of Expansion

Internal conflict: To quell conflicts between different social groups and economic classes, rulers have found it useful to extend the rights of political participation—to give the masses a bigger stake in the system so that they will be more inclined to support that system.

External conflict: In order to maintain a permanent army as a defense against other nation-states, governments needed popular support for military endeavors. The expansion of participation in government helped ensure enthusiasm for cause and country.

Promotion of national unity: Governments sometimes see local or regional loyalties as an obstacle to national unity; by expanding participation, they hope to tie people more strongly to the central government.

Consequences of Expansion

Citizens might use government for their own benefit (rather than watch it being used for the benefit of others).

The public believes it can control the government and therefore supports the continued expansion of government.

---

not allowing influence from below. The bourgeoisie embraced parliament as the means by which they could use their greater numbers and growing economic advantage against their aristocratic rivals.

Although motivated primarily by self-interest, the bourgeoisie advanced many of the principles that became the central underpinnings of individual freedom for *all* citizens—freedom of speech, of assembly, or conscience, and freedom from arbitrary search and seizure. It is important to note here that the bourgeoisie generally did not favor democracy as such. They were advocates of electoral and representative institutions, but they favored property requirements and other restrictions so as to limit participation to the middle classes. Yet, once the right to engage in politics was established, it was difficult to limit it just to the bourgeoisie. We will see time after time that principles first stated to justify a selfish interest can take on a life of their own, extending beyond those for whom the principles were designed.

The Expansion of Democratic Politics   Along with limits on government came an expansion of democratic government. Three factors explain why rulers were forced to give ordinary citizens a greater voice in public affairs: internal conflict, external threat, and the promotion of national unity and development.

First, during the eighteenth and nineteenth centuries, every nation was faced with intense conflict among the landed gentry, the bourgeoisie, lower-middle-class shopkeepers and artisans, the urban working class, and farmers. Many governments came to the conclusion that if they did not deal with basic class conflicts in some constructive way, disorder and revolution would result. One of the best ways of dealing with such conflict was to extend the rights of political participation, especially voting, to each new group as it grew more powerful.

Another form of internal threat is social disorder. Thanks to the Industrial Revolution, societies had become much more interdependent and therefore much more vulnerable to disorder. As that occurred, and as more people moved from rural areas to cities, disorder had to be managed, and one important approach to that management was to give the masses a bigger stake in the system itself. As one supporter of electoral reform put it, the alternative to voting was "the spoliation of property and the dissolution of social order."[4] In the modern world, social disorder helped to compel East European regimes and the republics of the former Soviet Union to take steps toward democratic reform.

The second factor that helped expand democratic government was external threat. The main external threat to governments' power is the existence of other nation-states. During the past three centuries, more and more tribes and nations—people tied together by a common culture and language—have formed into separate principalities, or *nation-states*, in order to defend their populations more effectively. But as more nation-states formed, the more likely it was that external conflicts would arise. War and preparation for war became constant rather than intermittent facts of national life, and the size and expense of military forces increased dramatically with the size of the nation-state and the size and number of its adversaries.

The cost of defense forced rulers to seek popular support to maintain military power. It was easier to raise huge permanent armies of citizen-soldiers and induce them to fight more vigorously and to make greater sacrifices if they were imbued with enthusiasm for cause and country. The expansion of participation and representation in government were key tactics used by the European regimes to raise that enthusiasm and support.

The third factor often associated with the expansion of democratic politics was the promotion of national unity and development. In some instances, governments seek to subvert local or regional loyalties by linking citizens directly to the central government via the ballot box. America's founders saw direct popular election of members of the House of Representatives as a means through which the new federal government could compete with the states for popular allegiance.

The Great Transformation: Tying Democracy to Strong Government

The expansion of democratic politics had two historic consequences. First, democracies opened up the possibility that citizens might use government for their own benefit rather than simply watching it being used for the benefit of others. This consequence is widely understood. But the second is not so well understood: Once citizens perceived that governments could operate in response to their demands, they became increasingly willing to support the expansion of government. The public's belief in its capacity to control the government's action is only one of the many factors responsible for the growth of government. But at the very least, this linkage of democracy and strong government set into motion a wave of governmental growth in the West that began in the middle of the nineteenth century and has continued to the present day.

nation-state A political entity consisting of a people with some common cultural experience (nation), who also share a common political authority (state), recognized by other sovereignties (nation-states).

---

[4]Quoted in John Cannon, *Parliamentary Reform, 1640–1832* (Cambridge: Cambridge University Press, 1973), p. 216.

DOES AMERICAN DEMOCRACY WORK?

The growth of democracy in the United States has led to wider participation, which in turn has fulfilled the democratic ideals of popular sovereignty and majority rule. Thus, democratization creates the possibility that citizens can use government for their own benefit. But what are the trade-offs involved in democracy? Are there unintended consequences of too much democracy?[5] The answers to these questions are complex. Despite over two hundred years of development, American democracy has still not worked out the inconsistencies and contradictions woven in its very fiber by the framers of the Constitution. Similarly, despite all that political scientists and political historians know about American government and politics, puzzles and anomalies reflective of the contradictions within American democracy remain for which we don't have fully satisfactory answers. We conclude this chapter by examining three of them.

Delegating Authority in a Representative Democracy

For over two centuries, we have expanded popular sovereignty to the point where a citizen, from the time he or she is roughly the age of a college freshman to the time that final breath is taken, can engage in political activity at various levels of government. Yet citizens often find it convenient to delegate many of these activities, sometimes (as when we don't pay attention, or vote, or even register to vote) conceding the field entirely to highly motivated individuals and groups ("special interests"). Ours is a ***representative democracy*** for very pragmatic reasons. Most citizens have lives to live and private concerns to attend to, and, therefore, acquiesce in an arrangement enabling them to economize on the effort they must devote to their own governance.

We think of our political representatives as our agents, whom we "hire" to act on our behalf. In this relationship, citizens are the principals—those with the authority—who delegate some of their authority to politicians. This ***principal-agent relationship*** means that citizens don't always get what they want, despite popular sovereignty, because, inadvertently or not, they allow agents to pursue their own self-interest or to be influenced unduly by those who care more or who have more at stake. Thus, popular sovereignty is qualified (some would say undermined) by our willingness to off-load governance responsibilities onto professional agents.

The Trade-off between Freedom and Order

If the imperfect fit between popular sovereignty and delegation of governance to a "political class" constitutes one anomaly, a second involves the trade-off between liberty and coercion. We have taken pains to suggest that governments are necessary to

representative democracy A system of government that provides the populace with the opportunity to make the government responsive to its views through the selection of representatives, who, in turn, play a significant role in governmental decision making.

principal-agent relationship The relationship between a principal and his or her agent; this relationship may be affected by the fact that each is motivated by their own self-interest.

---

[5]For a review and analysis of the detrimental consequences of the "opening up" of American democracy since the 1960s, see Morris P. Fiorina, "Parties, Participation, and Representation in America: Old Theories Face New Realities," in *Political Science: State of the Discipline,* ed. Ira Katznelson and Helen V. Milner (New York: Norton, 2002). For a more general and provocative analysis of the detrimental effects of too much democracy, see Fareed Zakaria, *The Future of Freedom: Illiberal Democracy at Home and Abroad* (New York: Norton, 2003).

maintain order, to protect property, and to provide public goods. All these activities require a degree of coercion. Laws, regulations, and rulings constrain behavior and restrict the uses of property. Taxes include claims on labor income, on gains in the value of capital, and on the transmission of estates from one generation to another. In short, all of these things constitute limits on liberty. The anomaly here is that liberty is one of the very purposes for which the coercion is necessary in the first place. So, a pinch of coercion is one of the ingredients in the stew of liberty. But where to draw the line? And, even if we had an answer to this question, there is another: how to arrange our political life to ensure just the right amount of coercion and no more. As the history of experiments in democratic self-government reveals, coercion is a slippery slope. Especially after the events of September 11, 2001, it is clear that a strong desire for public goods like security from terrorism lulls us into accepting extensive limitations on citizens' liberties.

The Instability of Majority Rule

A third anomaly involves the multitude of purposes pursued by different citizens. It is not always easy to add them up into a collective choice without doing damage to the interest of some. Majority rule, as we shall see in subsequent chapters, especially as manifested in the real institutions of constitutional democracies, is vulnerable to the powers of agenda setters, veto players, financial fat cats, and group leaders (political bosses, union heads, corporate CEOs, religious leaders). All democracies struggle with the fact that outcomes, because they entail disproportionate influence by some, are not always fair. In our American democracy, we put a great deal of faith in frequent elections, checks and balances among government institutions, and multiple levels of government. But again we may ask where to draw the line: Elections how frequent? How powerful the checks? How many governmental levels? At what point is something "broke enough" to need fixing? American political history is filled with instances of decisions, followed by reactions, followed by a revisiting of those decisions, followed by further reactions. The disproportionate influence of some would appear inescapable, despite our efforts to control it. We revisit decisions. We reform institutions. We alter political practices. But still perfection eludes us.

In all these puzzles and anomalies, normative principles sometimes clash. Popular sovereignty, individual liberty, delegation, and multiple purposes constitute the circle that cannot quite be squared. The great success of American democracy, we believe, is that at the end of the day our citizens are pragmatic, tolerant, and appear to avoid letting the best be the enemy of the good.

FOR FURTHER READING

Crenson, Matthew A., and Benjamin Ginsberg. *Downsizing Democracy*. Baltimore: Johns Hopkins University Press, 2002.

Downs, Anthony. *An Economic Theory of Democracy*. New York: Harper, 1957.

Dunn, John. *Democracy: A History*. New York: Atlantic Monthly Press, 2006.

Dworkin, Ronald. *Is Democracy Possible Here?* Princeton, N.J.: Princeton University Press, 2006.

Esman, Milton. *Government Works.* Cornell University Press, 2000.

Finer, S.E. *The History of Government.* New York: Oxford University Press, 1999.

Ginsberg, Benjamin. *The American Lie: Government By the People and Other Political Fables.* Boulder, Colo.: Paradigm, 2007.

Hartz, Louis. *The Liberal Tradition in America.* New York: Harcourt, 1955.

Higgs, Robert. *Neither Liberty Nor Safety: Fear, Ideology and the Growth of Government.* New York: Independent Institute Press, 2007.

Huntington, Samuel. *Who Are We? The Challenges to America's National Identity.* New York: Simon & Schuster, 2004.

ONLINE READING ○ Lupia, Arthur, and Mathew D. McCubbins. *The Democratic Dilemma: Can Citizens Learn What They Need to Know?* New York: Cambridge University Press, 1998.

ONLINE READING ○ Olson, Mancur, Jr. *The Logic of Collective Action: Public Goods and the Theory of Groups.* 1965. Reprinted with new preface and appendix. Cambridge, Mass.: Harvard University Press, 1971.

ONLINE READING ○ Shepsle, Kenneth A., and Mark S. Bonchek. *Analyzing Politics: Rationality, Behavior, and Institutions.* New York: Norton, 1997.

Skocpol, Theda. *Diminished Democracy.* Tulsa: University of Oklahoma Press, 2004.

Tilly, Charles. *Democracy.* New York: Cambridge University Press, 2007.

Tocqueville, Alexis de. *Democracy in America.* Ed. Isaac Kramnick. New York: Norton, 2007; orig. published 1835.

Wolfe, Alan. *Does American Democracy Still Work?* New Haven, Conn.: Yale University Press, 2006.

The Founding and the Constitution

The story of America's Founding and the Constitution is generally presented as something both inevitable and glorious: It was inevitable that the American colonies would break away from England to establish their own country successfully; and it was glorious in that it established the best of all possible forms of government under a new Constitution, which was easily adopted and quickly embraced, even by its critics. In reality, though, America's successful breakaway from England was by no means assured, and the Constitution that we revere today as one of the most brilliant creations of any nation was in fact highly controversial. Moreover, its ratification and durability were often in doubt. George Washington, the man venerated as the father of the country and the person chosen to preside over the Constitutional Convention of 1787, thought the document produced that hot summer in Philadelphia would probably last no more than twenty years, at which time leaders would have to convene again to come up with something new.

That Washington's prediction proved wrong is, indeed, a testament to the enduring strength of the Constitution. Nonetheless the Constitution was not carved in stone. It was a product of political bargaining and compromise, formed very much in the same way political decisions are made today. As this chapter will show, the Constitution reflects political self-interest and high principle, too. It also defines the relationship between American citizens and their government. To understand the character of the American Founding and the meaning of the American

● Core of the Analysis

● Both the American Revolution and the Constitution were expressions of competing interests.

● The Constitution laid the groundwork for a government sufficiently powerful to promote commerce and to protect private property.

● The Constitution and its amendments establish an institutional framework within which government and lawmaking can take place.

Constitution, it is essential to look beyond the myths and rhetoric and explore the conflicting interests and forces at work during the revolutionary and constitutional periods. Thus, we will first assess the political backdrop of the American Revolution, and then we will examine the Constitution that ultimately emerged as the basis for America's government.

THE FIRST FOUNDING: INTERESTS AND CONFLICTS

Competing ideals and principles often reflect competing interests, and so it was in revolutionary America. The American Revolution and the American Constitution were outgrowths of a struggle among economic and political forces within the colonies. Five sectors of society had interests that were important in colonial politics: (1) the New England merchants; (2) the Southern planters; (3) the "royalists"—holders of royal lands, offices, and patents (licenses to engage in a profession or business activity); (4) shopkeepers, artisans, and laborers; and (5) small farmers. Throughout the eighteenth century, these groups were in conflict over issues of taxation, trade, and commerce. For the most part, however, the Southern planters, the New England merchants, and the royal office and patent holders—groups that together made up the colonial elite—were able to maintain a political alliance that held in check the more radical forces representing shopkeepers, laborers, and small farmers. After 1750, however, British tax and trade policies split the colonial elite, permitting radical forces to expand their political influence and setting into motion a chain of events that culminated in the American Revolution.[1]

Political Strife and the Radicalizing of the Colonists

The political strife within the colonies was the background for the events of 1773–1774. In 1773, the British government granted the politically powerful East India Company a monopoly on the export of tea from Britain, eliminating a lucrative form of trade for colonial merchants. Together with their Southern allies, the merchants called upon their radical adversaries—shopkeepers, artisans, laborers, and small farmers—for support. The most dramatic result was the Boston Tea Party of 1773, led by Samuel Adams.

This event was of decisive importance in American history. The merchants had hoped to force the British government to rescind the Tea Act, but they did not support any demands beyond this one. They certainly did not seek independence from Britain. Samuel Adams and the other radicals, however, hoped to provoke the British government to take actions that would alienate its colonial supporters and pave the way for a rebellion. This was precisely the purpose of the Boston Tea Party, and it succeeded. By dumping the East India Company's tea into Boston Harbor, Adams and his followers goaded the British into enacting a number of harsh reprisals. The House of Commons closed the port of Boston to commerce, changed the provincial government of Massachusetts, provided for the removal of accused

---

[1]The social makeup of colonial America and some of the social conflicts that divided colonial society are discussed in Jackson Turner Main, *The Social Structure of Revolutionary America* (Princeton, N.J.: Princeton University Press, 1965).

persons to England for trial, and, most important, restricted movement to the West—further alienating the Southern planters who depended upon access to new western lands. These acts of retaliation confirmed the worst criticisms of England and helped radicalize the American colonists.

Thus, the Boston Tea Party set into motion a cycle of provocation and retaliation that in 1774 resulted in the convening of the First Continental Congress—an assembly consisting of delegates from all parts of the country—that called for a total boycott of British goods and, under the prodding of the radicals, began to consider the possibility of independence from British rule. The result was the Declaration of Independence.

The Declaration of Independence

In 1776, the Second Continental Congress appointed a committee consisting of Thomas Jefferson of Virginia, Benjamin Franklin of Pennsylvania, Roger Sherman of Connecticut, John Adams of Massachusetts, and Robert Livingston of New York to draft a statement of American independence from British rule. The Declaration of Independence, written by Jefferson and adopted by the Second Continental Congress, was an extraordinary document in both philosophical and political terms. Philosophically, the Declaration was remarkable for its assertion that certain rights, which it called "unalienable rights"—including life, liberty, and the pursuit of happiness—could not be abridged by governments. In the world of 1776, a world in which some kings still claimed to rule by divine right, this was a dramatic statement. The Declaration was remarkable as a political document because it identified and focused on problems, grievances, aspirations, and principles that might unify the various colonial groups. The Declaration was an attempt to identify and articulate a history and set of principles that might help to forge national unity.[2]

The Articles of Confederation

Having declared independence, the colonies needed to establish a government. In November 1777, the Continental Congress adopted the Articles of Confederation and Perpetual Union—the first written constitution of the United States. Although it was not ratified by all the states until 1781, it served as the country's constitution for almost twelve years, until March 1789.

The *Articles of Confederation* was concerned primarily with limiting the powers of the central government. It created no executive branch. Congress constituted the central government, but it had little power. Execution of its laws was to be left to the individual states. Its members were not much more than messengers from the state legislatures. They were chosen by the state legislature, their salaries were paid out of the state treasuries, and they were subject to immediate recall by state authorities. In addition, each state, regardless of its size, had only a single vote.

Congress was given the power to declare war and make peace, to make treaties and alliances, to coin or borrow money, and to regulate trade with Native Americans. It could also appoint the senior officers of the United States Army. But it could not levy

Articles of Confederation America's first written constitution. Adopted by the Continental Congress in 1777, the Articles of Confederation and Perpetual Union was the formal basis for America's national government until 1789, when it was supplanted by the Constitution.

---

[2]See Carl Becker, *The Declaration of Independence* (New York: Vintage, 1942).

Sources and Concepts of the Framers

One way to understand the American Revolution and the Constitution is to explore their intellecutal background, which has been debated among political scientists and historians. Some scholars have focused on the importance of *liberalism* in the founding period, while others have stressed the importance of *republicanism*. What do these terms mean, and how does examining the founding period in light of these concepts help us to understand it?

The term *liberalism* can be confusing because in the contemporary United States it implies the preference for *greater* government involvement in people's lives, whereas historically and in most of the world, liberalism implies *less* government involvement. It is important to note that in this discussion, we are referring to *classical* liberalism, which emphasizes individual freedom. Scholars who focus on the liberalism of colonial political thought point to the value placed on individual rights and freedom, including freedom from government—which is often termed a negative conception of liberty. This focus on the individual is evident in the conflict over representation and taxation. John Locke, a British thinker who influenced the American founders, argued that because government is formed to protect one's person, goods, and liberty, it "cannot take from any man any part of his property without his own consent."[1] Locke's influence is clear in the words of James Otis, a Massachusetts lawyer who wrote in a 1764 essay that Parliament "cannot take from any man any part of his property, without his consent . . .."[2] Similarly, in the Declaration of Independence, Thomas Jefferson noted the "imposing (of) taxes on us without our consent" as evidence of George III's tyranny.

liberalism	republicanism
↓	↓
negative liberty	positive liberty
government protects individual	government serves common good
securing individual rights	promoting virtue and checking corruption

Other scholars have emphasized the republican character of colonial thought. As with liberalism, we should clarify and note that in this context *republican* does not refer to the Republican party. Here, republicanism refers to a system that depends on the consent of the governed and emphasizes civic virtue. We can see these ideas in the framers' approach to government, as well as a connection between collective self-government and liberty—a conception of liberty that is often termed positive. Rather than viewing the Revolution as the product of Lockean liberalism, these writers see it as an effort to check British corruption and protect American virtue and liberty through the creation of a republican government. We can see such a conception in Article I, Section 8 of the Constitution, and its provision of many powers to secure the common good.

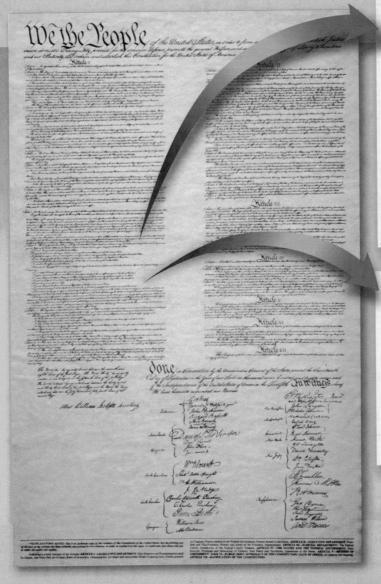

From Article I, Section 8 (republicanism)

"*To make all Laws which shall be necessary and proper for carrying into Execution the foregoing Powers and all other Powers vested by this Constitution in the Government of the United States, or in any Department or Officer thereof.*"

From Article I, Section 9 (liberalism)

"*The Privilege of the Writ of Habeas Corpus shall not be suspended, unless when in Cases or Rebellion or Invasion the public Safety may require it.*"

More recently, scholars have argued that the political thought of the founding period is best understood as a mixture of liberalism and republicanism. For instance, while Article I, Section 8 of the Constitution grants broad powers to the national government for securing the common good (republicanism), Article I, Section 9 provides for individual protections from the national government (liberalism).

---

[1] John Locke. *Second Treatise on Government.* C.B. MacPherson, ed. (Indianapolis: Hackett, 1980), p. 73.

[2] James Otis, "The Rights of the Colonies Asserted and Proved," in *Tracts of the American Revolution, 1763–1776,* ed. Merrill Jensen (Indianapolis: Hackett, 2003), p. 26.

taxes or regulate commerce among the states. Moreover, the army officers it appointed had no army to serve in because the nation's armed forces were composed of the state militias. Probably the most unfortunate part of the Articles of Confederation was that the central government could not prevent one state from discriminating against other states in the quest for foreign commerce.

In brief, the relationship between Congress and the states under the Articles of Confederation was much like the contemporary relationship between the United Nations and its member states, a relationship in which the states retain virtually all governmental powers. It was called a confederation because, as provided under Article II, "each state retains its sovereignty, freedom and independence, and every Power, Jurisdiction and right, which is not by this confederation expressly delegated to the United States, in Congress assembled." Not only was there no executive, there was also no judicial authority and no other means of enforcing Congress's will. If there was to be any enforcement at all, the states would have to do it.[3]

THE SECOND FOUNDING: FROM COMPROMISE TO CONSTITUTION

The Declaration of Independence and the Articles of Confederation were not sufficient to hold the nation together as an independent and effective nation-state. From almost the moment of armistice with the British in 1783, moves were afoot to reform and strengthen the Articles.

International Standing and Domestic Turmoil

There was a special concern for the country's international position. Competition among the states for foreign commerce allowed the European powers to play the states against one another, which created confusion on both sides of the Atlantic. At one point during the winter of 1786–1787, John Adams, a leader in the independence struggle, was sent to negotiate a new treaty with the British, one that would cover disputes left over from the war. The British government responded that, since the United States under the Articles of Confederation was unable to enforce existing treaties, it would negotiate with each of the thirteen states separately.

At the same time, well-to-do Americans—in particular the New England merchants and Southern planters—were troubled by the influence that "radical" forces exercised in the Continental Congress and in the governments of several of the states. The colonists' victory in the Revolutionary War had not only meant the end of British rule, but it had also significantly changed the balance of political power within the new states. As a result of the Revolution, one key segment of the colonial elite—the royal land, office, and patent holders—was stripped of its economic and political privileges. In fact, many of these individuals, along with tens of thousands of other colonists who considered themselves loyal British subjects, left for Canada after the British surrender. And while the elite was weakened, the radicals were now better organized than ever before. They controlled such states as Pennsylvania and

---

[3]See Merrill Jensen, *The Articles of Confederation* (Madison: University of Wisconsin Press, 1963).

Rhode Island, where they pursued economic and political policies that struck terror into the hearts of the prerevolutionary political establishment. The central government under the Articles of Confederation was powerless to intervene.

The new nation's weak international position and domestic turmoil led many Americans to consider whether a new version of the Articles might be necessary. In the fall of 1786, delegates from five states met in Annapolis, Maryland, and called on Congress to send commissioners to Philadelphia at a later time to devise adjustments to the constitution. Their resolution took on force as a result of an event that occurred the following winter in Massachusetts: Shays's Rebellion. Daniel Shays led a mob of farmers, who were protesting foreclosures on their land, in a rebellion against the state government. The state militia dispersed the mob within a few days, but the threat posed by the rebels scared Congress into action. The states were asked to send delegates to Philadelphia to discuss constitutional revision, and eventually delegates were sent from every state but Rhode Island.

The Constitutional Convention

Twenty-nine of a total of seventy-three delegates selected by the state governments convened in Philadelphia in May 1787, with political strife, international embarrassment, national weakness, and local rebellion fixed in their minds. Recognizing that these issues were symptoms of fundamental flaws in the Articles of Confederation, the delegates soon abandoned the plan to revise the Articles and committed themselves to a second founding—a second, and ultimately successful, attempt to create a legitimate and effective national system. This effort occupied the convention for the next five months.

The Great Compromise The proponents of a new government fired their opening shot on May 29, 1787, when Edmund Randolph of Virginia offered a resolution that proposed corrections and enlargements in the Articles of Confederation. His proposal was not a simple motion. It provided for virtually every aspect of a new government. Randolph later admitted it was intended to be an alternative draft constitution, and it did in fact serve as the framework for what ultimately became the Constitution.[4]

The portion of Randolph's motion that became most controversial was known as the ***Virginia Plan.*** This plan provided for a system of representation in the national legislature based upon the population of each state or the proportion of each state's revenue contribution, or both. (Randolph also proposed a second branch of the legislature, but it was to be elected by the members of the first branch.) Because the states varied enormously in size and wealth, the Virginia Plan was thought to be heavily biased in favor of the large states.

While the convention was debating the Virginia Plan, additional delegates arriving in Philadelphia were beginning to mount opposition to it. In particular,

Virginia Plan A framework for the Constitution, introduced by Edmund Randolph, which called for representation in the national legislature based upon the population of each state.

---

[4]There is no verbatim record of the debates, but James Madison, a Virginia delegate, was present during nearly all of the deliberations and kept full notes on them. Madison's notes are included in Max Farrand, ed., *The Records of the Federal Convention of 1787*, 4 vols., rev. ed. (New Haven, Conn.: Yale University Press, 1966).

delegates from the less populous states, which included Delaware, New Jersey, Connecticut, and New York, asserted that the more populous states, such as Virginia, Pennsylvania, North Carolina, Massachusetts, and Georgia, would dominate the new government if representation were to be determined by population. The smaller states argued that each state should be equally represented in the new regime regardless of its population. The proposal, called the **New Jersey Plan** (it was introduced by William Paterson of New Jersey), focused on revising the Articles rather than replacing them. Their opposition to the Virginia Plan's system of representation was sufficient to send the proposals back to committee for reworking into a common document.

The outcome was the Connecticut Compromise, also known as the **Great Compromise**. Under the terms of this compromise, in the first branch of Congress—the House of Representatives—the representatives would be apportioned according to the number of inhabitants in each state. This, of course, was what delegates from the large states had sought. But in the second branch—the Senate—each state would have an equal vote regardless of its size; this was to deal with the concerns of the small states. This compromise was not immediately satisfactory to all the delegates. In the end, however, both sets of forces preferred compromise to the breakup of the Union, and the plan was accepted.

The Question of Slavery: The Three-fifths Compromise   Many of the conflicts that emerged during the Constitutional Convention were reflections of the fundamental differences between the slave and the nonslave states—differences that pitted the Southern planters and the New England merchants against one another. This was the first premonition of a conflict that was almost to destroy the Republic in later years. In the midst of debate over large versus small states, Madison observed, "The great danger to our general government is the great southern and northern interests of the continent, being opposed to each other. Look to the votes in Congress, and most of them stand divided by the geography of the country, not according to the size of the states."[5]

Over 90 percent of all slaves resided in five states—Georgia, Maryland, North Carolina, South Carolina, and Virginia—where they accounted for 30 percent of the total population. In some places, slaves outnumbered nonslaves by as much as ten to one. Were they to be counted in determining how many congressional seats a state should have? Northerners and Southerners eventually reached agreement through the **Three-fifths Compromise**. The seats in the House of Representatives would be apportioned according to a "population" in which five slaves would count as three persons. The slaves would not be allowed to vote, of course, but the number of representatives would be apportioned accordingly. This arrangement was supported by the slave states, which included some of the biggest and some of the smallest states at that time. It was also accepted by delegates from nonslave states who strongly supported the principle of property representation, whether that property was expressed in slaves or in land, money, or stocks.

[5] Ibid., vol. 1, p. 476.

New Jersey Plan A framework for the Constitution, introduced by William Paterson, which called for equal representation in the national legislature regardless of a state's population.

Great Compromise Agreement reached at the Constitutional Convention of 1787 that gave each state an equal number of senators regardless of its population, but linked representation in the House of Representatives to population.

Three-fifths Compromise Agreement reached at the Constitutional Convention of 1787 that stipulated that for purposes of the appointment of congressional seats, every slave would be counted as three-fifths of a person.

The issue of slavery was the most difficult one faced by the framers, and it nearly destroyed the Union. Although some delegates believed slavery to be morally wrong, morality was not the issue that caused the framers to support or oppose the Three-fifths Compromise. Whatever they thought of the institution of slavery, most delegates from the northern states opposed counting slaves in the distribution of congressional seats. But southern delegates made it clear that if the Northerners refused to give in, they would never agree to the new government. William Davie of North Carolina heatedly asserted that the people of North Carolina would never enter the Union if slaves were not counted as part of the basis for representation. Without such an agreement, he asserted ominously, "the business was at an end." This conflict between the southern and the northern delegates was so divisive that many came to question the possibility of creating and maintaining a union of the two, and a compromise that acknowledged the legitimacy of slavery was probably necessary to keep the South from rejecting the Constitution.

THE CONSTITUTION

The political significance of the Great Compromise and the Three-fifths Compromise was to reinforce the unity of those who sought the creation of a new government. The Great Compromise reassured those who feared that the importance of their own local or regional influence would be reduced by the new governmental framework. The Three-fifths Compromise temporarily defused the rivalry between the merchants and the planters. Their unity secured, members of the alliance supporting the establishment of a new government moved to fashion a constitutional framework for this government that would be congruent with their economic and political interests.

In particular, the framers sought a new government that, first, would be strong enough to promote commerce and protect property from radical state legislatures such as Rhode Island's. This goal became the basis for the establishment of national control over commerce and finance, as well as the establishment of national judicial supremacy and a strong presidency. Second, the framers sought to prevent what they saw as the threat posed by the "excessive democracy" of the state and national governments under the Articles of Confederation. This led to such constitutional principles as *bicameralism* (division of the Congress into two chambers), checks and balances, staggered terms in office, and indirect election (selection of the president by an electoral college rather than by voters directly).

Third, hoping to secure support from the states or the public at large for the new form of government they proposed, the framers provided for direct popular election of representatives and, subsequently, for the addition of the Bill of Rights. Finally, to prevent the new government from abusing its power, the framers incorporated principles such as the separation of powers and federalism into the Constitution. Let us now assess the major provisions of the Constitution to see how each relates to these objectives.

bicameralism Division of a legislative body into two houses, chambers, or branches.

The Legislative Branch

The first seven sections of Article I of the Constitution provided for a Congress consisting of two chambers—a House of Representatives and a Senate. Members of the House of Representatives were given two-year terms in office and were to be subject to direct popular election—though generally only white males had the right to vote. State legislatures were to appoint members of the Senate (this was changed in 1913 by the Seventeenth Amendment, providing for direct election of senators) for six-year terms. These terms, moreover, were staggered so that the appointments of one-third of the senators would expire every two years. The Constitution assigned somewhat different tasks to the House and Senate. Though the approval of each body was required for the enactment of a law, the Senate alone was given the power to ratify treaties and approve presidential appointments. The House, on the other hand, was given the sole power to originate revenue bills.

The character of the legislative branch was directly related to the framers' major goals. The House of Representatives was designed to be directly responsible to the people in order to encourage popular consent for the new Constitution and, as we saw in Chapter 1, to help enhance the power of the new government. At the same time, to guard against "excessive democracy," the power of the House of Representatives was checked by the Senate, whose members were to be appointed for long (six-year) terms rather than elected directly by the people for short terms.

Staggered terms of service in the Senate were intended to make that body even more resistant to popular pressure. Because only one-third of the senators would be selected at any given time, the composition of the institution would be protected from changes in popular preferences transmitted by the state legislatures. Thus, the structure of the legislative branch was designed to contribute to governmental power, promote popular consent for the new government, and at the same time place limits on the popular political currents that many of the framers saw as a radical threat to the economic and social order.

The Powers of Congress and the States   The issues of power and consent were important throughout the Constitution. Section 8 of Article I specifically listed the powers of Congress, which include the authority to collect taxes, to borrow money, to regulate commerce, to declare war, and to maintain an army and navy. By granting it these powers, the framers indicated very clearly that they intended the new government to be far more influential than its predecessor. At the same time, by giving these important powers to Congress, the framers sought to reassure citizens that their views would be fully represented whenever the government exercised its new powers.

As a further guarantee to the people that the new government would pose no threat to them, the Constitution implied that any powers *not* listed were not granted at all. This is the doctrine of ***expressed power***. The Constitution grants only those powers specifically *expressed* in its text. But the framers intended to create an active and powerful government, and so they included the ***necessary and proper clause***, sometimes known as the elastic clause, which signified that the enumerated powers were meant to be a source of strength to the national government, not a limitation on it. Each power could be used with the utmost vigor, but no new powers could be

expressed power The notion that the Constitution grants to the federal government only those powers specifically named in its text.

necessary and proper clause Article I, Section 8, of the Constitution, which enumerates the powers of Congress and provides Congress with the authority to make all laws "necessary and proper" to carry them out; also referred to as the "elastic clause."

In Brief ✦ The Seven Articles of the Constitution

1. The Legislative Branch

House: two-year terms, elected directly by the people.

Senate: six-year terms (staggered so that only one-third of the Senate changes in any given election), appointed by state legislature (changed in 1913 to direct election).

Expressed powers of the national government: collecting taxes, borrowing money, regulating commerce, declaring war, and maintaining an army and a navy; all other power belongs to the states, unless deemed otherwise by the elastic (necessary and proper) clause.

Exclusive powers of the national government: states are expressly forbidden to issue their own paper money, tax imports and exports, regulate trade outside their own borders, and impair the obligation of contracts; these powers are the exclusive domain of the national government.

2. The Executive Branch

Presidency: four-year terms (limited in 1951 to a maximum of two terms), elected indirectly by the electoral college.

Powers: can recognize other countries, negotiate treaties, grant reprieves and pardons, convene Congress in special sessions, and veto congressional enactments.

3. The Judicial Branch

Supreme Court: lifetime terms, appointed by the president with the approval of the Senate.

Powers: include resolving conflicts between federal and state laws, determining whether power belongs to national government or the states, and settling controversies between citizens of different states.

4. National Unity and Power

Reciprocity among states: establishes that each state must give "full faith and credit" to official acts of other states, and guarantees citizens of any state the "privileges and immunities" of every other state.

5. Amending the Constitution

Procedures: requires two-thirds approval in Congress and three-fourths adoption by the states.

6. National Supremacy

The Constitution and national law are the supreme law of the land and cannot be overruled by state law.

7. Ratification

The Constitution became effective when approved by nine states.

---

seized upon by the national government without a constitutional amendment. Any power not enumerated was conceived to be "reserved" to the states (or the people).

The Executive Branch

The Constitution provided for the establishment of the presidency in Article II. As Alexander Hamilton put it, the presidential article sought "energy in the Executive." It did so in an effort to overcome the natural stalemate that was built into the bicameral legislature as well as into the separation of powers among the legislative, executive, and judicial branches. The Constitution afforded the president a measure of independence from the people and from the other branches of government—particularly Congress.

In line with the framers' goal of increased power to the national government, the president was granted the unconditional power to accept ambassadors from other countries; this amounted to the power to "recognize" other countries. He was also given the power to negotiate treaties, although their acceptance required the approval of the Senate. The president was given the unconditional right to grant reprieves and pardons, except in cases of impeachment. And he was provided with the power to appoint major departmental personnel, to convene Congress in special session, and to veto congressional enactments. (The veto power is formidable, but it is not absolute, since Congress can override it by a two-thirds vote.)

At the same time, the framers sought to help the president withstand (excessively) democratic pressures by making him subject to indirect rather than direct election (through his selection by a separate electoral college). The extent to which the framers' hopes were actually realized will be the topic of Chapter 6.

The Judicial Branch

Article III established the judicial branch. This provision reflects the framers' concern with giving more power to the national government and checking radical democratic impulses, while guarding against abuse of liberty and property by the new national government itself.

The framers created a court that was to be literally a supreme court of the United States, and not merely the highest court of the national government. The Supreme Court was given the power to resolve any conflicts that might emerge between federal and state laws and to determine to which level of government a power belonged. In addition, the Supreme Court was assigned jurisdiction over controversies between citizens of different states. The long-term significance of this was that as the country developed a national economy, it came to rely increasingly on the federal judiciary, rather than on the state courts, for resolution of disputes.

Judges were given lifetime appointments in order to protect them from popular politics and from interference by the other branches. But they would not be totally immune to politics or to the other branches, for the president was to appoint the judges and the Senate was to approve the appointments. Congress would also have the power to create inferior (lower) courts, to change the jurisdiction of the federal courts, to add or subtract federal judges, and even to change the size of the Supreme Court.

judicial review Power of the courts to declare actions of the legislative and executive branches invalid or unconstitutional. The Supreme Court asserted this power in *Marbury v. Madison.*

No direct mention is made in the Constitution of *judicial review*—the power of the courts to render the final decision when there is a conflict of interpretation of the Constitution or of laws. This conflict could be between the courts and Congress, the courts and the executive branch, or the courts and the states. Scholars generally feel that judicial review is implicit in the very existence of a written Constitution and in the power given directly to the federal courts over "all Cases . . . arising under this Constitution, the Laws of the United States, and Treaties made, or which shall be made, under their Authority" (Article III, Section 2). The Supreme Court eventually assumed the power of judicial review. Its assumption of this power, as we shall see in

Chapter 8, was based not on the Constitution itself but on the politics of later decades and the membership of the Court.

National Unity and Power

Various provisions in the Constitution addressed the framers' concern with national unity and power. Article IV provided for comity (reciprocity) among states, which we will discuss in more detail in Chapter 3. Each state was also prohibited from discriminating against the citizens of other states in favor of its own citizens, with the Supreme Court being the arbiter in each case.

The framers' concern with national supremacy was also expressed in Article VI, in the *supremacy clause*, which provided that national laws and treaties "shall be the supreme law of the land." This meant that all laws made under the "authority of the United States" would be superior to all laws adopted by any state or any other subdivision, and that the states would be expected to respect all treaties made under that authority. This was a direct effort to keep the states from dealing separately with foreign nations or businesses. The supremacy clause also bound the officials of all state and local as well as federal governments to take an oath of office to support the national Constitution. This meant that every action taken by the U.S. Congress would have to be applied within each state as though the action were in fact state law.

Amending the Constitution

The Constitution established procedures for its own revision in Article V. Its provisions are so difficult that Americans have succeeded in the amending process only seventeen times since 1791, when the first ten amendments were adopted. Many other amendments have been proposed in Congress, but fewer than forty of them have even come close to fulfilling the Constitution's requirement of a two-thirds vote in Congress, and only a fraction have gotten anywhere near adoption by three-fourths of the states. (A breakdown of these figures and further discussion of amending the Constitution appear in Chapter 3.) The Constitution could also be amended by a constitutional convention. Occasionally, proponents of particular measures, such as a balanced-budget amendment, have called for a constitutional convention to consider their proposals. Whatever the purpose for which it was called, however, such a convention would presumably have the authority to revise America's entire system of government.

Ratifying the Constitution

The rules for the ratification of the Constitution of 1787 made up Article VII of the Constitution. This provision actually violated the lawful procedure for constitutional change incorporated in the Articles of Confederation. For one thing, it adopted a nine-state rule in place of the unanimity among the states required by the Articles of Confederation. For another, it provided that ratification would occur in special state conventions called for that purpose rather than in the state legislatures. All the states except Rhode Island eventually did set up state conventions to ratify the Constitution, and none seemed to protest very loudly the extralegal character of the procedure.

supremacy clause
Article VI of the Constitution, which states that all laws passed by the national government and all treaties are the supreme laws of the land and superior to all laws adopted by any state or any subdivision.

In Brief ✦ Comparing the Articles of Confederation and the Constitution

	Articles of Confederation	Constitution
Legislative Branch	*Power to:* Declare war and make peace. Make treaties and alliances. Coin or borrow money. Regulate trade with Native Americans. Appoint senior officers of the United States Army. *Limits on power:* Cannot levy taxes, regulate commerce among the states, or create national armed forces.	*Power to:* Collect taxes. Borrow money. Regulate commerce. Declare war. Maintain an army and navy. *Limits on power:* All other powers belong to the states.
Executive Branch	*No executive branch was created.*	*Power to:* Recognize other countries. Negotiate treaties. Grant reprieves and pardons. Appoint major departmental personnel. Convene special sessions of Congress. Veto congressional actions. *Limits on power:* Senate must approve treaties. Congress can override a veto by a two-thirds vote.
Judicial Branch	*No judicial branch was created.*	*Power to:* Resolve conflicts between state and federal laws. Determine to which level of government a power belongs. Decide conflicts between citizens of different states. *Limits on power:* Judicial appointments are made by the president and approved by the Senate. Congress creates lower courts and can change the jurisdiction of the federal courts. Congress can add or subtract federal judges and can change the size of the Supreme Court.

Constitutional Limits on the National Government's Power

As we have indicated, though the framers sought to create a powerful national government, they also wanted to guard against possible misuse of that power. To that end, the framers incorporated two key principles into the Constitution—the *separation of powers* and *federalism* (see also Chapter 3). A third set of limitations, in the form of the *Bill of Rights*, was added to the Constitution to help secure its ratification when opponents of the document charged that it paid insufficient attention to citizens' rights.

The Separation of Powers   No principle of politics was more widely shared at the time of the 1787 Founding than the principle that power must be used to balance power. The French political theorist Montesquieu (1689–1755) believed that this balance was an indispensable defense against tyranny, and his writings, especially his major work, *The Spirit of the Laws*, "were taken as political gospel" at the Philadelphia Convention.[6] This principle is not stated explicitly in the Constitution, but it is clearly built on Articles I, II, and III, which provide for

1. Three separate branches of government (see Figure 2.1).

2. Different methods of selecting the top personnel, so that each branch is responsible to a different constituency. This is supposed to produce a "mixed regime," in which the personnel of each department will develop very different interests and outlooks on how to govern, and different groups in society will be assured some access to governmental decision making.

3. *Checks and balances,* a system under which each of the branches is given some power over the others. Familiar examples are the presidential veto power over legislation and the power of the Senate to approve high-level presidential appointments.

One clever formulation conceives of this system not as separated powers but as "separated institutions sharing power,"[7] thus diminishing the chance that power will be misused.

Federalism   Federalism was a step toward greater centralization of power. The delegates agreed that they needed to place more power at the national governmental level, without completely undermining the power of the state governments. Thus, they devised a system of two sovereigns—the states and the nation—with the hope that competition between the two would be an effective limitation on the power of both.

The Bill of Rights   Late in the Philadelphia Convention, a motion was made to include a bill of rights in the Constitution. After a brief debate in which hardly a word was said in its favor and only one speech was made against it, the motion to include it was almost unanimously turned down. Most delegates sincerely believed that since the federal government was already limited to its expressed powers, further

---

[6]Max Farrand, *The Framing of the Constitution of the United States* (New Haven, Conn.: Yale University Press, 1962), p. 49.

[7]Richard E. Neustadt, *Presidential Power* (New York: Wiley, 1960), p. 33.

separation of powers
The division of governmental power among several institutions that must cooperate in decision making.

federalism System of government in which power is divided by a constitution between a central government and regional governments.

Bill of Rights The first ten amendments to the U.S. Constitution, ratified in 1791. They ensure certain rights and liberties to the people.

checks and balances Mechanisms through which each branch of government is able to participate in and influence the activities of the other branches. Major examples include the presidential veto power over congressional legislation, the power of the Senate to approve presidential appointments, and judicial review of congressional enactments.

FIGURE 2.1 The Separation of Powers

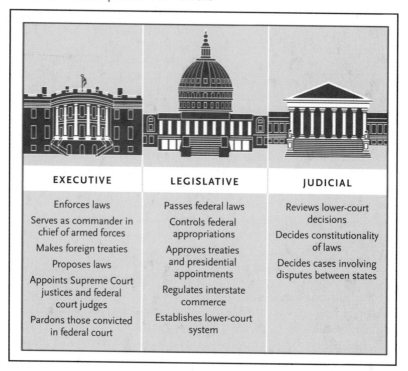

EXECUTIVE	LEGISLATIVE	JUDICIAL
Enforces laws	Passes federal laws	Reviews lower-court decisions
Serves as commander in chief of armed forces	Controls federal appropriations	Decides constitutionality of laws
Makes foreign treaties	Approves treaties and presidential appointments	Decides cases involving disputes between states
Proposes laws		
Appoints Supreme Court justices and federal court judges	Regulates interstate commerce	
Pardons those convicted in federal court	Establishes lower-court system	

protection of citizens was not needed. The delegates argued that the states should adopt bills of rights because their powers needed more limitations than those of the federal government. But almost immediately after the Constitution was ratified, there was a movement to adopt a national bill of rights. This is why the Bill of Rights, adopted in 1791, comprises the first ten amendments to the Constitution rather than being part of the body of it. We will have a good deal more to say about the Bill of Rights in Chapter 4.

THE FIGHT FOR RATIFICATION

The first hurdle faced by the new Constitution was ratification by state conventions of delegates elected by white, propertied males of each state. This struggle for ratification was carried out in thirteen separate campaigns. Each involved different individuals, moved at a different pace, and was influenced by local as well as national considerations. Two sides faced off throughout all the states, however, taking the names of Federalists and Antifederalists.[8] The *Federalists* supported the Constitution

---

Federalists Those who favored a strong national government and supported the constitution proposed at the American Constitutional Convention of 1787.

[8]An excellent analysis of the ratification campaigns—based on a quantitative assessment of the campaigners' own words as found in campaign documents, pamphlets, tracts, public letters, and the eighteenth-century equivalent of op-ed pieces (like the individual essays that make up the *Federalist Papers*)—is William H. Riker, *The Strategy of Rhetoric: Campaigning for the American Constitution* (New Haven, Conn.: Yale University Press, 1996).

and preferred a strong national government. The *Antifederalists* opposed the Constitution and preferred a more decentralized federal system of government; they took on their name by default, in reaction to their better-organized opponents. The Federalists were united in their support of the Constitution. The Antifederalists, although opposing this plan, were divided as to what they believed the alternative should be.

Under the name of "Publius," Alexander Hamilton, James Madison, and John Jay wrote eighty-five articles in the New York newspapers supporting ratification of the Constitution. These *Federalist Papers,* as they are collectively known today, defended the principles of the Constitution and sought to dispel the fears of a national authority.[9] The Antifederalists, however, such as Richard Henry Lee and Patrick Henry of Virginia and George Clinton of New York argued that the new Constitution betrayed the Revolution and was a step toward monarchy. They accused the Philadelphia Convention of being a "Dark Conclave" that had worked under a "thick veil of secrecy" to overthrow the law and spirit of the Articles of Confederation.[10]

By the end of 1787 and the beginning of 1788, five states had ratified the Constitution. Delaware, New Jersey, and Georgia ratified it unanimously; Connecticut and Pennsylvania ratified by wide margins. Opposition was overcome in Massachusetts by the inclusion of nine recommended amendments to the Constitution to protect human rights. Ratification by Maryland and South Carolina followed. In June 1788, New Hampshire became the ninth state to ratify. That put the Constitution into effect, but for the new national government to have real power, the approval of both Virginia and New York would be needed. After impassioned debate and a great number of recommendations for future amendment of the Constitution, especially for a bill of rights, the Federalists mustered enough votes for approval of the Constitution in June (Virginia) and July (New York) of 1788. North Carolina joined the new government in 1789, after a bill of rights actually was submitted to the states by Congress, and Rhode Island held out until 1790 before finally voting to become part of the new union.

CHANGING THE FRAMEWORK: CONSTITUTIONAL AMENDMENT

The Constitution has endured for two centuries as the framework of government. But it has not endured without change. Without change, the Constitution might have become merely a sacred text, stored under glass.

Amendments: Many Are Called, Few Are Chosen

The framers of the Constitution recognized the need for change. The provisions for amendment incorporated into Article V were thought to be "an easy, regular and Constitutional way" to make changes, which would occasionally be necessary because members of Congress "may abuse their power and refuse their consent on

Antifederalists Those who favored strong state governments and a weak national government and who were opponents of the constitution proposed at the American Constitutional Convention of 1787.

○   ONLINE READING

○   ONLINE READING

---

[9]Alexander Hamilton, James Madison, and John Jay, *The Federalist Papers,* ed. Isaac Kramnick (New York: Viking Press, 1987), esp. nos. 10 and 51.

[10]Herbert Storing, ed., *The Anti-Federalist* (Chicago: University of Chicago Press, 1985), "Brutus" letters pp. 108–21 and 133–38. Also, Herbert Storing, *What the Anti-Federalists Were For* (Chicago: University of Chicago Press, 1981).

In Brief ✦ Federalists versus Antifederalists

	Federalists	Antifederalists
Who were they?	Property owners, creditors, merchants.	Small farmers, frontiersmen, debtors, shopkeepers.
What did they believe?	Believed that elites were best fit to govern; feared "excessive democracy."	Believed that government should be closer to the people; feared concentration of power in the hands of the elites.
What system of government did they favor?	Favored strong national government; believed in "filtration" so that only elites would obtain governmental power.	Favored retention of power by state governments and protection of individual rights.
Who were their leaders?	Alexander Hamilton James Madison George Washington	Patrick Henry George Mason Elbridge Gerry George Clinton

that very account . . . to admit to amendments to correct the source of the abuse."[11] James Madison, again writing in *The Federalist Papers*, made a more balanced defense of the amendment procedures: "It guards equally against that extreme facility, which would render the Constitution too mutable; and that extreme difficulty, which might perpetuate its discovered faults."[12]

Experience since 1789 raises questions even about Madison's more modest claim. The Constitution has proven to be extremely difficult to amend. In the history of efforts to amend the Constitution, the most appropriate characterization is "many are called, few are chosen." Between 1789 and the present, more than eleven thousand amendments were formally offered in Congress. Of these, Congress officially proposed only twenty-nine, and only twenty-seven of these were eventually ratified by the states. But the record is even more severe than that. Since 1791, when the first ten amendments, the Bill of Rights, were added, only seventeen amendments have been adopted. And two of them—prohibition of alcohol (Eighteenth) and its repealer (Twenty-first)—cancel each other out, so that for all practical purposes, only

---

[11]Observation by Colonel George Mason, delegate from Virginia, early during the convention period. Quoted in Max Farrand, *The Records of the Federal Convention of 1787*, vol. 1, rev. ed. (New Haven, Conn.: Yale University Press, 1966), pp. 202–3.

ONLINE READING ○ [12]Clinton Rossiter, ed., *The Federalist Papers* (New York: New American Library, 1961), No. 43, p. 278.

fifteen amendments have been added to the Constitution since 1791. Despite vast changes in American society and its economy, only twelve amendments have been adopted since the Civil War amendments (Thirteenth, Fourteenth, and Fifteenth) in 1868.

As Figure 2.2 illustrates, Article V provides four methods of amendment:

1. Passage in House and Senate by two-thirds vote; then ratification by majority vote of the legislatures of three fourths (thirty-eight) of the states.

2. Passage in House and Senate by two-thirds vote; then ratification by conventions called for the purpose in three fourths of the states.

3. Passage in a national convention called by Congress in response to petitions by two-thirds of the states; ratification by majority vote of the legislatures of three fourths of the states.

4. Passage in a national convention, as in method 3; then ratification by conventions called for the purpose in three fourths of the states.

Because no amendment has ever been proposed by national convention, however, routes 3 and 4 have never been employed. And route 2 has only been employed once

FIGURE 2.2 Routes of Amendment

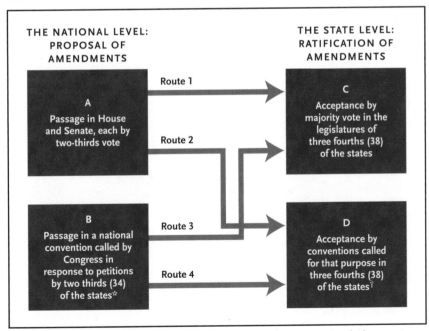

*This method of proposal has never been employed. Thus amendment routes 3 and 4 have never been attempted.

†In each amendment proposal, Congress has the power to choose the method of ratification, the time limit for consideration by the states, and other conditions of ratification.

(for the Twenty-first Amendment, which repealed the Eighteenth, or Prohibition, Amendment). Thus, route 1 has been used for all the others.

Now we should be better able to explain why it has been so difficult to amend the Constitution. The main reason is the requirement of a two-thirds vote in the House and the Senate, which means that any proposal for an amendment in Congress can be killed by only 34 senators *or* 136 members of the House. The amendment can also be killed by the refusal or inability of only thirteen state legislatures to ratify it. Since each state has an equal vote regardless of its population, the thirteen holdout states may represent a small fraction of the total American population. In the 1970s, the Equal Rights Amendment (ERA), granting protection from denial of rights on account of sex, got the necessary two-thirds vote in Congress but failed by three states to get the necessary three-fourths votes of the states, even after a three-year extension for its ratification.[13]

If the ERA was a defeat for liberal forces, conservatives have done no better. The school prayer amendment proposed in 2002 sought to restore power to the states to require selected religious observances, thereby reversing a whole series of earlier Supreme Court decisions.[14] The pro-life amendment proposed in 1981 sought to reverse *Roe v. Wade* in order to restore to the states the power to outlaw abortions. And Republicans have made frequent efforts to get Congress to adopt an amendment outlawing the burning or other desecration of the American flag. On four occasions—most recently in 2006—a resolution for a flag-burning amendment passed in the House of Representatives but never found enough support in the Senate. Republicans have also proposed an amendment to define marriage as a union of one man and one woman, but even some opponents of gay marriage are reluctant to change the Constitution to outlaw it.[15]

The Twenty-seven Amendments

All but two of the Constitution's twenty-seven amendments are concerned with the structure or composition of the government. This is consistent with the concept of a constitution as "higher law," because the whole point and purpose of a higher law is to establish a framework within which government and the process of making ordinary law can take place. Even those who would have preferred more changes in the Constitution would have to agree that there is great wisdom in this principle. A con-

---

[13]Marcia Lee, "The Equal Rights Amendment—Public Policy by Means of a Constitutional Amendment," in *The Politics of Policy Making in America*, ed. David Caputo (San Francisco: Freeman, 1977); Gilbert Steiner, *Constitutional Inequality: The Political Fortunes of ERA* (Washington, DC: Brookings Institution, 1985); and Jane Mansbridge, *Why We Lost the ERA* (Chicago: University of Chicago Press, 1986).

[14]For judicial action, see *Engel v. Vitale*, 370 U.S. 421 (1962). For the efforts of states to get around the Supreme Court requirement that public schools be secular, see John A. Murley, "School Prayer: Free Exercise of Religion or Establishment of Religion?" in *Social Regulatory Policy*, ed. Raymond Tatalovich and Byron Daynes (Boulder, Colo.: Westview Press, 1988), pp. 5–40.

[15]Evan Gerstmann, *Same Sex Marriage and the Constitution* (New York: Cambridge University Press, 2003).

TABLE 2.1 The Bill of Rights: Analysis of Its Provisions

Amendment	Purpose
I	*Limits on Congress:* Congress is not to make any law establishing a religion or abridging the freedom of speech, press, assembly, or the right to petition freedoms.
II, III, IV	*Limits on Executive:* The executive branch is not to infringe on the right of people to keep arms (II), is not to arbitrarily take houses for a militia (III), and is not to engage in the search or seizure of evidence without a court warrant swearing to a belief in the probable existence of a crime (IV).
V, VI, VII, VIII	*Limits on Courts:* The courts are not to hold trials for serious offenses without provision for a grand jury (V), a petit (trial) jury (VII), a speedy trial (VI), presentation of charges, confrontation of hostile witnesses (VI). Immunity from testimony against oneself (V), and immunity from trial more than once for the same offense (V). Neither bail nor punishment can be excessive (VIII), and no property can be taken without just compensation (V).
IX, X	*Limits on National Government:* All rights not enumerated are reserved to the states or the people.

stitution ought to enable legislation and public policies to take place, but it should not attempt to determine what that legislation or those policies ought to be.

The purpose of the ten amendments in the Bill of Rights was basically to give each of the three branches clearer and more restricted boundaries (see Table 2.1). The First Amendment clarified Congress's turf. Although the powers of Congress under Article I, Section 8, would not have justified laws regulating religion, speech, and the like, the First Amendment made this limitation explicit: "Congress shall make no law. . . . " The Second, Third, and Fourth Amendments similarly spelled out limits on the executive branch, a necessity given the abuses of executive power Americans had endured under British rule.

The Fifth, Sixth, Seventh, and Eighth Amendments contain some of the most important safeguards for individual citizens against the arbitrary exercise of government power. And these amendments sought to accomplish their goal by defining the judicial branch more concretely and clearly than had been done in Article III of the Constitution.

Five amendments adopted since 1791 are directly concerned with expansion of the electorate (see Table 2.2).[16] The founders were unable to establish a national electorate

---

[16]The Fourteenth Amendment is included in this table as well as in Tables 2.3 and 2.4 because it seeks not only to define citizenship but seems to intend also that this definition of citizenship included, along with the right to vote, all the rights of the Bill of Rights, regardless of the state in which the citizen resided. A great deal more will be said about this in Chapter 4.

TABLE 2.2 Amending the Constitution to Expand the Electorate

Amendment	Purpose	Year Proposed	Year Adopted
XIV	Section 1 provided national definition of citizenship*	1866	1868
XV	Extended voting rights to all races	1869	1870
XIX	Extended voting rights to women	1919	1920
XXIII	Extended voting rights to residents of the District of Columbia	1960	1961
XXIV	Extended voting rights to all classes by abolition of poll taxes	1962	1964
XXVI	Extended voting rights to citizens aged 18 and over	1971	1971

*In defining *citizenship*, the Fourteenth Amendment actually provided the constitutional basis for expanding the electorate to include all races, women, and residents of the District of Columbia. Only the "eighteen-year-olds' amendment" should have been necessary, since it changed the definition of citizenship. The fact that additional amendments were required after the Fourteenth suggests that voting is not considered an inherent right of U.S. citizenship. Instead, it is viewed as a privilege.

with uniform voting qualifications. They decided to evade the issue by providing in the final draft of Article I, Section 2, that eligibility to vote in a national election would be the same as "the Qualification requisite for Elector of the most numerous branch of the state Legislature." Article I, Section 4, added that Congress could alter state regulations as to the "Times, Places and Manner of holding Elections for Senators and Representatives," but this meant that any important expansion of the American electorate would almost certainly require a constitutional amendment.

Six more are also electoral in nature, although not concerned directly with voting rights and the expansion of the electorate. These six amendments are concerned with the elective offices themselves or with the relationship between elective offices and the electorate (see Table 2.3).

Another five have sought to expand or to limit the powers of the national and state governments (see Table 2.4). The Eleventh Amendment protected the states from suits by private individuals and took away from the federal courts any power to take suits by private individuals of one state (or a foreign country) against another state. The other three amendments in Table 2.4 are obviously designed to reduce state power (Thirteenth), to reduce state power and expand national power (Fourteenth), and to expand national power (Sixteenth). The Twenty-seventh put a moderate limit on Congress's ability to raise its own salary.

The Eighteenth, or Prohibition, Amendment underscores the meaning of the rest: This is the only amendment that the country used to try to *legislate*. In other

TABLE 2.3 Amending the Constitution to Change the Relationship between the Elected Offices and the Electorate

Amendment	Purpose	Year Proposed	Year Adopted
XII	Created separate ballot for vice president in the electoral college	1803	1804
XIV	Section 2 eliminated counting of slaves as "three-fifths" citizens for apportionment of House seats	1866	1868
XVII	Provided direct election of senators	1912	1913
XX	Eliminated "lame duck" session of Congress	1932	1933
XXII	Limited presidential term	1947	1951
XXV	Provided presidential succession in case of disability	1965	1967

words, it is the only amendment that was designed to deal directly with some substantive social problem. And it was the only amendment ever to have been repealed. Two other amendments—the Thirteenth, which abolished slavery, and the Sixteenth, which established the power to levy an income tax—can be said to have had the effect of legislation. But the purpose of the Thirteenth was to restrict the power of the states by forever forbidding them to treat any human being as property. As for the Sixteenth, it is certainly true that income tax legislation followed immediately; nevertheless, the amendment concerns itself strictly with establishing the power of Congress to enact such legislation. The legislation came later; and if down the line a majority in Congress had wanted to abolish the income tax, they could also have done this by legislation rather than through the arduous path of a constitutional amendment repealing the income tax.

DOES THE CONSTITUTION WORK?

The final product of the Constitutional Convention would have to be considered an extraordinary victory for those who wanted a new system of government to replace the Articles of Confederation. The new Constitution laid the groundwork for a government that would be sufficiently powerful to promote trade, to protect property, and to check the activities of radical state legislatures. Moreover, this new government was so constructed through internal checks and balances, indirect selection of officeholders, lifetime judicial appointments, and other similar provisions to preclude the "excessive democracy" feared by many of the founders. Some of the framers favored going even further in limiting popular influence, but the general

TABLE 2.4 Amending the Constitution to Expand or Limit the Power of Government

Amendment	Purpose	Year Proposed	Year Adopted
XI	Limited jurisdiction of federal courts over suits involving the states	1794	1798
XIII	Eliminated slavery and eliminated the right of states to allow property in persons	1865*	1865
XIV	(Part 2) Applied due process of Bill of Rights to the states	1866	1868
XVI	Established national power to tax incomes	1909	1913
XXVII	Limited Congress's power to raise its own salary	1789	1992

*The Thirteenth Amendment was proposed on 31 January 1865, and adopted less than a year later, on 18 December 1865.

consensus at the convention was that a thoroughly undemocratic document would never receive the popular approval needed to be ratified by the states.[17]

Though the Constitution was the product of a particular set of political forces, the principles of government it established have a significance that goes far beyond the interests of its authors. Two of these principles, federalism and civil liberties, will be discussed in Chapters 3 and 4. A third important constitutional principle that has affected America's government for the past two hundred years is the principle of checks and balances. As we saw earlier, the framers gave each of the three branches of government a means of intervening in and blocking the actions of the others. Often, checks and balances have seemed to prevent the government from getting much done. During the 1960s, for example, liberals were often infuriated as they watched Congress stall presidential initiatives in the area of civil rights. More recently, conservatives were outraged when President Clinton thwarted congressional efforts to enact legislation promised in the Republican "Contract with America." At various times, all sides have vilified the judiciary for invalidating legislation enacted by Congress and signed by the president.

Over time, checks and balances have acted as brakes on the governmental process. Groups hoping to bring about changes in policy or governmental institutions seldom have been able to bring about decisive and dramatic transformations in a short period of time. Instead, checks and balances have slowed the pace of change and increased the need for compromise and accommodation.

Groups able to take control of the White House, for example, must negotiate with their rivals who remain entrenched on Capitol Hill. New forces in Congress

---

[17]See Farrand, *The Records of the Federal Convention*, vol. 1, p. 132.

must reckon with the influence of other forces in the executive branch and in the courts. Checks and balances inevitably frustrate those who desire change, but they also function as a safeguard against rash action. During the 1950s, for example, Congress was caught up in a nearly hysterical effort to unmask subversive activities in the United States, which might have led to a serious erosion of American liberties if not for the checks and balances provided by the executive branch and the courts. Thus, a governmental principle that serves as a frustrating limitation one day may become a vitally important safeguard the next.

Yet, while the Constitution sought to lay the groundwork for a powerful government, the framers struggled to reconcile government power with freedom. The framers surrounded the powerful institutions of the new regime with a variety of safeguards—a continual array of checks and balances—designed to make certain that the power of the national government could not be used to undermine the states' power and their citizens' freedoms. Thus, the framers were the first Americans to confront head on the dilemma of coercion and power that we discussed briefly in Chapter 1. Whether their solutions to this dilemma were successful is the topic of the remainder of our chapters.

To Whose Benefit?

Of course, the groups whose interests were served by the Constitution in 1789, mainly the merchants and planters, are not the same groups that benefit from the Constitution's provisions today. Once incorporated into the law, political principles often take on lives of their own and have consequences that were never anticipated by their original champions. Indeed, many of the groups that benefit from constitutional provisions today did not even exist in 1789. Who would have thought that the principle of free speech would influence the transmission of data on the Internet? Who would have predicted that commercial interests that once sought a powerful government might come, two centuries later, to denounce governmental activism as "socialistic"? Perhaps one secret of the Constitution's longevity is that it did not confer permanent advantage upon any one set of economic or social forces.

Although they were defeated in 1789, the Antifederalists present us with an important picture of a road not taken and of an America that might have been. Would the country have been worse off if it had been governed by a confederacy of small republics linked by a national administration with severely limited powers? Were the Antifederalists correct in predicting that a government given great power in the hope that it might do good would, through "insensible progress," inevitably turn to evil purposes? Two hundred years of government under the federal Constitution are not necessarily enough to definitively answer these questions. Time must tell.

To What Ends?

The Constitution's framers placed individual liberty ahead of all other political values. Their concern for liberty led many of the framers to distrust both democracy and equality. They feared that democracy could degenerate into a majority tyranny in which the populace, perhaps led by a rabble-rousing demagogue, would trample on liberty. As to equality, the framers were products of their time and place; our contemporary ideas of racial and gender equality would have been foreign to them. The framers were concerned primarily with another manifestation of equality: They feared that those without property or position might be driven by what some called a "leveling spirit" to infringe upon liberty in the name of greater economic or social equality. Indeed, the framers believed that this leveling spirit was most likely to produce demagoguery and majority tyranny. As a result, the basic structure of the Constitution—separated powers, internal checks and balances, and federalism—was designed to safeguard liberty, and the Bill of Rights created further safeguards for liberty. At the same time, however, many of the Constitution's other key provisions, such as indirect election of senators and the president, as well as the appointment of judges for life, were designed to limit democracy and, hence, the threat of majority tyranny.

By championing liberty, however, the framers virtually guaranteed that democracy and even a measure of equality would sooner or later evolve in the United States. For liberty inevitably leads to the growth of political activity and the expansion of political participation. In James Madison's famous phrase, "Liberty is to faction as air is to fire."[18] Where they have liberty, more and more people, groups, and interests will almost inevitably engage in politics and gradually overcome whatever restrictions might have been placed upon participation. This is precisely what happened in the early years of the American Republic. During the Jeffersonian period, political parties formed. During the Jacksonian period, many state suffrage restrictions were removed and popular participation greatly expanded. Over time, liberty is conducive to democracy.

Liberty does not guarantee that everyone will be equal. It does, however, reduce the threat of inequality in one very important way. Historically, the greatest inequalities of wealth, power, and privilege have arisen where governments have used their power to allocate status and opportunity among individuals or groups. The most extreme cases of inequality are associated with the most tyrannical regimes. In the United States, however, by promoting a democratic politics, over time liberty unleashed forces that militated against inequality. As a result, over the past two hundred years, groups that have learned to use the political process have achieved important economic and social gains.

One limitation of liberty as a political principle, however, is that the idea of limits upon government action can also inhibit effective government. Take one of the basic tasks of government, the protection of citizens' lives and property. A government limited by concerns over the rights of those accused of crimes may be limited in its ability to maintain public order. Recently, the U.S. government has asserted that protecting the nation against terrorists requires law enforcement measures that seem at odds with legal and constitutional formalities. The conflict between liberty

---

[18]E. M. Earle, ed., *The Federalist* (New York: Modern Library, 1937), No. 10.

ONLINE READING

and governmental effectiveness is another tension at the heart of the American constitutional system.

CHAPTER REVIEW

Political conflicts between the colonies and England, and among competing groups within the colonies, led to the first Founding as expressed by the Declaration of Independence. The first constitution, the Articles of Confederation, was adopted one year later (1777). Under this document, the states retained their sovereignty. The central government, composed solely of Congress, had few powers and no means of enforcing its will. The national government's weakness soon led to the second Founding as expressed by the Constitution of 1787.

In this second Founding, the framers sought, first, to fashion a new government sufficiently powerful to promote commerce and protect property from radical state legislatures. Second, they sought to bring an end to the "excessive democracy" of the state and national governments under the Articles of Confederation. Third, they sought to introduce mechanisms that would secure popular consent for the new government. Finally, the framers sought to make certain that their new government would not itself pose a threat to liberty and property.

The Constitution consists of seven articles. In part, Article I provides for a Congress of two chambers (Sections 1–7), defines the powers of the national government (Section 8), and interprets the national government's powers as a source of strength rather than a limitation (necessary and proper clause). Article II describes the presidency and establishes it as a separate branch of government. Article III is the judiciary article. While there is no direct mention of judicial review in this article, the Supreme Court eventually assumed that power. Article IV addresses reciprocity among states and their citizens. Article V describes the procedures for amending the Constitution. Thousands of amendments have been offered but only twenty-seven have been adopted. With the exception of the two Prohibition amendments, all amendments were oriented toward some change in the framework or structure of government. Article VI establishes that national laws and treaties are "the supreme law of the land." And finally, Article VII specifies the procedure for ratifying the Constitution of 1787.

FOR FURTHER READING

Amar, Akhil Reed. *America's Constitution: A Biography*. New York: Random House, 2005.

Bailyn, Bernard. *The Ideological Origins of the American Revolution*. Cambridge, Mass.: Harvard University Press, 1967.

Beard, Charles A. *An Economic Interpretation of the Constitution of the United States*. New York: Macmillan, 1913.

Breyer, Stephen. *Active Liberty: Interpreting our Democratic Constitution*. New York: Knopf, 2005.

Chernow, Ron. *Alexander Hamilton*. New York: Penguin, 2004.

Ellis, Joseph. *Founding Brothers: The Revolutionary Generation*. New York: Knopf, 2000.

———. *His Excellency, George Washington*. New York: Knopf, 2004.

Farrand, Max, ed. *The Records of the Federal Convention of 1787.* Rev. ed. 4 vols. New Haven, Conn.: Yale University Press, 1966.

ONLINE READING ○ Hamilton, Alexander, James Madison, and John Jay. *The Federalist Papers.* Ed. Isaac Kramnick. New York: Viking Press, 1987.

Riker, William H. *The Strategy of Rhetoric: Campaigning for the American Constitution.* New Haven, Conn.: Yale University Press, 1996.

ONLINE READING ○ Storing, Herbert J., ed. *The Complete Anti-Federalist.* 7 vols. Chicago: University of Chicago Press, 1981.

Federalism and the
Separation of Powers

CHAPTER

3

HOW DO FEDERALISM AND THE SEPARATION OF POWERS WORK AS POLITICAL INSTITUTIONS?

Two of the most important elements of the American Constitution are federalism and the separation of powers. Federalism seeks to limit government by dividing it into two levels, national and state, each with sufficient independence, or sovereignty, to compete with the other, thereby restraining the power of both.[1] The separation of powers seeks to limit the power of the national government by dividing government against itself—by giving the legislative, executive, and judicial branches separate functions, thus forcing them to share power.

These two features of American's institutional structure have important consequences for politics and policy in the United States. Federalism means that the national government is not the only significant decision-making body in America. The fifty individual states are not agencies of the national government but instead have a good deal of power in their own rights. The separation of powers means that within the national government there is no neat decision-making hierarchy. Each of the three branches of government exercises power over the other two. Both federalism and the separation of powers complicate policy making in the United States. If governmental power were arranged neatly and simply in a single hierarchy, decisions could certainly be made more easily and more efficiently. But would they be better decisions? The framers thought that complexity, multiple checks, and institutionalized second-guessing while messy, would allow more interests to have a voice and would eventually produce better results. And along the way, messy decision processes might preserve liberty and prevent tyranny.

Institutional arrangements such as federalism and the separation of powers are part *script* and part *scorecard*. As two of the most important features of the

---

[1] The notion that federalism requires separate spheres of jurisdictions in which lower and higher levels of government are uniquely decisive is developed fully in William H. Riker, *Federalism: Origin, Operation, Significance* (Boston: Little, Brown, 1964). This American version of federalism is applied to the emerging federal arrangements in the People's Republic of China during the 1990s in a paper by Barry R. Weingast, "The Economic Role of Political Institutions: Market-Preserving Federalism and Economic Development," *Journal of Law, Economics, and Organization* 11 (1995): 1–32.

> ● **Core of the Analysis**
>
> ● Federalism limits national power by creating two sovereigns: the national government and the state governments.
>
> ● Under "dual federalism," which lasted from 1789 to 1937, the national government limited itself primarily to promoting commerce, while the state governments directly coerced citizens.
>
> ● After 1937, the national government exerted more influence, yet the states maintained many of their traditional powers.
>
> ● Checks and balances ensure the sharing of power among separate institutions of government. Within the system of separated powers, the framers of the Constitution provided for legislative supremacy.

constitutional structure, federalism and the separation of powers serve to channel and constrain political agents, first by limiting their jurisdictional authority and second by pitting them against one another as political competitors.

The amazing thing about these American political institutions is that they are not carved in granite (even if the official buildings that house them are!). While the Constitution initially set a broad framework for the division of authority between the national government and the states, and the division of labor among the branches of the national government, much adaptation and innovation took place as these institutions themselves were bent to the purposes of various political players. Politicians are goal-oriented and are constantly exploring the possibilities provided them by their institutional positions and political situations. As we shall see in this chapter, the Supreme Court has also been a central player in settling the ongoing debate over how power should be divided between the national government and the states and between Congress and the president.

FEDERALISM

Federalism can be defined as the division of powers and functions between the national government and the state governments. As we saw in Chapter 2, the states existed as former colonies before independence, and for nearly thirteen years they were virtually autonomous units under the Articles of Confederation. In effect, the states had retained too much power under the Articles, a problem that led directly to the Annapolis Convention in 1786 and the Constitutional Convention in 1787. Under the Articles, disorder within states was beyond the reach of the national government, and conflicts of interest between states were not manageable. For example, states were making their own trade agreements with foreign countries and companies, which might then play one state against another for special advantages. Some states adopted special trade tariffs, and further barriers to foreign commerce that were contrary to the interests of another

federalism System of government in which power is divided by a constitution between a central government and regional governments (in the United States, between the national government and state governments).

state.[2] Tax and other barriers were also being erected between the states.[3] But even after the ratification of the Constitution, the states continued to be more important than the national government. For nearly a century and a half, virtually all of the fundamental policies governing the lives of American citizens were made by the state legislatures, not by Congress.

Federalism in the Constitution

The United States was the first nation to adopt federalism as its governing framework. With federalism, the framers sought to limit the national government by creating a second layer of state governments. American federalism recognized two sovereigns in the original Constitution and reinforced the principle in the Bill of Rights by granting a few ***expressed powers*** to the national government and reserving all the rest to the states.

The Powers of the National Government   As we saw in Chapter 2, the expressed powers granted to the national government are found in Article I, Section 8, of the Constitution. These seventeen powers include the power to collect taxes, to coin money, to declare war, and to regulate commerce (which, as we will see, became a very important power for the national government). Article I, Section 8, also contains another important source of power for the national government: the ***implied powers*** that enable Congress "to make all Laws which shall be necessary and proper for carrying into Execution the foregoing Powers." Not until several decades after the founding did the Supreme Court allow Congress to exercise the power granted in this ***necessary and proper clause,*** but, as we shall see later in this chapter, this doctrine allowed the national government to expand considerably the scope of its authority, although the process was a slow one. In addition to these expressed and implied powers, the Constitution affirmed the power of the national government in the supremacy clause (Article VI), which made all national laws and treaties "the supreme Law of the Land."

The Powers of State Government   One way in which the framers sought to preserve a strong role for the states was through the Tenth Amendment to the Constitution. The Tenth Amendment states that the powers that the Constitution does not delegate to the national government or prohibit to the states are "reserved to the States respectively, or to the people." The Antifederalists, who feared that a strong central government would encroach on individual liberty, repeatedly pressed for such an amendment as a way of limiting national power. Federalists agreed to the amendment because they did not think it would do much harm, given the powers of the Constitution already granted to the national government. The Tenth Amendment is also called the ***reserved powers*** amendment because it aims to reserve powers to the states.

expressed powers (Congress) Specific powers granted to Congress under Article I, Section 8, of the Constitution.

implied powers Powers derived from the necessary and proper clause of Article I, Section 8, of the Constitution. Such powers are not specifically expressed but are implied through the expansive interpretation of delegated powers.

necessary and proper clause From Article I, Section 8, of the Constitution, it provides Congress with the authority to make all laws "necessary and proper" to carry out its expressed powers.

reserved powers Powers, derived from the Tenth Amendment of the Constitution, that are not specifically delegated to the national government or denied to the states.

---

[2]For a good treatment of these conflicts of interests between states, see Forrest McDonald, *E Pluribus Unum—The Formation of the American Republic, 1776–1790* (Boston: Houghton Mifflin, 1965), Chapter 7, especially pp. 319–38.

[3]See David O'Brien, *Constitutional Law and Politics,* vol. 1 (New York: Norton, 1997), pp. 602–3.

The most fundamental power that is retained by the states is that of coercion—the power to develop and enforce criminal codes, to administer health and safety rules, to regulate the family via marriage and divorce laws. The states have the power to regulate individuals' livelihoods; if you're a doctor or a lawyer or a plumber or a barber, you must be licensed by the state. Even more fundamentally, the states have the power to define private property—private property exists because state laws against trespassing define who is and is not entitled to use a piece of property. If you own a car, your ownership isn't worth much unless the state is willing to enforce your right to possession by making it a crime for anyone else to take your car. These are fundamental matters, and the powers of the states regarding these domestic issues are much greater than the powers of the national government, even today.

A state's authority to regulate these fundamental matters is commonly referred to as the ***police power*** of the state and encompasses the state's power to regulate the health, safety, welfare, and morals of its citizens. Policing is what states do—they coerce you in the name of the community in order to maintain public order. And this was exactly the type of power that the founders intended the states to exercise.

In some areas, the states share ***concurrent powers*** with the national government, wherein they retain and share some power to regulate commerce and to affect the currency—for example, by being able to charter banks, grant or deny corporate charters, grant or deny licenses to engage in a business or practice a trade, and regulate the quality of products or the conditions of labor. This issue of concurrent versus exclusive power has come up from time to time in our history, but wherever there is a direct conflict of laws between the federal and the state levels, the issue will most likely be resolved in favor of national supremacy.

State Obligations to One Another   The Constitution also creates obligations among the states. These obligations, spelled out in Article IV, were intended to promote national unity. By requiring the states to recognize actions and decisions taken in other states as legal and proper, the framers aimed to make the states less like independent countries and more like parts of a single nation.

Article IV, Section 1, calls for "Full Faith and Credit" among states, meaning that each state is normally expected to honor the "public Acts, Records, and judicial Proceedings" that take place in any other state. So, for example, if a couple is married in Texas—marriage being regulated by state law—Missouri must also recognize that marriage, even though they were not married under Missouri state law.

This ***full faith and credit clause*** has recently become embroiled in the controversy over same-sex marriage. In 1993, the Hawaii Supreme Court prohibited discrimination against same-sex marriage except in very limited circumstances. Many observers believed that Hawaii would eventually fully legalize gay marriage. In fact, after a long political battle, Hawaii passed a constitutional amendment in 1998 outlawing gay marriage. However, in December 1999, the Vermont Supreme Court ruled that gay couples should have the same rights as heterosexuals. The Vermont legislature responded with a new law that allowed gays to form "civil unions." Although not legally considered marriages, such unions allow same-sex couples most of the benefits of marriage, such as eligibility for the partner's health insurance, inheritance rights, and the right to transfer property. The Vermont statute and similar

police power Power reserved to the state to regulate the health, safety, and morals of its citizens.

concurrent powers Authority possessed by *both* state and national governments, such as the power to levy taxes.

full faith and credit clause Article IV, Section 1, of the Constitution provides that each state must accord the same respect to the laws and judicial decisions of other states that it accords to its own.

measures passed in Massachusetts and Connecticut could have broad implications for other states. More than thirty-five states have passed "defense of marriage acts" that define marriage as a union between men and women only. In 1996, Congress passed the Defense of Marriage Act, which declared that states will *not* have to recognize a same-sex marriage, even if it is legal in one state. The act also said that the federal government will not recognize gay marriage—even if it is legal under state law—and that gay marriage partners will not be eligible for the federal benefits, such as Medicare and Social Security, normally available to spouses.[4]

In 2004, a presidential election year, Alabama, Georgia, Kentucky, Michigan, Montana, North Dakota, Ohio, Oklahoma, and Utah approved state constitutional amendments strictly defining marriage as between a man and a woman. This large-scale approval of such amendments was probably prompted by a Massachusetts court decision permitting same-sex couples to wed, which was to go into effect in May 2004. In March 2005 a ruling by the San Francisco Superior Court said that California's state law banning same-sex marriage was a violation of the rights of gay men and lesbians. This ruling also nullified the state's Proposition 22, approved by referendum in 2000, limiting marriage to one man and one woman. These developments put fire back into President George W. Bush's pledge to support a constitutional amendment banning same-sex marriage, even though polls have shown substantial majorities favoring some form of same-sex union, whether marriage or "civil union."[5] In 2008, high courts in California and Connecticut ruled in favor of gay marriage. However, California voters overturned this ruling in November 2008 by voting to amend the state constitution. California was one of three states to pass ballot measures banning gay marriage in 2008, and the debate seemed certain to continue at the state and national levels.

Because of this controversy, the extent and meaning of the full faith and credit clause are sure to be considered by the Supreme Court. In fact, it is not clear that the clause requires states to recognize gay marriage because the Court's past interpretation of the clause has provided exceptions for "public policy" reasons: If states have strong objections to a law, they do not have to honor it. In 1997 the Court took up a case involving the full faith and credit clause. The case concerned a Michigan court order that prevented a former engineer for General Motors from testifying against the company. The engineer, who left the company on bad terms, later testified in a Missouri court about a car accident in which a woman died when her Chevrolet Blazer caught fire. General Motors challenged his right to testify, arguing that Missouri should give "full faith and credit" to the Michigan ruling. The Supreme Court ruled that the engineer could testify and that the court system in one state cannot hinder other state courts in their "search for the truth."[6]

---

[4]Ken I. Kersch, "Full Faith and Credit for Same-Sex Marriages?" *Political Science Quarterly* 112 (Spring 1997): 117–36; Joan Biskupic, "Once Unthinkable, Now under Debate," *Washington Post*, 3 September 1996, p. A1.

[5]This is a peculiar, albeit effective distinction because all marriages are "civil unions"—and nothing else.

[6]Linda Greenhouse, "Supreme Court Weaves Legal Principles from a Tangle of Legislation," *New York Times*, 30 June 1988, p. A20.

Article IV, Section 2, known as the "comity clause," also seeks to promote national unity. It provides that citizens enjoying the ***privileges and immunities*** of one state should be entitled to similar treatment in other states. What this has come to mean is that a state cannot discriminate against someone from another state or give special privileges to its own residents. For example, in the 1970s, when Alaska passed a law that gave residents preference over nonresidents in obtaining work on the state's oil and gas pipelines, the Supreme Court ruled the law illegal because it discriminated against citizens of other states.[7] This clause also regulates criminal justice among the states by requiring states to return fugitives to the states from which they have fled. Thus, in 1952, when an inmate escaped from an Alabama prison and sought to avoid being returned to Alabama on the grounds that he was being subjected to "cruel and unusual punishment" there, the Supreme Court ruled that he must be returned according to Article IV, Section 2.[8] This example highlights the difference between the obligations among states and those among different countries. In 1997, France refused to return an American fugitive because he might be subject to the death penalty, which does not exist in France.[9] The Constitution clearly forbids states from doing something similar.

States' relationships to one another are also governed by the interstate compact clause (Article I, Section 10), which states that "No State shall, without the Consent of Congress . . . enter into any Agreement or Compact with another State." The Court has interpreted the clause to mean that states may enter into agreements with one another, subject to congressional approval. Compacts are a way for two or more states to reach a legally binding agreement about how to solve a problem that crosses state lines. In the early years of the Republic, states turned to compacts primarily to settle border disputes. Today they are used for a wide range of issues but are especially important in regulating the distribution of river water, addressing environmental concerns, and operating transportation systems that cross state lines.[10]

Local Government and the Constitution   Local government occupies a peculiar but very important place in the American system. In fact, the status of American local government is probably unique in world experience. First, it must be pointed out that local government has no status in the American Constitution. *State* legislatures created local governments, and *state* constitutions and laws permit local governments to take on some of the responsibilities of the state governments. Most states amended their own constitutions to give their larger cities ***home rule***—a guarantee of noninterference in various areas of local affairs. But local governments enjoy no

privileges and immunities clause Provision from Article IV, Section 2, of the Constitution that a state cannot discriminate against someone from another state or give its own residents special privileges.

home rule Power delegated by the state to a local unit of government to manage its own affairs.

---

[7] *Hicklin v. Orbeck*, 437 U.S. 518 (1978).

[8] *Sweeny v. Woodall*, 344 U.S. 86 (1953).

[9] Marlise Simons, "France Won't Extradite American Convicted of Murder," *New York Times*, 5 December 1997, p. A9.

[10] Patricia S. Florestano, "Past and Present Utilization of Interstate Compacts in the United States," *Publius* 24 (Fall 1994): 13–26.

such recognition in the Constitution. Local governments have always been mere conveniences of the states.[11]

Local governments became administratively important in the early years of the Republic because the states possessed little administrative capability. They relied on local governments—cities and counties—to implement the laws of the state. Local government was an alternative to a statewide bureaucracy.

The Slow Growth of the National Government's Power

Before the 1930s, America's federal system was one of ***dual federalism***, a two-layered system—national and state—in which the states and their local principalities do most of the governing. This arrangement is demonstrated in Table 3.1. The items in each column (disregarding the local-level functions discussed in the previous section) are the important types of public policies that governed America for the first century and a half under the Constitution. We refer to it here as the traditional system precisely because almost nothing about our pattern of government changed during two thirds of our history. That is, of course, with the exception of the four years of the Civil War, after which we returned to the traditional system.

But there was more to dual federalism than merely the existence of two tiers. The two tiers were functionally quite different from each other. There have been debates every generation over how to divide responsibilities between the two tiers. As we have seen in this chapter, the Constitution delegated a list of specific powers to the national government and reserved all the rest to the states. That left a lot of room for interpretation, however, because of the final "elastic" clause of Article I, Section 8. The three formal words *necessary and proper* amounted to an invitation to struggle over the distribution of powers between national and state governments. We shall confront this struggle throughout the book. However, the most remarkable thing about the history of American federalism is that federalism remained dual for nearly two thirds of that history, with the national government remaining steadfastly within a "strict construction" of Article I, Section 8. The results are clear in Table 3.1.

The best example of the potential elasticity in Article I, Section 8, is in the ***commerce clause***, which delegates to Congress the power "to regulate Commerce with foreign Nations, and *among the several States* and with the Indian tribes" [emphasis added]. It is obvious that this clause can be interpreted broadly or narrowly, and in fact the Supreme Court embraced the broad interpretation throughout most of the nineteenth century. Yet Congress chose not to take the Court's invitation to be expansive. The first and most important case favoring national power was *McCulloch v. Maryland*.[12] The issue was whether Congress had the power to charter a bank, in particular the Bank of the United States (created by Congress in 1791 over Thomas

dual federalism The system of government that prevailed in the United States from 1789 to 1937 in which most fundamental governmental powers were shared between the federal and state governments.

commerce clause Article 1, Section 8, of the Constitution delegates to Congress the power "to regulate commerce with Foreign nations, and among the several States and with the Indian tribes. . . ." The Supreme Court interpreted this clause in favor of national power over the economy.

---

[11]A good discussion of the constitutional position of local governments is in York Y. Willbern, *The Withering Away of the City* (Bloomington: Indiana University Press, 1971). For more on the structure and theory of federalism, see Thomas R. Dye, *American Federalism: Competition among Governments* (Lexington, Mass.: Lexington Books, 1990), Chapter 1; and Martha Derthick, "Up-to-Date in Kansas City: Reflections on American Federalism," *PS: Political Science & Politics* 25 (December 1992): 671–75.

[12]*McCulloch v. Maryland*, 4 Wheaton 316 (1819).

○ ONLINE READING

TABLE 3.1 The Federal System: Specialization of Governmental Functions in the Traditional System, 1789–1937

National Government Policies (Domestic)	State Government Policies	Local Government Policies
Internal improvements	Property laws (including slavery)	Adaptation of state laws to local conditions (variances)
Subsidies	Estate and inheritance laws	Public works
Tariffs	Commerce laws	Contracts for public works
Public lands disposal	Banking and credit laws	Licensing of public accommodations
Patents	Corporate laws	Assessable improvements
Currency	Insurance laws	Basic public services
	Family laws	
	Morality laws	
	Public health laws	
	Education laws	
	General penal laws	
	Eminent domain laws	
	Construction codes	
	Land-use laws	
	Water and mineral laws	
	Criminal procedure laws	
	Electoral and political party laws	
	Local government laws	
	Civil service laws	
	Occupations and professions laws	

Jefferson's constitutional opposition), because no power to create banks was found anywhere in Article I, Section 8. Chief Justice John Marshall, speaking for the Supreme Court, answered that such a power could be "implied" from the other specific powers in Article I, Section 8, plus the final clause enabling Congress "to make all Laws which shall be necessary and proper for carrying into Execution the foregoing Powers." Thus the Court created the potential for significant increases in national governmental power.

A second question of national power arose in *McCulloch v. Maryland:* the question of whether Maryland's attempt to tax the bank was constitutional. Once again Marshall and the Supreme Court took the side of the national government, arguing that a legislature representing all the people (Congress) could not be taxed out of business by a state legislature (Maryland) representing only a small portion of the American people. This opinion was accompanied by Marshall's immortal dictum that "the power to tax is the power to destroy." It was also in this case that the Supreme Court recognized and reinforced the supremacy clause: Whenever a state law conflicts with a federal law, the state law should be deemed invalid because "the Laws of the United States . . . shall be the supreme Law of the Land." (This concept was introduced in Chapter 2 and will come up again in Chapter 8.)

This nationalistic interpretation of the Constitution was reinforced by another major case, that of *Gibbons v. Ogden* in 1824. The important but relatively narrow issue was whether the state of New York could grant a monopoly to Robert Fulton's steamboat company to operate an exclusive service between New York and New Jersey. Aaron Ogden had secured his license from Fulton's company, while Thomas Gibbons, a former partner of Ogden's, secured a competing license from the U.S. government. Chief Justice Marshall argued that Gibbons could not be kept from competing because the state of New York did not have the power to grant this particular monopoly. To reach his decision, it was necessary for Marshall to define what Article I, Section 8, meant by "Commerce . . . among the several States." Marshall insisted that the definition was "comprehensive" but added that the comprehensiveness was limited "to that commerce which concerns more states than one." This opinion gave rise to what later came to be called interstate commerce.[13]

Although *Gibbons* was an important case, the precise meaning of interstate commerce would remain uncertain for several decades of constitutional discourse. However, one thing was certain: "Interstate commerce" was a source of power for the national government as long as Congress sought to improve commerce through subsidies, services, and land grants (Table 3.1, col. 1). Later in the nineteenth century, when the national government sought to use its power to *regulate* the economy rather than merely promote economic development, the concept of interstate commerce began to operate as a restraint rather than as a source of national power. Any effort by the federal government to regulate commerce in such areas as fraud, the production of impure goods, the use of child labor, or the existence of dangerous working conditions or long hours was declared unconstitutional by the Supreme Court as a violation of the concept of interstate commerce. Regulation in these areas would mean the federal government was entering the factory and the workplace, areas inherently local because the goods produced there had not yet passed into commerce and crossed state lines. Any effort to enter these local workplaces was an exercise of police power, a power reserved to the states. No one questioned the power of the national government to regulate certain kinds of businesses, such as railroads, gas pipelines, and waterway transportation, because

---

[13]*Gibbons v. Ogden*, 9 Wheaton 1 (1824).

they intrinsically involved interstate commerce.[14] But well into the twentieth century, most other efforts by Congress to regulate commerce were blocked by the Supreme Court's interpretation of federalism, with the concept of interstate commerce as the primary barrier.

After 1937, the Supreme Court threw out the old distinction between interstate and intrastate commerce, converting the commerce clause from a barrier to a source of power. The Court began to refuse even to review appeals challenging acts of Congress that protected the rights of employees to organize and engage in collective bargaining, regulated the amount of farmland in cultivation, extended low-interest credit to small businesses and farmers, and restricted the activities of corporations dealing in the stock market, as well as many other laws that contributed to the construction of the "regulatory state" and the "welfare state."

Cooperative Federalism and Grants-in-Aid

If the traditional system of two sovereigns performing highly different functions could be called dual federalism, the system since the 1930s could be called ***cooperative federalism,*** which generally refers to supportive relations, sometimes partnerships, between national government and the state and local governments. It comes in the form of federal subsidization of special state and local activities; these subsidies are called ***grants-in-aid.*** But make no mistake about it: Although many of these state and local programs would not exist without the federal grant-in-aid, the grant-in-aid is also an important form of federal influence. (Another form of federal influence, the mandate, will be covered in the next section.)

A grant-in-aid is really a kind of bribe or "carrot"—Congress gives money to state and local governments, but with the condition that the money will be spent for a particular purpose as designed by Congress. Congress uses grants-in-aid because it does not usually have the political or constitutional power to command the cities to do its bidding directly.

This same approach was applied to cities beginning in the late 1930s. Congress set national goals such as public housing and assistance to the unemployed and provided grants-in-aid to meet these goals. The value of these ***categorical grants-in-aid*** increased from $2.3 billion in 1950 to $466.6 billion in 2008 (see Figure 3.1). Sometimes Congress requires the state or local government to match the national contribution dollar for dollar; but for some programs, such as the interstate highway system, the congressional grant-in-aid provides 90 percent of the cost of the program.

For the most part, the categorical grants created before the 1960s simply helped the states perform their traditional functions.[15] In the 1960s, however, the national role expanded and the number of categorical grants increased dramati-

---

cooperative federalism A type of federalism existing since the New Deal era in which grants-in-aid have been used strategically to encourage states and localities (without commanding them) to pursue nationally defined goals. Also known as intergovernmental cooperation.

grants-in-aid A general term for funds given by Congress to state and local governments.

categorical grants-in-aid Grants by Congress to states and localities, given with the condition that expenditures be limited to a problem or group specified by the national government.

---

[14]In *Wabash, St. Louis, and Pacific Railway Company v. Illinois,* 118 U.S. 557 (1886), the Supreme Court struck down a state law prohibiting rate discrimination by a railroad; in response, Congress passed the Interstate Commerce Act of 1887, creating the Interstate Commerce Commission (ICC), the first federal regulatory agency.

[15]Kenneth T. Palmer, "The Evolution of Grant Policies," in *The Changing Politics of Federal Grants,* by Lawrence D. Brown, James W. Fossett, and Kenneth T. Palmer (Washington, D.C.: Brookings Institution, 1984) p. 15.

FIGURE 3.1 The Historical Trend of Federal Grants-in-Aid, 1950–2008*

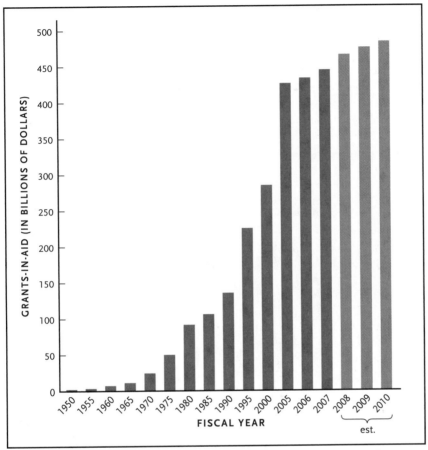

*Excludes outlays for national defense, international affairs, and net interest. 2008, 2009, and 2010 are estimates.

SOURCE: Office of Management and Budget, *Budget of the U.S. Government, Fiscal Year 2008, Analytical Perspectives* (Washington, D.C.: Government Printing Office, 2007).

cally. For example, during the Eighty-ninth Congress (1965–1966) alone, the number of categorical grant-in-aid programs grew from 221 to 379.[16] The grants authorized during the 1960s announced national purposes much more strongly than did earlier grants. Central to that national purpose was the need to provide opportunities to the poor.

Many of the categorical grants enacted during the 1960s were ***project grants,*** which require state and local governments to submit proposals to federal agencies. In contrast to the older ***formula grants,*** which used a formula (composed of such elements as need and state and local capacities) to distribute funds, the new project

project grants Grant programs in which state and local governments submit proposals to federal agencies and for which funding is provided on a competitive basis.

formula grants Grants-in-aid in which a formula is used to determine the amount of federal funds a state or local government will receive.

[16]Ibid., p. 6.

FIGURE 3.2 Evolving Federalism

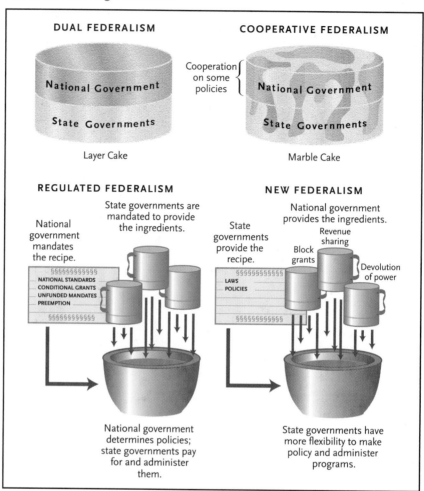

grants made funding available on a competitive basis. Federal agencies would give grants to the proposals they judged to be the best. In this way, the national government acquired substantial control over which state and local governments got money, how much they got, and how they spent it.

The most important scholar of the history of federalism, Morton Grodzins, characterized this as a move from "layer cake federalism" to "marble cake federalism" in which intergovernmental cooperation and sharing have blurred the line between where the national government ends and the state and local governments begin (see Figure 3.2).[17] Figure 3.3 demonstrates the financial basis of the marble

---

[17]Morton Grodzins, "The Federal System," in *Goals for Americans*, President's Commission on National Goals (Englewood Cliffs, N.J.: Prentice Hall, 1960), p. 265. In a marble cake, the white cake is distinguishable from the chocolate cake, but the two are streaked rather than in distinct layers.

FIGURE 3.3 The Rise, Decline, and Recovery of Federal Aid

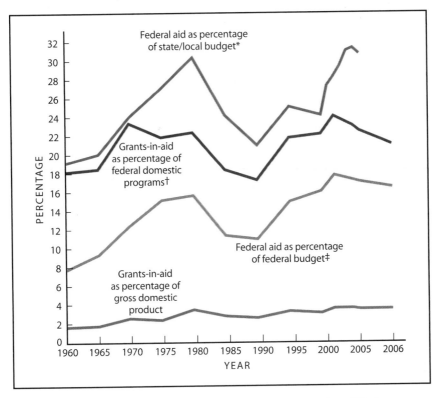

SOURCES: Office of Management and Budget, *Budget of the U.S. Government, Fiscal Year 2008, An-alytical Perspectives* (Washington, D.C.: Government Printing Office, 2006), table 8.3, p. 131; U.S. Bureau of the Census, *Statistical Abstract of the United States, 2007* (Washington, D.C.: Government Printing Office, 2007), table 421.

*Federal aid as a percentage of state and local expenditures after transfers.

†Federal aid as a percentage of federal expenditures from the federal government's own funds.

‡Excludes outlays for national defense, international affairs, and net interest.

cake idea. At the high point of grant-in-aid policies in the late 1970s, federal aid contributed about 25–30 percent of the operating budgets of all the state and local governments in the country. Table 3.2 represents federal aid to America's ten largest cities, which was significantly lower by 2004.

Regulated Federalism and National Standards Developments from the 1960s to the present have moved well beyond marble cake federalism to what might be called ***regulated federalism***.[18] In some areas the national government actually regulates the states by threatening to withhold grant money unless state and local govern-

regulated federalism
A form of federalism in which Congress imposes legislation on the states and localities requiring them to meet national standards.

---

[18]The concept and the best discussion of this modern phenomenon will be found in Donald F. Kettl, *The Regulation of American Federalism* (Baltimore: Johns Hopkins University Press, 1983 and 1987), especially pp. 33–41.

○ ONLINE READING

TABLE 3.2 Federal Aid to Cities

Federal aid as a percentage of general annual revenue in the nation's 10 largest cities, 2004			
New York	5.2	Phoenix	17.4
Los Angeles	4.6	San Antonio	3.1
Chicago	8.5	San Diego	10.5
Houston	6.6	Dallas	3.0
Philadelphia	14.7	San Jose	2.5

Source: U.S. Bureau of the Census, *Statistical Abstract of the United States, 2007* (Washington, D.C.: Government Printing Office, 2007), table 446.

ments conform to national standards. The most notable instances of this regulation are in the areas of civil rights, poverty programs, and environmental protection. In these instances, the national government provides grant-in-aid financing but sets conditions the states must meet in order to keep the grants. The national government refers to these policies as "setting national standards." Important cases of such efforts are in interstate highway use, in social services, and in education. The net effect of these national standards is that state and local policies are more uniform from coast to coast. However, there are a number of other programs in which the national government engages in regulated federalism by imposing obligations on the states *without providing any funding at all.* These have come to be called **unfunded mandates.**[19] States complained that mandates took up so much of their budgets that they were not able to set their own priorities.

These burdens became a major part of the rallying cry that produced the famous Republican Congress elected in 1994, with its Contract with America. One of the first measures adopted by the 104th Republican Congress was an act to limit unfunded mandates—the Unfunded Mandates Reform Act (UMRA). This was considered a triumph of lobbying efforts by state and local governments, and it was "hailed as both symbol and substance of a renewed congressional commitment to federalism."[20] Under this law, a point of order raised on the House or Senate floor can stop any mandate with an uncompensated state and local cost estimated at greater than $50 million a year as determined by the Congressional Budget Office

unfunded mandates Regulations or conditions for receiving grants that impose costs on state and local governments for which they are not reimbursed by the federal government.

---

[19] John DiIulio and Don Kettl report that in 1980 there were thirty-six laws that could be categorized as unfunded mandates. And despite the concerted opposition of the Reagan and Bush administrations, another twenty-seven laws qualifying as unfunded mandates were adopted between 1982 and 1991. See John DiIulio, Jr., and Donald F. Kettl, *Fine Print: The Contract with America, Devolution, and the Administrative Realities of American Federalism* (Washington, D.C.: Brookings Institution, 1995), p. 41.

[20] Paul Posner, "Unfunded Mandate Reform: How Is It Working?" *Rockefeller Institute Bulletin* (Albany, N.Y.: Nelson A. Rockefeller Institute of Government, 1998): 35.

(CBO). This was called a "stop, look, and listen" requirement, forcing Congress to take positive action to own up to the mandate and its potential costs. During 1996, its first full year of operation, only eleven bills included mandates that exceeded the $50 million threshold—from a total of sixty-nine estimates of actions in which mandates were included. Examples included minimum wage increase, parity for mental health and health insurance, mandated use of Social Security numbers on drivers' licenses, and extension of Federal Occupation Safety and Health to state and local employees. Most of them were modified in the House to reduce their costs. However, as one expert put it, "The primary impact of UMRA came not from the affirmative blockage of [mandate] legislation, but rather from its effect as a deterrent to mandates in the drafting and early consideration of legislation."[21]

As indicated by the first year of its operation, the effect of UMRA will not be revolutionary. UMRA does not prevent congressional members from passing unfunded mandates; it only makes them think twice before they do. Moreover, UMRA exempts several areas from coverage. And states must still enforce antidiscrimination laws and meet other requirements to receive federal assistance. But, on the other hand, UMRA does represent a serious effort to shift power in the national–state relationship a bit further toward the state side.

New Federalism and the National-State Tug of War   Presidents Nixon and Reagan called their efforts to reverse the trend toward national standards the new federalism. They helped craft policies to return more discretion to the states. Examples of these policies include Nixon's revenue sharing and Reagan's **block grants,** which consolidated a number of categorical grants into one larger category, leaving the state (or local) government more discretion to decide how to use the money. Presidents Nixon and Reagan, as well as former President George H. W. Bush, were sincere in wanting to return somewhat to a traditional notion of freedom of action for the states. They called it new federalism, but their concept and their goal were really much closer to the older, traditional federalism that predated the 1930s.

President Clinton adopted the new federalism of Nixon and Reagan even though he gave the appearance of expanding federal government activity. He signed the Unfunded Mandates Reform Act of 1995 as well as the Personal Responsibility and Work Opportunity Reconciliation Act of 1996 (PRA), which went further than any other act of Congress in the previous sixty years to relieve the states from both funded and unfunded national mandates. The PRA replaced the sixty-one-year-old Aid to Families with Dependent Children (AFDC) program with block grants to states for the Temporary Assistance to Needy Families program (TANF). Although some national standards remain, the place of the states in the national welfare system has been virtually revolutionized through **devolution,** the strategy of delegating to the states more and more authority over a range of policies that had been under national government authority, plus providing the states with a substantial portion of the cost of these programs. Since the mid-1990s, devolution has been quite consequential for the national-state tug of war.

block grants Federal grants-in-aid that allow states considerable discretion in how the funds should be spent.

devolution A policy to remove a program from one level of government by delegating it or passing it down to a lower level of government, such as from the national government to the states.

---

[21]Ibid., p. 36.

By changing welfare from a combined federal-state program into a block grant to the states, Congress gave the states more responsibility for programs that serve the poor. One argument in favor of devolution is that states can act as "laboratories of democracy" by experimenting with many different approaches to find one that best meets the needs of their citizens.[22] As states have altered their welfare programs in the wake of the new law, they have indeed designed diverse approaches. For example, Minnesota has adopted an incentive-based approach that offers extra assistance to families that take low-wage jobs. Other states, such as California, have more sticks than carrots in their new welfare programs.

President George W. Bush, though sometimes compared to Reagan, has not proven to be an unwavering supporter of new federalism and states' rights. On certain matters dear to his heart, Bush has been closer to the spirit of regulated federalism. Some of the expansions of national government under George W. Bush are clearly attributable to September 11 and the gigantic reaction to world terrorism, the creation of the Department of Homeland Security, the war in Iraq, and the cost of Hurricane Katrina, all complicated by failed implementation. But President Bush had other plans for the national government that he brought with him from his experience as a governor. His No Child Left Behind Act increased by 51 percent the budget of the Department of Education, a department that conservatives had vowed since the Reagan administration to abolish. The prescription drug benefit that he added to Medicare was another enormous national government commitment; its estimated cost is $534 billion, the largest expansion of the welfare state since Lyndon Johnson.[23] Bush's 2007 budget called for a 9 percent spending increase for the Department of Justice and another 12 percent increase for the Medicare program.

As these examples from the last decade show, assessments about "the right way" to divide responsibility in the federal system change over time.

The Supreme Court as Referee   For much of the nineteenth century, federal power remained limited. The Tenth Amendment was used to bolster arguments about **states' rights,** which in their extreme version claimed that the states did not have to submit to national laws when they believed the national government had exceeded its authority. These arguments in favor of states' rights were voiced less often after the Civil War. But the Supreme Court continued to use the Tenth Amendment to strike down laws that it thought exceeded national power, including the Civil Rights Act passed in 1875.

In the early twentieth century, however, the Tenth Amendment appeared to lose its force. Reformers began to press for national regulations to limit the power of large corporations and to preserve the health and welfare of citizens. The Supreme Court approved of some of these laws, but it struck others down, including a law combating child labor. The Court stated that the law violated the Tenth Amendment

---

states' rights The principle that states should oppose increasing authority of the national government. This view was most popular before the Civil War.

[22]The phrase "laboratories of democracy" was coined by Supreme Court Justice Louis Brandeis in his dissenting opinion in *New State Ice Co. v. Liebman,* 285 U.S. 262 (1932).

[23]The figures and judgments in this paragraph are provided by George F. Will, one of America's most distinguished conservative columnists and philosophers, in "The Last Word," *Newsweek,* 27 October 2005, p. 78.

because only states should have the power to regulate conditions of employment. By the late 1930s, however, the Supreme Court had approved such an expansion of federal power that the Tenth Amendment appeared irrelevant. In fact, in 1941, Justice Harlan Fiske Stone declared that the Tenth Amendment was simply a "truism," that it had no real meaning.[24]

Recent years have seen a revival of interest in the Tenth Amendment and important Supreme Court decisions limiting federal power. Much of the interest in the Tenth Amendment stems from conservatives who believe that a strong federal government encroaches on individual liberties. They believe such freedoms are better protected by returning more power to the states through the process of devolution. In 1996, Republican presidential candidate Bob Dole carried a copy of the Tenth Amendment in his pocket as he campaigned, pulling it out to read at rallies.[25] Around the same time, the Court revived the Eleventh Amendment concept of **state sovereign immunity.** This legal doctrine holds that states are immune from lawsuits by private persons or groups claiming that the state violated a statute enacted by Congress.

The Supreme Court's ruling in *United States v. Lopez* in 1995 fueled further interest in the Tenth Amendment. In that case, the Court, stating that Congress had exceeded its authority under the commerce clause, struck down a federal law that barred handguns near schools. This was the first time since the New Deal that the Court had limited congressional powers in this way. (The New Deal is discussed in Chapter 6.) The Court further limited the power of the federal government over the states in a 1996 ruling based on the Eleventh Amendment that prevented Native Americans from the Seminole tribe from suing the state of Florida in federal court. A 1988 law had given Indian tribes the right to sue a state in federal court if the state did not negotiate in good faith over issues related to gambling casinos on tribal land. The Supreme Court's ruling appeared to signal a much broader limitation on national power by raising new questions about whether individuals can sue a state if it fails to uphold federal law.[26]

Another significant decision involving the relationship between the federal government and state governments was the 1997 case *Printz v. United States* (joined with *Mack v. United States*),[27] in which the Court struck down a key provision of the Brady Bill, enacted by Congress in 1993 to regulate gun sales. Under the terms of the act, state and local law enforcement officers were required to conduct background checks on prospective gun purchasers. The Court held that the federal government cannot require states to administer or enforce federal regulatory programs. Since the states bear administrative responsibility for a variety of other federal programs, this decision could have far-reaching consequences. Finally, in another major ruling from the 1996–1997 term, in *City of Boerne v. Flores*,[28] the Court ruled

---

[24] *United States v. Darby Lumber Co.*, 312 U.S. 100 (1941).

[25] W. John Moore, "Pleading the 10th," *National Journal*, 29 July 1995, p. 1940.

[26] *Seminole Indian Tribe v. Florida*, 116 S. Ct. 1114 (1996).

[27] *Printz and Mack*, 521 U.S. 898, 117 S. Ct. 2365 (1997).

[28] *Boerne v. Flores*, 521 U.S. 507, 117 S. Ct. 2157 (1997).

state sovereign immunity Legal doctrine that holds that states cannot be sued for violating an act of Congress.

In Brief ✦ Federalism

Consequences of Federalism as Established in the Constitution

Existence of two sovereigns—the national government and the state governments, with state governments wielding more power for the first 150 years after the writing of the Constitution.
Particular restraint on the power of the national government to affect economic policy.
Great variations from state to state in terms of citizens' rights, role of government, and judicial activity.

Evolution of the Federal System

1789–1834	*Nationalization:* The Marshall Court interprets the Constitution broadly so as to expand and consolidate national power.
1835–1930s	*Dual federalism:* The functions of the national government are very specifically enumerated. States do much of the fundamental governing that affects citizens' day-to-day life. There is tension between the two levels of government, and the power of the national government begins to increase.
1930s–70s	*Cooperative federalism:* The national government uses grants-in-aid to encourage states and localities to pursue nationally defined goals.
1970s–	*Regulated federalism:* The national government sets conditions that states and localities must meet in order to keep certain grants. The national government also sets national standards in areas without providing funding to meet them.
	New federalism: The national government attempts to return more power to the states through block grants to the states.

that Congress had gone too far in restricting the power of the states to enact regulations they deemed necessary for the protection of public health, safety, or welfare. These rulings signal a move toward a much more restricted federal government.

In 1999, the Court's ruling on another Eleventh Amendment case further strengthened the doctrine of state sovereign immunity, finding that "The federal system established by our Constitution preserves the sovereign status of the States. . . . The generation that designed and adopted our federal system considered immunity from private suits central to sovereign dignity."[29] In 2000 in *United States v. Morrison,* the Supreme Court invalidated an important provision of the 1994 Violence against Women Act, which permitted women to bring private damage suits if their victimization was "gender-motivated." Although the 1994 act did not add any new national laws imposing liability or obligations on the states, the Supreme Court still held the act to be "an unconstitutional exercise" of Congress's power. And, although *Morrison* is a quite narrow federalism decision, when it is coupled with *United States v. Lopez* (1995)—the first modern holding against national authority to use commerce power to reach into the states—there is a definite trend toward strict scrutiny

---

[29] *Alden v. Maine.*

of the federal intervention aspects of all national civil rights, social, labor, and gender laws.[30] This trend had continued with the 2006 *Gonzales v. Oregon* case, in which the Court ruled that the federal government could not use federal drug laws to interfere with Oregon's assisted suicide law.

This tug of war between the states and national government will certainly continue, especially as the Roberts Court under Chief Justice John Roberts seems likely to pull us back further toward states' rights.

THE SEPARATION OF POWERS

James Madison quoted the French political thinker Baron de Montesquieu on the **separation of powers:**

> There can be no liberty where the legislative and executive powers are united in the same person . . . [or] if the power of judging be not separated from the legislative and executive powers.[31]

Using this same reasoning, many of Madison's contemporaries argued that there was not *enough* separation among the three branches, and Madison had to backtrack to insist that complete separation was not required:

> . . . unless these departments [branches] be so far connected and blended as to give each a constitutional control over the others, the degree of separation which the maxim requires, as essential to a free government, can never in practice be duly maintained.[32]

This is the secret of how we have made the separation of powers effective: We made the principle self-enforcing by giving each branch of government the means to participate in and partially or temporarily obstruct the workings of the other branches.

Checks and Balances

The means by which each branch of government interacts with each other branch is known informally as **checks and balances**. The best-known examples are shown in Figure 3.4. The framers sought to guarantee that the three branches would in fact use these checks and balances as weapons against one another by giving each branch a different political constituency and therefore a different perspective on what the government ought to do: direct, popular election for the members of the House; indirect election of senators (until the Seventeenth Amendment, adopted in 1913); indirect election of the president through the electoral college; and appointment of federal judges for life. All things considered, the best characterization of the separation of powers principle in action is "separated institutions sharing power."[33]

separation of powers The division of governmental power among several institutions that must cooperate in decision making.

checks and balances Mechanisms through which each branch of government is able to participate in and influence the activities of the other branches. Major examples include the presidential veto power over congressional legislation, the power of the Senate to approve presidential appointments, and judicial review of congressional enactments.

---

[30] *United States v. Morrison*, 529 U.S. 598 (2000).

[31] Clinton Rossiter, ed., *The Federalist Papers* (New York: New American Library, 1961), No. 47, p. 302.

[32] Ibid., No. 48, p. 308.

[33] Richard E. Neustadt, *Presidential Power* (New York: Wiley, 1960), p. 33.

ONLINE READING
ONLINE READING

Legislative Supremacy

Although each branch was to be given adequate means to compete with the other branches, it is also clear that within the system of separated powers the framers provided for *legislative supremacy* by making Congress the preeminent branch. Legislative supremacy made the provision of checks and balances in the other two branches all the more important.

The most important indication of the intentions of the framers were the provisions in Article I, to treat the powers of the national government as powers of Congress. The founders also provided for legislative supremacy in their decision to give Congress the sole power over appropriations.

Although "presidential government" seemed to supplant legislative supremacy after 1937, the relative power of the executive and legislative branches has varied. The power play between the president and Congress is especially intense during periods of *divided government,* when one party controls the White House and another controls Capitol Hill, as has been the case almost continuously since 1969.

The Role of the Supreme Court

The role of the judicial branch in the separation of powers has depended upon the power of judicial review, a power not provided for in the Constitution but asserted by Chief Justice Marshall in 1803:

> If a law be in opposition to the Constitution; if both the law and the Constitution apply to a particular case, so that the Court must either decide that case conformable to the law, disregarding the Constitution, or conformable to the Constitution, disregarding the law; the Court must determine which of these conflicting rules governs the case: This is of the very essence of judicial duty.[34]

Review of the constitutionality of acts of the president or Congress is relatively rare. For example, there were no Supreme Court reviews of congressional acts in the fifty plus years between *Marbury v. Madison* (1803) and *Dred Scott v. Sandford* (1857). In the century or so between the Civil War and 1970, eighty-four acts of Congress were held unconstitutional (in whole or in part), but there were long periods of complete Supreme Court deference to the Congress, punctuated by flurries of judicial review during periods of social upheaval. The most significant of these was 1935–1936, when twelve acts of Congress were invalidated, blocking virtually the entire New Deal program.[35] Then, after 1937, when the Court made its great reversals, no significant acts were voided until 1983, when the Court declared the legislative veto unconstitutional.[36] The Supreme Court became much more activist (that is, less deferential to Congress) after the elevation of Justice William H. Rehnquist to chief justice (1986–2005), and "a new program

legislative supremacy
The preeminence of Congress among the three branches of government, as established by the Constitution.

divided government
The condition in American government wherein one party controls the presidency while the opposing party controls one or both houses of Congress.

---

[34] *Marbury v. Madison,* 1 Cranch 137 (1803).

[35] C. Herman Pritchett, *The American Constitution* (New York: McGraw-Hill, 1959), pp. 180–86.

[36] *Immigration and Naturalization Service v. Chadha,* 462 U.S. 919 (1983). (See Chapter 7.)

FIGURE 3.4 Checks and Balances

Executive over Legislative
- President can veto acts of Congress.
- President can call a special session of Congress.
- President carries out, and thereby interprets, laws passed by Congress.
- Vice president casts tie-breaking vote in the Senate.

Legislative over Executive
- Congress can override presidential veto.
- Congress can impeach and remove president.
- Senate can reject president's appointments and refuse to ratify treaties.
- Congress can conduct investigations into president's actions.
- Congress can refuse to pass laws or provide funding that president requests.

Legislative over Judicial
- Congress can change size of federal court system and number of Supreme Court justices.
- Congress can propose constitutional amendments.
- Congress can reject Supreme Court nominees.
- Congress can impeach and remove federal judges.
- Congress can amend court jurisdictions.
- Congress controls appropriations.

Judicial over Legislative
- Court can declare laws unconstitutional.
- Chief Justice presides over Senate during hearing to impeach the president.

Executive over Judicial
- President nominates Supreme Court justices.
- President nominates federal judges.
- President can pardon those convicted in federal court.
- President can refuse to enforce the court's decisions.

Judicial over Executive
- Court can declare executive actions unconstitutional.
- Court has the power to issue warrants.
- Chief Justice presides over impeachment of president.

LEGISLATIVE

JUDICIAL

EXECUTIVE

of judicial activism"[37] seemed to be in place. Between 1995 and 2002, at least twenty-six acts or parts of acts of Congress were struck down on constitutional grounds.[38]

The Court has been far more deferential toward the president since the New Deal period, with only five significant confrontations. One was the so-called steel seizure case of 1952, in which the Court refused to permit President Truman to use

---

[37]Cass R. Sunstein, "Taking Over the Courts," *New York Times*, 9 November 2002, p. A19.

[38]Ibid.

Individual Interests and the Separation of Powers

In this chapter, we see how the different branches of government check and balance each other. James Madison feared the excessive concentration of power in government; part of the solution to this danger that he proposes in *Federalist* 51 is the separation of powers and federalism. But his solution did not rely on institutional checks alone; Madison also argued that "The interest of the man must be connected with the constitutional rights of the place." Why is it important that the interests of individual political actors be connected with the constitutional rights of their offices? Let us take a closer look at *Federalist* 51.

For Madison, human beings are "not angels" and political actors are no different. Recognizing that political actors are generally ambitious, Madison believed that this natural human tendency could be used to help thwart the ambitions of others. In addition to the presence of institutional checks and balances, then, we can also rely on human ambition to prevent the excessive accumulation of power in any single branch of government.

▼

Federalist 51

"...the great security against a gradual concentration of the several powers in the same department, consists in giving to those who administer each department the necessary constitutional means and personal motives to resist encroachments of the others. ...Ambition must be made to counteract ambition. **The interest of the man must be connected with the constitutional rights of the place.** It may be a reflection on human nature, that such devices should be necessary to control the abuses of government. But what is government itself, but the greatest of all reflections on human nature? If men were angels, no government would be necessary. If angels were to govern men, neither external nor internal controls on government would be necessary."

How does this work in practice? A threat to the power or prestige of the institution of the presidency, for example, is also a threat to the individual president's power and prestige. We can rely on the president's personal ambition to provide an incentive to resist efforts by the legislative or judicial branch to diminish or infringe on the rights of his office. Similarly, we can rely on the ambition of justices, judges, and members of Congress to link their individual interests to the constitutional rights of their offices.

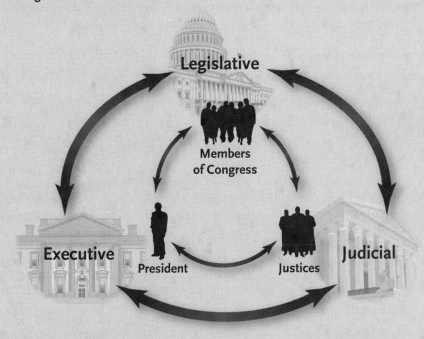

Recent events provide an illustration of Madison's idea in action. In May 2006, Louisiana congressman William J. Jefferson's office was searched by agents of the Justice Department (part of the executive branch) as part of a corruption probe. Although Jefferson was a Democrat seeking reelection at the time of the raid, the Republican Speaker of the House, J. Dennis Hastert, joined Democratic Minority Leader Nancy Pelosi and other Democrats in protesting the raid. In defending the institution of Congress from what they saw as unlawful interference by the executive branch, Hastert and Pelosi issued a joint statement, saying that "The Justice Department was wrong to seize records from Congressman Jefferson's office in violation of the constitutional principle of separation of powers."[1] Hastert's response can be seen as the product of his personal interests being linked to the interests of his office (Speaker of the House), with the goal of preventing the executive branch from overstepping its powers and infringing on the powers and prerogatives of Congress.

[1]Carl Hulse, "House Leaders Demand Return of Seized Files," *New York Times*, 25 May, 2006.

"emergency powers" to force workers back into the steel mills during the Korean War.[39] A second case was *United States v. Nixon,* in which the Court declared unconstitutional President Nixon's refusal to respond to a subpoena to make available the infamous White House tapes as evidence in a criminal prosecution. The Court argued that although **executive privilege** did protect confidentiality of communications to and from the president, this did not extend to data in presidential files or tapes varying upon criminal prosecutions.[40] During the heat of the scandal over President Clinton's relationship with intern Monica Lewinsky, the Supreme Court rejected the claim that the pressures and obligations of the office of president were so demanding that all litigation "but the most exceptional cases" should be deferred until his term ends.[41] The Supreme Court also struck down the Line-Item Veto Act of 1996 on the grounds that it violated Article I, Section 7, which prescribed procedures for congressional enactment and presidential acceptance or veto of statutes. Any such change in the procedures of adopting laws would have to be made by amendment to the Constitution, not by legislation.[42] Most recently, and of far greater importance, the Supreme Court repudiated the Bush administration's claims about the president's authority to detain enemy combatants without giving detainees an opportunity to defend themselves in an open court.[43]

DO FEDERALISM AND THE SEPARATION OF POWERS WORK?

Federalism and the separation of powers are two of the three most important constitutional principles upon which the United States' system of limited government is based. (The third is the principle of individual rights.) As we have seen, federalism limits the power of the national government in numerous ways. By its very existence, federalism recognizes the principle of two sovereigns, the national government and the state governments (hence the term "dual federalism"). In addition, the Constitution specifically restrained the power of the national government to regulate the economy. As a result, the states were free to do most of the fundamental governing for the first century and a half of American government. This began to change during and following the New Deal, as the national government began to exert more influence over the states through grants-in-aid and mandates. But even as the powers of the national government grew, so did the powers of the states. In the last decade, as well, we have noticed a counter-trend to the growth of national power as Congress has opted to devolve some of its powers to the states. The most recent notable instance of devolution was the welfare reform plan of 1996.

But the problem that arises with devolution is that programs that were once uniform across the country (because they were the national government's responsi-

executive privilege
The claim that confidential communications between a president and close advisers should not be revealed without the consent of the president.

---

[39] *Youngstown Sheet & Tube Co. v. Sawyer,* 343 U.S. 579 (1952).

[40] *United States v. Nixon,* 418 U.S. 683 (1974).

[41] *Clinton v. Jones,* 117 S. Ct. 1636 (1997).

[42] *Clinton v. City of New York,* 524 U.S. 417 (1998).

[43] *Hamdi v. Rumsfeld,* 124 S. Ct. 2633 (2004); *Rasul v. Bush,* 542 U.S. 466 (2004).

bility) can become highly variable, with some states providing benefits not available in other states. To a point, variation can be considered one of the virtues of federalism. But there are dangers inherent in large variations and inequalities in the provision of services and benefits in a democracy. For example, the Food and Drug Administration has been under attack in recent years. Could the government address the agency's perceived problems by devolving its regulatory tasks to the states? Would people care if drugs would require "caution" labels in some states but not in others? Would Americans want each state to set its own air and water pollution control policies without regard to the fact that pollution flows across state boundaries? Devolution, as attractive as it may be, is not an approach that can be applied across the board without analyzing carefully the nature of the program and of the problems it is designed to solve. Even the capacity of states to handle "devolved" programs will vary. According to the Washington research organization the Brookings Institution, the level of state and local government employment varies from state to state—from a low of 400 per 10,000 residents in some states to a high of 700 per 10,000 in others. "Such administrative diversity is bound to mediate the course and consequences of any substantial devolution of federal responsibility; no one-size-fits-all devolution [from federal to state and local government] can work."[44]

A key puzzle of federalism is deciding when differences across states represent the proper democratic decisions of the states and when such differences represent inequalities that should not be tolerated. Sometimes a decision to eliminate differences is made on the grounds of equality and individual rights, as in the Civil Rights Act of 1964, which outlawed segregation. At other times, a stronger federal role is justified on the grounds of national interest, as in the case of the oil shortage and the institution of a fifty-five mile per hour speed limit in the 1970s. Advocates of a more limited federal role often point to the value of democracy. Public actions can more easily be tailored to fit distinctive local or state desires if states and localities have more power to make policy. Viewed this way, variation across states can be an expression of democratic will.

In the 1990s, many Americans seemed to have grown disillusioned with the federal government and have supported efforts to give the states more responsibilities. A 1997 poll, for example, found that nearly two-thirds of those polled believed that shifting some responsibility to states and localities would help achieve excellence in government. After the terrorist attacks of September 11, 2001, however, support for the federal government soared. With issues of security topping the list of citizens' concerns, the federal government, which had seemed less important with the waning of the cold war, suddenly reemerged as the central actor in American politics. As one observer put it, "Federalism was a luxury of peaceful times."[45] Yet the newfound respect for the federal government is likely to be contingent on how well the government performs. If the federal government does not appear to be

---

[44]Eliza Newlin Carney, "Power Grab," *National Journal*, 11 April 1998, p. 798.

[45]Linda Greenhouse, "Will the Court Reassert National Authority?" *New York Times*, 30 September 2001, Sect. 4, p. 14.

effective in the fight against terrorism, its stature may once again decline in the minds of many Americans.

The second feature of limited government, separation of powers, is manifested in our system of checks and balances, whereby separate institutions of government share power with each other. Even though the Constitution clearly provided for legislative supremacy, checks and balances have functioned well. Some would say this system has worked too well. The last fifty years have witnessed long periods of divided government, when one party controls the White House while the other party controls Congress. During these periods, the level of conflict between the executive and legislative branches has been particularly divisive, resulting in what some analysts derisively call gridlock.[46]

During President George W. Bush's first six years in office, the separation of powers did not seem to work effectively. Congress gave Bush a free rein in such important matters as the war in Iraq and the war against terrorism. Of course during this period, Congress was controlled by the president's fellow Republicans. In 2006, Democrats won control of both houses and began to scrutinize the president's actions carefully. During the 2008 elections, Republicans argued that voters should be wary of electing a Democratic president and a Democratic Congress. However, any concerns among voters about how this would affect the separation of powers were apparently trumped by the economy and other issues.

CHAPTER REVIEW

In this chapter we have traced the development of two of the three basic principles of the U.S. Constitution: federalism and the separation of powers. Federalism involves a division between two layers of government, national and state. The separation of powers involves the division of the national government into three branches. These principles are limitations on the powers of government; Americans specified these principles as a condition of giving their consent to be governed. And these principles became the framework within which the government operates. The persistence of local government and of reliance of the national government on grants-in-aid to coerce local governments into following national goals demonstrates the continuing vitality of the federal framework. The intense competition among the president, Congress, and the courts dramatizes the continuing vitality of the separation of powers.

The purpose of a constitution is to organize the makeup or the composition of the government, the *framework* within which government and politics, including actual legislation, can take place. A country does not require federalism and the separation of powers to have a real constitutional government. And the country does not have to approach individual rights in the same manner as the American Constitution. But to be a true constitutional government, a government must have

---

[46]Not everybody will agree that divided government is all that less productive than government in which the same party controls both branches. See David Mayhew, *Divided We Govern: Party Control, Law Making and Investigations, 1946–1990* (New Haven, Conn.: Yale University Press, 1991). For another good evaluation of divided government, see Charles O. Jones, *Separate but Equal Branches—Congress and the Presidency* (Chatham, N.J.: Chatham House, 1995).

some kind of framework that consists of a few principles that cannot be manipulated by people in power merely for their own convenience. This is the essence of constitutionalism—principles that are above the reach of everyday legislatures, executives, bureaucrats, and politicians, yet that are not so far above their reach that these principles cannot sometimes be adapted to changing conditions.

FOR FURTHER READING

Bernstein, Richard B., with Jerome Agel. *Amending America—If We Love the Constitution So Much, Why Do We Keep Trying to Change It?* Lawrence: University Press of Kansas, 1993.

Campbell, Tom. *Separation of Powers in Practice.* Palo Alto, Calif.: Stanford University Press, 2004. ○ ONLINE READING

Crenson, Matthew, and Benjamin Ginsberg. *Presidential Power: Unchecked and Unbalanced.* New York: Norton, 2007.

Ferejohn, John A., and Barry R. Weingast, eds. *The New Federalism: Can the States Be Trusted?* Stanford, Calif.: Hoover Institution Press, 1997.

Fisher, Louis. *Congressional Abdication on War and Spending.* College Station: Texas A&M University Press, 2000.

Karmis, Dimitrios, and Wayne Norman. *Theories of Federalism: A Reader.* New York: Palgrave, Macmillan, 2005.

Kettl, Donald F. *The Regulation of American Federalism.* Baltimore: Johns Hopkins University Press, 1987. ○ ONLINE READING

Nagel, Robert. *The Implosion of American Federalism.* New York: Oxford University Press, 2001.

Noonan, John T. *Narrowing the Nation's Power: The Supreme Court Sides with the States.* Berkeley: University of California Press, 2002.

Peterson, Paul E. *The Price of Federalism.* Washington, D.C.: Brookings Institution, 1995.

Posner, Richard. *Not a Suicide Pact: The Constitution in a Time of National Emergency.* New York: Oxford University Press, 2006.

Riker, William H. *Federalism: Origin, Operation, Significance.* Boston: Little Brown, 1964. ○ ONLINE READING

Smith, Rogers M. *Civic Ideals: Conflicting Visions of Citizenship in U.S. History.* New Haven, Conn.: Yale University Press, 1997.

Winston, Pamela. *Welfare Policymaking in the States: The Devil in Devolution.* Washington, D.C.: Georgetown University Press, 2002.

Civil Liberties and Civil Rights

The first ten amendments of the United States Constitution, together called the ***Bill of Rights,*** are the basis for the freedoms we enjoy as American citizens. The Bill of Rights might well have been entitled the "Bill of Liberties," because the provisions that were incorporated in the Bill of Rights were seen as defining a private sphere of personal liberty, free of governmental restrictions. These freedoms include the right to free speech, the right to the free exercise of religion, prohibitions against unreasonable searches and seizures, and guarantees of due process of law.

As Jefferson had put it, a bill of rights "is what people are entitled to against every government on earth. . . . " ***Civil liberties*** are protections from improper government action. Thus, the Bill of Rights is a series of restraints imposed upon government. Some of these restraints are substantive liberties, which put limits on what the government shall and shall not have power to do—such as establishing a

● Core of the Analysis

● Civil liberties protect citizens from improper government action.

● Not until the 1960s were most of the civil liberties in the Bill of Rights nationalized, or applied to the states as well as the national government.

● Civil rights are obligations imposed on government to protect citizens from discrimination by other citizens and government agencies.

● Civil rights became part of the Constitution through the Fourteenth Amendment in 1868, but there was little advancement of equal rights until after World War II and the breakthrough case of *Brown v. Board of Education*.

● Since the passage of major civil rights legislation in 1964, the civil rights struggle has been expanded and universalized to include women, the disabled, gays, and other minority groups.

religion, quartering troops in private homes without consent, or seizing private property without just compensation. Other restraints are *procedural liberties,* which deal with how the government is supposed to act. These procedural liberties are usually grouped under the general category of *due process of law,* which first appears in the Fifth Amendment provision that "no person shall be . . . deprived of life, liberty, or property, without due process of law." For example, even though the government has the substantive power to declare certain acts to be crimes and to arrest and imprison persons who violate criminal laws, it may not do so without meticulously observing procedures designed to protect the accused person. The best-known procedural rule is that an accused person is presumed innocent until proven guilty. This rule does not question the government's power to punish someone for committing a crime; it questions only the way the government determines who committed the crime. Substantive and procedural restraints together identify the realm of civil liberties.

While civil liberties are phrased as negatives, ***civil rights*** are obligations imposed on government to guarantee equal citizenship and to protect citizens from discrimination by other private citizens and other government agencies. Civil rights did not become part of the Constitution until 1868 with the adoption of the Fourteenth Amendment, which addressed the issue of who was a citizen and provided for each citizen "equal protection of the laws." From that point on, we can see more clearly the distinction between civil liberties and civil rights, because civil liberties issues arise under the "due process of law" clause, and civil rights issues arise under the "equal protection of the laws" clause.[1]

The Fourteenth Amendment's guarantee to each citizen of the "equal protection of the laws" launched a century of political movements and legal efforts to press for racial equality. The African American quest for civil rights, in turn, inspired many other groups, including members of other racial and ethnic groups, women, the disabled, and gays and lesbians, to seek new laws and constitutional guarantees of their civil rights.

But even today, the question of what is meant by "equal rights" is hardly settled. While most Americans reject the idea that government should create equal outcomes for its citizens, they do widely endorse government action to prohibit public and private discrimination and they support the idea of equality of opportunity. However, even this concept is elusive. When past denial of rights creates unequal starting points for some groups, should government take additional steps to ensure equal opportunity? What kinds of groups should be specially protected against discrimination? Should the disabled receive special protection? Should gays and lesbians? Finally, what kinds of steps are acceptable to remedy discrimination, and who should bear the costs? These questions are at the heart of contemporary debates over civil rights.

Bill of Rights The first ten amendments to the U.S. Constitution.

civil liberties Areas of personal freedom with which governments are constrained from interfering.

civil rights Legal or moral claims that citizens are entitled to make upon the government to protect them from the illegal actions of other citizens and government agencies.

---

[1]For recent scholarship on the Bill of Rights and its development, see Geoffrey Stone, Richard Epstein, and Cass Sunstein, eds., *The Bill of Rights and the Modern State* (Chicago: University of Chicago Press, 1992); and Michael J. Meyer and William A. Parent, eds., *The Constitution of Rights* (Ithaca, N.Y.: Cornell University Press, 1992).

CIVIL LIBERTIES: NATIONALIZING THE BILL OF RIGHTS

The First Amendment provides that "Congress shall make no law respecting an establishment of religion . . . or abridging freedom of speech, or of the press; or the right of [assembly and petition]." But this is the only amendment in the Bill of Rights that addresses itself exclusively to the national government. For example, the Second Amendment provides that "the right of the people to keep and bear Arms shall not be infringed." The Fifth Amendment says, among other things, that "no person shall . . . be twice put in jeopardy of life or limb" for the same crime; that no person "shall be compelled in any Criminal Case to be a witness against himself"; that no person shall "be deprived of life, liberty, or property, without due process of law"; and that private property cannot be taken "without just compensation."[2]

Dual Citizenship

Since the First Amendment is the only part of the Bill of Rights that is explicit in its intention to put limits on the national government, a fundamental question inevitably arises: Do the remaining amendments of the Bill of Rights put limits on state governments or only on the national government? This question was settled in 1833 in a way that seems odd to Americans today. The case was *Barron v. Baltimore*, and the facts were simple. In paving its streets, the city of Baltimore had disposed of so much sand and gravel in the water near Barron's wharf that the value of the wharf for commercial purposes was virtually destroyed. Barron brought the city into court on the grounds that it had, under the Fifth Amendment, unconstitutionally deprived him of his property without just compensation. Barron took his case all the way to the Supreme Court. There Chief Justice Marshall, in one of the most significant Supreme Court decisions ever handed down, disagreed with Barron:

> The Constitution was ordained and established by the people of the United States for themselves, for their own government, and not for the government of the individual States. Each State established a constitution for itself, and in that constitution provided such limitations and restrictions on the powers of its particular government as its judgment dictated. . . . If these propositions be correct, the fifth amendment must be understood as restraining the power of the general government, not as applicable to the States.[3]

In other words, if an agency of the national government had deprived Barron of his property, there would have been little doubt about Barron's winning his case. But if the constitution of the state of Maryland contained no such provision protecting citizens of Maryland from such action, then Barron had no legal leg to stand on against Baltimore, an agency of the state of Maryland.

---

[2]It would be useful at this point to review all the provisions of the Bill of Rights (in the Appendix) to confirm this distinction between the wording of the First Amendment and the rest of the Bill of Rights. For a spirited and enlightening essay on the extent to which the entire Bill of Rights was about equality, see Martha Minow, "Equality and the Bill of Rights," in Meyer and Parent, *The Constitution of Rights*, pp. 118–28.

[3]*Barron v. Mayor and City of Baltimore*, 7 Peters 243 (1833).

Barron v. Baltimore confirmed dual citizenship—that is, that each American was a citizen of the national government and separately a citizen of one of the states. This meant that the Bill of Rights did not apply to decisions or procedures of state (or local) governments. Even slavery could continue, because the Bill of Rights could not protect anyone from state laws treating people as property. In fact, the Bill of Rights did not become a vital instrument for the extension of civil liberties for anyone until after a bloody Civil War and a revolutionary Fourteenth Amendment intervened. And even so, as we shall see, nearly a second century would pass before the Bill of Rights would truly come into its own.

The Fourteenth Amendment

From a constitutional standpoint, the defeat of the South in the Civil War settled one question and raised another. It probably settled forever the question of whether secession was an option for any state. After 1865, there was more "united" than "states" to the United States. But this left unanswered just how much the states were obliged to obey the Constitution, in particular, the Bill of Rights. Just reading the words of the Fourteenth Amendment, anyone might think it was almost perfectly designed to impose the Bill of Rights on the states and thereby to reverse *Barron v. Baltimore*. The very first words of the Fourteenth Amendment point in that direction:

> All persons born or naturalized in the United States, and subject to the jurisdiction thereof, are citizens of the United States and of the State wherein they reside.

This provides for a single national citizenship, and at a minimum that means that civil liberties should not vary drastically from state to state. That would seem to be the spirit of the Fourteenth Amendment: to nationalize the Bill of Rights by nationalizing the definition of citizenship.

This interpretation of the Fourteenth Amendment is reinforced by the next clause of the Amendment:

> No state shall make or enforce any law which shall abridge the privileges or immunities of citizens of the United States; nor shall any state deprive any person of life, liberty, or property, without due process of law.

All of this sounds like an effort to extend the Bill of Rights in its entirety to citizens wherever they might reside.[4] But this was not to be the Supreme Court's interpretation for nearly a hundred years. Within five years of ratification of the Fourteenth Amendment, the Court was making decisions as though it had never been adopted.[5] The shadow of Barron grew longer and longer. Table 4.1 outlines the major developments in the history of the Fourteenth Amendment against the backdrop of Barron, citing the particular provisions of the Bill of Rights as they were incorporated by Supreme Court decisions into the Fourteenth Amendment as limitations on all the states. This is a measure of the degree of "nationalization" of civil liberties.

The only change in civil liberties during the first sixty years after the adoption of the Fourteenth Amendment came in 1897, when the Supreme Court held that the due process clause of the Fourteenth Amendment did in fact prohibit states from taking property for a public use without just compensation.[6] This effectively overruled the specific holding in *Barron;* henceforth a citizen of Maryland or any state was protected from a "public taking" of property even if the state constitution did not provide such protection. The power of public agencies to seize private property is called eminent domain. According to the Fifth Amendment, private owners must be paid "just compensation" by the government if it decides that it needs their property. But in a broader sense, *Barron* still cast a shadow, because the Supreme Court had "incorporated" into the Fourteenth Amendment *only* the property protection provision of the Fifth Amendment, despite the fact that the **due process** clause applied to the taking of life and liberty as well as property.

No further expansion of civil liberties through incorporation occurred until 1925, when the Supreme Court held that freedom of speech is "among the fundamental personal rights and 'liberties' protected by the due process clause of the Fourteenth Amendment from impairment by the states."[7] In 1931, the Supreme Court added freedom of the press to that short list of civil rights protected by the Bill of Rights from state action; in 1939, it added freedom of assembly.[8]

---

[4]The Fourteenth Amendment also seems designed to introduce civil rights. The final clause of the all-important Section 1 provides that no state can "deny to any person within its jurisdiction the equal protection of the laws." It is not unreasonable to conclude that the purpose of this provision was to obligate the state governments as well as the national government to take *positive* actions to protect citizens from arbitrary and discriminatory actions, at least those based on race. This will be explored in the second half of the chapter.

[5]The Slaughter-House Cases, 16 Wallace 36 (1873); The Civil Rights Cases, 109 U.S. 3 (1883).

[6]*Chicago, Burlington and Quincy Railroad Company v. Chicago*, 166 U.S. 266 (1897).

[7]*Gitlow v. New York*, 268 U.S. 652 (1925)

[8]*Near v. Minnesota*, 283 U.S. 697 (1931); *Hague v. C.I.O.*, 307 U.S. 496 (1939).

due process To proceed according to law and with adequate protection for individual rights.

TABLE 4.1 Incorporation of the Bill of Rights into the Fourteenth Amendment

Selected Provisions and Amendments	Date "incorporated"	Key Cases
Eminent domain (V)	1897	*Chicago, Burlington and Quincy Railroad v. Chicago*
Freedom of speech (I)	1925	*Gitlow v. New York*
Freedom of the press (I)	1931	*Near v. Minnesota ex rel. Olson*
Free exercise of religion (I)	1934	*Hamilton v. Regents of the University of California*
Freedom of assembly (I)	1939	*Hague v. Committee for Industrial Organization*
Freedom from unnecessary search and seizure (IV)	1949	*Wolf v. Colorado*
Freedom from warrantless search and seizure ("exclusionary rule") (IV)	1961	*Mapp v. Ohio*
Freedom from cruel and unusual punishment (VIII)	1962	*Robinson v. California*
Right to counsel in any criminal trial (VI)	1963	*Gideon v. Wainwright*
Right against self-incrimination and forced confessions (V)	1964	*Mallory v. Hogan Escobedo v. Illinois*
Right to privacy (III, IV, and V)	1965	*Griswold v. Connecticut*
Right to remain silent (V)	1966	*Miranda v. Arizona*
Right against double jeopardy (V)	1969	*Benton v. Maryland*

For the following two decades, this was as far as the Supreme Court was willing to go in the effort to nationalize more of the rights in the Bill of Rights. And it should be made clear at this point that none of the rights in the Bill of Rights is absolute, including the most sacred right of all, freedom of speech. Figure 4.1 shows when free speech is protected and when it is not protected. A similar box could be constructed for each of the rights listed in Table 4.1. The only promise the Supreme Court is willing to make is that it will give "strict scrutiny" to any action taken by a

FIGURE 4.1 The Protection of Free Speech by the First Amendment

	PROTECTED SPEECH	UNPROTECTED SPEECH
If content is true:	All speech is protected by the First Amendment when it is the truth.	"True" speech can be regulated *only* if: • it fails the clear and present danger test, or • it falls below community standards of obscenity or pornography.
If content is false:	Defamatory speech is protected when: • it is spoken or written by a public official in the course of official business, or • it is spoken or written by a citizen or the press against someone in the public eye.	"False" speech can be regulated or punished *only* when it can be demonstrated that there was a reckless disregard for the truth (as in libel or slander).

state to limit or abridge a right. Again, no right is absolute; no right is protected at all times, regardless of the circumstances.

The shadow of *Barron* extended into its second century, despite adoption of the Fourteenth Amendment. At the time of World War II, the Constitution, as interpreted by the Supreme Court, left standing the framework in which the states had the power to determine their own law on a number of fundamental issues. It left states with the power to pass laws segregating the races. It also left states with the power to engage in searches and seizures without a warrant, to indict accused persons without benefit of a grand jury, to deprive persons of trial by jury, to force persons to testify against themselves, to deprive accused persons of their right to confront adverse witnesses, and to prosecute accused persons more than once for the same crime.[9] Few states exercised these powers, but the power was there for any state whose legislative majority chose to use it.

The Constitutional Revolution in Civil Liberties

Signs of change in the constitutional framework came after 1954, in *Brown v. Board of Education,* when the Court found state segregation laws for schools unconstitutional. Even though *Brown* was not a civil liberties case, it indicated rather clearly that the Supreme Court was going to be expansive about civil liberties, because with *Brown* the Court had effectively promised that it would actively subject the states and all actions affecting civil rights and civil liberties to **strict scrutiny.** In retrospect, one could say that this constitutional revolution was given a "jumpstart" in

strict scrutiny Higher standard of judicial protection for speech cases and other civil liberties and civil rights cases, in which the burden of proof shifts from the complainant to the government.

[9] All of these were implicitly identified in *Palko v. Connecticut,* 302 U.S. 319 (1937), as "not incorporated" into the Fourteenth Amendment as limitations on the powers of the states.

1954 by *Brown v. Board of Education*, even though the results were not apparent until after 1961, when the number of civil liberties incorporated increased (see Table 4.1).

Nationalizing the Bill of Rights   The constitutional revolution in federalism, as we saw in Chapter 3, began when the Supreme Court in 1937 interpreted "interstate commerce" in favor of federal government regulation.[10] Both revolutions, then, were movements toward nationalization, but they required opposite motions on the part of the Supreme Court. In the area of commerce (the first revolution), the Court had to decide to assume a *passive* role by not interfering as Congress expanded the meaning of the commerce clause of Article I, Section 8. This expansion has been so extensive that the national government can now constitutionally reach a single farmer growing twenty acres of wheat or a small restaurant selling barbecue to local "whites only" without being anywhere near interstate commerce routes. In the second revolution—involving the Bill of Rights and the Fourteenth Amendment— the Court had to assume an active role. It required close review of the laws of state legislatures and decisions of state courts in order to apply a single national Fourteenth Amendment standard to the rights and liberties of all citizens.

Table 4.1 shows that until 1961, only the First Amendment and one clause of the Fifth Amendment had been clearly incorporated into the Fourteenth Amendment.[11] After 1961, several other important provisions of the Bill of Rights were incorporated. Of the cases that expanded the Fourteenth Amendment's reach, the most famous was *Gideon v. Wainwright*, which established the right to counsel in a criminal trial, because it became the subject of a best-selling book and a popular movie.[12] In *Mapp v. Ohio*, the Court held that evidence obtained in violation of the Fourth Amendment ban on unreasonable searches and seizures would be excluded from trial.[13] This **exclusionary rule** was particularly irksome to the police and prosecutors because it meant that patently guilty defendants sometimes go free because the evidence that clearly incriminated them could not be used. In *Miranda*, the Court's ruling required that arrested persons be informed of the right to remain silent and to have counsel present during interrogation.[14] This is the basis of the **Miranda *rule*** of reading persons their rights. By 1969, in *Benton v. Maryland*, the Supreme Court had come full circle regarding the rights of the criminally accused, explicitly reversing a 1937 ruling and thereby incorporating double jeopardy.

During the 1960s and early 1970s, the Court also expanded another important area of civil liberties: rights to privacy. When the Court began to take a more activist

exclusionary rule The ability of the court to exclude evidence obtained in violation of the Fourth Amendment.

Miranda rule Principles developed by the Supreme Court in *Miranda v. Arizona* (1966) requiring those under arrest be informed of their legal rights, including right to counsel, prior to police interrogation.

○ **ONLINE READING**

○ **ONLINE READING**

---

[10] *NLRB v. Jones & Laughlin Steel Corp.*, 301 U.S. 1 (1937).

[11] The one exception was the right to public trial (Sixth Amendment), but a 1948 case (*In re Oliver*, 33 U.S. 257) did not actually mention the right to public trial as such; this right was cited in a 1968 case (*Duncan v. Louisiana*, 391 U.S. 145) as a precedent establishing the right to public trial as part of the Fourteenth Amendment.

[12] *Gideon v. Wainwright*, 372 U.S. 335 (1963); Anthony Lewis, *Gideon's Trumpet* (New York: Random House, 1964).

[13] *Mapp v. Ohio*, 367 U.S. 643 (1961).

[14] *Miranda v. Arizona*, 384 U.S. 436 (1966).

role in the mid-1950s and 1960s, the idea of a "right to privacy" was revived. In 1958, the Supreme Court recognized "privacy in one's association" in its decision to prevent the state of Alabama from using the membership list of the National Association for the Advancement of Colored People in the state's investigations.[15] As we shall see later in this chapter, legal questions about the right to privacy have come to the fore in more recent cases concerning birth control, abortion, homosexuality, and assisted suicide.

THE BILL OF RIGHTS TODAY

Since liberty requires restraining the power of government, the general status of civil liberties can never be considered fixed and permanent.[16] Every provision in the Bill of Rights is subject to interpretation, and in any dispute involving a clause of the Bill of Rights, interpretations will always be shaped by the interpreter's interest in the outcome. As we have seen, the Court continuously reminds everyone that if it has the power to expand the Bill of Rights, it also has the power to contract it.[17]

The First Amendment and Freedom of Religion

The Bill of Rights begins by guaranteeing freedom, and the First Amendment provides for that freedom in two distinct clauses: "Congress shall make no law [1] respecting an establishment of religion, or [2] prohibiting the free exercise thereof." The first clause is called the establishment clause, and the second is called the free exercise clause.

Separation between Church and State The **establishment clause** has been interpreted quite strictly to mean that a virtual wall of separation exists between church and state. Despite the absolute sound of the phrase *wall of separation*, there is ample room to disagree on how high the wall is or of what materials it is composed. For example, the Court has been consistently strict in cases of school prayer, striking down such practices as Bible reading,[18] nondenominational prayer,[19] a moment of silence for meditation, and pre-game prayer at public sporting events.[20] On the other hand, the Court has been quite permissive (and some would say inconsistent) about the public display of religious symbols, such as city-sponsored Nativity scenes in commercial or municipal areas.[21] In 1971, after thirty years of cases involving religious schools, the Court attempted to specify some criteria to guide its decisions and those of lower courts, indicating, for example, in a decision invalidat-

---

[15]*NAACP v. Alabama ex rel. Patterson*, 357 U.S. 449 (1958).

[16]This section is taken from Benjamin Ginsberg, Theodore J. Lowi, and Margaret Weir, *We the People: An Introduction to American Politics*, 6th ed. (New York: Norton, 2006).

[17]For a lively and readable treatment of the possibilities of restricting provisions of the Bill of Rights without actually reversing prior decisions, see David G. Savage, *Turning Right: The Making of the Rehnquist Supreme Court* (New York: Wiley, 1992).

[18]*Abington School District v. Schempp*, 374 U.S. 203 (1963).

[19]*Engel v. Vitale*, 370 U.S. 421 (1962).

[20]*Wallace v. Jaffree*, 472 U.S. 38 (1985).

[21]*Lynch v. Donnelly*, 465 U.S. 668 (1984).

establishment clause
The First Amendment clause that says, "Congress shall make no law respecting an establishment of religion." This law means that a wall of separation exists between church and state.

ing state payments for the teaching of secular subjects in parochial schools, circumstances under which the Court might allow certain financial assistance. The case was *Lemon v. Kurtzman;* in its decision, the Supreme Court established three criteria to guide future cases, in what came to be called the **Lemon *test.*** The Court held that government aid to religious schools would be accepted as constitutional if (1) it had a secular purpose, (2) its effect was neither to advance nor to inhibit religion, and (3) it did not entangle government and religious institutions in each other's affairs.[22]

More recently, the establishment clause has been put under pressure by the school-voucher and charter-school movements. Vouchers financed by public revenues are supporting tuition to religious schools, where common prayer and religious instruction are known parts of the curriculum. In 2004, the question of whether the phrase "under God" in the Pledge of Allegiance violates the establishment clause was brought before the Court, but the Court ruled that the plaintiff lacked a sufficient personal stake in the case to bring the complaint.[23] This inconclusive decision by the Court left "under God" in the Pledge while keeping the issue alive for possible resolution in a future case.

Free Exercise of Religion   The *free exercise clause* protects the right to believe and practice whatever religion one chooses; it also protects the right to be a nonbeliever. Although the Supreme Court has been fairly consistent and strict in protecting the free exercise of religious belief, it has taken pains to distinguish between religious beliefs and *actions* based on those beliefs. In one case, for example, two Native Americans had been fired from their jobs for smoking peyote, an illegal drug. They claimed they had been fired from their jobs illegally because smoking peyote was a religious sacrament protected by the free exercise clause. The Court disagreed with their claim in an important 1990 decision,[24] but Congress literally reversed the Court's decision with the enactment of the Religious Freedom Restoration Act (RFRA) of 1993, which forbids any federal agency or state government to restrict a person's free exercise of religion unless the federal agency or state government demonstrates that its action "furthers a compelling government interest" and "is the least restrictive means of furthering that compelling governmental interest." However in the *City of Boerne* case, the Supreme Court declared the RFRA unconstitutional, but on grounds rarely utilized, if not unique to this case: Congress had violated the separation-of-powers principle, infringing on the powers of the judiciary by going so far beyond its law-making powers.[25] The *City of Boerne* case did settle some matters of constitutional controversy over the religious exercise and the establishment clauses of the First Amendment, but it left a lot more unsettled.

---

[22] *Lemon v. Kurtzman,* 403 U.S. 602 (1971). The *Lemon* test is still good law, but as recently as the 1994 Court term, four justices urged that it be abandoned. Here is a settled area of law that may soon become unsettled.

[23] *Elk Grove Unified School District v. Newdow,* 542 U.S. 1 (2004).

[24] *Employment Division v. Smith,* 494 U.S. 872 (1990).

[25] *City of Boerne v. Flores,* 521 U.S. 507 (1997).

The First Amendment and Freedom of Speech and the Press

Because democracy depends on an open political process, freedom of speech and freedom of the press are considered critical. In 1938, freedom of speech (which in all important respects includes freedom of the press) was given extraordinary constitutional status when the Supreme Court established that any legislation that attempts to restrict these fundamental freedoms "is to be subjected to a more exacting judicial scrutiny . . . than are most other types of legislation."[26]

The Court was saying that the democratic political process must be protected at almost any cost. This higher standard of judicial review came to be called strict scrutiny. Strict scrutiny implies that speech—at least some kinds of speech—will be protected almost absolutely. But as it turns out, only some types of speech are fully protected against restrictions. As we shall see, many forms of speech are less than absolutely protected—even though they are entitled to strict scrutiny. This section will look at these two categories of speech: absolutely protected speech and conditionally protected speech.

Absolutely Protected Speech   Since the 1920s, political speech has been consistently protected by the courts even when it has been deemed "insulting" or "outrageous." Here is the way the Supreme Court put it in one of its most important statements on the subject:

> The constitutional guarantees of free speech and free press do not permit a State to forbid or proscribe advocacy of the use of force or of law violation *except where such advocacy is directed to inciting or producing imminent lawless action and is likely to incite or produce such action.*[27] [Emphasis added]

This statement was made in the case of a Ku Klux Klan leader, Charles Brandenburg, who had been arrested and convicted of advocating "revengent" action against the president, Congress, and the Supreme Court, among others, if they continued "to suppress the white, Caucasian race." Although Brandenburg was not carrying a weapon, some members of his audience were. Nevertheless, the Supreme Court reversed the state courts and freed Brandenburg while declaring Ohio's Criminal Syndicalism Act unconstitutional because it punished persons who "advocate, or teach the duty, necessity, or propriety [of violence] as a means of accomplishing industrial or political reform" or who publish materials or "voluntarily assemble . . . to teach or advocate the doctrines of criminal syndicalism." The Supreme Court argued that the statute did not distinguish "mere advocacy" from "incitement to imminent lawless action." It would be difficult to go much further in protecting freedom of speech.

Another area of recent expansion of political speech—the participation of wealthy persons and corporations in political campaigns—was opened up in 1976

---

[26] *United States v. Carolene Products Company*, 304 U.S. 144 (1938), 384. This footnote is one of the Court's most important doctrines. See Alfred H. Kelly, Winfred A. Harbison, and Herman Belz, *The American Constitution: Its Origins and Development*, 7th ed., 2 vols. (New York: Norton, 1991), II, pp. 519–23.

[27] *Brandenburg v. Ohio*, 395 U.S. 444 (1969).

with the Supreme Court's decision in *Buckley v. Valeo*.[28] Campaign finance reform laws of the early 1970s, arising out of the Watergate scandal, sought to put severe limits on campaign spending, and a number of important provisions were declared unconstitutional on the basis of a new principle that spending money by or on behalf of candidates is a form of speech protected by the First Amendment. The issue came up again in 2003, after passage of a new and more severe campaign finance law, the Bipartisan Campaign Reform Act (2002). In *McConnell v. Federal Election Commission*, the majority seriously reduced the area of speech protected by the *Buckley v. Valeo* decision by holding that Congress was well within its power to put limits on the amounts individuals could spend, plus severe limits on the amounts of "soft money" that could be spent by corporations and their PACs.

The First Amendment treats the freedoms of assembly and petition as equal to the freedoms of religion and political speech. Freedom of assembly and freedom of petition are closely associated with speech but go beyond it to speech associated with action. Since at least 1931, the Supreme Court has sought to protect actions that are designed to send a political message. Thus although the Court upheld a federal statute making it a crime to burn draft cards to protest the Vietnam War on the grounds that the government had a compelling interest in preserving draft cards as part of the conduct of the war itself, it considered the wearing of black armbands to school a protected form of assembly.

Another example is the burning of the American flag as a symbol of protest. In 1984, at a political rally held during the Republican National Convention in Dallas, a political protester burned an American flag in violation of a Texas statute that prohibited desecration of a venerated object. In a 5–4 decision, the Supreme Court declared the Texas law unconstitutional on the grounds that flag burning is expressive conduct protected by the First Amendment.[29] Since 1995, the House of Representatives has four times passed a resolution for a constitutional amendment to ban flag burning, but each time the Senate has failed to go along.[30] Further effort in Congress was probably killed by the Supreme Court's 2003 decision striking down a Virginia cross-burning statute.[31] In that case, the Court ruled that states could make cross burning a crime as long as the statute required prosecutors to prove that the act of setting fire to the cross was intended to intimidate.

Closer to the original intent of the assembly and petition clause is the category of ***speech plus***—following speech with physical activity such as picketing, distributing leaflets, and other forms of peaceful demonstration or assembly. Such assemblies are consistently protected by courts under the First Amendment; state and local laws regulating such activities are closely scrutinized and frequently overturned.

Freedom of the Press For all practical purposes, freedom of speech implies and includes freedom of the press. With the exception of the broadcast media, which are subject to federal regulation, the press is protected under the doctrine prohibiting

---

[28] *Buckley v. Valeo*, 424 U.S. 1 (1976).

[29] *Texas v. Johnson*, 491 U.S. 397 (1989).

[30] Carl Hulse, "Flag Amendment Narrowly Fails in Senate Vote," *New York Times*, 28 June 2006.

[31] *Virginia v. Black*, 538 U.S. 343 (2003).

speech plus Speech accompanied by activities such as sit-ins, picketing, and demonstrations. Protection of this form of speech under the First Amendment is conditional, and restrictions imposed by state or local authorities are acceptable if properly balanced by considerations of public order.

prior restraint. Beginning with the landmark 1931 case of *Near v. Minnesota,*[32] the Supreme Court has held that except under the most extraordinary circumstances, the First Amendment prohibits government agencies from seeking to prevent newspapers or magazines from publishing whatever they wish.

Conditionally Protected Speech   At least four forms of speech fall outside the absolute guarantees of the First Amendment and therefore outside the realm of absolute protection. Since they do enjoy some protection, they qualify as conditionally protected types of speech: libel and slander, obscenity and pornography, fighting words, and commercial speech.

Some speech is not protected at all. If a written statement is made in "reckless disregard of the truth" and is considered damaging to the victim because it is "malicious, scandalous, and defamatory," it can be punished as *libel.* If an oral statement of such nature is made, it can be punished as *slander.*

Today most libel suits involve freedom of the press, and the realm of free press is enormous. Historically, newspapers were subject to the law of libel, which provided that newspapers that printed false and malicious stories could be compelled to pay damages to those they defamed. In recent years, however, American courts have greatly narrowed the meaning of libel and made it extremely difficult, particularly for politicians or other public figures, to win a libel case against a newspaper.

If libel and slander cases can be difficult because of the problem of determining the truth of statements and whether those statements are malicious and damaging, cases involving pornography and obscenity can be even more sticky. It is easy to say that pornography and obscenity fall outside the realm of protected speech, but it is impossible to draw a clear line defining where protection ends and unprotected speech begins. All attempts by the courts to define pornography and obscenity have proved impractical because each instance required courts to screen thousands of pages of print material or feet of film alleged to be pornographic. In recent years, the battle against obscene speech has taken place in the realm of pornography on the Internet. Opponents of this form of expression argue that it should be banned because of the easy access children have to the Internet. The first major effort to regulate the content of the Internet occurred on February 1, 1996, when the 104th Congress passed major telecommunications legislation. Attached to the Telecommunications Act was an amendment, called the Communications Decency Act (CDA), that was designed to regulate the online transmission of obscene material. In the 1997 Supreme Court case of *Reno v. ACLU,* the Court struck down the CDA, ruling that it suppressed speech that "adults have a constitutional right to receive" and that governments may not limit the adult population to messages that are fit for children.[33] Congress again tried limiting children's access to Internet pornography with the 2001 Children's Internet Protection Act, which required public libraries to install anti-pornography filters on all library computers with Internet access. Though the act made cooperation a condition for receiving federal subsidies, it did

prior restraint An effort by a government agency to block the publication of material it deems libelous or harmful in some other way; censorship. In the United States, the courts forbid prior restraint except under the most extraordinary circumstances.

libel A written statement made in "reckless disregard of the truth" and considered damaging to a victim because it is "malicious, scandalous, and defamatory."

slander An oral statement made in "reckless disregard of the truth" and considered damaging to a victim because it is "malicious, scandalous, and defamatory."

---

[32] *Near v. Minnesota ex rel. Olson,* 283 U.S. 697 (1931).

[33] *Reno v. ACLU,* 521 U.S. 844 (1997).

permit librarians to unblock a site at the request of an adult patron. The law was challenged, and in 2003 the Court upheld it, asserting that its provisions did not violate library patrons' First Amendment rights.[34]

Speech can also lose its protected position when it moves toward the sphere of action. "Expressive speech," for example, is protected until it moves from the symbolic realm to the realm of actual conduct—to direct incitement of damaging conduct with the use of so-called *fighting words*. In 1942, the Supreme Court upheld the arrest and conviction of a man who had violated a state law forbidding the use of offensive language in public. He had called the arresting officer a "goddamned racketeer" and "a damn Fascist." When his case reached the Supreme Court, the arrest was upheld on the grounds that the First Amendment provides no protection for such offensive language because such words "are no essential part of any exposition of ideas."[35] Since that time, however, the Supreme Court has reversed almost every conviction based on arguments that the speaker had used "fighting words." But again, that does not mean this is an absolutely settled area.

Commercial speech, such as newspaper or television advertising, does not have full First Amendment protection because it cannot be considered political speech. Some commercial speech is still unprotected and therefore regulated. For example, the regulation of false and misleading advertising by the Federal Trade Commission is an old and well-established power of the federal government. The Supreme Court long ago approved the constitutionality of laws prohibiting the electronic media from carrying cigarette advertising.[36] However, the gains far outweigh the losses in the effort to expand the protection commercial speech enjoys under the First Amendment. As the scholar Louis Fisher explains, "In part, this reflects the growing appreciation that commercial speech is part of the free flow of information necessary for informed choice and democratic participation."[37] For example, in a 2001 case, the Court ruled that a Massachusetts ban on all cigarette advertising violated the First Amendment right of the tobacco industry to advertise its products to adult consumers.[38]

The Second Amendment and the Right to Bear Arms

The point and purpose of the Second Amendment is the provision for militias; they were to be the backing of the government for the maintenance of local public order. *Militia* was understood at the time of the founding to be a military or police resource for state governments, and militias were specifically distinguished from armies and troops, which came within the sole constitutional jurisdiction of Congress. The right of the people "to keep and bear Arms" is based on and associated with participation in state militias. Nonetheless, in the 2008 case of *District of Columbia v. Heller*,

---

[34] *United States v. American Library Association*, 539 U.S. 194 (2003).

[35] *Chaplinsky v. State of New Hampshire*, 315 U.S. 568 (1942).

[36] *Capital Broadcasting Company v. Acting Attorney General*, 405 U.S. 1000 (1972).

[37] Fisher, *American Constitutional Law*, p. 546.

[38] *Lorillard Tobacco v. Reilly*, 533 U.S. 525 (2001).

fighting words
Speech that directly incites damaging conduct.

the U.S. Supreme Court struck down a District of Columbia law that banned handgun possession by private citizens in the District.[39] The Court said that the Second Amendment protected the individual right to "keep and bear arms." The District of Columbia, however, is an agency of the federal government, and the Court specifically neglected to apply the *Heller* decision to the states. Hence, gun ordinances in such cities as New York and Chicago are not affected by the Court's decision.

Rights of the Criminally Accused

Except for the First Amendment, most of the battle to apply the Bill of Rights to the states was fought over the various protections granted to individuals who are accused of a crime, who are suspects in the commission of a crime, or who are brought before the court as a witness to a crime. The Fourth, Fifth, Sixth, and Eighth Amendments, taken together, are the essence of the due process of law, even though this fundamental concept does not appear until the very last words of the Fifth Amendment.

The Fourth Amendment and Searches and Seizures   The purpose of the Fourth Amendment is to guarantee the security of citizens against unreasonable (that is, improper) searches and seizures. In 1990, the Supreme Court summarized its understanding of the Fourth Amendment brilliantly and succinctly: "A search compromises the individual interest in privacy; a seizure deprives the individual of dominion over his or her person or property."[40]

The exclusionary rule, which prohibits evidence obtained during an illegal search from being introduced in a trial, is the most severe restraint ever imposed by the Constitution and the courts on the behavior of the police. The exclusionary rule is a dramatic restriction because it rules out precisely the evidence that produces a conviction; it frees those people who are *known* to have committed the crime of which they have been accused. Because it works so dramatically in favor of persons known to have committed a crime, the Court has since softened the application of the rule. In recent years, the federal courts have relied on a discretionary use of the exclusionary rule, whereby they make a judgment as to the "nature and quality of the intrusion." It is thus difficult to know ahead of time whether a defendant will or will not be protected from an illegal search under the Fourth Amendment.[41]

The Fifth Amendment   The first clause of the Fifth Amendment, the right to have a **grand jury** determine whether a trial is warranted, is considered "the oldest institution known to the Constitution."[42] Grand juries play an important role in federal criminal cases. However, the provision for a grand jury is the one important civil liberties provision of the Bill of Rights that was not incorporated by the Fourteenth Amendment to apply to state criminal prosecutions. Thus some states operate with-

grand jury A jury that determines whether sufficient evidence is available to justify a trial. Grand juries do not rule on the accused's guilt or innocence.

---

[39] *District of Columbia v. Heller* (2008).

[40] *Horton v. California,* 496 U.S. 128 (1990).

[41] For a good discussion of the issue, see Fisher, *American Constitutional Law,* pp. 884–89.

[42] E. S. Corwin and Jack Peltason, *Understanding the Constitution,* p. 286.

out grand juries. In such states, the prosecuting attorney simply files a "bill of information" affirming that there is sufficient evidence available to justify a trial.

The fifth amendment also provides the constitutional protection from double jeopardy, or being tried more than once for the same crime, and the guarantee that no citizen "shall be compelled in any criminal case to be a witness against himself." This protection against self-incrimination led to the *Miranda* case and the Miranda rules that police must follow when questioning an arrested criminal suspect.

Another fundamental clause of the Fifth Amendment is the "takings clause," which extends to each citizen a protection against the taking of private property "without just compensation." Although this part of the amendment is not specifically concerned with protecting persons accused of crimes, it is nevertheless a fundamentally important instance where the government and the citizen are adversaries. As discussed earlier in this chapter, the power of any government to take private property for a public use is called ***eminent domain***.

The Sixth Amendment and the Right to Counsel   Like the exclusionary rule of the Fourth Amendment and the self-incrimination clause of the Fifth Amendment, the "right to counsel" provision of the Sixth Amendment is notable for freeing defendants who seem to the public to be patently guilty as charged. Other provisions of the Sixth Amendment, such as the right to a speedy trial and the right to confront witnesses before an impartial jury, are less controversial in nature.

Gideon v. Wainwright is the perfect case study because it involved a disreputable person who seemed patently guilty of the crime for which he was convicted. In and out of jails for most of his fifty-one years, Clarence Earl Gideon received a five-year sentence for breaking into and entering a poolroom in Panama City, Florida. While serving time in jail, Gideon became a fairly well qualified "jailhouse lawyer," made his own appeal on a handwritten petition, and eventually won the landmark ruling on the right to counsel in all felony cases.[43] The right to counsel has been expanded rather than restricted during the past few decades, when the courts have become more conservative. For example, in 2003 the Supreme Court overturned the death sentence of a Maryland death-row inmate, holding that the defense lawyer had failed to fully inform the jury of the defendant's history of "horrendous childhood abuse."[44]

The Eighth Amendment and Cruel and Unusual Punishment   The Eighth Amendment prohibits "excessive bail," "excessive fines," and "cruel and unusual punishment." Virtually all the debate over Eighth Amendment issues focuses on the last clause of the amendment: the protection from "cruel and unusual punishment." One of the greatest challenges in interpreting this provision consistently is that what is considered "cruel and unusual" varies from culture to culture and from generation to generation. And unfortunately, it also varies by class and race.

By far the biggest issue in the inconsistency of class and race as constituting cruel and unusual punishment arises over the death penalty. In 1972, the Supreme

eminent domain The right of the government to take private property for public use, with reasonable compensation awarded for the property.

---

[43]For a full account of the story of the trial and release of Clarence Earl Gideon, see Lewis, *Gideon's Trumpet*. See also David M. O'Brien, *Storm Center*, 7th ed. (New York: Norton, 2005).

[44]*Wiggins v. Smith*, 539 U.S. 510 (2003).

Court overturned several state death-penalty laws not because they were cruel and unusual but because they were being applied in a capricious manner: blacks were much more likely than whites to be sentenced to death, the poor more likely than the rich, and men more likely than women.[45] Since 1976, the Court has consistently upheld state laws providing for capital punishment, although it also continues to review numerous death-penalty appeals each year.

Constitutional objections to the death penalty often invoke the Eighth Amendment's protection against punishments that are "cruel and unusual." Yet supporters of the death penalty say it can hardly be considered a violation of this protection, since it was commonly used in the eighteenth century and was supported by most early-American leaders.

The Right to Privacy

When the Court began to take a more activist role in the mid-1950s and 1960s, the idea of a **right to privacy** gained traction. In 1958, the Supreme Court recognized "privacy in one's association" in its decision to prevent the state of Alabama from using the membership list of the NAACP in the state's investigations. The sphere of privacy was drawn in earnest in 1965, when the Court ruled that a Connecticut statute forbidding the use of contraceptives violated the right of marital privacy. Justice William O. Douglas, author of the majority decision in the *Griswold* case, argued that this right of privacy is also grounded in the Constitution because it fits into a "zone of privacy" created by a combination of the Third, Fourth, and Fifth Amendments. The right to privacy was confirmed and extended in 1973 in the most important of all privacy decisions and one of the most important Supreme Court decisions in American history: *Roe v. Wade*. This decision established a woman's right to seek an abortion and prohibited states from making abortion a criminal act.[46]

In the last three decades, the right to be left alone began to include the privacy rights of homosexuals. One morning in Atlanta in the mid-1980s, Michael Hardwick was arrested by a police officer who discovered him in bed with another man. Hardwick was charged under Georgia's laws against heterosexual and homosexual sodomy. Hardwick filed a lawsuit against the state, challenging the constitutionality of the Georgia law, and won his case in the federal court of appeals. The state of Georgia, in an unusual move, appealed the court's decision to the Supreme Court. The majority of the Court reversed the lower-court decision, holding against Hardwick on the grounds that "the federal Constitution confers [no] fundamental right upon homosexuals to engage in sodomy" and that there was therefore no basis to invalidate "the laws of the many states that still make such conduct illegal and have done so for a very long time."[47] With *Lawrence v. Texas* in 2003, the Court overturned its 1986 decision in *Bowers v. Hardwick*, and state legislatures no longer had the authority to make private sexual behavior a crime.[48] Drawing from the tradition

right to privacy The right to be let alone, which has been interpreted by the Supreme Court to entail free access to birth control and abortions.

[45] *Furman v. Georgia*, 408 U.S. 238 (1972).

[46] *Roe v. Wade*, 410 U.S. 113 (1973).

[47] *Bowers v. Hardwick*, 478 U.S. 186 (1986). The dissenters were quoting an earlier case, *Olmstead v. United States*, 277 U.S. 438 (1928), to emphasize the nature of their disagreement with the majority in the *Bowers* case.

[48] *Lawrence and Garner v. Texas*, 539 U.S. 558 (2003).

ONLINE READING ○

ONLINE READING ○

of negative liberty, the Court maintained, "In our tradition the State is not omnipresent in the home. And there are other spheres of our lives and existence outside the home, where the State should not be a dominant presence." Explicitly encompassing lesbians and gay men within the umbrella of privacy, the Court concluded that the "petitioners are entitled to respect for their private lives. The State cannot demean their existence or control their destiny by making their private sexual conduct a crime." This decision added substance to the Ninth Amendment "right of privacy."

Another area ripe for litigation and public discourse is the so-called right to die. A number of highly publicized physician-assisted suicides have focused attention on whether people have a right to choose their own death and receive assistance in carrying it out. Can this become part of the privacy right, or is it a new substantive right? A tentative answer came in 1997, when the Court ruled that a Washington State law establishing a ban on "causing" or "aiding" a suicide did not violate the Fourteenth Amendment or any clauses of the Bill of Rights incorporated into the Fourteenth Amendment. Thus if a state can constitutionally adopt such a prohibition, there is no constitutional right to suicide or assisted suicide. However, the Court left open the narrower question of "whether a mentally competent person who is experiencing great suffering has a constitutionally cognizable interest in controlling the circumstances of his or her imminent death."

The War on Terrorism In response to the September 11, 2001, terrorist attacks on the United States, Congress enacted new legislation—the Patriot Act—designed to make it easier for federal law enforcement agencies to investigate and prosecute suspected terrorists. In addition, the president issued a series of orders allowing the National Security Agency to eavesdrop on domestic communications and the military to detain and try terrorism suspects. Civil libertarians have argued that the government's new surveillance and eavesdropping authority poses a threat to free speech and privacy. Critics have also declared that the open-ended military detention of terrorism suspects, along with the special military tribunals and procedures established by the president to try such suspects, violates many of the fundamental constitutional protections provided to those accused of criminal actions.

Some of these questions have been raised in the federal courts. In June 2004, the Supreme Court ruled in three cases involving the president's antiterrorism initiatives and claims of executive power and in two of those cases appeared to place some limit on presidential authority.[49] In these rulings, the Supreme Court asserted that presidential actions were subject to judicial scrutiny and placed some constraints on the president's unfettered power. At the same time, the Court affirmed the president's single most important claim: the unilateral power to declare individuals, including U.S. citizens, "enemy combatants," who can be detained by federal authorities under adverse legal circumstances. Future presidents are likely to cite the Court's decisions as precedents for, rather than limits on, the exercise of executive power. The same is likely to be true of the Court's June 2006 decision in the case

---

[49] *Hamdi v. Rumsfeld*, 542 U.S. 507 (2004); *Rasul v. Bush*, 542 U.S. 466 (2004); *Rumsfeld v. Padilla*, 542 U.S. 426 (2004).

of *Hamdan v. Rumsfeld.*[50] Salim Ahmed Hamdan, a Taliban fighter captured in Afghanistan in 2001 and held at Guantánamo since 2002, was slated for trial by a special military tribunal. Such tribunals, operating outside both the civilian and the military court systems, were created by the Bush administration to deal with suspected terrorists in the wake of the September 11 attacks and the U.S. invasion of Afghanistan. The Court found that President Bush's tribunals were not authorized by statute and were operating under procedures that provided defendants with fewer rights and safeguards than they would receive under the Uniform Code of Military Justice. But while invalidating these particular tribunals, the Supreme Court accepted the principle that the president could order persons he deemed unlawful combatants to be tried by military tribunals so long as the tribunals were lawfully constituted.

CIVIL RIGHTS

With the adoption of the Fourteenth Amendment in 1868, civil rights became part of the Constitution, guaranteed to each citizen through "equal protection of the laws." These words launched a century of political movements and legal efforts to press for racial equality. African Americans' quest for civil rights in turn inspired many other groups—including members of other racial and ethnic groups, women, people with disabilities, and gay men and lesbians—to seek new laws and constitutional guarantees of their civil rights.

Congress passed the Fourteenth Amendment and the states ratified it in the aftermath of the Civil War. Together with the Thirteenth Amendment, which abolished slavery, and the Fifteenth Amendment, which guaranteed voting rights to black men, it seemed to provide a guarantee of civil rights for the newly freed enslaved blacks. But the general language of the Fourteenth Amendment meant that its support for civil rights could be far reaching. The very simplicity of the ***equal protection clause*** of the Fourteenth Amendment left it open to interpretation:

> No State shall make or enforce any law which shall . . . deny to any person within its jurisdiction the equal protection of the laws.

Plessy v. Ferguson: "Separate but Equal"

Following its initial decision making "equal protection" a right, the Supreme Court was no more ready to enforce the civil rights aspects of the Fourteenth Amendment than it was to enforce the civil liberties provisions. The Court declared the Civil Rights Act of 1875 unconstitutional on the ground that the act sought to protect blacks against discrimination by private businesses, while the Fourteenth Amendment, according to the Court's interpretation, was intended to protect individuals only against discrimination by *public* officials of state and local governments.

In 1896, the Court went still further, in the infamous case of *Plessy v. Ferguson,* by upholding a Louisiana statute that required segregation of the races on

equal protection clause A clause in the Fourteenth Amendment that requires that states provide citizens "equal protection of the laws."

---

[50]*Hamdan v. Rumsfeld,* 548 U.S. (2006).

trolleys and other public carriers (and by implication in all public facilities, including schools). The Supreme Court held that the Fourteenth Amendment's "equal protection of the laws" was not violated by racial distinction as long as the facilities were equal.[51] People generally pretended they were equal as long as some accommodation existed. What the Court was saying, in effect, was that it was not unreasonable to use race as a basis of exclusion in public matters. This was the origin of the *"separate but equal" rule* that was not reversed until 1954.

Racial Discrimination after World War II

The Supreme Court had begun to change its position regarding racial discrimination just before World War II by being stricter about what the states would have to do to provide equal facilities under the "separate but equal" rule. In 1938, the Court rejected Missouri's policy of paying the tuition of qualified blacks to out-of-state law schools rather than admitting them to the University of Missouri Law School.[52] After the war, modest progress resumed. In 1950, the Court rejected Texas's claim that its new "law school for Negroes" afforded education equal to that of the all-white University of Texas Law School; without confronting the "separate but equal" principle itself, the Court's decision anticipated *Brown v. Board* by opening the question of whether *any* segregated facility could be truly equal.[53]

As the Supreme Court was ordering the admission of blacks to all-white state laws schools, it was also striking down the Southern practice of "white primaries," which legally excluded blacks from participation in the nominating process.[54] The most important pre-1954 decision was probably *Shelley v. Kraemer*,[55] in which the Court ruled against the practice of "restrictive convenants," whereby the seller of a home added a clause to the sales contract requiring the buyer to agree not to resell the home to a non-Caucasian, non-Christian, and so on.

Although none of those cases confronted "separate but equal" and the principle of racial discrimination as such, they were extremely significant to black leaders, and gave them encouragement enough to believe that there was at last an opportunity and enough legal precedent to change the constitutional framework itself. By the fall of 1952, the Court had on its docket cases from Kansas, South Carolina, Virginia, Delaware, and the District of Columbia challenging the constitutionality of school segregation. Of these, the Kansas case became the chosen one. It seemed to be ahead of the pack in its district court, and it had the special advantage of being located in a state outside the Deep South.[56]

"separate but equal" rule Doctrine that public accommodations could be segregated by race but still be equal.

○ ONLINE READING

---

[51] *Plessy v. Ferguson*, 163 U.S. 537 (1896).

[52] *Missouri ex rel. Gaines v. Canada*, 305 U.S. 337 (1938).

[53] *Sweatt v. Painter*, 339 U.S. 629 (1950).

[54] *Smith v. Allwright*, 321 U.S. 649 (1944).

[55] *Shelley v. Kraemer*, 334 U.S. 1 (1948).

[56] The District of Columbia case came up too, but since the District of Columbia is not a state, it did not directly involve the Fourteenth Amendment and its equal protection clause. It confronted the Court on the same grounds, however—that segregation is inherently unequal. Its victory in effect was "incorporation in reverse," with equal protection moving from the Fourteenth Amendment to become part of the Bill of Rights. See *Bolling v. Sharpe*, 347 U.S. 497 (1954).

Oliver Brown, the father of three girls, lived "across the tracks" in a low-income, racially mixed Topeka neighborhood. Every school-day morning, one of his daughters, Linda Brown, took the school bus to the Monroe School for black children about a mile away. In September 1950, Oliver Brown took Linda to the all-white Sumner School, which was actually closer to home, to enter her into the third grade in defiance of state law and local segregation rules. When they were refused, Brown took his case to the NAACP, and soon thereafter *Brown v. Board of Education* was born.

In deciding the case, the Court, to the surprise of many, rejected as inconclusive all the learned arguments about the intent of the Fourteenth Amendment and committed itself to considering only the consequences of segregation:

> Does segregation of children in public schools solely on the basis of race, even though the physical facilities and other "tangible" factors may be equal, deprive the children of the minority group of equal educational opportunities? We believe that it does. . . . We conclude that in the field of public education the doctrine of "separate but equal" has no place. Separate educational facilities are inherently unequal.[57]

The *Brown* decision altered the constitutional framework in two fundamental respects. First, after *Brown*, the states would no longer have the power to use race as a basis of discrimination in law. Second, the national government would from then on have the power (and eventually the obligation) to intervene with strict regulatory policies against the discriminatory actions of state or local governments, school boards, employers, and others in the private sector.

Civil Rights after *Brown v. Board of Education*

Although *Brown v. Board of Education* withdrew all constitutional authority to use race as a criterion of exclusion, this historic decision was merely a small opening move. First, most states refused to cooperate until sued, and many ingenious schemes were employed to delay obedience (such as paying the tuition for white students to attend newly created "private" academies). Second, even as Southern school boards began to cooperate by eliminating their legally enforced (**de jure**) school segregation, there remained extensive actual (**de facto**) school segregation in the North as well as the South. *Brown* could not affect *de facto* segregation, which was not legislated but happened as a result of racially segregated housing. Third, *Brown* did not directly touch discrimination in employment, public accommodations, juries, voting, and other areas of social and economic activity.

A decade of frustration following *Brown* made it fairly obvious to all that the goal of "equal protection" required positive, or affirmative, action by Congress and by administrative agencies. And given massive Southern resistance and a generally negative national public opinion toward racial integration, progress would not be made through courts, Congress, or agencies without intense, well-organized support.

de facto segregation Racial segregation that is not a direct result of law or government policy but is, instead, a reflection of residential patterns, income distributions, or other social factors.

de jure segregation Racial segregation that is a direct result of law or official policy.

ONLINE READING

[57] *Brown v. Board of Education of Topeka, Kansas*, 347 U.S. 483 (1954).

School Desegregation   Although the District of Columbia and some of the school districts in the border states began to respond almost immediately to court-ordered desegregation, the states of the Deep South responded with a well-planned delaying tactic. Southern legislatures passed laws ordering school districts to maintain segregated schools and state superintendents to withhold state funding from racially mixed classrooms. Some Southern states centralized public school authority to give them power to close the schools that might tend to obey the Court and to provide alternative private schooling.

Most of these plans of "massive resistance" were tested in the federal courts and were struck down as unconstitutional.[58] But Southern resistance was not confined to legislation. For example, in Arkansas in 1957, Governor Orval Faubus ordered the National Guard to prevent enforcement of a federal court order to integrate Central High School of Little Rock. President Eisenhower was forced to deploy U.S. troops and place the city under martial law. The Supreme Court handed down a unanimous decision requiring desegregation in Little Rock.[59] The end of massive resistance, however, became simply the beginning of still another Southern strategy. "Pupil placement" laws authorized school districts to place each pupil in a school according to a whole variety of academic, personal, and psychological considerations, never mentioning race at all. This put the burden of transferring to an all-white school on the nonwhite children and their parents.[60] It was thus almost impossible for a single court order to cover a whole district, let alone a whole state. This delayed desegregation a while longer. As Figure 4.2 shows, Southern schools remained largely segregated for a decade after *Brown.*

As new devices were invented by the Southern states to avoid desegregation, it was becoming unmistakably clear that the federal courts could not do the job alone.[61] The first modern effort to legislate in the field of civil rights was made in 1957, but the law contained only a federal guarantee of voting rights, without any powers of enforcement, although it did create the Civil Rights Commission to study abuses. Much more important legislation for civil rights followed during the 1960s, especially the Civil Rights Act of 1964 (see Time Line, page 98).

---

[58]The two most important cases were *Cooper v. Aaron*, 358 U.S. 1 (1958), which required Little Rock, Arkansas, to desegregate; and *Griffin v. Prince Edward County School Board*, 337 U.S. 218 (1964), which forced all the schools of that Virginia county to reopen after five years of being closed to avoid desegregation.

[59]In *Cooper v. Aaron*, the Supreme Court ordered immediate compliance with the lower court's desegregation order and went beyond that with a stern warning that it is "emphatically the province and duty of the judicial department to say what the law is." The justices also took the unprecedented action of personally signing the decisions.

[60]*Shuttlesworth v. Birmingham Board of Education*, 358 U.S. 101 (1958). This decision upheld a "pupil placement" plan purporting to assign pupils on various bases, with no mention of race. This case interpreted *Brown v. Board of Education* to mean that school districts must stop explicit racial discrimination but were under no obligation to take positive steps to desegregate. For a while, black parents were doomed to case-to-case approaches.

[61]For good treatments of that long stretch of the struggle of the federal courts to integrate the schools, see Brest and Levinson, *Processes of Constitutional Decisionmaking*, pp. 471–80; and Alfred Kelly, Winifred Harbison, and Herman Boltz, *The American Constitution: Its Origins and Development*, 7th ed. (New York: Norton, 1991), pp. 610–16.

Racial Equality

As we discuss in this chapter, civil rights is a major political issue in the United States. Especially since the 1960s, most forms of racial discrimination have been prohibited by law, and a large number of government programs have been designed to promote greater political, social, and economic equality between black and white Americans. Despite these efforts, progress in the direction of racial equality has been uneven. As we can see in the following figures and tables, some data suggest that the United States has made great strides toward the color-blind society envisioned by the early leaders of the civil rights movement. Other data, though, indicate that we have a long way to go.

In assessing racial equality in the United States, we could also consider numerous other statistics and other racial and ethnic groups. Depending upon which evidence is selected, one might argue that racial equality in the United States has increased substantially in recent years or that it has not.

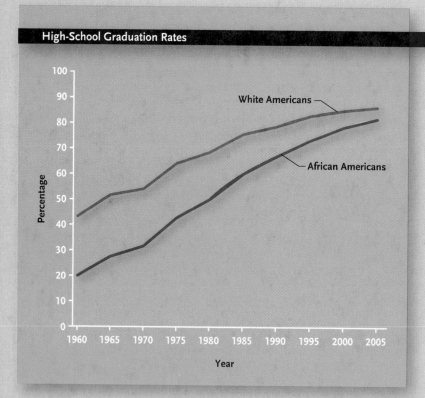

High-School Graduation Rates

One encouraging statistic is the change in black versus white levels of educational attainment over the past 45 years. In 1960, black Americans were less than half as likely to finish high school or graduate from college as whites. Today, the percentage of blacks graduating from high school is nearly identical to the percentage of whites who earn diplomas.

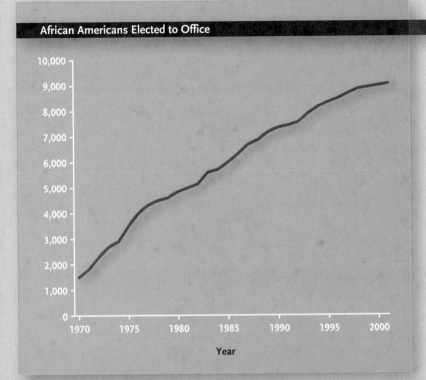

African Americans Elected to Office

(line graph; y-axis: 0 to 10,000 in increments of 1,000; x-axis: Year, 1970 to 2000)

Year

Progress has also been made in the political arena. As recently as 1970, only 1,469 African Americans held elected office in the United States—out of approximately half a million federal, state, and local offices. By 2001, the last year the government collected data, there were more than 9,000 black elected officials, an increase of more than 600 percent.

In the economic realm the gap between blacks and whites has decreased more slowly. In 2004, the average income of black men was only 67 percent of the average for white men. This represented only a slight increase since 1990. During the same period, the average income of black women actually fell relative to that of white women.

Median Income (2004 Dollars)

	Men			Women		
	1990	2000	2004	1990	2000	2004
White	29,668	**32,684**	31,335	14,459	**17,637**	17,648
Black	18,034	**23,411**	22,714	11,671	**17,420**	17,383

FIGURE 4.2 The Percentage of Southern Black Schoolchildren Attending School with Whites, 1955–73

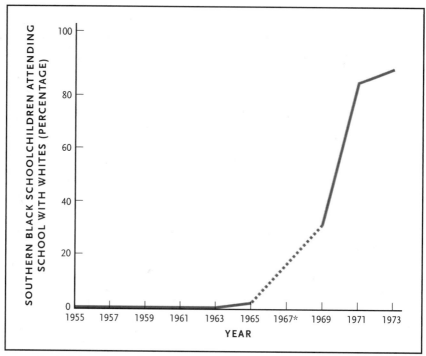

SOURCE: Gerald N. Rosenberg, *Hollow Hope: Can Courts Bring About Social Change?* (Chicago: University of Chicago Press, 1991), pp. 50–51.

NOTE: Dashed line indicates missing data.

Further progress in the desegregation of schools came in the form of busing[62] and redistricting, but it was slow and is likely to continue to be slow unless the Supreme Court decides to permit federal action against *de facto* segregation and against the varieties of private schools and academies that have sprung up for the purpose of avoiding integration.[63] A Supreme Court decision handed down in 1995, in which the Court signaled to the lower courts to "disengage from desegregation efforts," dimmed the prospects for further school integration. Moreover, school desegregation has been made more problematic by the Supreme Court's 2007 decision in the consolidated cases of *County Schools v. Seattle School District No. 1* and *Meredith v. Jefferson County Board of Education*. In both instances, school districts had categorized students by race and assigned them to schools partly on the basis of plans designed to

[62] *Swann v. Charlotte-Mecklenburg Board of Education*, 402 U.S. 1 (1971). See also Bernard Schwartz, *Swann's Way: The School Busing Case and the Supreme Court* (New York: Oxford University Press, 1986).

[63] For a good evaluation, see Gary Orfield, *Must We Bus? Segregated Schools and National Policy* (Washington, D.C.: Brookings Institution, 1978), pp. 144–46. See also Bob Woodward and Scott Armstrong, *The Brethren: Inside the Supreme Court* (New York: Simon and Schuster, 1979), pp. 426–27; and J. Anthony Lukas, *Common Ground* (New York: Random House, 1986).

achieve racial diversity in the districts' educational institutions. The Supreme Court, however, said that racial classifications were potentially "too pernicious" to be used except under the most compelling or extreme circumstances. While racial classifications can, indeed, be pernicious, rights activists pointed out that it is difficult to see how school systems might achieve greater racial diversity if they are prohibited from taking account of students' race when making school assignments.

The Rise of the Politics of Rights

Outlawing Discrimination in Employment   Despite the agonizingly slow progress of school desegregation, there was some progress in other areas of civil rights during the 1960s and 1970s. Voting rights were established and fairly quickly began to revolutionize Southern politics. Service on juries was no longer denied to minorities. But progress in the right to participate in politics and government dramatized the relative lack of economic progress, and it was in this area that battles over civil rights were increasingly fought.

The federal courts and the Justice Department entered this area through Title VII of the Civil Rights Act of 1964. Title VII outlawed job discrimination by all private and public employers, including governmental agencies (such as fire and police departments), that employed more than fifteen workers. We have already seen that the Supreme Court gave "interstate commerce" such a broad definition that Congress had the constitutional authority to outlaw discrimination by virtually any local employer.[64] Title VII made it unlawful to discriminate in employment on the basis of color, religion, sex, or national origin, as well as race.

One problem with Title VII was that the complaining party had to show that deliberate discrimination was the cause of the failure to get a job or a training opportunity. Rarely does an employer explicitly admit discrimination on the basis of race, sex, or any other illegal reason. For a time, courts allowed the complaining parties to make their case if they could show that an employer's hiring practices, whether intentional or not, had the *effect* of exclusion. Employers, in effect, had to justify their actions.[65] In recent years, though, the Supreme Court has placed a number of limits on employment discrimination suits. In 2007, for example, in the case of *Ledbetter v. Goodyear Tire and Rubber Co.* the court said that a complaint of gender discrimination must be brought within 180 days of the time the discrimination was alleged to have occurred.[66] This blocks suits based on events that might have taken place in the past.

---

[64] See especially *Katzenbach v. McClung*, 379 U.S. 294 (1964). Almost immediately after passage of the Civil Rights Act of 1964, a case was brought challenging the validity of Title II, which covered discrimination in public accommodations. Ollie's Barbecue was a neighborhood restaurant in Birmingham, Alabama. It was located eleven blocks away from an interstate highway and even farther from railroad and bus stations. Its table service was for whites only; there was only a take-out service for blacks. The Supreme Court agreed that Ollie's was strictly an intrastate restaurant, but since a substantial proportion of its food and other supplies were bought from companies outside the state of Alabama, there was sufficient connection to interstate commerce; therefore, racial discrimination at such restaurants would "impose commercial burdens of national magnitude upon interstate commerce." Although this case involved Title II, it had direct bearing on the constitutionality of Title VII.

[65] *Griggs v. Duke Power Company*, 401 U.S. 24 (1971).

[66] *Ledbetter v. Goodyear Tire and Rubber Co.*, 05-1074 (2007).

TIME LINE OF CAUSE AND EFFECT IN THE CIVIL RIGHTS MOVEMENT

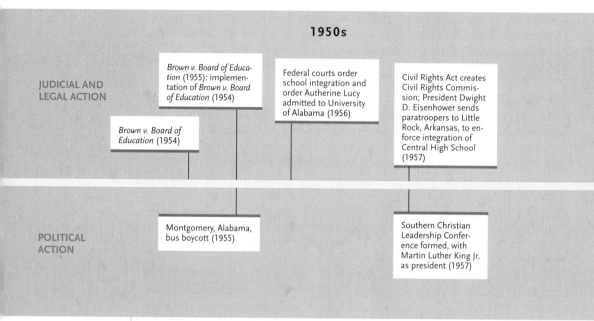

1950s

JUDICIAL AND LEGAL ACTION

Brown v. Board of Education (1955): implementation of *Brown v. Board of Education* (1954)

Federal courts order school integration and order Autherine Lucy admitted to University of Alabama (1956)

Civil Rights Act creates Civil Rights Commission; President Dwight D. Eisenhower sends paratroopers to Little Rock, Arkansas, to enforce integration of Central High School (1957)

Brown v. Board of Education (1954)

POLITICAL ACTION

Montgomery, Alabama, bus boycott (1955)

Southern Christian Leadership Conference formed, with Martin Luther King Jr. as president (1957)

Gender Discrimination Title VII provided a valuable tool for the growing women's movement in the 1960s and 1970s.[67] In fact, in many ways the law fostered the growth of the women's movement. The first major campaign of the National Organization for Women (NOW) involved picketing the Equal Employment Opportunity Commission (EEOC) for its refusal to ban sex-segregated employment advertisements. NOW also sued *The New York Times* for continuing to publish such ads after the passage of Title VII. Another organization, the Women's Equity Action League (WEAL), pursued legal action on a wide range of sex discrimination issues, filing lawsuits against law schools and medical schools for their discriminatory admission policies, for example.

Building on these victories and the growth of the women's movement, feminist activists sought an equal rights amendment (ERA) to the Constitution. The proposed amendment was short: Its substantive passage stated that "equality of rights under the law shall not be denied or abridged by the United States or by any State on account of sex." The amendment's supporters believed that such a sweeping guarantee of equal rights was a necessary tool for ending all discrimination against women and for making gender roles more equal. Opponents charged that it would be socially disruptive and would introduce changes—such as coed restrooms—that most Americans did not want. The amendment easily passed Congress in 1972 and

---

[67]This and the next five sections are from Ginsberg et al., *We the People.*

CHAPTER 4 CIVIL LIBERTIES AND CIVIL RIGHTS

1960s

CIAL AND AL ACTION

First substantive Civil Rights Act, primarily guaranteeing voting rights (1960)

Interstate Commerce Commission orders desegregation on all buses, on all trains, and in terminals; President John F. Kennedy favors executive action over civil rights legislation (1961)

President Kennedy shifts gears, supporting strong civil rights law; President Lyndon B. Johnson asserts strong support for civil rights (1963)

Congress passes historic Civil Rights Act covering voting, employment, public accommodations, education (1964)

War on poverty in full swing (1966)

Voting Rights Act (1965)

ITICAL ION

Student Nonviolent Coordinating Committee formed to organize protests, sit-ins, freedom rides (1960)

Nonviolent demonstrations in Birmingham, Alabama, lead to King's arrest and "Letter from Birmingham Jail"; March on Washington (1963)

King announces drive to register 3 million blacks in the South (1965)

Movement dissipates, with remnants focusing on litigation, community action programs, war protest, and more militant "black power" actions (1966)

won quick approval in many state legislatures but fell three states short of the thirty-eight needed to ratify the amendment by the 1982 deadline for its ratification.[68]

Despite the failure of the ERA, gender discrimination expanded dramatically as an area of civil rights law. In the 1970s, the conservative Burger Court helped to establish gender discrimination as a major and highly visible civil rights issue. Although the Burger Court refused to treat gender discrimination as the equivalent of racial discrimination,[69] it did make it easier for plaintiffs to file and win suits on the basis of gender discrimination by applying an "intermediate" level of review to these cases.[70] This ***intermediate scrutiny*** is midway between traditional rules of evidence, which put the burden of proof on the plaintiff, and the doctrine of strict scrutiny, which requires the defendant to show not only that a particular classification is reasonable but also that there is a need or compelling interest for it. Intermediate scrutiny shifts the burden of proof partially onto the defendant, rather than leaving it entirely on the plaintiff.

One major step was taken in 1992, when the Court decided in *Franklin v. Gwinnett County Public Schools* that violations of Title IX of the 1972 Education Act could

intermediate scrutiny
The test used by the Supreme Court in gender discrimination cases. Intermediate scrutiny places the burden of proof partially on the government and partially on the challengers to show that the law in question is constitutional.

---

[68]See Jane J. Mansbridge, *Why We Lost the ERA* (Chicago: University of Chicago Press, 1986); and Gilbert Steiner, *Constitutional Inequality* (Washington, D.C.: Brookings Institution, 1985).

[69]See *Frontiero v. Richardson*, 411 U.S. 677 (1973).

[70]See *Craig v. Boren*, 423 U.S. 1047 (1976).

be remedied with monetary damages.[71] Title IX forbids gender discrimination in education, but it initially sparked little litigation because of its weak enforcement provisions. The Court's 1992 ruling opened the door for more legal action in the area of education. The greatest impact has been in the areas of sexual harassment—the subject of the *Franklin* case—and in equal treatment of women's athletic programs. The potential for monetary damages has made universities and public schools take the problem of sexual harassment more seriously. Colleges and universities have also started to pay more attention to women's athletic programs. In the two years after the *Franklin* case, complaints to the Education Department's Office for Civil Rights about unequal treatment of women's athletic programs nearly tripled. In several high-profile legal cases, some prominent universities have been ordered to create more women's sports programs; many other colleges and universities have begun to add more women's programs in order to avoid potential litigation.[72] In 1997, the Supreme Court refused to hear a petition by Brown University challenging a lower-court ruling that the university establish strict sex equity in its athletic programs. The Court's decision meant that in colleges and universities across the country, varsity athletic positions for men and women must reflect their overall enrollment numbers.[73]

In 1996, the Supreme Court made another important decision about gender and education by putting an end to all-male schools supported by public funds. It ruled that the Virginia Military Institute's policy of not admitting women was unconstitutional.[74] Along with the Citadel, an all-male military college in South Carolina, Virginia Military Institute (VMI) had never admitted women. It argued that the unique educational experience it offered, including intense physical training and the harsh treatment of freshmen, would be destroyed if women were admitted. The Court, however, ruled that the male-only policy denied "substantial equality" to women. Two days after the Court's ruling, the Citadel announced that it would accept women. VMI considered becoming a private institution in order to remain all-male, but in September 1996 the school board finally voted to admit women. The legal decisions may have removed formal barriers to entry, but the experience of the female cadets at these schools has not been easy. The first female cadet at the Citadel, Shannon Faulkner, won admission in 1995 under a federal court order but quit after four days. Although four women were admitted to the Citadel after the Supreme Court decision, two of them quit several months later. They charged harassment by male students, including attempts to set the female cadets on fire.[75]

Courts began to find sexual harassment a form of sex discrimination during the late 1970s. Although sexual harassment law applies to education, most of the law of sexual harassment has been developed by courts through interpretation of Title VII

---

[71] *Franklin v. Gwinnett County Public Schools*, 503 U.S. 60 (1992).

[72] Jennifer Halperin, "Women Step Up to Bat," *Illinois Issues* 21 (September 1995): 11–14.

[73] Joan Biskupic and David Nakamura, "Court Won't Review Sports Equity Ruling," *Washington Post*, 22 April 1997, p. A1.

[74] *United States v. Virginia*, 518 U.S. 515 (1996).

[75] Judith Havemann, "Two Women Quit Citadel over Alleged Harassment," *Washington Post*, 13 January 1997, p. A1.

of the Civil Rights Act of 1964. In 1986, the Supreme Court recognized two forms of sexual harassment—the quid pro quo type, which involves sexual extortion, and the hostile-environment type, which involves sexual intimidation.[76] Employers and many employees have worried that hostile-environment sexual harassment is too ambiguous. When can an employee bring charges? When is the employer liable? In 1986, the Court said that sexual harassment may be legally actionable even if the employee did not suffer tangible economic or job-related losses in relation to it. And in 1993, the Court said that sexual harassment may be legally actionable even if the employee did not suffer tangible psychological costs as a result of it.[77] In two 1998 cases, the Court further strengthened the law when it said that whether or not sexual harassment results in economic harm to the employee, an employer is liable for the harassment if it was committed by someone with authority over the employee—by a supervisor, for example. But the Court also said that an employer may defend itself by showing that it had a sexual harassment prevention and grievance policy in effect.[78]

The development of gender discrimination as an important part of the civil rights struggle has coincided with the rise of women's politics as a discrete movement in American politics. As with the struggle for racial equality, the relationship between changes in government policies and political action suggests that changes in government policies to a great degree produce political action. Today the existence of a powerful women's movement derives in large measure from the enactment of Title VII of the Civil Rights Act of 1964 and from the Burger Court's vital steps in applying that law to the protection of women. The recognition of women's civil rights has become an issue that in many ways transcends the usual distinctions of American political debate. In the heavily partisan debate over the federal crime bill enacted in 1994, for instance, the section of the bill that enjoyed the widest support was the Violence against Women Act, whose most important feature was that it defined gender-biased violent crimes as a matter of civil rights and created a civil rights remedy for women who have been the victims of such crimes. But since the act was ruled unconstitutional by the Supreme Court in 2000, the struggle for women's rights will likely remain part of the political debate.

Latinos and Asian Americans   The labels "Latino" or "Hispanic" and "Asian American" encompass a wide range of groups with diverse national origins, distinctive cultural identities, and particular experiences. For example, the early political experiences of Mexican Americans were shaped by race and region. In 1898, Mexican Americans were given formal political rights, including the right to vote. In many places, however, and especially in Texas, Mexican Americans were segregated and prevented from voting by such means as the white primary and the poll tax.[79] Region made a difference too. In contrast to the northeastern and midwestern cities in

---

[76] *Meritor Savings Bank v. Vinson* (1986).

[77] *Harris v. Forklift Systems*, 510 U.S. 17 (1993).

[78] *Burlington Industries v. Ellerth*, 524 U.S. 742 (1998); *Faragher v. City of Boca Raton*, 524 U.S. 775 (1998).

[79] New Mexico had a different history because not many Anglos settled there initially. (*Anglo* is the term for a non-Hispanic white of European background.) Mexican Americans had considerable power in territorial legislatures between 1865 and 1912. See Lawrence H. Fuchs, *The American Kaleidoscope* (Hanover, N.H.: University Press of New England, 1990), pp. 239–40.

which most European immigrants settled, the Southwest did not have a tradition of ethnic mobilization associated with machine politics. Particularly after the political reforms enacted in the first decade of the twentieth century, city politics in the Southwest was dominated by a small group of white elites. In the countryside, when Mexican Americans participated in politics, it was often as part of a political organization dominated by a large white landowner, or *patron*.

The earliest independent Mexican American political organizations, the League of United Latin American Citizens (LULAC) and the American GI Forum, worked to stem discrimination against Mexican Americans in the years after World War II. By the late 1950s, the first Mexican American had been elected to Congress, and four others followed in the 1960s. In the late 1960s, a new kind of Mexican American political movement was born. Inspired by the black civil rights movement, Mexican American students launched boycotts of high-school classes in Los Angeles, Denver, and San Antonio. Students in colleges and universities across California joined in as well. Among their demands were bilingual education, an end to discrimination, and greater cultural recognition. In Crystal City, Texas, which had been dominated by Anglo politicians despite a population that was overwhelmingly Mexican American, the newly formed La Raza Unida party took over the city government.[80]

Since that time, Mexican American political strategy has developed along two tracks. One is a traditional ethnic-group path of voter registration and voting along ethnic lines. The second is a legal strategy using the various civil rights laws designed to ensure fair access to the political system. The Mexican American Legal Defense and Education Fund (MALDEF) has played a key role in designing and pursuing the latter strategy.

The early Asian experience in the United States was shaped by a series of naturalization laws dating back to 1790, the first of which declared that only white aliens were eligible for citizenship. Chinese immigrants had begun arriving in California in the 1850s, drawn by the boom of the gold rush. They were immediately met with hostility. The virulent antagonism toward Chinese immigrants in California led Congress in 1870 to declare Chinese immigrants ineligible for citizenship. In 1882, the first Chinese Exclusion Act suspended the entry of Chinese laborers.

At the time of the Exclusion Act, the Chinese community was composed predominantly of single male laborers, with few women and children. The few Chinese children in San Francisco were initially denied entry to the public schools; only after parents of American-born Chinese children pressed legal action were the children allowed to attend public school. Even then, however, they were made to attend a separate Chinese school. American-born Chinese children could not be denied citizenship, however; this right was confirmed by the Supreme Court in 1898, when it ruled in *United States v. Wong Kim Ark* that anyone born in the United States was entitled to full citizenship.[81] Still, new Chinese immigrants were barred from the

---

[80]On the La Raza Unida party, see Carlos Muñoz Jr. and Mario Barrera, "La Raza Unida Party and the Chicano Student Movement in California," in *Latinos and the Political System*, ed. F. Chris Garcia (Notre Dame, Ind.: University of Notre Dame Press, 1988), pp. 213–35.

[81]*United States v. Wong Kim Ark*, 169 U.S. 649 (1898).

United States until 1943; China by then had become a key wartime ally, and Congress repealed the Chinese Exclusion Act and permitted Chinese residents to become citizens.

Immigration climbed rapidly after the 1965 Immigration and Nationality Services Act, which lifted discriminatory quotas. In spite of this and other developments, limited English proficiency barred many Asian Americans and Latinos from full participation in American life. Two developments in the 1970s, however, established rights for language minorities. In 1974, the Supreme Court ruled in *Lau v. Nichols,* a suit filed on behalf of Chinese students in San Francisco, that school districts have to provide education for students whose English is limited.[82] It did not mandate bilingual education, but it established a duty to provide instruction that students could understand. The 1970 amendments to the Voting Rights Act of 1965 permanently outlawed literacy tests in all fifty states and mandated bilingual ballots or oral assistance for those who speak Spanish, Chinese, Japanese, Korean, Native American languages, or Eskimo languages.

Asian Americans and Latinos have also been concerned about the impact of immigration laws on their civil rights. Many Asian American and Latino organizations opposed the Immigration Reform and Control Act of 1986 because it imposes sanctions on employers who hire undocumented workers. Such sanctions, they feared, would lead employers to discriminate against Latinos and Asian Americans. These suspicions were confirmed in a 1990 report by the General Accounting Office that found employer sanctions had created a "widespread pattern of discrimination" against Latinos and others who appear foreign.[83] Organizations such as MALDEF and the Asian Law Caucus monitor and challenge such discrimination. These groups have turned their attention to the rights of legal and illegal immigrants as anti-immigrant sentiment has grown in recent years.

The Supreme Court has ruled that illegal immigrants are eligible for education and medical care but can be denied other social benefits; legal immigrants are to be treated much the same as citizens. But growing immigration—including an estimated 300,000 illegal immigrants per year—and mounting economic insecurity have undermined these practices. Groups of voters across the country now strongly support drawing a sharper line between immigrants and citizens. Not surprisingly, the movement to deny benefits to noncitizens began in California, which experienced sharp economic distress in the early 1990s and has the highest levels of immigration of any state. In 1994, Californians voted in favor of Proposition 187, which denied illegal immigrants all services except emergency medical care. Supporters of the measure hoped to discourage illegal immigration and pressure illegal immigrants already in the country to leave. Opponents contended that denying basic services to illegal immigrants risked creating a subclass of residents in the United States whose lack of education and poor health would threaten all Americans. In 1994 and 1997, a federal court declared most of Proposition 187 unconstitutional, affirming previous rulings that illegal immigrants should be granted

---

[82]*Lau v. Nichols,* 414 U.S. 563 (1974).

[83]Dick Kirschten, "Not Black and White," *National Journal,* 2 March 1991, p. 497.

public education. A booming economy helped to reduce public concern about illegal immigration, but supporters of Proposition 187 promised to reintroduce similar measures in the future.

In January 2004, President Bush released a plan to revamp American immigration laws to enable all undocumented immigrants "to obtain legal status as temporary workers." For illegal immigrants, the president proposed a new temporary-worker program, whereby every illegal immigrant could apply for a three-year work permit, which would be renewable for another three years provided the temporary, or "guest," worker already had a job. Those who failed to stay employed or who broke the law would be deported. Under the plan, employers would control the work permits so that the continued status of the guest worker would depend entirely on the discretion of the employer. In 2007, President Bush and a number of Democrats, including Senator Ted Kennedy of Massachusetts, supported a new immigration reform bill that would have offered legal status and the possibility of future citizenship to approximately 12 million illegal immigrants currently in the United States, while making it more difficult for new illegals to enter the country. However, the bill was defeated in June 2007, leaving the question of immigration reform unresolved.

The question of the rights of legal immigrants points to an even tougher problem. Congress has the power to deny public benefits to this group, but doing so would go against long-standing traditions in American political culture. Legal immigrants have traditionally enjoyed most of the rights and obligations of citizens (such as paying taxes). As the constitutional scholar Alexander Bickel points out, the Constitution begins with "We the People of the United States"; likewise the Bill of Rights refers to the rights of *people,* not the rights of citizens.

Native Americans   The political status of Native Americans was left unclear in the Constitution. But by the early 1800s, the courts had defined each of the Indian tribes as a nation. As members of an Indian nation, Native Americans were declared noncitizens of the United States. The political status of Native Americans changed in 1924, when congressional legislation granted citizenship to those who were born in the United States. A variety of changes in federal policy toward Native Americans during the 1930s paved the way for a later resurgence of their political power. Most important was the federal decision to encourage Native Americans on reservations to establish local self-government.[84]

The Native American political movement gathered force in the 1960s as Indians began to use protest, litigation, and assertion of tribal rights to improve their situation. In 1968, Dennis Banks co-founded the American Indian Movement (AIM), the most prominent Native American protest organization. AIM won national attention in 1969 when 200 of its members, representing twenty tribes, took over the famous prison island of Alcatraz in San Francisco Bay, claiming it for Native Americans. In 1973, AIM members took over the town of Wounded Knee, South Dakota, the site of the massacre of over 200 Sioux men, women, and children by the

---

[84]Not all Indian tribes agreed with this, including the Navajos. See Ronald Takaki, *A Different Mirror: A History of Multicultural America* (Boston: Little, Brown, 1993), pp. 238–48.

U.S. Army in December 1890. The federal government responded to the rise in Indian activism with the Indian Self-determination and Education Assistance Act (1975), which began to give Indians more control over their own land.[85]

As a language minority, Native Americans were also affected by the 1975 amendments to the Voting Rights Act and the *Lau* decision, which established the right of Native Americans to be taught in their own languages. This ruling marked quite a change from the boarding schools once run by the Bureau of Indian Affairs, at which members of Indian tribes were forbidden to speak their own languages. Native Americans have also sought to expand their rights on the basis of their sovereign status. Since the 1920s and 1930s, Native American tribes have sued the federal government for illegally seizing land, seeking monetary reparations and land as damages. Both types of damages have been awarded in such suits, but only in small amounts. Native American tribes have been more successful in winning federal recognition of their sovereignty. Sovereign status has, in turn, allowed them to exercise greater self-determination. Most significant economically was a 1987 Supreme Court decision that freed Native American tribes from most state regulations prohibiting gambling.[86] The establishment of casino gambling on Native American lands has brought a substantial flow of new income into desperately poor reservations.

Americans with Disabilities   The concept of rights for people with disabilities began to emerge in the 1970s as the civil rights model spread to other groups. The seed was planted in a little-noticed provision of the 1973 Rehabilitation Act that outlawed discrimination against individuals on the basis of disabilities. As in many other cases, the law itself helped give rise to the movement demanding rights.[87] Modeling itself on the NAACP's Legal Defense Fund, the disability movement founded a Disability Rights Education and Defense Fund to press its legal claims. The movement achieved its greatest success with the passage of the Americans with Disabilities Act (ADA) of 1990, which guarantees the disabled equal employment rights and access to public businesses. Claims of discrimination in violation of this act are considered by the EEOC. The impact of the law has been far-reaching as businesses and public facilities have installed ramps, elevators, and other devices to meet its requirements.[88]

In 1998, the Supreme Court interpreted the ADA to apply to people with HIV. Until then, ADA was interpreted as applying to people with AIDS but not people

---

[85]On the resurgence of Indian political activity, see Stephen Cornell, *The Return of the Native: American Indian Political Resurgence* (New York: Oxford University Press, 1990); and Dee Brown, *Bury My Heart at Wounded Knee (*New York: Holt, 1971).

[86]*California v. Cabazon Band of Mission Indians,* 480 U.S. 202 (1987).

[87]See the discussion in Robert A. Katzmann, *Institutional Disability: The Saga of Transportation Policy for the Disabled* (Washington, D.C.: Brookings Institution, 1986).

[88]For example, after pressure from the Justice Department, one of the nation's largest rental-car companies agreed to make special hand controls available to any customer requesting them. See "Avis Agrees to Equip Cars for Disabled," *Los Angeles Times,* 2 September 1994, p. D1.

with HIV. The case arose when a dentist was asked to fill a cavity for a woman with HIV; he would do it only if the procedure was done in a hospital setting. The woman sued, and her complaint was that HIV had already disabled her because it was discouraging her from having children. (The act prohibits discrimination in employment, housing, and health care.) Although there have been widespread concerns that the ADA was being expanded too broadly and the costs were becoming too burdensome, corporate America did not seem to be disturbed by the Court's ruling. Stephen Bokat, general counsel of the U.S. Chamber of Commerce, said businesses in general had already been accommodating people with HIV as well as those with AIDS and the case presented no serious problem.[89]

The Aged   The 1967 federal Age Discrimination in Employment Act (ADEA) makes age discrimination illegal when practiced by employers with at least twenty employees. Many states have added to the federal provisions with their own age discrimination laws, and some of the state laws are stronger than the federal provisions. The major lobbyist for seniors, AARP (formerly the American Association of Retired Persons), with its claim to more than 30 million members, has been active in keeping these laws on the books and making sure they are vigorously implemented.

Gay Men and Lesbians   In less than thirty years, the gay movement has become one of the largest civil rights movements in contemporary America. Beginning with street protests in the 1960s, it has grown into a well-financed and sophisticated lobby. The Human Rights Campaign is the primary national PAC focused on gay rights; it provides campaign financing and volunteers to work for candidates endorsed by the group. The movement has also formed legal rights organizations, including the Lambda Legal Defense and Education Fund.

Gay rights drew national attention in 1993, when President Bill Clinton confronted the question of whether gays should be allowed to serve in the military. As a candidate, Clinton had said he favored lifting the ban on homosexuals in the military. The issue set off a huge controversy in the first months of his presidency. After nearly a year of deliberation, the administration enunciated a compromise: its "don't ask, don't tell" policy, which allows gay men and lesbians to serve in the military as long as they do not openly proclaim their sexual orientation or engage in homosexual activity. The administration maintained that the ruling would protect gay men and lesbians from witch-hunting investigations, but many gay advocates expressed disappointment, charging the president with reneging on his campaign promise.

But until 1996, there was no Supreme Court ruling or national legislation explicitly protecting gay men and lesbians from discrimination. The first gay rights case that the Court decided, *Bowers v. Hardwick* (1986), ruled against a right to privacy that would protect consensual homosexual activity. After the *Bowers* decision, the gay rights movement sought suitable legal cases to test the constitutionality of discrimination against gay men and lesbians, much as the civil rights movement

---

[89] The case and the interview with Stephen Bokat were reported in Margaret Warner, "Expanding Coverage: Defining Disability," *Online NewsHour*, 30 June 1998 (www.pbs.org/newshour/bb/law/jan-june98/hiv_6-30.html).

had done in the late 1940s and 1950s. As one advocate put it, "lesbians and gay men are looking for their *Brown v. Board of Education*."[90] Among the cases tested were those stemming from local ordinances restricting gay rights (including the right to marry), job discrimination, and family-law issues such as adoption and parental rights. In 1996, in *Romer v. Evans*, the Supreme Court explicitly extended fundamental civil rights protections to gay men and lesbians by declaring unconstitutional a 1992 amendment to the Colorado state constitution that prohibited local governments from passing ordinances to protect gay rights.[91] The decision's forceful language highlighted the connection between gay rights and civil rights as it declared discrimination against gay people unconstitutional.

In *Lawrence v. Texas* (2003), the Court overturned *Bowers* and struck down a Texas statute criminalizing certain intimate sexual conduct between consenting partners of the same sex. A victory for lesbians and gay men every bit as significant as *Roe v. Wade* was for women, *Lawrence v. Texas* extends at least one aspect of civil liberties to sexual minorities: the right to privacy. However, this decision by itself does not undo the various exclusions that deprive lesbians and gay men of full civil rights, including the right to marry, which became a hot-button issue in 2004.

Early in that year, the Supreme Judicial Court of Massachusetts ruled that under that state's constitution gay men and lesbians were entitled to marry. The state senate then requested that the court rule on whether a civil-union statute would, as in Vermont, satisfy the court's ruling, in response to which the court ruled negatively, asserting that civil unions are too much like the "separate but equal" doctrine that maintained legalized racial segregation from 1896 to 1954. In San Francisco, meanwhile, mayor Gavin Newsom directed the city clerk to issue marriage licenses to same-sex couples in defiance of California law. At the same time, signs indicated that Massachusetts might move toward a state constitutional amendment that would ban gay unions by whatever name. Voters in Missouri, Louisiana, Alaska, Hawaii, Nebraska, and Nevada implemented bans on same-sex marriage. Voters in eleven other states approved similar bans in the November 2004 elections. In 2008, voters in Arizona, Florida, and California also passed bans on gay marriage, which in California overturned a recent court decision that it was unconstitutional to forbid gay marriage.

Affirmative Action

The politics of rights not only spread to increasing numbers of groups in the society but also expanded its goal. The relatively narrow goal of equalizing opportunity by eliminating discriminatory barriers had been developing toward the far broader goal of **affirmative action**—compensatory action to overcome the consequences of past discrimination and encourage greater diversity. An affirmative action policy tends to involve two novel approaches: (1) positive or benign discrimination in which race or some other status is taken into account, but for compensatory action

affirmative action A policy or program designed to redress historic injustices against specified groups by actively promoting equal access to educational and employment opportunities.

---

[90]Quoted in Joan Biskupic, "Gay Rights Activists Seek a Supreme Court Test Case," *Washington Post*, 19 December 1993, p. A1.

[91]*Romer v. Evans*, 517 U.S. 620 (1996).

rather than mistreatment, and (2) compensatory action to favor members of the disadvantaged group who themselves may never have been the victims of discrimination. Quotas may be—but are not necessarily—involved in affirmative action policies.

In 1965, President Lyndon Johnson attempted to inaugurate affirmative action by executive orders directing agency heads and personnel officers to pursue vigorously a policy of minority employment in the federal civil service and in companies doing business with the national government. But affirmative action did not become a prominent goal until the 1970s.

The Supreme Court and the Burden of Proof As this movement spread, it began to divide civil rights activists and their supporters. The whole issue of qualification versus minority preference was addressed in the case of Allan Bakke. Bakke, a white man with no minority affiliation, brought suit against the University of California Medical School at Davis on the grounds that in denying him admission the school had discriminated against him on the basis of his race (that year the school had reserved 16 of 100 available slots for minority applicants). He argued that his grades and test scores had ranked him well above many students who had been accepted at the school and that the only possible explanation for his rejection was that the others were black or Hispanic and he was white. In 1978, Bakke won his case before the Supreme Court and was admitted to the medical school, but he did not succeed in getting affirmative action declared unconstitutional. The Court rejected the procedures at the University of California because its medical school had used both a quota *and* a separate admissions system for minorities. The Court agreed with Bakke's argument that racial categorizations are suspect categories that place a severe burden of proof on those using them to show a "compelling public purpose." The Court went on to say that achieving "a diverse student body" was such a public purpose, but the method of a rigid quota of student slots assigned on the basis of race was incompatible with the equal protection clause. Thus the Court permitted universities (and other schools, training programs, and hiring authorities) to continue to take minority status into consideration but limited severely the use of quotas to situations in which previous discrimination had been shown and the quotas were used more as a guideline for social diversity than as a mathematically defined ratio.[92]

For nearly a decade after *Bakke*, the Supreme Court was tentative and permissive about efforts by corporations and governments to experiment with affirmative action programs in employment.[93] But in 1989, the Court returned to the *Bakke* position, ruling that any "rigid numerical quota" is suspect. In *Wards Cove v. Atonio*, the Court further weakened affirmative action by easing the way for employers to prefer white men, holding that the burden of proof of unlawful discrimination should be shifted from the defendant (the employer) to the plaintiff (the person

---

[92] *Regents of the University of California v. Bakke*, 438 U.S. 265 (1978).

[93] *United Steelworkers of America v. Weber*, 443 U.S. 193 (1979), and *Fullilove v. Klutznick*, 448 U.S. 448 (1980).

[94] *Wards Cove Packing Company v. Atonio*, 490 U.S. 642 (1989).

claiming to be the victim of discrimination).[94] This decision virtually overruled the Court's prior holding.[95] That same year, the Court ruled that any affirmative action program already approved by federal courts could be challenged by white men who alleged that the program discriminated against them.[96]

In 1995, the Supreme Court's ruling in *Adarand Constructors v. Pena* further weakened affirmative action. This decision stated that race-based policies, such as preferences given by the government to minority contractors, must survive strict scrutiny, placing the burden on the government to show that such affirmative action programs serve a compelling government interest and are narrowly tailored to address identifiable past discrimination.[97] President Clinton responded to the *Adarand* decision by ordering a review of all government affirmative action policies and practices. Although many observers suspected that the president would use the review as an opportunity to back away from affirmative action, the conclusions of the task force largely defended existing policies. Reflecting the influence of the Supreme Court's decision in *Adarand*, President Clinton acknowledged that some government policies would need to change. But on the whole, the review found that most affirmative action policies were fair and did not "unduly burden nonbeneficiaries."[98]

Although Clinton sought to "mend, not end" affirmative action, developments in the courts and the states continued to restrict it in important ways. One of the most significant was the *Hopwood* case, in which white students challenged admissions practices at the University of Texas Law School, charging that the school's affirmative action program discriminated against whites. In 1996, a federal court ruling on the case (the U.S. Court of Appeals for the Fifth Circuit) stated that race could never be considered in granting admissions and scholarships at state colleges and universities.[99] This decision effectively rolled back the use of affirmative action permitted by the 1978 *Bakke* case. In *Bakke*, as noted earlier, the Supreme Court had outlawed quotas but said that race could be used as one factor among many in admissions decisions. Many universities and colleges have since justified affirmative action as a way of promoting racial diversity among their student bodies. What was new in the *Hopwood* decision was the ruling that race could *never* be used as a factor in admissions decisions, even to promote diversity.

In 1996, the Supreme Court refused to hear a challenge to the *Hopwood* case. This meant that its ruling remains in effect in the states covered by the Fifth Circuit—Texas, Louisiana, and Mississippi—but does not apply to the rest of the country. The impact of the *Hopwood* ruling is greatest in Texas because Louisiana and Mississippi are under conflicting court orders to desegregate their universities. In Texas in the year after the *Hopwood* case, minority applications to state universities declined. Concerned about the ability of Texas public universities to serve the state's minority students, the Texas legislature quickly passed a new law granting

---

[95] *Griggs v. Duke Power Company* (1971).

[96] *Martin v. Wilks*, 490 U.S. 755 (1989).

[97] *Adarand Constructors v. Pena*, 515 U.S. 200 (1995).

[98] Ann Devroy, "Clinton Study Backs Affirmative Action," *Washington Post*, 19 July 1995, p. A1.

[99] *Hopwood v. State of Texas*, 78 F. 3d 932 (Fifth Cir., 1996).

students who graduate in the top 10 percent of their class automatic admission to the state's public universities. State officials hoped that this measure would ensure a racially diverse student body.[100]

The weakening of affirmative action in the courts was underscored in a case the Supreme Court agreed to hear in 1998. A white schoolteacher in New Jersey who had lost her job had sued her school district, charging that her layoff was racially motivated: A black colleague hired on the same day was not laid off. Under former president George H. W. Bush, the Justice Department had filed a brief on her behalf in 1989, but in 1994 the Clinton administration formally reversed course in a new brief supporting the school district's right to make distinctions based on race as long as they did not involve the use of quotas. Three years later, the administration, worried that the case was weak and could result in a broad decision against affirmative action, reversed course again and filed a brief with the Court urging a narrow ruling in favor of the dismissed worker. Because the school board had justified its actions on the grounds of preserving diversity, the administration feared that a broad ruling by the Supreme Court could totally prohibit the use of race in employment decisions, even as one factor among many designed to achieve diversity. But before the Court could issue a ruling, a coalition of civil rights groups brokered and arranged to pay for a settlement. This unusual move reflected the widespread fear of a sweeping negative decision. Cases involving dismissals, as the New Jersey case did, are generally viewed as much more difficult to defend than cases that concern hiring. In addition, the particular facts of the New Jersey case—two equally qualified teachers hired on the same day—were seen as unusual and unfavorable to affirmative action.[101]

This betwixt and between status of affirmative action was where things stood in 2003, when the Supreme Court took two cases against the University of Michigan that were virtually certain to clarify, if not put closure on, affirmative action. The first suit, *Gratz v. Bollinger,* alleged that by using a point-based ranking system that automatically awarded 20 points (out of 150) to African American, Latino, and Native American applicants, the university's undergraduate admissions policy discriminated unconstitutionally against white students with otherwise equal or superior academic qualifications. The Supreme Court agreed, 6–3, arguing that something tantamount to a quota was involved because undergraduate admissions lacked the necessary "individualized consideration," employing instead a "mechanical one," based too much on the favorable minority points.[102] The Court's ruling in *Gratz v. Bollinger* was not surprising, given *Bakke*'s holding against quotas and recent decisions calling for strict scrutiny of all racial classifications, even those that are intended to remedy past discrimination or promote future equality.

---

[100]See Lydia Lum, "Applications by Minorities Down Sharply," *Houston Chronicle,* 8 April 1997, p. A1; R. G. Ratcliffe, "Senate Approves Bill Designed to Boost Minority Enrollments," *Houston Chronicle,* 8 May 1997, p. A1.

[101]Linda Greenhouse, "Settlement Ends High Court Case on Preferences," *New York Times,* 22 November 1997, p. A1; Barry Bearak, "Rights Groups Ducked a Fight, Opponents Say," *New York Times,* 22 November 1997, p. A1.

[102]*Gratz v. Bollinger,* 539 U.S. 244 (2003).

The second case, *Grutter v. Bollinger,* broke new ground. Barbara Grutter sued the University of Michigan Law School on the grounds that it had discriminated in a race-conscious way against white applicants with grades and law boards equal or superior to those of minority applicants. A precarious vote of 5–4 aligned the majority of the Supreme Court with Justice Lewis Powell's opinion in *Bakke* for the first time. In *Bakke,* Powell had argued that diversity in education is a compelling state interest and that constitutionally race could be considered a positive factor in admissions decisions. In *Grutter,* the Court reiterated Powell's holding and, applying strict scrutiny to the law school's policy, found that its admissions process was narrowly tailored to the school's compelling state interest in diversity because it gave a "highly individualized, holistic review of each applicant's file," in which race counted but was not used in a "mechanical way."[103]

Throughout the 1990s, federal courts, including the Supreme Court, had subjected public affirmative action programs to strict scrutiny to invalidate them. *Adarand Constructors v. Pena* (1995) definitively established the Supreme Court's view that constitutionally permissible use of race must serve a compelling state interest. Between *Korematsu v. United States* (1944)[104] and *Grutter,* no consideration of race had survived strict scrutiny. Such affirmative action plans that had survived constitutional review did so before 1995, under a lower standard of review, one reserved for policies intended to remedy racial injustice. For affirmative action to survive under the post-1995 judicial paradigm, the Court needed to find that sometimes racial categories can be deployed to serve a compelling state interest. That the Court found exactly this in *Grutter* puts affirmative action on stronger ground—at least if its specific procedures pass the Supreme Court's muster and until the Court's majority changes.

Referendums on Affirmative Action   The courts have not been the only center of action: Challenges to affirmative action have also emerged in state and local politics, in the form of ballot initiatives or referendums that ask voters to decide the issue. One of the most significant state actions was the passage of the California Civil Rights Initiative, also known as Proposition 209, in 1996. Proposition 209 outlawed affirmative action programs in the state and local governments of California, thus prohibiting state and local governments from using race or gender preferences in their decisions about hiring, contracting, and university admissions. The political battle over Proposition 209 was heated, and supporters and defenders took to the streets and airwaves to make their case. When the referendum was held, the measure passed with 54 percent of the vote, including 27 percent of the black vote, 30 percent of the Latino vote, and 45 percent of the Asian American vote.[105] In 1997, the Supreme Court refused to hear a challenge to the new law.

---

[103] *Grutter v. Bollinger,* 539 U.S. 306 (2003).

[104] *Korematsu v. United States,* 323 U.S. 214 (1944).

[105] Michael A. Fletcher, "Opponents of Affirmative Action Heartened by Court Decision," *Washington Post,* 13 April 1997, p. A21.

ONLINE READING

Many observers predicted that the success of California's ban on affirmative action would provoke similar movements in states and localities across the country. But the political factors that contributed to the success of Proposition 209 in California may not exist in many other states. Winning a controversial state referendum takes leadership and lots of money. The popular California Republican governor Pete Wilson led with a strong anti–affirmative action stand (favoring Proposition 209), and his campaign had a lot of money for advertising. But similar conditions did not exist elsewhere. Few prominent Republican leaders in other states were willing to come forward to lead the anti–affirmative action campaign. Moreover, the outcome of any referendum, especially a complicated and controversial one, depends greatly on how the issue is drafted and placed on the ballot. California's Proposition 209 was framed as a civil rights initiative: "The state shall not discriminate against, or grant preferential treatment to, any individual or group on the basis of race, sex, color, ethnicity, or national origin." Different wording can produce quite different outcomes, as a 1997 vote on affirmative action in Houston revealed. There the ballot initiative asked voters whether they wanted to ban affirmative action in city contracting and hiring, not whether they wanted to end preferential treatment. In that city, 55 percent of voters decided in favor of affirmative action.[106]

CHAPTER REVIEW

Civil liberties and *civil rights* are two quite different phenomena and have to be treated legally and constitutionally in two quite different ways. We have defined civil liberties as that sphere of individual freedom of choice created by restraints on governmental power. The Bill of Rights explicitly placed an entire series of restraints on government. Some of these restraints were *substantive*, regarding *what* government could do; other restraints were *procedural*, regarding *how* the government was permitted to act. We call the rights listed in the Bill of Rights civil liberties because they are the rights of citizens to be free from arbitrary government interference.

But *which* government? This was settled in the *Barron v. Baltimore* case in 1833 when the Supreme Court held that the restraints in the Bill of Rights were applicable only to the national government and not to the states. The Court was recognizing "dual citizenship." At the time of its adoption in 1868, the Fourteenth Amendment was considered by many observers as a deliberate effort to reverse *Barron*, to put an end to the standard of dual citizenship, and to nationalize the Bill of Rights, applying its restrictions to state governments as well as to the national government. But the post–Civil War Supreme Court interpreted the Fourteenth Amendment otherwise. Dual citizenship remained almost as it had been before the Civil War, and the shadow of *Barron* extended across the rest of the nineteenth century and well into the twentieth century.

The slow process of nationalizing the Bill of Rights began in the 1920s, when the Court recognized that at least the restraints of the First Amendment had been

---

[106]See Sam Howe Verhovek, "Houston Vote Underlined Complexity of Rights Issue," *New York Times*, 6 November 1997, p. A1.

"incorporated" into the Fourteenth Amendment as restraints on the state govern-ments. But it was not until the 1960s that most of the civil liberties in the Bill of Rights were also incorporated into the Fourteenth Amendment.

The second aspect of protection of the individual, *civil rights*, stresses the ex-pansion of governmental power rather than restraints upon it. If the constitu-tional base of civil liberties is the due process clause of the Fourteenth Amendment, the constitutional base of civil rights is the equal protection clause. This clause imposes a positive obligation on government to advance civil rights, and its original motivation seems to have been to eliminate the gross injustices suffered by "the newly emancipated Negroes . . . as a class." But as with civil lib-erties, there was little advancement in the interpretation or application of the equal protection clause until after World War II. The major breakthrough came in 1954 with the case of *Brown v. Board of Education,* and advancements came in fits and starts during the succeeding ten years.

After 1964, Congress finally supported the federal courts with effective civil rights legislation. From that point, civil rights developed in two ways. First, the definition of civil rights was expanded to include victims of discrimination other than blacks. Second, the definition of civil rights became increasingly positive through affirmative action policies. Judicial decisions, congressional statutes, and administrative agency actions all have moved beyond the original goal of eliminating discrimination toward creating opportunities for minorities and, in some areas, compensating present individuals for the consequences of discrimi-natory actions against members of their group in the past. This kind of compen-sation has sometimes relied on quotas. The use of quotas, in turn, has given rise to intense debate over the constitutionality as well as the desirability of affirma-tive action.

The story has not ended and is not likely to end. The politics of rights will re-main an important part of American political discourse.

FOR FURTHER READING

Ackerman, Bruce. *Before the Next Attack: Preserving Civil Liberties in an Age of Terrorism.* New Haven, Conn.: Yale University Press, 2006.

Baer, Judith, and Leslie Goldstein. *The Constitutional and Legal Rights of Women.* Los Angeles: Roxbury, 2006.

Drake, W. Avon, and Robert D. Holsworth. *Affirmative Action and the Stalled Quest for Black Progress.* Urbana: University of Illinois Press, 1996.

Dworkin, Ronald. *Justice in Robes.* Cambridge, Mass.: Belknap Press, 2006.

Garrow, David J. *Bearing the Cross: Martin Luther King, Jr., and the Southern Christian Leader-ship Conference: A Personal Portrait.* New York: Morrow, 1986.

Gerstmann, Evan. *Same-Sex Marriage and the Constitution.* New York: Cambridge University Press, 2004.

Glendon, Mary Ann. *Rights Talk: The Impoverishment of Political Discourse.* New York: Free Press, 1991.

Greenberg, Jack. *Crusaders in the Courts: How a Dedicated Band of Lawyers Fought for the Civil Rights Revolution.* New York: Basic Books, 1994.

Jackson, Thomas. *From Civil Rights to Human Rights*. Philadelphia: University of Pennsylvania Press, 2006.

Klarman, Michael. *From Jim Crow to Civil Rights: The Supreme Court and the Struggle for Racial Equality*. New York: Oxford University Press, 2004.

Levy, Leonard W. *Freedom of Speech and Press in Early America: Legacy of Suppression*. New York: Harper & Row, 1963.

Lewis, Anthony. *Gideon's Trumpet*. New York: Random House, 1964.

Meltsner, Michael. *The Making of a Civil Rights Lawyer*. Charlottesville: University of Virginia Press, 2006.

ONLINE READING ○ Posner, Richard. *Not a Suicide Pact: The Constitution in a Time of National Emergency*. New York: Oxford University Press, 2006.

Rosenberg, Gerald N. *The Hollow Hope: Can Courts Bring About Social Change?* Chicago: University of Chicago Press, 1991.

Thernstrom, Abigail M. *Whose Votes Count? Affirmative Action and Minority Voting Rights*. Cambridge, Mass.: Harvard University Press, 1987.

ONLINE READING ○ Tushnet, Mark, and Michael Olivas. *Colored Men and Hombres Aqui: Hernandez v. Texas and the Emergence of Mexican American Lawyering*. Houston: Arte Publico Press, 2006.

Part Two | Institutions

Congress: The First Branch

HOW DOES CONGRESS WORK?

The U.S. Congress is the "first branch" of government under Article I of our Constitution and is also among the world's most important representative bodies. Congress is the only national representative assembly that can actually be said to govern. Many of the world's representative bodies only represent—that is, their governmental functions consist mainly of affirming and legitimating the national leadership's decisions. The only national representative body that actually possesses powers of governance is the U.S. Congress. For example, while the U.S. Congress never accedes to the president's budget proposals without making major changes, both the British House of Commons and the Japanese Diet always accept the budget exactly as proposed by the government.

In this chapter, we shall try to understand how the U.S. Congress is able to serve simultaneously as a representative assembly and a powerful agency of government. Congress controls a formidable battery of powers that it uses to shape policies and, when necessary, defend its prerogatives against the executive branch.

Congress has vast authority over the two most important powers given to any government: the power of force (control over the nation's military forces) and the power over money. Specifically, according to Article I, Section 8, Congress can "lay

Core of the Analysis

- Congress is the most important representative institution in American government.

- Constituents hold their representatives to account through elections.

- Congress also makes the law. Before a bill can become law, it must pass through the legislative process, a complex set of procedures in Congress.

- The legislative process is driven by numerous political forces: political parties, committees, staffs, caucuses, rules of lawmaking, and the president.

and collect Taxes," deal with indebtedness and bankruptcy, impose duties, borrow and coin money, and generally control the nation's purse strings. It also may "provide for the common Defence and general Welfare," regulate interstate commerce, undertake public works, acquire and control federal lands, promote science and "useful Arts" (pertaining mostly to patents and copyrights), and regulate the militia.

In the realm of foreign policy, Congress has the power to declare war, deal with piracy, regulate foreign commerce, and raise and regulate the armed forces and military installations. These powers over war and the military are supreme—even the president, as commander in chief of the military, must obey the laws and orders of Congress *if* Congress chooses to assert its constitutional authority. (In the past century, Congress has usually surrendered this authority to the president.) Further, the Senate has the power to approve treaties (by a two-thirds vote) and to approve the appointment of ambassadors. Capping these powers, Congress is charged to make laws "which shall be necessary and proper for carrying into Execution the foregoing Powers, and all other Powers vested by this Constitution in the Government of the United States, or in any Department or Officer thereof."

It is extraordinarily difficult for a large, representative assembly to formulate, enact, and implement the laws. The internal complexities of conducting business within Congress—the legislative process—are daunting. In addition, many individuals and institutions have the capacity to influence the legislative process. To exercise its power to make the law, Congress must first bring about something close to an organizational miracle. In this chapter, after a brief consideration of representation, we will examine the organization of Congress and the legislative process. Throughout, we point out the connections between these two aspects—the ways in which representation affects congressional operations (especially through "the electoral connection") and the ways in which congressional institutions enhance or diminish representation (especially Congress's division- and specialization-of-labor committee system).

REPRESENTATION

Congress is the most important representative institution in American government. Each member's primary responsibility is to the district, to his or her **constituency**, not to the congressional leadership, a party, or even Congress itself. Yet the task of representation is not a simple one. Views about what constitutes fair and effective representation differ, and constituents can make very different kinds of demands on their representatives. Members of Congress must consider these diverse views and demands as they represent their districts (Figure 5.1).

Some legislators see themselves as perfect agents of others: They have been elected to do the bidding of those who sent them to the legislature, and they act as *delegates.* Others see themselves as having been selected by their fellow citizens to do what they think is "right," and they act as **trustees.** Most legislators are a mix of these two types.

As we discussed in Chapter 1, *agency representation* takes place when constituents have the power to hire and fire their representatives. Frequent competitive

constituency Members of the district from which an official is elected.

delegate A representative who votes according to the preferences of his or her constituency.

trustee A representative who votes based on what he or she thinks is best for his or her constituency.

agency representation The type of representation by which representatives are held accountable to their constituents if they fail to represent them properly.

FIGURE 5.1 How Members of Congress Represent Their Districts

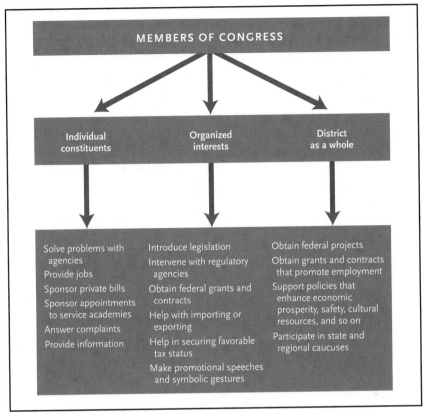

elections constitute an important means by which constituents hold their representatives to account and keep them responsive to constituency views and preferences. The idea of a representative as agent is similar to the relationship of lawyer and client. True, the relationship between the member of Congress and as many as 630,000 "clients" in the district or that between the senator and millions of clients in the state is very different from that of the lawyer and client. But the criteria of performance are comparable.

One expects at the very least that each representative will constantly be seeking to discover the interests of the constituency and will be speaking for those interests in Congress and other centers of government.[1] We expect this because we believe that members of Congress, like politicians everywhere, are ambitious. For many, this ambition is satisfied simply by maintaining a hold on their present office and advancing up the rungs of power in that legislative body. Some may be looking

---

[1] The classic description of interactions between politicians and "the folks back home" is given by Richard F. Fenno Jr., *Home Style: House Members in Their Districts* (Boston: Little, Brown, 1978). Essays elaborating on Fenno's classic are found in Morris P. Fiorina and David W. Rhode, eds., *Home Style and Washington Work* (Ann Arbor: University of Michigan Press, 1989).

ahead to the next level—to higher legislative office, as when a representative seeks a Senate seat, or to an executive office, as when a legislator returns home to run for the state's governorship, or at the highest level, when a legislator seeks the presidency.[2] In each of these cases the legislator is eager to serve the interests of constituents, either to enhance his or her prospects of contract renewal at the next election or to improve the chances of moving to another level.[3]

House and Senate: Differences in Representation

The framers of the Constitution provided for *bicameralism*—that is, a legislative body consisting of two chambers. As we saw in Chapter 2, the framers intended each of these chambers, the House and Senate, to serve a different constituency. Members of the Senate, appointed by state legislatures for six-year terms, were to represent the elite members of society and to be more attuned to the interests of property than to those of population. Today, members of the House and Senate are elected directly by the people. The 435 members of the House are elected from districts apportioned according to population: the 100 members of the Senate are elected by state, with two senators from each. Senators continue to have much longer terms in office and usually represent much larger and more diverse constituencies than do their counterparts in the House (see the In Brief Box on the following page).

The House and Senate play different roles in the legislative process. In essence, the Senate is the more deliberative of the two bodies—the forum in which any and all ideas can receive a thorough public airing. The House is the more centralized and organized of the two bodies—better equipped to play a routine role in the governmental process. In part, this difference stems from the different rules governing the two bodies. These rules give House leaders more control over the legislative process and provide for House members to specialize in certain legislative areas. The rules of the much-smaller Senate give its leadership relatively little power and discourage specialization.

Both formal and informal factors contribute to differences between the two chambers of Congress. Differences in the length of terms and requirements for holding office specified by the Constitution in turn generate differences in how members of each body develop their constituencies and exercise their powers of office. The result is that members of the House most effectively and frequently serve as the agents of well-organized local interests with specific legislative agendas—used car dealers seeking relief from regulation, labor unions seeking more favorable legislation, or farmers looking for higher subsidies. The small size and relative homogeneity of their constituencies and the frequency with which they must seek re-election make House members more attuned to the legislative needs of local

bicameralism Division of a legislative body into two houses, chambers, or branches.

ONLINE READING

[2]For more on political careers generally, see John R. Hibbing, "Lesiglative Careers: Why and How We Should Study Them," *Legislative Studies Quarterly* 24 (1999): 149–71. See also Cherie D. Maestas, Sarah Fulton, L. Sandy Maisel, and Walter J. Stone, "When to Risk It? Institutions, Ambitions, and the Decision to Run for the U.S. House," *American Political Science Review* 100, no. 2 (May 2006): 195–208.

[3]Constituents are not a legislative agent's only principals. He or she may also be beholden to party leaders and special interests, as well as to members and committees in the chamber. See Forrest Maltzman, *Competing Principals* (Ann Arbor: University of Michigan Press, 1997).

	House	Senate
Minimum age of member	25 years	30 years
U.S. citizenship	At least 7 years	At least 9 years
Length of term	2 years	6 years
Number per state	Depends on population: 1 per 30,000 in 1789; now 1 per 630,000	2 per state
Constituency	Tends to be local	Both local and national

interest groups. This, too, was the intent of the Constitution's drafters—namely, that the House of Representatives would be "the people's house" and that its members would reflect and represent public opinion in a timely manner.

Senators, on the other hand, serve larger and more heterogeneous constituencies. As a result, they are somewhat better able than members of the House to serve as the agents for groups and interests organized on a statewide or national basis. Moreover, with longer terms in office, senators have the luxury of considering "new ideas" or seeking to bring together new coalitions of interests, rather than simply serving existing ones. This is what the framers intended when they drafted the Constitution.

In recent years, the House has exhibited considerably more intense partisanship and ideological division than the Senate. Because of their diverse constituencies, senators are more inclined to seek compromises that will offend as few voters and interest groups as possible. Members of the House, in contrast, typically represent more homogeneous districts in which their own party is dominant. This situation has tended to make House members less inclined to seek compromises and more willing than their Senate counterparts to stick to partisan and ideological guns during the policy debates of the past several decades. In a similar vein, in 2006 and 2007 the House was considerably more partisan than the Senate in a number of votes on President Bush's policies in Iraq.

The Electoral System

In light of their role as agents for various constituencies in their states and districts, and the importance of elections as a mechanism by which principals (constituents) reward and punish their agents, representatives are very much influenced by electoral considerations. Three factors related to the U.S. electoral system affect who gets elected and what he or she does once in office. The first set of issues concerns who decides to run for office and which candidates have an edge over others. The second issue is that of the incumbency advantage. Finally, the way congressional district lines are drawn can greatly affect the outcome of an election. Let us examine more closely the impact of these considerations have on who serves in Congress.

Running for Office Voters' choices are restricted from the start by who decides to run for office. In the past, decisions about who would run for a particular elected office were made by local party officials. A person who had a record of service to the party, or who was owed a favor, or whose "turn" had come up might be nominated by party leaders for an office.[4] Today few party organizations have the power to slate candidates in that way. Instead, the decision to run for Congress is a more personal choice. One of the most important factors determining who runs for office is a candidate's individual ambition.[5] A potential candidate may also assess whether he or she can attract enough money to mount a credible campaign. The ability to raise money depends on connections to other politicians, interest groups, and the national party organization. In the past, the difficulty of raising campaign funds posed a disadvantage to female candidates. Since the 1980s, however, a number of political action committees (PACs) and other organizations have emerged to recruit women and fund their campaigns. The largest of them, EMILY's List, has become one of the most powerful fund-raisers in the nation. Recent research shows that money is no longer the barrier it once was to women running for office.[6]

Features distinctive to each congressional district also affect the field of candidates. For any candidate, decisions about running must be made early because once money has been committed to already declared candidates, it is harder for new candidates to break into a race. Thus the outcome of a November election is partially determined many months earlier, when decisions to run are finalized.[7]

Incumbency **Incumbency** plays a very important role in the American electoral system and in the kind of representation citizens get in Washington. Once in office, members of Congress are typically eager to remain in office and make politics a career. The career ambitions of members of Congress are helped by an array of

incumbency Holding a political office for which one is running.

ONLINE READING ○

[4]In the nineteenth century, it was often an *obligation*, not an honor, to serve in Congress. The real political action was back home in the state capital or a big city, not in Washington. So the practice of "rotation" was devised, according to which a promising local politician was to do a tour of duty in Washington before being slated for an important local office. This is not to say that electoral incentives—the so-called electoral connection in which a legislator's behavior was motivated by the desire to retain the seat for himself or his party—was absent in nineteenth-century America. See, for example, Jamie L. Carson and Erik J. Engstrom, "Assessing the Electoral Connection Evidence from the Early United States," *American Journal of Political Science* 49 (2005): 746–57. See also William T. Bianco, David B. Spence, and John D. Wilkerson, "The Electoral Connection in the Early Congress: The Case of the Compensation Act of 1816," *American Journal of Political Science* 40 (1996): 145–71.

[5]See Linda L. Fowler and Robert D. McClure, *Political Ambition: Who Decides to Run for Congress* (New Haven, Conn.: Yale University Press, 1989); and Alan Ehrenhalt, *The United States of Ambition: Politicians, Power, and the Pursuit of Office* (New York: Times Books, 1991).

[6]See Barbara C. Burrell, *A Woman's Place Is in the House: Campaigning for Congress in the Feminist Era* (Ann Arbor: University of Michigan Press, 1994), Chapter 6; and the essays in Elizabeth Adell Cook, Sue Thomas, and Clyde Wilcox, eds., *The Year of the Woman: Myths and Realities* (Boulder, Colo.: Westview, 1994).

[7]On the thesis of "strategic candidacy," see Gary C. Jacobson, *The Politics of Congressional Elections*, 6th ed. (New York: Pearson Longman, 2004).

tools that they can use to stack the deck in favor of their reelection. Through effective use of this arsenal of weapons, an incumbent establishes a reputation for competence, imagination, and responsiveness—the attributes most principals look for in an agent. One tool of incumbency is the franking privilege. Under a law enacted by the first U.S. Congress in 1789, members of Congress may send mail to their constituents free of charge to keep them informed of government business and public affairs. The franking privilege provides incumbents with a valuable resource for publicizing their activities and making themselves visible to voters.

A particularly important tool is the incumbent's reputation for constituency service: taking care of the problems and requests of individual voters. Through such services and their advertisement by word of mouth, the incumbent seeks to establish an attractive political reputation and a "personal" relationship with his or her constituents. Well over a quarter of the representatives' time and nearly two thirds of the time of their staff members is devoted to constituency service (termed **casework**). This service includes talking to constituents, providing them with minor services, presenting special bills for them, and attempting to influence decisions by regulatory commissions on their behalf.

One very direct way in which incumbent members of Congress serve as the agents of their constituencies is through the venerable institution of **patronage.** Patronage refers to a variety of forms of direct services and benefits that members provide for their districts. One of the most important forms of patronage is **pork-barrel legislation.** Through pork-barrel legislation, representatives seek to capture federal projects and federal funds for their own districts (or states in the case of senators) and thus "bring home the bacon" for their constituents. A common form of pork barreling is the "earmark," the practice through which members of Congress insert into otherwise pork-free bills language that provides special benefits for their own constituents.[8]

The incumbency advantage is evident in the high rates of reelection for congressional incumbents: over 95 percent for House members and nearly 90 percent for members of the Senate in recent years.[9] In 2006, 93 percent of House incumbents running in the general election were successful. The advantage is also evident in what is called sophomore surge—the tendency for candidates to win a higher percentage of the vote when seeking their second term in office than in their initial election victory. Once in office, members of Congress find it much easier to raise

casework An effort by members of Congress to gain the trust and support of constituents by providing them with personal service. One important type of casework consists of helping constituents obtain favorable treatment from the federal bureaucracy.

patronage The resources available to higher officials, usually opportunities to make partisan appointments to offices and to confer grants, licenses, or special favors to supporters.

pork-barrel legislation Appropriations made by legislative bodies for local projects that are often not needed but that are created so that local representatives can win reelection in their home district.

---

[8] For an excellent study of academic earmarking, see James D. Savage, *Funding Science in America: Congress, Universities, and the Politics of the Academic Pork Barrel* (New York: Cambridge University Press, 1999). For a general study of pork-barrel activity, see Diana Evans, *Greasing the Wheels: Using Pork-Barrel Projects to Build Majority Coalitions in Congress* (New York: Cambridge University Press, 2004).

[9] Norman J. Ornstein, Thomas E. Mann, and Michael J. Malbin, *Vital Statistics on Congress, 1995–1996* (Washington, D.C.: Congressional Quarterly Press, 1996), pp. 60–61 (see also subsequent editions); Robert S. Erickson and Gerald C. Wright, "Voters, Candidates, and Issues in Congressional Elections," in *Congress Reconsidered.* Lawrence C. Dodd and Bruce I. Oppenheimer, 5th ed., (Washington, D.C.: Congressional Quarterly Press, 1993), p. 99; John R. Alford and David W. Brady, "Personal and Partisan Advantage in U.S. Congressional Elections, 1846–1990," ibid., pp. 141–57.

FIGURE 5.2 The Power of Incumbency

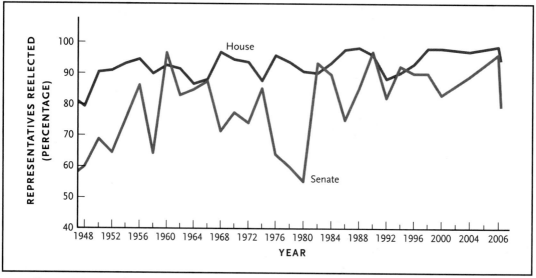

SOURCE: Norman J. Ornstein, Thomas E. Mann, and Michael J. Malbin, *Vital Statistics on Congress, 1995–1996* (Washington, D.C.: Congressional Quarterly Press, 1996), pp. 60–61, and authors' update.

campaign funds and are thus able to outspend their challengers (Figure 5.2).[10] Over the past quarter century, and despite many campaign-finance regulations to level the playing field, the gap between incumbent and challenger spending has grown (House) or held steady (Senate). Members of the majority party in the House and Senate are particularly attractive to donors who want access to those in power.[11] Incumbency can help a candidate by scaring off potential challengers. In many races, potential candidates may decide not to run because they fear that the incumbent simply has brought too many benefits to the district, has too much money, or is too well liked or too well known.[12]

The role of incumbency also has implications for the social composition of Congress. For example, the incumbency advantage makes it harder for women to increase their numbers in Congress because most incumbents are men. Women who run for open seats (for which there are no incumbents) are just as likely to win as male candidates.[13] Supporters of term limits argue that such limits are the only way to get new faces into Congress. They believe that the incumbency advantage and the

---

[10]Stephen Ansolabehere and James Snyder, "Campaign War Chests and Congressional Elections," *Business and Politics* 2 (2000): 9–34.

[11]Gary W. Cox and Eric Magar, "How Much Is Majority Status in the U.S. Congress Worth?" *American Political Science Review* 93, no. 2 (June 1999): 299–309.

[12]Kenneth Bickers and Robert Stein, "The Electoral Dynamics of the Federal Pork Barrel," *American Journal of Political Science* 40 (1996): 1300–26.

[13]See Burrell, *A Woman's Place Is in the House,* and David Broder, "Key to Women's Political Parity: Running," *Washington Post,* 8 September 1994, p. A17.

FIGURE 5.3 Apportionment of House Seats by Region, 1910 and 2000

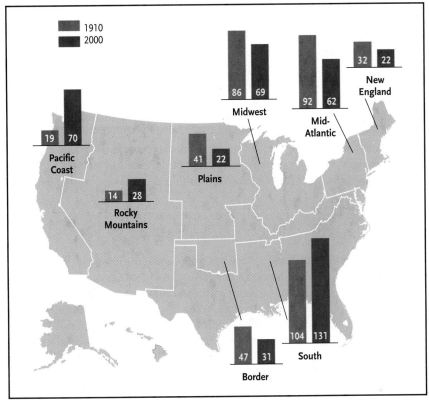

SOURCE: Norman J. Ornstein, Thomas E. Mann, and Michael J. Malbin, eds., *Vital Statistics on Congress, 2001–2002* (Washington, D.C.: American Enterprise Institute, 2002), p. 59.

tendency of many legislators to view politics as a career mean that very little turnover will occur in Congress unless limits are imposed on the number of terms a legislator can serve.

Congressional Districts   The final factor that affects who wins a seat in Congress is the way congressional districts are drawn. Every ten years, state legislatures must redraw congressional districts to reflect population changes. In 1929, Congress enacted a law fixing the total number of congressional seats at 435. As a result, when states with growing populations gain districts, they do so at the expense of states whose populations have remained stagnant or declined. In recent decades, this has meant that the nation's growth areas in the South and West have gained congressional seats at the expense of the Northeast and the Midwest (Figure 5.3). After the 2000 Census, for example, Arizona, Texas, Florida, and Georgia each gained two seats while New York and Pennsylvania each lost two seats. Redrawing congressional districts is a highly political process: Districts are shaped to create an advantage for the majority party in the state legislature, which controls the redistricting process. As we will see in Chapter 10, **gerrymandering** can have a major effect on the outcome of congressional elections.

Since the passage of the 1982 amendments to the 1965 Voting Rights Act, race has become a major—and controversial—consideration in drawing voting districts. These amendments, which encouraged the creation of districts in which members of racial minorities have decisive majorities, have greatly increased the number of minority representatives in Congress. After the 1991–92 redistricting, the number of predominantly minority districts doubled, rising from twenty-six to fifty-two. Among the most fervent supporters of the new minority districts were white Republicans, who used the opportunity to create more districts dominated by white Republican voters.[14] These developments raise thorny questions about representation. Some analysts argue that the system may grant minorities greater sociological representation, but it has made it more difficult for them to win substantive policy goals.[15]

THE ORGANIZATION OF CONGRESS

We shall now examine the organization of Congress and the legislative process, particularly the basic building blocks of congressional organization: political parties, the committee system, congressional staff, the caucuses, and the parliamentary rules of the House and Senate. Each of these factors plays a key role in the organization of Congress and in the process through which Congress formulates and enacts laws. We will also look at powers Congress has in addition to lawmaking and explore the future role of Congress in relation to the powers of the executive.

Party Leadership and Organization in the House and the Senate

One significant aspect of legislative life is not even part of the *official* organization: political parties. The legislative parties—primarily Democratic and Republican in modern times, but numerous others over the course of American history—are exemplars of organizations that foster cooperation, coalitions, and compromise. They are the vehicles of collective action, both for legislators sharing common policy objectives inside the legislature and for those very same legislators as candidates in periodic election contests back home.[16] In short, political parties in Congress are the

gerrymandering Apportionment of voters in districts in such a way as to give an unfair advantage to one political party.

ONLINE READING

[14]David Lublin, *The Paradox of Representation: Racial Gerrymandering and Minority Interests in Congress* (Princeton, N.J.: Princeton University Press, 1997).

[15]Lani Guinier, *The Tyranny of the Majority: Fundamental Fairness in Representative Democracy* (New York: Free Press, 1995). See also David Epstein and Sharyn O'Halloran, "Measuring the Electoral and Policy Impact of Majority-Minority Voting Districts," *American Journal of Political Science* 42 (1999): 36–95.

[16]For a historically grounded analysis of the development of political parties as well as a treatment of their general contemporary significance, see John H. Aldrich, *Why Parties? The Origin and Transformation of Political Parties in America* (Chicago: University of Chicago Press, 1995). For an analysis of the parties in the legislative process, see Gary W. Cox and Mathew D. McCubbins, *Legislative Leviathan: Party Government in the House* (Berkeley: University of California Press, 1993). A provocative essay questioning the role of parties is Keith Krehbiel, "Where's the Party?" *British Journal of Political Science* 23 (1993): 235–66.

fundamental building blocks from which policy coalitions are fashioned to pass legislation and monitor its implementation, thereby providing a track record on which members build electoral support.

Every two years, at the beginning of a new Congress, the members of each party gather to elect their House leaders. This gathering is traditionally called the *party caucus,* or, in the case of Republicans, the *party conference.*

The elected leader of the majority party is later proposed to the whole House and is automatically elected to the position of *Speaker of the House,* with voting along straight party lines. The House majority caucus (or conference) then also elects a *majority leader.* The minority party goes through the same process and selects the *minority leader.* Both parties also elect whips to line up party members on important votes and relay voting information to the leaders.

At one time, party leaders strictly controlled committee assignments, using them to enforce party discipline. Today, representatives expect to receive the assignments they want and resent leadership efforts to control assignments. For example, during the 104th Congress (1995–96) the chairman of the powerful Appropriations Committee, Robert Livingston, sought to remove freshman Mark Neumann (R-Wisc.) from the committee because of his lack of party loyalty. The entire Republican freshman class angrily opposed this move and forced the leadership to back down. Not only did Neumann keep his seat on the Appropriations Committee, but he was given a seat on the Budget Committee, as well, to placate the freshmen.[17] The leadership's best opportunities to use committee assignments as rewards and punishments come when more than one member seeks a seat on a committee.

Generally, representatives seek assignments that will allow them to influence decisions of special importance to their districts. Representatives from farm districts, for example, may request seats on the Agriculture Committee.[18] Seats on powerful committees such as Ways and Means, which is responsible for tax legislation, and Appropriations are especially popular.

Within the Senate, the president pro tempore exercises mainly ceremonial leadership. Usually, the majority party designates a member with the greatest seniority to serve in this capacity. Real power is in the hands of the majority leader and minority leader, each elected by party caucus or conference. The majority and minority leaders, together, control the Senate's calendar or agenda for legislation. In addition, the senators from each party elect a whip. (The whip system is discussed in the Party Discipline section of this chapter.)

In recent years, party leaders have sought to augment their formal powers by reaching outside Congress for resources that might enhance their influence within Congress. One aspect of this external strategy is the increased use of national communications media, including televised speeches and talk show appearances by party leaders. Former Republican House Speaker Newt Gingrich, for example, used television extensively to generate support for his programs among Republican

party caucus, or **party conference** A normally closed meeting of a political or legislative group to select candidates, plan strategy, or make decisions regarding legislative matters.

Speaker of the House The chief presiding officer of the House of Representatives. The speaker is elected at the beginning of every Congress on a straight party vote. The Speaker is the most important party and House leader, and can influence the legislative agenda, the fate of individual pieces of legislation, and members' positions within the House.

majority leader The elected leader of the party holding a majority of the seats in the House of Representatives or in the Senate. In the House, the majority leader is subordinate in the party hierarchy to the Speaker.

minority leader The elected leader of the party holding less than a majority of the seats in the House or Senate.

---

[17]Linda Killian, *The Freshmen: What Happened to the Republican Revolution* (Boulder, Colo.: Westview, 1998).

[18]Richard Fenno, Jr., *Home Style: House Members in Their Districts* (Boston: Little, Brown, 1978).

loyalists.[19] As long as it lasted, Gingrich's support among the Republican rank-and-file gave him an added measure of influence over Republican members of Congress.

A second external strategy involves fundraising. In recent years, congressional leaders have frequently established their own political action committees. Interest groups are usually eager to contribute to these "leadership PACs" to curry favor with powerful members of Congress. The leaders, in turn, use these funds to support the various campaigns of their party's candidates in order to create a sense of obligation. For example, in the 1998 congressional election, Majority Leader Dick Armey, who was running unopposed, raised more than $6 million, which he distributed to less well-heeled Republican candidates. Likewise, in the 2008 elections, Nancy Pelosi contributed extensively to the campaigns of fellow Democrats.

In addition to the tasks of organizing Congress, congressional party leaders may also seek to set the legislative agenda. Since the New Deal, presidents have taken the lead in creating legislative agendas. (This trend will be discussed in the next chapter.) But in recent years, congressional leaders, especially when facing a White House controlled by the opposing party, have attempted to devise their own agendas. The Analyzing the Evidence unit for this chapter takes a closer look at parties and agenda setting in Congress.

The Committee System

The committee system provides Congress with its second organizational structure, but it is more a division and specialization of labor than the hierarchy of power that determines leadership arrangements.

Six fundamental characteristics define the congressional committee system:

1. *The official rules give each* **standing committee** *a permanent status, with a fixed membership, officers, rules, staff, offices, and, above all, a jurisdiction that is recognized by all other committees and usually the leadership as well* (see Table 5.1).

2. *The jurisdiction of each standing committee is defined according to the subject matter of basic legislation.* Except for the House Rules Committee, all the important committees are organized to receive proposals for legislation and to process them into official bills. The House Rules Committee decides the order in which bills come up for a vote and determines the specific rules that govern the length of debate and the opportunity for amendments. Rules can be used to help or hinder particular proposals.

3. *Standing committees' jurisdictions usually parallel those of the major departments or agencies in the executive branch.* There are important exceptions—Appropriations (House and Senate) and Rules (House), for example—but by and large, the division of labor is self-consciously designed to parallel executive branch organization.

4. *Bills are assigned to standing committees on the basis of subject matter, but the speaker of the House and the Senate's presiding officer have some discretion in the allocation of bills to committees.* Most bills "die in committee"—that is, they are not reported out favorably. Ordinarily this ends a bill's life. There is only one way

standing committee
A permanent committee with the power to propose and write legislation that covers a particular subject such as finance or appropriations.

---

[19]Douglas Harris, *The Public Speaker* (Ph.D. diss., Johns Hopkins University, 1998).

TABLE 5.1 Standing Committees of Congress, 2008

House Committees	
Agriculture	Natural Resources
Appropriations	Oversight and Government Reform
Armed Services	Rules
Budget	Science and Technology
Education and Labor	Small Business
Energy and Commerce	Standards of Official Conduct (Ethics)
Financial Services	Transportation and Infrastructure
Foreign Affairs Homeland Security	Veterans' Affairs
House Administration	Ways and Means
Judiciary	

Senate Committees	
Agriculture, Nutrition, and Forestry	Foreign Relations
Appropriations	Health, Education, Labor, and Pensions
Armed Services	Homeland Security and Governmental Affairs
Banking, Housing, and Urban Affairs	
Budget	Judiciary
Commerce, Science, and Transportation	Rules and Administration
Energy and Natural Resources	Small Business and Entrepreneurship
Environment and Public Works	Veterans' Affairs
Finance	

for a legislative proposal to escape committee processing: A bill passed in one chamber may be permitted to go directly on to the calendar of the other chamber. Even here, however, the bill has received the full committee treatment before passage in the first chamber.

5. *Each standing committee is unique.* No effort is made to compose the membership of any committee to be representative of the total House or Senate membership. Members with a special interest in the subject matter of a committee are expected to seek membership on it. In both the House and the Senate, each party has established a Committee on Committees, which determines the committee assignments of new members and of established members who wish to change committees. Ordinarily, members can keep their committee assignments as long as they like.

Parties and Agenda Control in Congress

In assessing the influence of political parties on legislative politics, political scientists often ask how parties affect outcomes in Congress. One approach might be to look for evidence of arm twisting or promised favors by party leaders, both of which can be used to influence members' roll-call vote choices. Yet, increasingly, scholars have responded to this question by looking for evidence of agenda manipulation by the majority party. If the majority party can control *what* gets voted on—through its control of committees, including the Rules Committee, and the party leaders' scheduling power—then it can affect outcomes even when the party leaders cannot effectively twist arms or promise favors. Thus, a question that has taken center stage in congressional research is, Who controls the agenda in Congress?

REPUBLICAN AGENDA (104th Congress)	DEMOCRATIC AGENDA (110th Congress)
Balanced budget amendment	Budget reform
Welfare reform	Abortion, family planning
Tax cuts for families	Health care reform
Strong national defense	Homeland security enhancements
Strengthening families	Immigration
Rolling back government regulations	Iraq troop withdrawal
Legal reforms	Minimum wage increase
Congressional term limits	Retirement security

Sources: *Contract with America: The Bold Plan by Representative Newt Gingrich, Representative Dick Armey, and the House Republicans to Change the Nation* © 1994; Marilyn Werber Serafini, "Legislative Priorities: An issue-by-issue rundown on what's on the Democrats' wish list for the new Congress," *National Journal*, Nov. 11, 2006.

Why is agenda control so important in Congress? Whichever party controls a greater number of seats in either the House or the Senate decides which issues will come to the floor for consideration. To illustrate this point, consider the two most recent instances when majority control of Congress changed—in 1994, when Republicans assumed control of both chambers, and in 2006, when Democrats won control of both the House and the Senate. In addition to all the perks that come with majority control, each party was able to push items on it specific agenda. As we see from the table above, there are clear differences between Republicans and Democrats in terms of the legislative policies they chose to pursue.

HOUSE ROLLS ON FINAL-PASSAGE VOTES, 99TH–108TH CONGRESSES

Congress	Majority Party	Total Final Passage Votes	Majority Rolls	Majority Roll Rate (%)	Minority Rolls	Minority Roll Rate (%)
99th	Democrats	89	1	1.1	35	39.3
100th	Democrats	116	2	1.7	40	34.5
101th	Democrats	108	1	0.93	39	36.1
102th	Democrats	142	0	0	39	27.5
103th	Democrats	160	1	0.63	56	35
104th	Republicans	136	1	0.74	63	46.3
105th	Republicans	133	3	2.3	51	38.4
106th	Republicans	136	4	2.9	51	37.5
107th	Republicans	93	1	1.1	31	33.3
108th	Republicans	119	1	0.84	46	38.7

Source: Gary W. Cox and Mathew D. McCubbins
Setting the Agenda: Responsible Party Government in the U.S. House of Representatives © 2005, Cambridge University Press; calculated by author.

One specific way to think about agenda control in Congress is in terms of the winners and losers on particular pieces of legislation, because this may tell us how much influence the majority party actually has. The most prominent example of this approach has been to look at partisan roll rates. A party (or group of members) is "rolled" when it winds up on the losing side of a vote that passes. In focusing specifically on final passage votes in the U.S. House, political scientists Gary Cox and Mathew McCubbins have found that at the aggregate level, the majority party is essentially never rolled. In contrast, and as we see from the table above, the minority party is significantly more likely to be on the losing side of final-passage votes. This suggests that the majority party controls the agenda and prevents legislation that they oppose (and are likely to lose on) from coming to a vote.

6. *Each standing committee's hierarchy is based on seniority.* **Seniority** is determined by years of continuous service on a particular committee, not by years of service in the House or Senate. In general, each committee is chaired by the most senior member of the majority party. Although the power of committee chairs is limited, they play an important role in scheduling hearings, selecting subcommittee members, and appointing committee staff. Because Congress has a large number of subcommittees and has given each representative a larger staff, the power of the committee chairs has been diluted.

The Staff System: Staffers and Agencies

A congressional institution second in importance only to the committee system is the staff system. Every member of Congress employs a large number of staff members, whose tasks include handling constituency requests and, to a large and growing extent, dealing with legislative details and overseeing the activities of administrative agencies. Increasingly, staffers bear the primary responsibility for formulating and drafting proposals, organizing hearings, dealing with administrative agencies, and negotiating with lobbyists. Indeed, legislators typically deal with one another through staff rather than through direct, personal contact. Representatives and senators together employ nearly eleven thousand staffers in their Washington and home offices.

In addition to the personal staffs of individual senators and representatives, Congress also employs roughly two thousand committee staffers. These individuals are the permanent staff, who stay regardless of turnover in Congress, attached to every House and Senate committee, and who are responsible for organizing and administering the committee's work, including research, scheduling, organizing hearings, and drafting legislation.

Not only does Congress employ personal and committee staffs, but it has also established three *staff agencies* designed to provide the legislative branch with resources and expertise independent of the executive branch. These agencies enhance Congress's capacity to oversee administrative agencies and to evaluate presidential programs and proposals. They are the Congressional Research Service, which performs research for legislators who wish to know the facts and competing arguments relevant to policy proposals or other legislative business; the General Accounting Office, through which Congress can investigate the financial and administrative affairs of any government agency or program; and the Congressional Budget Office, which assesses the economic implications and likely costs of proposed federal programs, such as health care reform proposals.

Informal Organization: The Caucuses

In addition to the official organization of Congress, there also exists an unofficial organizational structure—the caucuses, formally known as *legislative service organizations* (*LSOs*). Caucuses are groups of senators or representatives who share certain opinions, interests, or social characteristics. They include ideological caucuses such as the liberal Democratic Study Group and the conservative Democratic Forum. There are also a large number of caucuses composed of legislators representing particular economic or policy interests, such as the Travel and Tourism Caucus, the Steel Caucus, the Mushroom Cau-

seniority Priority or status ranking given to an individual on the basis of length of continuous service in a committee in Congress.

cus, and the Concerned Senators for the Arts. Legislators who share common backgrounds or social characteristics have organized caucuses such as the Congressional Black Caucus, the Congressional Caucus for Women's Issues, and the Hispanic Caucus. All these caucuses seek to advance the interests of the groups they represent by promoting legislation, encouraging Congress to hold hearings, and pressing administrative agencies for favorable treatment.

RULES OF LAWMAKING: HOW A BILL BECOMES A LAW

The institutional structure of Congress is one key factor that helps to shape the legislative process. A second and equally important factor is the rules of congressional procedures. These rules govern everything from the introduction of a bill through its submission to the president for signing. Not only do these regulations influence the fate of each and every bill, they also help to determine the distribution of power in Congress.

Committee Deliberation

Even if a member of Congress, the White House, or a federal agency has spent months developing and drafting a piece of legislation, it does not become a bill until it is submitted officially by a senator or representative to the clerk of the House or Senate and referred to the appropriate committee for deliberation. No floor action on any bill can take place until the committee with jurisdiction over it has taken all the time it needs to deliberate. During the course of its deliberations, the committee typically refers the bill to one of its subcommittees, which may hold hearings, listen to expert testimony, and amend the proposed legislation before referring it to the full committee for its consideration. The full committee may accept the recommendation of the subcommittee or hold its own hearings and prepare its own amendments. Or, even more frequently, the committee and subcommittee may do little or nothing with a bill that has been submitted to them. Many bills are simply allowed to die in committee with little or no serious consideration ever given to them. In a typical congressional session, 85 to 90 percent of the roughly eight thousand bills introduced die in committee—an indication of the power of the congressional committee system.

Once a bill's assigned committee or committees in the House have reported it, the bill must pass one additional hurdle: the Rules Committee. This powerful committee determines the rules that will govern action on the bill on the House floor. In particular, the Rules Committee allots the time for debate and decides to what extent amendments to the bill can be proposed from the floor. A bill's supporters generally prefer what is called a **closed rule**, which severely limits floor debate and amendments. Opponents of a bill usually prefer an **open rule**, which permits potentially damaging floor debate and makes it easier to add amendments that may cripple the bill or weaken its chances for passage.

Debate

Party control of the agenda is reinforced by the rule giving the speaker of the House and the majority leader of the Senate the power of recognition during debate on a bill. Usually the chair knows the purpose for which a member intends to speak well

closed rule Provision by the House Rules Committee limiting or prohibiting the introduction of amendments during debate.

open rule Provision by the House Rules Committee that permits floor debate and the addition of amendments to a bill.

FIGURE 5.4 How a Bill Becomes a Law

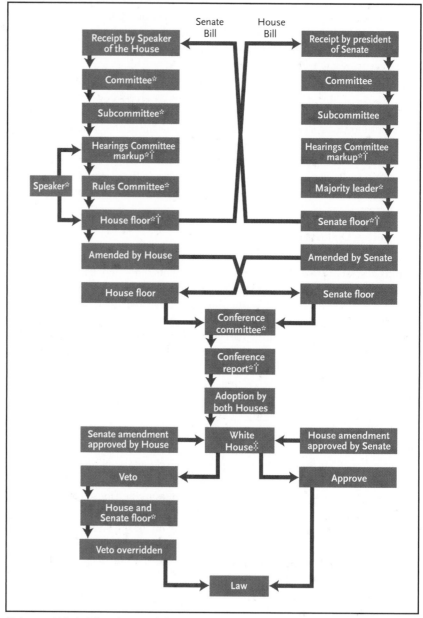

*Points at which the bill can be amended.

†Points at which the bill can die.

‡If the president neither signs nor vetoes the bill within ten days, it automatically becomes law.

in advance of the occasion. Spontaneous efforts to gain recognition are often foiled. For example, the speaker may ask, "For what purpose does the member rise?" before deciding whether to grant recognition.

In the House, virtually all of the time allotted by the Rules Committee for debate on a given bill is controlled by the bill's sponsor and by its leading opponent. In almost every case, these two people are the committee chair and the ranking minority member of the committee that processed the bill—or those they designate. These two participants are, by rule and tradition, granted the power to allocate most of the debate time in small amounts to members who are seeking to speak for or against the measure.

In the Senate, other than the power of recognition, the leadership has much less control over the floor debate. Indeed, the Senate is unique among the world's legislative bodies for its commitment to unlimited debate. Once given the floor, a senator may speak as long as he or she wishes. On a number of memorable occasions, senators have used this right to prevent action on legislation that they opposed. Through this tactic, called the *filibuster,* small minorities or even one individual in the Senate can force the majority to give in to their demands. During the 1950s and 1960s, for example, opponents of civil rights legislation often sought to block its passage by adopting the tactic of filibuster. The votes of three-fifths of the Senate, or sixty votes, are needed to end a filibuster. This procedure is called *cloture.*

In general, the party leadership in the House has total control over debate. In the Senate, each member has substantial power to block debate. This is one reason that the Senate tends to be a less partisan body than the House. A House majority can override opposition, while it takes a three-fifths vote in the Senate; thus the Senate tends to be more accommodating of various views.

Conference Committee: Reconciling House and Senate Versions of a Bill

Getting a bill out of committee and through one of the houses of Congress is no guarantee that a bill will be enacted into law. Frequently, bills that began with similar provisions in both chambers emerge with little resemblance to each other. Alternatively, a bill may be passed by one chamber but undergo substantial revision in the other chamber. In such cases, a *conference committee* composed of the senior members of the committees or subcommittees that initiated the bills may be required to iron out differences between the two pieces of legislation. Sometimes members or leaders will let objectionable provisions pass on the floor with the idea that they will get the change they want in conference. Usually, conference committees meet behind closed doors. Agreement requires a majority of each of the two delegations. Legislation that emerges from a conference committee is more often a compromise than a clear victory of one set of political forces over another.

When a bill comes out of conference, it faces one more hurdle. Before a bill can be sent to the president for signing, the House-Senate conference report must be approved on the floor of each chamber. Usually, such approval is given quickly. Occasionally, however, a bill's opponents use approval as one last opportunity to defeat a piece of legislation.

filibuster A tactic used by members of the Senate to prevent action on legislation they oppose by continuously holding the floor and speaking until the majority backs down. Once given the floor, senators have unlimited time to speak, and it requires a vote of three fifths of the Senate to end the filibuster.

cloture Rule allowing a majority, two thirds, or three fifths of the members in a legislative body to set a time limit on debate over a given bill.

conference committee A joint committee created to work out a compromise on House and Senate versions of a piece of legislation.

Presidential Action

Once adopted by the House and Senate, a bill goes to the president, who may choose to sign the bill into law or veto it. The *veto* is the president's constitutional power to reject a piece of legislation. To veto a bill, the president returns it within ten days to the house of Congress in which it originated, along with his objections to the bill. If Congress adjourns during the ten-day period, and the president has taken no action, the bill is also considered to be vetoed. This latter method is known as the **pocket veto.** The possibility of a presidential veto affects how willing members of Congress are to push for different pieces of legislation at different times. If they think the president is likely to veto a proposal, they might shelve it for a later time. Alternatively, the sponsors of a popular bill opposed by the president might push for passage in order to force the president to pay the political costs of vetoing it.[20]

A presidential veto may be overridden by a two-thirds vote in both the House and the Senate. A veto override says much about the support that a president can expect from Congress, and it can deliver a stinging blow to the executive branch. Presidents will often back down from a veto threat if they believe that Congress will override the veto.

HOW CONGRESS DECIDES

What determines the kinds of legislation that Congress ultimately produces? According to the most simple theories of representation, members of Congress would respond to the views of their constituency—the members of the district from which they are elected. In fact, the process of creating a legislative agenda, drawing up a list of possible measures, and deciding among them is very complex, and a variety of influences from inside and outside government play important roles. External influences include a legislator's constituency and various interest groups. Influences from inside government include party leadership, congressional colleagues, and the president. Let us examine each of these influences individually and then consider how they interact to produce congressional policy decisions.

Constituency

Because members of Congress, for the most part, want to be reelected, we would expect the views of their constituents to have a key influence on the decisions that legislators make. Yet constituency influence is not so straightforward. In fact, most constituents do not even know what policies their representatives support. The number of citizens who *do* pay attention to such matters—the attentive public—is usually very small. Nonetheless, members of Congress spend a lot of time worrying about what their constituents think, because these representatives realize that the choices they make may be scrutinized in a future election and used as ammunition by an opposing candidate. Because of this possibility, mem-

veto The president's constitutional power to turn down acts of Congress. A presidential veto may be overridden by a two-thirds vote of each house of Congress.

pocket veto A presidential veto of legislation wherein the president takes no formal action on a bill. If Congress adjourns within ten days of passing a bill, and the president does not sign it, the bill is considered to be vetoed.

---

[20]John Gilmour, *Strategic Disagreement* (Pittsburgh: University of Pittsburgh Press, 1995).

bers of Congress try to anticipate their constituents' policy views.[21] Legislators are more likely to act in accordance with their constituents' views if they think that voters will take them into account during elections. In this way, constituents may affect congressional policy choices even when there is little direct evidence of their influence.[22]

Interest Groups

Interest groups are another important external influence on the policies that Congress produces. When members of Congress are making voting decisions, those interest groups that have some connection to constituents in particular members' districts are most likely to be influential. For this reason, interest groups with the ability to mobilize followers in many congressional districts may be especially influential in Congress. The small-business lobby, for example, played an important role in defeating President Clinton's proposal for comprehensive health care reform in 1993–94. Because of the mobilization of networks of small businesses across the country, virtually every member of Congress had to take their views into account.

In the 2008 electoral cycle, interest groups and political action committees (PACs) donated many millions of dollars in campaign contributions to incumbent legislators and challengers. What does this money buy? A popular conception is that campaign contributions buy votes. In this view, legislators vote for whichever proposal favors the bulk of their contributors. Although the vote-buying hypothesis makes for good campaign rhetoric, it has little factual support. Empirical studies by political scientists show little evidence that contributions from large PACs influence legislative voting patterns.[23]

If contributions don't buy votes, what do they buy? Our claim is that campaign contributions influence legislative behavior in ways that are difficult for the public to observe and for political scientists to measure. The institutional structure of Congress provides opportunities for interest groups to influence legislation outside the public eye.

Committee proposal power enables legislators, if they are on the relevant committee, to introduce legislation that favors contributing groups. Gatekeeping power enables committee members to block legislation that harms contributing groups.

---

[21]See John W. Kingdon, *Congressmen's Voting Decisions* (New York: Harper & Row, 1973), chap. 3, and R. Douglas Arnold, *The Logic of Congressional Action* (New Haven, Conn.: Yale University Press, 1990). See also Joshua Clinton, "Representation in Congress: Constituents and Roll Calls in the 106th House," *Journal of Politics* 68 (2006): 397–409.   ○ ONLINE READING

[22]Interest groups from the state or district (which we discuss below) can be useful to legislators in this respect, when they provide information concerning the significance of particular issues for various constituency groups. See Kenneth W. Kollman, *Outside Lobbying: Public Opinion and Interest Group Strategies* (Princeton, N.J.: Princeton University Press, 1998).

[23]See Janet M. Grenke, "PACs and the Congressional Supermarket: The Currency Is Complex," *American Journal of Political Science* 33, no. 1 (February 1989): 1–24. More generally, see Jacobson, *The Politics of Congressional Elections*. For a view that too little, not too much, money is spent by interest groups, see Stephen Ansolabehere, John de Figueiredo, and James Snyder, "Why Is There So Little Money in U.S. Politics?" *Journal of Economic Perspectives* 17 (2003): 105–30.   ○ ONLINE READING

The fact that certain provisions are *excluded* from a bill is as much an indicator of PAC influence as the fact that certain provisions are *included*. The difference is that it is hard to measure what you don't see. Committee oversight powers enable members to intervene in bureaucratic decision making on behalf of contributing groups.

The point here is that voting on the floor, the alleged object of campaign contributions according to the vote-buying hypothesis, is a highly visible, highly public act, one that could get a legislator in trouble with his or her broader electoral constituency. The committee system, on the other hand, provides loads of opportunities for legislators to deliver to PAC contributors and other donors "services" that are more subtle and disguised from broader public view. Thus, we suggest that the most appropriate places to look for traces of campaign contribution influence on the legislative process are in the manner in which committees deliberate, mark up proposals, and block legislation from the floor; outside public view, these are the primary arenas for interest-group influence.

Party Discipline

In both the House and the Senate, party leaders have a good deal of influence over the behavior of their party members. This influence, sometimes called "party discipline," was once so powerful that it dominated the lawmaking process. At the turn of the century, because of their control of patronage and the nominating process, party leaders could often command the allegiance of more than 90 percent of their members. A vote on which 50 percent or more of the members of one party take a particular position while at least 50 percent of the members of the other party take the opposing position is called a ***party vote.*** At the beginning of the twentieth century, most ***roll-call votes*** in the House of Representatives were party votes. Today, primary elections have deprived party leaders of the power to decide who receives the party's official nomination. The patronage resources available to the leadership, moreover, have become quite limited. As a result, party-line voting happens less often. It is, however, fairly common to find at least a majority of Democrats opposing a majority of Republicans on any given issue.

Typically, party unity is greater in the House than in the Senate. House rules grant greater procedural control of business to the majority party leaders, which gives them more influence over their members. In the Senate, however, the leadership has few sanctions over its members. Former Senate Minority Leader Tom Daschle once observed that a Senate leader seeking to influence other senators has as incentives "a bushel full of carrots and a few twigs."[24] Party unity has increased in recent sessions of Congress as a consequence of the intense partisan struggles during the 1980s and 1990s (see Figure 5.5). On the whole, there was more party unity in the House during 1995 than in any year since 1954. By 1996, the level of party unity was back to average. In 1997, party unity diminished as House Republicans divided over budget and tax cut negotiations with President Clinton.

In 2001, George W. Bush called for an end to partisan squabbling in Congress. During his 2000 presidential campaign, Bush claimed that, as governor of Texas, he

party vote A roll-call vote in the House or Senate in which at least 50 percent of the members of one party take a particular position and are opposed by at least 50 percent of the members of the other party. Party votes are rare today, although they were fairly common in the nineteenth century.

roll-call vote A vote in which each legislator's yes or no vote is recorded as the clerk calls the names of the members alphabetically.

---

[24]Holly Idelson, "Signs Point to Greater Loyalty on Both Sides of the Aisle," *Congressional Quarterly Weekly Report*, 19 December 1992, p. 3849.

FIGURE 5.5 Party Unity Scores by Chamber, 1955–2007

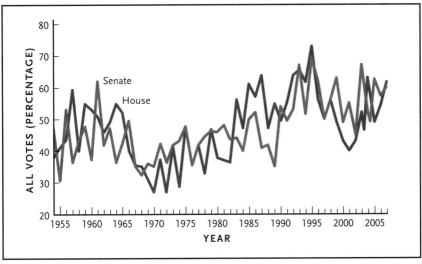

SOURCE: *Congressional Quarterly Weekly Report*

NOTE: The scores represent the percentage refers to recorded votes on which the majority of one party voted against the majority of the other party.

had built effective bipartisan coalitions that should serve as models for congressional activities as well. September 11, 2001, prompted almost every member of Congress to rally behind President Bush's military response. But Democrats and Republicans in the House divided sharply over the issue of airport security. Over the next several years, partisan differences emerged on a variety of issues, including taxation and foreign policy. On the issue of taxation, President Bush had sought to reduce federal taxes by as much as $700 billion over a period of several years. Many Democrats, on the other hand, opposed most or all of Bush's tax-cut proposals and called for increased federal spending on social programs, especially health care. On issues of foreign policy, many Democrats were deeply troubled by the president's willingness to use military force unilaterally when he deemed it necessary to do so. Prior to the 2003 Iraq war, Democratic leaders argued for giving UN weapons inspectors and diplomacy more time. Some Democrats accused the president of undermining America's relations with its allies.

To some extent, party divisions are based on ideology and background. Republican members of Congress are more likely than Democrats to be drawn from rural or suburban areas. Democrats are likely to be more liberal on economic and social questions than their Republican colleagues. This ideological gap has been especially pronounced since 1980 (see Figure 5.6). These differences certainly help to explain roll-call divisions between the two parties. Ideology and background, however, are only part of the explanation of party unity. The other part has to do with organization and leadership.

Although party organization has weakened since the turn of the century, today's party leaders still have some resources at their disposal: (1) committee assignments,

FIGURE 5.6 The Widening Ideological Gap between the Parties, 1947–2006

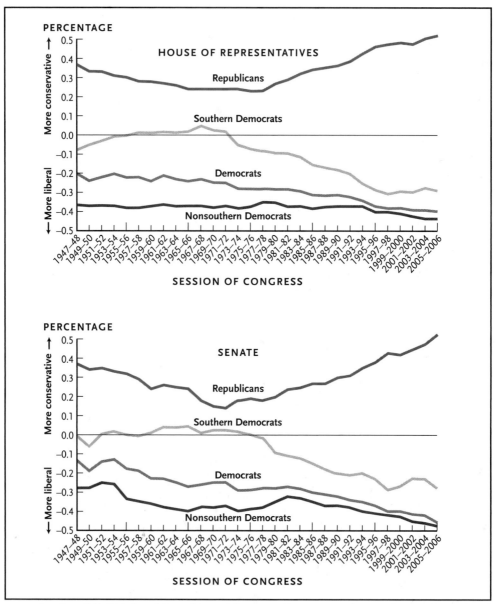

SOURCE: Data from Keith T. Poole and Howard Rosenthal, computed by Gary C. Jacobson, and reprinted in Poole and Rosenthal, *Congress: A Political-Economic History of Roll Call Voting* (New York: Oxford University Press, 1997); updates by Poole.

(2) access to the floor, (3) the whip system, (4) logrolling, and (5) the presidency. These resources are regularly used and are often very effective in securing the support of party members.

Committee Assignments   Leaders can create debts among members by helping them get favorable committee assignments. These assignments are made early in the congressional careers of most members and cannot be taken from them if they later balk at party discipline. Nevertheless, if the leadership goes out of its way to get the right assignment for a member, this effort is likely to create a bond of obligation that can be called upon without any other payments or favors.

Access to the Floor   The most important everyday resource available to the parties is control over access to the floor. With thousands of bills awaiting passage and most members clamoring for access in order to influence a bill or to publicize themselves, floor time is precious. In the House, the speaker, as head of the majority party (in consultation with the minority leader), allocates large blocks of floor time. More important, the speaker of the House and the majority leader in the Senate possess the power of recognition. Although this power may not appear to be substantial, it is a formidable authority and can be used to block a piece of legislation completely or to frustrate a member's attempts to speak on a particular issue. Because the power is significant, members of Congress usually attempt to stay on good terms with the speaker and the majority leader to ensure that they will continue to be recognized.[25]

The Whip System   Some influence accrues to party leaders through the **whip system,** which is primarily a communications network. Between twelve and twenty assistant and regional whips are selected by zones to operate at the direction of the majority or minority leader and the whip. They take polls of all the members in order to learn their intentions on specific bills. This tells the leaders whether they have enough support to allow a vote, as well as whether the vote is so close that they need to put pressure on a few swing votes. Leaders also use the whip system to convey their wishes and plans to the members, but only in very close votes do they actually exert pressure on a member. In those instances, the speaker or a lieutenant will go to a few party members who have indicated they will switch if their vote is essential. The whip system helps the leaders limit pressuring members to a few times per session.

The whip system helps maintain party unity in both houses of Congress, but it is particularly critical in the House of Representatives because of the large number of legislators whose positions and votes must be accounted for. The majority and minority whips and their assistants must be adept at inducing compromise among legislators who hold widely differing viewpoints. The whips' personal styles and their perception of their function significantly affect the development of legislative coalitions and influence the compromises that emerge.

whip system Primarily a communications network in each house of Congress, whips take polls of the membership in order to learn their intentions on specific legislative issues and to assist the majority and minority leaders in various tasks.

---

[25]A recent analysis of how floor time is allocated is found in Cox and McCubbins, *Setting the Agenda.*

ONLINE READING

The influence party leaders have over the behavior of their party members is maintained through a number of sources:

Committee assignments—By giving favorable committee assignments to members, party leaders create a sense of debt.

Access to the floor—Ranking committee members in the Senate and the speaker of the House control the allocation of floor time, so House and Senate members want to stay on good terms with these party leaders in order that their bills get time on the floor.

Whip system—The system allows party leaders to keep track of how many votes they have for a given piece of legislation; if the vote is close, they can try to influence members to switch sides.

Logrolling—Members who have nothing in common agree to support one another's legislation because each needs the vote.

Presidency—The president's legislative proposals are often the most important part of Congress's agenda. Party leaders use the president's support to rally members.

Logrolling   An agreement between two or more members of Congress who have nothing in common except the need for support is called ***logrolling***. The agreement states, in effect, "You support me on bill X and I'll support you on another bill of your choice." Since party leaders are the center of the communications networks in the two chambers, they can help members create large logrolling coalitions. Hundreds of logrolling deals are made each year, and while there are no official record-keeping books, it would be a poor party leader whose whips did not know who owed what to whom.

The Presidency   Of all the influences that maintain the clarity of party lines in Congress, the influence of the presidency is probably the most important. Indeed, it is a touchstone of party discipline in Congress. Since the late 1940s, under President Truman, presidents each year have identified a number of bills to be considered part of the administration's program. By the mid-1950s, both parties in Congress began to look to the president for these proposals, which became the most significant part of Congress's agenda. The president's support is a criterion for party loyalty, and party leaders in Congress are able to use it to rally some members.

Weighing Diverse Influences

logrolling A legislative practice wherein reciprocal agreements are made between legislators, usually in voting for or against a bill. In contrast to bargaining, parties to logrolling have nothing in common but their desire to exchange support.

Clearly, many factors affect congressional decisions. But at various points in the decision-making process, some factors are likely to be more influential than others. For example, interest groups may be more effective at the committee stage, when their expertise is especially valued and their visibility is less obvious. Because committees play a key role in deciding what legislation actually reaches the floor of the House or Senate, interest groups can often put a halt to bills they dislike, or they can ensure that the options that do reach the floor are those that the group's members support.

Once legislation reaches the floor, and members of Congress are deciding among alternatives, constituent opinion will become more important. Legislators are also influenced very much by other legislators: Many of their assessments about the substance and politics of legislation come from fellow members of Congress.

The influence of the external and internal forces described in the preceding section also varies according to the kind of issue being considered. On policies of great importance to powerful interest groups—farm subsidies, for example—those groups are likely to have considerable influence. On other issues, members of Congress may be less attentive to narrow interest groups and more willing to consider what they see as the general interest.

Finally, the mix of influences varies according to the historical moment. The 1994 electoral victory of Republicans allowed their party to control both houses of Congress for the first time in forty years. That fact, combined with an unusually assertive Republican leadership, meant that party leaders became especially important in decision making. The willingness of moderate Republicans to support measures they had once opposed indicated the unusual importance of party leadership in this period. As Former House Minority Leader Richard Gephardt put it, "When you've been in the desert 40 years, your instinct is to help Moses."[26] In a reversal of fortune, the Democrats bounced back in 2006 and 2008, winning control of the White House and majorities in both houses of Congress. The Democrats pledged to work with Republicans to bring about needed changes in the nation's foreign and domestic policies.

BEYOND LEGISLATION: ADDITIONAL CONGRESSIONAL POWERS

In addition to the power to make the law, Congress has at its disposal an array of other instruments through which to influence the process of government. The Constitution gives the Senate the power to approve treaties and appointments. And Congress has drawn to itself a number of other powers through which it can share with the other branches the capacity to administer the laws.

Oversight

Oversight, as applied to Congress, refers not to something neglected but to the effort to oversee or to supervise how the executive branch carries out legislation. Individual senators and members of the House can engage in a form of oversight simply by calling or visiting administrators, sending out questionnaires, or talking to constituents about programs. But in a more formal sense, oversight is carried out by committees or subcommittees of the Senate or House, which conduct hearings and investigations in order to analyze and evaluate bureaucratic agencies and the effectiveness of their programs. The purpose may be to locate inefficiencies or abuses of power, to explore the relationship between what an agency does and what a law intended, or to change or abolish a program. Most programs and agencies are subject to some oversight every year during the course of hearings on *appropriations,* that

oversight The effort by Congress, through hearings, investigations, and other techniques, to exercise control over the activities of executive agencies.

appropriations The amounts of money approved by Congress in statutes (bills) that each unit or agency of government can spend.

---

[26]David Broder, "At 6 Months, House GOP Juggernaut Still Cohesive," *Washington Post,* 17 July 1995, p. A1.

is, the funding of agencies and government programs. Committees or subcommittees have the power to subpoena witnesses, take oaths, cross-examine, compel testimony, and bring criminal charges for contempt (refusing to cooperate) and perjury (lying).

Hearings and investigations resemble each other in many ways, but they differ on one fundamental point. A hearing is usually held on a specific bill, and the questions asked there are usually intended to build a record with regard to that bill. In an investigation, the committee or subcommittee does not begin with a particular bill, but examines a broad area or problem and then concludes its investigation with one or more proposed bills. During an investigation into the abuse of prisoners in Iraq's Abu Ghraib prison, many Democrats and some Republicans complained that congressional oversight of the Iraq war had been too lax. Representative Christopher Shays (R-Conn.) stated, "I believe our failure to do proper oversight has hurt our country and the administration. Maybe they wouldn't have gotten into some of this trouble if our oversight had been better."[27]

Advice and Consent: Special Senate Powers

The Constitution has given the Senate a special power, one that is not based on law-making. The president has the power to make treaties and to appoint top executive officers, ambassadors, and federal judges—but only "with the Advice and Consent of the Senate" (Article II, Section 2). For treaties, two thirds of those present must concur; for appointments, a majority is required.

The power to approve or reject presidential requests also involves the power to set conditions. The Senate only occasionally exercises its power to reject treaties and appointments. The Senate has rejected only nine judicial nominees during the past century, while many times that number have been approved.

More common than Senate rejection of presidential appointees is a senatorial "hold" on an appointment. By Senate tradition, any member may place an indefinite hold on the confirmation of a mid- or lower-level presidential appointment. The hold is typically used by senators trying to wring concessions from the White House on matters having nothing to do with the appointment in question. After Bush took office in January 2001, the Democratic minority in the Senate has scrutinized judicial nominations and prevented final confirmation votes on a dozen especially conservative nominees, a matter about which the president frequently complained. Future judicial appointments also became an issue in the 2008 presidential election. Democrats charged that a Republican president would appoint judges who would overturn abortion rights and set back the clock on civil rights. Republicans, for their part, claimed that Democratic judges would expand access to abortion and promote same-sex marriage.

Most presidents make every effort to take potential Senate opposition into account in treaty negotiations and will frequently resort to ***executive agreements*** with foreign powers instead of treaties. The Supreme Court has held that such agree-

executive agreement
Agreement between the president and another country, which has the force of a treaty but does not require the Senate's "advice and consent."

---

[27]Carl Hulse, "Even Some in G.O.P. Call for More Oversight of Bush," *New York Times,* 31 May 2004, p. A13.

ments are equivalent to treaties, but they do not need Senate approval.[28] In the past, presidents sometimes concluded secret agreements without informing Congress of the agreements' contents, or even their existence. American involvement in the Vietnam War grew in part out of a series of secret arrangements made between American presidents and the South Vietnamese during the 1950s and 1960s. Congress did not even learn of these agreements until 1969.

In 1972, Congress passed the Case Act, which requires that the president inform Congress of any executive agreement within sixty days of its having been reached. This provides Congress with the opportunity to cancel agreements that it opposes. In addition, Congress can limit the president's ability to conduct foreign policy through executive agreement by refusing to appropriate the funds needed to implement an agreement. In this way, for example, Congress can modify or even cancel executive agreements to provide economic or military assistance to foreign governments.

Impeachment

The Constitution also grants Congress the power of **impeachment** over the president, vice president, and other executive officials. To impeach means to charge a government official (president or otherwise) with "Treason, Bribery, or other high Crimes and Misdemeanors," and bring him or her before Congress to determine guilt. Impeachment is thus like a criminal indictment in which the House of Representatives acts like a grand jury, voting (by simple majority) on whether the accused ought to be impeached. If a majority of the House votes to impeach, the impeachment trial moves to the Senate, which acts like a trial jury by voting whether to convict and forcibly remove the person from office (this vote requires a two-thirds majority).

Controversy over Congress's impeachment power has arisen over the grounds for impeachment, especially the meaning of "high Crimes and Misdemeanors." A strict reading of the Constitution suggests that the only impeachable offense is an actual crime. But a more commonly agreed upon definition is that an impeachable offense is whatever the majority of the House of Representatives considers it to be at a particular point in time. In other words, impeachment, especially the impeachment of a president, is a political decision.

During the course of American history, only two presidents have been impeached. In 1867, President Andrew Johnson, a Southern Democrat who had battled a congressional Republican majority over Reconstruction, was impeached by the House but saved from conviction by one vote in the Senate. In 1998, President Bill Clinton was impeached by the House for perjury and obstruction of justice arising from his sexual relationship with a former White House intern, Monica Lewinsky. At the conclusion of a Senate trial in 1999, Democrats, joined by a handful of Republicans, acquitted the president of both charges.

impeachment To charge a governmental official (president or otherwise) with "Treason, Bribery, or other high Crimes and Misdemeanors" and bring him or her before Congress to determine guilt.

---

[28] *U.S. v. Pink*, 315 U.S. 203 (1942). For a good discussion of the problem, see James W. Davis, *The American Presidency* (New York: Harper & Row, 1987), Chapter 8.

The impeachment power is an important one. The framers of the Constitution gave Congress the power to impeach in order to guard against executive tyranny.

DOES CONGRESS WORK?

Congress is both a representative assembly and a powerful institution of government. In assessing the effectiveness of Congress, we will focus on both its representative character and the efficiency by which Congress is able to get things done. Congress is the most important representative institution in American government. Each member's primary responsibility is to the district, to his or her constituency, not to the congressional leadership, a party, or even Congress itself. Yet the task of representation is not a simple one. Views about what constitutes fair and effective representation differ, and constituents can make very different kinds of demands on their representatives. Members of Congress must consider these diverse views and demands as they represent their districts (see Figure 5.1). A representative claims to act or speak for some other person or group. But how can one person be trusted to speak for another? How do we know that those who call themselves our representatives are actually speaking on our behalf, rather than simply pursuing their own interests?

As we saw earlier in the chapter, legislators vary in the weight given to personal priorities and the things desired by campaign contributors and past supporters. Some see themselves as delegates, elected to do the bidding of those who sent them to the legislature. Other legislators see themselves as trustees, selected by their fellow citizens to do what the legislator thinks is "right." Most legislators are mixes of these two types. Frequent competitive elections constitute an important means by which constituents hold their representatives in account and keep them responsive to constituency views and preferences.

Indeed, taking care of constituents explains a lot of the legislation that Congress produces. It is not too much of an exaggeration to suggest the following list of individuals whose support is necessary in order to get a measure through Congress and signed into law:

- A majority of the authorizing subcommittees in House and Senate (probably including the subcommittee chairs)
- A majority of the full authorizing committees in House and Senate (probably including committee chairs)
- A majority of the appropriations subcommittees in House and Senate (probably including the subcommittee chairs)
- A majority of the full appropriations committees in House and Senate (probably including committee chairs)
- A majority of the House Rules Committee (including its chair)
- A majority of the full House
- A majority—possibly as many as sixty votes, if needed to shut off a filibuster—of the Senate

- The Speaker and majority leader in the House
- The majority leader in the Senate
- The president

This list constitutes an extraordinarily large number of public officials.

With so many hurdles to clear for a legislative initiative to become a public law, the benefits must be spread broadly. It is as though a bill must travel on a toll road past a number of tollbooths, each one containing a collector with his or her hand out for payment. Frequently, features of the bill are drafted initially or revised so as to be more inclusive, spreading the benefits widely among beneficiaries. This is the ***distributive tendency.***

The distributive tendency is part of the American system of representative democracy. It is as American as apple pie! Legislators, in advocating the interests of their constituents, are eager to advertise their ability to deliver for their state or district. They maneuver to put themselves in a position to claim credit for good things that happen there and to duck blame for bad things. This is the way they earn trust back home, deter strong challengers in upcoming elections, and defeat those who run against them. This means that legislators must take advantage of every opportunity that presents itself. In some instances, as in our earlier discussion of the pork barrel, the results may seem bizarre. Nevertheless, the distributive tendency is a consequence of how Congress was designed to work.

Another consequence of Congress's design is almost the opposite of the distributive tendency: the tendency toward the status quo. The U.S. Congress has more veto points than any other legislative body in the world. If any of the individuals listed above says no, a bill dies. Some celebrate this design. As a result, the government is unlikely to change in response to superficial fluctuations in public sentiment. Congress's design does mean greater representation of minority interests in the legislative process (at least to say no to the majority). But it also creates the impression of gridlock, leading some to question Congress's effectiveness.

Critics of Congress want it to be both more representative and more effective. On the one hand, Congress is frequently criticized for falling victim to "gridlock" and failing to reach decisions on important issues like Social Security reform. This was one reason why, in 1995, the Republican House leadership reduced the number of committees and subcommittees in the lower chamber. Having fewer committees and subcommittees generally means greater centralization of power and more expeditious decision making. On the other hand, critics demand that Congress become more representative of the changing makeup and values of the American populace. In recent years, for example, some reformers have demanded limits on the number of terms that any member of Congress can serve. Term limits are seen as a device for producing a more rapid turnover of members and, hence, a better chance for new political and social forces to be represented in Congress. The problem, however, is that while reforms such as term limits and greater internal diffusion of power may make Congress more representative, they may also make it less efficient and effective. By the same token, reforms that may make Congress better able to act, such as strong central leadership, reduction of the number of committees and subcommittees, and retention of members

distributive tendency
The tendency of Congress to spread the benefits of a bill over a wide range of members' districts.

with seniority and experience, may make Congress less representative. This is the dilemma of congressional reform. Efficiency and representation are often competing principles in our system of government; we must be wary of gaining one at the expense of the other.

CHAPTER REVIEW

The legislative process must provide the order necessary for legislation to take place amid competing interests. It is dependent on a hierarchical organizational structure within Congress. Six basic dimensions of Congress affect the legislative process: (1) the parties, (2) the committees, (3) the staff, (4) the caucuses (or conferences), (5) the rules, and (6) the presidency.

Since the Constitution provides only for a presiding officer in each house, some method had to be devised for conducting business. Parties quickly assumed the responsibility for this. In the House, the majority party elects a leader every two years. This individual becomes speaker. In addition, a majority leader and a minority leader (from the minority party) and party whips are elected. Each party has a committee whose job it is to make committee assignments. Party structure in the Senate is similar, except that the vice president of the United States is the president of the Senate.

The committee system surpasses the party system in its importance in Congress. In the early nineteenth century, standing committees became a fundamental aspect of Congress. They have, for the most part, evolved to correspond to executive branch departments or programs and thus reflect and maintain the separation of powers.

The Senate has a tradition of unlimited debate, on which the various cloture rules it has passed have had little effect. Filibusters still occur. The rules of the House restrict talk and support committees; deliberation is recognized as committee business. The House Rules Committee has the power to control debate and floor amendments. The rules prescribe the formal procedure through which bills become law. Generally, the parties control scheduling and agenda, but the committees determine action on the floor. Committees, seniority, and rules all limit the ability of members to represent their constituents. Yet, these factors enable Congress to maintain its role as a major participant in government.

While party voting regularity remains strong, party discipline has declined. Still, parties do have several means of maintaining discipline: (1) Favorable committee assignments create obligations; (2) floor time in the debate on one bill can be allocated in exchange for a specific vote on another; (3) the whip system allows party leaders to assess support for a bill and convey their wishes to members; (4) party leaders can help members create large logrolling coalitions; and (5) presidents, by identifying pieces of legislation as their own, can muster support along party lines. In most cases, party leaders accept constituency obligations as a valid reason for voting against the party position.

This power of the post–New Deal presidency does not necessarily signify the decline of Congress and representative government. During the 1970s, Congress again became the "first branch" of government. During the early years of the Reagan administration, some of the congressional gains of the previous decade were diminished, but in the last two years of Reagan's second term, and in President G. W. Bush's term, Congress reasserted its role. At the start of the Clinton administration, congressional leaders promised to cooperate with the White House rather than confront it. But only two years later, confrontation was once again the order of the day.

FOR FURTHER READING

Adler, E. Scott. *Why Congressional Reforms Fail: Reelection and the House Committee System.* Chicago: University of Chicago Press, 2002. ○ ONLINE READING

Arnold, R. Douglas. *The Logic of Congressional Action.* New Haven, Conn.: Yale University Press, 1990. ○ ONLINE READING

Baker, Ross K. *House and Senate.* 3rd ed. New York: Norton, 2001.

Binder, Sarah. *Stalemate: Causes and Consequences of Legislative Gridlock.* Washington, D.C.: Brookings Institution, 2003.

———— and Paul Quirk, eds. *Institutions of Democracy: The Legislative Branch.* New York: Oxford University Press, 2004.

Brady, David, and Mathew D. McCubbins, eds. *Party, Process, and Political Change in Congress: New Perspectives on the History of Congress.* Palo Alto, Calif.: Stanford University Press, 2002.

Cox, Gary C., and Jonathon Katz, *Elbridge Gerry's Salamander: The Electoral Consequences of the Reapportionment Revolution.* Cambridge, England: Cambridge University Press, 2002. ○ ONLINE READING

————, and Mathew D. McCubbins. *Legislative Leviathan: Party Government in the House.* 2nd ed. Berkeley: University of California Press, 2006.

————. *Setting the Agenda: Responsible Party Government in the U.S. House of Representatives.* New York: Cambridge University Press, 2005. ○ ONLINE READING

Dodd, Lawrence C., and Bruce I. Oppenheimer, eds. *Congress Reconsidered.* 8th ed. Washington, D.C.: Congressional Quarterly Press, 2005.

Fenno, Richard F., Jr. *Home Style: House Members in Their Districts.* Boston: Little, Brown, 1978.

————. *The United States Senate: A Bicameral Perspective.* Washington, D.C.: American Enterprise Institute, 1982. ○ ONLINE READING

Fiorina, Morris P. *Congress: Keystone of the Washington Establishment.* 2nd ed. New Haven, Conn.: Yale University Press, 1989.

Frisch, Scott A., and Sean Q. Kelly. *Committee Assignment Politics in the U.S. House of Representatives.* Norman: University of Oklahoma Press, 2006.

Krehbiel, Keith. *Pivotal Politics: A Theory of U.S. Lawmaking.* Chicago: University of Chicago Press, 1998. ○ ONLINE READING

Mayhew, David. *Congress: The Electoral Connection.* New Haven, Conn.: Yale University Press, 1974. ○ ONLINE READING

Polsby, Nelson W. *How Congress Evolves.* New York: Oxford University Press, 2004.

Rohde, David W. *Parties and Leaders in the Post-reform House.* Chicago: University of Chicago Press, 1991.

Schickler, Eric. *Disjointed Pluralism*. Princeton, N.J.: Princeton University Press, 2001.

Sinclair, Barbara. *The Transformation of the U.S. Senate*. Baltimore: Johns Hopkins University Press, 1989.

Smith, Steven S., and Christopher J. Deering. *Committees in Congress*. 3rd ed. Washington, D.C.: Congressional Quarterly Press, 1997.

Stewart, Charles H. *Analyzing Congress*. New York: Norton, 2001.

Sundquist, James L. *The Decline and Resurgence of Congress*. Washington, D.C.: Brookings Institution, 1981.

The President

HOW DOES PRESIDENTIAL POWER WORK?

Presidential power generally seems to increase during times of war. For example, President Abraham Lincoln's 1862 declaration of martial law and Congress's 1863 legislation giving the president the power to make arrests and imprisonments through military tribunals amounted to a "constitutional dictatorship" that lasted through the war and Lincoln's reelection in 1864. But these measures were viewed as emergency powers that could be revoked once the crisis of union was resolved. In less than a year after Lincoln's death, Congress had reasserted its power, leaving the presidency in many respects the same as, if not weaker than, it had been before the war.

During World War II, Franklin D. Roosevelt, like Lincoln, did not bother to wait for Congress but took executive action first and expected Congress to follow. Roosevelt brought the United States into an undeclared naval war against Germany a year before Pearl Harbor, and he ordered the unauthorized use of wiretaps and other surveillance as well as the investigation of suspicious persons for reasons not clearly specified. The most egregious (and revealing) of these was his segregation and eventual confinement of 120,000 individuals of Japanese descent, many of whom were American citizens. Even worse, the Supreme Court

● Core of the Analysis

● Since the 1930s, the presidency has been the dominant branch of American government.

● Most of the real power of the modern presidency comes from the powers granted by the Constitution and the laws made by Congress. Mass public opinion, however, is also a source of presidential power.

● Contemporary presidents have also increased the power of the executive branch through "administrative strategies" that often allow them to achieve policy goals without congressional approval.

validated Roosevelt's treatment of the Japanese, on the flimsy grounds of military necessity. One dissenter on the Court called the president's assumption of emergency powers "a loaded weapon ready for the hand of any authority that can bring forward a plausible claim of an urgent need."[1]

The "loaded weapon" was seized again on September 14, 2001, when Congress defined the World Trade Center and Pentagon attacks as an act of war and proceeded to adopt a joint resolution authorizing the president to use "all necessary and appropriate force against those nations, organizations or persons he determines planned, authorized, committed or aided the terrorist attacks that occurred on September 11, 2001, or harbored such organizations or persons. . . ."[2] On the basis of this authorization, President Bush ordered the invasion of Afghanistan and began the reorganization of the nation's "homeland security."

In this chapter, we will examine the foundations of the American presidency and assess the origins and character of presidential power in the twenty-first century. National emergencies are one source of presidential power, but presidents are also empowered by democratic political processes and, increasingly, by their ability to control and expand the institutional resources of the office. The Supreme Court, to be sure, can sometimes check presidential power. For example, in the 2006 *Hamdan v. Rumsfeld* decision, the Court invalidated the military tribunals established by President Bush to try terror suspects. And, of course, through legislative investigations and its budgetary powers, Congress can oppose the president. With Democratic majorities in both houses of Congress after the 2006 elections, President Bush found it much more difficult to advance his policies on Iraq and the war on terrorism.

This chapter explains why the American system of government could be described as presidential government and how it got to be that way. We also explore how and why the president, however powerful, is nevertheless vulnerable to the popular will. But first, we begin with powers provided for in the Constitution.

THE CONSTITUTIONAL BASIS OF THE PRESIDENCY

The presidency was established by Article II of the Constitution. Article II begins by asserting, "The executive power shall be vested in a President of the United States of America." It goes on to describe the manner in which the president is to be chosen and defines the basic powers of the presidency. By vesting the executive power in a single president, the framers were emphatically rejecting proposals for various forms of collective leadership. Some delegates to the Constitutional Convention had argued in favor of a multiheaded executive or an "executive council" in order to avoid undue concentration of power in the hands of one individual. Most of the framers, however, were anxious to provide for "energy" in the executive. They hoped to have a president capable of taking

---

[1]Quoted from the dissenting opinion of Justice Robert Jackson in *Korematsu v. United States*, 323 U.S. 214 (1944).

[2]*Authorization for Use of Military Force*, Public Law 107-40, *U.S. Statutes at Large* 115 (2001): 224.

quick and aggressive action. They believed that a powerful executive would help to protect the nation's interests vis-à-vis other nations and promote the federal government's interests relative to the states.

Immediately following the first sentence, Section 1, Article II, defines the manner in which the president is to be chosen. This is an odd sequence, but it does say something about the struggle the delegates were having over how to give power to the executive and at the same time to balance that power with limitations. The struggle was between those delegates who wanted the president to be selected by Congress, and thus responsible to it, and those delegates who preferred that the president be elected directly by the people. Direct popular elections would create a more independent and more powerful presidency. The framers finally agreed on a scheme of indirect election through an electoral college, in which the electors would be selected by the state legislatures (and close elections would be resolved in the House of Representatives). In this way, the framers hoped to achieve a "republican" solution: a strong president who would be responsible to state and national legislators rather than directly to the electorate.

THE CONSTITUTIONAL POWERS OF THE PRESIDENCY

While Section 1 of Article II explains how the president is to be chosen. Sections 2 and 3 outline the powers and duties of the president. These two sections identify two sources of presidential power. Some presidential powers are specifically established by the language of the Constitution. For example, the president is authorized to make treaties, grant pardons, and nominate judges and other public officials. These specifically defined powers are called the **expressed powers** of the office and cannot be revoked by the Congress or any other agency without an amendment to the Constitution. Other expressed powers include the power to receive ambassadors and command of the military forces of the United States.

In addition to establishing the president's expressed powers, Article II declares that the president "shall take Care that the Laws be faithfully executed." Since the laws are enacted by Congress, this language implies that Congress is to delegate to the president the power to implement or execute its will. Powers given to the president by Congress are called **delegated powers.** In principle, Congress delegates to the president only the power to identify or develop the means to carry out Congressional decisions. So, for example, if Congress determines that air quality should be improved, it might delegate to the executive branch the power to determine the best means of improvement as well as the power to implement the cleanup process. In practice, of course, decisions about how to clean the air are likely to have an enormous impact on businesses, organizations, and individuals throughout the nation. As it delegates power to the executive, Congress substantially enhances the importance of the presidency and the executive branch. In most cases, Congress delegates power to executive agencies rather than to the president. As we shall see, however, contemporary presidents have found ways to capture a good deal of this delegated power for themselves.

Presidents have claimed a third source of power beyond expressed and delegated powers. These are powers not specified in the Constitution or the law but

expressed powers (president) Specific powers granted to the president under Article II, Sections 2 and 3, of the Constitution.

delegated powers Constitutional powers that are assigned to one governmental agency but that are exercised by another agency with the express permission of the first.

said to stem from "the rights, duties and obligations of the presidency."[3] They are referred to as the *inherent powers* of the presidency and are most often asserted by presidents in times of war or national emergency. For example, after the fall of Fort Sumter and the outbreak of the Civil War, President Abraham Lincoln issued a series of executive orders for which he had no clear legal basis. Without even calling Congress into session, Lincoln combined the state militias into a ninety-day national volunteer force, called for forty thousand new volunteers, enlarged the regular army and navy, diverted $2 million in unspent appropriations to military needs, instituted censorship of the U.S. mails, ordered a blockade of Southern ports, suspended the writ of *habeas corpus* in the border states, and ordered the arrest by military police of individuals whom he deemed to be guilty of engaging in or even contemplating treasonous actions.[4] Lincoln asserted that these extraordinary measures were justified by the president's inherent power to protect the nation.[5] Subsequent presidents, including Franklin D. Roosevelt and George W. Bush, have had similar views.

Expressed Powers

The president's expressed powers, as defined by Sections 2 and 3 of Article II, fall into several categories:

1. *Military.* Article II, Section 2, provides for the power as "Commander in Chief of the Army and Navy of the United States, and of the Militia of the several States, when called in to the actual Service of the United States."

2. *Judicial.* Article II, Section 2, also provides the power to "grant Reprieves and Pardons for Offenses against the United States, except in Cases of Impeachment."

3. *Diplomatic.* Article II, Section 3, provides the power to "receive Ambassadors and other public Ministers."

4. *Executive.* Article II, Section 3, authorizes the president to see to it that all the laws are faithfully executed; Section 2 gives the chief executive the power to appoint, remove, and supervise all executive officers and to appoint all federal judges.

5. *Legislative.* Article I, Section 7, and Article II, Section 3, give the president the power to participate authoritatively in the legislative process.

Military The president's military powers are among the most important that the chief executive exercises. The position of *commander in chief* makes the president the highest military officer in the United States, with control of the entire military establishment. The president is also the head of the nation's intelligence hierarchy, which includes not only the Central Intelligence Agency (CIA) but also the National Security Council (NSC), the National Security Agency (NSA), the

inherent powers
Powers claimed by a president that are not expressed in the Constitution, but are inferred from it.

commander in chief
The position of the president as commander of the national military and the state National Guard units (when they are called into service).

---

[3] *In re Neagle,* 135 U.S. 1 (1890).

[4] James G. Randall, *Constitutional Problems under Lincoln* (New York: Appleton, 1926), Chapter 1.

[5] Edward S. Corwin, *The President: Office and Powers,* 4th rev. ed. (New York: New York University Press, 1957), p. 229.

Federal Bureau of Investigation (FBI), and a host of lesser-known but very powerful international and domestic security agencies.

War and Inherent Presidential Power The Constitution, of course, gives Congress the power to declare war. Presidents, however, have gone a long way toward capturing this power for themselves. Congress has not declared war since December 1941, yet since then American military forces have engaged in numerous campaigns throughout the world under the orders of the president. When North Korean forces invaded South Korea in June 1950, Congress was prepared to declare war but President Harry S. Truman decided not to ask for congressional action. Instead, Truman asserted the principle that the president and not Congress could decide when and where to deploy America's military might. He dispatched American forces to Korea without a congressional declaration, and in the face of the emergency, Congress felt it had to acquiesce. It passed a resolution approving the president's actions, and this became the pattern for future congressional-executive relations in the military realm. The wars in Vietnam, Bosnia, Afghanistan, and Iraq, as well as a host of smaller scale conflicts, were all fought without declarations of war.

In 1973, Congress responded to presidential unilateralism by passing the ***War Powers Resolution*** over President Nixon's veto. This resolution reasserted the principle of congressional war power, required the president to inform Congress of any planned military campaign, and stipulated that forces must be withdrawn within sixty days in the absence of a specific congressional authorization for their continued deployment. Presidents, however, have generally ignored the War Powers Resolution, claiming inherent executive power to defend the nation. Thus, for example, in 1989, President George H. W. Bush ordered an invasion of Panama without consulting Congress. In 1990 the same President Bush received congressional authorization to attack Iraq but had already made it clear that he was prepared to go to war with or without congressional assent. President Clinton ordered a massive bombing campaign against Serbian forces in the former nation of Yugoslavia without congressional authorization. And, of course, President George W. Bush responded to the 2001 attacks by Islamic terrorists by organizing a major military campaign to overthrow the Taliban regime in Afghanistan, which had sheltered the terrorists. In 2002, Bush ordered a major American campaign against Iraq, which he accused of posing a threat to the United States. U.S. forces overthrew the government of Iraqi dictator Saddam Hussein and occupied the country. In both instances, Congress passed resolutions approving the president's actions, but the president was careful to assert that he did not need congressional authorization. The War Powers Resolution was barely mentioned on Capital Hill and was ignored by the White House.

Military Sources of Domestic Power The president's military powers extend into the domestic sphere although Article IV, Section 4, provides that the "United States shall [protect] . . . every State . . . against Invasion . . . and . . . domestic Violence," Congress has made this an explicit presidential power through statutes directing the president as commander in chief to discharge these obligations.[6]

War Powers Resolution A resolution of Congress that the president can send troops into action only by authorization of Congress, or if American troops are already under attack or serious threat.

---

[6]These statutes are contained mainly in Title 10 of the United States Code, Sections 331, 332, and 333.

The Constitution restrains the president's use of domestic force by providing that a state legislature (or governor when the legislature is not in session) must request federal troops before the president can send them into the state to provide public order. Yet this proviso is not absolute. First, presidents are not obligated to deploy national troops merely because the state legislature or governor makes such a request. And more important, presidents may deploy troops in a state or city without a specific request if they consider it necessary to maintain an essential national service, to enforce a federal judicial order, or to protect federally guaranteed civil rights.

A famous example of the unilateral use of presidential power to protect the states against domestic disorder occurred in 1957 under President Eisenhower. He decided to send troops into Little Rock, Arkansas, against the wishes of the state of Arkansas, to enforce court orders to integrate Little Rock's Central High School. Arkansas Governor Orval Faubus had posted the Arkansas National Guard at the entrance of the school to prevent the court-ordered admission of nine black students. After an effort to negotiate with Governor Faubus failed, President Eisenhower reluctantly sent to Little Rock a thousand paratroopers, who stood watch while the black students took their places in the all-white classrooms. This case makes quite clear that the president does not have to wait for a request by a state legislature or governor before acting as domestic commander in chief.[7] However, in most instances of domestic disorder—whether from human or from natural causes—presidents tend to exercise unilateral power justified by declaring a "state of emergency," thereby making available federal grants, insurance, and direct assistance as well as troops. After hurricanes Katrina and Rita struck the Gulf Coast in fall 2005, President Bush declared a state of emergency, using both state militias and federal troops for rescue operations, the prevention of looting and violence, and the delivery of medical, health, and food services.

Military emergencies have typically also led to expansion of the domestic powers of the executive branch. This was true during World Wars I and II and has been true during the "war on terrorism" as well. Within a month of the 9/11 attacks, the White House drafted and Congress enacted the USA Patriot Act, expanding the power of government agencies to engage in domestic surveillance activities, including electronic surveillance, and restricting judicial review of such efforts. The act also gave the attorney general greater authority to detain and deport aliens suspected of having terrorist affiliations. The following year, Congress created the Department of Homeland Security, combining offices from twenty-two federal agencies into one huge new cabinet department responsible for protecting the nation from attack. The new agency, with a tentative budget of $40 billion, includes the Coast Guard, Transportation Safety Administration, Federal Emergency Management Administration, Immigration and Naturalization Service, and offices from the departments of Agriculture, Energy, Transportation, Justice, Health and Human Services, Commerce, and the General Services Administration. The White House drafted the reorganization plan, but Congress weighed in to make certain that the new agency's workers had civil service and union protections.

---

[7]An excellent study covering all aspects of the domestic use of the military is that of Adam Yarmolinsky, *The Military Establishment* (New York: Harper & Row, 1971).

Judicial Power The presidential power to grant reprieves, pardons, and amnesties as well as to "commute" or reduce the severity of sentences, literally gives the president the power of life and death over individuals. Presidents may use this power on behalf of a particular individual, as did Gerald Ford when he pardoned Richard Nixon in 1974 "for all offenses against the United States which he . . . has committed or may have committed." Similarly, in 2007, President George W. Bush commuted the sentence handed down to Lewis "Scooter" Libby, one of Vice President Cheney's top aides. Libby had been found guilty of perjury and obstruction of justice and was sentenced to several years in prison as well as ordered to pay a steep fine. President Bush declared that Libby would not go to prison, though he would still have to pay the fine.

Sometimes presidents use their power on a large scale, as did President Andrew Johnson in 1868, when he gave full amnesty to all Southerners who had participated in the "Late Rebellion," and President Carter in 1977, when he declared an amnesty for all the draft evaders of the Vietnam War. President George H. W. Bush used this power before his retirement in mid-December 1992, when he pardoned former Secretary of Defense Caspar Weinberger and five other participants in the Iran-Contra affair. This power of life and death over others has helped elevate the president to the level of earlier conquerors and kings by establishing the president as the person before whom supplicants might come to make their pleas for mercy.

Diplomatic Power The president is America's "head of state"—its chief representative in dealings with other nations. As head of state, the president has the power to make treaties for the United States (with the advice and consent of the Senate). When President George Washington received Edmond Genêt ("Citizen Genêt") as the formal emissary of the revolutionary government of France in 1793, he transformed the power to "receive Ambassadors and other public Ministers" into the power to "recognize" other countries. That power gives the president the almost unconditional authority to review the claims of any new ruling groups to determine whether they indeed control the territory and population of their country, so that they can commit it to treaties and other agreements.

In recent years, presidents have expanded the practice of using executive agreements to conduct foreign policy.[8] An ***executive agreement*** is like a treaty because it is a contract between two countries, but an executive agreement does not require a two-thirds vote of approval by the Senate. Ordinarily, executive agreements are used to carry out commitments already made in treaties, or to arrange for matters well below the level of policy. But when presidents have found it expedient to use an executive agreement in place of a treaty, Congress has typically acquiesced.

Executive Power The most important basis of the president's power as chief executive is to be found in the sections of Article II, which stipulate that the president must see that all the laws are faithfully executed and which provide that the president will appoint all executive officers and all federal judges. In this manner, the Constitution focuses executive power and legal responsibility upon the president. The famous sign

executive agreement
An agreement between the president and another country, which has the force of a treaty but does not require the Senate's "advice and consent."

---

[8]In *United States v. Pink*, 315 U.S. 203 (1942), the Supreme Court confirmed that an executive agreement is the legal equivalent of a treaty, despite the absence of Senate approval.

on President Truman's desk, "The buck stops here," was not merely an assertion of Truman's personal sense of responsibility. It acknowledged his acceptance of the constitutional imposition of that responsibility upon the president. The president is subject to some limitations, because the appointment of all the top officers, including ambassadors and ministers and federal judges, is subject to a majority approval by the Senate. But these appointments are at the discretion of the president. Although the Constitution is silent on the power of the president to remove such officers, the federal courts have filled this silence with a series of decisions that grant the president this power.[9]

Another component of the president's power as chief executive is **executive privilege,** which is the claim that confidential communications between a president and close advisers should not be revealed without the consent of the president. Presidents have made this claim ever since George Washington refused a request from the House of Representatives to deliver documents concerning negotiations of an important treaty. Washington refused (successfully) on the grounds that, first, the House was not constitutionally part of the treaty-making process, and, second, that diplomatic negotiations required secrecy.

Executive privilege became a popular part of the "checks and balances" counterpart between president and Congress, and presidents have usually had the upper hand when invoking it. The expansion of executive privilege into a claim of "uncontrolled discretion" to refuse Congress's request for information came when President Nixon was beginning to get into political trouble over the Vietnam War in 1971. During the investigation of the Watergate break-in, it was President Nixon's claim to an almost absolute immunity to congressional inquiry that led to a Supreme Court rejection of the doctrine as a constitutional feature of the presidency in *United States v. Nixon.*[10] Although succeeding presidents continued to invoke the doctrine, they usually did so when they had something to hide that was of questionable legality (Iran-Contra) or potentially scandalous (Clinton's various scrapes). The exercise of presidential power through the executive-privilege doctrine has been all the more frequent in the past twenty years, when we lived nearly 90 percent of the time under conditions of divided government, where the party not in control of the White House controlled one or both of the chambers of Congress.[11]

ONLINE READING ○

[9]*Myers v. U.S.*, 272 U.S. 52 (1926); modified by *Humphrey's Executor v. U.S.*, 295 U.S. 602 (1935), *Wiener v. U.S.*, 357 U.S. 349 (1958), *Bowsher v. Synar*, 478 U.S. 714 (1986), and *Morrison v. Olson*, 108 S. Ct. 2597 (1988). See also Michael Nelson, ed., "The Removal Power," in *Congressional Quarterly's Guide to the Presidency* (Washington, D.C.: Congressional Quarterly Press, 1989), pp. 414–15.

[10]*United States v. Nixon*, 418 U.S. 683 (1974).

[11]A recent extension of executive power by President George W. Bush is the "signing statement." During each ceremony in which he signs a bill into law, President Bush has claimed the prerogative not to enforce those portions of the bill he believes to be unconstitutional. Thus he has asserted "the power to set aside any statute passed by Congress when it conflicts with his interpretation of the Constitution." This highly controversial assertion remains unsettled as a constitutional matter and surely will reach the Supreme Court in the near future. See Charlie Savage, "Bush Challenges Hundreds of Laws: President Cites Powers of His Office," *Boston Globe*, 30 April 2006.

The President's Legislative Power   The president plays a role not only in the administration of government but also in the legislative process. Two constitutional provisions are the primary sources of the president's power in the legislative arena. Article II, Section 3, provides that the president "shall from time to time give to the Congress Information of the State of the Union, and recommend to their Consideration such Measures as he shall judge necessary and expedient." This first legislative power has been important especially since Franklin Delano Roosevelt began to use the provision to initiate proposals for legislative action in Congress. Roosevelt established the presidency as the primary initiator of legislation.

The second of the president's legislative powers is the "*veto* power" assigned by Article I, Section 7. The veto power is the president's constitutional power to turn down acts of Congress. This power alone makes the president the most important single legislative leader. No bill vetoed by the president can become law unless both the House and the Senate override the veto by a two-thirds vote. In the case of a *pocket veto,* Congress does not even have the option of overriding the veto, but must reintroduce the bill in the next session. The president may exercise a pocket veto when presented with a bill during the last ten days of a legislative session. Usually, if a president does not sign a bill within ten days, it automatically becomes law. But this is true only while Congress is in session. If a president chooses not to sign a bill within the last ten days that Congress is in session, then the ten-day limit does not expire until Congress is out of session, and instead of becoming law, the bill is vetoed. Figure 6.1 illustrates the president's veto option. In 1996, a new power was added—the *line-item veto*—giving the president power to strike specific spending items from appropriations bills passed by Congress, unless reenacted by a two-thirds vote of both the House and Senate. In 1997, President Clinton used this power eleven times to strike eighty-two items from the federal budget. But, as we saw in Chapter 5, in 1998 the Supreme Court ruled that the Constitution does not authorize the line-item veto power.[12] Only a constitutional amendment would restore this power to the president.

The Games Presidents Play: The Veto   Use of the veto varies according to the political situation that each president confronts. During Bill Clinton's first two years in office, when Democrats controlled both houses of Congress, he vetoed no bills. After the congressional elections of 1994, however, Clinton confronted a Republican-controlled Congress with a definite agenda, and he began to use his veto power more vigorously. Likewise, George W. Bush vetoed no bill during his first term, a period in which his party controlled both houses of Congress. In general, presidents have used the veto to equalize or perhaps upset the balance of power with Congress. While the simple power to reject or accept legislation in its entirety might seem like a crude tool for making sure that legislation adheres to a president's preferences, the politics surrounding the veto is complicated, and it is rare that vetoes are used simply as bullets to kill legislation. Instead, vetoes are usually part of an intricate bargaining process between the president and Congress, involving threats of vetoes, repassing

veto The president's constitutional power to turn down acts of Congress. A presidential veto may be overridden by a two-thirds vote of each house of Congress.

pocket veto A presidential veto of legislation wherein the president takes no formal action on a bill. If Congress adjourns within ten days of passing a bill, and the president does not sign it, the bill is considered to be vetoed.

line-item veto Power that allows a governor (or the president) to strike out specific provisions (lines) of bills that the legislature passes. Without a line-item veto, the governor (or president) must accept or reject an entire bill. The line-item veto is no longer in effect for the president.

---

[12]*Clinton v. City of New York*, 524 U.S. 417 (1998).

ONLINE READING

FIGURE 6.1 The Veto Process

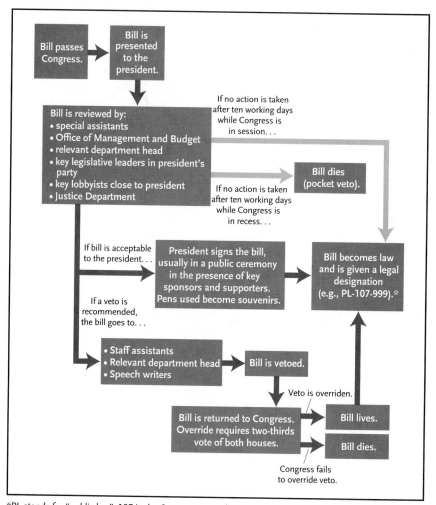

*PL stands for "public law"; 107 is the Congress (e.g., the 107th Congress was in session in 2001–2); 999 is the number of the law.

legislation, re-vetoes.[13] The Analyzing the Evidence unit in this chapter takes a closer look at veto politics.

Although presidents rarely veto legislation, this does not mean vetoes and veto bargaining have an insignificant influence over the policy process. The fact that presidents vetoed only 434 of the 17,000 public bills that Congress sent to them between 1945 and 1992 belies the centrality of the veto to presidential power. Many of these bills were insignificant and not worth the veto effort. Thus it is important to separate "significant"

[13]Charles M. Cameron, *Veto Bargaining: Presidents and the Politics of Negative Power* (New York: Cambridge University Press, 2000). See also David W. Rohde and Dennis Simon, "Presidential Vetoes and Congressional Response: A Study of Institutional Conflict," *American Journal of Political Science* 29 (1985): 397–427.

ONLINE READING ○

legislation, for which vetoes frequently occur, from insignificant legislation.[14] Vetoes can also be effective—even though they are rarely employed because of a concept known as "the second face of power"—that is, individuals will condition their actions based on how they think others will respond.[15] With respect to vetoes, this means that members of Congress will alter the content of a bill to make it more to a president's liking to pre-empt a veto. Thus the veto power can be influential even when the veto pen rests in its inkwell. This second face of power works to influence the content of legislation. The Analyzing the Evidence unit on the following page takes a closer look at veto politics.

What about the relationship between mass public support for the president and the use of the veto? At least for the modern presidency, a crucial resource for the president in negotiating with Congress has been his public approval as measured by opinion polls.[16] In some situations, members of Congress pass a bill not because they want to change policy but because they want to force the president to veto a popular bill that he disagrees with in order to hurt his approval ratings.[17] The key is that the public, uncertain of the president's policy preferences, uses information conveyed by vetoes to reassess what it knows about his preferences. As a result, vetoes may come at a price to the president.

Legislative Initiative Although not explicitly stated, the Constitution provides the president with the power of *legislative initiative.* To initiate means to originate, and in government that can mean power. The framers of the Constitution clearly saw legislative initiative as one of the keys to executive power. Initiative obviously implies the ability to formulate proposals for important policies, and the president, as an individual with a great deal of staff assistance, is able to initiate decisive action more frequently than Congress, with its large assemblies that have to deliberate and debate before taking action. With some important exceptions, Congress banks on the president to set the agenda of public policy. And quite clearly, there is power in initiative; there is power in being able to set the terms of discourse in the making of public policy.

For example, during the weeks immediately following September 11, 2001, George W. Bush took many presidential initiatives to Congress, and each was given almost unanimous support—from commitments to pursue al Qaeda to the removal of the Taliban, the reconstitution of the Afghanistan regime, all the way to almost unlimited approval for mobilization of both military power and power over the regulation of American civil liberties. Bush's second term, however, was difficult. Growing problems (and casualties) in Iraq, administrative scandals, and charges of incompetence in responding to the aftermath of Hurricanes Katrina and Rita plagued Bush. One could almost feel a shift in momentum, with Congress seizing back some of the initiative in dealing with the president. Presidential bargaining advantages ebb and flow—as presidential popularity ebbed in the polls in 2005, so too did Bush's agenda power.

---

[14]David R. Mayhew, *Divided We Govern: Party Control, Lawmaking, and Investigations, 1946–1990* (New Haven, Conn.: Yale University Press, 1991).

[15]Jack H. Nagel, *The Descriptive Analysis of Power* (New Haven, Conn.: Yale University Press, 1975).

[16]Theodore J. Lowi, *The Personal President: Power Invested, Promise Unfulfilled* (Ithaca, N.Y.: Cornell University Press, 1985).

[17]Timothy Groseclose and Nolan McCarty, "The Politics of Blame: Bargaining before an Audience," *American Journal of Political Science* 45 (2001): 100–19.

legislative initative
The president's inherent power to bring a legislative agenda before Congress.

○ ONLINE READING

Veto Politics

Although vetoes are relatively rare in the legislative process, scholars are drawn to study them because vetoes carry clear policy implications. Indeed, a president's use of the veto is an ideal example of negative agenda control—it creates an opportunity to block legislative action, but does not give the executive the power to alter proposed legislation after the fact. Nonetheless, chief executives regularly use the threat of a veto in their attempts to shape legislative outcomes.[1] In many cases, a credible veto threat may be sufficient to force compliance on the part of reluctant legislators who would like to avoid a prolonged legislative battle over a controversial bill or resolution, especially near the end of a legislative session. Instead of "losing" to the president, one or both chambers of the legislature may be willing to make concessions if the price of passage necessitates it.

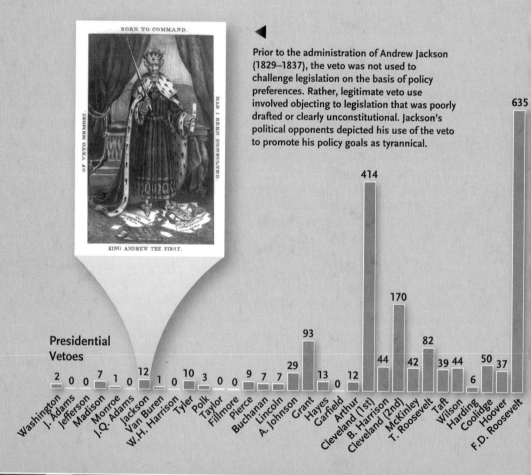

Prior to the administration of Andrew Jackson (1829–1837), the veto was not used to challenge legislation on the basis of policy preferences. Rather, legitimate veto use involved objecting to legislation that was poorly drafted or clearly unconstitutional. Jackson's political opponents depicted his use of the veto to promote his policy goals as tyrannical.

BORN TO COMMAND.

OF VETO MEMORY.

HAD I BEEN CONSULTED.

KING ANDREW THE FIRST.

Presidential Vetoes

President	Vetoes
Washington	2
J. Adams	0
Jefferson	0
Madison	7
Monroe	1
J.Q. Adams	0
Jackson	12
Van Buren	1
W.H. Harrison	0
Tyler	10
Polk	3
Taylor	0
Fillmore	0
Pierce	9
Buchanan	7
Lincoln	7
A. Johnson	29
Grant	93
Hayes	13
Garfield	0
Arthur	12
Cleveland (1st)	414
B. Harrison	44
Cleveland (2nd)	170
McKinley	42
T. Roosevelt	82
Taft	39
Wilson	44
Harding	6
Coolidge	50
Hoover	37
F.D. Roosevelt	635

Veto power is by no means absolute. Consistent with the Madisonian notion of checks and balances, the legislature has the opportunity to override a veto if legislators can muster the necessary votes. In the U.S. Congress, two thirds of both chambers must successfully vote to override a presidential veto. While many override attempts fail as a result of this supermajority requirement, the risk of a successful override attempt provides an important check on unilateral executive power.[2]

PRESIDENTIAL VETOES AND CONGRESSIONAL OVERRIDES, 1945–2007

	Years in Office	Vetoes	Divided Government	Override Attempts		Successes	
Truman	1945–1953	250	1947–1949	22	8.8%	12	54.5%
Eisenhower	1953–1961	181	1955–1961	11	6.1%	2	18.2%
Kennedy	1961–1963	21		0	0.0%	0	0.0%
Johnson	1963–1969	30		0	0.0%	0	0.0%
Nixon	1969–1974	43	1969–1974	21	48.8%	7	33.3%
Ford	1974–1977	66	1974–1977	28	42.4%	12	42.9%
Carter	1977–1981	31		4	12.9%	2	50.0%
Reagan	1981–1989	78	1981–1989	15	19.2%	9	60.0%
G.H.W. Bush	1989–1993	44	1989–1993	21	47.7%	1	4.8%
Clinton	1993–2001	38	1995–2001	14	36.8%	2	14.3%
G.W. Bush	2001–	5	2007–	5	100.0%	1	20.0%

(as of 12/5/07)

Sources: "Congressional Bills Vetoed: 1789–2001." Contributed by John P. McIver. *Historical Statistics of the United States*, Millennial Edition On Line, edited by Susan B. Carter, Scott S. Gartner, Michael R. Haines, Alan L. Olmstead, Richard Sutch, and Gavin Wright. © Cambridge University Press, 2006; calculated by author.

Veto override attempts and success are more likely to occur under divided government than unified government, which is most likely a function of divergent preferences across the institutions. Note that few or no overrides were attempted during presidencies that enjoyed unified government, with the president's party controlling at least one chamber of Congress.

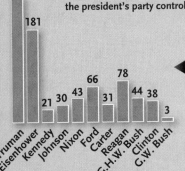

Since Jackson left office in 1837, presidents have routinely vetoed legislation for political reasons. During the twentieth century, for instance, the incidence of presidential vetoes was almost always greater under divided government, in which the executive is controlled by one political party and at least one chamber of Congress by the other.

[1]Charles M. Cameron, *Veto Bargaining: Presidents and the Politics of Negative Power*. (New York: Cambridge University Press, 2000).
[2]David W. Rohde and Dennis W. Simon. 1985. "Presidential Vetoes and Congressional Response: A Study of Institutional Conflict." *American Journal of Political Science* 29: 397–427.

The president's initiative does not end with policy making involving Congress and the making of laws in the ordinary sense of the phrase. The president has still another legislative role (in all but name) within the executive branch. This is designated as the power to issue *executive orders*. The executive order is first and foremost simply a management tool, a power possessed by virtually any CEO to make "company policy"—rules setting procedures, etiquette, chains of command, functional responsibilities, and so on. But evolving out of this normal management practice is a recognized presidential power to promulgate rules that have the effect and the formal status of legislation. Most of the executive orders of the president provide for the reorganization of structures and procedures or otherwise direct the affairs of the executive branch—either to be applied across the board to all agencies or applied in some important respect to a single agency or department. The power to issue executive orders illustrates that although reputation and persuasion are typically required in presidential policy making, the practice of issuing executive orders, within limits, allows a president to govern without the necessity to persuade.[18]

THE RISE OF PRESIDENTIAL GOVERNMENT

Most of the real influence of the modern presidency derives from the powers granted by the Constitution and the laws made by Congress. Thus, any person properly elected and sworn in as president will possess all of the power held by the strongest presidents in American history. But what variables account for a president's success in exercising these powers? Why are some presidents considered to be great successes and others colossal failures? This relates broadly to the very concept of presidential power. Is it a reflection of the attributes of the person or is it more characteristic of the political situations that a president encounters?

The personal view of presidential power dominated political scientists' view for several decades,[19] but recent scholars have argued that presidential power should be analyzed in terms of the strategic interactions that a president has with other political actors. The veto, which we reviewed in the last section, is one example of this sort of strategic interaction, but there are many other "games" that presidents play: the Supreme-Court-nomination and treaty-ratification games with the Senate, the executive-order game, the agency-supervision-and-management game with the executive branch. As the political scientist Charles M. Cameron has argued, "Understanding the presidency means understanding these games."[20] Success in these "games" translates into presidential power.

executive order A rule or regulation issued by the president that has the effect and formal status of legislation.

ONLINE READING ○

ONLINE READING ○

---

[18] This point is developed in both Kenneth R. Mayer, *With the Stroke of a Pen: Executive Orders and Presidential Power* (Princeton, N.J.: Princeton University Press, 2001), and William G. Howell, *Power without Persuasion: The Politics of Direct Presidential Action* (Princeton, N.J.: Princeton University Press, 2003).

[19] Richard Neustadt, *Presidential Power: The Politics of Leadership* (New York: Wiley, 1960).

[20] Charles M. Cameron, "Bargaining and Presidential Power," in Robert Y. Shapiro, Martha Joynt Kumar, and Lawrence R. Jacobs, eds., *Presidential Power: Forging the Presidency for the Twenty-first Century* (New York: Columbia University Press, 2000), p. 47.

We must not forget, however, the tremendous resources that a president can rely on in his strategic interactions with others. Remember that the presidency is a democratic institution with a national constituency. Its broad popular base is a presidential resource that can be deployed strategically in the various bargaining games just discussed; a president's success depends on the qualities of the person in office and the situations that arise. For example, political scientist Samuel Kernell suggests that presidents may rally public opinion and put pressure on Congress by "going public."[21] With the occasional exception, however, it took more than a century, perhaps as much as a century and a half, before presidents came to be seen as consequential players in these strategic encounters. A bit of historical review will be helpful in understanding how the presidency has risen to its current level of influence.

The Legislative Epoch, 1800–1933

In 1885, a then-obscure political science professor named Woodrow Wilson entitled his general textbook *Congressional Government* because American government was just that, "congressional government." The clear intent of the framers of the Constitution was for legislative supremacy. The strongest evidence of this original intent is the fact that the powers of the national government were listed in Article I, the legislative article. Madison had laid it out explicitly in *The Federalist*, No. 51: "In republican government, the legislative authority necessarily predominates."[22]

By the second term of President Jefferson (1805–09), the executive branch was beginning to play the secondary role anticipated by the Constitution. The quality of presidential performance and then of presidential personality and character declined accordingly. The president was seen by some observers as little more than America's "chief clerk." It was said of President James Madison, who had been the principal author of the Constitution, that he knew everything about government except how to govern. Indeed, after Jefferson and until the beginning of the twentieth century, most historians agree that Presidents Jackson and Lincoln were the only exceptions to what was the rule of weak presidents.

---

[21] Samuel Kernell, *Going Public: New Strategies of Presidential Leadership*, 3rd ed. (Washington, D.C.: Congressional Quarterly Press, 1998).

[22] The Library of Congress believes that *Federalist* No. 51 could have been written by Hamilton or by Madison, and it is true that the authorship of certain of the *Federalist Papers* is still in dispute. But we insist on Madison's authorship of *Federalist* No. 51 for two important reasons: First, the style of the essay and the political theory underlying the essay are, to us, clearly Madisonian. Second, Madison's authorship of *Federalist* No. 51 seems to be the consensus among academic political scientists and historians, and we find our strongest support in three of the most esteemed and admirable students of the Founding: historian Forrest McDonald, *Novus Ordo Seclorum—The Intellectual Origins of the Constitution* (Lawrence: University Press of Kansas, 1985), p. 258; political theorist Isaac Kramnick in his edition of *The Federalist Papers* (New York: Viking Penguin, 1987), Editor's Introduction, especially p. 53; and the late Clinton Rossiter, *The Federalist Papers* (New York: New American Library, 1961), pp. xiii–xiv.

One reason that so few great men became presidents in the nineteenth century is that there was only occasional room for greatness in such a weak office.[23] As Chapter 3 indicated, the national government of that period was not particularly powerful. Another reason is that during this period, the presidency was not closely linked to major national political and social forces. Federalism had taken very good care of this by fragmenting political interests and diverting the energies of interest groups toward state and local governments, where most key decisions were being made.

The presidency was strengthened somewhat in the 1830s with the introduction of the national convention system of nominating presidential candidates. Until then, presidential candidates had been nominated by their party's congressional delegates. This was the caucus system of nominating candidates, and it was derisively called "King Caucus" because any candidate for president had to defer to the party's leaders in Congress in order to get the party's nomination and the support of the party's congressional delegation in the election. The national nominating convention arose outside Congress in order to provide some representation for a party's voters who lived in districts where they weren't numerous enough to elect a member of Congress. The political party in each state made its own provisions for selecting delegates to attend the presidential nominating convention, and in virtually all states, the selection was dominated by the party leaders (called "bosses" by the opposition party). Only in recent decades have state laws intervened to regularize the selection process and provide (in all but a few instances) for open election of delegates.

In the nineteenth century, the national nominating convention was seen as a victory for democracy against the congressional elite. And the national convention gave the presidency a base of power independent of Congress. Eventually, though more slowly, the presidential selection process began to be further democratized, with the adoption of primary elections through which millions of ordinary citizens were given an opportunity to take part in the presidential nominating process by popular selection of convention delegates.

This independence did not immediately transform the presidency into the office we recognize today, because Congress was able to keep tight reins on the president's power. The real turning point came during the administration of Franklin Delano Roosevelt. The New Deal was a response to political forces that had been gathering national strength and focus for fifty years. What is remarkable is not that they gathered but that they were so long gaining influence in Washington.

The New Deal and the Presidency

The "First Hundred Days" of the Roosevelt administration in 1933 have no parallel in U.S. history. But this period was only the beginning. The policies proposed by President Roosevelt and adopted by Congress during the first thousand days of

---

[23]For related appraisals, see Jeffrey Tulis, *The Rhetorical Presidency* (Princeton, N.J.: Princeton University Press, 1988); Stephen Skowronek, *The Politics Presidents Make: Presidential Leadership from John Adams to George Bush* (Cambridge, Mass.: Harvard University Press, 1993); and Robert Spitzer, *President and Congress: Executive Hegemony at the Crossroads of American Government* (New York: McGraw-Hill, 1993).

his administration so changed the size and character of the national government that they constitute a moment in American history equivalent to the Founding or to the Civil War. The president's constitutional obligation to see "that the laws be faithfully executed" became, during Roosevelt's presidency, virtually a responsibility to shape the laws before executing them.

New Programs Expand the Role of National Government   Many of the New Deal programs were extensions of the traditional national government approach, which was described in Chapter 3 (see especially Table 3.1, p. 49). But the New Deal also adopted policies never before tried on a large scale by the national government. It began intervening into economic life in ways that had hitherto been reserved to the states. In other words, the national government discovered that it, too, had "police power" and that it could directly regulate individuals as well as provide roads and other services.

The new programs were such dramatic departures from the traditional policies of the national government that their constitutionality was in doubt. The turning point came in 1937 with *National Labor Relations Board v. Jones & Laughlin Steel Corporation*. At issue was the National Labor Relations Act, or Wagner Act, which prohibited corporations from interfering with the efforts of employees to engage in union activities. The newly formed National Labor Relations Board (NLRB) had ordered Jones & Laughlin to reinstate workers fired because of their union activities. The appeal reached the Supreme Court because Jones & Laughlin had made a constitutional issue over the fact that its manufacturing activities were local and therefore beyond the national government's reach. The Supreme Court rejected this argument with the response that a big company with subsidiaries and suppliers in many states was innately involved in interstate commerce.[24] Since the end of the New Deal, the Supreme Court has never again seriously questioned the constitutionality of an important act of Congress broadly authorizing the executive branch to intervene into the economy or society.[25]

Delegation of Power   The most important constitutional effect of Congress's actions and the Supreme Court's approval of those actions during the New Deal was

---

[24]*NLRB v. Jones & Laughlin Steel Corporation*, 301 U.S. 1 (1937). Congress had attempted to regulate the economy before 1933, as with the Interstate Commerce Act and Sherman Antitrust Act of the late nineteenth century and with the Federal Trade Act and the Federal Reserve in the Wilson period. But these were rare attempts, and each was restricted very carefully to a narrow and acceptable definition of "interstate commerce." The big break did not come until after 1933.

[25]Some will argue that there are some exceptions to this statement. One was the 1976 case declaring unconstitutional Congress's effort to supply national minimum wage standards to state and local government employees (*National League of Cities v. Usery*, 426 U.S. 833 [1976]). But the Court reversed itself on this nine years later, in 1985 (*Garcia v. San Antonio Metropolitan Transit Authority*, 469 U.S. 528 [1985]). Another was the 1986 case declaring unconstitutional the part of the Gramm-Rudman law authorizing the comptroller general to make "across the board" budget cuts when total appropriations exceeded legally established ceilings (*Bowsher v. Synar*, 478 U.S. 714 [1986]). In 1999, executive authority was compromised somewhat by the Court's decision to question the Federal Communication Commission's authority to supervise telephone deregulation under the Telecommunications Act of 1996. But cases such as these are rare, and they only touch on part of a law, not the constitutionality of an entire program.

the enhancement of presidential power. Most major acts of Congress in this period involved significant exercises of control over the economy. But few programs specified the actual controls to be used. Instead, Congress authorized the president or, in some cases, a new agency to determine what the controls would be. Some of the new agencies were independent commissions responsible to Congress. But most of the new agencies and programs of the New Deal were placed in the executive branch directly under presidential authority.

This form of congressional act is called the "delegation of power." In theory, the delegation of power works as follows: (1) Congress recognizes a problem; (2) Congress acknowledges that it has neither the time nor the expertise to deal with the problem; and (3) Congress therefore sets the basic policies and then delegates to an agency the power to "fill in the details." But in practice, Congress was delegating not merely the power to "fill in the details," but actual and real policy-making powers, that is, real legislative powers, to the executive branch.

No modern government can avoid the delegation of significant legislative powers to the executive branch. But the fact remains that these delegations of power cumulatively produced a fundamental shift in the American constitutional framework. During the 1930s, the growth of the national government through acts delegating legislative power tilted the American national structure away from a Congress-centered government toward a president-centered government. Congress continues to be the constitutional source of policy, and Congress can rescind these delegations of power or restrict them with later amendments, committee oversight, or budget costs. But since Congress has continued to enact large new programs involving very broad delegations of legislative power to the executive branch, and since the Court has gone along with such actions,[26] we can say that presidential government has become an established fact of American life.

PRESIDENTIAL GOVERNMENT

There was no great mystery in the shift from Congress-centered government to president-centered government. Congress simply delegated its own powers to the executive branch. Congressional delegations of power, however, are not the only resources available to the president. Presidents have at their disposal a variety of other formal and informal resources that enable them to govern. Indeed, without these other resources, presidents would lack the tools needed to make much use of the power and responsibility given to them by Congress. Let us first consider the president's formal or official resources (see Figure 6.2). Then, in the section following, we will turn to the more informal resources that affect a president's capacity to govern, in particular the president's popular support.

---

[26]The Supreme Court did in fact *dis*approve broad delegations of legislative power by declaring the National Industrial Recovery Act of 1933 unconstitutional on the grounds that Congress did not accompany the broad delegations with sufficient standards or guidelines for presidential discretion (*Panama Refining Co. v. Ryan*, 293 U.S. 388 [1935], and *Schechter Poultry Corp. v. U.S.*, 295 U.S. 495 [1935]). The Supreme Court has never reversed those two decisions, but it has also never really followed them. Thus, broad delegations of legislative power from Congress to the executive branch can be presumed to be constitutional.

FIGURE 6.2 The Institutional Presidency, 2008

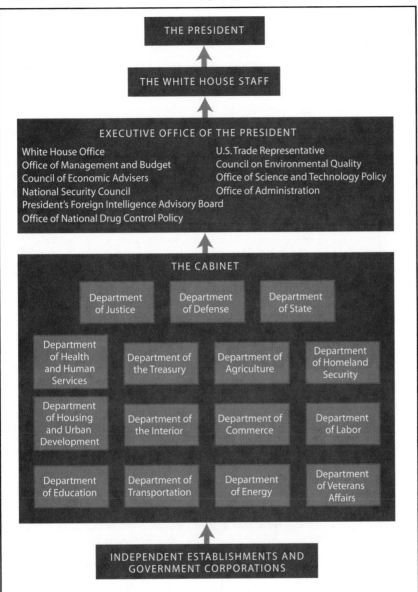

Note: Arrows are used to indicate lines of legal responsibility.

Source: Office of the Federal Register, National Archives and Records Administration, *The United States Government Manual, 1995–1996* (Washington, D.C.: Government Printing Office, 1995), p. 22.

Formal Resources of Presidential Power

The Cabinet In the American system of government, the ***cabinet*** is the traditional but informal designation for the heads of all the major federal government departments. The cabinet has no constitutional status. Unlike that of England and many other parliamentary countries, where the cabinet *is* the government, the American cabinet is not a collective body. It meets but makes no decisions as a group. Each appointment must be approved by the Senate, but the person appointed is not responsible to the Senate or to Congress at large. Cabinet appointments help build party and popular support, but the cabinet is not a party organ. The cabinet is made up of directors but is not a board of directors.

Presidents tend to develop an impatience with and a mild distrust of cabinet members. Presidents seek to make the cabinet a rubber stamp for actions already decided on, demanding results, or the appearance of results, more immediately and more frequently than most department heads can provide. Since cabinet appointees generally come from differing careers, the formation of an effective, governing group out of this motley collection of appointments is very unlikely.

Some presidents have relied heavily on an "inner cabinet," the ***National Security Council (NSC).*** The NSC, established by law in 1947, is composed of the president; the vice president; the secretaries of state, defense, and treasury; the attorney general; and other officials invited by the president. It has its own staff of foreign policy specialists run by the special assistant to the president for national security affairs. George W. Bush created an "inner cabinet" composed largely of former and proven senior staffers and cabinet members of former Republican administrations, most particularly Vice President Richard Cheney and former Defense Secretary Donald Rumsfeld.

Presidents have obviously been uneven and unpredictable in their reliance on the NSC and other subcabinet bodies, because executive management is inherently a personal matter. However, despite all the personal variations, one generalization can be made: Presidents have increasingly preferred the White House staff to the cabinet as their means of managing the gigantic executive branch.

The White House Staff The White House staff is composed mainly of analysts and advisers. Although many of the top White House staffers are given the title "special assistant" for a particular task or sector, the types of judgments they are expected to make and the kinds of advice they are supposed to give are a good deal broader and more generally political than those that come from the cabinet departments or the Executive Office of the President. The White House staff has grown substantially under recent presidents (see Table 6.1).[27]

The White House staff is a crucial information source and management tool for the president. But it may also insulate the president from other sources of information. Managing this trade-off between in-house expertise and access to independ-

---

[27]All the figures since 1967, and probably 1957, are understated; additional White House staff members who were on "detailed" service from the military and other departments are not counted here because they were not on the White House payroll.

TABLE 6.1 The Expanding White House Staff

Year	President	Full-time Employees	Year	President	Full-time Employees*
1937	Franklin D. Roosevelt	45	1980	Jimmy Carter	488
1947	Harry S. Truman	190	1984	Ronald Reagan	575
1957	Dwight D. Eisenhower	364	1992	George H. W. Bush	605
1967	Lyndon B. Johnson	251	1996	Bill Clinton	511
1972	Richard M. Nixon	550	2001	George W. Bush	507
1975	Gerald R. Ford	533			

*The vice president employs over twenty staffers, and there are at least one hundred on the staff of the National Security Council. These people work in and around the White House and Executive Office but are not included in the preceding totals.

SOURCES: Thomas E. Cronin, "The Swelling of the Presidency: Can Anyone Reverse the Tide?" in *American Government: Readings and Cases*, 8th ed., ed. Peter Woll (Boston: Little, Brown, 1984), p. 347. Copyright © 1984 by Thomas E. Cronin. Reproduced with the permission of the author. For 1990: U.S. Office of Personnel Management, *Federal Civilian Workforce Statistics, Employment and Trends as of January 1990* (Washington, D.C.: Government Printing Office, 1990), p. 29. For 1992, 1996, and 2001: OMB and the White House.

ent outside opinion is a major challenge for the president. Sometimes it is botched, as when President George W. Bush depended too heavily on his staff for information about WMDs in Iraq, leading him to erroneous conclusions.[28]

The Executive Office of the President   The development of the White House staff can be appreciated only in relation to the still larger Executive Office of the President (EOP). Created in 1939, the EOP is what is often called the "institutional presidency"—the permanent agencies that perform defined management tasks for the president. The most important and the largest EOP agency is the Office of Management and Budget (OMB). Its roles in preparing the national budget, designing the president's program, reporting on agency activities, and overseeing regulatory proposals make OMB personnel part of virtually every conceivable presidential responsibility. The status and power of the OMB within the EOP has grown in importance from president to president.

The process of budgeting was at one time a bottom-up procedure, with expenditure and program requests passing from the lowest bureaus through the departments to "clearance" in OMB and hence to Congress, where each agency could be called in to reveal what its original request had been before OMB got hold of it. Now the process is top-down, with OMB setting the budget guidelines for agencies as well as for Congress.

---

[28]See George Krause, "The Secular Decline in Presidential Domestic Policymaking: An Organizational Perspective," *Presidential Studies Quarterly* 34 (2004): 779–92. On the general issue, see James P. Pfiffner, ed., *The Managerial Presidency*, 2nd ed. (College Station: Texas A&M University Press, 1999).

The Vice Presidency   The Constitution created the vice presidency along with the presidency, and the office exists for two purposes only: to succeed the president in the case of a vacancy[29] and to preside over the Senate, casting the tie-breaking vote when necessary.[30] Traditionally, a presidential candidate's most important rule for the choice of a running mate is that he or she bring the support of at least one state (preferably a large one) not otherwise likely to support the ticket. Another rule holds that the vice-presidential nominee should come from a region and, where possible, from an ideological or ethnic subsection of the party differing from the presidential nominee's. It is very doubtful that John Kennedy would have won in 1960 without his vice-presidential candidate, Lyndon Johnson, and the contribution Johnson made to carrying Texas. George W. Bush's choice of Dick Cheney in 2000 was completely devoid of direct electoral value since Cheney came from one of our least populous states (Wyoming, which casts only three electoral votes). But given Cheney's stalwart right-wing record both in Congress and as President George H. W. Bush's secretary of defense, his inclusion on the Republican ticket was clearly an effort to consolidate the support of the restive right wing of his party. In 2008, Barack Obama named Senator Joseph Biden of Delaware to serve as his running mate. Biden chaired the Senate Foreign Relations committee and was seen as compensating for Obama's own lack of foreign policy experience. Biden is also Catholic and from a working-class background, which Democrats hoped would help their ticket appeal to blue-collar voters in battleground states like Ohio and Pennsylvania. John McCain chose Alaska governor Sarah Palin as his running mate. Palin was very popular among the GOP's religious conservatives and helped to energize the party's "base." The governor's inexperience and apparent lack of familiarity with national issues, however, led many voters to question her qualifications and probably hurt the McCain ticket.

As the institutional presidency has grown in size and complexity, most presidents of the past twenty-five years have sought to use their vice presidents as a management resource after the election. George H. W. Bush, as vice president, was "kept within the loop" of decision making because President Reagan delegated so much power. A copy of virtually everything made for Reagan was made for Bush, especially during the first term, when Bush's close friend James Baker was chief of staff. Former President Bush did not take such pains to keep Dan Quayle "in the loop," but President Clinton relied greatly on his vice president, Al Gore, who emerged as one of the most trusted and effective figures in the Clinton White House. Gore's most important task was to oversee the National Performance Review (NPR), an ambitious program to "reinvent" the way the federal government conducts its affairs. The presidency of George W. Bush resulted in unprecedented power and responsibility for his vice president, Cheney.

---

[29]This provision was clarified by the Twenty-fifth Amendment (1967), which provides that the president (with majority confirmation of House and Senate) must appoint someone to fill the office of vice president if the vice president should die or should fill a vacancy in the presidency. This procedure has been invoked twice—once in 1973 when President Nixon nominated Gerald Ford, and the second time in 1974 when President Ford, having automatically succeeded the resigned President Nixon, filled the vice presidential vacancy with Nelson Rockefeller.

[30]Article I, Section 3, provides that the vice president "shall be President of the Senate, but shall have no Vote, unless they be equally divided."

The Contemporary Bases of Presidential Power

Generally, presidents can expand their power in three ways: party, popular mobilization, and administration. In the first instance, presidents may construct or strengthen national partisan institutions with which to exert influence in the legislative process and through which to implement their programs. Alternatively, or in addition to the first tactic, presidents may use popular appeals to create a mass base of support that will allow them to subordinate their political foes. This tactic has sometimes been called the strategy of "going public" or the "rhetorical" presidency.[31] Third, presidents may seek to bolster their control of established executive agencies or to create new administrative institutions and procedures that will reduce their dependence on Congress and give them a more independent governing and policy-making capability. Presidents' use of executive orders to achieve their policy goals in lieu of seeking to persuade Congress to enact legislation is, perhaps, the most obvious example.

Party as a Source of Power   All presidents have relied on the members and leaders of their own party to implement their legislative agendas. President George W. Bush, for example, worked closely with congressional GOP leaders on such matters as energy policy and Medicare reform. But the president does not control his own party; party members have considerable autonomy. Moreover, in America's system of separated powers, the president's party may be in the minority in Congress and unable to do much for the chief executive's programs (Figure 6.3). Consequently, although their party is valuable to chief executives, it has not been a fully reliable presidential tool. The more unified the president's party is behind his legislative requests, the more unified the opposition party is also likely to be. Unless the president's party majority is very large, he must also appeal to the opposition to make up for the inevitable defectors within the ranks of his own party. Thus the president often poses as being above partisanship to win "bipartisan" support in Congress. But to the extent that he pursues a bipartisan strategy, he cannot throw himself fully into building the party loyalty and the party discipline that would maximize the value of his own party's support in Congress. This is a dilemma for every president, particularly those faced with an opposition-controlled Congress.

Going Public   Popular mobilization as a technique of presidential power has its historical roots in the presidencies of Theodore Roosevelt and Woodrow Wilson and has, subsequently, became a weapon in the political arsenals of most presidents since the mid-twentieth century. During the nineteenth century, it was considered inappropriate for presidents to engage in personal campaigning on their own behalf or in support of programs and policies. When Andrew Johnson broke this unwritten rule and made a series of speeches vehemently seeking public support for his

---

[31]Samuel Kernell, *Going Public: New Strategies of Presidential Leadership*, 3rd ed. (Washington, D.C.: Congressional Quarterly Press, 1997); also, Jeffrey Tulis, *The Rhetorical Presidency* (Princeton, N.J.: Princeton University Press, 1987).

FIGURE 6.3 The Presidential Batting Average: Presidential Success on Congressional Votes, 1953–2004

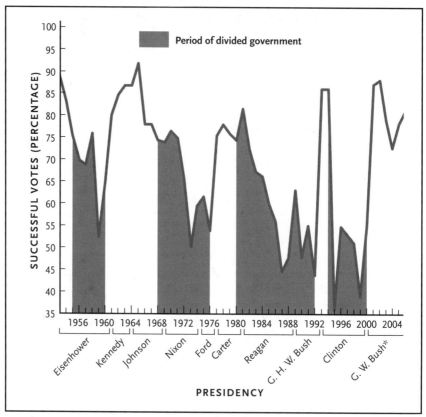

SOURCE: *Congressional Quarterly Weekly Report*, 3 January 2004, p. 18.

NOTE: Percentages are based on votes on which presidents took a position.

*In 2001, the government was divided for only part of the year.

Reconstruction program, even some of Johnson's most ardent supporters were shocked at what was seen as his lack of decorum.

The president who used public appeals most effectively was Franklin D. Roosevelt. Political scientist Sidney Milkis observes that FDR was "firmly persuaded of the need to form a direct link between the executive office and the public."[32] FDR developed a number of tactics aimed at forging such a link. Like his predecessors, he often embarked on speaking trips around the nation to promote his programs. In addition, FDR made limited but important use of the new electronic medium, the radio, to reach millions of Americans. In his famous "fireside chats," the president, or at least his voice, came into every living room in the country to discuss programs

---

[32]Sidney M. Milkis, *The President and the Parties* (New York: Oxford, 1993), p. 97.

and policies and generally to assure Americans that Franklin Delano Roosevelt was aware of their difficulties and working diligently toward solutions.

Roosevelt also made himself available for biweekly press conferences, during which he offered candid answers to reporters' questions and made certain to make important policy announcements that would provide the reporters with significant stories to file with their papers.[33] Roosevelt was the first president to designate a press secretary (Stephen Early) who was charged with organizing the press conferences and making certain that reporters observed the informal rules distinguishing presidential comments that were off the record from those that could be attributed directly to the president.

Every president since FDR has sought to craft a public relations strategy that would emphasize the incumbent's strengths and maximize his popular appeal. One Clinton innovation was to make the White House Communications Office an important institution within the EOP. In a practice continued by George W. Bush, the Communications Office became responsible not only for responding to reporters' queries but for developing and implementing a coordinated communications strategy—promoting the president's policy goals, developing responses to unflattering news stories, and making certain that a favorable image of the president would, insofar as possible, dominate the news. George W. Bush's first communications director, Karen Hughes, sought to put the office "ahead of the news," constantly developing stories that would dominate the headlines, present the president in a favorable light, and deflect criticism.

In addition to using the media, recent presidents have reached out directly to the American public to gain its approval. This is an expression of the presidency as a ***permanent campaign*** for reelection. A study by political scientist Charles O. Jones shows that President Bill Clinton engaged in campaignlike activity throughout his presidency and was the most-traveled American president in history. In his first twenty months in office, he made 203 appearances outside of Washington, compared to 178 for George H. W. Bush and 58 for Ronald Reagan. President George W. Bush might outdo them all. During his first hundred days, Bush gave speeches and other public appearances in twenty-six states; Clinton's and former president Bush's records during their first hundred days were fifteen states each.

However, popular support has not been a firm foundation for presidential power. To begin with, popular support is notoriously fickle. President George W. Bush maintained an approval rating of over 70 percent for more than a year after the September 11 terrorist attacks. By 2003, however, his approval rating had fallen nearly twenty points as American casualties in Iraq mounted; by the end of 2005 it had fallen almost another twenty points, to the high-30s range. Such declines in popular approval during a president's term in office are nearly inevitable and follow a predictable pattern (see Figure 6.4).[34] Presidents generate popular support by promising to undertake important programs that will contribute directly to the

[33]Kernell, *Going Public*, p. 79.

[34]Theodore J. Lowi, *The Personal President: Power Invested, Promise Unfulfilled* (Ithaca, N.Y.: Cornell University Press, 1985).

permanent campaign Description of presidential politics in which all presidential actions are taken with reelection in mind.

FIGURE 6.4 Public Appearances by Presidents

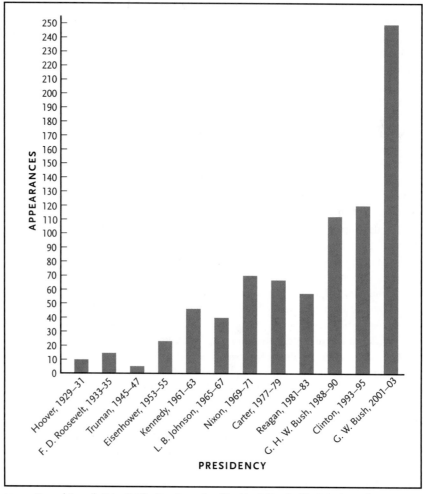

SOURCE: Samuel Kernell, *Going Public: New Strategies of Presidential Leadership*, 3rd ed. (Washington, D.C.: Congressional Quarterly Press, 1998), p. 118.

NOTE: Only the first two years of each term are included, because the last two years include many purely political appearances for the president's reelection campaign.

well-being of large numbers of Americans. Almost inevitably, presidential performance falls short of those promises and popular expectations, leading to a sharp decline in public support and an ensuing collapse of presidential influence.[35]

Presidents have certainly not abandoned "going public," but they no longer do so as frequently as they once did—there has been, for example, a decline in presidential appearances on prime-time television.[36] Instead, presidents have employed

---

[35] Lowi, *The Personal President*, p. 11.

[36] Kernell, *Going Public*, p. 114.

institutionalized public and media relations efforts more to create a generally favorable public image than to promote specific policies. Thus, in 2002, President George W. Bush made several speeches to boost the proposed creation of the Homeland Security department. At the same time, however, the White House Communications Office was engaged in a nonstop, seven-day-a-week effort to promote news and feature stories aimed at bolstering the president's more general public image. Stories emphasized the president's empathy for retirees hurt by the downturn of stock prices, the president's anger over corporate abuses, the president's concern for the environment, the president's determination to prevent terrorism, the president's support for Israel, and so forth. These are all examples of image-polishing rather than going public on behalf of specific programs. Confronted with the limitations of a strategy of popular mobilization, presidents have shifted from an offensive strategy to a more defensive mode in this domain. The limitations of going public as a route to presidential power have also led contemporary presidents to make use of a third technique: expansion of their administrative capabilities.

The Administrative State

Contemporary presidents have increased the administrative capabilities of their office in three ways. First, they have enhanced the reach and power of the EOP. Second, they have sought to increase White House control over the federal bureaucracy. Third, they have expanded the role of executive orders and other instruments of direct presidential governance. Taken together, these components of what might be called the White House "administrative strategy" have given presidents a capacity to achieve their programmatic and policy goals even when they are unable to secure congressional approval. Indeed, some recent presidents have been able to accomplish quite a bit without much congressional, partisan, or even public support.

The Executive Office of the President has grown from six administrative assistants in 1939 to today's 400 employees working directly for the president in the White House office along with some 1,400 individuals staffing the several (currently eight) divisions of the Executive Office.[37] The growth of the White House staff gives the president an enormously enhanced capacity to gather information, plan programs and strategies, communicate with constituencies, and exercise supervision of the executive branch. In particular, the OMB serves as a potential instrument of presidential control over federal spending and hence as a mechanism through which the White House has greatly expanded its power. The OMB has the capacity to analyze and approve all legislative proposals, not only budgetary requests, emanating from all federal agencies before being submitted to Congress. Thus in one White House agency, the president has the means to exert major influence over the flow of money as well as the shape and content of national legislation.

A second tactic that presidents have used to increase their power and reach is the process of regulatory review, through which presidents have sought to seize control of rule making by the agencies of the executive branch. Whenever Congress enacts a

---

[37] Harold W. Stanley and Richard G. Niemi, *Vital Statistics on American Politics, 2001–2002* (Washington, D.C.: Congressional Quarterly Press, 2001), pp. 250–51.

statute, its actual implementation requires the promulgation of hundreds of rules by the agency charged with administering the law and giving effect to the will of Congress. Some congressional statutes are quite detailed and leave agencies with relatively little discretion. Typically, however, Congress enacts a relatively broad statement of legislative intent and delegates to the appropriate administrative agency the power to fill in many important details.[38] In other words, Congress typically says to an administrative agency, "Here is the problem: deal with it."[39]

The discretion Congress delegates to administrative agencies has provided recent presidents with an important avenue for expanding their power. For example, Clinton ordered the Food and Drug Administration (FDA) to develop rules designed to restrict the marketing of tobacco products to children. White House and FDA staffers then spent several months preparing nearly 1,000 pages of new regulations affecting tobacco manufacturers and vendors.[40] Republicans denounced Clinton's actions as a usurpation of power.[41] However, after he took office, President George W. Bush made no move to surrender the powers Clinton had claimed.

A third mechanism through which contemporary presidents have sought to enhance their power to govern unilaterally is through the use of executive orders and other forms of presidential decrees, including executive agreements, national security findings and directives, proclamations, reorganization plans, the signing of statements, and a host of others.[42] Presidents may not use executive orders to issue whatever commands they please. The use of such decrees is bound by law. If a president issues an executive order, proclamation, directive, or the like, in principle he does so pursuant to the powers granted to him by the Constitution or delegated to him by Congress, usually through a statute. When presidents issue such orders, they generally state the constitutional or statutory basis for their actions. For example, when President Truman ordered the desegregation of the armed services, he did so pursuant to his constitutional powers as commander in chief. In a similar vein, when President Johnson issued Executive Order No. 11246, he asserted that the order was designed to implement the 1964 Civil Rights Act, which prohibited employment discrimination. Where an executive order has no statutory or constitutional basis, the courts have held it to be void. The most important case illustrating this point is *Youngstown Sheet & Tube Co. v. Sawyer*, the so-called steel seizure case of 1952.[43] Here the Supreme Court ruled that President Truman's seizure of the nation's steel mills during the Korean War had no statutory or constitutional basis and was thus invalid.

A number of court decisions, though, have established broad boundaries that leave considerable room for presidential action. By illustration, the courts have

---

[38]The classic critique of this process is Theodore J. Lowi, *The End of Liberalism* (New York: Norton, 1979).

[39]Kenneth Culp Davis, *Administrative Law Treatise* (St. Paul, Minn.: West Publishing, 1958), p. 9.

[40]Elena Kagan, "Presidential Administration," *Harvard Law Review* 2245 (2001): 2265.

[41]For example, Douglas W. Kmiec, "Expanding Power," in *The Rule of Law in the Wake of Clinton*, ed. Roger Pilon (Washington, D.C.: Cato Institute Press, 2000), pp. 47–68.

[42]A complete inventory is provided in Harold C. Relyea, "Presidential Directives: Background and Review," The Library of Congress, *Congressional Research Service Report 98–611*, 9 November 2001.

ONLINE READING ○ [43]*Youngstown Sheet & Tube Co. v. Sawyer*, 346 U.S. 579 (1952).

FIGURE 6.5 Significant Executive Orders, 1900–1995

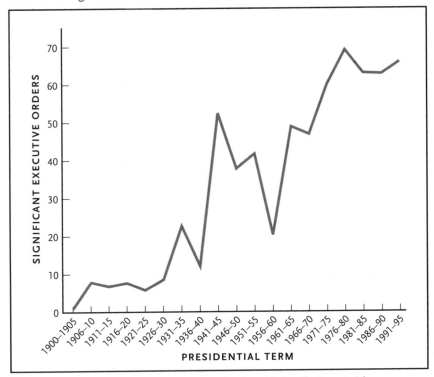

SOURCE: William G. Howell, "The President's Powers of Unilateral Action: The Strategic Advantages of Acting Alone" (Ph.D. diss., Stanford University, 1999).

held that Congress might approve a presidential action after the fact or, in effect, ratify a presidential action through "acquiescence"—for example, by not objecting for long periods of time or by continuing to provide funding for programs established by executive orders. In addition, the courts have indicated that some areas, most notably the realm of military policy, are presidential in character and have allowed presidents wide latitude to make policy by executive decree. Thus, within the very broad limits established by the courts, presidential orders can be and have been important policy tools (see Figure 6.5). President George W. Bush has not hesitated to use executive orders, issuing more than forty during his first year in office and continuing to employ this device (along with signing statements) regularly during his presidency.

IS THE PRESIDENCY TOO STRONG?

The framers of the Constitution, as we saw, created a unitary executive branch because they thought this would make the presidency a more energetic institution.

At the same time, they checked the powers of the executive branch by creating a system of separated powers. Did the framers' work make the presidency a strong or weak institution?

At one time, historians and journalists liked to debate the question of strong versus weak presidents. Some presidents, such as Lincoln and FDR, were called "strong" for their leadership and ability to guide the nation's political agenda. Others, like James Buchanan and Calvin Coolidge, were seen as "weak" for failing to develop significant legislative programs and seeming to observe rather than shape political events. Today, the strong versus weak categorization has become moot. *Every president is strong.* This strength is not so much a function of personal charisma as it is a reflection of the increasing powers of the institution of the presidency. Of course, as we noted earlier, political savvy in strategic interactions with other politicians and mobilizing public opinion can account for a president's success in exercising these powers. But contemporary presidents all possess a vast array of resources and powers.

Indeed, presidents seek to dominate the policy-making process and claim the inherent power to lead the nation in time of war. The expansion of presidential power over the past century has not come about by accident but as the result of an ongoing effort by successive presidents to expand the power of the office. Some presidential efforts have succeeded and others have failed. One recent president, Nixon, was forced to resign and others have left office under clouds. Most presidents, nevertheless, have sought to increase the office's power. As the framers of the Constitution predicted, presidential ambition has been a powerful and unrelenting force in American politics. Why has presidential ambition gone virtually unchecked? What are the consequences of such a development?

As is often noted by the media and in the academic literature, popular participation in American political life has declined precipitously since its nineteenth-century apogee. Voter turnout in national presidential elections barely exceeds the 50 percent mark, while hardly a third of those eligible participate in off-year congressional races. Turnout in state and local contests is typically even lower. These facts are well known and their implications for the representative character of American government frequently deplored.

The decay of popular political participation, however, also has profoundly important institutional implications that are not often fully appreciated. To put the matter succinctly, the decline of voting and other forms of popular involvement in American political life reduce congressional influence while enhancing the power of the presidency. This is a development with which we should be deeply concerned. For all its faults and foibles, the Congress is the nation's most representative political institution and remains the only entity capable of placing limits on unwise or illegitimate presidential conduct. Certainly, the courts have seldom been capable of thwarting a determined president, especially in the foreign policy realm. Unfortunately, however, in recent decades our nation's undemocratic politics has undermined the Congress while paving the way for aggrandizement of power by the executive and the presidential unilateralism that inevitably follows.

The framers of the Constitution created a system of government in which the Congress and the executive branch were to share power. In recent years, however, the powers of Congress have waned while those of the presidency have expanded dramatically. To begin with a recent instance of congressional retreat in the face of presidential assertiveness, in October 2002, pressed by President George W. Bush, both houses of Congress voted overwhelmingly to authorize the White House to use military force against Iraq. The resolution adopted by Congress allowed the president complete discretion to determine whether, when, and how to attack Iraq. The president had rejected language that might have implied even the slightest limitations on his prerogatives. Indeed, Bush's legal advisers had pointedly declared that the president did not actually need specific congressional authorization to attack Iraq if he deemed such action to be in America's interest. "We don't want to be in the legal position of asking Congress to authorize the use of force when the president already has that full authority," said one senior administration official. Few members of Congress even bothered to object to this apparent rewriting of the U.S. Constitution.

There is no doubt that Congress continues to be able to harass presidents and even, on occasion, to hand the White House a sharp rebuff. In the larger view, however, presidents' occasional defeats—however dramatic—have to be seen as temporary setbacks in a gradual and decisive shift toward increased presidential power in the twenty-first century. Louis Fisher, America's leading authority on the separation of powers, recently observed that in what are arguably the two most important policy arenas, national defense and the federal budget, the powers of Congress have been in "precipitous decline" for at least the past fifty years. The last occasion on which Congress exercised its constitutional power to declare war was December 8, 1941, yet since that time American forces have been committed to numerous battles on every continent by order of the president. The much-hailed 1973 War Powers Resolution, far from limiting presidential power, actually allowed the president considerably more discretionary authority than he was granted by the Constitution. The War Powers Act gave the president the authority to deploy forces abroad without congressional authority for sixty days. The Constitution, though, seems to require congressional authorization before troops can be deployed for even one day.

As to spending powers, the framers of the Constitution conceived the "power of the purse" to be Congress's most fundamental prerogative, and for more than a century this power was jealously guarded by powerful congressional leaders like William Howard Taft–era House Speaker "Uncle" Joe Cannon, who saw congressional control of the budget as a fundamental safeguard against "Prussian-style" militarism and autocracy. Since the New Deal, however, successive Congresses have yielded to steadily increasing presidential influence over the budget process. In 1939, Congress allowed Franklin D. Roosevelt to take a giant step toward presidential control of the nation's purse strings when it permitted FDR to bring the Bureau of the Budget (BoB) into the newly created Executive Office of the President. Roosevelt and his successors used the BoB (now called the White House Office of Management and Budget) effectively to seize the nation's legislative and budgetary agenda. In 1974, Congress attempted to respond to Richard Nixon's efforts to further enhance presidential control of spending when it enacted the Budget and Impoundment Control Act. This piece of legislation centralized Congress's own budgetary process and seemed to reinforce congressional power. Yet, less than ten years later, Congress watched as President Ronald Reagan essentially seized control over the congressional budget process. Subsequently, as Fisher observes, lacking confidence in its own ability to maintain budgetary discipline, Congress has surrendered more and more power to the president, even attempting to hand the chief executive a line-item veto in 1995.

Representative assemblies like the U.S. Congress derive their influence from the support of groups and forces in civil society that believe these institutions serve their interests. Britain's Parliament ultimately overcame the Crown because it gradually won the confidence and support of the most important forces in civil society. Chief executives such as the president of the United States, on the other hand, fundamentally derive their power from their command of bureaucracies, armies, and the general machinery of the state. Presidents can certainly benefit from popular support. If we imagine, however, a fully demobilized polity in which neither institution could count on much support from forces in civil society, the president would still command the institutions of the state while Congress would be without significant resources. In a fully mobilized polity, on the other hand, Congress might have a chance to counterbalance the president's institutional powers with the support of significant social forces.

A powerful presidency, a weak Congress, and a partially demobilized electorate are a dangerous mix. Presidents have increasingly asserted the right to govern unilaterally and now appear able to overcome most institutional and political constraints. Presidential power, to be sure, can be a force for good. To cite one example from the not-so-distant past, it was President Lyndon Johnson, more than Congress or the judiciary, who faced up to the task of smashing America's segregationist system. Yet, as the framers knew, unchecked power is always dangerous. Americans of the Founding generation feared that unchecked presidential power would lead to *monocracy*—a republican form of monarchy without a king or queen. Have we not taken more than one step in that direction? Inevitably, there is a price to be paid for our undemocratic politics.

CHAPTER REVIEW

The foundations for presidential government were set down in the Constitution, which provided for a unitary executive and made the president head of state as well as head of government. The first section of this chapter reviewed the powers of each: the head of state with its military, judicial, and diplomatic powers; and the head of government with its executive, military, and legislative powers. But the presidency was subordinated to congressional government during the nineteenth century and part of the twentieth, as the national government took part in few domestic functions and was inactive or sporadic in foreign affairs.

The second section of the chapter showed the rise of modern presidential government following the long period of congressional government. There is no mystery in the shift to government centered on the presidency. Congress built the modern presidency essentially in the 1930s by delegating to it not only the power to implement the vast new programs of the New Deal but also by delegating its own legislative power to make policy. The cabinet, the other top presidential appointments, the White House staff, and the Executive Office of the President are some of the impressive formal resources of presidential power.

The third section focused on the president's informal resources, in particular the president's political party, the supportive group coalitions, access to the media, and, through that, access to the millions of Americans who make up the general public. These resources are not cost-free or risk-free. A good relationship with the public is the president's most potent modern resource, but the polls reveal that the public's rating of presidential performance tends to go down with time. Only international actions or events can boost presidential performance ratings, and then only briefly. This means that presidents may be tempted to use foreign policy for domestic purposes.

FOR FURTHER READING

Cameron, Charles M. *Veto Bargaining: Presidents and the Politics of Negative Power.* New York: Cambridge University Press, 2000.

Canes-Wrone, Brandice. *Who Leads Whom? Presidents, Policy, and the Public.* Chicago: University of Chicago Press, 2006. ○ ONLINE READING

Deering, Christopher, and Forrest Maltzman. "The Politics of Executive Orders: Legislative Constraints on Presidential Power." *Political Research Quarterly* 52 (1999): 767–83.

Greenstein, Fred I. *The Presidential Difference: Leadership Style from FDR to Clinton.* Princeton, N.J.: Princeton University Press, 2001.

Kernell, Samuel. *Going Public: New Strategies of Presidential Leadership.* 3rd ed. Washington, D.C.: Congressional Quarterly Press, 1997.

Lowi, Theodore J. *The Personal President: Power Invested, Promise Unfulfilled.* Ithaca, N.Y.: Cornell University Press, 1985.

Milkis, Sidney M. *The President and the Parties: The Transformation of the American Party System since the New Deal.* New York: Oxford University Press, 1993.

———, and Michael Nelson. *The American Presidency: Origins and Development, 1776–2002.* 4th ed. Washington, D.C.: Congressional Quarterly Press.

Nelson, Michael, ed. *The Presidency and the Political System.* 8th ed. Washington, D.C.: Congressional Quarterly Press, 2005.

Neustadt, Richard E. *Presidential Power and the Modern Presidents: The Politics of Leadership from Roosevelt to Reagan.* 1960. Rev. ed., New York: Free Press, 1990. ○ ONLINE READING

Pfiffner, James P. *The Modern Presidency.* 4th ed. Belmont, Calif.: Wadsworth, 2005.

Skowronek, Stephen. "Leadership by Definition: First Term Reflection on George W. Bush's Political Stance." *Perspectives on Politics* 3 (2005): 817–31.

———. *The Politics Presidents Make: Leadership from John Adams to Bill Clinton.* Cambridge, Mass.: Harvard University Press, 1997.

Tulis, Jeffrey. *The Rhetorical Presidency.* Princeton, N.J.: Princeton University Press, 1987.

CHAPTER

The Executive Branch

WHY BUREAUCRACY?

Bureaucracies are commonplace because they touch so many aspects of daily life. Government bureaucracies implement the decisions made by the political process. Bureaucracies are full of routine because that assures the regular delivery of services and ensures that each agency fulfills its mandate. Public bureaucracies are powerful because legislatures and chief executives, and indeed the people, delegate to them vast power to make sure a particular job is done, enabling the rest of us to be more free to pursue our private ends. The public sentiments that emerged after September 11, 2001, revealed this underlying appreciation of public bureaucracies. When faced with the challenge of making air travel safe again, the public strongly supported giving the federal government responsibility for airport security, even though this meant increasing the size of the federal bureaucracy by making the security screeners federal workers. Former House majority whip Tom DeLay

● Core of the Analysis

● Despite its problems, the bureaucracy is necessary for the maintenance of order in a large society.

● The size of the federal bureaucracy is large, but it has not been growing any faster than the economy or the population as a whole.

● Government agencies vary in their levels of responsiveness to the president and his political appointees, congressional members and committees, and commercial and private interests.

● Responsible bureaucracy requires more than presidential power and management control.

● Congress has delegated much of its legislative power to the president and the bureaucracy; congressional committees use oversight to make the bureaucracy accountable.

FIGURE 7.1 The Public Thinks There Is a Lot of Waste in Government

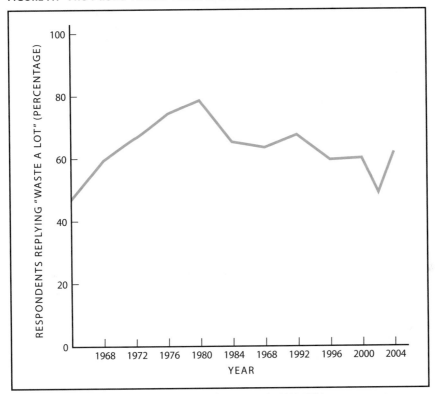

SOURCE: American National Election Studies, Cumulative Data File, 1948–2004
(www.electionstudies.org/index.htm).

sought to forestall this growth in the federal government, declaring that "the last thing we can afford to do is erect a new bureaucracy that is unaccountable and unable to protect the American public."[1] But the antibureaucratic language that had been so effective prior to September 11 no longer resonated with a fearful public. Instead, there was a widespread belief that a public bureaucracy would provide more effective protection than the cost-conscious private security companies that had been charged with airport security in the past. Bureaucrats across the federal government felt a new appreciation for their work. Moreover, as an economic crisis loomed in 2008, politicians found that many Americans—though not all—wanted the government to do more to resolve the crisis and regulate the economy. In particular, Americans seemed to expect the executive branch agencies responsible for economic matters, such as the Federal Reserve System and the Treasury Department, to take strong action.

In this chapter, we will focus on the federal bureaucracy—the administrative structure that on a day-to-day basis *is* the American government. We will first seek to define and describe bureaucracy as a social and political phenomenon.

---

[1]Janet Hook, "U.S. Strikes Back; Political Landscape; GOP Bypasses the Bipartisan Truce," *Los Angeles Times,* 14 October 2001, p. A8.

Second, we will look in detail at American bureaucracy in action by examining the government's major administrative agencies, their role in the governmental process, and their political behavior. These details of administration are the very heart and soul of modern government and will provoke the questions of the third and final section of the chapter: Can bureaucracy be made accountable to the president and Congress? Can bureaucracy and democracy coexist?

HOW DOES BUREAUCRACY WORK?

Despite the tendency to criticize bureaucracy, most Americans recognize that maintaining order in a large society is impossible without some sort of large governmental apparatus staffed by professionals with some expertise in public administration. When we approve of what a government agency is doing, we give the phenomenon a positive name, *administration;* when we disapprove, we call the phenomenon *bureaucracy.*

bureaucracy The complex structure of offices, tasks, rules, and principles of organization that are employed by all large-scale institutions to coordinate the work of their personnel.

Although the terms "administration" and "bureaucracy" are often used interchangeably, it is useful to distinguish between the two. Administration is the more general of the two terms; it refers to all the ways human beings might rationally coordinate their efforts to achieve a common goal. This applies to private as well as public organizations. **Bureaucracy** refers to the actual offices, tasks, and principles of organization that are employed in the most formal and sustained administration. The In Brief Box on the previous page defines bureaucracy by identifying its basic characteristics.

Bureaucratic Organization Enhances Efficiency

The core of bureaucracy is the *division of labor*. The key to bureaucratic effectiveness is the coordination of experts performing complex tasks. If each job is specialized in order to gain efficiencies, then each worker must depend upon the output of other workers, and that requires careful *allocation* of jobs and resources. Inevitably, bureaucracies become hierarchical, often approximating a pyramid in form. At the base of the organization are workers with the fewest skills and specializations; one supervisor can deal with a relatively large number of these workers. At the next level of the organization, where there are more highly specialized workers, the supervision and coordination of work involves fewer workers per supervisor. Toward the top of the organization, a very small number of high-level executives engages in the "management" of the organization, meaning the coordination and oversight of all the tasks and functions, plus the allocation of the appropriate supplies, and the distribution of the outputs of the organization to the market (if it is a "private sector" organization) or to the public.

Bureaucracies Allow Governments to Operate

Bureaucracy, when used pejoratively, conjures up images of endless paperwork, red tape, and lazy, uncaring employees. In fact, the term refers to a rather spectacular human achievement. By dividing up tasks, matching tasks to a labor force that develops appropriately specialized skills, routinizing procedures, and providing the incentive structure and oversight arrangements to get large numbers of people to operate in a coordinated, purposeful fashion, bureaucracies accomplish tasks and missions in a manner that would otherwise be unimaginable. The provision of "government goods" as broad as the defense of people, property, and national borders or as narrow as a subsidy to a wheat farmer, beef rancher, or manufacturer of specialty steel requires organization, routines, standards, and, at the end of the day, the authority for someone to cut a check and put it in the mail. Bureaucracies are created to do these things. No large organization would be larger than the sum of its parts, and many would be smaller, without bureaucratizing its activities.

Bureaucracy also consolidates a range of complementary programs and insulates them from the predatory ambitions of out-of-sympathy political forces. Nothing in this world is permanent, but bureaucracies come close. By creating clienteles—in the legislature, the world of interest groups, and public opinion—a bureaucracy establishes a coalition of supporters, some of whom will fight to the end to keep it in place. It is a well-known rule of thumb that everyone in the political world cares deeply and intensely about a subset of policies and the agencies that produce them, and opposes other policies and agencies but not with nearly the same passion. Opponents, to succeed, must clear many hurdles, while proponents, to maintain the status quo, must only marshall their forces at a few veto points. In the final analysis, opponents typically meet obstacle after obstacle and eventually give up their uphill battles and concentrate on protecting and expanding that about which they care most deeply. In a complex political system such as that of the United States, it is much easier to do the latter. Politicians appreciate this fact of life. Consequently, both opponents and proponents of a particular set of government activities wage the fiercest battles at the time programs are enacted and a bureaucracy is created. Once created, these organizations assume a position of relative permanence.

So, in response to the question of how bureaucracy makes government possible, there is an *efficiency* part to the answer and a *credibility* part. The creation of a bureau is a way to deliver government goods efficiently *and* a device by which to "tie one's hands," thereby providing a credible commitment to the long-term existence of a policy.

Bureaucrats Fulfill Important Roles

"Government by offices and desks" conveys to most people a picture of hundreds of office workers shuffling millions of pieces of paper. There is a lot of truth in that image, but we have to look more closely at what papers are being shuffled and why. More than fifty years ago, an astute observer defined bureaucracy as "continuous routine business."[2] Almost any organization succeeds by reducing its work to routines, with each routine being given to a different specialist. But specialization separates people from each other; one worker's output becomes another worker's input. The timing of such relationships is essential, and this requires that these workers stay in communication with each other. Communication is the key. In fact, bureaucracy was the first information network. Routine came first; voluminous routine came as bureaucracies grew and specialized.

Bureaucrats Implement Laws   Bureaucrats, whether in public or in private organizations, communicate with each other in order to coordinate all the specializations within their organization. This coordination is necessary to carry out the primary task of bureaucracy, which is **implementation**, that is, implementing the objectives of the organization as laid down by its board of directors (if a private company) or by law (if a public agency). In government, the "bosses" are ultimately the legislature and the elected chief executive.

Bureaucrats Make and Enforce Rules   When the bosses—Congress, in particular, when it is making the law—are clear in their instructions to bureaucrats, implementation is a fairly straightforward process. Bureaucrats translate the law into specific routines for each of the employees of an agency. But what happens to routine administrative implementation when there are several bosses who disagree as to what the instructions ought to be? This requires yet a fourth job for bureaucrats: interpretation. Interpretation is a form of implementation, in that the bureaucrats still have to carry out what they believe to be the intentions of their superiors. But when bureaucrats have to interpret a law before implementing it, they are in effect engaging

implementation The efforts of departments and agencies to translate laws into specific bureaucratic routines.

[2]Arnold Brecht and Comstock Glaser, *The Art and Techniques of Administration in German Ministries* (Cambridge, Mass.: Harvard University Press, 1940), p. 6.

in lawmaking.[3] Congress often deliberately delegates to an administrative agency the responsibility of lawmaking. Members of Congress often conclude that some area of industry needs regulating or some area of the environment needs protection, but they are unwilling or unable to specify just how that should be done. In such situations, Congress delegates to the appropriate agency a broad authority within which the bureaucrats have to make law, through the procedures of rulemaking and administrative adjudication.

Rulemaking is exactly the same as legislation; in fact it is often referred to as quasi-legislation. The rules issued by government agencies provide more detailed and specific indications of what the policy actually will mean. For example, the Forest Service is charged with making policies that govern the use of national forests. Just before President Clinton left office, the agency issued rules that banned new road building and development in the forests. This was a goal long sought by environmentalists and conservationists. In 2005, the Forest Service relaxed the rules, allowing states to make proposals for building new roads within the national forests. Just as the timber industry opposed the Clinton rule banning road building, environmentalists have challenged the new ruling and have sued the Forest Service in federal court for violating clean-water and endangered-species legislation.

New rules proposed by an agency take effect only after a period of public comment. Reaction from the people or businesses that are subject to the rules may cause an agency to modify the rules they first issue. The rule-making process is thus highly political. Once rules are approved, they are published in the *Federal Register* and have the force of law.

Bureaucrats Settle Disputes   Administrative adjudication is very similar to what the judiciary ordinarily does: applying rules and precedents to specific cases in order to settle disputes. In administrative adjudication, the agency charges the person or business suspected of violating the law. The ruling in an adjudication dispute applies only to the specific case being considered. Many regulatory agencies use administrative adjudication to make decisions about specific products or practices. For example, product recalls are often the result of adjudication.

In sum, government bureaucrats do essentially the same things that bureaucrats in large private organizations do. But because of the authoritative, coercive nature of government, far more constraints are imposed on public bureaucrats than on private bureaucrats, even when their jobs are the same. Public bureaucrats are required to maintain a far more thorough paper trail. Public bureaucrats are also subject to a great deal more access from the public. Newspaper reporters, for example, have access to public bureaucrats. Public access has been vastly facilitated in the past thirty years; the adoption of the Freedom of Information Act (FOIA) in 1966 gave ordinary citizens the right of access to agency files and agency data to determine whether derogatory information exists in the file about citizens themselves and to learn about what the agency is doing in general.

---

[3]When bureaucrats engage in interpretation, the result is what political scientists call bureaucratic drift. Bureaucratic drift occurs because, as we've suggested, the "bosses" (in Congress) and the agents (within the bureaucracy) don't always share the same purposes. Bureaucrats also have their own agendas to fulfill.

Moreover, citizens are given far more opportunities to participate in the decision-making processes of public agencies. There are limits of time, money, and expertise to this kind of access, but it does exist, and it occupies a great deal of the time of mid-level and senior public bureaucrats. This public exposure and access serves a purpose, but it also cuts down significantly on the efficiency of public bureaucrats. Thus, much of the lower efficiency of public agencies can be attributed to the political, judicial, legal, and publicity restraints put on public bureaucrats.

Legislatures Find It Valuable to Delegate

In principle, the legislature could make all bureaucratic decisions itself, writing very detailed legislation each year, dotting every *i* and crossing every *t*. In some jurisdictions—tax policy, for example—this is in fact done. Tax policy is promulgated in significant detail by the House Ways and Means Committee, the Senate Finance Committee, and the Joint Committee on Taxation. The Internal Revenue Service, the administrative agency charged with implementation, engages in relatively less discretionary activity than many other regulatory and administrative agencies. But this is the exception.

The norm is for statutory authority to be delegated to the bureaucracy, sometimes with specificity but often in relatively vague terms. The bureaucracy is expected to fill in the gaps. This, however, is not a blank check to exercise unconstrained discretion. The bureaucracy is expected to be guided by legislative intent, and it will be held to account by the legislature's oversight of bureaucratic performance. The latter is monitored by the staffs of relevant legislative committees, which also serve as repositories for complaints from affected parties.[4] Poor performance or the exercise of discretion inconsistent with the preferences of the important legislators invites sanctions ranging from the browbeating of senior bureaucrats to the trimming of budgets and the clipping of authority.

The delegation relationship will be revisited later in this chapter. For now, simply note that over and above the more conventional reasons for bureaucracy, politicians find it convenient to delegate many of the nuts-and-bolts decisions to bureaucratic agents. We will take up the reasons shortly.

HOW IS THE EXECUTIVE BRANCH ORGANIZED?

Cabinet departments, agencies, and bureaus are the operating parts of the bureaucratic whole. These parts can be separated into four general types: 1) cabinet departments, 2) independent agencies, 3) government corporations, and 4) independent regulatory commissions.

Although Figure 7.2 is an "organizational chart" of the Department of Agriculture, any other department could have been used as an illustration. At the top is the head of the department, who in the United States is called the "secretary" of the department. Below the department head are several top administrators, such as the general counsel and the chief financial officer, whose responsibilities cut across the various departmental functions and enable the secretary to manage the entire

ONLINE READING [4]See Mathew D. McCubbins and Thomas Schwartz, "Congressional Oversight Overlooked: Police Patrols versus Fire Alarms," *American Journal of Political Science* 28 (1984): 165–79.

FIGURE 7.2 Organizational Chart of the Department of Agriculture

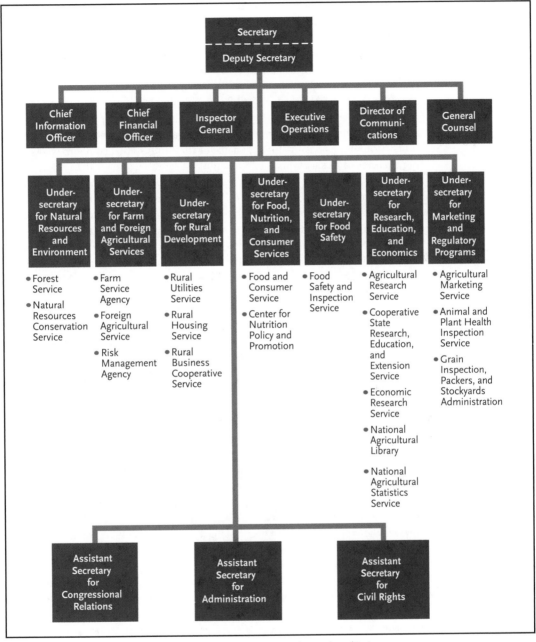

SOURCE: U.S. Department of Agriculture (www.usda.gov/img/content/org_chart_enlarged.jpg).

organization. Of equal status are the assistant and undersecretaries, each of whom has management responsibilities for a group of operating agencies, which are arranged vertically below each of the undersecretaries.

The next tier, generally called the bureau level, is the highest level of responsibility for specialized programs. The names of these bureau-level agencies are often very well known to the public: The Forest Service and the Food Safety and Inspection Service are two examples. Sometimes they are officially called bureaus, as in the Federal Bureau of Investigation (FBI), which is a bureau in the Department of Justice. Nevertheless, "bureau" is also the generic term for this level of administrative agency. Within the bureaus, there are divisions, offices, services, and units—sometimes designating agencies of the same status, sometimes designating agencies of lesser status.

Not all government agencies are part of cabinet departments. Some independent agencies are set up by Congress outside the departmental structure altogether, even though the president appoints and directs the heads of these agencies. Independent agencies usually have broad powers to provide public services that are either too expensive or too important to be left to private initiatives. Some examples of independent agencies are the National Aeronautics and Space Administration (NASA), the Central Intelligence Agency (CIA), and the Environmental Protection Agency (EPA). Government corporations are a third type of government agency, but are more like private businesses performing and charging for a market service, such as delivering the mail (the United States Postal Service) or transporting railroad passengers (Amtrak).

Yet a fourth type of agency is the independent regulatory commission, given broad discretion to make rules. The first regulatory agencies established by Congress, beginning with the Interstate Commerce Commission in 1887, were set up as independent regulatory commissions because Congress recognized that regulatory agencies are "mini-legislatures," whose rules are the same as legislation but require the kind of expertise and full-time attention that is beyond the capacity of Congress. Until the 1960s, most of the regulatory agencies that were set up by Congress, such as the Federal Trade Commission (1914) and the Federal Communications Commission (1934), were independent regulatory commissions. But beginning in the late 1960s and the early 1970s, all new regulatory programs, with two or three exceptions (such as the Federal Election Commission), were placed within existing departments and made directly responsible to the president. Since the 1970s, no major new regulatory programs have been established, independent or otherwise.

There are too many agencies in the executive branch to identify, much less to describe, so a simple classification of agencies will be helpful. Instead of dividing the bureaucracy into four general types, as we did previously, this classification is organized by the mission of each agency, as defined by its jurisdiction: clientele agencies, agencies for maintenance of the Union, regulatory agencies, and redistributive agencies. We shall examine each of these types of agencies, focusing on both their formal structure and their place in the political process.

Clientele Agencies Serve Particular Interests

clientele agencies Departments or bureaus of government whose mission is to promote, serve, or represent a particular interest.

The entire Department of Agriculture is an example of a *clientele agency*. So are the departments of the Interior, Labor, and Commerce. Although all administrative agencies have clienteles, certain agencies are singled out and called by that name because they are directed by law to foster and promote the interests of their clientele. For example, the Department of Commerce and Labor was founded in 1903 as a single department "to foster, promote, and develop the foreign and domestic commerce, the mining, the manufacturing, the shipping, and fishing industries, and the transportation facilities of the United States."[5] It remained a single department until 1913, when the law created the two separate departments of Commerce and Labor, with each statute providing for the same obligation: to support and foster their respective clienteles.[6] The Department of Agriculture serves the many farming interests that, taken together, are the United States' largest economic sector (agriculture accounts for one fifth of the U.S. total domestic output).

Most clientele agencies locate a relatively large proportion of their total personnel in field offices dealing directly with the clientele. The Extension Service of the Department of Agriculture is among the most familiar, with its numerous local "extension agents" who consult with farmers on farm productivity. These same agencies also seek to foster the interests of their clientele by providing "functional representation"; that is, they try to learn what their clients' interests and needs are and then operate almost as a lobby in Washington on their behalf. In addition to the Department of Agriculture, other clientele agencies include the Department of Interior and the five newest cabinet departments. Housing and Urban Development (HUD), created in 1966; Transportation (DOT), created in 1966; Energy (DOE), created in 1977; and Education (ED) and Health and Human Services (HHS), both created in 1979.[7]

Agencies for Maintenance of the Union Keep the Government Going

These agencies could be called public order agencies were it not for the fact that the Constitution entrusts so many of the vital functions of public order, such as the police, to the state governments. But some agencies vital to maintaining *national* bonds do exist in the national government, and they can be grouped for convenience into three categories: (1) agencies for control of the sources of government revenue, (2) agencies for control of conduct defined as a threat to internal national security, and (3) agencies for defending American security from external threats. The departments of greatest power in these three areas are Treasury, Justice, Defense, State, and Homeland Security.

Revenue Agencies   The Internal Revenue Service (IRS) is the most important revenue agency. The IRS is also one of the federal government's largest bureaucracies. Over one hundred thousand employees are spread through four regions, sixty-three districts, ten service centers, and hundreds of local offices.

---

[5]32 Stat. 825; 15 USC 1501.

[6]For a detailed account of the creation of the Department of Commerce and Labor and its split into two separate departments, see Theodore J. Lowi, *The End of Liberalism* (New York: Norton, 1979), pp. 78–84.

[7]The departments of Education and of Health and Human Services until 1979 were joined in a single department, the Department of Health, Education, and Welfare (HEW), which had been established by Congress in 1953.

Agencies for Internal Security   As long as the country is not in a state of insurrection, most of the task of maintaining the Union takes the form of legal work, and the main responsibility for that lies with the Department of Justice. It is indeed a luxury, and rare in the world, when national unity can be maintained by routines of civil law rather than imposed by an army with guns. The largest and most important agency in the Justice Department is the Criminal Division, which is responsible for enforcing all the federal criminal laws except a few specifically assigned to other divisions. Criminal litigation is actually done by the U.S. attorneys. There is a presidentially appointed U.S. attorney assigned to each federal judicial district, and he or she supervises the work of assistant U.S. attorneys. The work or jurisdiction of the Antitrust and Civil Rights Divisions is described by their official names. Although it looms so very large in American folklore, the FBI is simply another bureau of the Department of Justice. The FBI handles no litigation but instead serves as the information-gathering agency for all the other divisions.

In 2002, Congress created the Department of Homeland Security to coordinate the nation's defense against the threat of terrorism. The new department is responsible for a number of tasks, including protecting commercial airlines from would-be hijackers.

Agencies for External National Security   Two departments occupy center stage here, State and Defense. There are a few key agencies outside State and Defense that also have external national-security functions. They are treated in this chapter only as bureaucratic phenomena and as examples of the political problems relevant to administration.

Although diplomacy is generally considered the primary task of the State Department, diplomatic missions make up only one of its organizational dimensions. The State Department is also composed of geographic, or regional, bureaus concerned with all problems within the defined regions of the world; "functional" bureaus, which handle such things as economic and business affairs, intelligence, and research; and international organizations and bureaus of internal affairs, which handle such areas as security, finance and management, and legal issues.

Despite the importance of the State Department in foreign affairs, fewer than 20 percent of all U.S. government employees working abroad are directly under its authority. By far the largest number of career government professionals working abroad are under the authority of the Defense Department.

The creation of the Department of Defense by legislation enacted between 1947 and 1949 was an effort to unify the two historic military departments, the War Department and the Navy Department, and integrate into them a new department, the Air Force Department. Real unification did not occur, however. Instead, the Defense Department added more pluralism to national security.

America's primary political problem with its military has not been the historic one of how to keep the military out of the politics of governing, a problem that has plagued so many countries in Europe and Latin America. The American military problem is instead one of the lower politics of the pork barrel. President Clinton's long list of proposed military-base closings, a major part of his budget-cutting drive for 1993, caused a firestorm of opposition even in his own party, with some of the opposition coming from members of Congress who otherwise prominently favored significant reductions in the Pentagon budget. Emphasis on jobs rather than strategy and policy means pork-barrel use of the military for political purposes. This is a classic way for a bureaucracy to defend itself politically in a democracy. It is the distributive tendency, in which the bureaucracy ensures political support among elected officials by making sure to distribute things—military bases, contracts, facilities, and jobs—to the states and districts that elected the legislators. As is commonly known, it is hard to bite the hand that feeds you! Thus the best way to understand the military in American politics is to study it wihin the bureaucratic framework that is used to explain the domestic agencies.

Regulatory Agencies Guide Individual Conduct

The United States has no Department of Regulation but has many ***regulatory agencies.*** Some of these are bureaus within departments, such as the Food and Drug Administration (FDA) in the Department of Health and Human Services, the Occupational Safety and Health Administration (OSHA) in the Department of Labor, and the Animal and Plant Health and Inspection Service (APHIS) in the Department of Agriculture. Other regulatory agencies are independent regulatory commissions. An example is the Federal Trade Commission (FTC). But whether departmental or independent, an agency or commission is regulatory if Congress delegates to it relatively broad powers over a sector of the economy or a type of commercial activity and authorizes it to make rules governing the conduct of people and businesses within that jurisdiction. Rules made by regulatory agencies have the force and effect of legislation; indeed, the rules they make are referred to as ***administrative legislation.*** And when these agencies make decisions or orders settling disputes between parties or between the government and a party, they are really acting like courts.

Agencies for Redistribution Implement Fiscal/Monetary and Welfare Policies

Welfare agencies and fiscal/monetary agencies are responsible for the transfer of hundreds of billions of dollars annually between the public and the private spheres, and through such transfers these agencies influence how people and corporations spend and invest trillions of dollars annually. We call them agencies of redistribution because they influence the amount of money in the economy and because they directly influence who has money, who has credit, and whether people will want to invest or save their money rather than spend it.

Fiscal and Monetary Agencies   The best generic term for government activity affecting or relating to money is fiscal policy. However, we choose to make a further distinction, reserving *fiscal* for taxing and spending policies and using *monetary* for policies having to do with banks, credit, and currency. And the third, *welfare*, deserves to be treated as an equal member of this redistributive category.

Administration of fiscal policy is primarily performed in the Treasury Department. It is no contradiction to include the Treasury here as well as with the

regulatory agencies Departments, bureaus, or independent agencies whose primary mission is to impose limits, restrictions, or other obligations on the conduct of individuals or companies in the private sector.

administrative legislation Rules made by regulatory agencies and commissions.

agencies for maintenance of the Union. This indicates that (1) the Treasury is a complex department performing more than one function of government, and (2) traditional controls have had to be adapted to modern economic conditions and new technologies.

Today, in addition to administering and policing income tax and other tax collections, the Treasury is responsible for managing the enormous federal debt. The Treasury Department is responsible for printing the currency that we use, but currency represents only a tiny proportion of the entire money economy. Most of the trillions of dollars used in the transactions that compose the private and public sectors of the U.S. economy exist on printed accounts and computers, not in currency.

Another important fiscal agency (although for technical reasons it is called an agency of monetary policy) is the **Federal Reserve System,** headed by the Federal Reserve Board. The Federal Reserve System (the Fed) has authority over the credit rates and lending activities of the nation's most important banks. Established by Congress in 1913, the Fed is responsible for adjusting the supply of money to the needs of banks in the different regions and of the commerce and industry in each. The Fed helps shift money from where there is too much to where it is needed. It also ensures that the banks do not overextend themselves by having lending policies that are too liberal, out of fear that if there is a sudden economic scare, a run on a few banks might be contagious and cause another terrible stock market crash like the one in 1929. The Federal Reserve Board sits at the top of the pyramid of twelve district Federal Reserve Banks, which are "bankers' banks," serving the monetary needs of the hundreds of member banks in the national bank system (see also Chapter 13).

Welfare Agencies   No single government agency is responsible for all the programs comprising the "welfare state." The largest agency in this field is the Social Security Administration (SSA), which manages the social insurance aspects of Social Security and SSI. Other agencies in the Department of Health and Human Services administer Temporary Assistance to Needy Families (TANF) and Medicaid, and the Department of Agriculture is responsible for the food stamp program. With the exception of Social Security, these are means-tested programs, requiring applicants to demonstrate that their total annual cash earnings fall below an officially defined poverty line. These public assistance programs compose a large administrative burden.

In 1996, Congress adopted the Personal Responsibility and Work Opportunity Reconciliation Act (PRA), which abolished virtually all *national means-tested* public assistance programs, thereby terminating virtually all "entitlements" to welfare benefits to the poor, including single mothers and their children. This was without question the largest single "devolution" of national power to state governments in U.S. history. However, those who expected revolutionary savings of government expenditures and responsibilities were in for a big disappointment. The national government continues to fund welfare programs, even though the money is allocated to the states in block grants, leaving maximum discretion to the states. Additional costs are involved in the fact that national and state governments are required by law to regulate these grants, because the 1996 law laid down some severe national standards for eligibility—for example, limits on years of eligibility for benefits.

Federal Reserve System (Fed) Consisting of twelve Federal Reserve Banks, an agency that facilitates exchanges of cash, checks, and credit; it regulates member banks, and it uses monetary policies to fight inflation and deflation.

THE PROBLEM OF BUREAUCRATIC CONTROL

Two centuries, millions of employees, and trillions of dollars after the founding, we must return to James Madison's observation that "you must first enable the government to control the governed; and in the next place oblige it to control itself."[8] Today the problem is the same, but the form has changed. Our problem today is bureaucracy and our inability to keep it accountable to elected political authorities.

Bureaucrats Have Their Own Motivational Considerations

The economist William Niskanen proposed that we consider a bureau or department of government as analogous to a division of a private firm and conceive of the bureaucrat just as we would the manager who runs that division.[9] In particular, Niskanen stipulated that a bureau chief or department head can be thought of as trying to maximize his or her budget (just as the private-sector counterpart tries to maximize his or her division's profits).

There are quite a number of motivational bases on which bureaucratic budget maximizing might be justified. A cynical (though some would say realistic) basis for budget maximizing is that the bureaucrat's own compensation is often tied to the size of his or her budget. A second, related motivation for large budgets is nonmaterial personal gratification. An individual understandably enjoys the prestige and respect that comes from running a major enterprise. You can't take these things to the bank or put them on your family's dinner table, but your sense of esteem and your stature are surely buoyed by the conspicuous fact that your bureau or division has a large budget.

But salary and power tripping are not the only forces driving a bureaucrat toward gaining as large a budget as possible. Some bureaucrats, perhaps most, actually *care* about their mission.[10] They initially choose to go into public safety, or the military, or health care, or social work, or education because they believe in the importance of helping people in their community. As they rise through the ranks of a public bureaucracy and assume management responsibilities, they take this mission orientation with them. Thus they try to secure as large a budget as they can to succeed in achieving the mission to which they have devoted their professional lives.

Critics of the budget-maximizing theory call into question its assumption about the passivity of the legislature. The legislature, the only customer of the bureau's product, in essence tells the bureau how much it is willing to pay for various production levels. The critics suggest that this is akin to a customer walking onto a used-car lot and telling the salesman precisely how much he or she is willing to spend for each vehicle.[11]

---

[8]Alexander Hamilton, James Madison, and John Jay, *The Federalist Papers,* ed. Clinton L. Rassiter (New York: New American Library, 1961), no. 51.

[9]William A. Niskanen Jr., *Bureaucracy and Representative Government* (Chicago: Aldine, 1971).

[10]John Brehm and Scott Gates, *Working, Shirking, and Sabotage: Bureaucratic Response to a Democratic Public* (Ann Arbor: University of Michigan Press, 1997).   ○ ONLINE READING

[11]This and other related points are drawn from Gary J. Miller and Terry M. Moe, "Bureaucrats, Legislators, and the Size of Government," *American Political Science Review 77,* no. 2 (June 1983): 297–323.

In a representative democracy, it may be difficult for the legislature to keep silent about its own willingness to pay. The bureau, at any rate, can do some research to judge the preferences of various legislators based on who their constituents are. But legislators can do research, too. Indeed, we suggested in Chapter 5 that the collection, evaluation, and dissemination of information are precisely the things in which specialized legislative committees engage. After the fact, the committees engage in oversight, making sure that what the legislature was told at the time when authorization and appropriations were voted actually holds in practice. In short, the legislature can be much more proactive than the Niskanen budget-maximizing theory gives it credit for.

Before leaving motivational considerations, it should be remarked that budget maximizing is not the only objective that bureaucrats pursue. It needs to be emphasized and reemphasized that career civil servants and high-level political appointees are *politicians*. They spend their professional lives pursuing political goals, bargaining, forming alliances and coalitions, solving cooperation and collective-action problems, making policy decisions, operating within and interfacing with political institutions—in short, doing what other politicians do. As politicians subject to the oversight and authority of others, bureaucrats must be strategic and forward thinking. Whichever party wins control of the House or the Senate, whichever candidate wins the presidency, whoever becomes chair of the legislative committee with authorization or appropriation responsibility over their agency, life will go on and bureau chiefs will have to adjust to the prevailing political winds. To protect and expand authority and resources, bureaucratic politicians seek, in the form of autonomy and discretion, insurance against political change. They don't always succeed in acquiring this freedom, but they do try to insulate themselves from changes in the broader political world.[12] So bureaucratic motivations include budget-maximizing behavior, to be sure, but bureaucrats also seek the autonomy to weather changes in the political atmosphere and the discretion and flexibility to achieve their goals.

Control of the Bureaucracy Is a Principal-Agent Problem

How does the principal-agent problem apply to the president's and Congress's control of the bureaucracy? Suppose the legislation that created the EPA required that after ten years new legislation be passed renewing its existence and mandate. The issue facing the House, the Senate, and the president in their consideration of renewal involves how much authority to give this agency and how much money to permit it to spend. Eventually relevant majorities in the House and the Senate (including the support of relevant committees) and the president agree on a policy reflecting a compromise among their various points of view.

The bureaucrats are not particularly pleased with this compromise because it gives them considerably less authority and funding than they had hoped for. If they flout the wishes of their principals and implement a policy exactly to their liking,

---

[12]For an expanded view of bureaucratic autonomy and insulation with historical application to the U.S. Department of Agriculture and the Post Office Department, see Daniel P. Carpenter, *The Forging of Bureaucratic Autonomy: Reputations, Networks, and Policy Innovation in Executive Agencies, 1862–1928* (Princeton, N.J.: Princeton University Press, 2001).

they risk the unified wrath of the House, the Senate, and the president. Undoubtedly the politicians would react with new legislation (and they would also presumably find other political appointees and career bureaucrats at the EPA to replace the current bureaucratic leadership). If, however, the EPA implements some policy located between its own preferences and the preferences of its principals, it might be able to get away with it.

Thus we have a principal-agent relationship in which a political principal—a collective principal consisting of the president and coalitions in the House and Senate—formulates policy and creates an implementation agent to execute its details. The agent, however, has policy preferences of its own and, unless subjected to further controls, will inevitably implement a policy that drifts toward its ideal.

A variety of controls might conceivably restrict this *bureaucratic drift*. Indeed, legislative scholars often point to congressional hearings in which bureaucrats may be publicly humiliated, annual appropriations decisions that may be used to punish out-of-control bureaus, and watchdog agents, like the Government Accountability Office, that may be used to monitor and scrutinize the bureau's performance. But these all come after the fact and may be only partially credible threats to the agency. The most powerful before-the-fact political weapon is the appointment process. The adroit control of the political stance of a given bureau by the president and Congress, through their joint powers of nomination and confirmation (especially if they can arrange for appointees who closely share the political consensus on policy) is a self-enforcing mechanism for ensuring reliable agent performance. A second powerful before-the-fact weapon is procedural controls. The general rules and regulations that direct the manner in which federal agencies conduct their affairs are contained in the Administrative Procedure Act. This act is almost always the boilerplate of legislation creating and renewing federal agencies. It is not uncommon, however, for an agency's procedures to be tailored to suit particular circumstances.

The President as Chief Executive Can Direct Agencies

In 1937, President Franklin Roosevelt's Committee on Administrative Management gave official sanction to an idea that had been growing increasingly urgent: "The president needs help." The national government had grown rapidly during the preceding twenty-five years, but the structures and procedures necessary to manage the burgeoning executive branch had not yet been established. The response to the call for help for the president initially took the form of three management policies: (1) All communications and decisions that related to executive policy decisions must pass through the White House; (2) to cope with such a flow, the White House must have an adequate staff of specialists in research, analysis, legislative and legal writing, and public affairs; and (3) the White House must have additional staff to follow through on presidential decisions—to ensure that those decisions are made, communicated to Congress, and carried out by the appropriate agency.

Establishing a management capacity for the presidency began in earnest with FDR, but it did not stop there. The story of the modern presidency can be told largely as a series of responses to the plea for managerial help. Indeed, each expansion of the national government into new policies and programs in the twentieth century was accompanied by a parallel expansion of the president's management

bureaucratic drift
The oft-observed phenomenon of bureaucratic implementation that produces policy more to the liking of the bureaucracy than to the original intention of the legislation that created it, but without triggering a political reaction from elected officials.

authority. This pattern began even before FDR's presidency, with the policy innovations of President Woodrow Wilson between 1913 and 1920. Congress responded to Wilson's policies with the 1921 Budget and Accounting Act, which conferred on the White House agenda-setting power over budgeting. The president, in his annual budget message, transmits comprehensive budgetary recommendations to Congress. Because Congress retains ultimate legislative authority, a president's proposals are sometimes said to be dead on arrival on Capitol Hill. Nevertheless, the power to frame deliberations is potent and constitutes an important management tool. Each successive president has continued this pattern of setting the congressional agenda, creating what we now know as the managerial presidency.

For example, President Clinton inaugurated one of the most systematic efforts to change the way government does business in his National Performance Review. Heavily influenced by the theories of management consultants who prize decentralization, customer responsiveness, and employee initiative, Clinton sought to infuse these new practices into government.[13] George W. Bush was the first president with a graduate degree in business. His management strategy followed a standard business-school dictum: Select skilled subordinates and delegate responsibility to them. Bush followed this model closely in his appointment of highly experienced officials to cabinet positions.

The story of the modern presidency can be told largely as a series of responses to the rise of big government. Each expansion of the national government in the twentieth century was accompanied by a parallel expansion of presidential management authority. The executive bureaucracy and the institutional presidency are right in the middle of the separation-of-powers administrative state (Figure 7.3).

Congress Can Promote Responsible Bureaucracy through Oversight and Incentives

Congress is constitutionally essential to responsible bureaucracy because, in a "government of laws," legislation is the key to government responsibility. When a law is passed and its intent is clear, the president knows what to "faithfully execute," and the agency understands its guidelines. But when Congress enacts vague legislation, everybody, from president to agency to courts to interest groups, gets involved in the interpretation of legislation. In that event, to whom is the agency responsible?

The answer lies in **oversight**. The more legislative power Congress delegates to the executive branch, the more power it seeks to regain through committee and subcommittee oversight of executive branch agencies. The standing committee system of Congress is well-suited for oversight, inasmuch as most congressional committees and subcommittees have jurisdictions roughly parallel to one or more executive departments or agencies. Appropriations committees and authorization committees have oversight powers—and delegate their respective oversight powers to their subcommittees. In addition, there is a committee on government operations both in the House and the Senate, and these committees have oversight powers not limited by departmental jurisdiction.

oversight The effort by Congress, through hearings, investigations, and other techniques, to exercise control over the activities of executive agencies.

---

[13]See John Micklethwait, "Managing to Look Attractive," *New Statesman*, 8 November 1996, p. 24.

FIGURE 7.3 Congress, the President, and the Executive Branch

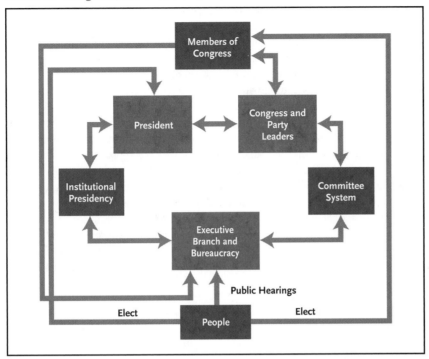

Committees and subcommittees oversee agencies through public hearings. Representatives from each agency, the White House, major interest groups, and other concerned citizens are called as witnesses to present testimony at these hearings. These are printed in large volumes and are widely circulated. Detailed records of the recent activities and expenditures of each and every agency can be found in these volumes. The number of hearings and equivalent public meetings (sometimes called investigations) rose steadily from 1950 to 1980, as Congress tried through oversight to keep pace with the expansion of the executive branch.[14] However, around 1980 the number began to decline. New questions about the ability of Congress to exercise oversight arose when the Republicans took over Congress in 1995. Reductions in committee staffing and an emphasis on using investigative oversight to uncover scandal meant much less time spent on programmatic oversight. Moreover, congressional Republicans complained that they could not get sufficient information about programs from the White House to conduct effective

[14]For figures on the frequency and character of oversight, see Lawrence Dodd and Richard Schott, *Congress and the Administrative State* (New York: Wiley, 1979), p. 169. See also Norman Ornstein et al., *Vital Statistics on Congress, 1987–88* (Washington, D.C.: Congressional Quarterly Press, 1987), pp. 161–62. For a valuable and skeptical assessment of legislative oversight of administration, see James W. Fesler and Donald F. Kettl, *The Politics of the Administrative Process* (Chatham, N.J.: Chatham House, 1991), Chapter 11.

oversight. Congressional records show that in 1991–92, when Democrats controlled the House, they issued reports on fifty-five federal programs, while in 1997–98, the Republican Congress issued only fourteen.[15] On issues of major national importance, multiple committees may initiate oversight hearings simultaneously. No less than a dozen congressional committees (along with the Justice Department and the Securities and Exchange Commission) launched investigations into the 2001 collapse of the giant energy company Enron.

Although congressional oversight is potent because of Congress's power to make—and, therefore, to change—the law, often the most effective and influential lever over bureaucratic accountability is "the power of the purse"—the ability of the House and Senate committees and subcommittees on appropriations to look at agency performance through the microscope of the annual appropriations process. This annual process makes bureaucrats attentive to Congress because they know that Congress has a chance each year to reduce their funding.[16] A more recent evaluation of the budget and appropriations process by NPR expressed one serious concern about oversight through appropriation: Pressure to cut appropriations "has put a premium on preserving particular programs, projects, and activities from Executive Branch as well as congressional action." This may be another explanation for why there may be some downsizing but almost no terminations of federal agencies.

Congressional Oversight: Abdication or Strategic Delegation? Congress often grants the executive-branch bureaucracies discretion in determining certain features of a policy during the implementation phase. Although the complexities of governing a modern industrialized democracy make the granting of discretion necessary, some argue that Congress not only gives unelected bureaucrats too much discretion but also delegates too much policy-making authority to them. By enacting vague statutes that give bureaucrats broad discretion, so the argument goes, members of Congress effectively abdicated their constitutionally designated roles and effectively removed themselves from the policy-making process.

Others claim that even though Congress may possess the tools to engage in effective oversight, it fails to use them simply because we do not see Congress actively engaging in much oversight activity.[17] However, Mathew McCubbins and Thomas Schwartz argue that these critics have focused on the wrong type of oversight and have missed a type of oversight that benefits members of Congress in their bids for reelection.[18] McCubbins and Schwartz distinguish between two types of oversight: police patrol and fire alarm. Under the police-patrol variety, Congress systematically

[15]Richard E. Cohen, "Crackup of the Committees," *National Journal*, 31 July 1999, p. 2214.

[16]See Aaron Wildavsky, *The New Politics of the Budgetary Process*, 2nd ed. (New York: HarperCollins, 1992), pp. 15–16.

[17]Morris S. Ogul, *Congress Oversees the Bureaucracy: Studies in Legislative Supervision* (Pittsburgh: University of Pittsburgh Press, 1976); and Peter Woll, *American Bureaucracy*, 2nd ed. (New York: Norton, 1977).

[18]See Mathew D. McCubbins and Thomas Schwartz, "Congressional Oversight Overlooked: Police Patrols versus Fire Alarms," *American Journal of Political Science* 28 (1984): 165–79.

ONLINE READING ○

initiates investigation into the activity of agencies. Under the fire-alarm variety, members of Congress do not initiate investigations but wait for adversely affected citizens or interest groups to bring bureaucratic perversions of legislative intent to the attention of the relevant congressional committee. To make sure that individuals and groups bring these violations to members' attention—to set off the fire alarm, so to speak—Congress passes laws that help individuals and groups make claims against the bureaucracy, granting them legal standing before administrative agencies and federal courts.

McCubbins and Schwartz argue that given the incentives of elected officials, it makes sense that we would see Congress engaging more in fire-alarm oversight than police-patrol oversight. Why should members spend their scarce resources (mainly time) to initiate investigations without having any evidence that they will reap electoral rewards? Police-patrol oversight can waste taxpayers' dollars too, because many investigations will not turn up any evidence of violations of legislative intent. It is much more cost-effective for members to conserve their resources and then claim credit for fixing the problem (and saving the day) after the fire alarms have been sounded. The Analyzing the Evidence unit on the following page takes a closer look at the problem of congressional oversight.

On the other hand, bureaucratic drift might be contained if Congress spent more of its time clarifying its legislative intent and less of its time on oversight activity. If its original intent in the law were clearer, Congress could then afford to defer to presidential management to maintain bureaucratic responsibility. Bureaucrats are more responsive to clear legislative guidance than to anything else. But when Congress and the president are at odds (or coalitions within Congress are at odds), bureaucrats have an opportunity to evade responsibility by playing one branch off against the other.

HOW CAN BUREAUCRACY BE REDUCED?

Americans like to complain about bureaucracy. Americans don't like big government because big government means Big Bureaucracy, and bureaucracy means the federal service—about 2.7 million civilian and 1.5 million military employees.[19] Promises to cut the bureaucracy are popular campaign appeals; "cutting out the fat" with big reductions in the number of federal employees is held out as a sure-fire way of cutting the deficit.

Despite fears of bureaucratic growth getting out of hand, however, the federal service has hardly grown at all during the past thirty years; it reached its peak postwar level in 1968 with 2.9 million civilian employees plus an additional 3.6 million military personnel (a figure swollen by Vietnam). The number of civilian federal executive-branch employees has since remained close to that figure. The growth of the federal service is even less imposing when placed in the context of the total workforce and when compared to the size of state and local public employment which was 15,789,000 in

---

[19] This is just under 99 percent of all national government employees. About 2 percent work for the legislative branch and for the federal judiciary. U.S. Bureau of the Census, *Statistical Abstract of the U.S.* 2007.

Oversight of the Executive Branch

Although we often think of the Congress as a lawmaking body, it also carries out another important task—checking the executive branch through the oversight process. If Congress thinks the bureaucracy is no longer serving the public's interest as defined by the legislative branch, it can use its oversight powers to put the agency back on track. In recent years, it has been suggested that Congress may be neglecting its oversight responsibilities. Let us consider how oversight has varied over time, and why measuring the effectiveness of oversight may be difficult.

GOVERNMENT EFFICIENCY AND BUREAUCRATIC OVERSIGHT HEARINGS[1]

Congressional hearings are an important tool used to oversee the bureaucracy. The House holds more hearings than the Senate: On average during this period, the House held 9.6 hearings per year while the Senate held only 6.1. We also see two periods where the number of hearings increased dramatically. Both chambers began to hold more hearings in the mid- to late 1970s in the wake of the Watergate scandal and the Vietnam War, and hearings in the House increased significantly after a new Republican majority was elected in 1994.

According to congressional scholars Norman Ornstein and Thomas Mann, in recent years oversight of the bureaucracy across a range of policies has virtually collapsed.[2] Since the 1990s, the Senate has lagged well behind the House in holding oversight hearings. In fact, there were no Senate oversight hearings in 2001 and only two each in 2003 and 2004.

[1]Source: Policy Agendas Project, Center for American Politics and Public Policy, University of Washington.
[2]Norman J. Ornstein and Thomas Mann. 2006. "When Congress Checks Out." *Foreign Affairs* 85(6): 67–82.

Measuring the effectiveness of oversight may be difficult because it depends on the type of oversight Congress is using. Mathew McCubbins and Thomas Schwartz define two types of oversight: Police Patrols and Fire Alarms.

Under the police-patrol method, Congress systematically initiates investigations into the activity of agencies. The goal is to catch and punish enough violators so that the rest of the bureaucracy will be discouraged from straying too far from legislative intent. However, Congress cannot monitor all agencies at once. Police-patrol oversight is especially difficult because of the vast number of employees spread out over many government departments and agencies. The table below lists the number of employees in each of the fifteen executive Cabinet departments and the six largest independent agencies.

EXECUTIVE BRANCH EMPLOYEES

Executive Departments		Independent Agencies	
Defense	616,000	Social Security Administration	65,000
Veterans Affairs	234,000	National Aeronautics and Space Administration	20,000
Homeland Security	149,000		
Justice	103,000	Environmental Protection Agency	18,000
Agriculture	102,000		
Treasury	95,000	Tennessee Valley Authority	13,000
Interior	71,000	General Services Administration	13,000
Health and Human Services	61,000		
Transportation	57,000	Federal Deposit Insurance Corporation	5,000
Commerce	36,000		
Labor	16,000		
Energy	15,000		
State	13,000		
Housing and Urban Development	10,000		
Education	4,000		

Source: Bureau of Labor Statistics, U.S. Department of Labor, *Career Guide to Industries, 2006–07 Edition*, Federal Government, Excluding the Postal Service, www.bls.gov/oco/cg/cgs041.htm (accessed June 11, 2007).

The fire-alarm method relies on the public. Members of Congress do not initiate investigations but wait for adversely affected citizens or interest groups to bring bureaucratic perversions of legislative intent to the attention of the relevant congressional committee. McCubbins and Schwartz argue that this method is more effective because, "Instead of sniffing for fires, Congress places fire-alarm boxes on street corners, builds neighborhood fire houses and sometimes dispatches its own hook-and-ladder in response to an alarm."[3] Since concerned citizens are out looking for bureaucratic fires, members of Congress will have more time to engage in other activities, such as securing reelection.

[3]Mathew McCubbins and Thomas Schwartz. 1984. "Congressional Oversight Overlooked: Police Patrols and Fire Alarms." *American Journal of Political Science* 28(1): 165–179.

FIGURE 7.4 Employees in the Federal Service

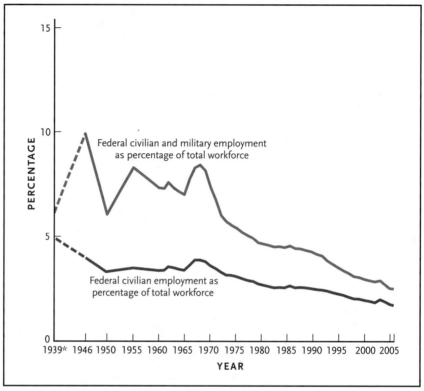

SOURCE: Tax Foundation, *Facts and Figures on Government Finance* (Baltimore: Johns Hopkins University Press, 1990), pp. 22, 44; Office of Management and Budget, *Budget of the U.S. Government, Fiscal Year 2002, Historical Tables* (Washington, D.C.: Government Printing Office, 2001), p. 304; and U.S. Bureau of Labor Statistics, "Employment Status of the Civilian Population by Sex and Age," *Labor Force Statistics from the Current Population Survey* (stats.bls.gov/webapps/legacy/cpsatab1.htm), table A1.

NOTE: Workforce includes unemployed persons.

*Lines between 1939 and 1946 are broken because they connect the last prewar year with the first postwar year, disregarding the temporary ballooning of federal employees, especially in the military, during the war years.

2004.[20] Figure 7.4 indicates that, since 1950, the ratio of federal service employment to the total workforce has been steady and in fact has declined slightly in the past twenty-five years. Another useful comparison is to be found in Figure 7.5. Although the dollar increase in federal spending shown by the bars looks very impressive, the horizontal line indicates that even here the national government has simply kept pace with the growth of the economy.

---

[20]Ibid.

FIGURE 7.5 Annual Federal Outlays

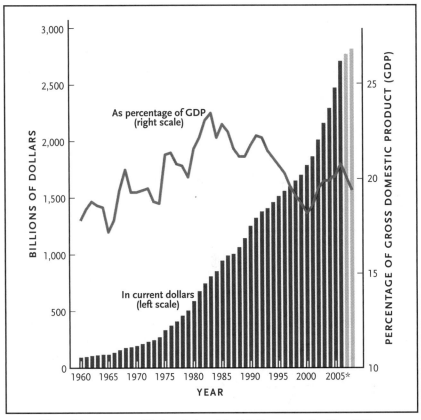

SOURCE: Office of Management and Budget, *Budget of the U.S. Government, Fiscal Year 2007, Historical Tables* (Washington, D.C.: Government Printing Office, 2007), p. 55.

*Data for 2007–8 are estimated.

In sum, the national government is indeed "very large," but the federal service has not been growing any faster than the economy or the society. The same is roughly true of the growth pattern of state and local public personnel. Bureaucracy keeps pace with our society, despite our seeming dislike for it, because we can't operate the control towers, the prisons, the Social Security system, and other essential elements without bureaucracy. And we certainly could not have gone to war in Iraq without a gigantic military bureaucracy.

Nevertheless some Americans continue to argue that bureaucracy is too big and should be reduced. In the 1990s, Americans seemed particularly enthusiastic about reducing (or to use the popular contemporary word, "downsizing") the federal bureaucracy.

Termination

The only *certain* way to reduce the size of the bureaucracy is to eliminate programs. Variations in the levels of federal personnel and expenditures demonstrate the futility of trying to make permanent cuts in existing agencies. Furthermore, most agencies have a supportive constituency that will fight to reinstate any cuts that are made. Termination is the only way to ensure an agency's reduction, and it is a rare occurrence.

The Republican-led 104th Congress (1995–96) was committed to the termination of programs. Newt Gingrich, speaker of the House, took Congress by storm with his promises of a virtual revolution in government. But when the dust had settled at the end of the first session of the first Gingrich-led Congress, no significant progress had been made toward downsizing through termination of agencies and programs.[21] The only two agencies eliminated were the Office of Technology Assessment, which provided research for Congress, and the Advisory Council on Intergovernmental Relations, which studied the relationship between the federal government and the state. Significantly, neither of these agencies had a strong constituency to defend it.

The overall lack of success in terminating bureaucracy is a reflection of Americans' love/hate relationship with the national government. As antagonistic as Americans may be toward bureaucracy in general, they grow attached to the services being rendered and protections being offered by particular bureaucratic agencies—that is, they fiercely defend their favorite agencies while perceiving no inconsistency between that defense and their antagonistic attitude toward the bureaucracy in general. A good case in point was the agonizing problem of closing military bases in the wake of the end of the cold war with the former Soviet Union, when the United States no longer needed so many bases. Since every base is in some congressional member's district, it proved impossible for Congress to decide to close any of them. Consequently, between 1988 and 1990, Congress established a Defense Base Closure and Realignment Commission to decide on base closings, taking the matter out of Congress's hands altogether.[22] And even so, the process has been slow and agonizing.

Elected leaders have come to rely on a more incremental approach to downsizing the bureaucracy. Much has been done by budgetary means, reducing the budgets of all agencies across the board by small percentages, and cutting some less-supported agencies by larger amounts. Yet these changes are still incremental, leaving the existence of agencies unaddressed.

An additional approach has been taken to thwart the highly unpopular regulatory agencies, which are so small (relatively) that cutting their budgets contributes virtually nothing to reducing the deficit. This approach is called ***deregulation,*** simply defined as a reduction in the number of rules promulgated by regulatory agencies. But deregulation by rule reduction is still incremental and has certainly not satisfied the hunger of the American public in general and Washington representatives in particular for a genuine reduction of bureaucracy.

---

deregulation A policy of reducing or eliminating regulatory restraints in the conduct of individuals or private institutions.

[21]A thorough review of the first session of the 104th Congress will be found in "Republican's Hopes for 1996 Lie in Unfinished Business," *Congressional Quarterly Weekly Report,* 6 January 1996, pp. 6–18.

[22]Public Law 101-510, Title XXIX, Sections 2,901 and 2,902 of Part A (Defense Base Closure and Realignment Commission).

FIGURE 7.6 Government Employment

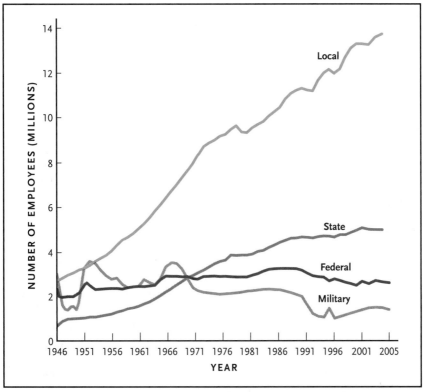

SOURCE: U.S. Bureau of the Census, *Statistical Abstract of the United States 2006* (Washington, D.C.: Government Printing Office, 2006), pp. 297, 330.

NOTE: Federal government employment figures include civilians only. Military employment figures include only active-duty personnel.

Devolution

The next best approach to genuine reduction of the size of the bureaucracy is *devolution*—downsizing the federal bureaucracy by delegating the implementation of programs to state and local governments. Indirect evidence for this is seen in Figure 7.6, which shows the increase in state and local government employment against a backdrop of flat or declining federal employment. This evidence suggests a growing share of governmental actions taking place on the state and local levels. Devolution often alters the pattern of who benefits most from government programs. In the early 1990s, a major devolution of transportation policy sought to open up decisions about transportation to a new set of interests. Since the 1920s, transportation policy had been dominated by road-building interests in the federal and state governments. Many advocates for cities and many environmentalists believed that the emphasis on road building hurt cities and harmed the environment. The 1992

devolution A policy to remove a program from one level of government by delegating it or passing it down to a lower level of government, such as from the national government to the states.

reform, initiated by environmentalists, put more power in the hands of metropolitan planning organizations and lifted many federal restrictions on how the money should be spent. Reformers hoped that these changes would open up the decision-making process so those advocating alternatives to road building, such as mass transit, bike paths, and walking, would have more influence over how federal transportation dollars were spent. Although the pace of change has been slow, devolution has indeed brought new voices into decisions about transportation spending, and alternatives to highways have received increasing attention.

Often the central aim of devolution is to provide more efficient and flexible government services. Yet, by its very nature, devolution entails variation across the states. In some states, government services may improve as a consequence of devolution. In other states, services may deteriorate as the states use devolution as an opportunity to cut spending and reduce services. This has been the pattern in the implementation of the welfare reform passed in 1996, the most significant devolution of federal government social programs in many decades. Some states, such as Wisconsin, have used the flexibility of the reform to design innovative programs that respond to clients' needs; other states, such as Idaho, have virtually dismantled their welfare programs. Because the legislation placed a five-year lifetime limit on receiving welfare, the states will take on an even greater role in the future as existing clients lose their eligibility for federal benefits. Welfare reform has been praised by many for reducing welfare rolls and responding to the public desire that welfare be a temporary program. At the same time, it has placed more low-income women and their children at risk for being left with no form of assistance at all, depending on the state in which they live.

This variation is the dilemma that devolution poses. To a point, variation can be considered one of the virtues of federalism. But there are dangers inherent in large variations in the provisions of services and benefits in a democracy.

Privatization

Privatization, another downsizing option, seems like a synonym for termination, but that is true only at the extreme. Most of what is called "privatization" is not termination at all but the provision of government goods and services by private contractors under direct government supervision. Except for top-secret strategic materials, virtually all of the production of military hardware, from boats to bullets, is done on a privatized basis by private contractors. Billions of dollars of research services are bought under contract by governments; these private contractors are universities as well as ordinary industrial corporations and private "think tanks." *Privatization* simply means that a formerly public activity is picked up under contract by a private company or companies. But such programs are still very much government programs; they are paid for and supervised by government. Privatization downsizes the government only in that the workers providing the service are no longer counted as part of the government bureaucracy.

privatization Removing all or part of a program from the public sector to the private sector.

The central aim of privatization is to reduce the cost of government. When private contractors can perform a task as well as government but for less money, taxpayers win. Often the losers in such situations are the workers. Government workers are generally unionized and, therefore, receive good pay and benefits. Private sector workers are less likely to be unionized, and private firms often provide lower pay and fewer benefits. For this reason, public sector unions have been one of the strongest voices arguing against privatization. Other critics of privatization observe that private firms may not be more efficient or less costly than government. This is especially likely when there is little competition among private firms and when public bureaucracies are not granted a fair chance to bid in the contracting competition. When private firms have a monopoly on service provision, they may be less efficient than government and more expensive. This problem raises important questions about how private contractors can be held accountable. As one analyst of Pentagon spending put it, "The Pentagon is supposed to be representing the taxpayer and the public interest—its national security. So it's really important to have transparency, to be able to see these competitions and hold people accountable."[23] As security has become the nation's paramount concern, new worries about privatization have surfaced. Some Pentagon officials fear that too many tasks vital to national security may have already been contracted out and that national security might best be served by limiting privatization.

The new demands of domestic security have altered the thrust of bureaucratic reform. The emphasis on reducing the size of government that was so prominent during the previous two decades is gone. Instead, there is an acceptance that the federal government will grow as needed to ensure the safety of American citizens. The administration's effort to focus the entire federal bureaucracy on a single central mission will require unprecedented levels of coordination among federal agencies. Despite the strong agreement on the goal of fighting terrorism, the effort to streamline the bureaucracy around a single purpose is likely to face considerable obstacles along the way. Reform of public bureaucracies is always complex because strong constituencies may attempt to block changes that they believe will harm them. Initiatives that aim to improve coordination among agencies can easily provoke political disputes if the proposed changes threaten to alter the access of groups to the bureaucracy. And groups that oppose bureaucratic changes can appeal to Congress to intervene on their behalf. As respected reform advocate Donald Kettl said of the effort to reinvent government, "Virtually no reform that really matters can be achieved without at least implicit congressional support."[24] In wartime, many obstacles to bureaucratic reform are lifted. But the war on terrorism is an unusual war that will be fought over an extended period of time. Whether the unique features of this war improve or limit the prospects for bureaucratic reform remains to be seen.

DOES BUREAUCRACY WORK?

Our concern in the first two sections of this chapter was to present a picture of bureaucracy, its necessity as well as the particular uses to which the national

---

[23]Ellen Nakashima, "Defense Balks at Contract Goals; Essential Services Should Not Be Privatized, Pentagon Tells OMB," *Washington Post*, 30 January 2002, p. A21.

[24]Quoted in Stephen Bar, "Midterm Exam for 'Reinvention': Study Cites 'Impressive Results' but Calls for Strategy to Win Congressional Support," *Washington Post*, 19 August 1994, p. A25.

government puts it. We then explored how the American system of government has tried to accommodate this vast apparatus to the requirements of representative democracy. We then turned this issue on its head and looked at how democratic processes have sought to make this bureaucratic apparatus somewhat smaller. And we now conclude by analyzing whether bureaucracy can work by being both democratic and efficient.

The subtitle of the chapter, "Bureaucracy in a Democracy," was intended to convey the sense that the two are contradictory. We cannot live without bureaucracy—it is the most efficient way to organize people to get a large collective job done. But we can't live comfortably with bureaucracy either. Bureaucracy requires hierarchy, appointed authority, and professional expertise. Those requirements make bureaucracy the natural enemy of representation, which requires discussion and reciprocity among equals. Yet the task is not to retreat from bureaucracy but to take advantage of its strengths while trying to make it more accountable to the demands that democratic policies and representative government make upon it.

Indeed, as the president and Congress seek to translate the ideal of democratic accountability into practice, they struggle to find the proper balance between administrative discretion and the public's right to know. An administration whose every move is subject to intense public scrutiny may be hamstrung in its efforts to carry out the public interest. On the other hand, a bureaucracy that is shielded from the public eye may wind up pursuing its own interests rather than those of the public. The last century has seen a double movement toward strengthening the managerial capacity of the presidency and making bureaucratic decision making more transparent. The purpose of these reforms has been to create an effective, responsive bureaucracy. But reforms alone cannot guarantee democratic accountability. Presidential and congressional vigilance in the defense of the public interest is essential.

Another approach to bureaucratic accountability is for Congress to spend more of its time clarifying its legislative intent and less of its time on committee or individual oversight. If the intent of the law were clear, Congress could then count on the president to maintain a higher level of bureaucratic responsibility, because bureaucrats are more responsive to clear legislative guidance than to anything else. Nevertheless, this is not a neat and sure solution, because Congress and the president can still be at odds, and when they are at odds, bureaucrats have an opportunity to evade responsibility by playing one branch off against the other.

As to the vast apparatus, bureaucracy is here to stay. The administration of myriad government functions and responsibilities in a large, complex society will always require "rule by desks and offices" (the literal meaning of *bureaucracy*). No "reinvention" of government, however well conceived or executed, can alter that basic fact, nor can it resolve the problem of reconciling bureaucracy in a Democracy. President Clinton's National Performance Review accomplished some impressive things: The national bureaucracy has become somewhat smaller, and in the next few years, it will become smaller still; government procedures are being streamlined and are under tremendous pressure to become even more efficient. But these efforts are no guarantee that the bureaucracy itself will become more malleable. Congress will not suddenly change its practice of loose and vague leg-

The president may	appoint and remove agency heads.
	reorganize the bureaucracy (with congressional approval).
	make changes in agencies' budget proposals.
	initiate or adjust policies that would alter the bureaucracy's activities.
Congress may	pass legislation that alters the bureaucracy's activities.
	abolish existing programs.
	investigate bureaucratic activities and force bureaucrats to testify about them.
	influence presidential appointments of agency heads and other officials.
The judiciary may	rule on whether bureaucrats have acted within the law and require policy changes to comply with the law.
	force the bureaucracy to respect the rights of individuals through hearings and other proceedings.
	rule on the constitutionality of all rules and regulations.

islative draftsmanship. Presidents will not suddenly discover new reserves of power or vision to draw more tightly the reins of responsible management. No deep solution can be found in quick fixes. As with all complex social and political problems, the solution lies mainly in a sober awareness of the nature of the problem. This awareness enables people to avoid fantasies and myths about the abilities of a democratized presidency—or the potential of a reform effort, or the powers of technology, or the populist rhetoric of a new Congress—to change the nature of governance by bureaucracy.

CHAPTER REVIEW

Most American citizens possess less information and more misinformation about bureaucracy than about any other feature of government. We therefore began the chapter with an elementary definition of bureaucracy, identifying its key characteristics and demonstrating the extent to which bureaucracy is not only a phenomenon but an American phenomenon. In the second section of the chapter, we showed how all essential government services and controls are carried out by bureaucracies—or to be more objective, administrative agencies. Following a very general description of the different general types of bureaucratic agencies in the executive branch, we divided the agencies of the executive branch into four categories according to mission: the clientele agencies, the agencies for maintaining the Union, the regulatory agencies, and the agencies for redistribution. These illustrate the varieties of administrative experience in American government. Although the bureaucratic phenomenon is universal, not all the bureaucracies are the same in the way they are organized, in the degree of their responsiveness, or in the way they participate in the political process.

Finally, the chapter concluded with a review of all three of the chapters on "representative government" in order to assess how well the two political branches (the legislative and the executive) do the toughest job any government has to do: making the bureaucracy accountable to the people it serves and controls. "Bureaucracy in a Democracy" is the subtitle and theme of the chapter not because we have succeeded in democratizing bureaucracies but because it is the neverending task of politics in a democracy.

FOR FURTHER READING

Aberbach, Joel, and Bert A. Rockman. *In the Web of Politics: Three Decades of the U.S. Federal Executive*. Washington, D.C.: Brookings Institution, 2000.

Arnold, Peri E. *Making the Managerial Presidency: Comprehensive Reorganization Planning, 1905–1980*. Princeton, N.J.: Princeton University Press, 1986.

Downs, Anthony. *Inside Bureaucracy*. Boston: Little, Brown, 1966.

Esman, Milton J. *Government Works: Why Americans Need the Feds*. Ithaca, N.Y.: Cornell University Press, 2000.

Goodsell, Charles. *The Case for Bureaucracy*. 4th ed. Washington, D.C.: Congressional Quarterly Press, 2003.

Heclo, Hugh. *On Thinking Institutionally*. Boulder, Colo.: Paradigm, 2007.

Kerwin, Cornelius M. *Rulemaking*. 3rd ed. Washington, D.C.: Congressional Quarterly Press, 2003.

Kettl, Donald F., and James Fesler. *The Politics of the Administrative Process*. 3rd ed. Washington, D.C.: Brookings Institution, 2005.

Light, Paul C. *The True Size of Government*. Washington, D.C.: Brookings Institution, 1999.

Meier, Kenneth J., and John Bohte. *Politics and the Bureaucracy*. 5th ed. Belmont, Calif.: Wadsworth, 2006.

Seidman, Harold. *Politics, Position, and Power: The Dynamics of Federal Organization*. 5th ed. New York: Oxford University Press, 1998.

ONLINE READING ○ Wilson, James Q. *Bureaucracy: What Government Agencies Do and Why They Do It*. New York: Basic Books, 1989.

The Federal Courts

George W. Bush won the 2000 national election. The final battle in the race, however, was not decided in the electoral arena and did not involve the participation of ordinary Americans. Instead, the battle was fought in the courts, in the Florida state legislature, and in the executive institutions of the Florida state government by small groups of attorneys and political activists. During the course of the dispute, some forty lawsuits were filed in the Florida circuit and supreme courts, the U.S. District Court, the U.S. Court of Appeals, and the U.S. Supreme Court.[1] Together, the two campaigns ran up nearly $10 million in legal fees during the month of litigation. In most of the courtroom battles, the Bush campaign prevailed. Despite two setbacks before the all-Democratic Florida supreme court, Bush attorneys won most of the circuit court cases and the ultimate clash before the U.S. Supreme Court in a narrow 5–4 vote. The next day, Al Gore made a speech conceding the election, and on December 18, 2000, 271 presidential electors—the constitutionally prescribed majority—cast their votes for George W. Bush.

The court battle over Florida's twenty-five electoral votes in 2000 illustrates the political power that the courts now exercise. The past fifty years have seen a sharp increase in the number of major policy issues that have been fought and decided in the judicial realm. But since judges are not elected and accountable to the people, what does this shift in power mean for American democracy?

In this chapter, we will first examine the judicial process, including the types of cases that the federal courts consider. Second, we will assess the organization and structure of the federal court system as well as the flow of cases through the courts. Third, we will consider judicial review and how it makes the Supreme Court a "lawmaking body." Fourth, we will examine various influences on the Supreme Court. Finally, we will analyze the role and power of the federal courts in the American political process, looking in particular at the growth of judicial power in the United States. The framers of the American Constitution called the Court the "least dangerous branch" of American government. Today, it is not unusual to hear friends and foes of the Court alike refer to it as the "imperial judiciary."[2] Before we

---

[1]"In the Courts," *San Diego Union Tribune,* 7 December 2000, p. A14.

[2]See Richard Neely, *How Courts Govern America* (New Haven, Conn.: Yale University Press, 1981).

can understand this transformation and its consequences, however, we must look in some detail at America's judicial process.

HOW COURTS WORK

Court cases in the United States proceed under three broad categories of law: criminal law, civil law, and public law.

Cases of **criminal law** are those in which the government charges an individual with violating a statute that has been enacted to protect the public health, safety, morals, or welfare. In criminal cases, the government is always the **plaintiff** (the party that brings charges) and alleges that a criminal violation has been committed by a named **defendant.** Most criminal cases arise in state and municipal courts and involve matters ranging from traffic offenses to robbery and murder. While the great bulk of criminal law is still a state matter, a growing body of federal criminal law deals with such matters as tax evasion, mail fraud, and the sale of narcotics. Defendants found guilty of criminal violations may be fined or sent to prison.

Cases of **civil law** involve disputes among individuals or between individuals and the government where no criminal violation is charged. But unlike criminal cases, the losers in civil cases cannot be fined or sent to prison, although they may be required to pay monetary damages for their actions. In a civil case, the one who brings a complaint is the plaintiff and the one against whom the complaint is brought is the defendant. The two most common types of civil cases involve contracts and torts. In a typical contract case, an individual or corporation charges that it has suffered because of another's violation of a specific agreement between the two. For example, the Smith Manufacturing Corporation may charge that Jones Distributors failed to honor an agreement to deliver raw materials at a specified time, causing Smith to lose business. Smith asks the court to order Jones to compensate it for the damage allegedly suffered. In a typical tort case, one individual charges that he or she has been injured by another's negligence or malfeasance. Medical malpractice suits are one example of tort cases.

In deciding cases, courts apply statutes (laws) and legal **precedents** (prior decisions). State and federal statutes, for example, often govern the conditions under which contracts are and are not legally binding. Jones Distributors might argue

criminal law The branch of law that deals with disputes or actions involving criminal penalties (as opposed to civil law). It regulates the conduct of individuals, defines crimes, and provides punishment for criminal acts.

plaintiff The individual or organization who brings a complaint in court.

defendant The individual or organization against whom a complaint is brought in criminal or civil cases.

civil law A system of jurisprudence, including private law and governmental actions, to settle disputes that do not involve criminal penalties.

precedents Prior cases whose principles are used by judges as the bases for their decisions in present cases.

Type of law	Type of case or dispute	Form of case
Criminal law	Cases arising out of actions that violate laws protecting the health, safety, and morals of the community. The government is always the plaintiff.	*U.S. (or state) v. Jones* *Jones v. U.S. (or state)*, if Jones lost and is appealing
Civil law	"Private law," involving disputes between citizens or between government and citizen where no crime is alleged. Two general types are contract and tort. *Contract cases* are disputes that arise over voluntary actions. *Tort cases* are disputes that arise out of obligations inherent in social life. Negligence and slander are examples of torts.	*Smith v. Jones* *New York v. Jones* *U.S. v. Jones* *Jones v. New York*
Public law	All cases where the powers of government or the rights of citizens are involved. The government is the defendant. *Constitutional law* involves judicial review of the basis of a government's action in relation to specific clauses of the Constitution as interpreted in Supreme Court cases. *Administrative law* involves disputes of the statutory authority, jurisdiction, or procedures of administrative agencies.	*Jones v. U.S. (or state)* *In re Jones* *Smith v. Jones*, if a license or statute is at issue in their private dispute

that it was not obliged to fulfill its contract with the Smith Corporation because actions by Smith, such as the failure to make promised payments, constituted fraud under state law. Attorneys for a physician being sued for malpractice, on the other hand, may search for prior instances in which courts ruled that actions similar to those of their client did not constitute negligence. Such precedents are applied under the doctrine of **stare decisis**, a Latin phrase meaning "let the decision stand."

A case becomes a matter of the third category, **public law**, when plaintiffs or defendants in a civil or criminal case seeks to show that their case involves the powers of government or rights of citizens as defined under the Constitution or by statute. One major form of public law is constitutional law, under which a court will examine the government's actions to see if they conform to the Constitution as it has been interpreted by the judiciary. Thus, what began as an ordinary criminal case may enter the realm of public law if a defendant claims that the police violated his or her constitutional rights. Another important arena of public law is administrative law, which involves disputes over the jurisdiction, procedures, or authority

stare decisis Literally "let the decision stand." A previous decision by a court applies as a precedent in similar cases until that decision is overruled.

public law Cases in private law, civil law, or criminal law in which one party to the dispute argues that a license is unfair, a law is inequitable or unconstitutional, or an agency has acted unfairly, violated a procedure, or gone beyond its jurisdiction.

of administrative agencies. Under this type of law, civil litigation between an individual and the government may become a matter of public law if the individual asserts that the government is violating a statute or abusing its power under the Constitution. For example, land owners have asserted that federal and state restrictions on land use constitute violations of the Fifth Amendment's restrictions on the government's ability to confiscate private property. Recently, the Supreme Court has been very sympathetic to such claims, which effectively transform an ordinary civil dispute into a major issue of public law.

Most of the important Supreme Court cases we will examine in this chapter involve judgments concerning the constitutional or statutory basis of the actions of government agencies. As we shall see, it is in this arena of public law that the Supreme Court's decisions can have significant consequences for American politics and society.

Types of Courts

In the United States, systems of courts have been established both by the federal government and by the governments of the individual states. Both systems have several levels, as shown in Figure 8.1. More than 99 percent of all court cases in the United States are heard in state courts. The overwhelming majority of criminal cases, for example, involves violations of state laws prohibiting such actions as murder, robbery, fraud, theft, and assault. If such a case is brought to trial, it will be heard in a state *trial court,* in front of a judge and sometimes a jury, who will determine whether the defendant violated state law. If the defendant is convicted, he or she may appeal the conviction to a higher court, such as a state *court of appeals,* and from there to a state's *supreme court.* Similarly, in civil cases, most litigation is brought in the courts established by the state in which the activity in question took place. For example, a patient bringing suit against a physician for malpractice would file the suit in the appropriate court in the state where the alleged malpractice occurred. The judge hearing the case would apply state law and state precedent to the matter at hand. (It should be noted that in both criminal and civil matters, most cases are settled before trial through negotiated agreements between the parties. In criminal cases, these agreements are called *plea bargains.*)

Although each state has its own set of laws, these laws have much in common from state to state. Murder and robbery, obviously, are illegal in all states, although the range of possible punishments for those crimes varies from state to state. Some states, for example, provide for capital punishment (the death penalty) for murder and other serious offenses; other states do not. As we saw in Chapter 4, however, some acts that are criminal offenses in one state may be legal in another state. Prostitution, for example, is legal in some Nevada counties, although it is outlawed in all other states. Considerable similarity among the states is also found in the realm of civil law. In the case of contract law, most states have adopted the *Uniform Commercial Code* in order to reduce interstate differences. In areas such as family law, however, which covers such matters as divorce and child custody arrangements, state laws vary greatly.

trial court The first court to hear a criminal or civil case.

court of appeals A court that hears the appeals of trial court decisions.

supreme court The highest court in a particular state or in the United States. This court primarily serves an appellate function.

plea bargains Negotiated agreements in criminal cases in which a defendant agrees to plead guilty in return for the state's agreement to reduce the severity of the criminal charge the defendant is facing.

Uniform Commercial Code A set of standards for contract law, recognized by all states, that greatly reduces interstate differences in the practice of contract law.

FIGURE 8.1 The U.S. Court System

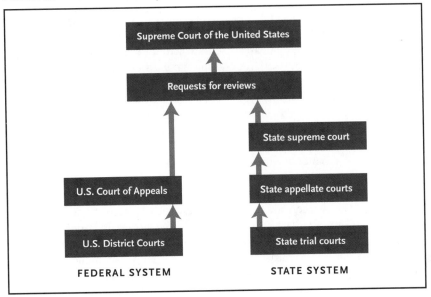

Cases are heard in the federal courts if they involve federal laws, treaties with other nations, or the U.S. Constitution; these areas are the official *jurisdiction* of the federal courts. In addition, any case in which the U.S. government is a party is heard in the federal courts. If, for example, an individual is charged with violating a federal criminal statute, such as evading the payment of income taxes, a federal prosecutor would bring charges before a federal judge. Civil cases involving the citizens of more than one state and in which more than fifty thousand dollars is at stake may be heard in either the federal or the state courts, usually depending upon the preference of the plaintiff.

Federal courts serve another purpose in addition to trying cases within their jurisdiction: that of hearing appeals from state-level courts. Individuals found guilty of breaking a state criminal law, for example, can appeal their convictions to a federal court by raising a constitutional issue and asking a federal court to determine whether the state's actions were consistent with the requirements of the U.S. Constitution. An appellant might assert, for example, that the state court denied him or her the right to counsel, imposed excessive bail, or otherwise denied the appellant *due process*. Under such circumstances, an appellant can ask the federal court to overturn his or her conviction. Federal courts are not obligated to accept such appeals and will do so only if they feel that the issues raised have considerable merit and if the appellant has exhausted all possible remedies within the state courts. (This procedure is discussed in more detail later in this chapter.) The decisions of state supreme courts may also be appealed to the U.S. Supreme Court if the state court's decision has conflicted with prior U.S. Supreme Court rulings or has raised some important question of federal law. Such appeals are accepted by the U.S. Supreme Court at its discretion.

jurisdiction The authority of a court to consider a case initially. Distinguished from appellate jurisdiction, which is the authority to hear appeals from a lower court's decision.

due process To proceed according to law and with adequate protection for individual rights.

FEDERAL JURISDICTION

Cases are heard in the federal courts if they involve federal laws, treaties with other nations, or the U.S. Constitution; these areas are the official jurisdiction of the federal courts. In addition, any case in which the U.S. government is a party is heard in the federal courts. If, for example, an individual is charged with violating a federal criminal statute, such as evading the payment of income taxes, charges would be brought before a federal judge by a federal prosecutor. Civil cases involving the citizens of more than one state and in which more than $70,000 is at stake may be heard in either the federal or the state courts, usually depending on the preference of the plaintiff.

But even if a matter belongs in federal court, how do we know which federal court should exercise jurisdiction over the case? The answer to this seemingly simple question is somewhat complex. The jurisdiction of each federal court is derived from the U.S. Constitution and federal statutes. Article III of the Constitution gives the Supreme Court appellate jurisdiction in all federal cases and original jurisdiction in cases involving foreign ambassadors and issues in which a state is a party. Article III assigns original jurisdiction in all other federal cases to the lower courts that Congress was authorized to establish. Over the years, as Congress enacted statutes creating the federal judicial system, it specified the jurisdiction of each type of court it established. For the most part, Congress has assigned jurisdictions on the basis of geography. The nation is currently, by statute, divided into ninety-four judicial districts, including one court for each of three U.S. territories: Guam, the U.S. Virgin Islands, and the Northern Marianas. Each of the ninety-four U.S. district courts exercises jurisdiction over federal cases arising within its territorial domain. The judicial districts are, in turn, organized into eleven regional circuits and the District of Columbia circuit. Each circuit court exercises appellate jurisdiction over cases heard by the district courts within its region.

Geography is not the only basis for federal court jurisdiction. Congress has also established several specialized courts that have nationwide original jurisdiction in certain types of cases. These include the U.S. Court of International Trade, created to deal with trade and customs issues, and the U.S. Court of Federal Claims, which handles damage suits against the United States. Congress has, in addition, established a court with nationwide appellate jurisdiction. This is the U.S. Court of Appeals for the Federal Circuit, which hears appeals involving patent law and those arising from the decisions of the trade and claims courts.

The appellate jurisdiction of the federal courts also extends to cases originating in the state courts. In both civil and criminal cases, a decision of the highest state court can be appealed to the U.S. Supreme Court by raising a federal issue. Appellants might assert, for example, that they were denied the right to counsel or otherwise deprived of the due process guaranteed by the federal Constitution, or they might assert that important issues of federal law were at stake in the case. The U.S. Supreme Court is not obligated to accept such appeals and will accept them only if it believes that the matter has considerable national significance. (We shall return to this topic later in this chapter.) In addition, in criminal cases defendants who have been convicted in a state court may request a writ of **habeas corpus** from

habeas corpus A court order demanding that an individual in custody be brought into court and shown the cause for detention. *Habeas corpus* is guaranteed by the Constitution and can be suspended only in cases of rebellion or invasion.

a federal district court. *Habeas corpus* is a court order to the authorities to release a prisoner deemed to be held in violation of his or her legal rights. Generally speaking, state defendants seeking a federal writ of *habeas corpus* must show that they have exhausted all available state remedies and raise issues not previously raised in their state appeals. Federal courts of appeals and, ultimately, the U.S. Supreme Court have appellate jurisdiction over federal district court *habeas* decisions.

Although the federal courts hear only a small fraction of all the civil and criminal cases decided each year in the United States, their decisions are extremely important. It is in the federal courts that the Constitution and federal laws that govern all Americans are interpreted and their meaning and significance established. Moreover, it is in the federal courts that the powers and limitations of the increasingly powerful national government are tested. Finally, through their power to review the decisions of the state courts, it is ultimately the federal courts that dominate the American judicial system.

The Federal Trial Courts

The federal district courts handle most of the cases of original federal jurisdiction. These trial courts have general jurisdiction, and their cases are, in form, indistinguishable from cases in the state trial courts.

There are eighty-nine district courts in the fifty states, plus one in the District of Columbia and one in Puerto Rico, and three territorial courts. These courts are staffed by 678 federal district judges. District judges are assigned to district courts according to the workload; the busiest of these courts may have as many as twenty-eight judges. The routines and procedures of the federal district courts are essentially the same as those of the lower state courts, except that federal procedural requirements tend to be stricter. States, for example, do not have to provide a grand jury, a twelve-member trial jury, or a unanimous jury verdict. Federal courts must provide all of these.

Federal Appellate Courts

Roughly 20 percent of all lower court cases along with appeals from some federal agency decisions are subsequently reviewed by a federal appeals court. The country is divided into twelve judicial circuits, each of which has a U.S. Court of Appeals. A thirteenth appellate court, the U.S. Court of Appeals for the Federal Circuit, is defined by subject matter rather than geographical jurisdiction. This court accepts appeals regarding patents, copyrights, and international trade.

Except for cases selected for review by the Supreme Court, decisions made by the appeals courts are final. Because of this finality, certain safeguards have been built into the system. The most important is the provision of more than one judge for every appeals case. Each court of appeals has three to twenty-eight permanent judgeships, depending on the workload of the circuit. Although normally three judges hear appealed cases, in some instances a larger number of judges sit together *en banc*.

Another safeguard is provided by the assignment of a Supreme Court justice as the circuit justice for each of the eleven circuits. The circuit justice deals with requests for special action by the Supreme Court. The most frequent and best-known action of circuit justices is that of reviewing requests for stays of execution when the full Court is unable to do so—mainly during the summer, when the Court is in recess.

The Supreme Court

The Supreme Court is America's highest court. Article III of the Constitution vests "the judicial power of the United States" in the Supreme Court, and this court is supreme in fact as well as form. The Supreme Court is made up of a chief justice and eight associate justices. The ***chief justice*** presides over the Court's public sessions and conferences. In the Court's actual deliberations and decisions, however, the chief justice has no more authority than his or her colleagues. Each justice casts one vote. The chief justice, though, is always the first to speak and the last to vote when the justices deliberate. In addition, if the chief justice has voted with the majority, he decides which of the justices will write the formal opinion for the court. The character of the opinion can be an important means of influencing the evolution of the law beyond the mere affirmation or denial of the appeal at hand. To some extent, the influence of the chief justice is a function of his or her own leadership ability. Some chief justices, such as the late Earl Warren, have been able to lead the court in a new direction. In other instances, a forceful associate justice, such as the late Felix Frankfurter, is the dominant figure on the Court.

The Constitution does not specify the number of justices who should sit on the Supreme Court; Congress has the authority to change the Court's size. In the early nineteenth century, there were six Supreme Court justices; later there were seven. Congress set the number of justices at nine in 1869, and the Court has remained that size ever since. In 1937, President Franklin D. Roosevelt, infuriated by several Supreme Court decisions that struck down New Deal programs, asked Congress to enlarge the court so that he could add a few sympathetic justices to the bench. Although Congress balked at Roosevelt's "court packing" plan, the Court gave in to FDR's pressure and began to take a more favorable view of his policy initiatives. The president, in turn, dropped his efforts to enlarge the Court. The Court's surrender to FDR came to be known as "the switch in time that saved nine."

How Judges Are Appointed

Federal judges are appointed by the president and are generally selected from among the more prominent or politically active members of the legal profession. Many federal judges previously served as state court judges or state or local prosecutors. Before the president makes a formal nomination, however, the senators from the candidate's own state must indicate that they support the nominee. This is an informal but seldom violated practice called ***senatorial courtesy***. If one or both senators from a prospective nominee's home state belong to the president's political party, the president will almost invariably consult them and secure their blessing for the nomination. Because the president's party in the Senate will rarely support a nominee opposed by a home-state senator from their ranks, this arrangement gives these senators virtual veto power over appointments to the federal bench in their own states. Senators often see such a nomination as a way to

chief justice Justice on the Supreme Court who presides over the Court's public sessions.

senatorial courtesy The practice whereby the president, before formally nominating a person for a federal judgeship, will seek approval of the nomination from the senators who represent the candidate's own state.

reward important allies and contributors in their states. If the state has no senator from the president's party, the governor or members of the state's House delegation may make suggestions. In general, presidents endeavor to appoint judges who possess legal experience and good character and whose partisan and ideological views are similar to the president's own. During the presidencies of Ronald Reagan and George H. W. Bush, most federal judicial appointees were conservative Republicans. Bush established an advisory committee to screen judicial nominees to make certain that their legal and political philosophies were sufficiently conservative. Bill Clinton's appointees to the federal bench, on the other hand, tended to be liberal Democrats. Clinton also made a major effort to appoint women and African Americans to the federal courts. He drew nearly half of his nominees from these groups.

Once the president has formally nominated an individual, the nominee must be considered by the Senate Judiciary Committee and confirmed by a majority vote in the full Senate. In recent years, the Senate Judiciary Committee has sought to signal the president when it has had qualms about a judicial nomination. After the Republicans won control of the Senate in 1994, for example, Judiciary Committee Chair Orrin Hatch of Utah let President Clinton know that he considered two of Clinton's nominees to be too liberal. The president withdrew the nominations.

Federal appeals court nominations follow much the same pattern. Since appeals court judges preside over jurisdictions that include several states, however, senators do not have as strong a role in proposing potential candidates. Instead, the Justice Department or important members of the administration usually suggest potential appeals court candidates to the president. The senators from the nominee's own state are still consulted before the president will formally act.

During President George W. Bush's first two years in office, Democrats controlled the Senate and used their majority on the Judiciary Committee to block eight of the president's first eleven federal court nominations. After the GOP won a narrow Senate majority in the 2002 national elections, Democrats used a filibuster to block action on several other Bush federal appeals court nominees. Both Democrats and Republicans saw struggles over lower court slots as practice and preparation for all-out partisan warfare over the next Supreme Court vacancy.

If political factors play an important role in the selection of district and appellate court judges, they are decisive when it comes to Supreme Court appointments. For example, presidents Ronald Reagan and George H. W. Bush appointed five justices whom they believed to have conservative perspectives: Justices Sandra Day O'Connor, Antonin Scalia, Anthony Kennedy, David Souter, and Clarence Thomas. Reagan also elevated William Rehnquist to the position of chief justice. Reagan and Bush sought appointees who believed in reducing government intervention in the economy and who supported the moral positions taken by the Republican Party in recent years, particularly opposition to abortion. However, not all the Reagan and Bush appointees have fulfilled their sponsors' expectations. Bush appointee David Souter, for example, has been attacked by conservatives as a turncoat for his decisions on school prayer and abortion rights. Nevertheless, through their appointments, Reagan and Bush were able to create a far more conservative Supreme Court. For his part, President Bill Clinton named Ruth Bader Ginsburg and Stephen Breyer to the Court, hoping to counteract the influence of the Reagan and Bush appointees.

In 2005, President George W. Bush was presented with an opportunity to put his own stamp on the Supreme Court as Justice Sandra Day O'Connor announced her decision to retire and Chief Justice Rehnquist died of the cancer that had limited his judicial activities for the past year. Bush quickly nominated federal appeals court judge John G. Roberts, Jr., initially to replace O'Connor but then as Chief Justice when Rehnquist died while the Senate was still considering the appointment. Roberts, a moderate conservative with a brilliant legal record, provoked some Democratic opposition but won confirmation without much difficulty. Bush's next nominee, though, sparked an intense battle within the president's own party. To the surprise of most observers, the president named one of his long-time associates, White House Counsel Harriet Miers, to replace Justice O'Connor. Many Republicans viewed Miers as merely a Bush crony lacking judicial qualifications and insufficiently supportive of conservative causes. Opposition to Miers within the GOP was so intense that Democrats remained gleefully silent as the president was forced to allow her to withdraw her name from consideration. In the wake of the Miers debacle, President Bush turned to a more conventional nominee, federal appeals court judge Samuel Alito. This nomination pleased Republican conservatives who saw Alito as cut from the same mold as arch-conservative Justice Antonin Scalia. Indeed, Alito had sometimes been called "Scalito" because of the similarities between his views and Scalia's. After a brief Democratic filibuster failed, Alito was confirmed in January of 2006 by a slim margin. (Table 8.1 shows more information about the current Supreme Court justices.)

Typically, in recent years, after the president has named a nominee, interest groups opposed to the nomination have mobilized opposition in the media, the public, and the Senate. When former President George H. W. Bush proposed conservative judge Clarence Thomas for the Court, for example, liberal groups launched a campaign to discredit Thomas. After extensive research into his background, opponents of the nomination were able to produce evidence suggesting that Thomas had sexually harassed a former subordinate, Anita Hill. Thomas denied the charge. After contentious Senate Judiciary Committee hearings, highlighted by testimony from both Thomas and Hill, Thomas narrowly won confirmation.

Likewise, conservative interest groups carefully scrutinized Bill Clinton's somewhat more liberal nominees, hoping to find information about them that would sabotage their appointments. During his two opportunities to name Supreme Court justices, Clinton was compelled to drop several potential appointees because of information unearthed by political opponents.

These struggles over judicial appointments indicate the growing intensity of partisan struggle in the United States today. They also indicate how much importance competing political forces attach to Supreme Court appointments. Because these contending forces see the outcome as critical, they are willing to engage in a fierce struggle when Supreme Court appointments are at stake.

TABLE 8.1 Supreme Court Justices, 2007

Name	Year of Birth	Prior Experience	Appointment by	Year of Appointment
John G. Roberts, Jr. *Chief Justice*	1955	Federal judge	G. W. Bush	2005
John Paul Stevens	1920	Federal judge	Ford	1975
Antonin Scalia	1936	Law professor, federal judge	Reagan	1986
Anthony Kennedy	1936	Federal judge	Reagan	1988
David Souter	1939	Federal judge	G. H. W. Bush	1990
Clarence Thomas	1948	Federal judge	G. H. W. Bush	1991
Ruth Bader Ginsburg	1933	Federal judge	Clinton	1993
Stephen Breyer	1938	Federal judge	Clinton	1994
Samuel Alito	1950	Federal judge	G. W. Bush	2006

JUDICIAL REVIEW

The phrase *judicial review* refers to the power of the judiciary to examine and, if necessary, invalidate actions undertaken by the legislative and executive branches (see Figure 8.2). The phrase is sometimes used, as well, to describe the scrutiny that appeals courts give to the actions of trial courts, but, strictly speaking, this is an improper usage. A higher court's examination of a lower court's decision might be called "appellate review" but it is not "judicial review."

Judicial Review of Acts of Congress

Because the Constitution does not give the Supreme Court the power of judicial review of congressional enactments, the Court's exercise of it may be seen as something of a usurpation. Among the proposals debated at the Constitutional Convention was one to create a council composed of the president and the judiciary that would share the veto power over legislation. Another proposal was to route all legislation through both the Court and the president; overruling a veto by either one would have required a two-thirds vote of the House and the Senate. Those and other proposals were rejected by the delegates, and no further effort was made to give the Supreme Court review power over the other branches. This does not prove that the framers of the Constitution opposed judicial review, but it does indicate that "if they intended to provide for it in the Constitution, they did so in a most obscure fashion."[3]

judicial review Power of the courts to declare actions of the legislative and executive branches invalid or unconstitutional. The Supreme Court asserted this power in *Marbury v. Madison*.

---

[3]C. Herman Pritchett, *The American Constitution* (New York: McGraw-Hill, 1959), p. 138.

FIGURE 8.2 Judicial Review

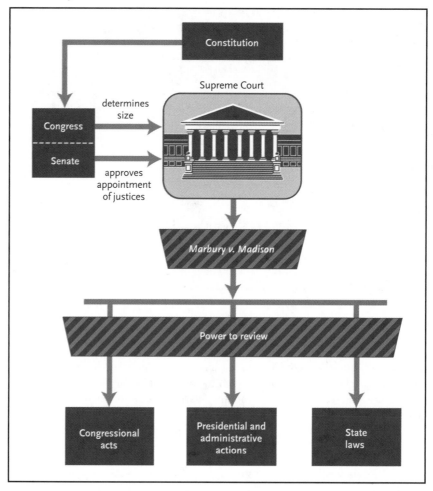

Disputes over the intentions of the framers were settled in 1803 in the case of *Marbury v. Madison*.[4] In that case, William Marbury sued Secretary of State James Madison for Madison's failure to complete Marbury's appointment to a lower judgeship that had been initiated by the outgoing administration of President John Adams. Quite apart from the details of the case, Chief Justice John Marshall, speaking on behalf of the court, used the case to declare a portion of a law unconstitutional. In effect, he stated that while the substance of Marbury's request was not unreasonable, the Court's jurisdiction in the matter was based on a section of the Judiciary Act of 1789, which the Court declared unconstitutional.

Although Congress and the president have often been at odds with the Court, its legal power to review acts of Congress has not been seriously questioned since

ONLINE READING ○ [4]*Marbury v. Madison*, 1 Cranch 137 (1803).

1803. One reason is that judicial power has been accepted as natural, if not intended. Another reason is that during the early years of the Republic, the Supreme Court was careful to use its power sparingly, striking down only two pieces of legislation during the first seventy-five years of its history. In recent years, with the power of judicial review securely accepted, the Court has been more willing to use it. Just since 1995, the Supreme Court has struck down more than forty acts of Congress, in part or in their entirety.

Judicial Review of State Actions

The power of the Supreme Court to review state legislation or other state action and to determine its constitutionality is neither granted by the Constitution nor inherent in the federal system. But the logic of the *supremacy clause* of Article VI of the Constitution, which declares it and laws made under its authority to be the supreme law of the land, is very strong. Furthermore, in the Judiciary Act of 1789, Congress conferred on the Supreme Court the power to reverse state constitutions and laws whenever they are clearly in conflict with the U.S. Constitution, federal laws, or treaties.[5] This power gives the Supreme Court jurisdiction over all of the millions of cases handled by American courts each year.

The supremacy clause of the Constitution not only established the federal Constitution, statutes, and treaties as the "supreme law of the land," but also provided that "the Judges in every State shall be bound thereby, any Thing in the Constitution or Laws of the State to the Contrary notwithstanding." Under this authority, the Supreme Court has frequently overturned state constitutional provisions or statutes and state court decisions that it feels are counter to rights or privileges guaranteed under the Constitution or federal statutes.

Judicial Review of Federal Agency Actions

Although Congress makes the law, as we saw in Chapters 5 and 7, it can hardly administer the thousands of programs it has enacted and must delegate power to the president and to a huge bureaucracy to achieve its purposes. For example, if Congress wishes to improve air quality, it cannot possibly anticipate all the conditions and circumstances that may arise with respect to that general goal. Inevitably, Congress must delegate to the executive substantial discretionary power to make judgments about the best ways to improve air quality in the face of changing circumstances. Thus, over the years, almost any congressional program will result in thousands of pages of administrative regulations developed by executive agencies nominally seeking to implement the will of the Congress.

The issue of delegation of power has led to a number of court decisions over the past two centuries generally revolving around the question of the scope of the delegation. Courts have also been called upon to decide whether the rules and regulations adopted by federal agencies are consistent with Congress's express or implied intent.

supremacy clause
Article VI of the Constitution, which states that laws passed by the national government and all treaties are the supreme laws of the land and superior to all laws adopted by any state or any subdivision.

---

[5]This review power was affirmed by the Supreme Court in *Martin v. Hunter's Lessees,* 1 Wheaton 304 (1816).

As presidential power expanded during the New Deal era, one measure of increased congressional subordination to the executive was the enactment of laws that contained few, if any, principles limiting executive discretion. Congress enacted legislation, often at the president's behest, that gave the executive virtually unfettered authority to address a particular concern. For example, the Emergency Price Control Act of 1942 authorized the executive to set "fair and equitable" prices without offering any indication of what those terms might mean.[6] While the Court initially challenged these delegations of power to the president during the New Deal, a confrontation with President Franklin D. Roosevelt caused the Court to retreat from its position. Perhaps as a result, no congressional delegation of power to the president has been struck down as impermissibly broad in more than six decades. In the last two decades in particular, the Supreme Court has found that as long as federal agencies developed rules and regulations "based upon a permissible construction" or "reasonable interpretation" of Congress's statute, the judiciary would accept the views of the executive branch.[7] Generally, the courts give considerable deference to administrative agencies as long as those agencies have engaged in a formal rule-making process and can show that they have carried out the conditions prescribed by the various statutes governing agency rule making. These include the 1946 Administrative Procedure Act, which requires agencies to notify parties affected by proposed rules as well as allow them ample time to comment on such rules before they go into effect.

Judicial Review and Presidential Power

The federal courts are also called on to review the actions of the president. As we saw in Chapter 6, presidents increasingly make use of unilateral executive powers rather than rely on congressional legislation to achieve their objectives. On many occasions, presidential orders and actions have been challenged in the federal courts by members of Congress and by individuals and groups opposing the president's policies. In recent years, assertions of presidential power in such realms as foreign policy, war and emergency powers, legislative power, and administrative authority have, more often than not, been upheld by the federal bench. Indeed, the federal judiciary has sometimes taken extraordinary presidential claims made for limited and temporary purposes and rationalized them, that is, converted them into routine and permanent instruments of presidential government. Take, for example, Richard Nixon's sweeping claims of executive privilege. In *U.S. v. Nixon*, the Court, to be sure, rejected the president's refusal to turn over tapes to congressional investigators. For the first time, though, the justices also recognized the validity of the principle of executive privilege and discussed the situations in which such claims might be appropriate.[8] This judicial recognition of the principle encouraged Presidents Bill Clinton and George W. Bush to make broad claims of executive priv-

---

[6] 56 Stat. 23 (30 January 1942).

[7] *Chevron v. Natural Resources Defense Council*, 467 U.S. 837 (1984).

[8] *U.S. v. Nixon*, 418 U.S. 683 (1974).

ilege during their terms in office.[9] Executive privilege has recently been invoked to protect even the deliberations of the vice president from congressional scrutiny in the case of Dick Cheney's consultations with representatives of the energy industry.

This pattern of judicial deference to presidential authority is also manifest in the Supreme Court's recent decisions regarding suspects in terrorism cases. In June 2004, the Supreme Court ruled in three cases involving the president's antiterrorism initiatives and claims of executive power and in two of the three cases appeared to place some limits on presidential authority. Indeed, the justices had clearly been influenced by revelations that U.S. troops had abused prisoners in Iraq and sought in these cases to make a statement against the absolute denial of procedural rights to individuals in the custody of American military authorities. But while the Court's decisions were widely hailed as reining in the executive branch, they actually fell far short of stopping presidential power in its tracks.

The most important case decided by the Court was *Hamdi v. Rumsfeld*.[10] Yaser Esam Hamdi, apparently a Taliban soldier, was captured by American forces in Afghanistan and brought to the United States, where he was incarcerated at the Norfolk Naval Station. Hamdi was classified as an enemy combatant and denied civil rights, including the right to counsel, despite the fact that he had been born in Louisiana and held American citizenship. A federal district court scheduled a hearing on Hamdi's *habeas corpus* petition and ordered that he be given unmonitored access to counsel. This ruling, however, was reversed by the Fourth Circuit Court of Appeals. In its opinion the court held that in the national security realm, the president wields "plenary and exclusive power." This power was even greater, said the court, when the president acted with statutory authority from Congress. The court did not indicate which statute, in particular, might have authorized the president's actions, but went on to affirm the president's constitutional power, as supported in many prior rulings, to conduct military operations, decide who is and is not an enemy combatant, and determine the rules governing the treatment of such individuals. In essence, said the court, the president had virtually unfettered discretion to deal with emergencies and it was inappropriate for the judiciary to saddle presidential decisions with what the court called the "panoply of encumbrances associated with civil litigation."

In June 2004, the Supreme Court ruled that Hamdi was entitled to a lawyer and "a fair opportunity to rebut the government's factual assertions." However, the Supreme Court affirmed that the president possessed the authority to declare a U.S. citizen to be an enemy combatant and to order such an individual held in federal detention. Several of the justices intimated that once designated an enemy combatant, a U.S. citizen might be tried before a military tribunal and the normal presumption of innocence suspended. In 2006, in *Hamdan v. Rumsfeld*, the Court ruled that the military commissions established to try enemy combatants and

---

[9]On Clinton, see Jonathan Turley, "Paradise Lost: The Clinton Administration and the Erosion of Executive Privilege," 60 *Maryland Law Review* 205 (2001). On Bush, see Jeffrey P. Carlin, "*Walker v. Cheney*: Politics, Posturing and Executive Privilege," 76 *Southern California Law Review* 235 (November 2002).

[10]2004 Westlaw 1431951.

other detainees violated both the Uniform Code of Military Justice and the Geneva Conventions.[11]

Thus, the Supreme Court did assert that presidential actions were subject to judicial scrutiny and placed some constraints on the president's power. But at the same time the Court affirmed the president's single most important claim—the unilateral power to declare individuals, including U.S. citizens, "enemy combatants" who could be detained by federal authorities under adverse legal circumstances.

Judicial Review and Lawmaking

Much of the work of the courts involves the application of statutes to the particular case at hand. Over the centuries, however, judges have developed a body of rules and principles of interpretation that are not grounded in specific statutes. This body of judge-made law is called common law.

The appellate courts are in another realm. When a court of appeals hands down its decision, it accomplishes two things. First, of course, it decides who wins—the person who won in the lower court or the person who lost in the lower court. But at the same time, it expresses its decision in a manner that provides guidance to the lower courts for handling future cases in the same area. Appellate judges try to give their reasons and rulings in writing so the "administration of justice" can take place most of the time at the lowest judicial level. They try to make their ruling or reasoning clear, so as to avoid confusion, which can produce a surge of litigation at the lower levels. These rulings can be considered laws, but they are laws governing the behavior only of the judiciary. Decisions by appellate courts affect citizens by giving them a cause of action or by taking it away from them. That is, they open or close access to the courts.

THE SUPREME COURT IN ACTION

How Cases Reach the Supreme Court

Given the millions of disputes that arise every year, the job of the Supreme Court would be impossible if it were not able to control the flow of cases and its own case load. The Supreme Court has original jurisdiction in a limited variety of cases defined by the Constitution. The original jurisdiction includes (1) cases between the United States and one of the fifty states, (2) cases between two or more states, (3) cases involving foreign ambassadors or other ministers, and (4) cases brought by one state against citizens of another state or against a foreign country. The most important of these cases are disputes between states over land, water, or old debts. Generally, the Supreme Court deals with these cases by appointing a "special master," usually a retired judge, to actually hear the case and present a report. The Supreme Court then allows the states involved in the dispute to present arguments for or against the master's opinion.[12]

---

[11] *Hamdan v. Rumsfeld*, 548 U.S. (2006).

[12] Walter F. Murphy, "The Supreme Court of the United States," in *Encyclopedia of the American Judicial System*, ed. Robert J. Janosik (New York: Scribner's, 1987).

FIGURE 8.3 Reaching the Supreme Court through *Certiorari*

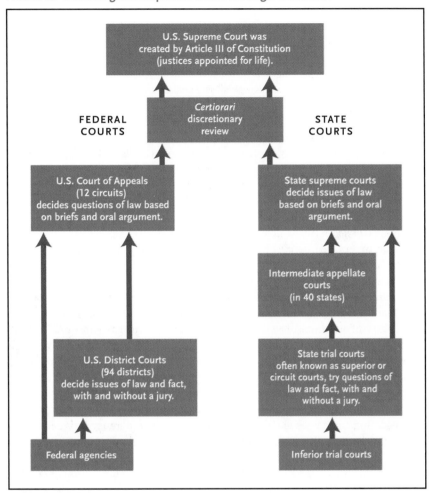

Rules of Access   Over the years, the courts have developed specific rules that govern which cases within their jurisdiction they will and will not hear. To have access to the courts, cases must meet certain criteria that are initially applied by the trial court but may be reconsidered by appellate courts. These rules of access can be broken down into three major categories: case or controversy, standing, and mootness.

Article III of the Constitution and Supreme Court decisions define judicial power as extending only to "cases and controversies." This means that the case before a court must be an actual controversy, not a hypothetical one, with two truly adversarial parties. The courts have interpreted this language to mean that they do not have power to render advisory opinions to legislatures or agencies about the constitutionality of proposed laws or regulations. Furthermore, even after a law is enacted, the courts will generally refuse to consider its constitutionality until it is actually applied.

Parties to a case must also have **standing**, that is, they must show that they have a substantial stake in the outcome of the case. The traditional requirement for standing has been to show injury to oneself; that injury can be personal, economic, or even aesthetic, for example. For a group or class of people to have standing (as in class action suits), each member must show specific injury. This means that a general interest in the environment, for instance, does not provide a group with sufficient basis for standing.

The Supreme Court also uses a third criterion in determining whether it will hear a case: that of **mootness**. In theory, this requirement disqualifies cases that are brought too late—after the relevant facts have changed or the problem has been resolved by other means. The criterion of mootness, however, is subject to the discretion of the courts, which have begun to relax the rules of mootness, particularly in cases where a situation that has been resolved is likely to come up again. In the abortion case *Roe v. Wade*, for example, the Supreme Court rejected the lower court's argument that because the pregnancy had already come to term, the case was moot. The Court agreed to hear the case because no pregnancy was likely to outlast the lengthy appeals process.

Putting aside the formal criteria, the Supreme Court is most likely to accept cases that involve conflicting decisions by the federal circuit courts, cases that present important questions of civil rights or civil liberties, and cases in which the federal government is the appellant.[13] Ultimately, however, the question of which cases to accept can come down to the preferences and priorities of the justices. If a group of justices believes that the Court should intervene in a particular area of policy or politics, they are likely to look for a case or cases that will serve as vehicles for judicial intervention. For many years, for example, the Court was not interested in considering challenges to affirmative action or other programs designed to provide particular benefits to minorities. In recent years, however, several of the Court's more conservative justices have been eager to push back the limits of affirmative action and racial preference, and have therefore accepted a number of cases that would allow them to do so. In 1995, the Court's decision in *Adarand Constructors v. Peña, Missouri v. Jenkins,* and *Miller v. Johnson* placed new restrictions on federal affirmative action programs, school desegregation efforts, and attempts to increase minority representation in Congress through the creation of "minority districts" (see Chapter 10).[14] Similarly, because some justices have felt that the Court had gone too far in the past in restricting public support for religious ideas, the Court accepted the case of *Rosenberger v. University of Virginia*. This case was brought by a Christian student group against the University of Virginia, which had refused to provide student activities fund support for the group's magazine, *Wide Awake*. Other student publications received subsidies from the activities fund, but

standing The right of an individual or organization to initiate a court case.

mootness A criterion used by courts to screen cases that no longer require resolution.

[13]Gregory A. Caldeira and John R. Wright, "Organized Interests and Agenda Setting in the U.S. Supreme Court," *American Political Science Review*, 82 (1988):1109–27.

[14]*Adarand Constructors, Inc. v. Pena,* 115 S. Ct. 2097 (1995); *Missouri v. Jenkins,* 115 S. Ct. 2038 (1995); *Miller v. Johnson,* 115 S. Ct. 2475 (1995).

university policy prohibited grants to religious groups. Lower courts supported the university, finding that support for the magazine would violate the Constitution's prohibition against government support for religion. The Supreme Court, however, ruled in favor of the students' assertion that the university's policies amounted to support for some ideas but not others. The Court said this violated the First Amendment right of freedom of expression.[15]

Writs   Most cases reach the Supreme Court through a ***writ of* certiorari.** Certiorari is an order to a lower court to deliver the records of a particular case to be reviewed for legal errors. The term certiorari is sometimes shortened to *cert* and cases deemed to merit certiorari are referred to as "certworthy." An individual who loses in a lower federal court or state court and wants the Supreme Court to review the decision has 90 days to file a petition for a writ of certiorari with the clerk of the U.S. Supreme Court. There are two types of petitions, paid petitions and petitions *in forma pauperis* (in the form of a pauper). The former requires payment of filing fees, submission of a certain number of copies and compliance with a variety of other rules. For *in forma pauperis* petitions, usually filed by prison inmates, the Court waives the fees and most other requirements.

Since 1972, most of the justices have participated in a "certiorari pool" in which they pool their law clerks to evaluate the petitions. Each petition is reviewed by one clerk who writes a memo for all the justices participating in the pool summarizing the facts and issues and making a recommendation. Clerks for the other justices add their comments to the memo. After they review the memos, any justice may place any case on the "Discuss List." This is a list circulated by the Chief Justice of all the petitions to be talked about and voted on at the Court's conference. If a case is not placed on the discuss list it is automatically denied *certiorari*. Cases placed on the discuss list are considered and voted on during the justices' closed-door conference.

For *certiorari* to be granted four justices must be convinced that the case satisfies Rule 10 of the Rules of the U.S. Supreme Court. Rule 10 states that *certiorari* is not a matter of right but is to be granted only where there are special and compelling reasons. These include conflicting decisions by two or more circuit courts; conflicts between circuit courts and state courts of last resort; conflicting decisions by two or more state courts of last resort; decisions by circuit courts on matters of federal law that should be settled by the Supreme Court; or a circuit court decision on an important question that conflicts with Supreme Court decisions. It should be clear from this list that the Court will usually take action only under the most compelling circumstances—where there are conflicts among the lower courts about what the law should be; where an important legal question has been raised in the lower courts but not definitively answered; and where a lower court deviates from the principles and precedents established by the High Court. The support of four justices is needed for *certiorari* and few cases are able to satisfy this requirement. In recent sessions, though thousands of petitions have been filed

writ of *certiorari* A decision of at least four of the nine Supreme Court justices to review a decision of a lower court; from the Latin "to make more certain."

---

[15] *Rosenberger v. University of Virginia*, 115 S. Ct. 2510 (1995).

FIGURE 8.4 Cases Filed in the U.S. Supreme Court, 1938–2005

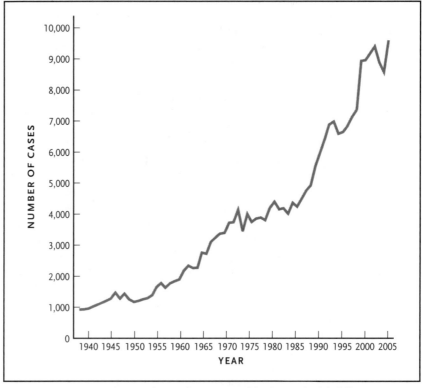

SOURCE: Years 1938–69: successive volumes of U.S. Bureau of the Census, *Statistical Abstract of the United States* (Washington, D.C.: Government Printing Office); 1970–83: Office of the Clerk of the Supreme Court; 1984–99: reprinted with permission from *The United States Law Week* (Washington, D.C.: Bureau of National Affairs), vol. 56, 3102; vol. 59, 3064; vol. 61, 3098; vol. 63, 3134; vol. 65, 3100; vol. 67, 3167; vol. 69, 3134 (copyright © Bureau of National Affairs Inc.); 2000–2002: successive volumes of U.S. Bureau of the Census, *Statistical Abstract of the United States.*

NOTE: Graph indicates the number of cases filed in the term beginning in the year indicated.

(see Figure 8.4), the Court has granted *certiorari* to hardly more than 80 petitioners each year—about 1 percent of those seeking a Supreme Court review.

A handful of cases reach the Supreme Court through avenues other than certiorari. One of these is the "writ of certification." This writ can be used when a U.S. Court of Appeals asks the Supreme Court for instructions on a point of law that has never been decided. A second avenue is the "writ of appeal," used to appeal the decision of a three-judge district court.

Controlling the Flow of Cases: The Role of the Solicitor General

solicitor general The top government lawyer in all cases before the appellate courts where the government is a party.

If any single person has greater influence than the individual justices over the work of the Supreme Court, it is the **solicitor general** of the United States. The solicitor general is third in status in the Justice Department (below the attorney general and the deputy attorney general, who serve as the government's chief prosecutors) but is the top government defense lawyer in almost all cases before the appellate courts where the government is a party. Although others can regulate the flow of cases, the solicitor general has the greatest control, with no review of his or her actions by any higher authority in the executive branch. More than half the Supreme Court's total workload consists of cases under the direct charge of the solicitor general.

The solicitor general exercises especially strong influence by screening cases long before they approach the Supreme Court; the justices rely on the solicitor general to "screen out undeserving litigation and furnish them with an agenda to government cases that deserve serious consideration."[16] Agency heads may lobby the president or otherwise try to circumvent the solicitor general, and a few of the independent agencies have a statutory right to make direct appeals, but without the solicitor general's support, these are seldom reviewed by the Court.

The solicitor general can enter a case even when the federal government is not a direct litigant by writing an **amicus curiae** ("friend of the court") brief. A "friend of the court" is not a direct party to a case but has a vital interest in its outcome. Thus, when the government has such an interest, the solicitor general can file an *amicus curiae*, or the Court can invite such a brief because it wants an opinion in writing. Other interested parties may file briefs as well.

The Supreme Court's Procedures

The Preparation   The Supreme Court's decision to accept a case is the beginning of what can be a lengthy and complex process (see Figure 8.5). First, the attorneys on both sides must prepare ***briefs***—written documents in which the attorneys explain why the Court should rule in favor of their client. The document filed by the individual bringing the case is called the petitioner's brief. This brief summarizes the facts of the case and presents the legal basis upon which the Supreme Court is being asked to overturn the lower court's decision. The document filed by the side that prevailed in the lower court is called the respondent's brief. This brief explains why the Supreme Court should affirm the lower court's verdict. The petitioners will then file a brief answering and attempting to refute the points made in the respondent's brief. This document is called the petitioner's reply brief. Briefs are filled with referrals to precedents specifically chosen to show that other courts have frequently ruled in the same way that the Supreme Court is being asked to rule.

As the attorneys prepare their briefs, they often ask sympathetic interest groups for their help. Groups are asked to file *amicus curiae* briefs that support the claims of one or the other litigant. In a case involving separation of church and state, for example, liberal groups such as the ACLU and Citizens for the American Way are likely to file *amicus* briefs in support of strict separation, whereas conservative religious groups are likely to file *amicus* briefs advocating increased public support for religious ideas. Often, dozens of briefs will be filed on each side of a major case.

amicus curiae Literally, "friend of the court"; individuals or groups who are not parties to a lawsuit but who seek to assist the court in reaching a decision by presenting additional briefs.

brief A written document in which attorneys explain why a court should rule in favor of their client.

---

[16]Robert Scigliano, *The Supreme Court and the Presidency* (New York: Free Press, 1971), p. 162. For an interesting critique of the solicitor general's role during the Reagan administration, see Lincoln Caplan, "Annals of the Law," *New Yorker,* 17 August 1987, pp. 30–62.

FIGURE 8.5 The Supreme Court's Decision-Making Process

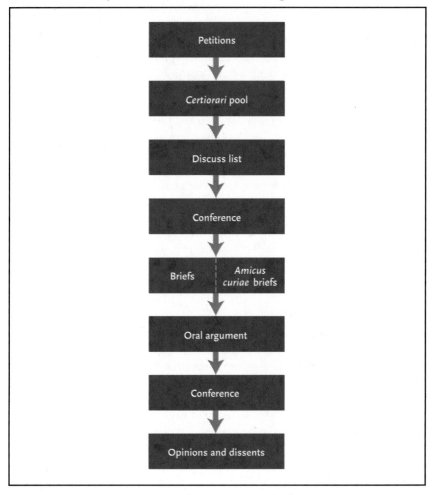

Oral Argument The next stage of a case is ***oral argument,*** in which attorneys for both sides appear before the Court to present their positions and answer the justices' questions. Each attorney has only a half hour to present his or her case, and this time includes interruptions for questions. Certain members of the Court, such as Justice Antonin Scalia, are known to interrupt attorneys dozens of times. Others, such as Justice Clarence Thomas, seldom ask questions. For an attorney, the opportunity to argue a case before the Supreme Court is a singular honor and a mark of professional distinction. It can also be a harrowing experience, as justices interrupt a carefully prepared presentation. Nevertheless, oral argument can be very important to the outcome of a case. It allows justices to better understand the heart of the case and to raise questions that might not have been addressed in the opposing side's briefs. It is not uncommon for justices to go beyond the strictly legal issues and ask opposing counsel to discuss the implications of the case for the Court and the nation at large.

oral argument Oral presentations to a court made by attorneys for both sides in a dispute.

The Conference Following oral argument, the Court discusses the case in its Wednesday or Friday conference. The chief justice presides over the conference and speaks first; the other justices follow in order of seniority. The Court's conference is secret, and no outsiders are permitted to attend. The justices discuss the case and eventually reach a decision on the basis of a majority vote. As the case is discussed, justices may try to influence or change one another's opinions. At times, this may result in compromise decisions.

Opinion Writing After a decision has been reached, one of the members of the majority is assigned to write the **opinion.** This assignment is made by the chief justice, or by the most senior justice in the majority if the chief justice is on the losing side. The assignment of the opinion can make a significant difference to the interpretation of a decision. Every opinion of the Supreme Court sets a major precedent for future cases throughout the judicial system. Lawyers and judges in the lower courts will examine the opinion carefully to ascertain the Supreme Court's meaning. Differences in wording and emphasis can have important implications for future litigation. Thus, in assigning an opinion, serious thought must be given to the impression the case will make on lawyers and on the public, as well as to the probability that one justice's opinion will be more widely accepted than another's.

One of the more dramatic instances of this tactical consideration occurred in 1944, when Chief Justice Harlan F. Stone chose Justice Felix Frankfurter to write the opinion in the "white primary" case *Smith v. Allwright.* The chief justice believed that this sensitive case, which overturned the Southern practice of prohibiting black participation in nominating primaries, required the efforts of the most brilliant and scholarly jurist on the Court. But the day after Stone made the assignment, Justice Robert H. Jackson wrote a letter to Stone urging a change of assignment. In his letter, Jackson argued that Frankfurter, a foreign-born Jew from New England, would not win the South with his opinion, regardless of its brilliance. Stone accepted the advice and substituted Justice Stanley Reed, an American-born Protestant from Kentucky and a Southern Democrat in good standing.[17]

Once the majority opinion is drafted it is circulated to the other justices. Some members of the majority may agree with both the outcome and the rationale but wish to emphasize or highlight a particular point and so will draft a concurring opinion for that purpose. In other instances, one or more justices may agree with the majority but may disagree with the rationale presented in the majority opinion. These justices may draft special concurrences, explaining their disagreements with the majority.

Dissent Justices who disagree with the majority decision of the Court may choose to publicize the character of their disagreement in the form of a **dissenting opinion.** The dissenting opinion is generally assigned by the senior justice among the dissenters. Dissents can be used to express irritation with an outcome or to signal to defeated political forces in the nation that at least some members

---

[17] *Smith v. Allwright,* 321 U.S. 649 (1944).

opinion The written explanation of the Supreme Court's decision in a particular case.

dissenting opinion Decision written by a justice in the minority in a particular case in which the justice wishes to express his or her reasoning in the case.

of the Court support their position. Ironically, the most dependable way an individual justice can exercise a direct and clear influence on the Court is to write a dissent. Because there is no need to please a majority, dissenting opinions can be more eloquent and less guarded than majority opinions. The current Supreme Court often produces five-to-four decisions, with dissenters writing long and detailed opinions that, they hope, will help them convince a swing justice to join their side on the next round of cases dealing with a similar topic. Thus, for example, Justice Souter wrote a thirty-four-page dissent in a 2002 case upholding the use of government-funded school vouchers to pay for parochial school tuition. Souter called the decision "a dramatic departure from basic Establishment Clause principle," which he hoped a "future court will reconsider."[18]

Dissent plays a special role in the work and impact of the Court because it amounts to an appeal to lawyers all over the country to keep bringing cases of the sort at issue. Therefore, an effective dissent influences the flow of cases through the Court as well as the arguments that will be used by lawyers in later cases.

Judicial Decision Making

The judiciary is conservative in its procedures, but its impact on society can be radical. That impact depends on a variety of influences, two of which stand out above the rest. The first influence is the individual members of the Supreme Court, their attitudes, and their relationships with each other. The second is the other branches of government, particularly Congress.

The Supreme Court Justices The Supreme Court explains its decisions in terms of law and precedent. But although law and precedent do have an effect on the Court's deliberations and eventual decisions, it is the Supreme Court that decides what laws actually mean and what importance precedent will actually have. Throughout its history, the Court has shaped and reshaped the law. If any individual judges in the country influence the federal judiciary, they are the Supreme Court justices.

From the 1950s to the 1980s, the Supreme Court took an activist role in such areas as civil rights, civil liberties, abortion, voting rights, and police procedures. For example, the Supreme Court was more responsible than any other governmental institution for breaking down America's system of racial segregation. The Supreme Court virtually prohibited states from interfering with the right of a woman to seek an abortion and sharply curtailed state restrictions on voting rights. And it was the Supreme Court that placed restrictions on the behavior of local police and prosecutors in criminal cases.

But since the early 1980s, resignations, deaths, and new judicial appointments have led to many shifts in the mix of philosophies and ideologies represented on the Court. In a series of decisions between 1989 and 2001, the conservative justices appointed by Ronald Reagan and George H. W. Bush were

---

[18]Warren Richey, "Dissenting Opinions as a Window on Future Rulings," *Christian Science Monitor,* 1 July 2002, p. 1.

able to swing the Court to a more conservative position on civil rights, affirmative action, abortion rights, property rights, criminal procedure, voting rights, desegregation, and the power of the national government.

However, precisely because the Court has been so evenly split in recent years, the conservative bloc has not always prevailed. Among the justices serving at the beginning of 2005, Rehnquist, Scalia, and Thomas took conservative positions on most issues and were usually joined by O'Connor and Kennedy. Breyer, Ginsburg, Souter, and Stevens were reliably liberal. This produced many 5-4 splits. On some issues, though, Justice O'Connor or Justice Kennedy tended to side with the liberal camp, producing a 5-4 and sometimes a 6-3 victory for the liberals. In the case of *McConnell v. Federal Election Commission,* for example, Justice O'Connor joined the liberal bloc to uphold the validity of the Bipartisan Campaign Reform Act.[19] The Analyzing the Evidence unit on the following page examines the trend toward more 5–4 decisions in recent years.

On abortion, women's rights, and affirmative action, O'Connor often joined the liberal justices. With the departure of O'Connor and her replacment by Alito in 2006, many anticipated a series of new 5–4 decisions favoring the conservatives.[20] In 2007, for example, the Court upheld the Partial Birth Abortion Act—a law favored by conservatives—by a 5–4 majority. However, the Court's policy influence comes not from these "horse race" results often trumpeted by the media, but rather from the written opinions providing the constitutional or statutory rationale for policy in the future; these establish the guidelines that govern how federal courts must decide similar cases in the future. The departure of Justice O'Connor moves the center of the Court (the part that proves pivotal in formulating these opinions) to Justice Anthony Kennedy, who, by many measures, is not significantly different from O'Connor in his jurisprudence. So the Court's policies will probably drift rightward, but only from O'Connor's position to Kennedy's, not as dramatic as the difference between O'Connor and Alito.[21]

Activism and Restraint   One element of judicial philosophy is the issue of activism versus restraint. Over the years, some justices have believed that courts should interpret the Constitution according to the stated intentions of its framers and defer to the views of Congress when interpreting federal statutes. The late justice Felix Frankfurter, for example, advocated judicial deference to legislative bodies and avoidance of the "political thicket," in which the Court would entangle itself by deciding questions that were essentially political rather than legal in character. Advocates of *judicial restraint* are sometimes called "strict constructionists," because they look strictly to the words of the Constitution in interpreting its meaning.

The alternative to restraint is *judicial activism.* Activist judges such as the former Chief Justice Earl Warren believed that the Court should go beyond the words of the Constitution or a statute to consider the broader societal implications of its

judicial restraint Judicial deference to the views of legislatures and adherence to strict jurisdictional standards.

judicial activism Proclivity of a court to select cases because of their importance to society rather than adhere to strict legal standards of jurisdiction.

---

[19]02-1674 (2003).

[20]Adam Liptak, "Entrances and Exits: The New 5-to-4 Supreme Court," *New York Times,* 22 April 2007.

[21]For a development of this argument, see David W. Rohde and Kenneth A. Shepsle, "Advising and Consenting in the 60-Vote Senate," *Journal of Politics,* 69, no. 3 (August 2007): 664–77.

Consensus on the U.S. Supreme Court

For much of the nineteenth century and through the early part of the twentieth century, the Supreme Court publicly operated under what many considered to be a "norm of consensus." Justices believed that unanimity in decision making would serve to strengthen the authority of the Court and its rulings, even if disagreements persisted in private.[1] Over time, however, this behavioral norm appears to have declined among the justices serving on the Court.

▶

The proportion of unanimous decisions handed down by the Court declined sharply between 1930 and 1950, dropping from 90 percent of the cases heard to less than 20 percent. While a number of changes occurred within the judiciary during this period, no definitive explanation exists to account for this trend. Since the 1950s, there has been a modest increase in the proportion of unanimous decisions, but not to anywhere near the level that was common prior to the 1930s.

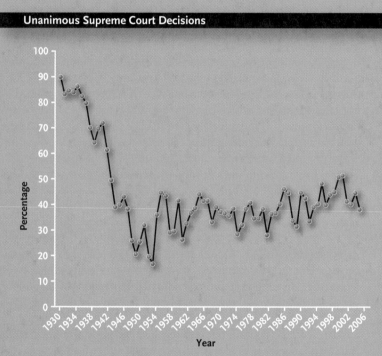

Unanimous Supreme Court Decisions

Source: Lee Epstein, Jeffrey A. Segal, Harold J. Spaeth, and Thomas G. Walker. 2003. *The Supreme Court Compendium: Data Decisions, and Developments.* 3rd edition. (Washington, DC: CQ Press, 2003).

[1]On these points, see Lee Epstein, Jeffrey A. Segal, and Harold J. Spaeth. 2001. "The Norm of Consensus on the U.S. Supreme Court." *American Journal of Political Science* 45 (April): 362–377.

As Alexander Hamilton observed in *Federalist* 78, the federal judiciary was designed to be the weakest of the three branches of government. Given that the Supreme Court is reliant upon the other branches of government to enforce its decisions, it is much easier to defend a unanimous Court decision than one that reveals a sharp divide among the justices.

Federalist 78

The judiciary...has no influence over either the sword or the purse; no direction either of the strength or of the wealth of the society; and can take no active resolution whatever. It may truly be said to have neither FORCE nor WILL, but merely judgment; and must ultimately depend upon the aid of the executive arm even for the efficacy of its judgments.[2]

Cases Decided by a One-Vote Margin

Percentage (y-axis: 0, 10, 20, 30, 40, 50)

Year (x-axis: 1930, 1934, 1938, 1942, 1946, 1950, 1954, 1958, 1962, 1966, 1970, 1974, 1978, 1982, 1986, 1990, 1994, 1998, 2002, 2006)

Source: Lee Epstein, Jeffrey A. Segal, Harold J. Spaeth, and Thomas G. Walker. *The Supreme Court Compendium: Data Decisions, and Developments*. 3rd edition. (Washington, DC: CQ Press, 2003).

What are the implications of the precipitous decline in unanimous decisions after 1930? Unanimously decided cases are less likely to be interpreted differently by lower court judges who consider these decisions to be established precedents, whereas decisions supported by a bare majority of justices may not be followed as strictly. Indeed, the proportion of Supreme Court cases decided by a one-vote margin has been steadily increasing since 1930.

[2]Alexander Hamilton, *Federalist* No. 78, in *The Federalist Papers*, edited by Clinton Rossiter. (New York, Penguin: 1961).

decisions. Activist judges sometimes strike out in new directions, promulgating new interpretations or inventing new legal and constitutional concepts when they believe these to be socially desirable. For example, Justice Harry Blackmun's opinion in *Roe v. Wade* was based on a constitutional right to privacy that is not found in the words of the Constitution. Blackmun and the other members of the majority in the *Roe* case argued that other constitutional provisions implied the right to privacy. In this instance of judicial activism, the Court knew the result it wanted to achieve and was not afraid to make the law conform to the desired outcome.

Political Ideology   The second component of judicial philosophy is political ideology. The liberal or conservative attitudes of justices play an important role in their decisions.[22] Indeed, the philosophy of activism versus restraint is, to a large extent, a smokescreen for political ideology. In the past, liberal judges have often been activists, willing to use the law to achieve social and political change, whereas conservatives have been associated with judicial restraint. Interestingly, however, in recent years some conservative justices who have long called for restraint have actually become activists in seeking to undo some of the work of liberal jurists over the past three decades.

Other Institutions of Government

Congress   At both the national and state level in the United States, courts and judges are "players" in the policy game because of the separation of powers. Essentially, this means that the legislative branch formulates policy (defined constitutionally and institutionally by a legislative process); that the executive branch implements policy (according to well-defined administrative procedures, and subject to initial approval by the president or the legislative override of his veto); and that the courts, when asked, rule on the faithfulness of the legislated and executed policy either to the substance of the statute or to the Constitution itself. The courts, that is, may strike down an administrative action either because it exceeds the authority granted in the relevant statute (statutory rationale) or because the statute itself exceeds the authority granted the legislature by the Constitution (constitutional rationale).

If the court declares the administrative agent's act as outside the permissible bounds prescribed by the legislation, we suppose the court's majority opinion can declare whatever policy it wishes. If the legislature is unhappy with this judicial action, then it may either recraft the legislation (if the rationale for striking it down were statutory)[23] or initiate a constitutional amendment that would enable the stricken-down policy to pass constitutional muster (if the rationale for originally striking it down were constitutional).

In reaching their decisions, Supreme Court justices must anticipate Congress's response. As a result, judges will not always vote according to their true preferences because doing so may provoke Congress to enact legislation that

---

[22]C. Herman Pritchett, *The Roosevelt Court* (New York: Macmillan, 1948).

[23]William N. Eskridge, Jr., "Overriding Supreme Court Statutory Interpretation Decisions," *Yale Law Journal* 101 (1991): 331–55.

moves the policy further away from what the judges prefer. By voting for a lesser preference, the justices can get something they prefer to the status quo without provoking congressional action to overturn their decision. The most famous example of this phenomenon is the "switch in time that saved nine," when several justices voted in favor of New Deal legislation, the constitutionality of which they doubted, in order to diminish congressional support for President Roosevelt's plan to "pack" the Court by increasing the number of justices. In short, the interactions between the Court and Congress are part of a complex strategic "game."[24]

The President   The president's most direct influence on the Court is the power to nominate justices. Presidents typically nominate judges who they believe are close to their policy preferences and close enough to the preferences of a majority of senators, who must confirm the nomination.

Yet the efforts by presidents to reshape the federal judiciary are not always successful. Often in American history, judges have surprised and disappointed the presidents who named them to the bench. Justice Souter, for example, has been far less conservative than President George H. W. Bush and the Republicans who supported Souter's appointment in 1990 thought he would be. Likewise, Justices O'Connor and Kennedy have disappointed conservatives by opposing limitations on abortion.

JUDICIAL POWER AND POLITICS

One of the most important institutional changes to occur in the United States during the past half-century has been the striking transformation of the role and power of the federal courts, those of the Supreme Court in particular. Understanding how this transformation came about is the key to understanding the contemporary role of the courts in America.

Traditional Limitations on the Federal Courts

For much of American history, the power of the federal courts was subject to five limitations.[25] First, courts were constrained by judicial rules of standing that limited access to the bench. Claimants who simply disagreed with governmental action or inaction could not obtain access. Access to the courts was limited to individuals who could show that they were directly affected by the government's behavior in some area. This limitation on access to the courts diminished the judiciary's capacity to forge links with important political and social forces. Second, courts were traditionally limited in the kind of relief they could provide. In general, courts acted

---

[24]A fully strategic analysis of the maneuvering among legislative, executive, and judicial branches in the separation-of-powers arrangement choreographed by the U.S. Constitution may be found in William Eskridge and John Ferejohn, "The Article I, Section 7 Game," *Georgetown Law Review* 80 (1992):523–65. The entire issue of this journal is devoted to the theme of strategic behavior in American institutional politics.

[25]For limits on judicial power, see Alexander Bickel, *The Least Dangerous Branch* (Indianapolis: Bobbs-Merrill, 1962).

ONLINE READING

only to offer relief to individuals and not to broad social classes, again inhibiting the formation of alliances between the courts and important social forces. Third, courts lacked enforcement powers and were compelled to rely on executive or state agencies to ensure compliance. If the executive or state agencies were unwilling to assist the courts, judicial enactments could go unheeded.

Fourth, federal judges are appointed by the president (with the consent of the Senate). As a result, the president and Congress can shape the composition of the federal courts and ultimately, perhaps, the character of judicial decisions. Finally, Congress has the power to change both the size and the jurisdiction of the Supreme Court and other federal courts. In many areas, federal courts obtain their jurisdiction not from the Constitution but from the congressional statutes. On a number of occasions, Congress has threatened to take matters out of the Court's hands when it was unhappy with the Court's rulings on certain cases.[26]

As a result of these five limitations on judicial power, through much of their history, the chief function of the federal courts has been to provide judicial support for executive agencies and to legitimate acts of Congress by declaring them to be consistent with constitutional principles. Only on rare occasions did the federal courts actually dare to challenge Congress or the executive.[27]

Two Judicial Revolutions

Since the Second World War, however, the role of the federal judiciary has been strengthened and expanded through two judicial revolutions in the United States. The first and most visible of these was the substantive revolution in judicial policy. In policy areas, including school desegregation, legislative apportionment, and criminal procedure, as well as obscenity, abortion, and voting rights, the Supreme Court was at the forefront of a series of sweeping changes in the role of the U.S. government and, ultimately, in the character of American society.[28]

At the same time that the courts were introducing important policy innovations, they were also bringing about a second, less visible revolution. During the 1960s and 1970s, the Supreme Court and other federal courts instituted a series of institutional changes in judicial procedure that had major consequences by fundamentally expanding the power of the courts in the United States. First, the federal courts liberalized the concept of standing to permit almost any group to bring its case before the federal bench. This change has given the courts a far greater role in the administrative process than ever before. Many federal judges are concerned that federal legislation in areas such as health care reform would create new rights and entitlements that would give rise to a deluge of court cases. "Any time you create a new right, you create a host of disputes and claims," warned Barbara Rothstein, chief judge of the federal district court in Seattle, Washington.[29]

---

[26]See Walter Murphy, *Congress and the Court* (Chicago: University of Chicago Press, 1962).

[27]Robert Dahl, "The Supreme Court and National Policy Making," *Journal of Public Law* 6 (1958), p. 279.

[28]Martin Shapiro, "The Supreme Court: From Warren to Burger," in *The New American Political System*, ed. Anthony King (Washington, D.C.: American Enterprise Institute, 1978).

[29]Toni Locy, "Bracing for Health Care's Caseload," *Washington Post*, 22 August 1994, p. A15.

In a second institutional change, the federal courts broadened the scope of relief to permit action on behalf of broad categories or classes of persons in "class action" cases, rather than just on behalf of individuals.[30] A *class action suit* permits large numbers of persons with common interests to join together under a representative party to bring or defend a lawsuit.

In the third major judicial change, the federal courts began to employ so-called structural remedies, in effect retaining jurisdiction of cases until the court's mandate had actually been implemented to its satisfaction.[31] The best known of these instances was Federal Judge W. Arthur Garrity's effort to operate the Boston school system from his bench in order to ensure its desegregation. Between 1974 and 1985, Judge Garrity issued fourteen decisions relating to different aspects of the Boston school desegregation plan that had been developed under his authority and put into effect under his supervision.[32]

Through these three judicial mechanisms, the federal courts paved the way for an unprecedented expansion of national judicial power. In essence, liberalization of the rules of standing and expansion of the scope of judicial relief drew the federal courts into linkages with important social interests and classes, while the introduction of structural remedies enhanced the courts' abilities to serve these constituencies. Thus, during the 1960s and 1970s, the power of the federal courts expanded in the same way that the power of the executive expanded during the 1930s—through links with constituencies, such as civil rights, consumer, environmental, and feminist groups, that staunchly defended the Supreme Court in its battles with Congress, the executive, or other interest groups.

During the 1980s and early 1990s, the Reagan and first Bush administrations sought to end the relationship between the Court and liberal political forces. The conservative judges appointed by these Republican presidents modified the Court's position in areas such as abortion, affirmative action, and judicial procedure—though not as completely as some conservatives had hoped. In June 2003, for example, the Court handed down a series of decisions that pleased many liberals and outraged conservative advocacy groups. Within a period of one week, the Supreme Court affirmed the validity of affirmative action, reaffirmed abortion rights, strengthened gay rights, offered new protection to individuals facing the death penalty, and issued a ruling in favor of a congressional apportionment plan that dispersed minority voters across several districts—a practice that appeared to favor the Democrats.[33] Interestingly, however, the Court has not been eager to surrender the expanded powers carved out by its liberal predecessors. In a number of decisions during the 1980s and 1990s, the

class action suit A lawsuit in which large numbers of persons with common interests join together under a representative party to bring or defend a lawsuit, such as hundreds of workers together suing a company.

---

[30]See "Developments in the Law—Class Actions," *Harvard Law Review* 89 (1976), p. 1318.

[31]See Donald Horowitz, *The Courts and Social Policy* (Washington, D.C.: Brookings Institution, 1977).

[32]*Moran v. McDonough*, 540 F. 2nd 527 (1 Cir., 1976; *cert denied* 429 U.S. 1042 [1977]).

[33]David Van Drehle, "Court That Liberals Savage Proves to Be Less of a Target," *Washington Post*, 29 June 2003, p. A18.

Court was willing to make use of its expanded powers on behalf of interests it favored.[34] As we saw at the start of this chapter, the role and power of the federal courts, particularly the Supreme Court, was especially evident after the 2000 presidential election.

There can be little doubt that the contemporary Supreme Court exercises considerably more power than the framers of the Constitution intended. In the original conception of the framers, the judiciary was to be the institution that would protect individual liberty from the government. As we saw in Chapter 2, the framers believed that in a democracy, the great danger was what they termed "tyranny of the majority"—the possibility that a popular majority, "united or actuated by some common impulse or passion," would "trample on the rules of justice."[35] The framers hoped that the courts would protect liberty from the potential excesses of democracy. And for most of American history, this was precisely the role played by the federal courts. The courts' most important decisions were those that protected the freedoms—to speak, worship, publish, vote, and attend school— of groups and individuals whose political views, religious beliefs, or racial or ethnic backgrounds made them unpopular.

In recent years, however, the courts have been changing their role in the political process. Rather than serving simply as a bastion of individual liberty against the excessive power of the majority, the judiciary has tried to play an active role in helping groups and forces in American society bring about social and political change. In a sense, the judiciary has entered the political process and has begun to behave more like the democratic institutions whose sometimes misdirected impulses toward tyranny the courts were supposed to keep in check.

CHAPTER REVIEW

Millions of cases come to trial every year in the United States. The great majority— nearly 99 percent—are tried in state and local courts. The types of law are civil law, criminal law, and public law. Cases are heard at the state level before three types of courts: trial court, appellate court, and (state) supreme court.

There are three kinds of federal cases: (1) civil cases involving diversity of citizenship, (2) civil cases where a federal agency is seeking to enforce federal laws that provide for civil penalties, and (3) cases involving federal criminal statutes or where state criminal cases have been made issues of public law.

Each district court is in one of the twelve appellate districts, called circuits, presided over by a court of appeals. Appellate courts admit no new evidence; their rulings are based solely on the records of the court proceedings or agency hearings that led to the original decision. Appeals court rulings are final unless the Supreme Court chooses to review them.

---

[34]Mark Silverstein and Benjamin Ginsberg, "The Supreme Court and the New Politics of Judicial Power," *Political Science Quarterly* 102 (Fall 1987), pp. 371–88.

[35]Clinton Rossiter, ed., *The Federalist Papers* (New York: New American Library, 1961), No. 10, p. 78.

The Supreme Court has some original jurisdiction, but its major job is to review lower court decisions involving substantial issues of public law. Congress and the state legislatures can reverse Supreme Court decisions, but seldom do. There is no explicit constitutional authority for the Supreme Court to review acts of Congress. Nonetheless, the 1803 case of *Marbury v. Madison* established the Court's right to review congressional acts. The supremacy clause of Article VI and the Judiciary Act of 1789 give the Court the power to review state constitutions and laws.

Cases reach the Court mainly through the writ of *certiorari*. The Supreme Court controls its case load by issuing few writs and by handing down clear leading opinions that enable lower courts to resolve future cases without further review.

Judge-made law is like a statute in that it articulates the law as it relates to future controversies. It differs from a statute in that it is intended to guide judges rather than the citizenry in general.

The judiciary as a whole is subject to two major influences: (1) the individual members of the Supreme Court, who have lifetime tenure; and (2) the Justice Department—particularly the solicitor general, who regulates the flow of cases.

The influence of an individual member of the Supreme Court is limited when the Court is polarized, and close votes in a polarized Court impair the value of the decision rendered. Writing the majority opinion for a case gives a justice an opportunity to influence the judiciary. But the need to frame an opinion in such a way as to develop majority support on the Court may limit such opportunities. Dissenting opinions can have more impact than the majority opinion; they stimulate a continued flow of cases around that issue. The solicitor general is the most important single influence outside the Court itself because he or she controls the flow of cases brought by the Justice Department and also shapes the argument in those cases.

In recent years, the importance of the federal judiciary—the Supreme Court in particular—has increased substantially as the courts have developed new tools of judicial power and forged alliances with important forces in American society.

FOR FURTHER READING

Abraham, Henry J. *The Judicial Process: An Introductory Analysis of the Courts of the United States, England, and France.* 7th ed. New York: Oxford University Press, 1998.

Baum, Lawrence. *Judges and Their Audiences: A Perspective on Judicial Behavior.* Princeton, N. J.: Princeton University Press, 2006. ○ ONLINE READING

Bickel, Alexander M. *The Least Dangerous Branch: The Supreme Court at the Bar of Politics.* Indianapolis: Bobbs-Merrill, 1962. ○ ONLINE READING

Epstein, Lee, and Jack Knight. *The Choices Justices Make.* Washington, D.C.: Congressional Quarterly Press, 1998.

Kahn, Ronald. *The Supreme Court and Constitutional Theory, 1953–1993.* Lawrence: University Press of Kansas, 1994.

O'Brien, David M. *Storm Center: The Supreme Court in American Politics.* 8th ed. New York: Norton, 2008.

Perry, H. W., Jr. *Deciding to Decide: Agenda Setting in the United States Supreme Court.* Cambridge, Mass.: Harvard University Press, 1991. ○ ONLINE READING

Segal, Jeffrey A., and Harold J. Spaeth. *The Supreme Court and the Attitudinal Model Revisited.* New York: Cambridge University Press, 2002.

Silverstein, Mark. *Judicious Choices: The New Politics of Supreme Court Confirmations.* 2nd ed. New York: Norton, 2007.

Tribe, Laurence H. *Constitutional Choices.* Cambridge, Mass.: Harvard University Press, 1985.

Public Opinion and the Media

In March 2003, American and British military forces invaded Iraq with the express intent of disarming Iraq's military and driving Iraqi President Saddam Hussein from power. The invasion followed months of diplomatic wrangling and an ultimately unsuccessful effort by President George W. Bush and British Prime Minister Tony Blair to win United Nations support for military action against Iraq. In the months prior to the war, many Americans were dubious about the need to attack Iraq. For example, according to a CBS News poll taken during the first week in March 2003, only 50 percent of those responding thought removing Suddam Hussein from power was worth the potential costs of war, while 43 percent thought it was not worth it. The same poll reported that only 55 percent of Americans approved of the way President Bush was handling the situation with Iraq. Once the American and British invasion of Iraq began, however, popular support for U.S. military action rose by 24 points to 77 percent.

Many commentators attributed support for the war to a rally-round-the-flag effect that is commonly seen when a president leads Americans into battle. Pundits predicted that support for the war and the president would drop if fighting turned out to be prolonged or inconclusive. And the pundits were right. A week after the 2006 midterm elections, a CNN poll reported that only 33 percent of those surveyed approved of U.S. policy in Iraq, and 63 percent were opposed to it. In a CBS poll at

● Core of the Analysis

● Opinions are shaped by individuals' characteristics but also by institutional, political, and governmental forces.

● Among the most important influences shaping public opinion are the media. The media have tremendous power to shape the public agenda and our images of politicians and policies.

● In general, the government's actions are consistent with public preferences.

FIGURE 9.1 President Bush's Falling Approval Rating

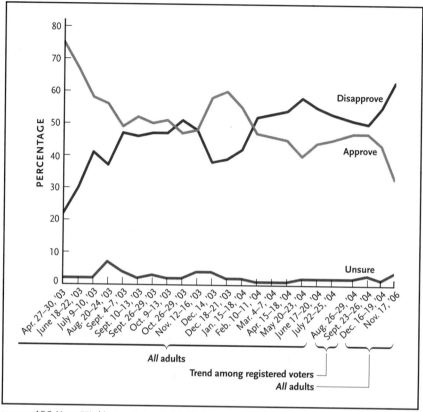

SOURCE: ABC News/*Washington Post* poll, 16–19 December 2004 (www.pollingreport.com), CNN poll 17 November 2006.

NOTE: *N* = 1,004 adults nationwide. Margin of error is ±3.

about the same time, only 34 percent approved of President Bush's job performance, and 61 percent disapproved of it (Figure 9.1).

It also quickly became apparent that support for the president and his war policy varied considerably according to demographic and political factors. Men were more supportive than women of the president's policies, indicating a continuation of the gender gap that has been a persistent feature of American public opinion. Race was also a factor, with African Americans much more critical than whites of President Bush and his goals. In addition, partisanship was important. Republicans were nearly unanimous in their approval of President Bush's policies, while Democrats were more closely divided on the wisdom of going to war. Partisan politics, it seems, did not stop at the water's edge.

Even as popular support for his policies eroded, President Bush remained steadfast. The president won reelection in 2004 despite doubts about his handling of the Iraq situation, and he was determined to bring about the creation of a pro-

American regime in that nation. The president attempted to halt the downward trend of popular approval for his policies by hinting that American forces might be reduced after the 2005 Iraqi elections and by continuously restating the need to promote democracy in the Middle East. At the same time, though, President Bush made it clear that his policies would not respond to shifts in popular opinion. The president reminded Americans that he planned to do his duty as he saw it, regardless of the vicissitudes of public sentiment. Even after a stinging rebuke in the 2006 midterm congressional elections, President Bush insisted on "staying the course" in Iraq, though support for that policy even among politicians had begun to waver.

These events underline many of the issues raised in this chapter. Do Americans know enough to form meaningful opinions about important policy issues? What factors account for differences in opinion? To what extent can the government manipulate popular sentiment? To what extent do—or should—the government's policies respond to public opinion?

Public opinion is the term used to denote the values and attitudes that people have about issues, events, and personalities. Although the terms are sometimes used interchangeably, it is useful to distinguish between values and beliefs on the one hand, and attitudes or opinions on the other. ***Values*** (or ***beliefs***) are a person's basic orientations to politics. Values represent deep-rooted goals, aspirations, and ideals that shape an individual's perceptions of political issues and events. Liberty, equality, and democracy are basic political values that most Americans hold.

Another useful term for understanding public opinion is *ideology*. ***Political ideology*** refers to a complex and interrelated set of beliefs and values that, as a whole, form a general philosophy about government. As we shall see, liberalism and conservatism are important ideologies in America today. For example, many Americans believe that governmental solutions to problems are inherently inferior to solutions offered by the private sector. This general belief, in turn, may lead individuals to have negative views about specific government programs even before they know much about them. An ***attitude*** (or ***opinion***) is a specific view about a particular issue, personality, or event. An individual may have an opinion about George W. Bush or an attitude toward American policy in Iraq. The attitude or opinion may have emerged from a broad belief about Republicans or military interventions, but an attitude itself is very specific. Some attitudes may be short-lived.

One reason that public policy and public opinion may not always coincide is that our government is a representative one, not a direct democracy. The framers of the Constitution thought that our nation would be best served by a system of government that allowed elected representatives of the people an opportunity to reflect and consider their decisions rather than bow immediately to shifts in popular sentiment. A century after the Founding, however, the Populist movement averred that government was too far removed from the people and introduced procedures for direct popular legislation through the initiative and referendum. A number of states allow policy issues to be placed on the ballot, where they are resolved by a popular vote. Some modern-day populists believe that initiative and referendum processes should be adopted at the national level as well. Whether this would lead to greater responsiveness, however, is an open question to which we shall return.

public opinion Citizens' attitudes about political issues, personalities, institutions, and events.

values (or beliefs) Basic principles that shape a person's opinions about political issues and events.

political ideology A cohesive set of beliefs that form a general philosophy about the role of government.

attitude (or opinion) A specific preference on a particular issue.

In this chapter, we will examine the role of public opinion in American politics. First, we will examine the political values and beliefs that help Americans form their perceptions of the political process. After reviewing basic American political values, we will analyze how values and beliefs are formed and how certain processes and institutions influence their formation. We conclude this section by considering the ways in which values and beliefs can cumulate to comprise political ideologies. Second, we will see how general values and beliefs help to shape more specific attitudes and opinions. In this discussion we will consider the role of political knowledge and the influence of political leaders, private groups, and the media. We will see why there appear to be so many differences of opinion among Americans. Third, we will assess the science of gathering and measuring public opinion. Finally, we will assess the impact of public opinion on the government and its policies. Is the U.S. government responsive to public opinion? Should it be?

WHAT ARE THE ORIGINS OF PUBLIC OPINION?

Opinions are products of individuals' personalities, social characteristics, and interests. But opinions are also shaped by institutional, political, and governmental forces that make it more likely that citizens will hold some beliefs and less likely that they will hold others.

Common Fundamental Values   Today most Americans share a common set of political beliefs. First, Americans generally believe in *equality of opportunity*. That is, they assume that all individuals should be allowed to seek personal and material success. Moreover, Americans generally believe that such success should be linked to personal effort and ability rather than family, "connections," or other forms of special privilege. Second, Americans strongly believe in individual freedom. They typically support the notion that governmental interference with individuals' lives and property should be kept to the minimum consistent with the general welfare (although in recent years Americans have grown accustomed to greater levels of governmental intervention than would have been deemed appropriate by the founders of liberal theory). Third, most Americans believe in democracy. They presume that every person should have the opportunity to take part in the nation's governmental and policy-making processes and to have some "say" in determining how they are governed (see Figure 9.2).[1]

Agreement on fundamental political values, though certainly not absolute, is probably more widespread in the United States than anywhere else in the Western world. During the course of Western political history, competing economic, social, and political groups put forward a variety of radically divergent views, opinions, and political philosophies. America was never socially or economically homogeneous. But two forces that were extremely powerful and important sources of ideas and beliefs elsewhere in the world were relatively weak or absent in the United States.

equality of opportunity A universally shared American ideal that all people should have the freedom to use whatever talents and wealth they have to reach their fullest potential.

[1]For a discussion of the political beliefs of Americans, see Everett Carll Ladd, *The American Ideology* (Storrs, Conn.: Roper Center, 1994).

FIGURE 9.2 Americans' Support for Fundamental Values

| EQUALITY OF OPPORTUNITY | LIBERTY | DEMOCRACY |

89%
agree

70%
disagree

69%
agree

Homosexuals should have equal rights in terms of job opportunities

The First Amendment goes too far.

Any group should be allowed to hold a rally for a cause.

SOURCES: Gallup Poll, 2001, 2007; Roper Poll, 2002; and New England Survey Research Associates, 2007.

First, the United States never had the feudal aristocracy like the one that dominated so much of European history. Second, for reasons including America's prosperity and the early availability of political rights, no socialist movements comparable to those that developed in nineteenth-century Europe were ever able to establish themselves in the United States. As a result, during the course of American history, there existed neither an aristocracy to assert the virtues of inequality, special privilege, and a rigid class structure, nor a powerful American communist or socialist party to challenge the desirability of limited government and individualism.[2]

Obviously, the principles that Americans espouse have not always been put into practice. For two hundred years, Americans were able to believe in the principles of equality of opportunity and individual liberty while denying them in practice to generations of African Americans. Yet it is important to note that the strength of the principles ultimately helped to overcome practices that deviated from those principles. Proponents of slavery and, later, of segregation were defeated in the arena of public opinion because their practices differed so sharply from the fundamental principles accepted by most Americans. Ironically, in contemporary politics, Americans' fundamental commitment to equality of opportunity has led to divisions over racial policy. In particular, both proponents and opponents of affirmative action programs cite their belief in equality of opportunity as the justification for their

---

[2]See Louis Hartz, *The Liberal Tradition in America* (New York: Harcourt, Brace, 1955).

position. Proponents see these programs as necessary to ensure equality of opportunity, while opponents believe that affirmative action is a form of preferential treatment that violates basic American values.[3]

Political Socialization

The attitudes that individuals hold about political issues and personalities tend to be shaped by their underlying political beliefs and values. For example, someone who has basically negative feelings about government intervention into America's economy and society would probably be predisposed to oppose the development of new health care and social programs. Similarly, someone who distrusts the military would likely be suspicious of any call for the use of American troops. The processes through which these underlying political beliefs and values are formed are collectively called *political socialization.*

The process of political socialization is important. Probably no nation, and certainly no democracy, could survive if its citizens did not share some fundamental beliefs. If Americans had few common values or perspectives, it would be very difficult for them to reach agreement on particular issues. In contemporary America, some elements of the socialization process tend to produce differences in outlook, whereas others promote similarities. Four of the most important *agencies of socialization* that foster differences in political perspectives are the family, membership in social groups, education, and prevailing political conditions.

Although these factors cannot fully explain the development of any given individual's political outlook, let us look at some of the most important ways in which they tend to influence most people.

The Family   Most people acquire their initial orientation to politics from their families. As might be expected, differences in family background tend to produce divergent political outlooks. Although relatively few parents spend much time teaching their children about politics, political conversations occur in many households and children tend to absorb the political views of parents and other caregivers, perhaps without realizing it. Studies have suggested, for example, that party preferences are initially acquired at home. Children raised in households in which the primary caregivers are Democrats tend to become Democrats themselves, whereas children raised in homes where their caregivers are Republicans tend to favor the GOP (Grand Old Party, a traditional nickname for the Republican Party).[4] Similarly, children reared in politically liberal households are more likely than not to develop a liberal outlook, whereas children raised in politically conservative settings are prone to see the world through conservative lenses. Obviously, not all children absorb their parents' political views. Two of conservative Republican President Ronald Reagan's three children, for instance, rejected their parents' conservative values. Moreover, even those children whose views are initially shaped by parental values may change their minds as they

political socialization
The induction of individuals into the political culture; learning the underlying beliefs and values upon which the political system is based.

agencies of socialization Social institutions, including families and schools, that help to shape individuals' basic political beliefs and values.

---

[3]Paul M. Sniderman and Edward G. Carmines, *Reaching beyond Race* (Cambridge, Mass.: Harvard University Press, 1997).

[4]See Angus Campbell, Philip E. Converse, Warren E. Miller, and Donald E. Stokes, *The American Voter* (New York: Wiley, 1960), p. 147.

mature and experience political life for themselves. Nevertheless, the family is an important initial source of political orientation for everyone.

Social Groups   Another important source of divergent political orientations and values are the social groups to which individuals belong. Social groups include those to which individuals belong involuntarily—gender and racial groups, for example—as well as those to which people belong voluntarily—such as political parties, labor unions, and educational and occupational groups. Some social groups have both voluntary and involuntary attributes. For example, individuals are born with a particular social-class background, but as a result of their own efforts people may move up—or down—the class structure.

Membership in social groups can affect political values in a variety of ways. Membership in a particular group can give individuals important experiences and perspectives that shape their view of political and social life. In American society, for example, the experiences of blacks and whites can differ significantly. Blacks are a minority and have been victims of persecution and discrimination throughout American history. Blacks and whites also have different educational and occupational opportunities, often live in separate communities, and many attend separate schools. Such differences tend to produce distinctive political outlooks. For example, in 1995 blacks and whites had very different reactions to the murder trial of former football star O. J. Simpson, who was accused of killing his ex-wife and one of her friends. Seventy percent of the white Americans surveyed believed that Simpson was guilty, based on the evidence presented by the police and prosecutors. But an identical 70 percent of the black Americans surveyed immediately after the trial believed that the police had fabricated evidence and had sought to convict Simpson of a crime he had not committed; these beliefs were presumably based on blacks' experiences with and perceptions of the criminal justice system.[5]

According to other recent surveys, blacks and whites in the United States differ on a number of issues. For example, in surveys conducted by the Pew Research Center, clear majorities of whites supported the ideas that government should do more to guarantee food and shelter (62 percent in a 2003 survey) and generally help the needy (55 percent in a 2005 survey). Much larger majorities of blacks expressed support for the guarantee of food and shelter (80 percent) and the provision of help for the needy (72 percent).[6] Other issues show a similar pattern of disagreement, reflecting the differences in experience, background, and interests between blacks and whites in America (Figure 9.3).

Of course, disagreements between blacks and whites are not the only important racial or ethnic differences to be found in contemporary America. Latinos are another major American subgroup with distinctive opinions on some public issues. For example, 54 percent of Latinos surveyed in 2004 by the Pew Hispanic Center viewed education as the most important issue facing America. In the general population, however, only 5 percent of those surveyed attached such importance to education.

---

[5]Richard Morin, "Poll Reflects Division over Simpson Case," *Washington Post*, 8 October 1995, p. A31.

[6]Pew Research Center for the People and the Press, "The Black and White of Public Opinion," 31 October 2005 (people-press.org/commentary).

FIGURE 9.3 Disagreement among Blacks and Whites

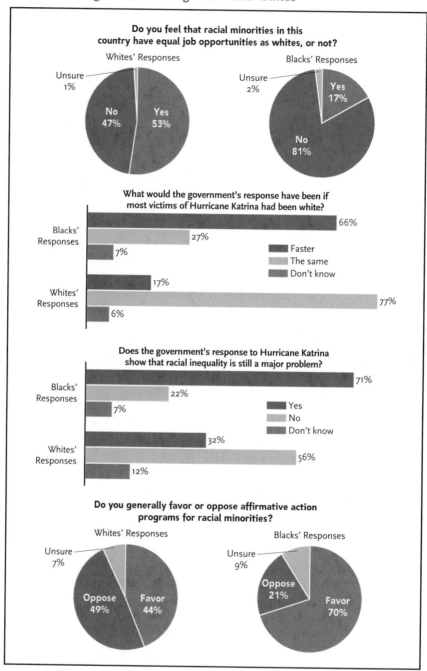

SOURCE: Gallup polls, 8–25 June 2006 and 12–15 June 2003 (www.pollingreport.com); Pew Research Center for the People and the Press, "The Black and White of Public Opinion," 31 October 2005 (people-press.org/commentary).

TABLE 9.1 Should Same-Sex Marriage Be Legalized?

Religious Group	In Favor (%)	Opposed (%)
White evangelical Protestant	14	78
White nonevangelical Protestant	42	47
White non-Hispanic Catholic	33	58
Black Protestant	19	74
Secular	63	27

SOURCE: Pew Research Center for the People and the Press, "Pragmatic Americans Liberal and Conservative on Social Issues: Most Want Middle Ground on Abortion," 3 August 2006 (people-press.org/reports).

Often immigrants or the children of immigrants, Hispanics view education as the ticket to a better life in America and attach great value to educational opportunity. As a population currently moving to the United States, Latinos also have a distinctive view of immigration. A 2004 Pew Hispanic Center survey found that more than 60 percent of Latinos believe that immigration is good for America. Among non-Latinos, though, more than 60 percent believe that immigration poses a major threat to the country. The Latino community is itself divided into subgroups based on national origin. Latinos of Mexican, Puerto Rican, Cuban, and Central American descent have distinctive opinions and even partisan loyalties. Cuban Americans, for example, tend to be Republican and conservative, whereas Puerto Rican Americans are more likely to be liberal and Democratic. These differences, in turn, are related to each group's level of education, economic status, and history. Cubans tend to be wealthier and better educated than other Latinos and have traditionally viewed the Republican party as a foe of the Communist regime that forced them (or their parents or grandparents) to flee Cuba. Puerto Ricans, by contrast, tend to be poorer and to depend more on the social services championed by the Democratic party.

Religion has become another important source of variation in opinion. In recent years, contending political forces have placed a number of religious and moral issues on the national political agenda. The Republican party, in particular, has emphasized its support for traditional "family values" and its opposition to abortion, same-sex marriage, and other practices opposed by conservative religious leaders. It is not surprising that public opinion on these issues differs along religious lines, with evangelical Protestants being most supportive of traditional values and respondents identifying themselves as "secular" manifesting the least support for them. Take the issue of same-sex marriage, for example (Table 9.1).

Men and women have important differences of opinion as well. Reflecting differences in social roles, political experience, and occupational patterns, women tend to be less militaristic than men on issues of war and peace, more likely than men to favor measures to protect the environment, and more supportive than men of government social and health-care programs (Table 9.2). Perhaps because of these

TABLE 9.2 Disagreements among Men and Women on Issues of War and Peace

	Approve of Action (%)	
Government Action	**Men**	**Women**
Continued troop commitment in Iraq (2005)	57	48
Brokering a cease-fire in Yugoslavia instead of using NATO air strikes (1999)	44	51
Ending the ban on homosexuals in the military (1993)	34	51
Engaging in a military operation against a Somali warlord (1993)	72	60
Going to war against Iraq (1991)	72	53

SOURCE: Gallup polls, 1991, 1993, and 1999; *Washington Post*, 2003; Pew Research Center, 2005.

differences on issues, women are more likely than men to vote for Democratic candidates, while men have become increasingly supportive of the GOP.[7] This tendency for men's and women's opinions to differ is called the **gender gap.** Perhaps surprisingly, the gender gap has virtually vanished on the abortion issue. An August 2006 Pew Research Center poll indicated that men and women are nearly identical—52 percent versus 51 percent—on the issue of allowing abortion in general or on a limited basis, and 46 percent of both men and women believe abortion should always or almost always be illegal.[8]

As we shall see in Chapter 11, political party membership can be another factor affecting political orientation. Partisans tend to rely on party leaders and spokespersons for cues on the appropriate position to take on major political issues. In recent years, congressional redistricting and partisan realignment in the South have reduced the number of conservative Democrats and all but eliminated liberal Republicans from Congress and positions of prominence in the party. As a result, the leadership of the Republican party has become increasingly conservative and that of the Democratic party has become more and more liberal. These changes in the positions of party leaders have been reflected in the views of party adherents and sympathizers in the general public. According to recent studies, differences between Democratic and Republican partisans on a variety of political and policy questions are greater today than they were during any other period for which data are available. On issues of national security, for example, Republicans have become very "hawkish," whereas Democrats have become quite "dovish." This polarization was

---

gender gap A distinctive pattern of voting behavior reflecting the differences in views between women and men.

[7]For data, see Center for American Women and Politics, Eagleton Institute of Politics, Rutgers, State University of New Jersey, "Sex Differences in Voter Turnout," 2005 (www.cawp.rutgers.edu/Facts5.html).

[8]Pew Research Center for the People and the Press, "Pragmatic Americans Liberal and Conservative on Social Issues: Most Want Middle Ground on Abortion," 3 August 2006 (people-press.org/reports).

most evident in October 2006, just before the midterm congressional elections, when 67 percent of conservative Republicans but only 10 percent of liberal Democrats thought the war effort in Iraq was "going very/fairly well."[9]

Membership in a social group can affect individuals' political orientations in another way: through the efforts of groups themselves to influence their members. Labor unions, for example, often seek to "educate" their members through meetings, rallies, and literature. These activities are designed to shape union members' understanding of politics and to make them more amenable to supporting the political positions favored by union leaders. Similarly, organization can sharpen the impact of membership in an involuntary group. Women's groups, black groups, religious groups, and the like usually endeavor to structure their members' political views through intensive educational programs. The importance of such group efforts can be seen from the impact of group membership on political opinion. Women who belong to women's organizations, for example, are likely to differ more from men in their political views than women without such group affiliation.[10] Other analysts have found that African Americans who belong to black organizations are more likely than blacks who lack such affiliations to differ from whites in their political orientations.[11]

In many cases, no particular efforts are required by groups to affect their members' beliefs and opinions. Often, individuals will consciously or unconsciously adapt their views to those of the groups with which they identify. For example, an African American who is dubious about affirmative action is likely to come under considerable peer pressure and internal pressure to modify his or her views. In this and other cases, dissenters are likely gradually to shift their own views to conform to those of the group. Political psychologist Elisabeth Noelle-Neumann has called this process the "spiral of silence."[12]

Another way that membership in social groups can affect political beliefs is through what might be called objective political interests. On many economic issues, for example, the interests of the rich and poor differ significantly. Inevitably, these differences of interest will produce differences of political outlook. James Madison and other framers of the Constitution thought that the inherent gulf between the rich and the poor would always be the most important source of conflict in political life. Certainly today, struggles over tax policy, welfare policy, health care policy, and so forth are fueled by differences of interest between wealthier and poorer Americans. In a similar vein, objective differences of interest between "senior citizens" and younger Americans can lead to very different views on such diverse issues as health care policy, Social Security, and criminal justice.

---

[9]Pew Research Center for the People and the Press, "Iraq Looms Large in Nationalized Election," 5 October 2006 (people-press.org/reports).

[10]Pamela Johnston Conover, "The Role of Social Groups in Political Thinking," *British Journal of Political Science* 18 (1988): 51–78.

[11]See Michael C. Dawson, "Structure and Ideology: The Shaping of Black Opinion," paper presented to the 1995 annual meeting of the Midwest Political Science Association, Chicago, Illinois, 7–9 April 1995. See also Michael C. Dawson, *Behind the Mule: Race and Class in African-American Politics* (Princeton, N.J.: Princeton University Press, 1994).

[12]Elisabeth Noelle-Neumann, *The Spiral of Silence: Public Opinion, Our Social Skin* (Chicago: University of Chicago Press, 1984).

It is worth pointing out again that, like the other agencies of socialization, group membership can never fully explain a given individual's political views. One's unique personality and life experiences may produce political views very different from those of the group to which one might nominally belong. Group membership is conducive to particular outlooks, but it is not determinative.

Differences in Education A third important source of differences in political perspectives comes from a person's education. In some respects, of course, schooling is a great equalizer. Governments use public education to try to teach all children a common set of civic values. It is mainly in school that Americans acquire their basic belief in liberty, equality, and democracy. In history classes, students are taught that the founders fought for the principle of liberty. Through participation in class elections and student government, students are taught the virtues of democracy. In the course of studying such topics as the Constitution, the Civil War, and the civil rights movement, students are taught the importance of equality. These lessons are repeated in every grade in a variety of contexts. No wonder they are such an important element in Americans' beliefs.

At the same time, however, differences in educational attainment are strongly associated with differences in political outlook. In particular, those who attend college are often exposed to philosophies and modes of thought that will forever distinguish them from their friends and neighbors who do not pursue college diplomas. Table 9.3 outlines some general differences of opinion found in one survey taken in 2000 comparing college graduates and other Americans. One of the major differences between college graduates and other Americans can be seen in levels of political participation. College graduates vote, write "letters to the editor," join campaigns, take part in protests, and, generally, make their voices heard.

Political Conditions A fourth set of factors that shape political orientations and values are the conditions under which individuals and groups are recruited into and involved in political life. Although political beliefs are influenced by family background and group membership, the precise content and character of these views is, to a large extent, determined by political circumstances. For example, many Americans who came of political age during the Great Depression and World War II developed an intense sense of loyalty to President Franklin D. Roosevelt and became permanently attached to his Democratic Party. In a similar vein, the Vietnam War and social upheavals of the 1960s produced lasting divisions among Americans of the "baby boomer" generation. Indeed, arguments over Vietnam persisted into the 2004 presidential election, some thirty years after American troops left Southeast Asia. Perhaps the 9/11 terrorist attacks and ongoing threats to America's security will have a lasting impact on the political orientations of contemporary Americans.

In a similar vein, the views held by members of a particular group can shift drastically over time, as political circumstances change. For example, American white Southerners were staunch members of the Democratic Party from the Civil War through the 1960s. As members of this political group, they became key supporters of liberal New Deal and post–New Deal social programs that greatly ex-

TABLE 9.3 Education and Public Opinion

Issue	Level of Education			
	Grade School	High School	Some College	College Graduate
Women and men should have equal roles.	38%	75%	83%	86%
Abortion should never be allowed.	21	10	7	4
The government should adopt national health insurance.	35	47	42	39
The United States should not concern itself with other nations' problems.	45	26	20	8
Government should see to fair treatment in jobs for African Americans.	49	28	30	45
Government should provide fewer services to reduce government spending.	8	17	19	27

SOURCE: American National Election Studies, 2004 data, Center for Political Studies, University of Michigan (electionstudies.org).

NOTE: The figures show the percentage of respondents in each category agreeing with the statement.

panded the size and power of the American national government. Since the 1960s, however, Southern whites have shifted in large numbers to the Republican Party. Now they provide a major base of support for efforts to scale back social programs and sharply reduce the size and power of the national government. The South's move from the Democratic to the Republican camp took place because of white Southern opposition to the Democratic Party's racial policies and because of determined Republican efforts to win white Southern support. It was not a change in the character of white Southerners but a change in the political circumstances in which they found themselves that induced this major shift in political allegiances and outlooks in the South.

The moral of this story is that a group's views cannot be inferred simply from the character of the group. College students are not inherently radical or inherently conservative. Jews are not inherently liberal. Southerners are not inherently conservative. Men are not inherently supportive of the military. Any group's political outlooks and orientations are shaped by the political circumstances in which that group finds itself, and those outlooks can change as circumstances change. Quite probably, the generation of American students now coming of political age will have a very different view of the use of American military power than their parents—members of a generation that reached political consciousness during the 1960s, when opposition to the Vietnam War and military conscription were important political phenomena.

Agreement on fundamentals, however, by no means implies that Americans do not differ with one another on a wide variety of issues. As we shall see, American political life is characterized by vigorous debate on economic, foreign policy, and social policy issues; race relations; environmental affairs; and a host of other matters.

Political Ideology

As we have seen, people's beliefs about government can vary widely. But for some individuals, this set of beliefs can fit together into a coherent philosophy about government. This set of underlying orientations, ideas, and beliefs through which we come to understand and interpret politics is called a political ideology.

In America today, people often describe themselves as liberals or conservatives. Liberalism and conservatism are political ideologies that include beliefs about the role of the government, ideas about public policies, and notions about which groups in society should properly exercise power. Historically these terms were defined somewhat differently than they are today. As recently as the nineteenth century, a liberal was an individual who favored freedom from state control, while a conservative was someone who supported the use of governmental power and favored continuation of the influence of church and aristocracy in national life.

Today, the term *liberal* has come to imply support for political and social reform; support for extensive governmental intervention in the economy; the expansion of federal social services; more vigorous efforts on behalf of the poor, minorities, and women; and greater concern for consumers and the environment. In social and cultural areas, liberals generally support abortion rights and oppose state involvement with religious institutions and religious expression. In international affairs, liberal positions are usually seen as including support for aid to poor nations, opposition to the use of American troops to influence the domestic affairs of developing nations, and support for international organizations such as the United Nations.

Of course, liberalism is not monolithic. For example, among individuals who view themselves as liberal, many support American military intervention when it is tied to a humanitarian purpose, as in the case of America's military action in Kosovo in 1998–99. Most liberals supported President George W. Bush's war on terrorism, even when some of the president's actions seemed to curtail civil liberties.

By contrast, the term *conservative* today is used to describe those who generally support the social and economic status quo and are suspicious of efforts to introduce new political formulae and economic arrangements. Conservatives believe strongly that a large and powerful government poses a threat to citizens' freedom. Thus, in the domestic area, conservatives generally oppose the expansion of governmental activity, asserting that solutions to social and economic problems can be developed in the private sector. Conservatives particularly oppose efforts to impose government regulation on business, pointing out that such regulation is frequently economically inefficient and costly and can ultimately lower

liberal A liberal today generally supports political and social reform; extensive governmental intervention in the economy; the expansion of federal social services; more vigorous efforts on behalf of the poor, minorities, and women; and greater concern for consumers and the environment.

conservative Today this term refers to one who generally supports the social and economic status quo and is suspicious of efforts to introduce new political formulae and economic arrangements. Conservatives believe that a large and powerful government poses a threat to citizens' freedom.

the entire nation's standard of living. As to social and cultural positions, many conservatives oppose abortion and support school prayer. In international affairs, conservatism has come to mean support for the maintenance of American military power.

Like liberalism, conservatism is far from a monolithic ideology. Some conservatives support many government social programs. George W. Bush calls himself a "compassionate conservative" to indicate that he favors programs that assist the poor and needy. Other conservatives oppose efforts to outlaw abortion, arguing that government intrusion in this area is as misguided as government intervention in the economy. Such a position is sometimes called "libertarian." In a similar vein, Pat Buchanan has angered many fellow conservatives by opposing most American military intervention in other regions. Many conservatives charge Buchanan with advocating a form of American "isolationism" that runs counter to contemporary conservative doctrine. The real political world is far too complex to be seen in terms of a simple struggle between liberals and conservatives.

To some extent, contemporary liberalism and conservatism can be seen as differences of emphasis with regard to the fundamental American political values of liberty and equality. For liberals, equality is the most important of the core values. Liberals are willing to tolerate government intervention in such areas as college admissions and business decisions when these seem to result in high levels of race, class, or gender inequality. For conservatives, on the other hand, liberty is the core value. Conservatives oppose most efforts by the government, however well intentioned, to intrude into private life or the marketplace. This simple formula for distinguishing liberalism and conservatism, however, is not always accurate, because political ideologies seldom lend themselves to neat or logical characterizations.

Often political observers search for logical connections among the various positions identified with liberalism or with conservatism, and they are disappointed or puzzled when they are unable to find a set of coherent philosophical principles that define and unite the several elements of either of these sets of beliefs. On the liberal side, for example, what is the logical connection between opposition to U.S. government intervention in the affairs of foreign nations and calls for greater intervention in America's economy and society? On the conservative side, what is the logical relationship between opposition to governmental regulation of business and support for a ban on abortion? Indeed, the latter would seem to be just the sort of regulation of private conduct that conservatives claim to abhor.

Frequently, the relationships among the various elements of liberalism or the several aspects of conservatism are *political* rather than *logical*. One underlying basis of liberal views is that all or most represent criticisms of or attacks on the foreign and domestic policies and cultural values of the business and commercial strata that have been prominent in the United States for the past century. In some measure, the tenets of contemporary conservatism represent this elite's defense of its positions against its enemies, who include organized labor, minority groups, and some intellectuals and professionals. Thus, liberals attack business and commercial elites by advocating more governmental regulation, including consumer protection and environmental regulation, opposition to military weapons programs, and support for expensive social programs. Conservatives counterattack by

How Polarized Is Public Opinion?

In the past several years, Americans have heard a lot about how divided they are. The American public is portrayed as increasingly "polarized"—with two camps, red and blue, that are far apart on key political questions. In particular, some have argued that America is experiencing a "culture war" over hot-button social issues, such as abortion and gay marriage. But how accurate is this characterization?

▶

In this map, red states are those won by President Bush in 2004, and blue states are those won by John Kerry. Here, the United States looks very polarized. The South and much of the Midwest appear Republican. The West Coast and the Northeast appear Democratic. But this map is misleading.

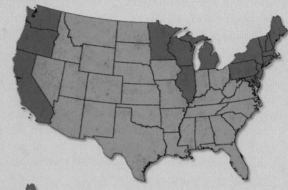

◀

What happens if we break down the map by counties instead of states? Even within red and blue states, there are areas where the majority votes differently. There are pockets of "blue" even in the Deep South and lots of "red" on the West Coast.

▶

Even more importantly, every state and county includes both Democrats and Republicans, making its true partisan color a shade of purple. If we color each county not based on whether Bush or Kerry won, but based on the percent of the vote that each of them received, the country hardly looks divided. Instead, much of the country is neither red nor blue.

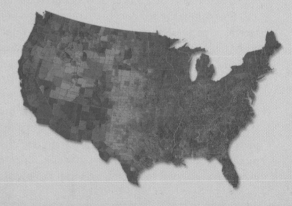

The portrayal of a "culture war" between Democrats and Republicans is also misleading. While Americans have different opinions on issues such as abortion and gay marriage, these differences have increased only a little, if at all. For example, consider abortion. For over twenty-five years, the American National Election Study has asked the following question:

▶

Which one of these opinions best agrees with your view?

1. By law, abortion should never be permitted.

2. The law should permit abortion only in cases of rape, incest, or when the woman's life is in danger.

3. The law should permit abortion for reasons other than rape, incest, or danger to the woman's life, but only after the need for the abortion has been clearly established.

4. By law, a woman should always be able to obtain an abortion as a matter of personal choice.

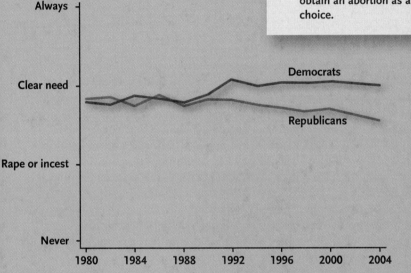

◀

The average opinions of Democrats and Republicans have diverged somewhat over time, but both groups are still quite close to the middle. Democrats do not unanimously support abortion under all circumstances, and Republicans do not unanimously oppose abortion under any circumstance. The term "culture war" seems an exaggeration.

Americans have not become more polarized on many issues, but there are two big exceptions: attitudes about President George W. Bush and attitudes toward the Iraq War. In the immediate aftermath of the September 11 terrorist attacks, both Republicans and Democrats tended to approve of President Bush. Over time, however, the gap between Republicans and Democrats increased dramatically. The gap with regard to the Iraq War also increased.

	October 2001	October 2003	June 2007
Approve of Bush			
Democrats	88%	53%	10%
Independents	92%	68%	32%
Republicans	99%	92%	74%
Believe Iraq War was worth fighting			
Democrats	–	50%	14%
Independents	–	70%	35%
Republicans	–	91%	70%

asserting that governmental regulation of the economy is ruinous and that military weapons are needed in a changing world.[13]

Of course, it is important to note that many people who call themselves liberals or conservatives accept only part of the liberal or conservative ideology. During the 1980s, many political commentators asserted that Americans were becoming increasingly conservative in their political orientations. Indeed, it was partly in response to this view that the Democrats in 1992 selected a presidential candidate, Bill Clinton, drawn from the party's moderate wing. Although it appears that Americans have adopted more conservative outlooks on some issues, their views in other areas have remained largely unchanged or even become more liberal in recent years. Thus, many individuals are liberal on social issues but conservative on economic issues. There is nothing illogical about these mixed positions. They indicate the relatively open and fluid character of American political debate. The Analyzing the Evidence unit in this chapter explores the question of how divided Democrats and Republicans are in their opinions.

HOW ARE POLITICAL OPINIONS FORMED?

An individual's opinions on particular issues, events, and personalities emerge as he or she evaluates these phenomena through the lenses of the beliefs and orientations that, taken together, compose his or her political ideology. Thus, if a conservative is confronted with a plan to expand federal social programs, he or she is likely to express opposition to the endeavor without spending too much time pondering the specific plan. Similarly, if a liberal is asked to comment on former President Ronald Reagan, he or she is not likely to hesitate long before offering a negative view. Underlying beliefs and ideologies tend to automatically color people's perceptions and opinions about politics.

Opinions on particular issues, however, are seldom fully shaped by underlying ideologies. It is true that most people have underlying beliefs that help to shape their opinions on particular issues,[14] but other factors are also important: a person's knowledge of political issues, and outside influences on that person's views.

Knowledge and Information

As they read newspapers, listen to the radio, watch television, and chat with their friends and associates, citizens are constantly confronted by new political events, issues, and personalities. Often they will be asked what they think about a particular issue or whether they plan to support a particular candidate. Indeed, in our democracy we expect every citizen to have views about the major problems of the day as well as opinions about who should be entrusted with the nation's leadership.

Some Americans know quite a bit about politics, and many have general views and hold opinions on several issues. Few Americans, though, devote sufficient time,

---

[13]For a discussion of this conflict, see Benjamin Ginsberg and Martin Shefter, "A Critical Realignment? The New Politics, the Reconstituted Right, and the Election of 1984," in *The Elections of 1984*, ed. Michael Nelson (Washington, D.C.: Congressional Quarterly Press, 1985), pp. 1–26.

[14]R. Michael Alvarez and John Brehm, *Hard Choices, Easy Answers: Values, Information, and American Public Opinion* (Princeton, N.J.: Princeton University Press, 2002).

energy, or attention to politics to really understand or evaluate the myriad issues with which they are bombarded on a regular basis. In fact, many studies have shown that the average American knows very little about politics. In one major study, for example, only 25 percent of respondents could name their two senators, only 29 percent could name their U.S. representative, and fewer than half knew that the Constitution's first ten amendments are called the Bill of Rights.[15] Evidence that half of America's citizens—particularly those who have not attended college—are so unaware of the nation's history and politics is troubling.

Yet ignorance is probably a predictable and inevitable fact of political life. Some analysts have argued that political attentiveness is costly; it means spending time at the very least, and often money as well, to collect, organize, and digest political information.[16] Balanced against this cost to an individual is the very low probability that he or she will, on the basis of this costly information, take an action that would not otherwise have been taken *and* that such a departure in behavior would make a beneficial difference to him or her *and* that such a difference, if it existed, would exceed the cost of acquiring the information in the first place. Because individuals anticipate that informed actions taken by them will rarely make much difference while the costs of informing oneself are often not trivial, especially for those with little education to begin with, it is rational to remain ignorant. In other words, the rationality principle suggests that many people should more profitably devote their personal resources— particularly their time—to more narrowly personal matters. This idea is in turn suggested by the collective-action principle, in which the bearing of burdens—such as the cost of becoming informed—is not likely to have much impact in a mass political setting. A more moderate version of "rational" ignorance recognizes that some kinds of information are inexpensive to acquire, such as sound bites from the evening news, or can be pleasant, such as reading the front page of the newspaper while drinking a cup of coffee. In such cases, an individual may become partially informed, but usually not in detail.

Precisely because becoming truly knowledgeable about politics requires a substantial investment of time and energy, many Americans seek to acquire political information and to make political decisions on the cheap, using shortcuts that seem to relieve them of having to engage in information gathering and evaluation. One "inexpensive" way to become informed is to take cues from trusted others—the local minister, the television commentator or newspaper editorialist, an interest-group leader, friends, and relatives.[17] Sometimes the cue giver is distrusted, in which case the cue leads the receiver in the opposite direction. For example, if a liberal is told that Republican leaders are backing a major overhaul of the Social Security system, he or she will probably not read thousands of pages of economic projections before exhibiting suspicion of the president's efforts. Along the same lines, a common shortcut for political evaluation and decision making is to assess new issues and

---

[15]Michael X. Delli Carpini and Scott Keeter, *What Americans Know about Politics and Why It Matters* (New Haven, Conn.: Yale University Press, 1996), pp. 307–28.

[16]Anthony Downs, *An Economic Theory of Democracy* (New York: Harper & Row, 1957).

[17]For a discussion of the role of information in democratic politics, see Arthur Lupia and Mathew D. McCubbins, *The Democratic Dilemma: Can Citizens Learn What They Need to Know?* (New York: Cambridge University Press, 1998).

○ ONLINE READING

events through the lenses of one's general beliefs and orientation. Thus if a conservative learns of a plan to expand federal social programs, he or she might express opposition to the endeavor without carefully pondering the specifics of the proposal.

Neither of these shortcuts is entirely reliable, however. Taking cues from others may lead individuals to accept positions that they would not support if they had more information. And general ideological orientations are usually poor guides to decision making in concrete instances. For one thing, especially when applied to discrete issues, most individuals' beliefs turn out to be filled with contradictions. For example, what position should a liberal take on immigration? Should a liberal favor keeping America's borders open to poor people from all over the world, or should he or she be concerned that America's open borders create a pool of surplus labor that permits giant corporations to drive down the wages of poor American workers? Many other issues defy easy ideological characterization. What should conservatives think about the financial rescue plan enacted by Congress in 2008? How should liberals view America's military actions in Iraq? Each of these policies combines a mix of issues and is too complex to lend itself to simple ideological interpretation.

While understandable and perhaps inevitable, widespread inattentiveness to politics weakens American democracy in two ways. First, those who lack political information or resort to inadequate shortcuts to acquire and assess information cannot effectively defend their political interests and can easily become victims or losers in political struggles. Second, the presence of large numbers of politically inattentive or ignorant individuals means that the political process can be more easily manipulated by the various institutions and forces that seek to shape public opinion.

As to the first of these problems, in our democracy millions of ordinary citizens take part in political life, at least to the extent of voting in national elections. Those with little knowledge of the election's issues or candidates or procedures can find themselves acting against their own preferences and interests. One example is U.S. tax policy. Over the past several decades, the United States has substantially reduced the rate of taxation for its wealthiest citizens.[18] Tax cuts signed into law by President Bush in 2001 and mostly maintained throughout the decade provided a tax break mainly for the top 1 percent of the nation's wage earners, and further tax cuts proposed by the president offered additional benefits to this privileged stratum. It is surprising, however, that polling data showed that millions of middle-class and lower-middle-class Americans who did not stand to benefit from the president's tax cuts seemed to favor them nonetheless. The explanation for this odd state of affairs appeared to be a lack of political knowledge. Millions of individuals who were unlikely to derive much advantage from President Bush's tax policy thought they would. The political scientist Larry Bartels has called this phenomenon "misplaced self-interest."[19] Upper-bracket taxpayers, who are usually served by an army of financial advisers,

---

[18]One of the most detailed analyses of the distribution of the tax burden in advanced industrial democracies in the past half century is Thomas Piketty and Emmanuel Saez, "How Progressive Is the U.S. Federal Tax System? Historical and International Perspectives," working paper 12404, National Bureau of Economic Research, 2006 (www.nber.org/papers/w12404).

[19]Larry M. Bartels, "Homer Gets a Tax Cut: Inequality and Public Policy in the American Mind," *Perspectives on Politics* 3 (2005): 15–31.

are unlikely to suffer from this problem. Knowledge may not always translate into political power, but lack of knowledge is almost certain to translate into political weakness. And according to the policy principle, the lack of knowledge and concomitant political weakness mean policy disappointment.

Government and Political Leaders

All governments attempt, to a greater or lesser extent, to influence, manipulate, or manage their citizens' beliefs. But the extent to which public opinion is actually affected by governmental public relations efforts is probably limited. The government—despite its size and power—is only one source of information and evaluation in the United States. Very often, governmental claims are disputed by the media, by interest groups, and at times by opposing forces within the government itself.

Often, too, governmental efforts to manipulate public opinion backfire when the public is made aware of the government's tactics. Thus, in 1971, the United States government's efforts to build popular support for the Vietnam War were hurt when CBS News aired its documentary "The Selling of the Pentagon," which revealed the extent and character of government efforts to sway popular sentiment. In this documentary, CBS demonstrated the techniques, including planted news stories and faked film footage, that the government had used to misrepresent its activities in Vietnam. These revelations, of course, had the effect of undermining popular trust in all government claims.

A hallmark of the Clinton administration was the steady use of campaign techniques such as those used in election campaigns to bolster popular enthusiasm for White House initiatives. The president established a "political war room" in the Executive Office Building similar to the one that operated in his campaign headquarters. Representatives from all departments met in the war room every day to discuss and coordinate the president's public relations efforts. Many of the same consultants and pollsters who directed the successful Clinton campaign were employed in the selling of the president's programs.[20]

After he assumed office in 2001, President George W. Bush asserted that political leaders should base their programs upon their own conception of the public interest rather than the polls. This, however, did not mean that Bush ignored public opinion. Bush relied on pollster Jan van Lohuizen to conduct a low-key operation, sufficiently removed from the limelight to allow the president to renounce polling while he continued to make use of survey data.[21] At the same time, the Bush White House developed an extensive public relations program, led by former presidential aide Karen P. Hughes, to bolster popular support for the president's policies. Hughes, working with conservative Republican strategist Mary Matalin, coordinated White House efforts to maintain popular support for the administration's war against terrorism. These efforts included presidential speeches, media appearances by administration officials, numerous press conferences, and thousands of press releases presenting the administration's views. The White House also made a substantial effort to sway opinion in foreign

---

[20]Gerald F. Seib and Michael K. Frisby, "Selling Sacrifice," *Wall Street Journal*, 5 February 1993, p. 1.

[21]Joshua Green, "The Other War Room," *Washington Monthly*, April 2002.

countries, even sending officials to present the administration's views on television networks serving the Arab world.

Another example of a Bush administration effort to shape public opinion is a series of commercials it produced at taxpayer expense in 2004 to promote the new Medicare prescription drug program. The commercials, prominently featuring the president, were designed to look like actual news stories and were aired in English and Spanish by hundreds of local television stations. Called a "video news release," this type of commercial is designed to give viewers the impression that they are watching a real news story. The presumption is that viewers are more likely to believe what they think is news coverage than material they know to be advertising. Democrats, of course, accused the administration of conducting a partisan propaganda campaign with public funds, but Republicans pointed out that the Clinton administration had engaged in similar practices.

Private Groups

We have already seen how the government tries to shape opinion. But the ideas that become prominent in political life are also developed and spread by important economic and political groups searching for issues that will advance their causes. In some instances, private groups espouse values in which they truly believe in the hope of bringing others over to their side. Take, for example, the campaign against so-called partial birth abortion that resulted in the Partial Birth Abortion Ban Act of 2003. Proponents of the act believed that prohibiting particular sorts of abortions would be a first step toward eliminating all abortions—something they viewed as a moral imperative.[22] In other cases, groups will promote principles designed mainly to further hidden agendas of political and economic interests. One famous example is the campaign against cheap, imported handguns—the so-called Saturday night specials—covertly financed by domestic manufacturers of more expensive firearms. The campaign's organizers claimed that cheap handguns posed a grave risk to the public and should be outlawed. The real goal, though, was not safeguarding the public but protecting the economic well-being of the domestic gun industry. A more recent example is the campaign against the alleged "sweatshop" practices of some American companies manufacturing products in third-world countries. This campaign is mainly financed by U.S. labor unions seeking to protect their members' jobs by discouraging American firms from manufacturing products abroad.

Typically, ideas are best marketed by groups with access to financial resources, public or private institutional support, and sufficient skill or education to select, develop, and draft ideas that will attract interest and support. Thus, the development and promotion of conservative themes and ideas in recent years has been greatly facilitated by the millions of dollars that conservative corporations and business organizations, such as the Chamber of Commerce and the Public Affairs Council, spend each year on public information and what is now called in corporate circles "issues management." In addition, conservative businesses have contributed mil-

---

[22]Cynthia Gorney, "Gambling with Abortion," *Harper's Magazine*, November 2004, pp. 33–46.

lions of dollars to such conservative institutions as the Heritage Foundation, the Hoover Institution, and the American Enterprise Institute.[23]

Although they often do not have access to financial assets that match those available to their conservative opponents, liberal intellectuals and professionals have ample organizational skills, access to the media, and practice in creating, communicating, and using ideas. During the past three decades, the chief vehicle through which liberal intellectuals and professionals have advanced their ideas has been the "public interest group," an institution that relies heavily upon voluntary contributions of time, effort, and interest on the part of its members. Through groups such as Common Cause, the National Organization for Women, the Sierra Club, Friends of the Earth, and Physicians for Social Responsibility, intellectuals and professionals have been able to use their organizational skills and educational resources to develop and promote ideas.[24]

Journalist and author Joe Queenan correctly observed that although political ideas can erupt spontaneously, they almost never do. Instead,

> . . . issues are usually manufactured by tenured professors and obscure employees of think tanks. . . . It is inconceivable that the American people, all by themselves, could independently arrive at the conclusion that the depletion of the ozone layer poses a dire threat to our national well-being, or that an immediate, across-the-board cut in the capital-gains tax is the only thing that stands between us and the economic abyss. The American people do not have that kind of sophistication. *They have to have help.*[25]

THE MEDIA

Among the most important forces shaping public opinion are the national news media. The content and character of news and public affairs programming—what the media choose to present and how they present it—can have the most far-reaching political consequences. Media disclosures can greatly enhance—or fatally damage—the careers of public officials. Media coverage can rally support for—or intensify opposition to—national policies. When American and British forces attacked Iraq in 2003, reporters accompanied the troops into battle and provided real-time broadcasts from the battlefront twenty-four hours a day, seven days a week. The reporters' presence was of course no accident. Allowing journalists to accompany the troops was part of a purposeful Defense Department strategy. Military planners believed that the so-called embedded reporters would quickly identify with the troops, whose hardships they shared, and write positive accounts of their activities. Here was a cause where U.S. military policies were shaped by the desire to obtain favorable news coverage rather than by the anticipation of combat effectiveness. And for the most part, this Defense Department

---

[23]See David Vogel, "The Power of Business in America: A Reappraisal," *British Journal of Political Science* 13 (January 1983): 19–44.

[24]See David Vogel, "The Public Interest Movement and the American Reform Tradition," *Political Science Quarterly* 96 (Winter 1980): 607–27.

[25]Joe Queenan, "Birth of a Notion," *Washington Post*, 20 September 1992, p. C1. [Emphasis in original.]

strategy was successful. The journalists' identification with the troops was so complete that writers often used the pronoun *we* when discussing military operations.

While the embedded reporters generally provided favorable accounts of U.S. military activities, their colleagues behind the lines reporting from U.S. headquarters in Kuwait or commenting from New York and Washington were not always as kind. By 2006, daily media accounts of the continuing violence and chaos in Iraq persuaded many American voters that it was time for a change and helped the Democrats win control of both houses of Congress. And in 2007, when President Bush announced that he planned to stabilize Iraq by sending more American troops to that country, the media treated his ideas with skepticism while giving extensive and respectful coverage to congressional critics who asserted that the president's efforts were destined to fail.

The media can shape and modify, if not fully form, public perceptions of events, issues, and institutions. In this section, we examine the role and increasing power of the media in American politics.

Types of Media

Americans obtain their news from three main sources: broadcast media (radio, television), print media (newspapers and magazines), and, increasingly, the Internet. Each of these sources has distinctive institutional characteristics that help to shape the character of their coverage of political events.

Broadcast Media   Television news reaches more Americans than any other single news source. Tens of millions of individuals watch national and local news programs every day. Television news, however, covers relatively few topics and provides little depth of coverage. Television news is more like a series of newspaper headlines connected to pictures. It serves the extremely important function of alerting viewers to issues and events but provides little else.

The twenty-four-hour news stations like Cable News Network (CNN) offer more detail and commentary than the networks' half-hour evening news shows. In 2003, at the start of the war in Iraq, CNN, Fox, and MSNBC provided twenty-four-hour-a-day coverage of the war, including on-the-scene reports from embedded reporters, expert commentary, and interviews with government officials. In this instance, these networks' depth of coverage rivaled that of the print media. Normally, however, CNN and the others offer more headlines than analysis, especially during their prime-time broadcasts. In recent years, cable has been growing in importance as a news source (Table 9.4).

Politicians generally view the local broadcast news as a friendlier venue than the national news. National reporters are often inclined to criticize and question, whereas local reporters often accept the pronouncements of national leaders at face value. For this reason, presidents often introduce new proposals in a series of short visits to a number of cities—indeed, sometimes flying from airport stop to airport stop—in addition to or instead of making a national presentation. For example, in February 2002, President Bush introduced his idea for a new national volunteer corps during his State of the Union message and then made a number

TABLE 9.4 The Trend in Regular News Consumption

	1993 (%)	1996 (%)	2000 (%)	2002 (%)	2004 (%)	2006 (%)
Local TV news	77	65	56	57	59	54
Cable TV news	—	—	—	33	38	34
Nightly network news	60	42	30	32	34	28
Radio*	47†	44	43	41	40	36
Newspaper*	58†	50	47	41	42	40
Online news‡	—	2§	23	25	29	31

SOURCE: Pew Research Center for the People and the Press, "Maturing Internet News Audience—Broader Than Deep: Online Papers Modestly Boost Newspaper Readership," 30 July 2006 (people-press.org/reports/pdf/282.pdf).

*Based on use the previous day.

†Data from 1994.

‡Viewed at least three days per week.

§Data from 1995.

of local speeches around the country promoting the theme. While national reporters questioned the president's plans, local news coverage was overwhelmingly positive.

Radio news is also essentially a headline service without pictures. In the short time—usually five minutes per hour—that they devote to news, radio stations announce the day's major events without providing much detail. In major cities, all-news stations provide a bit more coverage of major stories, but for the most part these stations fill the day with repetition rather than detail. All-news stations like WTOP (Washington, D.C.) and WCBS (New York City) assume that most listeners are in their cars and that, as a result, the people who constitute the audience change markedly throughout the day as they reach their destination. Thus, rather than use their time to flesh out a given set of stories, these stations repeat the same stories each hour to present them to new listeners.

In recent years, much of the content of the news, especially local news, has shifted away from politics and public affairs toward "soft news"—coverage focusing on celebrities, health tips, advice to consumers, and other topics more likely to provide entertainment than enlightenment. Even a good deal of political coverage is soft. For example, media coverage of the 2005 presidential inauguration devoted nearly as much attention to the dresses worn by President Bush's daughters as it did to the content of the president's address.

Softer even than soft news is a category of programming sometimes called infotainment. This neologism refers to material that purports to combine information with entertainment. For example, in 2003, Arnold Schwarzenegger appeared on *The*

Tonight Show, exchanged jokes with the host, Jay Leno, and announced that he would be a candidate for governor of California. A currently popular infotainment program is *The Daily Show,* which presents comedic parodies of political figures and calls itself America's "most trusted name in fake news." While purveyors of the "true" news often sneer at *The Daily Show* and other infotainment programs, one recent survey suggested that *Daily Show* viewers do receive a surprising quantity of correct information along with their fake news.

Print Media   Newspapers remain an important source of news even though they are not the primary news source for most Americans. The print media are important for two reasons. First, as we shall see later in this chapter, the broadcast media rely on leading newspapers such as *The New York Times* and *The Washington Post* to set their news agenda. The broadcast media engage in very little actual reporting; they primarily cover stories that have been "broken," or initially reported, by the print media. For example, sensational charges that President Bill Clinton had an affair with a White House intern were reported first by *The Washington Post* and *Newsweek* before being trumpeted around the world by the broadcast media. It is only a slight exaggeration to observe that if an event is not covered in *The New York Times,* it is not likely to appear on the *CBS Evening News.* One important exception, obviously, is the case of "breaking" news, which can be carried by the broadcast media as it unfolds or soon after, while the print media are forced to catch up later in the day. Recall the dramatic real-time videos of the collapsing Twin Towers seen by tens of millions of Americans. Second, the print media provide more detailed and more complete information, offering a better context for analysis. Third, the print media are also important because they are the prime source of news for educated and influential individuals. The nation's economic, social, and political elites rely on the detailed coverage provided by the print media to inform and influence their views about important public matters. The print media may have a smaller audience than their cousins in broadcasting, but they have an audience that matters.

The Internet   A relatively new source of news is the Internet. Every day several million Americans, especially younger Americans, scan one of many news sites on the Internet for coverage of current events. For the most part, however, the Internet provides electronic versions of coverage offered by print sources. One great advantage of the Internet is that it allows frequent updating. It can potentially combine the depth of coverage of a newspaper with the timeliness of television and radio and probably will become a major news source in the next decade. Already most political candidates and interest groups have sites on the World Wide Web. Some of the more sensational aspects of President Clinton's relationship with Monica Lewinsky were first reported on a Web site maintained by Matt Drudge, who specializes in posting sensational charges about public figures. Though many deny it, most reporters scan Drudge's site regularly, hoping to pick up a bit of salacious gossip. Many Americans relied on Web sites such as CNN.com for up-to-the-minute election news in the days after the 2000 presidential election, the dramatic post-election battle in Florida, the 2001 terrorist attacks on New York City and Washington, D.C., the war in Iraq, and

Hurricane Katrina.[26] Acknowledging the growing importance of the Internet as a political communications medium, the U.S. Supreme Court posted its decisions in the Florida election cases as soon as they were issued. The full potential of the Internet as a campaign tool began to be realized in 2008. The Obama campaign harnessed the power of social networking technologies to build an Internet community of millions of supporters who mobilized support for the ticket and generated several hundred million dollars in campaign funds, mostly in small contributions, for Obama and the Democrats.

In addition, hundreds of thousands of readers turn to more informal sources of Internet news and commentary: Web logs, or blogs. Blogs are intermittently published online by thousands of individuals and generally feature personal opinion and commentary on national and world events. In recent years, some news stories first discussed by bloggers have been picked up by mainstream journalists and have had a major impact on political events. In December 2002, for example, bloggers criticized Senator Trent Lott for praising the one-time segregationist Senator Strom Thurmond at a birthday party for Thurmond. A few days later the mainstream press focused on the story, and Lott was forced to resign his post as Senate majority leader. In 2004, after CBS aired a story claiming that George W. Bush had received preferential treatment while serving in the Air National Guard, conservative bloggers mounted a campaign charging that the documents presented by CBS had been forged. The network ultimately admitted that the documents had not been properly authenticated, and CBS anchor Dan Rather was forced to resign. In 2006, bloggers and other avid Internet users, sometimes called netroot activists, helped bring about the defeat of the Virginia Republican senator and presidential hopeful, George Allen. After it was shown on the YouTube Web site, a video clip of Allen directing what appeared to be a racial slur at a Democratic campaign worker was downloaded to hundreds of thousands of computers and discussed by thousands of bloggers. The story was then featured by the television networks. Allen was defeated in his bid for reelection and saw his presidential hopes destroyed.

Regulation of the Media

In some countries, the government controls media content. In other countries, the government owns the broadcast media but does not tell the media what to say (as is the case with the BBC in Great Britain). In the United States, the government neither owns nor controls the communications networks, but it does regulate the content and ownership of the broadcast media. The print media, on the other hand, are essentially free from government interference.

Broadcast Media   American radio and television are regulated by the Federal Communications Commission (FCC), an independent regulatory agency established in 1934. Radio and TV stations must renew their FCC licenses every five years. Through regulations prohibiting obscenity, indecency, and profanity, the FCC has

---

[26]For a discussion of the growing role of the Internet, see Leslie Wayne, "On Web, Voters Reinvent Grass-Roots Activism," *New York Times*, 21 May 2000, p. 22. See also James Fallows, "Internet Illusions," *New York Review of Books*, 16 November 2000, p. 28.

also sought to prohibit radio and television stations from airing explicit sexual and excretory references between 6 A.M. and 10 P.M., the hours when children are most likely to be in the audience. The FCC has enforced these rules haphazardly. Since 1990, nearly half the $5 million in fines levied by the agency have involved Howard Stern, the "shock jock" whose programs are often built around sexually explicit material. In 2004, after another set of FCC fines, Stern's program was dropped by a major outlet, Clear Channel Communications. Stern charged that the Bush administration had singled him out for censure because of his known opposition to the president.

For more than sixty years, the FCC also sought to regulate and promote competition in the broadcast industry, but in 1996 Congress passed the Telecommunications Act, a broad effort to do away with most regulations in effect since 1934. The act loosened restrictions on media ownership and allowed for telephone companies, cable television providers, and broadcasters to compete with one another for the provision of telecommunication services. Following the passage of the act, several mergers between telephone and cable companies and between different segments of the entertainment media produced an even greater concentration of media ownership.

The federal government has used its licensing power to impose several regulations that can affect the political content of radio and TV broadcasts. The first of these is the **equal time rule,** under which broadcasters must provide candidates for the same political office equal opportunities to communicate their messages to the public. The second regulation affecting the content of broadcasts is the **right of rebuttal,** which requires that individuals be given the opportunity to respond to personal attacks. For many years, a third important federal regulation was the **fairness doctrine**—under which broadcasters who aired programs on controversial issues were required to provide air time for opposing views. In 1985, the FCC stopped enforcing the fairness doctrine on the grounds that there were so many radio and television stations—to say nothing of newspapers and newsmagazines—that in all likelihood many different viewpoints were being presented even without the requirement that each station present all sides of an argument.

Freedom of the Press   Unlike the broadcast media, the print media are not subject to federal regulation. Indeed, the great principle underlying the federal government's relationship with the press is the doctrine against **prior restraint.** Beginning with the landmark 1931 case of *Near v. Minnesota,* the U.S. Supreme Court has held that, except under the most extraordinary circumstances, the First Amendment of the Constitution prohibits government agencies from seeking to prevent newspapers or magazines from publishing whatever they wish.[27]

Even though newspapers may not be restrained from publishing whatever they want, they may be subject to sanctions after the fact. Historically, newspapers have been subject to the law of libel, which provides that newspapers that print false and malicious stories can be compelled to pay damages to those they defame. In recent

---

[27] *Near v. Minnesota ex rel.,* 283 U.S. 697 (1931).

equal time rule The requirement that broadcasters provide candidates for the same political office an equal opportunity to communicate their messages to the public.

right of rebuttal An FCC regulation giving individuals the right to have the opportunity to respond to personal attacks made on a radio or TV broadcast.

fairness doctrine An FCC requirement that broadcasters who air programs on controversial issues provide time for opposing views.

prior restraint An effort by a government agency to block the publication of material it deems libelous or harmful in some other way; censorship. In the United States, the courts forbid prior restraint except under the most extraordinary circumstances.

Setting the agenda for political discussion: Groups wishing to generate support for policy proposals or political candidacies must secure media coverage. The media must be persuaded that an item is newsworthy.

Framing: The media's interpretation of an event or political action can sometimes determine how people perceive the event or result.

Priming: Most citizens will never meet their political leaders, but will base opinions of these leaders on their media images. The media have a great deal of control over how a person is portrayed or whether an individual even receives public attention.

years, however, American courts have greatly narrowed the meaning of libel and made it extremely difficult, particularly for politicians and other public figures, to win a libel case against a newspaper.

Sources of Media Power

Agenda Setting   The power of the media stems from several sources. The first is *agenda setting,* which means that the media help determine which political issues become part of the public debate. Groups and forces that wish to bring their ideas before the public to generate support for policy proposals or political candidacies must somehow secure media coverage. If the media are persuaded that an idea is newsworthy, then they may declare it an issue that must be resolved or a problem to be solved, thus clearing the first hurdle in the policy-making process. On the other hand, if an idea lacks or loses media appeal, its chance of resulting in new programs or policies is diminished. Some ideas seem to surface, gain media support for a time, lose media appeal, and then resurface.

In most instances, the media serve as conduits for agenda-setting efforts by competing groups and forces. Occasionally, however, journalists themselves play an important role in setting the agenda of political discussion. For example, whereas many of the scandals and investigations surrounding President Clinton were initiated by his political opponents, the Watergate scandal that destroyed Nixon's presidency was in some measure initiated and driven by *The Washington Post* and the national television networks.

Priming   A second important media power is *priming.* This occurs when media coverage affects the way the public evaluates political leaders or candidates for office. For example, nearly unanimous media praise for President Bush's speeches to the nation in the wake of the September 11 terrorist attacks prepared, or "primed," the public to view Bush's subsequent response to terrorism in an extremely positive light even though some aspects of the administration's efforts were problematic.

In the case of political candidates, the media have considerable influence over whether a particular individual will receive public attention, whether a particular individual will be taken seriously as a viable contender, and whether the public will

agenda setting The power of the media to bring public attention to particular issues and problems.

priming When media coverage affects public perception and evaluation of political leaders and candidates.

evaluate a candidate's performance favorably. Thus if the media find a candidate interesting, they may treat him or her as a serious contender even though the facts of the matter seem to suggest otherwise. Similarly, the media may declare that a candidate has "momentum," a mythical property that the media confer on candidates, if the candidate happens to exceed the media's expectations. Momentum has no substantive meaning—it is simply a media prediction that a particular candidate will do better in the future than he or she has done in the past. Such media prophecies can become self-fulfilling as contributors and supporters jump on the bandwagon of the candidate possessing this "momentum." In 1992, when Bill Clinton's poll standings surged in the wake of the Democratic National Convention, the media determined that Clinton had enormous momentum. In fact, nothing that happened during the remainder of the race led the media to change its collective judgment.

Framing   A third source of the media's power, known as *framing,* is their power to decide how political events and results are interpreted by the American people. For example, during the 1995–96 struggle between President Clinton and congressional Republicans over the nation's budget—a struggle that led to several partial shutdowns of the federal government—the media's interpretation of events forced the Republicans to back down and agree to a budget on Clinton's terms. At the beginning of the crisis, congressional Republicans, led by House Speaker Newt Gingrich, were confident that they could compel Clinton to accept their budget, which called for substantial cuts in domestic social programs. Republicans calculated that Clinton would fear being blamed for lengthy government shutdowns and would quickly accede to their demands. The Republicans reasoned that once Americans saw that life went on with government agencies closed, they would support the Republicans in asserting that the United States could get along with less government.

However, the media did not fully cooperate with the GOP's plans. Media coverage of the several government shutdowns during this period emphasized the hardships imposed on federal workers who were being furloughed in the weeks before Christmas. Indeed, Newt Gingrich, who was generally portrayed as the villain who caused the crisis, came to be called the Gin*grinch* who stole Christmas from the children of hundreds of thousands of federal workers. Rather than suggest that the shutdown demonstrated that America could carry on with less government, media accounts focused on the difficulties encountered by Washington tourists unable to visit the capital's monuments, museums, and galleries. The woes of American travelers whose passports were delayed were also given considerable attention. This sort of coverage eventually convinced most Americans that the government shutdown was bad for the country. In the end, Gingrich and the congressional Republicans were forced to surrender and accept a new budget reflecting many of Clinton's priorities. The Republicans' defeat in the budget showdown contributed to the unraveling of the GOP's legislative program and, ultimately, to the Republicans' poor showing in the 1996 presidential elections. The character of media coverage of an event thus had enormous repercussions on how Americans interpreted it.

In 2001, the Bush White House recognized the importance of framing when presidential aides held extensive discussions with television networks and Hollywood

framing The power of the media to influence how events and issues are interpreted.

filmmakers about the portrayal of America's war on terrorism. The White House asked the media to sound a patriotic note and frame the "war" as a patriotic duty.

The Rise of Adversarial Journalism   The political power of the news media has increased greatly in recent years through the growing prominence of "adversarial journalism," a form of journalism in which the media adopt a hostile posture toward the government and public officials.

During the nineteenth century, American newspapers were completely subordinate to the political parties. Newspapers depended on official patronage—legal notice and party subsidies—for their financial survival and were controlled by party leaders. (A vestige of that era survived into the twentieth century in such newspaper names as the *Springfield Republican* and the *St. Louis Globe-Democrat*.) At the turn of the century, with the development of commercial advertising, newspapers became financially independent, making possible the emergence of a formally nonpartisan press.

Presidents were the first national officials to see the opportunities in this development. By communicating directly with the electorate through newspapers and magazines, Theodore Roosevelt and Woodrow Wilson established political constituencies independent of party organizations and strengthened their own power relative to Congress. President Franklin D. Roosevelt used the radio, most notably in his famous fireside chats, to reach out to voters and make himself the center of American politics. FDR was also adept at developing close personal relationships with reporters, which enabled him to obtain favorable news coverage despite the fact that in his day a majority of newspaper owners and publishers were staunch conservatives. Following Roosevelt's example, subsequent presidents have sought to use the media to enhance their popularity and power. For example, through televised news conferences, President John F. Kennedy mobilized public support for his domestic- and foreign-policy initiatives.

During the 1950s and early 1960s, a few members of Congress also made successful use of the media—especially television—to mobilize national support for their causes. Senator Estes Kefauver of Tennessee became a major contender for the presidency and won a place on the 1956 Democratic national ticket as a result of his dramatic televised hearings on organized crime. Senator Joseph McCarthy of Wisconsin made himself a powerful national figure through his well-publicized investigations of alleged Communist infiltration of key American institutions. These senators, however, were more exceptional than typical. Through the mid-1960s, the executive branch continued to generate the bulk of the news coverage, and the media served as a cornerstone of presidential power.

The Vietnam War shattered this relationship between the press and the presidency. During the early stages of U.S. involvement, American officials in Vietnam who disapproved of the way the war was being conducted leaked to reporters information critical of administrative policy. Publication of this material infuriated the White House, which pressured publishers to block its release; on one occasion, President Kennedy went so far as to ask *The New York Times* to reassign its Saigon correspondent. The national print and broadcast media discovered, however, that there was an audience for critical coverage and investigative reporting among segments of the public skeptical of administration policy. As the Vietnam conflict dragged on, critical media coverage fanned antiwar sentiment. Moreover, growing opposition to the war among liberals encouraged some members of Congress, most notably Senator J. William Fulbright, chair of the Senate Foreign Relations Committee, to break with the president. In turn, these shifts in popular and congressional sentiment emboldened journalists and publishers to continue to present critical news reports. Through this process, journalists developed a commitment to adversarial journalism, while a constituency emerged that would rally to the defense of the media when it came under White House attack.

This pattern endured through the 1970s and into the present. Political forces opposed to presidential policies, many members of Congress, and the national news media began to find that their interests often overlapped. Adversarial, or "attack," journalism has become commonplace in America, and some critics have suggested that the media have contributed to popular cynicism and the low levels of citizen participation that characterize contemporary American political processes. Of course in October 2001, the adversarial relationship between the government and the media was at least temporarily transformed into a much more supportive association as the media helped rally the American people for the fight against terrorism. And, indeed, some commentators have suggested that segments of the media, the more conservative media in particular, became far less adversarial in their tone during the Bush presidency than they had been in prior years.

The adversarial relationship between the government and segments of the press resumed, however, during the war in Iraq. Such newspapers as *The Washington Post* and *The New York Times* castigated President Bush for going to war without winning the support of some of America's major allies. When American forces failed to uncover evidence that Iraq possessed weapons of mass destruction—a major reason cited by the administration for launching the war—these newspapers intimated that the war had been based on intelligence failures, if not outright deceptions by the Bush administration. The president, as noted earlier, denounced the media for distorting his record. Thus after a brief interlude of post–September 11 harmony, the customary hostilities between the government and the press seemed to manifest themselves once again.

MEASURING PUBLIC OPINION

As we have considered the impact of the media and other forces upon public opinion, we have generally relied upon the data reported by public opinion polls to gauge popular beliefs and preferences. Politicians, the news media, advertisers, and others constantly bombard us with information from surveys. During election campaigns, for example, the news media report on a daily basis poll results designed to indicate which candidates are running ahead and which seem to be falling behind. Typically, news stories and political analyses make extensive use of poll data as reporters and pundits seek to assess the public's mood and to predict future political outcomes.

Through we take opinion polling for granted today, as recently as fifty years ago, American political leaders gauged public opinion by people's applause or cheers and by the presence of crowds in meeting places. This direct exposure to the people's views did not necessarily produce accurate knowledge of public opinion. It did, however, give political leaders confidence in their public support—and therefore confidence in their ability to govern by consent.

Abraham Lincoln and Stephen Douglas debated each other seven times in the campaign for the Illinois Senate seat during the summer and autumn of 1858, two years before they became presidential nominees. Their debates took place before audiences in parched cornfields and courthouse squares. More than a century later, the presidential debates, although seen by millions, take place before a few reporters and technicians in television studios that might as well be on the moon. The public's response cannot be experienced directly. This distance between leaders and followers is one of the agonizing problems of modern democracy. The media send information to millions of people, but they are not yet as efficient at getting information back to leaders. Is government by consent possible where the scale of communication is so large and so impersonal? To compensate for the decline in their ability to experience public opinion for themselves, leaders have turned to science, in particular to the science of opinion polling.

It is no secret that politicians and public officials make extensive use of **public opinion polls** to help them decide whether to run for office, what policies to support, how to vote on important legislation, and what types of appeals to make in their campaigns. President Lyndon Johnson was famous for carrying the latest Gallup and Roper poll results in his hip pocket, and it is widely believed that he began to withdraw from politics because the polls reported losses in public support. All recent presidents and other major political figures have worked closely with polls and pollsters.

Constructing Public Opinion from Surveys

The population in which pollsters are interested is usually quite large. To conduct their polls, they choose a **sample** of the total population. The selection of this sample is important. Above all, it must be representative; the views of those in the sample must accurately and proportionately reflect the views of the whole. To a large extent, the validity of the poll's results depends on the sampling procedure used.

Sampling Techniques and Selection Bias   The most common techniques for choosing such a sample are probability sampling and random digit dialing. In the case of **probability sampling**, the pollster begins with a listing of the population to be surveyed. This listing is called the sampling frame. After assigning each member of the population a number, the pollster uses a table of random numbers or a computerized random selection process to select those to be surveyed. This technique is appropriate when the entire population can be identified. For example, all students registered at Texas colleges and universities can be identified from college records and a sample of them can easily be drawn. When the pollster is interested in a national sample of Americans, however, this technique is not feasible, as no complete list of Americans exists.[28] National samples are usually drawn using a

---

[28]Herbert Asher, *Polling and the Public* (Washington, D.C.: Congressional Quarterly Press, 2001), p. 64.

public opinion polls Scientific instruments for measuring public opinion.

sample A small group selected by researchers to represent the most important characteristics of an entire population.

probability sampling A method used by pollsters to select a representative sample in which every individual in the population has an equal probability of being selected as a respondent.

technique called ***random digit dialing***. A computer random number generator is used to produce a list of as many ten-digit numbers as the pollster deems necessary. Since more than 95 percent of American households have telephones, this technique usually results in a random national sample.

The importance of sampling was brought home early in the history of political polling. A 1936 *Literary Digest* poll predicted that Republican presidential candidate Alf Landon would defeat Democrat Franklin D. Roosevelt in that year's presidential election. The actual election, of course, ended in a Roosevelt landslide. The main problem with the survey had been what is called ***selection bias*** in drawing the sample. The pollsters relied on telephone directories and automobile registration rosters to produce a sampling frame. During the Great Depression, only wealthier Americans owned telephones and automobiles. Thus, the millions of working-class Americans who constituted Roosevelt's principal base of support were excluded from the sample.

In recent years, the issue of selection bias has been further complicated by the fact that growing numbers of individuals refuse to answer pollsters' questions or use such devices as answering machines and caller ID to screen unwanted callers. If pollsters could be certain that those who responded to their surveys simply reflected the views of those who refused to respond, there would be no problem. Some studies, however, suggest that the views of respondents and nonrespondents can differ, especially along social-class lines. Middle- and upper-middle-class individuals are more likely to be willing to respond to surveys than their working-class counterparts.[29] Thus far, "nonresponse bias" has not undermined a major national survey, but the possibility of a future *Literary Digest* fiasco should not be ignored.

Sample Size   The degree of reliability in polling is also a function of sample size. For polls of citizens of the United States, the typical size of a sample ranges from 450 to 1,500 respondents. This number reflects a trade-off between cost and degree of precision desired. A larger and hence more costly sample size is associated with greater precision in making generalizations to the full population than is a smaller sample size.

The chance that the sample used does not accurately represent the population from which it is drawn is called the ***sampling error***, or *margin of error*. The sampling error measures the range of possibilities for a particular characteristic of a population based on the estimate of that characteristic in the sample drawn. The margin of error acknowledges that any given sample may not be perfectly representative of the full population. A typical survey of 1,500 respondents, for example, will have a sampling error of approximately 3 percent. When a preelection poll indicates that 51 percent of voters surveyed favor the Republican candidate and 49 percent support the Democratic candidate, the outcome is in fact too close to call because it is within the margin of error of the survey. A figure of 51 percent means that between 54 and 48 percent of voters in the population favor the Republicans, while a figure of 49 percent indicates that between 52 and 46 percent of all voters support the Democrats. Thus in this example, any outcome ranging from a 54–46 Republican victory

[29]John Goyder, Keith Warriner, and Susan Miller, "Evaluating Socio-economic Status Bias in Survey Nonresponse," *Journal of Official Statistics* 18, no. 1 (2002).

random digit dialing Polls in which respondents are selected at random from a list of ten-digit telephone numbers, with every effort made to avoid bias in the construction of the sample.

selection bias Polling error that arises when the sample is not representative of the population being studied, which creates errors in overrepresenting or underrepresenting some opinions.

sampling error A polling error that arises on account of the small size of the sample.

to a 48–52 Republican loss is consistent with the survey evidence. The precision of the poll in this case does not permit a clear prediction of a winner.

Table 9.5 shows how accurate two of the major national polling organizations have been in predicting the outcome of presidential elections. In both the 2000 and the 2004 presidential elections, for example, in light of a 3 percent margin of error, both the Harris and the Gallup organizations predicted a "dead heat." Pollsters have been mostly correct in their predictions.[30]

Survey Design   Even with reliable sample procedures, surveys may fail to reflect the true distribution of opinion within a target population. One frequent source of **measurement error** is the wording of survey questions. The precise words used in a question can have an enormous effect on the answers a survey elicits. The validity of survey results can also be adversely affected by poorly formatted questions, a faulty ordering of questions, inappropriate vocabulary, ambiguous questions, or questions with built-in biases. Often seemingly minor differences in the wording of a question can convey vastly different meanings to respondents and thus produce quite different response patterns. For example, for many years the University of Chicago's National Opinion Research Center has asked respondents whether they think the federal government is spending too much, too little, or about the right amount of money on "assistance for the poor." Answering the question posed this way, about two thirds of all respondents seem to believe that the government is spending too little. However, the same survey also asks whether the government spends too much, too little, or about the right amount for "welfare." When the word *welfare* is substituted for *assistance for the poor*, about half of all respondents indicate that too much money is being spent.[31]

Push Polling   In recent years, another form of bias has been introduced into surveys by the use of a technique called **push polling.** This technique involves asking a respondent a loaded question about a political candidate, with the question designed to elicit the response sought by the pollster and, simultaneously, to shape the respondent's perception of the candidate in question. For example, during the 1996 New Hampshire presidential primary, push pollsters employed by the campaign of one of Lamar Alexander's rivals called thousands of voters to ask, "If you knew that Lamar Alexander had raised taxes six times in Tennessee, would you be less inclined or more inclined to support him?"[32] More than 100 consulting firms across the nation now specialize in push polling, which is not a conventional use of legitimate survey methods and has been condemned by the American Association for Public

measurement error Failure to identify the true distribution of opinion within a population because of errors such as ambiguous or poorly worded questions.

push polling A polling technique in which the questions are designed to shape the respondent's opinion.

---

[30]For a recent paper on the difficulties with polls, especially in trying to assess the preferences of specific subgroups in the population, see David Leal, Matt Barreto, Jongho Lee, and Rodolfo O. de la Garza, "The Latino Vote in the 2004 Election," *PS: Political Science and Politics* 38 (January 2005): 41–49.

[31]Michael Kagay and Janet Elder, "Numbers Are No Problem for Pollsters, Words Are," *New York Times,* 9 August 1992, p. E6.

[32]Donn Tibbetts, "Draft Bill Requires Notice of Push Polling," *Manchester Union Leader,* 3 October 1996, p. A6.

TABLE 9.5 Two Pollsters and Their Records

Year	Presidential Candidates	Harris	Gallup	Actual Outcome
2008	Obama	50	51	53
	McCain	44	43	46
2004	Bush, G. W.	49	49	51
	Kerry	48	49	48
	Nader	1	1	0
2000	Bush, G. W.	47	48	48
	Gore	47	46	49
	Nader	5	4	3
1996	Clinton	51	52	49
	Dole	39	41	41
	Perot	9	7	8
1992	Clinton	44	44	43
	Bush, G. H. W.	38	37	38
	Perot	17	14	19
1988	Bush, G. H. W.	51	53	54
	Dukakis	47	42	46
1984	Reagan	56	59	59
	Mondale	44	41	41
1980	Reagan	48	47	51
	Carter	43	44	41
	Anderson		8	
1976	Carter	48	48	51
	Ford	45	49	48
1972	Nixon	59	62	61
	McGovern	35	38	38
1968	Nixon	40	43	43
	Humphrey	43	42	43
	Wallace	13	15	14
1964	Johnson	62	64	61
	Goldwater	33	36	39
1960	Kennedy	49	51	50
	Nixon	41	49	49
1956	Eisenhower	NA*	60	58
	Stevenson		41	42
1952	Eisenhower	47	51	55
	Stevenson	42	49	44
1948	Truman	NA*	44.5	49.6
	Dewey		49.5	45.1

SOURCE: Data from the Harris survey and the Gallup poll, Chicago Tribune–New York News Syndicate, various press releases, 1964–2008. Courtesy of Louis Harris & Associates and the Gallup Organization.

NOTE: Figures are percentages. All except those for 1948 are rounded.
*Not asked

Opinion Researchers.[33] Calling push polling the "political equivalent of a drive-by shooting," Representative Joe Barton (R-Tex.) launched a congressional investigation into the practice.[34] Push polls may be one reason why Americans are becoming increasingly skeptical of the practice of polling and increasingly unwilling to answers pollsters' questions.[35]

Illusion of Salience　In the early days of a political campaign, when voters are asked which candidates they do or do not support, the answer they give often has little salience or significance because the choice is not yet important to them. Their preferences may change many times before the election. This is part of the explanation for the phenomenon of the postconvention "bounce" in the popularity of presidential candidates, which is observed after Democratic and Republican national nominating conventions. Respondents' preferences reflected the amount of attention a candidate had received during the conventions rather than strongly held views.

Truly ***salient interests*** are those that stand out beyond others, interests that are of more than ordinary concern to respondents in a survey or to voters in the electorate. Politicians, social scientists, journalists, or pollsters who assume that something is important to the public when in fact it is not are creating an ***illusion of salience.*** This illusion can be created and fostered by polls despite careful controls in sampling, interviewing, and data analysis. In fact, the illusion is strengthened by the credibility that science gives survey results.

The problem of salience has become especially acute as a result of the proliferation of media polls. The television networks and major national newspapers all make heavy use of opinion polls. Polls are also commissioned by local television stations and local and regional newspapers. On the positive side, polls allow journalists to make independent assessments of political realities, assessments not influenced by the partisan claims of politicians.

At the same time, however, media polls can allow journalists to make news when none exists. Polling diminishes journalists' dependence on news makers. A poll commissioned by a news agency can provide the basis for a good story even when candidates, politicians, and other news makers are not engaging in especially newsworthy activities. Thus on days when little or nothing is taking place in a political campaign, poll results, especially apparent changes in candidates' popularity margins, can provide exciting news. Several times during the 2004 presidential campaign, for example, small changes in the relative standing of the Democratic and Republican candidates produced banner headlines around the country. Stories about what the candidates actually did or said often took second place to reporting the "horse race."

Because rapid and dramatic shifts in candidates' margins tend to take place when voters' preferences are least fully formed, it is interesting that horse-race news

salient interests Attitudes and views that are especially important to the individual holding them.

illusion of salience Impression conveyed by polls that something is important to the public when actually it is not.

[33]See www.aapor.org.pdfs/2003/2003pushpollstatement.pdf.

[34]Amy Keller, "Subcommittee Launches Investigation of Push Polls," *Roll Call*, 3 October 1996, p. 1.

[35]For a discussion of the growing difficulty of persuading people to respond to surveys, see John Brehm, *Phantom Respondents* (Ann Arbor: University of Michigan Press, 1993).

is most likely to make the headlines when it is least significant. In other words, media interest in poll results is inversely related to the salience of voters' opinions and the significance of the polls' findings. However, by influencing perceptions, especially those of major contributors, media polls can influence political realities.

Bandwagon Effect   One of the most noted polling problems is the **bandwagon effect,** which occurs when polling results influence people to support the candidate marked as the probable victor. Some scholars argue that the bandwagon effect can be offset by an "underdog effect," in favor of the candidate who is trailing in the polls.[36] However, a candidate who demonstrates a lead in the polls usually finds it considerably easier to raise campaign funds than does a candidate whose poll standing is poor. With these additional funds, poll leaders can often afford to pay for television time and other campaign activities that will cement their advantage.

PUBLIC OPINION AND GOVERNMENT POLICY

In democratic nations, leaders should pay attention to public opinion, and most evidence suggests that they do. There are many instances in which public policy and public opinion do not coincide, but in general the government's actions are consistent with citizens' preferences. One study, for example, found that between 1935 and 1979, in about two-thirds of all cases, significant changes in public opinion were followed within one year by changes in government policy consistent with the shift in the popular mood.[37] Other studies have come to similar conclusions about public opinion and government policy at the state level.[38] Do these results suggest that politicians pander to the public? The answer is no. Elected leaders don't always pander to the results of public opinion polls, but instead use polling to sell their policy proposals and shape the public's views.[39]

In addition, there are always areas of disagreement between opinion and policy. For example, the majority of Americans favored stricter governmental control of handguns for years before Congress finally adopted the modest restrictions on firearms purchases embodied in the 1994 Brady Bill and the Crime Control Act. Similarly, most Americans—blacks as well as whites—oppose school busing to achieve racial balance, yet such busing continues to be used extensively throughout the nation. Most Americans are far less concerned with the rights of the accused than the federal courts seem to be. Most Americans oppose U.S. military interven-

---

[36]See Michael Traugott, "The Impact of Media Polls on the Public," in *Media Polls in American Politics*, ed. Thomas E. Mann and Gary Orren (Washington, D.C.: Brookings Institution, 1992), pp. 125–49.

[37]Benjamin I. Page and Robert Y. Shapiro, "Effects of Public Opinion on Policy," *American Political Science Review* 77 (March 1983): 175–90.

[38]Robert A. Erikson, Gerald Wright, and John McIver, *Statehouse Democracy: Public Opinion and Democracy in the American States* (New York: Cambridge University Press, 1994).

[39]The results of separate studies by the political scientists Lawrence Jacobs, Robert Shapiro, and Alan Monroe were reported by Richard Morin in "Which Comes First, the Politician or the Poll?" *Washington Post National Weekly Edition*, 10 February 1997, p. 35.

bandwagon effect A situation wherein reports of voter or delegate opinion can influence the actual outcome of an election or a nominating convention.

tion in other nations' affairs, yet interventions continue to take place and often win public approval after the fact.

Several factors can contribute to a lack of consistency between opinion and governmental policy. First, the national majority on a particular issue may not be as intensely committed to its preference as the adherents of the minority viewpoint. An intensely committed minority may often be more willing to commit its time, energy, efforts, and resources to the affirmation of its opinions than an apathetic, even if large, majority. In the case of firearms, for example, although the proponents of gun control are in the majority by a wide margin, most do not regard the issue as one of critical importance to themselves and are not willing to commit much effort to advancing their cause. The opponents of gun control, by contrast, are intensely committed, well organized, and well financed, and as a result are usually able to carry the day.

A second important reason that public policy and public opinion may not coincide has to do with the character and structure of the American system of government. The framers of the American Constitution, as we saw in Chapter 2, sought to create a system of government that was based upon popular consent but that did not invariably and automatically translate shifting popular sentiments into public policies. As a result, the American governmental process includes arrangements such as an appointed judiciary that can produce policy decisions that may run contrary to prevailing popular sentiment—at least for a time.

Perhaps the inconsistencies between opinion and policy could be resolved if broader use were made of the initiative and referendum. This procedure allows propositions to be placed on the ballot and voted into law by the electorate thereby eliminating most of the normal machinery of representative government. In recent years, several important propositions sponsored by business and conservative groups have been enacted by voters in the states.[40] For example, California's Proposition 209, approved by the state's voters in 1996, prohibited the state and local government agencies in California from using race or gender preferences in the processes of hiring, contracting, or admitting university students. In 2000, conservative groups in such states as Virginia, South Dakota, South Carolina, Tennessee, and Idaho sponsored successful referenda to ban same-sex marriage while liberal forces in Missouri, Montana, Nevada, and Ohio promoted equally successful if nonbinding initiatives to raise the federal minimum wage. At the same time, gambling interests in Ohio waged an unsuccessful campaign to legalize slot machines, while promoters of marijuana use failed to convince their fellow citizens in Colorado, Nevada, and South Dakota of the virtues of cannabis.

Initiatives such as these seem to provide the public with an opportunity to express its will. The major problem, however, is that government by initiative offers little opportunity for reflection and compromise. Voters are presented with a proposition, usually sponsored by a special interest group, and are asked to take it or leave it. Perhaps the true will of the people, not to mention their best interest, might lie

---

[40]David S. Broder, *Democracy Detailed: Initiative Campaigns and the Power of Money* (New York: Harcourt, 2000).

somewhere between the positions taken by various interest groups. Perhaps, for example, California voters might have wanted affirmative action programs to be modified but not scrapped altogether as Proposition 209 mandated. In a representative assembly, as opposed to a referendum campaign, a compromise position might have been achieved that was more satisfactory to all the residents of the state. This is one reason the framers of the U.S. Constitution strongly favored representative government rather than direct democracy.

When all is said and done, however, there can be little doubt that in general the actions of the American government do not remain out of line with popular sentiment for very long. A major reason for this is, of course, the electoral process, to which we shall next turn.

CHAPTER REVIEW

All governments claim to obey public opinion, and in the democracies politicians and political leaders actually try to do so.

The American government does not directly regulate opinions and beliefs in the sense that dictatorial regimes often do. Opinion is regulated by an institution that the government constructed and that it maintains—the marketplace of ideas. In this marketplace, opinions and ideas compete for support. In general, opinions supported by upper-class groups have a better chance of succeeding than those views that are advanced mainly by the lower classes.

Americans share a number of values and viewpoints but often classify themselves as liberal or conservative in their basic orientations. The meaning of these terms has changed greatly over the past century. Once liberalism meant opposition to big government. Today liberals favor an expanded role for the government. Once conservatism meant support for state power and aristocratic rule. Today conservatives oppose almost all government regulation.

Although the United States relies mainly on market mechanisms, our government does intervene to influence particular opinions and, more important, the general climate of political opinion, often by trying to influence media coverage of events.

Another important force shaping public opinion is the news media, which help to determine the agenda or focus of political debate and to shape popular understanding of political events. The power of the media stems from their having the freedom to present information and opinion critical of government, political leaders, and policies. Free media are essential ingredients of popular government.

The scientific approach to learning public opinion is called polling. Through polling, elections can be accurately predicted; polls also provide information on the bases and conditions of voting decisions and make it possible to assess trends in attitudes and the influence of ideology on attitudes.

FOR FURTHER READING

Althaus, Scott. *Collective Preferences and Democratic Politics.* New York: Cambridge University Press, 2003.

Arnold, R. Douglas. *Congress, the Press, and Political Accountability.* Princeton, N.J.: Princeton University Press, 2004.

Bagdikian, Ben. *The New Media Monopoly.* Boston: Beacon Press, 2004.

Cook, Timothy. *Governing with the News: The News Media as a Political Institution.* Chicago: University of Chicago Press, 1997. ○ ONLINE READING

Erikson, Robert S., and Kent L. Tedin. *American Public Opinion: Its Origins, Content, and Impact.* 6th ed. New York: Longman, 2001.

Fenton, Tom. *Bad News: The Decline of Reporting, the Business of News, and the Danger to Us All.* New York: HarperCollins, 2005.

Fritz, Ben, Bryan Keefer, and Brendan Nyhan. *All the President's Spin.* New York: Touchstone Books, 2004.

Gallup, George, and Saul Forbes Rae. *The Pulse of Democracy: The Public-Opinion Poll and How It Works.* New York: Simon & Schuster, 1940.

Ginsberg, Benjamin. *The Captive Public: How Mass Opinion Promotes State Power.* New York: Basic Books, 1986.

Goldberg, Bernard. *Bias: A CBS Insider Exposes How the Media Distort the News.* New York: Regnery, 2002.

Hamilton, James. *All the News That's Fit to Sell.* Princeton, N.J.: Princeton University Press, 2004.

Kellner, Douglas. *Media Spectacle and the Crisis of Democracy: Terrorism, War, and Election Battles.* Boulder, Colo.: Paradigm, 2005. ○ ONLINE READING

Key, V. O. *Public Opinion and American Democracy.* New York: Knopf, 1961.

Lee, Taeku. *Mobilizing Public Opinion.* Chicago: University of Chicago Press, 2002. ○ ONLINE READING

Lippmann, Walter. *Public Opinion.* New York: Harcourt, Brace, 1922.

Merritt, Davis. *Knightfall: Knight Ridder and How the Erosion of Newspaper Journalism Is Putting Democracy at Risk.* New York: Amacom Books, 2005.

Norris, Pippa, Montague Kern, and Marion R. Just, eds. *Framing Terrorism: The News Media, the Government, and the Public.* New York: Routledge, 2003. ○ ONLINE READING

Rutherford, Paul. *Weapons of Mass Persuasion.* Toronto: University of Toronto Press, 2004.

Shogan, Robert. *Bad News: Where the Press Goes Wrong in the Making of the President.* Chicago: Dee, 2001.

Starr, Paul. *The Creation of the Media.* New York: Basic Books, 2004.

Stimson, James A. *Public Opinion in America: Moods, Cycles, and Swings.* 2nd ed. Boulder, Colo.: Westview Press, 1998. ○ ONLINE READING

Trippi, Joe. *The Revolution Will Not Be Televised: Democracy, the Internet, and the Overthrow of Everything.* New York: Regan Books, 2004.

Zaller, John R. *The Nature and Origins of Mass Opinion.* New York: Cambridge University Press, 1992.

Elections

HOW ELECTIONS WORK

Over the past two centuries, elections have come to play a significant role in the political processes of most nations. Democratic electoral systems, such as those that have evolved in the United States and western Europe, allow opposing forces to compete against and even to replace current officeholders. In democracies, elections can also serve as institutions of legitimation and as safety valves for social discontent. But beyond these functions, democratic elections facilitate popular influence, promote leadership accountability, and offer groups in society a measure of protection from the abuse of governmental power. Citizens exercise influence through elections by determining who should control the government. The chance to decide who will govern serves as an opportunity for ordinary citizens to make choices about the policies, programs, and directions of government action. In the United States, for example, recent Democratic and Republican candidates have differed significantly on issues of taxing, social spending, and governmental regulation. As American voters have chosen between the two parties' candidates, they have also made choices about these issues.

● Core of the Analysis

● Elections are important because they promote accountability in elected officials and facilitate popular influence in the governmental process.

● The government exerts a measure of control over the electoral process by regulating the composition of the electorate, translating voters' choices into electoral decisions, and insulating day-to-day government from the impact of those decisions.

● The strongest influences on voters' decisions are partisan loyalty, issue and policy concerns, and candidate characteristics.

● The increasing importance of money in elections has profound consequences for American democracy.

Elections promote leadership accountability because the threat of defeat at the polls exerts pressure on those in power to conduct themselves responsibly and to take account of popular interests and wishes when they make their decisions. As James Madison observed in the *Federalist Papers*, elected leaders are "compelled to anticipate the moment when their power is to cease, when their exercise of it is to be reviewed, and when they must descend to the level from which they were raised, there forever to remain unless a faithful discharge of their trust shall have established their title to a renewal of it."[1] It is because of this need to anticipate that elected officials constantly monitor public opinion polls as they decide what positions to take on policy issues.

In this chapter, we shall look first at the formal structure and setting of American elections. Second, we shall see how—and what—voters decide when they take part in elections. Third, we shall focus on recent national elections, including the 2008 presidential race. Fourth, we shall discuss the role of money in the election process, particularly in recent elections. Finally, we shall assess the place of elections in the American political process, raising the important question "Do elections matter?"[2]

REGULATING THE ELECTORAL PROCESS

In earlier chapters, we suggested that the relationship between citizens and elected politicians is an instance of a principal-agent relationship (see Chapter 1). There are two basic approaches to this relationship: the consent approach and the agency approach. The consent approach emphasizes the historical reality that the right of the citizen to participate in his or her own governance, mainly through the act of voting or other forms of consent, arises from an existing governmental order aimed at making it easier for the governors to govern by legitimating their rule. By giving their consent, citizens provide this legitimation. The agency approach treats the typical citizen as someone who would much rather devote scarce time and effort to his or her own private affairs than spend that time and effort on governance. He or she therefore chooses to delegate governance to agents—politicians—who are controlled through elections. In this approach, the control of agents is emphasized.

Whether they are seen as a means to control delegates (the agency approach) or legitimate governance by politicians (the consent approach), elections allow citizens to participate in political life on a routine and peaceful basis. Indeed, American voters have the opportunity to select and, if they so desire, depose some of their most important leaders. In this way, Americans have a chance to intervene in and influence the government's programs and policies. Yet it is important to recall that elections are not spontaneous affairs. Instead, they are formal governmental institutions. Although elections allow citizens a chance to participate in politics, they also allow the government a chance to exert a good deal of control over when,

---

[1]Clinton Rossiter, ed., *The Federalist Papers* (New York: New American Library, 1961), No. 57, p. 352.

[2]For up-to-date research on analyzing elections, see Rebecca B. Morton, *Analyzing Elections* (New York: Norton, 2006).

where, how, and which of its citizens will participate. Electoral processes are governed by a variety of rules and procedures that provide those in power with a significant opportunity to regulate the character—and perhaps also the consequences—of mass political participation.

Thus elections provide governments with an excellent opportunity to regulate and control popular involvement. Three general forms of regulation have played especially important roles in the electoral history of the Western democracies. First, governments often attempt to regulate the composition of the electorate to diminish the electoral weight of groups they deem undesirable. Second, governments frequently seek to manipulate the translation of voters' choices into electoral outcomes. Third, virtually all governments attempt to insulate policy-making processes from electoral intervention through regulation of the relationship between electoral decisions and the composition or organization of the government.

Electoral Composition

Perhaps the oldest and most obvious device used to regulate voting and its consequences is manipulation of the electorate's composition. In the first elections in western Europe, for example, the suffrage was generally limited to property owners and others who could be trusted to vote in a way acceptable to those in power. Property qualifications in France prior to 1848 limited the electorate to 240,000 of some 7 million men over the age of twenty-one.[3] No women were permitted to vote. During the same era, other nations manipulated the electorate's composition by assigning unequal electoral weights to different classes of voters. The 1831 Belgian constitution, for example, assigned individuals anywhere from one to three votes depending on their property holdings, education, and position.[4] But even in the context of America's ostensibly universal and equal suffrage in the twentieth century, the composition of the electorate is still subject to manipulation. Until recent years, some states tried to manipulate the vote by the discriminatory use of *poll taxes* and literacy tests or by such practices as the placement of polls and the scheduling of voting hours to depress participation by one or another group. In the aftermath of the 2004 presidential elections, in which Ohio proved a pivotal state for George W. Bush's victory, it was alleged that Republicans engaged in this sort of manipulation. In the county in which Kent State University (a Democratic stronghold) is located, very few voting machines were made available, producing long lines and up to nine-hour waiting times. Republican suburban locations, on the other hand, were more than adequately provisioned with voting machines. Similar stories about Democratic manipulations also circulated in the aftermath of the election. Today the most important example of the regulation of the American electorate's composition is the unique personal registration requirement.

Levels of voter participation in twentieth-century American elections are quite low by comparison to those of the other Western democracies (see Figure 10.1).[5] In-

poll tax A state-imposed tax on voters as a prerequisite for registration. Poll taxes were rendered unconstitutional in national elections by the Twenty-fourth Amendment, and in state elections by the Supreme Court in 1966.

---

[3]Stein Rokkan, *Citizens, Elections, Parties* (New York: David McKay, 1970), p. 149.

[4]John A. Hawgood, *Modern Constitutions since 1787* (New York: D. Van Nostrand, 1939), p. 148.

[5]See Walter Dean Burnham, "The Changing Shape of the American Political Universe," *American Political Science Review* 59 (1965), pp. 7–28.

FIGURE 10.1 Voter Turnout around the World, 1945–2006

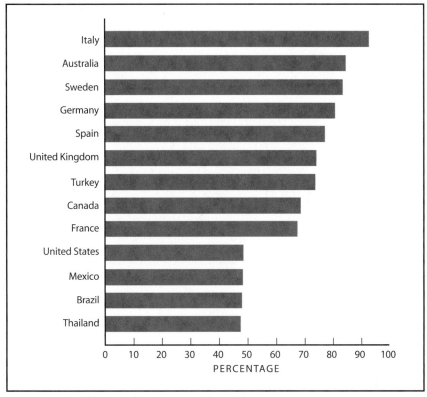

SOURCE: International Institute of Democracy and Electoral Assistance.

NOTE: Average between 1945 and 2006.

deed, voter participation in U.S. presidential elections has barely averaged 50 percent in recent years. Turnout in the 2000 presidential election was 51 percent. In 2004, major efforts to get out the vote brought turnout to over 59 percent. This was the first significant increase in voting in recent years, and further efforts brought turnout to over 60 percent in 2008. During the nineteenth century, however, voter turnout in the United States was much higher. Records, in fact, indicate that in some counties as many as 105 percent of those eligible voted in presidential elections. Some proportion of this total obviously was artificial—a result of the widespread corruption that characterized American voting practices during that period. Nevertheless, it seems clear that the proportion of eligible voters actually going to the polls was considerably greater in nineteenth-century America than it is today.

As Figure 10.2 indicates, the critical years during which voter turnout declined across the United States were between 1890 and 1910 (see page 295). These years coincide with the adoption of laws across much of the nation requiring eligible citizens to appear personally at a registrar's office to register to vote some time prior to the actual date of an election. Personal registration was one of several "progressive"

Manipulation of the electorate's composition is a device used to regulate voting and its consequences.

Past methods by which voter participation was limited	Current limits on participation
Property ownership and literacy requirements	There are numerous restrictions on the voting rights of convicted felons that vary from state to state. Prison inmates serving a felony sentence are prohibited from voting in 48 states and the District of Columbia.
Poll taxes	
Race and gender restrictions	
Placement of polls and scheduling of polling hours	
Voter registration rules	There are no other official limits (other than the age requirement), except that voter must be an American citizen. However, any voter registration rules tend to depress participation on the part of the poor and uneducated.

reforms initiated at the turn of the century. The ostensible purpose of registration was to discourage fraud and corruption. But to many Progressive reformers, "corruption" was a code word referring to the politics practiced in large cities where political parties had organized immigrant and ethnic populations. Reformers not only objected to this corruption but also opposed the growing political power of these urban populations and their leaders.

Personal registration imposed a new burden upon potential voters and altered the format of American elections. Under the registration systems adopted after 1890, it became the duty of individual voters to secure their own eligibility. This duty could prove to be a significant burden for potential voters. During a personal appearance before the registrar, individuals seeking to vote were (and are) required to furnish proof of identity, residence, and citizenship. While the inconvenience of registration varied from state to state, usually voters could register only during business hours on weekdays. Many potential voters could not afford to lose a day's pay in order to register. Second, voters were usually required to register well before the next election, in some states up to several months earlier. Third, since most personal registration laws required a periodic purge of the election rolls to keep them up to date, voters often had to reregister to maintain their eligibility. Thus, although personal registration requirements helped to diminish the widespread electoral corruption that accompanied a completely open voting process, they also made it much more difficult for citizens to participate in the electoral process.

Registration requirements particularly depress participation on the part of those with little education and low incomes, for two reasons. First, the simple obstacle of registering on weekdays during business hours is difficult for working-class persons to overcome. Second, and more important, registration requires a greater

FIGURE 10.2 Voter Turnout in Presidential Elections

SOURCES: For 1860–1928, U.S. Bureau of the Census, *Historical Statistics of the United States, Colonial Times to 1970* (www.census.gov/prod/www/abs/statab.html); pt. 2, p. 1071; for 1932–92, U.S. Bureau of the Census, *Statistical Abstract of the United States,* 1993 (Washington, D.C.: Government Printing Office, 1993), p. 284; for 1996–2008, Federal Election Commission data.

NOTE: Data reflect the population of eligible voters; the percentage of the voting-age population that voted would be smaller.

degree of political involvement and interest than does the act of voting itself. To vote, a person need only be concerned with the particular election campaign at hand. Requiring individuals to register before the next election forces them to make a decision to participate on the basis of an abstract interest in the electoral process rather than a simple concern with a specific campaign. Such an abstract interest in electoral politics is largely a product of education. Those with relatively little education may become interested in political events because of a particular campaign, but by that time it may be too late to register. As a result, personal registration requirements not only diminish the size of the electorate but also tend to create an electorate that is, in the aggregate, less representative of the voting-age population. The electorate becomes better educated, higher in income and social status, and composed of fewer African Americans and other minorities than the citizenry as a whole.

Over the years, voter registration restrictions have been modified somewhat to make registration easier. In 1993, for example, Congress approved and President Clinton signed the ***Motor Voter bill*** to ease voter registration by allowing individuals to register when they applied for driver's licenses as well as in public assistance and military recruitment offices.[6] In Europe, there is typically no registration burden on the individual voter; the government handles voter registration automatically. This is

Motor Voter bill A legislative act passed in 1993 that requires all states to allow voters to register by mail when they renew their drivers' licenses and provides for the placement of voter registration forms in motor vehicle, public assistance, and military recruitment offices.

---

[6]Helen Dewar, "'Motor Voter' Agreement Is Reached," *Washington Post,* 28 April 1993, p. A6.

one reason that voter turnout rates in Europe are higher than those in the United States.

Another factor explaining low rates of voter turnout in the United States is the weakness of the American party system. During the nineteenth century, American political party machines employed hundreds of thousands of workers to organize and mobilize voters and bring them to the polls. The result was an extremely high rate of turnout, typically more than 90 percent of eligible voters.[7] But political party machines began to decline in strength in the early twentieth century and by now have largely disappeared. Without party workers to encourage them to go to the polls and even to bring them there if necessary, many eligible voters will not participate. In the absence of strong parties, participation rates drop the most among poorer and less-educated citizens. Because of the absence of strong political parties, the American electorate is smaller and skewed more toward the middle class than toward the population of all those potentially eligible to vote.

Translating Voters' Choices into Electoral Outcomes

With the exception of America's personal registration requirements, contemporary governments generally do not try to limit the composition of their electorates. Instead, they prefer to allow everyone to vote and then to manipulate the outcome of the election. This is possible because there is more than one way to decide the relationship between individual votes and electoral outcomes. Any number of possible rules can be used to determine how individual votes will be translated into collective electoral decisions. Two types of regulations are especially important: the rules that set the criteria for victory, and the rules that define electoral districts.

The Criteria for Winning In some nations, to win a seat in the parliament or other representative body, a candidate must receive a simple majority (50% + 1) of all the votes cast in the relevant district. This type of electoral system is called a

---

[7] Erik Austin and Jerome Chubb, *Political Facts of the United States since 1789* (New York: Columbia University Press, 1986), pp. 378–79.

majority system and was used in the primary elections of most Southern states until recent years. Generally, majority systems have a provision for a second or "runoff" election among the two top candidates if the initial contest drew so many contestants that none received an absolute majority of the votes cast.

In other nations, candidates for office need not receive an absolute majority of the votes cast to win an election. Instead, victory is awarded to the candidate who receives the most votes in a given election regardless of the actual percentage of votes this represents. Thus, a candidate who receives 40 percent, 30 percent, or 20 percent of the votes cast may win the contest so long as no rival receives more votes. This type of electoral process is called a *plurality system,* and it is the system used in almost all general elections in the United States.

In some political systems, multiple representatives are chosen from each district, constituency, or region, according to a third electoral system, called *proportional representation.* Under proportional rules, competing political parties are awarded legislative seats roughly in proportion to the percentage of the popular vote that they receive. For example, a party that won 30 percent of the votes would receive roughly 30 percent of the seats in the parliament or other representative body. In the United States, many states use proportional representation in presidential primary elections. In these primaries, candidates for the Democratic and Republican nominations are awarded convention delegates in rough proportion to the percentage of the popular vote they receive in the primary.

Electoral Districts Congressional district boundaries in the United States are redrawn by governors and state legislatures every ten years, after the decennial census determines the number of House seats to which each state is entitled (see Figure 10.3). Rather than seeking to manipulate the criteria for victory, American politicians have usually sought to influence electoral outcomes by manipulating the organization of electoral districts. This is called *gerrymandering* in honor of nineteenth-century Massachusetts Governor Elbridge Gerry, who was alleged to have drawn district boundaries in the shape of a salamander to capture a disproportionate number of his party's votes within the district. The principle is simple. Different distributions of voters among districts produce different electoral outcomes; those in a position to control the arrangements of districts are also in a position to manipulate the results. For example, until recent years, gerrymandering to dilute the voting strength of racial minorities was a tactic of many state legislatures. One of the more common strategies involved redrawing congressional boundary lines in such a way as to divide and disperse a black population that otherwise would have constituted a majority within the original district.

This form of racial gerrymandering, sometimes called "cracking," was used in Mississippi during the 1960s and 1970s to prevent the election of an African American to Congress. Historically, the black population in Mississippi was clustered in the western half of the state, along the Mississippi Delta. From 1882 until 1966, the delta was one congressional district. Although blacks constituted a clear majority within the district (66 percent in 1960), the continuing election of white representatives was assured simply because blacks were denied the right to register and vote. With Congress's passage of the Voting Rights Act of 1965, however, the Mississippi

majority system Type of electoral system in which, to win a seat in the parliament or other representative body, a candidate must receive a majority of all the votes cast in the relevant district.

plurality system Type of electoral system in which, to win a seat in the parliament or other representative body, a candidate need only receive the most votes in the election, not necessarily a majority of votes cast.

proportional representation A multiple-member district system that awards seats based on the percentage of the vote won by each candidate. By contrast, the "winner-take-all" system of elections awards the seat to the one candidate who wins the most votes.

gerrymandering Apportionment of voters in districts in such a way as to give unfair advantage to one political party.

state legislature moved swiftly to minimize the potential voting power of African Americans by redrawing congressional district lines to fragment the African American population in the delta into four of the state's five congressional districts. Mississippi's gerrymandering scheme was preserved in the state's redistricting plans in 1972 and 1981 and helped to prevent the election of any African American representative until 1986, when Mike Espy became the first African American since Reconstruction to represent Mississippi in Congress.

Recently, the federal government has encouraged what is sometimes called benign gerrymandering, designed to increase minority representation in Congress. The 1982 amendments to the Voting Rights Act of 1965 foster the creation of legislative districts with predominantly African American or Hispanic American populations by requiring states, when possible, to draw district lines that take account of concentrations of African American and Hispanic American voters. These amendments were initially supported by Democrats who assumed that minority-controlled districts would guarantee the election of Democratic members of Congress. Republicans championed them, too, hoping that if minority voters were concentrated in particular districts, Republican prospects in other districts would be enhanced.[8]

The 1993 Supreme Court in decision in *Shaw v. Reno,* however, opened the way for challenges by white voters to the drawing of these districts. In the five-to-four majority opinion, Justice Sandra Day O'Connor wrote that if district boundaries were so "bizarre" as to be inexplicable on any grounds other than an effort to ensure the election of minority group members to office, white voters would have reason to assert that they had been the victims of unconstitutional racial gerrymandering.[9] In the 1995 case of *Miller v. Johnson,* the Supreme Court put further limits on "benign" gerrymandering by asserting that the use of race as a "predominant factor" in creating election districts was presumptively unconstitutional. However, the Court held open the possibility that race could be *one* of the factors influencing legislative redistricting.[10]

Traditionally, district boundaries have been redrawn only once a decade, following the decennial national census. In recent years, however, the Republican Party has adopted an extremely aggressive redistricting strategy, in some instances not waiting for a new census before launching a redistricting effort that could serve its political interests. In Texas, for example, after the GOP took control of both houses of the state legislature in the 2002 elections, Republican lawmakers sought to enact a redistricting plan that promised to shift as many as five congressional seats to the Republican column. This Republican effort was masterminded by U.S. House Majority Leader at the time, Tom DeLay, who is himself a Texan. DeLay saw an opportunity to increase the Republican majority in the House and reduce Democratic prospects for regaining control of Congress. In an effort to block DeLay's plan, fifty-one Democratic legislators refused to attend state legislative sessions, leaving the Texas legislature without a quorum and unable to conduct its business. The legislature's Republican leadership ordered the state police to apprehend the missing

---

[8]Roberto Suro, "In Redistricting, New Rules and New Prizes," *New York Times,* 6 May 1990, sec. 4, p. 5.

[9]*Shaw v. Reno,* 113 S. Ct. 2816 (1993); Linda Greenhouse, "Court Questions Districts Drawn to Aid Minorities," *New York Times,* 29 June 1993, p. 1.

[10]*Miller v. Johnson,* 63 USLW 4726 (1995).

FIGURE 10.3 Congressional Redistricting

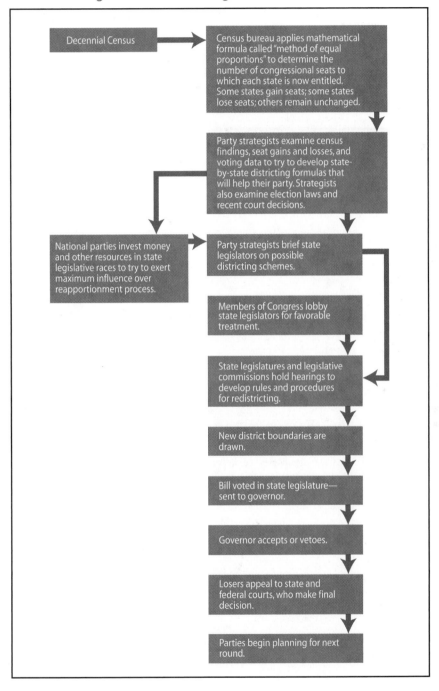

Decennial Census

Census bureau applies mathematical formula called "method of equal proportions" to determine the number of congressional seats to which each state is now entitled. Some states gain seats; some states lose seats; others remain unchanged.

Party strategists examine census findings, seat gains and losses, and voting data to try to develop state-by-state districting formulas that will help their party. Strategists also examine election laws and recent court decisions.

National parties invest money and other resources in state legislative races to try to exert maximum influence over reapportionment process.

Party strategists brief state legislators on possible districting schemes.

Members of Congress lobby state legislators for favorable treatment.

State legislatures and legislative commissions hold hearings to develop rules and procedures for redistricting.

New district boundaries are drawn.

Bill voted in state legislature—sent to governor.

Governor accepts or vetoes.

Losers appeal to state and federal courts, who make final decision.

Parties begin planning for next round.

The Electoral Impact of Congressional Redistricting

The method by which electoral districts are drawn may directly impact who gets elected from those districts. Recent decades have witnessed more states utilizing independent commissions or panels to redraw congressional districts in an attempt to limit partisanship in the districting process, but the majority of states still rely on state legislatures to reapportion House seats. At the same time, technological innovations such as Geographic Information Systems (GIS) software allow mapmakers to be extremely precise in terms of how individual voters are allocated among districts. As a result, congressional redistricting has become a focal point for party strategy.

◀ Consider a hypothetical state where Republicans represent 60% of voters and Democrats represent the remaining 40% of voters. As a result of population changes during the preceding decade, this state now has five congressional districts. Assuming members of the state legislature want to create congressional districts with approximately the same number of people, there are several ways to draw district boundaries.

▶ For instance, a state legislature controlled by a Republican majority could draw congressional districts so that Republican voters clearly dominate three of the five districts and Democratic voters dominate the remaining two. In this scenario, the Republicans could expect their candiates to win three of the five House districts.

R	R	R	R	R
R	R	R	R	R
R	R	R	R	R
D	D	D	D	D
D	D	D	D	D

SCENARIO 1

R	R	R	R	R
R	R	R	R	R
R	R	R	R	R
D	D	D	D	D
D	D	D	D	D

◀ Another possibility might arise if the Republican state legislature decides to make the districts slightly more competitive, but also attempts to gain control of all five House districts in the upcoming election.

SCENARIO 2

Suppose that the Democrats are in control of the state legislature. With the same distribution of voters in the state, they could draw the districts to favor Democrats as much as possible (with Democratic voters dominating three of the districts).

R	R	R	R	R
R	R	R	R	R
R	R	R	R	R
D	D	D	D	D
D	D	D	D	D

SCENARIO 3

IOWA DISTRICTS, 2000

5

2

1

Des Moines ★

Iowa City

4

3

By contrast, a non-partisan independent commission or panel may draw more-competitive districts, with a more even distribution of Republican and Democratic voters. A real-world example from Iowa (which employs an independent commission) shows district boundaries before and after the 2002 redistricting cycle.

Note how the district boundaries changed in an effort to promote greater levels of competition throughout the state. This is reflected by the incumbent vote share in the subsequent election. The more-competitive districts created after 2002 meant that incumbents could be challenged more easily, and as a result, Iowa incumbents received a smaller share of votes in the 2004 elections.

IOWA DISTRICTS, 2002

4

1

5

Des Moines ★

Iowa City

3

2

THE OUTCOME

Incumbent vote share, 2000 House races in Iowa **62.4%**

Incumbent vote share, 2004 House races in Iowa **56%**

30   40   50   60   70

Democrats and return them to the Capitol. The Democrats responded by escaping to Oklahoma, beyond the jurisdiction of the Texas police. Eventually, the Democrats capitulated and the GOP was able to enact its redistricting plan. In 2006, the U.S. Supreme Court upheld the legality of most of the DeLay plan. A similar GOP redistricting effort in Pennsylvania was also upheld by the U.S. Supreme Court in 2004.

Insulating Decision-Making Processes

Virtually all governments attempt at least partially to insulate decision-making processes from electoral intervention. The most obvious ways of doing this are confining popular elections to only some governmental positions, using various modes of indirect election, and setting lengthy terms of office. In the United States, the framers of the Constitution intended that only members of the House of Representatives would be subject to direct popular election. The president and senators were to be indirectly elected for longer terms to allow them, as the *Federalist Papers* put it, to avoid "an unqualified complaisance to every sudden breeze of passion, or to every transient impulse which the people may receive."[11]

The Electoral College   In the early history of popular voting, nations often made use of indirect elections. In these elections, voters would choose the members of an intermediate body. These members would, in turn, select public officials. The assumption underlying such processes was that ordinary citizens were not really qualified to choose their leaders and could not be trusted to do so directly. The last vestige of this procedure in America is the ***electoral college,*** the group of electors who formally select the president of the United States.

When Americans go to the polls on election day, they are technically not voting directly for presidential candidates. Instead, voters within each state are choosing among slates of electors who have been elected or appointed to their positions some months earlier. The electors are pledged to support their own party's presidential candidate chosen in the presidential race. In each state (except for Maine and Nebraska), the slate that wins casts all the state's electoral votes for its party's candidate.[12] Each state is entitled to a number of electoral votes equal to the number of the state's senators and representatives combined, for a total of 538 electoral votes for the fifty states and the District of Columbia. Occasionally, an elector breaks his or her pledge and votes for the other party's candidate. For example, in 1976, when the Republicans carried the state of Washington, one Republican elector from that state refused to vote for Gerald Ford, the Republican presidential nominee. Many states have now enacted statutes formally binding electors to their pledges, but some constitutional authorities doubt whether such statutes are enforceable.

electoral college The presidential electors from each state who meet in their respective state capitals after the popular election to cast ballots for president and vice president.

---

[11]Rossiter, ed., *The Federalist Papers*, No. 71, p. 432.

[12]State legislatures determine the system by which electors are selected and almost all states use this "winner-take-all" system. Maine and Nebraska, however, provide that one electoral vote goes to the winner in each congressional district and two electoral votes go to the winner statewide.

In each state, the electors whose slate has won proceed to the state's capital on the Monday following the second Wednesday in December and formally cast their ballots. These are sent to Washington, tallied by Congress in January, and the name of the winner is formally announced. If no candidate receives a majority of all electoral votes, the names of the top three candidates are submitted to the House, where each state can cast one vote. Whether a state's vote is decided by a majority, plurality, or some other fraction of the state's delegates is determined under rules established by the House.

In 1800 and 1824, the electoral college failed to produce a majority for any candidate. In the election of 1800, Thomas Jefferson, the Jeffersonian Republican Party's presidential candidate, and Aaron Burr, that party's vice-presidential candidate, received an equal number of votes in the electoral college, throwing the election into the House of Representatives. (The Constitution at that time made no distinction between presidential and vice-presidential candidates, specifying only that the individual receiving a majority of electoral votes would be named president.) Some members of the Federalist Party in Congress suggested that they should seize the opportunity to damage the Republican cause by supporting Burr and denying Jefferson the presidency. Federalist leader Alexander Hamilton put a stop to this mischievous notion, however, and made certain that his party supported Jefferson. Hamilton's actions enraged Burr and helped lead to the infamous duel between the two men, in which Hamilton was killed. The Twelfth Amendment, ratified in 1804, was designed to prevent a repetition of such a situation by providing for separate electoral college votes for president and vice president.

In the 1824 election, four candidates—John Quincy Adams, Andrew Jackson, Henry Clay, and William H. Crawford—divided the electoral vote; no one of them received a majority. The House of Representatives eventually chose Adams over the others, even though Jackson had won more electoral and popular votes. This choice resulted from the famous "corrupt bargain" between Adams and Henry Clay. After 1824, the two major political parties had begun to dominate presidential politics to such an extent that by December of each election year, only two candidates remained for the electors to choose between, thus ensuring that one would receive a majority. This freed the parties and the candidates from having to plan their campaigns to culminate in Congress, and Congress very quickly ceased to dominate the presidential selection process.

On all but three occasions since 1824, the electoral vote has simply ratified the nationwide popular vote. Since electoral votes are won on a state-by-state basis, it is mathematically possible for a candidate who receives a nationwide popular plurality to fail to carry states whose electoral votes would add up to a majority. Thus, in 1876, Rutherford B. Hayes was the winner in the electoral college despite receiving fewer popular votes than his rival, Samuel Tilden. In 1888, Grover Cleveland received more popular votes than Benjamin Harrison, but received fewer electoral votes. And in 2000, Al Gore outpolled his opponent, George W. Bush, but narrowly lost the electoral college by a mere four electoral votes.

In the modern era, the electoral college has a profound effect on the nature of campaigning. Imagine an election with no electoral college, in which the winner of the popular vote is elected. Campaigns in this scenario would focus on votes wherever they may be found. Resources—for television ads, candidates' visits, or securing local endorsements—would be invested wherever the vote yield was expected to be fruitful. In a world *with* an electoral college, on the other hand, votes in a state matter only if they can move that state into the candidate's column. There was no point in 2008, for example, for either McCain or Obama to devote scarce campaign resources to Massachusetts (a sure Obama state) or Texas (a sure McCain state); instead, they focused on places that were contestable: Ohio, Florida, and Pennsylvania. A contest with no electoral college would entail a wide-open national campaign with votes sought out everywhere. A contest with an electoral college, in contrast, concentrates campaign activity in contestable states.

Frequency of Elections   Less obvious are the insulating effects of electoral arrangements that permit direct, and even frequent, popular election of public officials, but tend to fragment the impact of elections upon the government's composition. In the United States, for example, the constitutional provision of staggered terms of service in the Senate was designed to diminish the impact of shifts in electoral sentiment upon the Senate as an institution. Since only one-third of its members were to be selected at any time, the composition of the institution would be partially protected from changes in electoral preferences.

Size of Electoral Districts   The division of the nation into relatively small, geographically based constituencies for the purpose of selecting members of the House of Representatives was, in part, designed to have a similar effect. Representatives were to be chosen frequently. And although not prescribed by the Constitution, the fact that each was to be selected by a discrete constituency was thought by Madison and others to diminish the government's vulnerability to mass popular movements.

In a sense, the House of Representatives was compartmentalized in the same way that a submarine is divided into watertight sections to confine the impact of any damage to the vessel. First, dividing the national electorate into small districts increased the importance of local issues. Second, because of the salience of local issues, a representative's electoral fortunes were more closely tied to factors peculiar to his or her own district than to national responses to issues. Third, given a geographical principle of representation, national groups were somewhat fragmented while the formation of local forces that might or might not share common underlying attitudes were encouraged. No matter how well represented individual constituencies might be, the influence of voters on national policy questions would be fragmented.

Australian ballot An electoral format that presents the names of all the candidates for any given office on the same ballot. Introduced at the turn of the twentieth century, the Australian ballot replaced the partisan ballot and facilitated split-ticket voting.

The Ballot   Prior to the 1890s, voters cast ballots according to political parties. Each party printed its own ballots, listed only its own candidates for each office, and employed party workers to distribute its ballots at the polls. This ballot format virtually prevented split-ticket voting. Because only one party's candidates appeared on any ballot, it was very difficult for a voter to cast anything other than a straight party vote.

The advent of a new, neutral ballot (known as the ***Australian ballot***) represented a significant change in electoral procedure. The new ballot was prepared and administered by the state rather than the parties. Each ballot was identical and included the names of all candidates for office. This ballot reform made it possible for voters to make their choices on the basis of the individual rather than the collective merits of a party's candidates. Because all candidates for the same office now appeared on the same ballot, voters were no longer forced to choose a straight party ticket. This gave rise to the phenomenon of split-ticket voting in American elections.

Prior to the reform of the ballot, it was not uncommon for an entire incumbent administration to be swept from office and replaced by an entirely new set of officials. In the absence of a real possibility of split-ticket voting, any desire on the part of the electorate for change could be expressed only as a vote against all candidates of the party in power. Because of this, there always existed the possibility, particularly at the state and local levels, that an insurgent slate committed to policy change could be swept into power. The party ballot thus increased the potential impact of elections upon the government's composition. Although this potential may not always have been realized, the party ballot at least increased the chance that electoral decisions could lead to policy changes. By contrast, because it permitted choice on the basis of candidates' individual appeals, ticket splitting led to increasingly divided partisan control of government.

The actual ballots used by voters vary from county to county across the United States. Some counties employ paper ballots; others use mechanical voting machines. Some use punch-card systems; still others have introduced electronic and computerized systems. Not surprisingly, the controversy surrounding Florida's presidential vote in 2000 led to a closer look at the different balloting systems, and it became apparent that some of them produced unreliable results. Indeed, faulty ballots in Florida and other states may have changed the outcome of the 2000 election. Many counties moved to introduce computerized voting systems, which they hoped would lessen the chance of spoiled or incorrectly counted ballots. Some critics of computerized systems, however, warn that they may be vulnerable to unauthorized use or "hacking," which could call the result of an entire election into question.

Taken together, regulation of the electorate's composition, the translation of voters' choices into electoral decisions, and the impact of those decisions upon the government's composition allow those in power a measure of control over mass participation in political life. These techniques do not necessarily have the effect of diminishing citizens' capacity to influence their rulers' conduct. Rather, these techniques are generally used to influence *electoral influence*.

Direct Democracy: The Referendum and Recall

In addition to voting for candidates, voters in some states also vote on referenda. The **referendum** process allows citizens to vote directly on proposed laws or other governmental actions. In recent years, voters in several states have voted to set limits on tax rates, to block state and local spending proposals, and to prohibit social services for illegal immigrants. Although it involves voting, a referendum is not an election. The election is an institution of representative government. Through an election, voters choose officials to act for them. The referendum, by contrast, is an institution of direct democracy; it allows voters to govern directly without intervention by government officials. The validity of referenda results, however, is subject to judicial action. If a court finds that a referendum outcome violates the state or

referendum The practice of referring a measure proposed by a legislature to the vote of the electorate for approval or rejection.

national constitution, it can overturn the result. This happened in the case of a 1995 California referendum curtailing social services to illegal aliens.[13]

Twenty-four states permit various forms of the ***initiative.*** Whereas the referendum described above allows citizens to affirm or reject a policy produced by legislative action, the initiative provides citizens with a way forward in the face of legislative inaction. This is done by placing a policy proposal (legislative or state constitutional amendment) on the ballot to be approved or disapproved by the electorate. In order to reserve a place on the ballot, a petition must be accompanied by a minimum number of voter signatures—a requirement that varies from state to state—that are certified by the state's Secretary of State.

The initiative is also vulnerable to adverse selection. Ballot propositions involve policies the state legislature cannot (or does not want to) resolve. Like referendum issues, these are often highly emotional and, consequently, not always well-suited to resolution in the electoral arena. One of the "virtues" of the initiative is that it may be *action-forcing*. Legislative leaders can induce recalcitrant legislators to move ahead on controversial issues in the knowledge that a possibly worse outcome will result from inaction.[14]

Eighteen states also have legal provisions for ***recall*** elections. The recall is an electoral device introduced by turn-of-the-century Populists to allow voters to remove governors and other state officials from office prior to the expiration of their terms. Federal officials such as the president and members of Congress are not subject to recall. Generally, a recall effort begins with a petition campaign. For example, in California, the site of a tumultuous recall battle in 2003, if 12 percent of those who voted in the last general election sign petitions demanding a special recall election, the state board of elections must schedule one. Such petition campaigns are relatively common, but most fail to garner enough signatures to bring the matter to a statewide vote. In the California case, however, a conservative Republican member of Congress, Darrell Issa, led a successful effort to recall Democratic Governor Gray Davis. Voters were unhappy about the state's economy, dissatisfied with Davis's performance, and blamed Davis for the state's $38 billion budget deficit. Under California law, voters in a special recall election are also asked to choose a replacement for the official whom they dismiss. Californians in 2003 elected movie star Arnold Schwarzenegger to be their governor. In 2008, a number of politicians faced recall elections. For example, voters in Montana's Big Horn County were given an opportunity to recall Sheriff Lawrence "Pete" Big Hair, who had been charged by his wife with domestic assault. Michigan voters pondered whether to recall House Speaker Andy Dillon, who made enemies when he backed a state income tax increase. And, in an ironic twist, the California prison guards union launched an effort (unsuccessful) to recall Governor Arnold Schwarzenegger.

The referendum, initiative, and recall all entail shifts in agenda-setting power. The referendum gives an impassioned electoral majority the opportunity to reverse

initiative The process that allows citizens to propose new laws and submit them for approval by the state's voters.

recall Procedure to allow voters an opportunity to remove state officials from office before their terms expire.

---

[13] *League of United Latin American Citizens v. Wilson*, CV-94-7569 (C.D. Calif.) (1995).

[14] This point is developed in Mordon Bennedsen and Sven Fledmann, "Lobbying Legislatures," *Journal of Political Economy* 110 (2002).

legislation that displeases them, thus affecting the initial strategic calculations of institutional agenda setters (who want to get as much of what they want without its being subsequently reversed). The initiative has a similar effect on institutional agenda setters, but here it inclines them toward action rather than inaction. Combining the two, an institutional agenda setter is caught on the two horns of an institutional dilemma: Do I act, risking a reversal via referendum, or do I maintain the status quo, risking an overturn via initiative? The recall complements both of these, keeping institutional agenda setters on their toes to avoid being ousted. As the institution principle implies, these arrangements do not just provide citizens with governance tools. They also affect the strategic calculations of institutional politicians—legislators and governors.

HOW DO VOTERS DECIDE?

Thus far, we have focused on the election as an institution. But the election is also a process in which millions of individuals make decisions and choices. Three types of factors influence voters' decisions at the polls: partisan loyalty, issues, and candidates' characteristics.

Partisan Loyalty

Many studies have shown that most Americans identify more or less strongly with one of the two major political parties. Partisan loyalty was strong during the 1940s and 1950s, declined for the next five decades, and has recently ticked up, reaching the levels it enjoyed in the 1950s. Most voters today feel a certain sense of identification or kinship with the Democratic or Republican party. This sense of identification is often handed down from parents to children and is reinforced by social and cultural ties. Partisan identification predisposes voters in favor of their party's candidates and against those of the opposing party. Partisanship is most likely to assert itself in the less-visible races, where issues and candidates are not very well known. Races for state legislatures, for example, are often decided by voters' party ties. However, even at the level of the presidential contest, in which issues and candidates' personalities become very important, many Americans supported John McCain or Barack Obama in 2008 largely because of partisan loyalty. Once formed, partisan loyalties are resistant to change. But sufficiently strong events and experiences may have the effect of eroding or even reversing them. White men in the South, for example, have been transformed over the last fifty years from strong partisans of the Democratic party to independents and even supporters of the Republican party. Voters tend to keep their party affiliations unless some crisis causes them to reexamine the bases of their loyalties and conclude that they have not given their support to the appropriate party. During these relatively infrequent periods, millions of voters can change their party ties. For example, at the beginning of the New Deal era, between 1932 and 1936, millions of former Republicans transferred their allegiance to Franklin Roosevelt and the Democratic party.

Partisan loyalty should be understood as more than a psychological attachment (although it certainly is that as well). It is also an informational shortcut—a way for voters to economize on information collection and processing. In many circumstances, it may be "enough" simply to know what party label a particular candidate wears. Any extra information—issue positions or personal attributes—may not influence the voter's choice once the partisan content has been taken on board. For example, once a particular voter learns that a candidate is a Democrat, he or she knows that the candidate is likely to be the preferred alternative; for another voter, however, that simple fact may be enough to cause him or her to vote for the other guy! In the second half of the twentieth century, party labels began losing their capacity to signal likely characteristics of candidates, with the result that more and more voters found their partisan attachments weakening or disappearing altogether. The rise in the proportion of the electorate now identifying only weakly with a party or declaring themselves independents is testimony to this fact.[15]

The Analyzing the Evidence unit in Chapter 11 takes a closer look at trends in partisanship. Accompanying the long-term trend in party attachments, however, are ebbs and flows. As voters sorted themselves out between the parties, with more southerners becoming Republicans and moderates and liberals moving toward the Democrats, there was an uptick in partisan attachment in the 1990s. Parties, it would seem, by clarifying themselves ideologically, have become useful informational shortcuts again.[16]

Issues

Issues and policy preferences are a second factor influencing voters' choices at the polls. Voters may cast their ballots for the candidate whose position on economic issues they believe to be closest to their own. Similarly, they may select the candidate who has what they believe to be the best record on foreign policy. Issues are more important in some races than others. If candidates actually "take issue" with one another—that is, articulate and publicize very different positions on important public questions—then voters are more likely to be able to identify and act upon whatever policy preferences they may have.

The ability of voters to make choices on the bases of issue or policy preferences is diminished if competing candidates do not differ substantially or do not focus their campaigns on policy matters. Very often, candidates deliberately take the safe course and emphasize topics that will not be offensive to any voters. Thus, candidates often trumpet their opposition to corruption, crime, and inflation. Presumably, few voters favor these things. While it may be perfectly reasonable for candidates to take the safe course and remain as inoffensive as possible, this candidate strategy makes it extremely difficult for voters to make their issue or policy preferences the bases for their choices at the polls.

---

[15] For a detailed assessment of the political use of information-economizing devices like party labels, see Arthur Lupia and Mathew D. McCubbins, *The Democratic Dilemma: Can Citizens Learn What They Need to Know?* (New York: Cambridge University Press, 1998). For the classic argument that party loyalty is a *variable*, not a constant, and that the voter updates party loyalty on the basis of his or her experience with the parties and their candidates, see Morris P. Fiorina, *Retrospective Voting in American National Elections* (New Haven, Conn.: Yale University Press, 1981).

ONLINE READING ○ [16] See Larry M. Bartels, "Partisanship and Voting Behavior, 1952–1956," *American Journal of Political Science* 44 (2000): 35–50; and Marc Hetherington, "Resurgent Mass Partisanship: The Role of Elite Polarization," *American Political Science Review* 95, no. 3 (September 2001): 619–31.

Similarly, a paucity of information during a campaign can influence the decisions of "knowledge-challenged" voters. Some analysts claimed that in 2000 Al Gore snatched defeat from the jaws of victory in just this way. In his efforts to distance himself from his scandal-plagued predecessor, he also failed to remind voters of his great successes—eight years of peace and prosperity as Clinton's vice president. Consequently, voters, such as moderate Republicans, who may have been prepared to overlook Gore's party label because of his achievements, were not given much opportunity to do so.[17]

Voters' issue choices usually involve a mix of their judgments about the past behavior of competing parties and candidates and their hopes and fears about candidates' future behavior. Political scientists call choices that focus on future behavior *prospective voting,* while those based on past performance are called *retrospective voting.* To some extent, whether prospective or retrospective evaluation is more important in a particular election depends on the strategies of competing candidates. Candidates always endeavor to define the issues of an election in terms that will serve their interests. Incumbents running during a period of prosperity will seek to take credit for the economy's happy state and define the election as revolving around their record of success. This strategy encourages voters to make retrospective judgments. By contrast, an insurgent running during a period of economic uncertainty will tell voters it is time for a change and ask them to make prospective judgments. Thus, Bill Clinton focused on change in 1992 and prosperity in 1996, and through well-crafted media campaigns was able to define voters' agenda of choices.

In 2004, President Bush emphasized his efforts to protect the nation from terrorists and his strong commitment to religious and moral values. Democratic candidate John Kerry, on the other hand, attacked Bush's decision to invade Iraq, questioned the president's leadership in the war on terror, and charged that the president's economic policies had failed to produce prosperity. When asked by exit pollsters which issue mattered most in deciding how they voted for president, 22 percent of all voters cited moral values as their chief concern. More than 80 percent of these voters supported President Bush. The economy was cited as the most important issue by 20 percent of those who voted and 80 percent of these Americans voted for Senator Kerry. The 2006 midterm elections were portrayed by Democrats as a referendum on President Bush's conduct of the war in Iraq. There was a considerable swing of votes to the Democrats, even in districts that had supported Bush over Kerry in 2004, with the result that the Democrats picked up twenty-five seats in the House and six in the Senate.[18] In 2008, the economy was at the fore again, and voters expressed their dissatisfaction with the Republicans' economic policies by electing a Democratic president and increasing the Democrats' majorities in Congress.

prospective voting
Voting based on the imagined future performance of a candidate.

retrospective voting
Voting based on the past performance of a candidate.

---

[17]This argument is spelled out in Morris P. Fiorina, Samuel Abrams, and Jeremy Pope, "The 2000 U.S. Presidential Election: Can Retrospective Voting Be Saved?" *British Journal of Political Science* 33 (2003): 163–87.

[18]William F. Connelly Jr., "Wall vs. Wave?" *The Forum 4,* no. 3 (www.bepress.com/forum/vol4/1553/art3).

Partisan loyalty—Most Americans identify with either the Democratic or Republican party and will vote for candidates accordingly. Party loyalty rarely changes and is most influential in less visible electoral contests, such as on the state or local level where issues and candidates are less well known.

Issues—Voters may choose a candidate whose views they agree with on a particular issue that is very important to them, even if they disagree with the candidate in other areas. It is easier for voters to make choices based on issues if candidates articulate very different positions and policy preferences.

Candidate characteristics—Voters are more likely to identify with and support a candidate who shares their background, views, and perspectives; therefore, race, ethnicity, religion, gender, geography, and social background are characteristics that influence how people vote. Personality characteristics such as honesty and integrity have become more important in recent years.

The Economy

As we identify the strategies and tactics employed by opposing political candidates and parties, we should keep in mind that the best-laid plans of politicians often go awry. Election outcomes are affected by a variety of forces that candidates for office cannot fully control. Among the most important of these is the condition of the economy. If voters are satisfied with their economic prospects, they tend to support the party in power, while voters' unease about the economy tends to favor the opposition. Thus George H. W. Bush lost in 1992 during an economic downturn even though his victory in the Persian Gulf War had briefly given him a 90 percent favorable rating in the polls. And Bill Clinton won in 1996 during an economic boom even though voters had serious concerns about his moral fiber. Over the past quarter century, the Consumer Confidence Index, calculated by the Conference Board, a business research group, has been a fairly accurate predictor of presidential outcomes. The index is based on surveys asking voters how optimistic they are about the future of the economy. It would appear that a generally rosy view, indicated by a score greater than 100, augers well for the party in power. An index score of less than 100, suggesting that voters are pessimistic about the economy's trend, suggests that incumbents should worry about their job prospects (Figure 10.4).

Candidate Characteristics

Candidates' personal attributes always influence voters' decisions. Some analysts claim that voters prefer tall candidates to short candidates, candidates with shorter names to candidates with longer names, and candidates with lighter hair to candidates with darker hair. Perhaps these rather frivolous criteria do play some role. But the more important candidate characteristics that affect voters' choices are race, ethnicity, religion, gender, geography, and social background. Voters presume that can-

FIGURE 10.4 Consumer Confidence and Presidential Elections

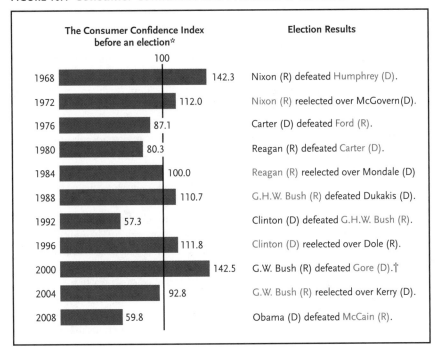

The Consumer Confidence Index before an election*	Election Results
1968 — 142.3	Nixon (R) defeated Humphrey (D).
1972 — 112.0	Nixon (R) reelected over McGovern (D).
1976 — 87.1	Carter (D) defeated Ford (R).
1980 — 80.3	Reagan (R) defeated Carter (D).
1984 — 100.0	Reagan (R) reelected over Mondale (D)
1988 — 110.7	G.H.W. Bush (R) defeated Dukakis (D).
1992 — 57.3	Clinton (D) defeated G.H.W. Bush (R).
1996 — 111.8	Clinton (D) reelected over Dole (R).
2000 — 142.5	G.W. Bush (R) defeated Gore (D).†
2004 — 92.8	G.W. Bush (R) reelected over Kerry (D).
2008 — 59.8	Obama (D) defeated McCain (R).

SOURCE: *Bloomberg Markets.*

NOTE: The candidate representing the incumbent party appears in red.

*Survey was bimonthly before 1977, so figures for 1968, 1972, and 1976 are for October; from 1980 on, they are for September.

†Gore won the popular vote but Bush was elected by the Electoral College.

didates with similar backgrounds to their own are likely to share their views and perspectives. Moreover, they may be proud to see someone of their ethnic, religious, or geographic background in a position of leadership. This is why for many years politicians sought to "balance the ticket," making certain that their party's ticket included members of as many important groups as possible.

Just as a candidate's personal characteristics may attract some voters, they may repel others. Many voters are prejudiced against candidates of certain ethnic, racial, or religious groups. And many voters—both men and women—continue to be reluctant to support the political candidacies of women, although this appears to be changing.

Voters also pay attention to candidates' personality characteristics, such as their "decisiveness," "honesty," and "vigor." In recent years, integrity has become a key election issue. In the 2004 presidential race, President Bush and the Republicans accused Senator Kerry of being inconsistent, a "flip-flopper" who continually changed his positions when it was expedient to do so. Bush, on the other hand, emphasized his own constancy. "I say what I mean, and I do what I say" was the president's frequent refrain. The president also pointed to his strong religious commitment as evidence of exemplary character. For their part, Democrats emphasized Senator Kerry's intelligence, empathy for ordinary Americans, and record of wartime heroism, which, they said, stood in sharp contrast to Bush's own somewhat blemished military record. In the end, the GOP's characterization of Kerry as a "flip-flopper" and Bush as an individual with deep moral and religious commitments seemed to resonate with voters. Among those who said that it was important for the president to take a clear stand on issues, 80 percent voted for President Bush; among those for whom strong religious faith was important, 90 percent voted for Bush; and among those who cited honesty as the candidate quality that mattered most, more than 70 percent gave their votes to Bush. In 2008, Republicans frequently questioned Barack Obama's character, pointing to his association with 1960s radical William Ayers and with outspoken black minister Rev. Jeremiah Wright. Democrats, for their part, attacked vice-presidential candidate Sarah Palin for alleged abuses of power in Alaska. However, voters seemed less concerned with these matters than with the ability of the candidates to deal with the nation's economic woes. In hard times, the electorate tends to become impatient with partisan mudslinging.

All candidates seek, through polling and other mechanisms, to determine the best image to project to the electorate. At the same time, the communications media—television in particular—exercise a good deal of control over how voters perceive candidates. Candidates have developed a number of techniques designed to take control of the image-making process away from the media. Among the chief instruments of this "spin control" is the candidate talk-show appearance. Talk-show appearances allow candidates to reach the public, while avoiding tough questions from reporters for traditional news sources.

THE 2008 ELECTION

The 2008 presidential election was in some ways predictable—voters wanted a change from a very unpopular Republican administration and, perhaps predictably, elected a Democrat—but in many ways the 2008 race was a groundbreaking departure from politics as usual. In 2008, for the first time in the nation's history, Americans elected an African American to the White House as Illinois senator Barack Obama led the Democratic party to a solid electoral victory, securing 53 percent of the popular vote versus 46 percent for Republican candidate Senator John McCain. Obama won a 365 to 173 majority in the Electoral College (see Figure 10.5), far more than the 270 electoral votes needed to claim the presidency. The 2008 presidential election was also notable because of the prominence of women candidates. Hillary Clinton's strong campaign for the Democratic nomination shattered the notion that a woman couldn't compete seriously for the nation's highest office, and John McCain's selection of Sarah Palin as his running mate seemed based at least partly on the advantages of having a woman on the ticket. The 2008 campaigns also brought about a significant shift in the electoral map, as states like Virginia and North Carolina that hadn't supported a Democratic candidate in decades went from "red" to "blue."

As noted above, the Democrats increased their strength in both houses of Congress, adding at least six seats in the Senate, giving them a larger majority, with four

FIGURE 10.5 Distribution of Electoral Votes in the 2008 Presidential Election

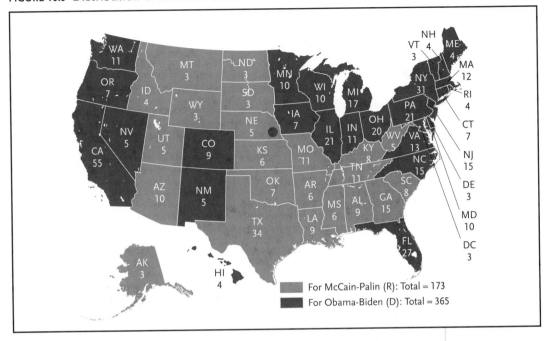

For McCain-Palin (R): Total = 173
For Obama-Biden (D): Total = 365

more seats still up for grabs pending recounts in the days after the election. Democrats had hoped to reach the magical sixty-seat total that would prevent GOP filibusters from blocking votes on Democratic bills. Democrats also gained at least twenty-two seats in the House of Representatives (eight were still undecided at the end of the night) to win a 254-to-173 majority in the lower chamber, with more seats possible. Further embarrassing the Republicans, incumbent GOP senators in New Hampshire (John Sununu) and North Carolina (Elizabeth Dole) were ousted by Democratic challengers. Because of enormous interest in the campaign, the increasing use of absentee and pre-Election Day voting, and well-financed voter registration drives conducted mainly by the Democrats, more than 120 million Americans cast ballots in 2008, a number comparable to the level of turnout reached in 2004.

The 2008 Primaries

The 2008 Democratic and Republican primaries and caucuses to select the parties' candidates for the presidency began January 3 with the Iowa Democratic caucuses. The actual campaigns, of course, began early in 2007, as ambitious politicians assessed their chances and started the long process of raising the tens of millions of dollars required to launch a presidential candidacy. On the Republican side, the front-runner was John McCain. The Arizona senator had campaigned for the Republican nomination in 2000 only to be defeated by Bush in a primary contest remembered for the victor's smear tactics. McCain, the son and grandson of U.S. Navy admirals, was a Vietnam War hero. McCain had a distinguished career in the Senate and was the chief sponsor of several major pieces of legislation, including the McCain-Feingold campaign reform law. Despite his national prominence, McCain was generally not well liked in Republican circles. Traditional business-oriented Republicans might have preferred Mitt Romney, a successful businessperson and former governor of Massachusetts, but the GOP's evangelical Protestant cadres did not like the idea of Romney, a Mormon, as their party's candidate. Social conservatives supported former Arkansas governor and evangelical minister Mike Huckabee, an articulate politician whose sense of humor made him a successful guest on *Saturday Night Live*. Establishment Republicans, however, thought Huckabee was too closely associated with the party's religious element and would have no chance in a national campaign. Other Republicans, Ron Paul, Rudy Giuliani, and Fred Thompson, excited little interest. After losing the Iowa caucuses to Huckabee and struggling to raise money, McCain regained his political and financial footing and was able to drive his opponents from the race. McCain had effectively secured the Republican nomination by the beginning of March.

Clinton versus Obama   On the Democratic side, the early front-runner for the presidential nomination was New York senator and former first lady Hillary Rodham Clinton. Senator Clinton was famous, her husband was extraordinarily popular among Democrats, and her contacts and position as a New York senator meant that she would be able to count on tens of millions of dollars in campaign contributions. Most pundits predicted an easy Clinton victory, and many leading Democrats quickly endorsed Clinton to make sure that the probable future nominee and likely next president of the United States would remember their early support. Other Democratic contenders included former North Carolina senator and 2004 vice-presidential candidate John Edwards, former New Mexico governor Bill Richardson, Congressman Dennis Kucinich, former Alaska senator Mike Gravel, and senators Joe Biden, Chris Dodd, and Barack Obama. Biden, Dodd, and Richardson, along with Gravel and Kucinich, generated relatively little interest and quickly dropped out. Edwards was popular among his fellow trial lawyers, who contributed enough money to his campaign to keep him in through the end of January, though with little chance of success. The surprise of the Democratic primary contest was, of course, Illinois senator Barack Obama.

Obama was a first-term senator, having arrived in Washington in 2004. He had won a measure of national celebrity by delivering a rousing keynote address at the 2004 Democratic national convention. While Senator Clinton was resolutely marching toward what was widely assumed to be an almost certain victory, Obama was making his own plans. Just before announcing his candidacy in February 2007, Obama had retained the services of a little-known consultancy named Blue State Digital. Blue State had learned how to make use of the new technologies of social networking introduced by such companies as Facebook. For a fee reported to be little more than $1 million, Blue State agreed to undertake an Internet campaign on

Obama's behalf. The results were spectacularly successful. Blue State created a social networking site for Obama, called "MyBO," which allowed Obama supporters to communicate directly with one another, organize events, trade ideas, and raise money for the campaign. More than a million Democrats eventually became members of MyBO and gave hundreds of millions of dollars, mostly in small contributions, to the Obama campaign.

However, MyBO and Obama's powerful supporters could not have succeeded if the candidate himself had not been able to inspire and energize the voters who saw him. Obama proved to be an intelligent campaigner and an especially gifted speaker who could hold his own against any competing politician. Many Democrats' first opportunity to see Obama as a serious contender came in the Democratic debates. The Illinois senator was not necessarily more articulate, more knowledgeable, or more passionate about important issues than Clinton, Edwards, and the others, but observers were impressed that at debate after debate the virtually unknown senator stood toe to toe with his more seasoned and famous opponents and held his own. Obama's impressive performance electrified liberal Democrats, excited young voters, intrigued the media, and ignited the enthusiasm of black Democrats, even if most were initially dubious that Obama could succeed. This enthusiastic response to Obama's debate appearances swelled the ranks of MyBO members, inspired donors to write checks, and gave Obama the means to compete against Clinton.

Throughout the primaries, Clinton and Obama battled furiously in state after state. Obama was particularly popular with younger voters and with liberals who resented what they saw as Clinton's early equivocation on the Iraq war. Black politicians—many of whom had considered Bill Clinton an important ally during his presidency—initially supported Hillary Clinton, assuming she would win. But, as their constituents rallied to Obama, and it became clear that Obama's candidacy actually had a chance, the Illinois senator was able to garner overwhelming black support. Some pundits said it was ironic that the first woman to mount a serious presidential bid and the first black person to mount such a bid were pitted against one another. For the news media, however, in this battle of the firsts, Obama's candidacy was the more important first. Clinton was seen as an established figure on the political scene—a powerful senator from New York, former first lady, and wife of perhaps the most powerful figure in the Democratic party. Clinton's status in some ways worked against her. To some commentators it appeared that Clinton had already been co-president for eight years and was no longer a first.

By late spring, it became clear that Obama would be the Democratic presidential nominee. The result was close. Under Democratic rules, 2,118 delegates were needed to win the nomination. In the various primaries and caucuses, Obama had won 1,763 delegates to Clinton's 1,640. This effectively left the decision to the party's 796 "superdelegates," party officials and notables chosen to attend the convention. At the outset, most superdelegates had backed Clinton. As the race wore on, however, sentiment shifted toward Obama. Some saw Obama as the better candidate, while others worried that black Democrats—20 percent of the party's electoral strength—would stay home on Election Day if Obama was denied the nomination.

With 438 superdelegates supporting Obama, he could count on 2,201 votes. Clinton briefly weighed taking her candidacy to the floor of the convention to be decided there, but ultimately, on June 3, withdrew and announced that she and her husband would staunchly support Obama in the general election.

The General Election

At the August 2008 Democratic national convention, speaker after speaker extolled Obama's virtues, and even Bill Clinton gave a strong speech supporting Obama, though some still doubted the former president's sincerity. Obama chose Delaware senator Joseph Biden as his vice-presidential running mate. Biden, chair of the Senate Foreign Relations Committee, was selected at least partly in response to questions about Obama's scant foreign policy experience. In addition, Biden had working-class roots in Pennsylvania. Democrats hoped that Biden would appeal to the so-called Joe Six-pack voters, blue-collar workers whom the Democrats needed in such battleground states as Ohio and Pennsylvania.

The Republican convention, which opened a few days after the Democratic convention ended, began without much fanfare. Although John McCain had won the primary battle and was respected for his military service, he was not an especially beloved figure among rank-and-file Republicans. Nevertheless, McCain excited and energized Republicans when he chose little-known Alaska governor Sarah Palin as his vice-presidential running mate and "introduced" her to the GOP base at the convention. Palin, a religious conservative who opposed abortion, excited many Republicans who had been cool toward McCain. Unfortunately for the GOP, Palin's star faded rapidly as the inexperienced governor proved unequal to the demands of a national campaign. In television interviews, including one with Katie Couric on CBS, Palin seemed to know little about current political issues and problems and could do no more than repeat Republican talking points that she seemed to have committed to memory. Despite her reasonable performance in the nationally televised vice-presidential debate, Palin was declared "clearly out of her league," even by staunchly Republican commentators, who wondered aloud if Palin could seriously be entrusted with the presidency if anything happened to McCain.

Despite the brief surge of enthusiasm generated by the selection of Palin, the McCain ticket struggled throughout the campaign. From the beginning, the deck seemed stacked against the Republicans. Despite his assertions of independence, the fact remained that McCain was a Republican and, hence, was tied to the Bush administration. Obama and the Democrats, moreover, held an enormous fund-raising advantage over McCain and the Republicans. Knowing that he would have difficulty raising money from traditional GOP donors, McCain had decided to accept public funding for the general election. This would give his campaign some $84 million to spend on organizing, advertising, and voter registration. McCain hoped Republican party fund-raising would add considerably to this figure. Obama, on the other hand, became the first major party candidate since the law was enacted to forgo general election public funding. As a consequence, Obama was able to step up his Internet and conventional fund-raising, which eventually produced in the neighborhood of $700 million, an astonishing total that more than doubled the previous record, which had been set by the Republicans in 2004. His campaign's extraordinary fund-raising prowess gave Obama and the Democrats some $200 million more to spend than was available to McCain and the Republicans.

Lack of money was not McCain's only problem. In September 2008, the nation experienced a serious financial crisis that began with a decline in home sales and a wave of mortgage foreclosures and continued with billions of dollars of losses in mortgage-based securities. Toward the end of September, the stock market lost more than a third of its value, wiping out trillions of dollars in investments. Some of the nation's leading financial institutions, such as the venerable Lehman Brothers, failed, and a host of others seemed poised to close their doors. Since all these events took place while the Republicans controlled the White House, the Democrats were quick to blame the Bush administration's economic policies for the crisis.

The Debates   Obama helped his cause enormously in the three televised presidential debates held in September and October. He responded with evident knowledge and intelligence to questions of domestic and foreign policy. So, for that matter, did McCain. But McCain, the Washington veteran, was expected to have answers to policy questions. Obama was the newcomer who had been chided for his inexperience. Like Kennedy, Reagan, and Clinton before him, Obama bore the burden of reassuring voters that he measured up to the job of being president. In the debates, Obama spoke clearly and incisively on education, economic policy, health policy, and the wars in Iraq and Afghanistan. Even more important was Obama's manner. By contrast with the often twitchy McCain, Obama was smooth, calm, and reassuring. Many commentators observed that Obama appeared "presidential" and that this helped more and more Americans feel comfortable with his candidacy. Following the debates, Obama's approval ratings rose steadily and the McCain campaign faltered.

Obama's Victory   Throughout October, Obama consistently led by single-digit margins in the national polls. Given the faltering economy, an unpopular president, and the Democrats' enormous financial advantage, the GOP should have been heading for a train wreck of epic proportions, and yet, until Obama's lead increased in late October, McCain trailed by only three to five points in the polls. Some analysts of opinion data thought the problem was race. A white Democratic candidate, according to some mathematical models of public opinion, would have enjoyed a much stronger lead in the polls, perhaps an additional six or seven points. Some analysts worried whether Obama's lead was even as strong as it looked. These analysts pointed to the so-called Bradley effect, a phantom lead produced when white voters, reluctant to display overt signs of racism, lie to pollsters about their intentions. This is allegedly what happened in 1982, when Los Angeles mayor Tom Bradley lost the California gubernatorial race after leading his white opponent in the polls. While asserting that race would not be a factor in the 2008 election, Obama cautioned his supporters not to be overconfident.

In the end, racial antipathy did not determine the outcome of the 2008 presidential election. Some voters undoubtedly opposed Obama because of his race while others supported him on the same grounds. But, given America's long history of slavery, segregation, and racial antagonism, the most important fact of the election was that tens of millions of white voters—some reluctantly—voted for a black man for the presidency of the United States. Though many forces were at work in 2008, Obama's victory was made possible by the softening of racial antagonisms in the United States over the past half-century and the delegitimization of overtly racist rhetoric in the public forum. But the election of a black president does not mean the end of racism in America. Obama is an exceptional individual—a graduate of the Harvard Law School with a white mother, an African rather than an African American father, and raised by white grandparents. Some Democratic canvassers emphasized these facts to white voters, describing their candidate as a man from a multiracial background whose father was an African intellectual, not an American from the inner city. Does Obama's victory represent the end of racism and the birth of a new America? Or is Obama an exception? Only time will help us to fully understand the significance of the 2008 election.

CAMPAIGN FINANCE

Modern national political campaigns are fueled by enormous amounts of money. In 2008, incumbent candidates in competitive House races typically spent close to $2 million to hold on to their seats. In Senate races, the average winner spent more than $4 million. In recent years, some Senate contests have cost $25 million or more. In the 2008 presidential race, the two parties and their presidential candidates spent more than $1.5 billion. Hundreds of millions more were spent by individuals and groups who ran independent ads seeking to influence the outcome of the presidential contest.

Sources of Campaign Funds

In 2008, according to the Center for Responsive Politics, roughly $3 billion was spent by candidates for federal offices. About 10 percent of this total came from political action committees (PACs), mainly in support of congressional races, and the remainder from individual donors. Several million individuals donated money to political campaigns in 2008, some in contributions of as little as $5 or $10. One of the sources of Barack Obama's fund-raising advantage in the 2008 campaign was his ability to generate more than two million small and medium-size contributions to his campaign. Another $500 million in 2008 was raised and spent by individuals and advocacy groups—the so-called 527s and 501c(4) groups operating outside the structure of the Democratic and Republican campaigns.

Individual Donors   Politicians spend a great deal of time asking people for money. Money is solicited via direct mail, over the phone, via the Internet, and in numerous face-to-face meetings. Under federal law, individual donors may donate as much as $2,300 per candidate per election, $5,000 per PAC per calendar year (to a maximum of $65,000), $28,500 per national party committee per calendar year, and $10,000 to state and local party committees per calendar year (to a maximum of $42,700). Federal rules also impose an overall limit on individual contributors of $108,200 per election cycle. Individuals may also contribute freely to 527 committees and to

501c(4) groups. 527 donations are a matter of public record, but 501c(4)s are not required to disclose their donor lists. Individuals may also attempt to enhance their influence by raising and "bundling" their contributions with those of friends and associates. Many Washington lobbyists curry favor with politicians through vigorous bundling efforts.

Political Action and 527 Committees   *Political action committees (PACs)* are organizations established by corporations, labor unions, or interest groups to channel the contributions of their members into political campaigns. Under the terms of the 1971 Federal Elections Campaign Act, which governs campaign finance in the United States, PACs are permitted to make larger contributions to any given candidate than individuals are allowed to make. Individuals may donate a maximum of $2,300 to any single candidate, but a PAC may donate as much as $5,000 to each candidate. Moreover, allied or related PACs often coordinate their campaign contributions, greatly increasing the amount of money a candidate actually receives from the same interest group. More than 4,500 PACs are registered with the Federal Election Commission, which oversees campaign finance practices in the United States. Nearly two thirds of all PACs represent corporations, trade associations, and other business and professional groups. Labor unions also sponsor PACs, as do ideological, public interest, and nonprofit groups. The National Rifle Association sponsors a PAC, as does the Sierra Club. Many congressional and party leaders have established PACs, known as leadership PACs, to provide funding for their political allies.

527 committees have been another important source of money during elections. These nonprofit fundraising groups, which are named after the section of the tax code that defines them, have raised and spent millions of dollars attempting to influence recent elections. Expenditures by these committees are "soft" because they are not subject to FEC regulations, and technically they are not given to or coordinated with any specific candidate's campaign. Indeed 527 advertisements cannot directly endorse a candidate. But by registering voters with serious Democratic propensities in 2004, as did the 527 committee financed by billionaire George Soros, or attacking John Kerry's Vietnam service record, as did the Swift Boat Veterans for Truth 527 committee, these soft money expenditures had clear and significant candidate- and party-specific effects.

The Candidates   On the basis of the Supreme Court's 1976 decision in *Buckley v. Valeo*, the right of individuals to spend their own money to campaign for office is a constitutionally protected matter of free speech and is not subject to limitation.[19] Thus, extremely wealthy candidates often contribute millions of dollars to their own campaigns. Jon Corzine, for example, spent approximately $60 million of his own funds in a successful New Jersey Senate bid in 2000, launching a political career that has included his election as governor in 2005.

political action committee (PAC) A private group that raises and distributes funds for use in election campaigns.

527 committees Nonprofit independent groups that receive and disburse funds to influence the nomination, election, or defeat of candidates. Named after Section 527 of the Internal Revenue Code, which defines and provides tax-exempt status for nonprofit advocacy groups.

---

[19] *Buckley v. Valeo*, 424 U.S. 1 (1976).

ONLINE READING

Independent Spending   Independent spending is also free from regulation; private groups and wealthy individuals, engaging in what is called *issue advocacy,* may spend as much as they wish to help elect one candidate or defeat another, as long as these expenditures are not coordinated with any political campaign. Many business and ideological groups engage in such activities. Some estimates suggest that groups and individuals spend as much as $500 million on issue advocacy—generally through television advertising—during a presidential election year.[20] During the 2008 national elections, issue ads were sponsored by pro- and anti-abortion groups, gun rights and gun control groups, environmental groups, labor unions, business groups, and a host of other forces.

Some groups are careful not to mention particular candidates in their issues ads to avoid any suggestion that they might merely be fronts for a candidate's campaign committee. Most issue ads, however, are attacks on the opposing candidate's record or character. Organized labor spent more than $35 million in 1996 to attack a number of Republican candidates for the House of Representatives. Business groups launched their own multimillion-dollar issues campaign to defend the GOP House members targeted by labor.[21] In 2004, pro-Republican groups sponsored a series of ads portraying President George W. Bush as protecting the nation by fighting terrorism while his political opponents tried to undermine him (and the nation) for selfish political reasons. Democratic groups, for their part, attacked Bush's economic policies and handling of the Iraq war.

Public Funding   The Federal Election Campaign Act also provides for public funding of presidential campaigns. As they seek a major party presidential nomination, candidates become eligible for public funds by raising at least $5,000 in individual contributions of $250 or less in each of twenty states. Candidates who reach this threshold may apply for federal funds to match, on a dollar-for-dollar basis, all individual contributions of $250 or less that they receive. The funds are drawn from the Presidential Election Campaign Fund. Taxpayers can contribute $1 to this fund, at no additional cost to themselves, by checking a box on the first page of their federal income-tax returns. Major party presidential candidates receive a lump sum (currently nearly $90 million) during the summer before the general election. They must meet all their campaign expenses from this money—that is, they may not accept other contributions. Under current law, no candidate is required to accept public funding for either the nominating races or the presidential election. Candidates who do not accept public funding are not affected by any expenditure limits. Thus in 1992, Ross Perot financed his own presidential bid and was not bound by the $55 million limit to which the Democratic and Republican candidates were held

issue advocacy Independent spending by individuals or interest groups on a campaign issue but not directly tied to a particular candidate.

---

[20]Kathleen Hall Jamieson, "Issue Advertising in the 1999–2000 Election Cycle," Annenberg Public Policy Center, University of Pennsylvania, 1 February 2001.

[21]David Broder and Ruth Marcus, "Wielding Third Force in Politics," *Washington Post,* 20 September 1997, p. 1.

that year. Perot did accept public funding in 1996. In 2008, John McCain accepted public funding for the general election campaign, receiving $84 million, but Barack Obama declined, choosing to rely on his own fund-raising prowess. Obama was ultimately able to outspend McCain by a wide margin. As a result, many observers believe that the 2008 race may be the last time that a major-party candidate will forgo fund-raising in favor of public funding. Candidates who accept public funding may not engage in fund-raising for their own campaigns with one exception: Publicly funded candidates may raise money to meet the costs of complying with federal campaign laws and other legal and accounting costs, up to a total of 5 percent of their campaign expenditures. Hence in 2008, John McCain raised more than $4 million for the "McCain-Palin Compliance Fund."

Third-party candidates are eligible for public funding only if they received at least 5 percent of the vote in the previous presidential race. This stipulation effectively blocks preelection funding for third-party or independent candidates, although a third party that wins more than 5 percent of the vote can receive public funding after the election. In 1980, John Anderson convinced banks to lend him money for an independent candidacy on the strength of poll data showing that he would receive more than 5 percent of the vote and would thus obtain public funds with which to repay the loans.

Campaign Finance Reform

The United States is one of the few advanced industrial nations that permit individual candidates to accept large private contributions from individual or corporate donors. Most other countries either mandate public funding of campaigns or, as in the case of Great Britain, require that large private donations be made to political parties rather than to individual candidates. The logic of such a requirement is that a contribution that might seem very large to an individual candidate would weigh much less heavily if made to a national party. Thus the chance of a donor's buying influence would be reduced.

After the 1996 and 2000 national elections, efforts were made to enact reform measures, but these failed. In 2002, however, a scandal involving contributions made by Enron, the giant Texas energy company that was subsequently embroiled in a much bigger scandal and collapsed in bankruptcy, gave reformers the ammunition they needed to bring about a set of changes in election law in the form of the Bipartisan Campaign Reform Act (BCRA). One of the changes brought about by BCRA was a ban on campaign spending by the national party organizations, which had previously used hundreds of millions of dollars in soft-money contributions from corporations, unions, and individuals to influence electoral contests. The long-term effects of this reform remain to be seen. Perhaps banning soft money will reduce the influence of wealthy donors, but at the same time eliminating soft money is likely to weaken the national parties—now among the few sources of coherence in America's fragmented political process. In the short term at least, the Democratic party seems to be suffering from the soft-money ban more than the Republican party is. The Democratic party had come to depend on a relatively small number of well-heeled contributors who wrote large checks to the national

TABLE 10.1 Federal Campaign Finance Regulation

The Rules for Campaign Contributions

Who	may contribute . . .	to . . .	if . . .
Individuals	up to $2,300	a candidate	they are contributing to a single candidate in a single election.
Individuals	up to $28,500	a national party committee.	
Individuals	up to $5,000	a PAC.	
PACs	up to $5,000	a candidate	they contribute to the campaigns of at least five candidates.
Individuals and PACs	unlimited funds	a 527 committee	the funds are used for issue advocacy and the 527 committee's efforts are not coordinated with any political campaign.
Individuals and PACs	up to $10,000	a state party committee	the money is used for voter registration and get-out-the-vote efforts.

The Rules for Campaign Advertising

Who	may not finance . . .	if . . .
Unions, corporations, and nonprofit organizations	broadcast issue ads mentioning federal candidates	they occur within sixty days of a general election or thirty days of a primary.

party. The Republicans, on the other hand, have developed a broader base of smaller contributors who are accustomed to sending money directly to individual candidates. These hard-money contributions are not affected by the new law.[22] In

[22]Adam Nagourney, "McCain Feingold School Finds Many Bewildered," *New York Times,* 19 February 2003, p. A23.

The Rules for Presidential Primaries and Elections

Candidates . . .	may receive . . .	if . . .
In primaries	federal matching funds, dollar for dollar, up to $5 million	they raise at least $5,000 in each of twenty states in contributions of $250 or less.
In general elections	full federal funding (but may spend no more than their federal funding)	they belong to a major party (minor-party candidates may receive partial funding).
In any election	money from independent groups (PACs and 527 committees)	the groups' efforts are not tied directly to the official campaign.

Important Definitions for Campaign Finance Regulation

- **Political action committee (PAC):** Private group that raises and distributes funds for use in election campaigns.

- **527 committee:** Tax-exempt organization that engages in political activities, often through unlimited "soft-money" contributions. The committee is not restricted by current law on campaign finance, thus exploiting a loophole in the Internal Revenue Service code.

- **501(c)4:** Not-for-profit groups that may engage in unlimited political spending so long as amount spent does not exceed 50 percent of its budget. Unlike the 527s, 501(c)4s are not required to disclose contributor and recipient information.

- **Federal matching funds:** Federal funds that match, dollar for dollar, all individual contributions of $250 or less received by a candidate. To qualify, the candidate must raise at least $5,000 in individual contributions of $250 or less in each of twenty states.

- **Federal Election Commission:** The commission that oversees campaign finance practices in the United States.

the 2004 election, 527 committees, though not able to spend directly on particular campaigns, took up some of this slack, with Democrats outspending Republicans via this route.

Implications for Democracy

The important role played by private funds in American politics affects the balance of power among contending social groups. Politicians need large amounts of money to campaign successfully for major offices. This fact inevitably ties their interests to the interests of the groups and forces that can provide this money. In a nation as large and diverse as the United States, to be sure, campaign contributors represent many different groups and often represent clashing interests. Business groups, labor groups, environmental groups, and pro-choice and right-to-life forces all contribute millions of dollars to political campaigns. Through such PACs as EMILY's List, women's groups contribute millions of dollars to women running for political office. One set of trade associations may contribute millions to win politicians' support for telecommunications reform, while another set may contribute just as much to block the same reform efforts. Insurance companies may contribute millions of dollars to Democrats to win their support for changes in the health care system, while physicians may contribute equal amounts to prevent the same changes from becoming law.

Interests that donate large amounts of money to campaigns expect, and often receive, favorable treatment from the beneficiaries of their largesse. For example, in 2000 a number of major interest groups with specific policy goals made substantial donations to the Bush presidential campaign. These interests included airlines, energy producers, banks, tobacco companies, and a number of others. After Bush's election, these interests pressed the new president to promote their legislative and regulatory agendas.

Despite this diversity of contributors, however, not all interests play a role in financing political campaigns. Only those interests that have a good deal of money to spend can make their interests known in this way. These interests are not monolithic, but they do not completely reflect the diversity of American society. The poor, the destitute, and the downtrodden also live in America and have an interest in the outcome of political campaigns. Who is to speak for them?

DO ELECTIONS MATTER?

What is the place of elections in the American political process? Unfortunately, recent political trends raise real questions about the continuing ability of ordinary Americans to influence their government through electoral politics.

Why Is Voter Turnout So Low?

Despite the sound and fury of contemporary American politics, one very important fact stands out: Participation in the American political process is still relatively low. Even with increases in turnout in 2004 and 2008, fewer Americans participate in elections today than at the end of the nineteenth century. Moreover, as we saw earlier in the chapter, voting rates are much lower in the United States than in most other advanced democracies.

Competition and Voter Turnout   Throughout much of American history, the major parties have been the principal agents responsible for giving citizens the motivation and incentive to vote. One of the most interesting pieces of testimony to the lengths to which parties have been willing to go to induce citizens to vote is a list of Chicago precinct captains' activities in the 1920s and 1930s. Among other matters, these party workers helped constituents obtain food, coal, and money for rent; gave advice in dealing with juvenile and domestic problems; helped constituents obtain government and private jobs; adjusted taxes; aided with permits, zoning, and building-code problems; served as liaisons with social, relief, and medical agencies; provided legal assistance and help in dealing with government agencies; handed out Christmas baskets; and attended weddings and funerals.[23] Obviously, all these services were provided in the hope of winning voters' support at election time.

The parties' competitive efforts to attract citizens to the polls are not their only influence on voting. Individual voters tend to form psychological ties with parties. Although the strength of partisan ties in the United States has declined in recent years, a majority of Americans continue to identify with either the Republican or Democratic party. Party loyalty gives citizens a stake in election outcomes that encourages them to take part with considerably greater regularity than those lacking partisan ties.[24] Even where both legal facilitation and competitiveness are weak, party loyalists vote with great regularity.

In recent decades, as we will see in Chapter 11, the importance of party as a political force in the United States appears to have diminished in some respects. The change in party influence is undoubtedly one of the factors responsible for the relatively low rates of voter turnout that characterize American national elections. To an extent, the federal and state governments and even PACs, 527 committees, and individual candidates' organizations have directly assumed some of the burden of voter mobilization once assigned to the parties. For example, the 1993 Motor Voter bill was a step, though a hesitant one, in the direction of expanded voter participation. This act requires all states to allow voters to register by mail when they renew their driver's licenses (twenty-eight states already had similar mail-in procedures) and provides for the placement of voter registration forms in motor vehicle, public assistance, and military recruitment offices. Motor Voter did result in some increases in voter registration. However, in 1996, the percentage of newly registered voters who appeared at the polls actually dropped.[25] More interesting and more promising is the fact that many states have liberalized absentee balloting and allowed early voting, reducing the cost (in terms of time, missed work, etc.) of voting. An increasing percentage of all votes are now cast via absentee ballots.

A number of other simple institutional reforms could increase voter turnout. Same-day registration, currently used in several states including Minnesota, could boost turnout. Making Election Day a federal holiday would make it easier for Americans to go to the polls. Weekend voting in a number of European nations has increased turnout by as much as 10 percentage points.

Another reform that has been proposed is abolition of the electoral college, which would affect campaigning and the two-party system. Candidates would be

[23]Harold F. Gosnell, *Machine Politics, Chicago Model,* rev. ed. (Chicago: University of Chicago Press, 1968), Chapter 4.

[24]See Angus Campbell et al., *The American Voter* (New York: Wiley, 1960).

[25]Peter Baker, "Motor Voter Apparently Didn't Drive Up Turnout," *Washington Post,* 6 November 1996, p. B7.

compelled to campaign throughout the nation rather than in the small number of states they currently see as the key "battlegrounds" for electoral college victory. The abolition of the electoral college might also make way for new parties which might breathe new life into the political process, add to the confusion of presidential elections, or both.

Why Should Citizens Vote?   Compared to that of other democracies, voter turnout in national elections is extremely low in the United States. In defense of American citizens, it should be pointed out that occasions for voting as a form of civic activity occur more frequently in the United States than in other democracies. There are more offices filled by election in the United States than elsewhere—indeed, more offices per capita, which is somewhat startling given how large a democracy the United States is. Many of these are posts that are filled by appointment in other democracies. Especially unusual in this respect are elected judges in many jurisdictions and elected local "bureaucrats" (like the local sheriff and the proverbial town dog catcher). In addition, there are primaries as well as general elections, and, in many states, there are initiatives and referenda to vote on, too. It is a wonder that American citizens don't suffer from some form of democratic fatigue! Though many scholars have tried to answer the question "Why is turnout so low?" others have argued that the real question should be "Why is turnout so high?" That is, why does anyone turn out to vote at all?

There are many costs to voting. People must take time out of their busy schedules, possibly incurring a loss of wages, in order to show up at the polls. In many states, voters have to overcome numerous hurdles just to register. If an individual wants to cast an informed vote, he or she must also spend time learning about the candidates and their positions.

Voters must bear these costs no matter the outcome of the election, yet it is extremely unlikely that an individual's vote will actually affect the outcome, unless the vote makes or breaks a tie. Just making a close election one vote closer by voting for the loser, or the winner one vote more secure by voting for her, doesn't matter much. As the old saw has it, "Closeness only counts in horseshoes and dancing." It is almost certain that if an individual did not incur the costs of voting and stayed home instead, the election results would be the same. The probability of a single vote being decisive in a presidential election is about one in 10 million.[26]

One possible solution to this puzzle is that people are motivated by more than just their preferences for electing a particular candidate—they are, in fact, satisfying their duty as citizens, and this benefit exceeds the costs of voting.[27]

ONLINE READING

[26]Andrew Gelman, Gary King, and John Boscardin, "Estimating the Probability of Events That Have Never Occurred: When Is Your Vote Decisive?" *Journal of the American Statistical Association* 93, no. 441 (March 1998): 1–9.

[27]In effect, there is an experiential as well as an instrumental rationale for voting. In more economic terms, this is the view that voting is a form of consumption as much as it is a type of investment. For a brief and user-friendly development of this logic, see Kenneth A. Shepsle and Mark S. Bonchek, *Analyzing Politics: Rationality, Behavior, and Institutions* (New York: Norton, 1997) pp. 251–59.

John Aldrich offers another possible solution: he looks at the question from the politician's point of view.[28] Candidates calculate how much to invest in campaigns based on their probability of winning. In the unlikely event that an incumbent appears beatable, the challengers often invest heavily in their own campaigns because they believe the investment has a good chance of paying off. In response to these strong challenges, incumbents will not only work harder to raise campaign funds but also spend more of what they raise.[29] Parties seeking to maximize the number of positions in the government they control may also shift resources to help out the candidates in these close races.

More vigorous campaigns will generally lead to increased turnout. The increase is not necessarily due to citizens reacting to the closeness of the race (that is, the perception that their vote may affect the outcome) but to the greater effort and resources that candidates put into close races, which, in turn, reduce the costs of voting. Candidates share some of the costs of voting by helping citizens register and by getting them to the polls on Election Day. Heated advertising campaigns reduce the voters' costs of becoming informed (since candidates flood the public with information about themselves). This decrease in costs to individual voters in what strategic politicians perceive to be a close race at least partially explains why citizens would turn out to vote.

Why Do Elections Matter as Political Institutions?

Voting choices and electoral outcomes can be extremely important in the United States. Yet, to observe that there can be relationships among voters' choices, leadership composition, and policy outputs is only to begin to understand the significance of democratic elections, rather than to exhaust the possibilities. Important as they are, voters' choices and electoral results may still be less consequential for government and politics than the simple fact of voting itself. Electoral participation has important consequences in that it socializes and institutionalizes political action.

First, democratic elections socialize political activity. Voting is not a natural or spontaneous phenomenon. It is an institutionalized form of mass political involvement. That individuals vote rather than engage in some other form of political behavior is a result of national policies that create the opportunity to vote and discourage other political activities relative to voting. Elections transform what might otherwise consist of sporadic, citizen-initiated acts into a routine public function. This transformation expands and democratizes mass political involvement. At the same time, however, elections help to preserve the government's stability by containing and channeling away potentially more disruptive or dangerous forms of mass political activity. By establishing formal avenues for mass participation and accustoming citizens to their use, government reduces the threat that volatile, unorganized involvement can pose to the established order.

---

[28]John H. Aldrich, "Rational Choice and Turnout," *American Journal of Political Science* 37 (February 1993): 246–78.

[29]Gary C. Jacobson and Samuel Kernell, *Strategy and Choice in Congressional Elections*, 2nd ed. (New Haven, Conn.: Yale University Press, 1983).

Second, elections bolster the government's power and authority. Elections help to increase popular support for political leaders and for the regime itself. The formal opportunity to participate in elections serves to convince citizens that the government is responsive to their needs and wishes. Moreover, elections help to persuade citizens to obey. Electoral participation increases popular acceptance of taxes and military service upon which the government depends. Even if popular voting can influence the behavior of those in power, voting serves simultaneously as a form of cooptation. Elections—particularly democratic elections—substitute consent for coercion as the foundation of governmental power.

Finally, elections institutionalize mass influence in politics. Democratic elections permit citizens to select and depose public officials routinely, and elections can serve to promote popular influence over officials' conduct. But however effective this electoral sanction may be, it is hardly the only means through which citizens can reward or punish public officials for their actions. Spontaneous or privately organized forms of political activity, or even the threat of their occurrence, can also induce those in power to heed the public's wishes. The alternative to democratic elections is not clearly and simply the absence of popular influence; it can be unregulated and unconstrained popular intervention into government. It is often precisely because spontaneous forms of mass political activity can have too great an impact upon the actions of government that elections are introduced. Walter Lippmann, a journalist who helped to pioneer the idea of public opinion voicing itself through the press via the "opinion-editorial," or op-ed, page, once observed that "new numbers were enfranchised because they had power, and giving them the vote was the least disturbing way of letting them exercise their power."[30] The vote can provide the "least disturbing way" of allowing ordinary people to exercise power. If the people had been powerless to begin with, elections would never have been introduced.

Thus, although citizens can secure enormous benefits from their right to vote, government secures equally significant benefits from allowing them to do so.

CHAPTER REVIEW

Allowing citizens to vote represents a calculated risk on the part of power holders. On the one hand, popular participation can generate consent and support for the government. On the other hand, the right to vote may give ordinary citizens more influence in the governmental process than political elites would like.

Voting is only one of the many possible types of political participation. The significance of voting is that it is an institutional and formal mode of political activity. Voting is organized and subsidized by the government. This makes voting both more limited and more democratic than other forms of participation.

---

[30]Walter Lippmann, *The Essential Lippmann*, eds. Clinton Rossiter and James Lare (New York: Random House, 1965), p. 12.

All governments regulate voting to influence its effects. The most important forms of regulation include regulation of the electorate's composition, regulation of the translation of voters' choices into electoral outcomes, and insulation of policy-making processes from electoral intervention.

Voters' choices are based on partisanship, issues, and candidates' personalities. Which of these criteria will be most important varies over time and depends upon the factors and issues that opposing candidates choose to emphasize in their campaigns.

Whatever voters decide, elections are important because they socialize political activity, increase governmental authority, and institutionalize popular influence in political life.

FOR FURTHER READING

ONLINE READING ○ Bartels, Larry M. "What's the Matter with *What's the Matter with Kansas?*" *Quarterly Journal of Political Science* 1 (2006): 201–26.

Brady, David W. *Critical Elections and Congressional Policy Making.* Palo Alto, Calif.: Stanford University Press, 1988.

Carmines, Edward G., and James A. Stimson. *Issue Evolution: Race and the Transformation of American Politics.* Princeton, N.J.: Princeton University Press, 1989.

Conway, M. Margaret. *Political Participation in the United States.* 3rd ed. Washington, D.C.: Congressional Quarterly Press, 2000.

Fowler, Linda L. *Candidates, Congress, and the American Democracy.* Ann Arbor: University of Michigan Press, 1994.

Ginsberg, Benjamin, and Martin Shefter. *Politics by Other Means: Politicians, Prosecutors, and the Press from Watergate to Whitewater.* 3rd ed. New York: Norton, 2002.

ONLINE READING ○ Green, Donald, and Alan Gerber. *Get Out the Vote!: How to Increase Voter Turnout.* Washington, D.C.: Brookings Institution, 2004.

Lau, Richard, and David Redlawsk. *How Voters Decide.* New York: Cambridge University Press, 2006.

Morton, Rebecca B. *Analyzing Elections.* New York: Norton, 2006.

Piven, Frances Fox, and Richard A. Cloward. *Why Americans Don't Vote.* New York: Pantheon, 1988.

Reichley, A. James, ed. *Elections American Style.* Washington, D.C.: Brookings Institution, 1987.

Tate, Katherine. *From Protest to Politics: The New Black Voters in American Elections.* Cambridge, Mass.: Harvard University Press, 1994.

Witt, Linda, Karen M. Paget, and Glenna Matthews. *Running as a Woman: Gender and Power in American Politics.* New York: Free Press, 1994.

Political Parties

HOW PARTIES WORK

We often refer to the United States as a nation with a "two-party system." By this we mean that in the United States the Democratic and Republican parties compete for office and power. Most Americans believe that party competition contributes to the health of the democratic process.

In recent years, however, electoral politics has become a "candidate-centered" affair in which individual candidates for office build their own campaign organizations, while voters make choices based more upon their reactions to the candidates than upon loyalty to the parties. Party organization, as we saw in Chapter 5, continues to be an important factor within Congress. Even in Congress, however, the influence of party leaders is based more upon ideological affinity and agenda control than any direct power over party members. In general, the party system in American politics, in its role in organizing both elections and government, has fluctuated in importance.[1]

In this chapter, we examine the realities underlying changing conceptions of **political parties**. As long as political parties have existed, they have been criticized for introducing selfish, "partisan" concerns into public debate and national policy. Yet political parties are extremely important to the proper functioning of a democracy. As we shall see, parties expand popular political participation, promote more effective choice in elections, and smooth the flow of public business in the Congress. Our problem in America today is not that political life is too partisan but that our parties are not strong enough to function effectively. This is one reason why America has such low levels of popular political involvement. Nevertheless, parties continue to play an important if uneven role in the American political process. For one thing, tens of millions of Americans identify strongly with one or the other major party.[2] Many Republican partisans would not dream of voting for a Democrat,

---

[1]For an excellent discussion of the fluctuating role of political parties in the United States and the influence of government on that role, see John J. Coleman, *Party Decline in America: Policy, Politics, and the Fiscal State* (Princeton, N.J.: Princeton University Press, 1996).

[2]For an analysis of partisanship in the second half of the twentieth century, see Larry M. Bartels, "Partisanship and Voting Behavior, 1952–1996," *American Journal of Political Science* 44 (2000): 35–50.

● Core of the Analysis

● Today the Democratic and Republican parties dominate the American two-party political system.

● The most important functions of American political parties are facilitating nominations and elections and organizing the institutions of national government.

● By some measures, the role of parties in electoral politics has declined in the United States over the last thirty years.

and many Democratic partisans viewed the 2004 reelection of George W. Bush as a national tragedy. The 2006 midterm elections, however, in which the Democrats captured both houses of Congress, revealed a preference of many voters to strip the Republicans of unified control of the government. In the final days of the 2008 campaign, when it seemed clear that Barack Obama would defeat Republican presidential candidate John McCain, Republicans urged voters to support the GOP Senate and House candidates in order to safeguard the system of checks and balances. This argument seemed not to sway many voters.

What should become clear in this chapter is that the role of parties in the electoral arena and the halls of government is constantly changing, flowing in some eras but ebbing in others, stronger in some arenas but weaker in others. In our examination of political parties in America, we look first at party functions and organization and at the place of parties in the American political process. Second, we discuss the role of parties in election campaigns and the policy process. Third, we consider why America has a two-party system, we trace the history of the major parties, and we look at some of the third parties that have come and gone over the past two centuries. Finally, we address the significance and changing role of parties in American politics today.

FUNCTIONS OF THE PARTIES

Parties are mainly involved in nominations and elections—providing the candidates for office, getting out the vote, and facilitating mass electoral choice. They also influence the institutions of government—providing the leadership and organization of the various congressional committees.

Recruiting Candidates

One of the most important but least noticed party activities is the recruitment of candidates for local, state, and national office. Each election year, candidates must be found for thousands of state and local offices as well as congressional seats. Where they do not have an incumbent running for reelection, party leaders attempt to identify strong candidates and to interest them in entering the campaign. One reason for the great success of the Democrats in the 2006 midterm elections was the heightened role played by their campaign committees in the House and Senate and, especially,

political parties Organized groups that attempt to influence the government by electing their members to important government offices.

the active recruitment of new candidates by Rahm Emanuel (D-Ill.) and Charles Schumer (D-N.Y.), chairs respectively of the Democratic Congressional Campaign Committee and the Democratic Senatorial Campaign Committee. Emanuel and Schumer recruited quality candidates, steered campaign resources their way, and have begun to focus on protecting them in their first reelection campaigns.[3]

An ideal candidate will have an unblemished record and the capacity to raise enough money to mount a serious campaign. Party leaders are usually not willing to provide financial backing to candidates who are unable to raise substantial funds on their own. For a House seat, this can mean several hundred thousand dollars; for a Senate seat, a serious candidate must be able to raise several million dollars. Often, party leaders have difficulty finding attractive candidates and persuading them to run. Candidate recruitment is problematic in an era when political campaigns often involve mudslinging, and candidates must assume that their personal lives will be intensely scrutinized in the press.[4]

Nominations

Nomination is the process of selecting one party candidate to run for each elective office. The nominating process can precede the election by many months, as it does when the many candidates for the presidency are eliminated from consideration through a grueling series of debates and state primaries until there is only one survivor in each party—the party's nominee. Figure 11.1 summarizes the three types of nominating processes described below.

Nomination by Convention   A nominating convention is a formal caucus bound by a number of rules that govern participation and nominating procedures. Conventions are meetings of delegates elected by party members from the relevant county (county convention) or state (state convention). Delegates to each party's national convention (which nominates the party's presidential candidate) are chosen by party members on a state-by-state basis; there is no single national delegate selection process.

Nomination by Primary Election   In primary elections, party members select the party's nominees directly rather than selecting convention delegates who then select the nominees. Primaries are far from perfect replacements for conventions, since it is rare that more than 25 percent of the enrolled voters participate in them. Nevertheless, they are replacing conventions as the dominant method of nomination.[5] Currently, only a few states, including Connecticut, Delaware, and Utah, provide for state conventions to nominate candidates for statewide offices, and even these states

---

[3]See Adam Nagourney, "Eyeing '08: Democrats Nurse Freshmen at Risk," *New York Times*, 22 December 2006.

[4]For an excellent analysis of the parties' role in recruitment, see Paul Herrnson, *Congressional Elections: Campaigning at Home and in Washington* (Washington, D.C.: Congressional Quarterly Press, 1995).

[5]For a discussion of some of the effects of primary elections, see Peter F. Galderisi and Benjamin Ginsberg, "Primary Elections and the Evanescence of Third Party Activity in the United States," in *Do Elections Matter?* eds. Benjamin Ginsberg and Alan Stone (Armonk, N.Y.: M. E. Sharpe, 1986), pp. 115–30.

nomination The process through which political parties select their candidate for election to public office.

FIGURE 11.1 Types of Nominating Processes

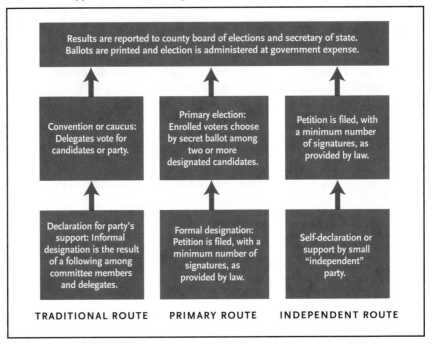

Results are reported to county board of elections and secretary of state. Ballots are printed and election is administered at government expense.

Convention or caucus: Delegates vote for candidates or party.

Primary election: Enrolled voters choose by secret ballot among two or more designated candidates.

Petition is filed, with a minimum number of signatures, as provided by law.

Declaration for party's support: Informal designation is the result of a following among committee members and delegates.

Formal designation: Petition is filed, with a minimum number of signatures, as provided by law.

Self-declaration or support by small "independent" party.

TRADITIONAL ROUTE   **PRIMARY ROUTE**   **INDEPENDENT ROUTE**

combine them with primaries whenever a substantial minority of delegates vote for one of the defeated aspirants.

Primary elections are of two types: closed and open. In a *closed primary*, participation is limited to individuals who have declared their affiliation by registering with the party. In an *open primary*, individuals declare their party affiliation on the actual day of the primary election—they simply go to the polling place and ask for the ballot of a particular party. The open primary allows each voter an opportunity to consider candidates and issues before deciding whether to participate and in which party's contest to participate. Open primaries, therefore, are less conducive than closed contests to strong political parties. But in either case, primaries are more open then conventions or caucuses to new issues and new candidates.

Getting Out the Vote

The election period begins immediately after the nominations. Historically, this has been a time of glory for the political parties, whose popular base of support is fully displayed. All the paraphernalia of party committees and all the committee members are activated into local party work forces.

The first step in the electoral process involves voter registration. This aspect of the process takes place all year round. There was a time when party workers were responsible for virtually all of this kind of electoral activity, but they have been supple-

closed primary A primary election in which voters can participate in the nomination of candidates, but only of the party in which they are enrolled for a period of time prior to primary day.

open primary A primary election in which the voter can wait until the day of the primary to choose which party to enroll in to select candidates for the general election.

mented (and in many states virtually displaced) by civic groups such as the League of Women Voters, unions, and chambers of commerce.

Those who have registered have to decide on Election Day whether to go to the polling place, stand in line, and actually vote for the various candidates and referenda on the ballot. Political parties, candidates, and campaigning can make a big difference in convincing the voters to vote. Because it is costly for voters to participate in elections and because many of the benefits that winning parties bestow are public goods (that is, parties cannot exclude any individual from enjoying them), people will often free ride by enjoying the benefits without incurring the costs of electing the party that provided the benefits. This is the *free-rider problem* (see Chapter 1), and parties are important because they help overcome it by mobilizing the voters to support the candidates.

In recent years, not-for-profit groups like America Votes have made an effort to register and mobilize voters. To comply with election law, these groups are nominally independent of the political parties. In reality, though, such not-for-profits are shadow appendages of the two parties, with liberal groups working to mobilize Democratic voters and conservative groups laboring to mobilize Republicans. In 2004, Republican and conservative registration and get-out-the-vote efforts helped secure George W. Bush's reelection. In 2008, the Democrats, with the support of liberal groups like ACORN, registered several million new voters—many members of minority groups and young people—who helped Democratic candidates sweep to power.

On any general election ballot, there are likely to be only two or three candidacies for which the nature of the office and the characteristics and positions of the candidates are well-known to voters. But what about the choices for judges, the state comptroller, the state attorney general, and many other elective positions? Without partisan cues, voters are likely to find it extremely difficult to make informed choices about these candidates. And what about referendums? This method of making policy choices is being used more and more as a means of direct democracy. The typical referendum question is one on which few voters have a clear and knowledgeable position. Parties and campaigns help most by giving information when voters must choose among obscure candidates and vote on unclear referendums.

Facilitating Mass Electoral Choice

Parties facilitate mass electoral choice. It is often argued that we should vote for the "best person" regardless of his or her party affiliation. But as the late Harvard political scientist V. O. Key pointed out, in the absence of party labels, voters would be constantly confronted by a bewildering array of "new faces, new choices" and might have considerable difficulty making informed decisions. Without a doubt, their own party identifications and candidates' party affiliations help voters make reasonable choices.

Parties lower the information costs of participating by providing a kind of "brand-name" recognizability—that is, voters know with a substantial degree of accuracy what positions a candidate will take just by identifying the candidate's party affiliation. In addition, parties give elections a kind of sporting-event atmosphere, with voters treating parties like teams that they can support and cheer on to victory. This enhances the entertainment value of participating in elections. Parties also direct the flow of government benefits, such as patronage jobs, to those who put the party in power. These and other activities encourage individuals to identify with and support one of the two parties.[6]

Although political parties continue to be significant in the United States, the role of party organizations in electoral politics has clearly declined over the past three decades. This decline, and the partial replacement of the party by new forms of electoral technology (discussed later in this chapter), is one of the most important developments in twentieth- and twenty-first-century American politics.

Influence on National Government

The ultimate test of the party system is its relationship to and influence on the institutions of national government and the policy-making process. Thus, it is important to examine the party system in relation to Congress and the president.

Parties and Policy   One of the most familiar observations about American politics is that the two major parties try to be all things to all people and are therefore indistinguishable from each other. Data and experience give some support to this observation. Parties in the United States are not programmatic or ideological, as they have sometimes been in Britain or in other parts of Europe. But this does not mean there are no differences between them. During the Reagan era, important differences emerged between the positions of Democratic and Republican party leaders on a number of key issues, and these differences are still apparent today. For example, the national leadership of the Republican Party supports maintaining high levels of military spending, cuts in social programs, tax relief for middle- and upper-income voters, tax incentives to businesses, and the "social agenda" backed by members of conservative religious denominations. The national Democratic leadership, on the other hand, supports expanded social welfare spending, cuts in military spending, increased regulation of business, and a variety of consumer and environmental programs.

These differences reflect differences in philosophy as well as differences in the core constituencies to which the parties seek to appeal. The Democratic Party at the national level seeks to unite organized labor, the poor, members of racial minorities, and liberal upper-middle-class professionals. The Republicans, by contrast, appeal to business, upper-middle- and upper-class groups in the private sector, and social conservatives. Often, party leaders will seek to develop issues they hope will add new groups to their party's constituent base. During the 1980s, for example, under the leadership of Ronald Reagan, the Republicans devised a series of "social issues," including support for school prayer, opposition to abortion, and opposition to affirmative action, designed to cultivate the support of white Southerners. This effort was extremely successful in increasing Republican strength in the once solidly Democratic South. In the 1990s, under the leadership of Bill Clinton, who called himself a "new Democrat," the Democratic Party sought to develop new social programs de-

---

[6]On the concept of party as brand name, see Gary W. Cox and Mathew D. McCubbins, *Legislative Leviathan: Party Government in the House* (Berkeley: University of California Press, 1993).

signed to solidify the party's base among working-class and poor voters, and new, somewhat more conservative economic programs aimed at attracting the votes of middle- and upper-middle-class voters.

As these examples suggest, parties do not always support policies because they are favored by their constituents. Instead, party leaders can play the role of policy entrepreneurs, seeding ideas and programs that will expand their party's base of support while eroding that of the opposition. In recent years, for example, leaders of both major political parties have sought to develop ideas and programs they hoped would appeal to America's most rapidly growing electoral bloc: Latino voters. Thus President George W. Bush has recommended a number of proposals designed to help Latinos secure U.S. residence and employment. Democrats, for their part, have proposed education and social service programs designed to appeal to the needs of Latino immigrants. Both parties promoted their ideas extensively within the Latino community in the 2004 presidential campaign, and although the Democrats won more Latino votes in 2004, each party claimed to be satisfied with its long-term strategy for building Latino support. The 2006 election campaign, however, produced much more one-sided results. A hard-line view on immigration, especially from Latin America, put Republicans at a competitive disadvantage. Democratic support among Latinos rose dramatically in the midterm elections, and several prominent Republican incumbents in the southwest lost their seats as a result.

It is one of the essential characteristics of party politics in America that a party's programs and policies often lead, rather than follow, public opinion. Like their counterparts in the business world, party leaders seek to identify and develop "products" (programs and policies) that will appeal to the public. The public, of course, has the ultimate voice. With its votes it decides whether or not to "buy" new policy offerings.

Through members elected to office, both parties have made efforts to translate their general goals into concrete policies. Republicans, for example, implemented tax cuts, increased defense spending, cut social spending, and enacted restrictions on abortion during the 1980s and 1990s. Democrats were able to defend consumer and environmental programs against GOP attacks and sought to expand domestic social programs in the late 1990s. During his two terms in office, President George W. Bush sought substantial cuts in federal taxes, "privatization" of the social security system, and a larger role for faith-based organizations allied with the Republican party in the administration of federal social programs. In the context of the nation's campaign against terrorism, Bush also sought to shift America's defense posture from an emphasis on deterrence to a doctrine of preemptive strikes against perceived threats.

The Parties and Congress   Congress, in particular, depends more on the party system than is generally recognized. First, the speakership of the House is a party office. All the members of the House take part in the election of the speaker. But the actual selection is made by the majority party. When the *majority party* caucus presents a nominee to the entire House, its choice is then invariably ratified in a straight party-line vote.

The committee system of both houses of Congress is also a product of the two-party system. Although the rules organizing committees and the rules defining the

majority party The party that holds the majority of legislative seats in either the House or the Senate.

jurisdiction of each committee are adopted like ordinary legislation by the whole membership, parties shape all other features of the committees. For example, each party is assigned a quota of members for each committee, depending upon the percentage of total seats held by the party. On the rare occasions when an independent or third-party candidate is elected, the leaders of the two parties must agree against whose quota this member's committee assignments will count.

The assignment of individual members to committees is a party decision. Each party has a "committee on committees" to make such decisions. Permission to transfer from one committee to another is also a party decision. Moreover, advancement up the committee ladder toward the chair is a party decision. Since the late nineteenth century, most advancements have been automatic—based upon the length of continual service on the committee. This seniority system has existed only because of the support of the two parties, and each party can depart from it by a simple vote. During the 1970s, both parties reinstituted the practice of reviewing each chair—voting anew every two years on whether each chair would be continued. In 2001, Republicans lived up to their 1995 pledge to limit House committee chairs to three terms. Existing chairpersons were forced to step down, but were replaced generally by the most senior Republican member of each committee.

President and Party

As we saw earlier, the party that wins the White House is led, in title anyway, by the president. The president normally depends upon fellow party members in Congress to support legislative initiatives. At the same time, members of the party in Congress hope that the president's programs and personal prestige will help them raise campaign funds and secure reelection.

When he assumed office in 2001, President George W. Bush called for a new era of bipartisan cooperation, and the new president did receive the support of some Democratic conservatives. Generally, however, Bush depended on near-unanimous backing from his own party in Congress to implement his plans for cutting taxes as well as other elements of his program. After the terrorist attacks of September 11, both parties united behind Bush's military response. By the end of the president's first term, however, the parties were sharply divided on the administration's policies in Iraq, economic policy, Social Security reform, abortion, other social issues, and the need for enhanced governmental law-enforcement powers to combat terrorism. Ultimately, Bush relied mainly on Republican support to achieve his goals.

THE TWO-PARTY SYSTEM IN AMERICA

Although George Washington deplored partisan politics, the two-party system emerged early in the history of the new Republic. Beginning with the Federalists and the Jeffersonian Republicans in the early 1800s, two major parties would dominate national politics, although which particular two parties they were would change with the times and issues. This two-party system has culminated in today's Democrats and Republicans. The evolution of American political parties is shown in Figure 11.2.

FIGURE 11.2 How the U.S. Party System Evolved

*In some cases, there was even a fourth party. Most of the parties listed here existed for only one term.

†The Anti-Masonics not only had the distinction of being the first third party but also were the first party to hold a national nominating convention and the first to announce a party platform.

The Democrats

When the Jeffersonian party splintered in 1824, Andrew Jackson emerged as the leader of one of its four factions. In 1830, Jackson's group became the Democratic Party. This new party had the strongest national organization of its time and presented itself as the party of the common man. Jacksonians supported reductions in the price of public lands and a policy of cheaper money and credit. Laborers, immigrants, and settlers west of the Alleghenies were quickly attracted to it.

From 1828, when Jackson was elected president, to 1860, the Democratic Party was the dominant force in American politics. For all but eight of those years, the Democrats held the White House. In addition, a Democratic majority controlled the Senate for twenty-six years and the House for twenty-four years during the same time period. Nineteenth-century Democrats emphasized the importance of interpreting the Constitution literally, upholding states' rights, and limiting federal spending.

In 1860, the issue of slavery split the Democrats along geographic lines. In the South, many Democrats served in the Confederate government. In the North, one faction of the party (the Copperheads) opposed the war and advocated negotiating a peace with the South. Thus, for years after the war, Republicans denounced the Democrats as the "party of treason."

The Democratic Party was not fully able to regain its political strength until the Great Depression. In 1933, Democrat Franklin D. Roosevelt entered the White House, and the Democrats won control of Congress as well. Roosevelt's New Deal coalition, composed of Catholics, Jews, African Americans, farmers, intellectuals, and members of organized labor, dominated American politics until the 1970s and served as the basis for the party's expansion of federal power and efforts to remedy social problems.

The Democrats were never fully united. In Congress, Southern Democrats often aligned with Republicans in the "conservative coalition" rather than with members of their own party. But the Democratic Party remained America's majority party, usually controlling Congress and the White House, for nearly four decades after 1932. By the 1980s, the Democratic coalition faced serious problems. The once-solid South often voted for the Republicans, along with many blue-collar Northern voters. On the other hand, the Democrats increased their strength among African American voters and women. The Democrats maintained a strong base in the bureaucracies of the federal government and the states, in labor unions, and in the not-for-profit sector of the economy. During the 1980s and 1990s, moderate Democrats were able to take control of the party nominating process and sought to broaden middle-class support for the party. This helped the Democrats elect a president in 1992. In 1994, however, the unpopularity of Democratic President Bill Clinton led to the loss of the Democrats' control of both houses of Congress for the first time since 1946. In 1996, Clinton was able to win reelection to a second term over the weak opposition of Republican candidate Robert Dole. Democrats were, however, unable to dislodge their GOP rivals from the leadership of either house of Congress. During the 2000 national presidential elections, Vice President Al Gore won the nomination despite a serious challenge from former New Jersey Senator Bill Bradley. In the general presidential election, Gore outpolled Republican candidate George W. Bush but lost the electoral vote after Bush won a long battle over Florida's votes.

Disagreements between the two wings of the party were evident during the campaign for the Democratic presidential nomination in 2004 and 2008. In 2004, moderate Democrat Joseph Lieberman, for example, supported President Bush's decision to launch a war against Iraq, while liberal Democrats such as Howard Dean and Al Sharpton strongly criticized the president's military policies. The party's eventual nominee, Senator John Kerry of Massachusetts, had originally supported the war but sought to stake out a position in opposition to Bush's policies that would satisfy liberal Democrats but not appear to be indecisive. Similarly, in 2007, antiwar Democrats castigated front-runners Clinton and Obama for not demanding an immediate withdrawal of American forces from Iraq.

The Republicans

The 1854 Kansas-Nebraska Act overturned the Missouri Compromise of 1820 and the Compromise of 1850, which had both barred the expansion of slavery in the American territories. The Kansas-Nebraska Act gave each territory the right to decide whether or not to permit slavery. Opposition to this policy galvanized antislavery groups and led them to create a new party, the Republicans. It drew its membership from existing political groups—former Whigs, Know-Nothings, Free Soilers, and antislavery Democrats. In 1856, the party's first presidential candidate, John C. Frémont, won one-third of the popular vote and carried eleven states.

The early Republican platforms appealed to commercial as well as antislavery interests. The Republicans favored homesteading, internal improvements, the construction of a transcontinental railroad, and protective tariffs, as well as the containment of slavery. In 1858, the Republican Party won control of the House; in 1860, the Republican presidential candidate, Abraham Lincoln, was victorious.

From the Civil War to the Great Depression, the Republicans were America's dominant political party, especially after 1896. In the seventy-two years between 1860 and 1932, Republicans occupied the White House for fifty-six years, controlled the Senate for sixty years, and controlled the House for fifty. During these years, the Republicans came to be closely associated with big business. The party of Lincoln became the party of Wall Street.

The Great Depression, however, ended Republican supremacy. The voters held Republican President Herbert Hoover responsible for the economic catastrophe, and by 1936 the party's popularity was so low that Republicans won only eighty-nine seats in the House and seventeen in the Senate. The Republican presidential candidate, Governor Alfred M. Landon of Kansas, carried only two states. The Republicans won only four presidential elections between 1932 and 1980, and they controlled Congress for only four of those years (1947–1949 and 1953–1955).

The Republican Party has widened its appeal over the last four decades. Groups previously associated with the Democratic Party—particularly blue-collar workers and Southern Democrats—have been increasingly attracted to Republican presidential candidates (for example, Dwight D. Eisenhower, Richard Nixon, Ronald Reagan, and George Bush). But Republicans generally did not do as well at the state and local levels and had little chance of capturing a majority in either the House or Senate. Yet in 1994, the Republican Party finally won a majority in both houses of Congress, in large part because of the party's growing strength in the South.

During the 1990s, conservative religious groups, who had been attracted to the Republican camp by its opposition to abortion and support for school prayer, made a concerted effort to expand their influence within the party. This effort led to conflict between these members of the "religious Right" and more traditional "country-club" Republicans, whose major concerns were matters such as taxes and federal regulation of business. This coalition swept the polls in 1994 and maintained its control of both houses of Congress in 1996, despite President Clinton's reelection. In 1998, however, severe strains began to show in the GOP coalition. In 2000, George W. Bush sought to unite the party's centrist and right wings behind a program of tax cuts, education reform, military strength, and family values. Bush avoided issues that divided the GOP camp, like abortion. In 2004, he adopted a similar strategy. Bush's candidacy seemed to bode well for the future of the GOP insofar as he was able to find a political formula that could unite the party. By 2008, however, conflicts over the Iraq war undermined Republican unity and the GOP's electoral chances.

Electoral Alignments and Realignments

In the United States, party politics has followed a pattern (see Figure 11.3). Typically, during the course of American political history, the national electoral arena has been dominated by one party for a period of roughly thirty years. At the conclusion of this period, a new party has supplanted the dominant party in what political scientists call an *electoral realignment.* The realignment is typically followed by a long period in which the new party is the dominant political force in the United States—not necessarily winning every election but generally maintaining control of the Congress and usually of the White House as well.[7]

Although there are some disputes among scholars about the precise timing of these critical realignments, there is general agreement that at least five have occurred since the founding of the American Republic. The first took place around 1800 when the Jeffersonian Republicans defeated the Federalists and became the dominant force in American politics. The second realignment occurred in about 1828, when the Jacksonian Democrats took control of the White House and the Congress. The third period of realignment centered on 1860. During this period, the newly founded Republican Party led by Abraham Lincoln won power, in the process destroying the Whig Party, which had been one of the nation's two major parties since the 1830s. During the fourth critical period, centered on the election of 1896, the Republicans reasserted their dominance of the national government, which had been weakening since the 1880s. The fifth realignment took place during the period 1932–1936 when the Democrats, led by Franklin Delano Roosevelt, took control of the White House and Congress and, despite sporadic interruptions, maintained

electoral realignment The point in history when a new party supplants the ruling party, becoming in turn the dominant political force. In the United States, this has tended to occur roughly every thirty years.

---

[7]See Walter Dean Burnham, *Critical Elections and the Mainsprings of American Electoral Politics* (New York: Norton, 1970). See also James L. Sundquist, *Dynamics of the Party System* (Washington, D.C.: Brookings Institution, 1983).

FIGURE 11.3 Electoral Realignments

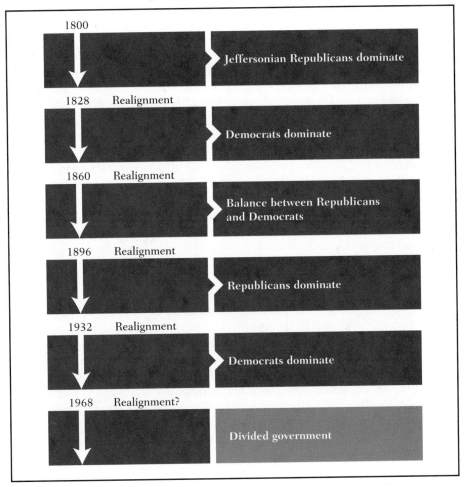

control of both through the 1960s. Since that time, American party politics has been characterized primarily by ***divided government***, wherein one party controls the presidency while the other party controls one or both houses of Congress.

Historically, realignments occur when new issues combined with economic or political crises persuade large numbers of voters to reexamine their traditional partisan loyalties and permanently shift their support from one party to another. For example, in the 1850s, diverse regional, income, and business groups supported one of the two major parties, the Democrats or the Whigs, on the basis of their positions on various economic issues, such as internal improvements, the tariff, monetary policy, and banking. This economic alignment was shattered during the 1850s. The newly formed Republican Party campaigned on the basis of opposition to slavery and, in particular, opposition to the expansion of slavery into the territories. The issues of

divided government
The condition in American government in which one party controls the presidency while the opposing party controls one or both houses of Congress.

slavery and sectionalism produced divisions within both the Democratic and the Whig parties, ultimately leading to the dissolution of the latter, and these issues compelled voters to reexamine their partisan allegiances. Many Northern voters who had supported the Whigs or the Democrats on the basis of their economic stands shifted their support to the Republicans as slavery replaced tariffs and economic concerns as the central item on the nation's political agenda. Many Southern Whigs shifted their support to the Democrats. The new sectional alignment of forces that emerged was solidified by the trauma of the Civil War and persisted almost to the turn of the century.

In 1896, this sectional alignment was at least partially supplanted by an alignment of political forces based on economic and cultural factors. During the economic crises of the 1880s and 1890s, the Democrats forged a coalition consisting of economically hard-pressed Midwestern and Southern farmers, as well as small-town and rural economic interests. These groups tended to be descendants of British Isles, Dutch, and Hessian fundamentalist Protestants. The Republicans, on the other hand, put together a coalition comprising most of the business community, industrial workers, and city dwellers. In the election of 1896, Republican candidate William McKinley, emphasizing business, industry, and urban interests, decisively defeated Democrat William Jennings Bryan, who spoke for sectional interests, farmers, and fundamentalism. Republican dominance lasted until 1932.

Such periods of critical realignment in American politics have had extremely important institutional and policy results. Realignments occur when new issue concerns coupled with economic or political crises weaken the established political elite and permit new groups of politicians to create coalitions of forces capable of capturing and holding the reins of governmental power. The construction of new governing coalitions during these realigning periods has effected major changes in American governmental institutions and policies. Each period of realignment represents a turning point in American politics. The choices made by the national electorate during these periods have helped shape the course of American political history for generations.[8]

American Third Parties

Although the United States is said to possess a two-party system, we have always had more than two parties. Typically, *third parties* in the United States have represented social and economic protests that, for one or another reason, were not given voice by the two major parties.[9] Such parties have had a good deal of influence on ideas and elections in the United States. The Populists, a party centered in the rural areas of the West and the Midwest during the late nineteenth century, and the Progressives, spokesmen for the urban middle classes in the late nineteenth and early twentieth centuries, are among the most important examples. More recently, Ross Perot, who ran in 1992 and 1996 as an independent, impressed some voters with his folksy style in the presidential debates and garnered almost 19 percent of the votes

third parties Parties that organize to compete against the two major American political parties.

---

[8]Benjamin Ginsberg, *The Consequences of Consent* (New York: Random House, 1982), Chapter 4.

[9]For a discussion of third parties in the United States, see Daniel A. Mazmanian, *Third Parties in Presidential Elections* (Washington, D.C.: Brookings Institution, 1974).

TABLE 11.1 Parties and Candidates, 2008

Candidate	Party	Vote Total	Percentage of Vote
Barack Obama	Democratic	64,629,649	53
John McCain	Republican	56,887,996	46
Ralph Nader	Independent	667,045	0.5
Robert L. Barr, Jr.	Libertarian	493,987	0.4
Charles O. Baldwin	Independent	177,690	0.1
Alan Keyes	Independent	35,299	0

SOURCE: elections.foxnews.com/tracker.html (accessed 11/6/08).

cast in the 1992 presidential election. Earlier, George Wallace received almost 10 percent of the vote in 1968, and John Anderson received about 5 percent in 1980.

Table 11.1 lists the top candidates in the presidential election of 2008, including third-party and independent candidates who ran. In addition to the candidates listed in Table 11.1, the Green Party, the Socialist Party, the Prohibition Party, and several other parties nominated candidates for the presidency in 2008. In order to have any realistic chance of winning, a candidate needs to appear on the ballot in at least enough states to reach a total of 270 electoral votes. However, most of the third-party and independent candidates in 2008 did not appear on the ballot in enough states to have any hope of winning. The third-party and independent candidates gained no electoral votes for president, and most of them disappeared immediately after the presidential election. Third-party candidates also arise at the state and local levels. In New York, the Liberal and Conservative parties have been on the ballot for decades. In 1998, Minnesota elected a third-party governor, former professional wrestler Jesse Ventura. In 2002, the Green Party candidate for governor in Massachusetts, Jill Stein, may have affected the race between Mitt Romney and his Democratic rival by drawing votes away from the Democrat in a close race. And in 2006, the entertainer Kinky Friedman mounted a somewhat credible campaign running as an independent candidate for the governorship of Texas.

Although the Republican Party was only the third American political party ever to make itself permanent (by replacing the Whigs), other third parties have enjoyed an influence far beyond their electoral size. This was because large parts of their programs were adopted by one or both of the major parties, who sought to appeal to the voters mobilized by the new party, and so to expand their own electoral strength. The Democratic Party, for example, became a great deal more liberal when it adopted most of the Progressive program early in the twentieth century. Many Socialists felt that President Roosevelt's New Deal had adopted most of their party's program, including old-age pensions, unemployment compensation, an agricultural marketing program, and laws guaranteeing workers the right to organize into unions.

This kind of influence explains the short lives of third parties. Their causes are usually eliminated by the ability of the major parties to absorb their programs and to draw their supporters into the mainstream. There are, of course, additional reasons that most third parties are short-lived. One is the usual limitation of their electoral support to one or two regions. Populist support, for example, was primarily Midwestern. The 1948 Progressive Party, with Henry Wallace as its candidate, drew nearly half its votes from the state of New York. The American Independent Party polled nearly 10 million popular votes and 45 electoral votes for George Wallace in 1968—the most electoral votes ever polled by a third-party candidate. But all of Wallace's electoral votes and the majority of his popular vote came from the states of the Deep South.

Americans usually assume that only the candidates nominated by one of the two major parties have any chance of winning an election. Thus, a vote cast for a third-party or independent candidate is often seen as a wasted vote. Voters who would prefer a third-party candidate may feel compelled to vote for the major party candidate whom they regard as the lesser of two evils to avoid wasting their vote in a futile gesture. Third-party candidates must struggle—usually without success—to overcome the perception that they cannot win. Thus in 2004, many liberals who admired Ralph Nader nevertheless urged him not to mount an independent bid for the presidency for fear he would siphon liberal votes from the Democrats, as he had in 2000. Some former Naderites participated in efforts to keep Nader off the ballot in a number of states. Ultimately Nader did mount a presidential campaign but received 2.5 million fewer votes in 2004 than in 2000. Most of his former adherents, knowing he could not win, voted for John Kerry. In 2008, Nader was on the ballot again, but received just over half a million votes. The other leading third-party and independent candidates in 2008 seemed more likely to siphon votes from the Republicans. For example, Bob Barr, the Libertarian candidate, ran on a platform of smaller government, lower taxes, and more individual freedom. Independent candidates Charles Baldwin and Alan Keyes were social conservatives. However, none won more than half a million votes, so their direct impact on the outcome was negligible.

single-member district An electorate that is allowed to elect only one representative from each district; the normal method of representation in the United States.

As many scholars have pointed out, third-party prospects are also hampered by America's *single-member-district* plurality election system. In many other nations, several individuals can be elected to represent each legislative district. This is called a system of *multiple-member districts.* With this type of system, the candidates of weaker parties have a better chance of winning at least some seats. For their part, voters are less concerned about wasting ballots and usually more willing to support minor-party candidates.

multiple-member district An electorate that selects all candidates at large from the whole district; each voter is given the number of votes equivalent to the number of seats to be filled.

Reinforcing the effects of the single-member district, plurality voting rules (as was noted in Chapter 10) generally have the effect of setting what could be called a high threshold for victory. To win a plurality race, candidates usually must secure many more votes than they would need under most European systems of proportional representation. For example, to win an American plurality election in a single-member district where there are only two candidates, a politician must win more than 50 percent of the votes cast. To win a seat from a European multiple-member district under proportional rules, a candidate may need to win only 15 or 20 percent of the votes cast. This high American threshold discourages minor parties and encourages the various political factions that might otherwise form minor parties to minimize their differences and remain within the major-party coalitions.

It would nevertheless be incorrect to assert (as some scholars have maintained) that America's single-member plurality election system is the major cause of our historical two-party pattern. All that can be said is that American election law depresses the number of parties likely to survive over long periods of time in the United States. There is no requirement that there be even two strong parties. Indeed, the single-member plurality system of election can also discourage second parties. After all, if one party consistently receives a large plurality of the vote, people may eventually come to see their vote *even for the second party* as a wasted effort. This happened to the Republican Party in the Deep South before World War II.

Despite these obstacles, every presidential election brings out a host of minor-party hopefuls (see Table 11.1). Few survive until the next contest.

POLITICAL PARTIES TODAY

As a result of Progressive reform, American party organizations entered the twentieth century with rickety substructures. As the use of civil service, primary elections, and other Progressive innovations spread, the strength of party organizations eroded. By the end of World War II, political scientists were already bemoaning the absence of party discipline and "party responsibility" in the United States.

High-Tech Politics

This erosion of the parties' organizational strength set the stage for the introduction of new political techniques that represented radical departures from the campaign practices perfected during the nineteenth century. In place of workers and organization, contending forces began to employ intricate electronic communications techniques to attract supporters. Contemporary political technology includes six basic elements.

1. *Polling.* Surveys of voter opinion provide the information that candidates and their staffs use to craft campaign strategies. Candidates use polls to select issues, to assess their own strengths and weaknesses (as well as those of the opposition), to check voter response to the campaign, and to determine the degree to which various constituent groups are susceptible to campaign appeals. Virtually all contemporary campaigns for national and statewide office, as well as many local campaigns, make extensive use of opinion surveys. As we saw in Chapter 9, President Clinton used polling extensively both during and after the 1996 presidential election, using the results to shape his rhetoric and to guide his policy initiatives.

2. *The broadcast media.* Extensive use of the electronic media, television in particular, has become the hallmark of the modern political campaign. Generally, media campaigns attempt to follow the guidelines indicated by a candidate's polls, emphasizing issues and personal characteristics that appear important in the poll data.

Is Partisanship in Decline?

Since 1948, researchers at the University of Michigan have collected survey data during election years as part of the American National Election Studies (ANES). The purpose of these surveys is to offer systematic explanations of election outcomes through individual-level surveys of ordinary citizens who participate in these elections. Because these data have been collected over an extended period, they have contributed to a much better understanding of changes in voting behavior over time.

Among the survey questions is a measure of how strongly voters and non-voters identify with a particular political party. Rather than using just three broad categories (Democrat, Republican, independent), the ANES uses a seven-point scale to assess partisanship. By separating out "strong" and "weak" partisan identifiers from independent "leaners" and "pure" independents, we gain a more nuanced understanding of trends in partisanship.

Democrat			Independent		Republican	
Strongly Democrat	Weakly Democrat	Independent Leans Democrat	Pure Independent	Independent Leans Republican	Weakly Republican	Strongly Republican

Interestingly, in the ANES data we observe a sizeable decline in the number of strong partisan identifiers beginning in the 1960s and continuing into the 1970s and 1980s. This trend has been documented elsewhere by scholars, who suggest that large segments of the American public have steadily been drifting away from the major parties since the 1950s.[1]

[1] Martin P. Wattenberg. *The Decline of American Political Parties: 1952–1994*. (Cambridge, Mass.: Harvard University Press, 1996).

But is partisanship really in decline? By 1996, the proportion of citizens strongly identifying with the two major parties was almost as high as it was during the 1950s. When we factor in the proportion of weak identifiers and independent leaners over this entire period, we observe that the aggregate number of Americans identifying with the parties has remained fairly constant since the 1950s, even if the intensity of citizen preferences for the parties has clearly changed over time.

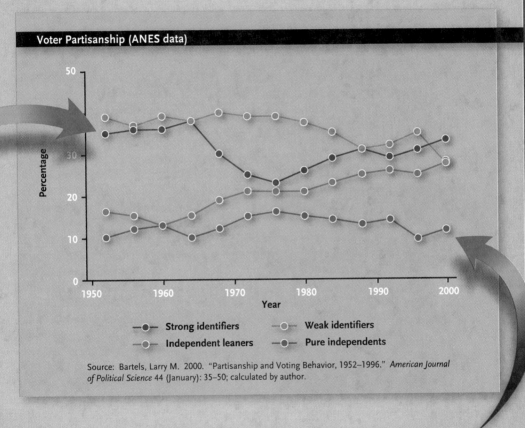

Source: Bartels, Larry M. 2000. "Partisanship and Voting Behavior, 1952–1996." *American Journal of Political Science* 44 (January): 35–50; calculated by author.

There has not been a marked increase in the number of "pure" independents over this period, suggesting that parties may be as relevant today as they were 50 years ago. The lesson here is how one thinks about the seven-point scale of partisanship affects the types of conclusions one draws about American political behavior.

The broadcast media are now so central to modern campaigns that most candidates' activities are tied to their media strategies.[10] Candidate activities are designed expressly to stimulate television news coverage. For instance, members of Congress running for reelection or for president almost always sponsor committee or subcommittee hearings to generate publicity.

3. *Phone banks.* Through the broadcast media, candidates communicate with voters en masse and impersonally. Phone banks, on the other hand, allow campaign workers to make personal contact with hundreds of thousands of voters. Personal contacts of this sort are thought to be extremely effective. Again, poll data serve to identify the groups that will be targeted for phone calls. Computers select phone numbers from areas in which members of these groups are concentrated. Staffs of paid or volunteer callers, using computer-assisted dialing systems and prepared scripts, place calls to deliver the candidate's message. The targeted groups are generally those identified by polls as either uncommitted or weakly committed to the candidate, or they may be strong supporters of the candidate who are contacted simply to encourage them to vote.

4. *Direct mail.* Direct mail serves both as a vehicle for communicating with voters and as a mechanism for raising funds. The first step in any direct-mail campaign is the purchase or rental of a computerized mailing list of voters deemed to have some particular perspective or social characteristic. Often sets of magazine subscription lists or lists of donors to various causes are employed. For example, a candidate interested in reaching conservative voters might rent subscription lists from the *National Review;* a candidate interested in appealing to liberals might rent subscription lists from the *New York Review of Books* or the *New Republic.* Considerable fine-tuning is possible. After obtaining the appropriate mailing lists, candidates usually send pamphlets, letters, and brochures describing themselves and their views to voters believed to be sympathetic. Different types of mail appeals are made to different electoral subgroups.

In addition to its use as a political advertising medium, direct mail has also become an important source of campaign funds. Computerized mailing lists permit campaign strategists to pinpoint individuals whose interests, background, and activities suggest that they may be potential donors to the campaign. Letters of solicitation are sent to these potential donors. Some of the money raised is then used to purchase additional mailing lists. Direct-mail solicitation can be enormously effective.[11]

5. *Professional public relations.* Modern campaigns and the complex technology upon which they rely are typically directed by professional public relations consultants. Virtually all serious contenders for national and statewide office retain the services of professional campaign consultants. Increasingly, candidates for local office, too, have come to rely upon professional campaign managers. Consultants offer candidates the expertise necessary to conduct accurate opinion polls, produce effective television commercials, organize direct-mail campaigns, and make use of sophisticated computer analyses.

---

[10]Larry J. Sabato, *The Rise of Political Consultants* (New York: Basic Books, 1981).

[11]Ibid., p. 250.

Polling—Candidates use polls to select issues, to assess their own strengths and weaknesses, and to check voter response.

Broadcast media—Television spot ads are the most common use of television by candidates. Ads establish name recognition, communicate the candidate's stand on issues, and link the candidate to desirable groups in the community. The televised debate is another long-standing use of the media. New media techniques include the talk-show interview, the "electronic town hall" meeting, and the "infomercial."

Phone banks—Through phone banks, campaign workers make personal contact with hundreds of thousands of voters.

Direct mail—Direct mail serves as a fund-raising tool and as a means of communicating a candidate's ideas. The choice of mailing lists is very important.

Professional public relations—Professional campaign consultants offer expertise in how best to utilize the above-mentioned methods. Virtually all national and statewide candidates and more and more local political candidates rely on consultants.

Internet—Candidates use Web sites as a point of contact with voters.

6. *The Internet.* A more recent form of new technology has been the Internet. Most candidates for office set up a Web site as an inexpensive means to establish a public presence. The 1998 election saw increased use of the Internet by political candidates. Virtually all statewide candidates, as well as many candidates for Congress and local offices, developed Web sites providing contact information, press releases, speeches, photos, and information on how to volunteer, contact the candidate, or donate money to the campaign.

In 2000, the politician who made the most extensive use of the Internet was John McCain. McCain used his Web site to mobilize volunteers and to raise hundreds of thousands of dollars for his bid for the Republican presidential nomination. In the future, all politicians will use the Web to collect information about potential voters and supporters; this will, in turn, allow them to personalize direct mailings and telephone calls and develop direct e-mail advertising. One consultant now refers to politics on the Internet as "netwar," and asserts that "small, smart attackers" can defeat more powerful opponents in the new, information-age "battlespace."[12]

The political impact of the Internet may be limited by the fact that, unlike a TV commercial that comes to viewers without any action on their part, a Web site requires citizens to take the initiative to visit it. In general, this means that only those already supporting a candidate are likely to visit the site, limiting its political utility. However, during the 2004 presidential primaries, Democratic hopeful Howard

---

[12]Dana Milbanks, "Virtual Politics," *New Republic,* 5 July 1999, p. 22.

Dean made extensive use of the Internet as a communication and fund-raising tool. Thousands of bloggers maintained discussion forums that promoted Dean's candidacy and solicited funds. By the end of 2003, Dean had amassed a war chest of more than $15 million, much of it raised on the Internet, for his presidential bid. Dean Internet guru Joe Trippi hoped to persuade 2 million Americans to each give "one hundred dollars online," to match the funds President Bush was expected to accumulate through traditional fund-raising methods. In 2004, both Kerry and Bush used the Internet to raise money and mobilize voters. In 2008, the Internet played a vital role in Barack Obama's presidential campaign. As discussed in Chapter 10, the Obama campaign harnessed the power of social networking as a communication, mobilization, and fund-raising device, generating hundreds of millions of dollars in small contributions that helped Obama win the Democratic nomination and the general election.

Contemporary Party Organizations

In the United States, party organizations exist at virtually every level of government (see Figure 11.4). These organizations are usually committees made up of a number of active party members. State law and party rules prescribe how such committees are constituted. Usually, committee members are elected at local party meetings—called *caucuses*—or as part of the regular primary election. The best-known examples of these committees are at the national level—the Democratic National Committee and the Republican National Committee.

The National Convention   At the national level, the party's most important institution is the quadrennial national convention. The convention is attended by delegates from each of the states; as a group, they nominate the party's presidential and vice-presidential candidates, draft the party's campaign platform for the presidential race, and approve changes in the rules and regulations governing party procedures. Before World War II, presidential nominations occupied most of the time, energy, and effort expended at the national convention. The nomination process required days of negotiation and compromise among state party leaders and often required many ballots before a nominee was selected. In recent years, however, presidential candidates have essentially nominated themselves by winning enough delegate support in primary elections to win the official nomination on the first ballot. The actual convention has played little or no role in selecting the candidates.

The convention's other two tasks, establishing the party's rules and platform, remain important. Party rules can determine the relative influence of competing factions within the party and can also increase or decrease the party's chances for electoral success. In 1972, for example, the Democratic National Convention adopted a new set of rules favored by the party's liberal wing. Under these rules, state delegations to the Democratic convention were required to include women and members of minority groups in rough proportion to those groups' representation among the party's membership in that state. Liberals correctly calculated that women and African Americans would generally support liberal ideas and candidates. The convention also approves the party platform. Platforms are often dismissed as documents filled with platitudes that are seldom read by voters.

caucus (political) A normally closed meeting of a political or legislative group to select candidates, plan strategy, or make decisions regarding legislative matters.

FIGURE 11.4 How American Parties Are Organized

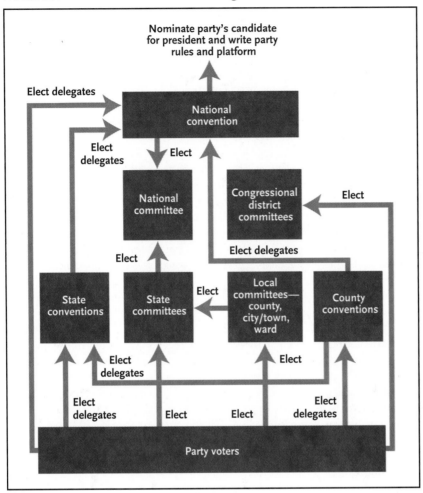

Furthermore, the parties' presidential candidates make little use of the platforms in their campaigns; usually they prefer to develop and promote their own themes. Nonetheless, the platform should be understood as a "treaty" in which the various factions attending the convention state their terms for supporting the ticket.

The National Committee Between conventions, each national political party is technically headed by its national committee. For the Democrats and Republicans, these are called the Democratic National Committee (DNC) and the Republican National Committee (RNC), respectively. These national committees raise campaign funds, head off factional disputes within the party, and endeavor to enhance the party's media image. Since 1972, the size of staff and the amount of money raised have increased substantially for both national committees. The work of each national committee is overseen by its chairperson. Other committee members are generally major party contributors or fund-raisers and serve in a largely ceremonial capacity.

For the party that controls the White House, the national committee chair is appointed by the president. Typically, this means that that party's national committee becomes little more than an adjunct to the White House staff. For a first-term president, the committee devotes the bulk of its energy to the reelection campaign. The national committee chair of the party not in control of the White House is selected by the committee itself and usually takes a broader view of the party's needs, raising money and performing other activities on behalf of the party's members in Congress and in the state legislatures.

Congressional Campaign Committees   Each party forms House and Senate campaign committees to raise funds for House and Senate election campaigns. Their efforts may or may not be coordinated with the activities of the national committees. For the party that controls the White House, the national committee and the congressional campaign committees are often rivals since both groups are seeking donations from the same people but for different candidates: The national committee seeks funds for the presidential race while the congressional campaign committees approach the same contributors for support for the congressional contests. In recent years, the Republican Party has attempted to coordinate the fund-raising activities of all its committees. Republicans have sought to give the GOP's national institutions the capacity to invest funds in those close congressional, state, and local races where they can do the most good. The Democrats have been slower to coordinate their various committee activities, and this may have placed them at a disadvantage in recent congressional and local races. The efforts of the parties to centralize and coordinate fund-raising activities have helped bring about greater party unity in Congress. As members have come to rely upon the leadership for campaign funds, they have become more likely to vote with the leadership on major issues.

All in all, campaign committees have begun to resemble large-scale campaign consulting firms, hiring full-time political operatives and evolving into professional organizations.

State and Local Party Organizations   Each of the two major parties has a central committee in each state. The parties traditionally also have county committees and, in some instances, state senate district committees, judicial district committees, and, in the case of larger cities, citywide party committees and local assembly district "ward" committees as well. Congressional districts also may have party committees.

State and local party organizations are very active in recruiting candidates and conducting voter registration drives. Under current federal law, state and local party organizations can spend unlimited amounts of money on "party-building" activities such as voter registration and get-out-the-vote drives (though in some states such practices are limited by state law). As a result, for many years the national party organizations, which have enormous fund-raising abilities but were restricted by law in how much they could spend on candidates, transferred millions of dollars to the state and local organizations. The state and local parties, in turn, spent these funds, sometimes called soft money, to promote the candidacies of national, as well as state and local, candidates. In this process, as local organizations have become linked financially to the national parties, American political parties became somewhat more integrated and nationalized than ever before. At the same time, the state and local party organizations came to control large financial resources and play important roles in elections despite the collapse of the old patronage machines.[13]

The Contemporary Party as Service Provider to Candidates　Party leaders have adapted parties to the modern age. Parties as organizations are more professional, better financed, and more organized than ever before.[14] Political scientists argue that parties have evolved into "service organizations," which, though they no longer hold a monopoly over campaigns, still provide services to candidates, without which it would be extremely difficult for candidates to win and hold office. Parties have not declined but have simply adapted to serve the interests of political actors.[15]

Many politicians, however, are able to raise funds, attract volunteers, and win office without much help from local party organizations. Once in office, these politicians often refuse to submit to party discipline; instead they steer independent courses. They are often supported by voters who see independence as a virtue and party discipline as "boss rule." Analysts refer to this pattern as a "candidate-centered" politics to distinguish it from a political process in which parties are the dominant forces. The problem with a candidate-centered politics is that it tends to be associated with low turnout, high levels of special-interest influence, and a lack of effective decision making. In short, many of the problems that have plagued American politics in recent years can be traced directly to the independence of American voters and politicians and the candidate-centered nature of American national politics.

The Role of the Parties in Contemporary Politics

Political parties make democratic government possible. We often do not appreciate that democratic government is a contradiction in terms. Government implies policies, programs, and decisive action. Democracy, on the other hand, implies an opportunity for all citizens to participate fully in the governmental process. The contradiction is that full participation by everyone is often inconsistent with getting anything done. At what point should participation stop and governance begin? How can we make certain that popular participation will result in a government capable of making decisions and developing needed policies? The problem of democratic government is especially acute in the United States because of the system of separated powers bequeathed to us by the Constitution's framers. Our system of separated powers means that it is very difficult to link popular participation and

---

[13]For a useful discussion, see John Bibby and Thomas Holbrook, "Parties and Elections," in *Politics in the American States: A Comparative Analysis,* eds. Virginia Gray and Herbert Jacob, 6th ed. (Washington, D.C.: Congressional Quarterly Press, 1996), pp. 78–121.

[14]See John H. Aldrich, *Why Parties? The Origin and Transformation of Party Politics in America* (Chicago: University of Chicago Press, 1995), Chapter 8.　　○　ONLINE READING

[15]See Paul S. Herrnson, *Party Campaigning in the 1980s* (Cambridge, Mass.: Harvard University Press, 1988).

effective decision making. Often, after the citizens have spoken and the dust has settled, no single set of political forces has been able to win control of enough of the scattered levers of power to actually do anything. Instead of government, we have a continual political struggle.

Strong political parties are a partial antidote to the inherent contradiction between participation and government. Strong parties can both encourage popular involvement and convert participation into effective government. More than fifty years ago, a committee of the academic American Political Science Association (APSA) called for the development of a more "responsible" party government. By **responsible party government,** the committee meant political parties that mobilized voters and were sufficiently well organized to develop and implement coherent programs and policies after the election. Strong parties can link democratic participation and government.

Although they are significant factors in politics and government, American political parties today are not as strong as the "responsible parties" advocated by the APSA. Can political parties be strengthened? The answer is, in principle, yes. For example, political parties could be strengthened if the rules governing campaign finance were revised to make candidates more dependent financially upon state and local party organizations rather than on personal resources or private contributors. Such a reform, to be sure, would require more strict regulation of party fund-raising practices to prevent soft money abuses. The potential benefit, however, of a greater party role in political finance could be substantial. If parties controlled the bulk of the campaign funds, they would become more coherent and disciplined, and might come to resemble the responsible parties envisioned by the APSA. In 2002, Congress enacted campaign finance reforms that diminished the role of the national party organizations in financing campaigns. Time will tell what consequences will be brought about by this change. Political parties have been such important features of American democratic politics that we need to think long and hard about how to preserve and strengthen them.

CHAPTER REVIEW

Political parties seek to control government by controlling its personnel. Elections are their means to this end. Thus, parties take shape from the electoral process. The formal principle of party organization is this: For every district in which an election is held—from the entire nation to the local county or precinct—there should be some kind of party unit.

The two-party system dominates U.S. politics. Today, on individual issues, the two parties differ little from each other. In general, however, Democrats lean more to the left on issues and Republicans lean more to the right. Even though party affiliation means less to Americans than it once did, partisanship remains important. What ticket-splitting there is occurs mainly at the national level between Congress and the presidency.

Voters' choices have had particularly significant consequences during periods of critical electoral realignment. During these periods, which have occurred roughly every thirty years, new electoral coalitions have formed, new groups have come to power, and

responsible party government A set of principles that idealizes a strong role for parties in defining their stance on issues, mobilizing voters, and fulfilling their campaign promises once in office.

important institutional and policy changes have occurred. The last such critical period was associated with Franklin Roosevelt's New Deal.

Third parties are short-lived for several reasons. They have limited electoral support, the tradition of the two-party system is strong, and a major party often adopts their platforms. Single-member districts with two competing parties also discourage third parties.

Nominating and electing are the basic functions of parties. Originally nominations were made in party caucuses, and individuals who ran as independents had a difficult time getting on the ballot. In the 1830s, dissatisfaction with the cliquish caucuses led to nominating conventions. In 2002, Congress enacted campaign finance reforms that diminished the role of the national party organizations in financing campaigns. Time will tell what consequences will be brought about by this change. Although these ended the "King Caucus" that controlled the nomination of the presidential candidates, and thereby gave the presidency a popular base, they too proved unsatisfactory. Primaries have now more or less replaced the conventions. There are both closed and open primaries. Closed primaries are more supportive of strong political parties than open primaries. Contested primaries sap party strength and financial resources, but they nonetheless serve to resolve important social conflicts and recognize new interest groups. Winning at the top of a party ticket usually depends on the party regulars at the bottom getting out the vote. At all levels, the mass communications media are important. Mass mailings, too, are vital in campaigning. Thus, campaign funds are crucial to success.

Congress is organized around the two-party system. The House speakership is a party office. Parties determine the makeup of congressional committees, including their chairs, which are no longer based entirely on seniority.

In recent years, the role of parties in political campaigns has been partially supplanted by the use of new political technologies. These include polling, the broadcast media, phone banks, direct-mail fund-raising and advertising, professional public relations, and the Internet. These techniques are enormously expensive and have led to a shift from labor-intensive to capital-intensive politics. This shift works to the advantage of political forces representing the well-to-do. The parties currently have also entrenched themselves in government agencies and sectors of the national economy.

FOR FURTHER READING

Aldrich, John H. *Why Parties? The Origin and Transformation of Party Politics in America.* Chicago: University of Chicago Press, 1995. ○ ONLINE READING

Beck, Paul Allen, and Marjorie Randon Hershey. *Party Politics in America.* 10th ed. New York: Longman, 2003.

Chambers, William N., and Walter Dean Burnham, eds. *The American Party Systems: Stages of Political Development.* 2nd ed. New York: Oxford University Press, 1975.

Coleman, John J. *Party Decline in America: Policy, Politics, and the Fiscal State.* Princeton, N.J.: Princeton University Press, 1996.

Cox, Gary W., and Mathew D. McCubbins. *Legislative Leviathan: Party Government in the House.* Berkeley: University of California Press, 1993.

ONLINE READING ○ ————. *Setting the Agenda: Responsible Party Government in the U.S. House of Representatives.* New York: Cambridge University Press, 2005.

Hofstadter, Richard. *The Idea of a Party System: The Rise of Legitimate Opposition in the United States, 1780–1840.* Berkeley: University of California Press, 1969.

Kayden, Xandra, and Eddie Mahe Jr. *The Party Goes On: The Persistence of the Two-Party System in the United States.* New York: Basic Books, 1985.

Milkis, Sidney M. *The President and the Parties: The Transformation of the American Party System since the New Deal.* New York: Oxford University Press, 1993.

Rohde, David W. *Parties and Leaders in the Post-reform House.* Chicago: University of Chicago Press, 1991.

Shafer, Byron, ed. *Beyond Realignment? Interpreting American Electoral Eras.* Madison: University of Wisconsin Press, 1991.

ONLINE READING ○ Sundquist, James L. *Dynamics of the Party System: Alignment and Realignment of Political Parties in the United States.* Washington, D.C.: Brookings Institution, 1983.

ONLINE READING ○ Wattenberg, Martin P. *The Decline of American Political Parties, 1952–1996.* Cambridge, Mass.: Harvard University Press, 1998.

Groups and Interests

HOW DO INTEREST GROUPS WORK?

For more than two decades, lobbyists for senior citizens, led by the AARP (formerly called the American Association of Retired Persons), have sought to add a prescription drug benefit to the Medicare program on which most seniors depend for their health care. Many members of Congress have opposed such a benefit because it would cost hundreds of billions of dollars. The pharmaceutical industry also feared that such a Medicare prescription plan would open the way for government regulation of drug prices as well as other aspects of the industry. Through its political arm, the Pharmaceutical Research and Manufacturers of America (PhRMA), the pharmaceutical industry is one of the most powerful lobby groups in Washington. Drug company executives and corporate PACs have contributed tens of millions of dollars to political campaigns since 2000, and a number of drug industry lobbyists and executives were major donors to and fund-raisers for George W. Bush's presidential campaign. The drug industry's political clout was, for years, an enormous impediment to the enactment of a Medicare prescription drug plan.

By the early 2000s, however, the industry had begun to face a number of economic and political problems. To begin with, the high prices charged for prescription drugs were producing enormous pressure in Congress to reduce the patent

● Core of the Analysis

● Interest groups are organized to influence government decisions.

● Interest groups have proliferated over the last thirty years as a result of the expansion of the federal government and the "New Politics" movement.

● Interest groups use various strategies to promote their goals, including lobbying, gaining access to key decision makers, using the courts, going public, and influencing electoral politics.

● Though interest groups sometimes promote public concerns, they more often represent narrow interests.

protection enjoyed by drug company products; this would allow cheaper generic drugs to enter the marketplace more rapidly. Second, many consumers had discovered that they could purchase drugs in Canada and Europe for as much as 75 percent less than what they cost in the United States. These foreign purchases, while illegal, are difficult to monitor and are costing the drug companies millions of dollars in profits. Finally, growing numbers of senior citizens were not able to afford their prescription drugs at all and so were simply not buying medicine—another source of lost profit for the industry.

In the face of these problems, PhRMA changed its lobbying strategy. Rather than continue to resist a Medicare drug plan, the industry moved to craft a plan of its own. In 2002, the pharmaceutical industry formed an alliance with several other health industry groups, including nursing home and hospital interests, to develop a new Medicare bill. The AARP had a number of misgivings about the bill but lent its support, calculating that once a law was enacted, the "senior lobby" could secure favorable amendments over the ensuing years. The resulting legislation, enacted by Congress in November 2003, after the drug industry spent nearly $40 million lobbying on its behalf, appeared to be perfectly tailored to suit the industry's needs. Under the new plan, Medicare will subsidize drug purchases for all seniors who agree to pay a modest monthly fee. The plan prohibits the government from attempting to force the companies to lower drug prices, leaves in place the ban on imported drugs, and does not address the issue of generic drugs. Since it began operation in 2006, the Medicare prescription plan has increased industry profits at a cost of tens of billions of dollars a year to the federal treasury.[1] PhRMA's nursing home and hospital allies also won favorable treatment under the plan.[2] Seniors at long last got their drug plan but in a form that cost the nation an enormous amount of money, funds that are being transferred from the pockets of taxpayers into the coffers of an already fabulously wealthy industry.

After the 2006 elections gave the Democrats control of both houses of Congress, Democratic leaders promised to take a new look at the prescription drug plan. In particular, they talked about undoing the provisions of the law that ban imported drugs and prohibit the government from attempting to lower drug prices. Some Democrats said the drug industry should be forced to give up some of its patent protection to allow more generics to enter the marketplace. The pharmaceutical industry responded quickly by hiring dozens of new Democratic lobbyists, whom they expected to have influence with the new leadership in Congress.

In this chapter, we will examine some of the antecedents and consequences of interest-group politics in the United States. First, we will seek to understand the character of the interests promoted by interest groups. Second, we will assess the growth of interest-group activity in recent American political history, including the emergence of "public interest" groups. Finally, we will review and evaluate the strategies that competing groups use in their struggle for influence.

---

[1]Ceci Connolly, "Drugmakers Protect Their Turf," *Washington Post*, 21 November 2003, p. A4.

[2]Thomas B. Edsall, "2 Bills Would Benefit Top Bush Fundraisers," *Washington Post*, 22 November 2003, p. 1.

THE CHARACTERISTICS OF INTEREST GROUPS

An ***interest group*** is an organized group of people that makes policy-related appeals to government. Individuals form groups in order to increase the chance that their views will be heard and their interests treated favorably by the government. Interest groups are organized to influence governmental decisions. They are often referred to as lobbies.

Interest groups are sometimes confused with political action committees. The difference is that PACs focus on influencing elections, and interest groups focus on influencing elected officials. One final distinction that we should make is that interest groups are also different from political parties: interest groups tend to concern themselves with the *policies* of government; parties tend to concern themselves with the *personnel* of government.

Enhancing Democracy

There are an enormous number of interest groups in the United States, and millions of Americans are members of one or more groups, at least to the extent of paying dues or attending an occasional meeting. By representing the interests of such large numbers of people and encouraging political participation, organized groups can and do enhance American democracy. Organized groups educate their members about issues that affect them. Groups lobby members of Congress and the executive, engage in litigation, and generally represent their members' interests in the political arena. Groups mobilize their members for elections and grassroots lobbying efforts, thus encouraging participation. Interest groups also monitor government programs to make certain that their members are not adversely affected by these programs. In all these ways, organized interests can be said to promote democratic politics. But because not all interests are represented equally, interest-group politics works to the advantage of some and the disadvantage of others.

"The Evils of Faction"

The framers of the Constitution feared the power that could be wielded by organized interests and that the public good would be "disregarded in the conflict of rival [factions]."[3] Yet they believed that interest groups thrived because of freedom—the freedom that all Americans enjoyed to organize and express their views. To the framers, this problem presented a dilemma—indeed, the dilemma of freedom versus power that is central to our text. If the government were given the power to regulate or in any way to forbid efforts by organized interests to interfere in the political process, the government would in effect have been given the power to suppress freedom. The solution to this dilemma was presented by James Madison:

> . . . Take in a greater variety of parties and interest [and] you make it less probable that a majority of the whole will have a common motive to invade the rights of other citizens. . . . [Hence the advantage] enjoyed by a large over a small republic.[4]

interest group A group of people organized around a shared belief or mutual concern who try to influence the government to make policies promoting their belief or concerns.

---

[3]Clinton Rossiter, ed., *The Federalist Papers* (New York: New American Library, 1961), No. 10, p. 78.
[4]Ibid. p. 83.

○ **ONLINE READING**

What Interests Are Represented

    Economic interests—American Farm Bureau Federation

    Labor organizations—AFL-CIO, United Mine Workers, Teamsters

    Professional lobbies—American Bar Association, American Medical Association

    Financial institutions—American Bankers Association, National Savings & Loan League

    Public interest groups—Common Cause, Union of Concerned Scientists

    Public sector lobby—National League of Cities

Organizational Components

    Attracting and keeping members

    Fund-raising to support their infrastructure and their lobbying efforts

    Leadership and decision-making structure

    Agency that carries out the group's tasks

Characteristics of Members

    Interest groups tend to attract members from the middle and upper-middle classes because these people are more likely to have the time, the money, and the inclination to take part in such associations. People from less advantaged socioeconomic groups need to be organized on the massive scale of political parties.

According to Madisonian theory, a good constitution encourages multitudes of interests so that no single interest can ever tyrannize the others. The basic assumption is that competition among interests will produce balance and compromise, with all the interests regulating each other.[5] Today, this Madisonian principle of regulation is called ***pluralism.***

There are tens of thousands of organized groups in the United States, but the huge number of interest groups competing for influence in the United States does not mean that all interests are fully and equally represented in the American political process. As we shall see, the political deck is heavily stacked in favor of those interests able to organize and to wield substantial economic, social, and institutional resources on behalf of their cause. This means that within the universe of interest-group politics it is political power—not some abstract conception of the public good—that is likely to prevail. Moreover, this means that interest-group politics, taken as a whole, is a political format that works more to the advantage of some types of interests than others. In general, a politics in which interest groups predominate is a politics with a distinctly upper-class bias.

What Interests Are Represented

When most people think about interest groups, they immediately think of groups with a direct economic interest in governmental actions (see Table 12.1). These

pluralism The theory that all interests are and should be free to compete for influence in the government. The outcome of this competition is balance and compromise.

[5]Ibid.

TABLE 12.1 Who Is Represented by Organized Interests?

Economic Role of the Individual	U.S. Adults (%)	Orgs. (%)	Type of Org. in Washington	Ratio of Orgs. to Adults
Managerial/administrative	7	71.0	Business association	10.10
Professional/technical	9	17.0	Professional association	1.90
Student/teacher	4	4.0	Educational organization	1.00
Farmworker	2	1.5	Agricultural workers' organization	0.75
Unable to work	2	0.6	Organization for the handicapped	0.30
Other nonfarm workers	41	4.0	Union	0.10
Homemaker	19	1.8	Women's organization	0.09
Retired	12	0.8	Senior citizens' organization	0.07
Looking for work	4	0.1	Unemployment organization	0.03

groups are generally supported by groups of producers or manufacturers in a particular economic sector. Examples of this type of group include the National Petroleum Refiners Association, the American Farm Bureau Federation, and the National Federation of Independent Business, which represents small business owners. At the same time that broadly representative groups like these are active in Washington, specific companies—like Disney, Shell Oil, IBM, and General Motors—may be active on certain issues that are of particular concern to them.

Labor organizations are equally active lobbyists. The AFL-CIO, the United Mine Workers, and the Teamsters are all groups that lobby on behalf of organized labor. In recent years, lobbies have arisen to further the interests of public employees, the most significant among these being the American Federation of State, County, and Municipal Employees.

Professional lobbies like the American Bar Association and the American Medical Association have been particularly successful in furthering their own interests in state and federal legislatures. Financial institutions, represented by organizations like the American Bankers Association and the National Savings & Loan League, although frequently less visible than other lobbies, also play an important role in shaping legislative policy.

Recent years have witnessed the growth of a powerful "public interest" lobby purporting to represent interests whose concerns are not likely to be addressed by traditional lobbies. These groups have been most visible in the consumer protection and environmental policy areas, although public interest groups cover a broad range of issues. The National Resources Defense Council, the Union of Concerned Scientists, and Common Cause are all examples of public interest groups.

The perceived need for representation on Capitol Hill has generated a public sector lobby in the past several years, including the National League of Cities and the "research" lobby. The latter group comprises think tanks and universities that have an interest in obtaining government funds for research and support, and it includes such prestigious institutions as Harvard University, the Brookings Institution, and the American Enterprise Institute. Indeed, many universities have expanded their lobbying efforts even as they have reduced faculty positions and course offerings and increased tuition.[6]

Organizational Components

Although there are many interest groups, most share certain key organizational components. First and most important, all groups must attract and keep members. Somehow, groups must persuade individuals to invest the money, time, energy, or effort required to take part in the group's activities. Members play a larger role in some groups than in others. In membership associations, group members actually serve on committees and engage in projects. In the case of labor unions, members may march on picket lines, and in the case of political or ideological groups, members may participate in demonstrations and protests. In another set of groups, staff organizations, a professional staff conducts most of the group's activities; members are called on only to pay dues and make other contributions. Among the well-known public interest groups, some—such as the National Organization for Women (NOW)—are membership groups; others—such as Defenders of Wildlife and the Children's Defense Fund—are staff organizations.

Usually, groups appeal to members not only by promoting political goals or policies they favor but also by offering them direct *informational, material,* or *social benefits*. Thus, for example, the AARP, which promotes the interests of senior citizens, offers members information, insurance benefits, and commercial discounts. In many organizations information is provided through conferences, training programs, and newsletters and other periodicals sent automatically to those who have paid membership dues. Material benefits can be discount purchasing, shared advertising, and perhaps most valuable of all, health and retirement insurance. Another benefit that can attract members is social interaction, networking, and good fellowship. Thus, the local chapters of many national groups provide their members with a congenial social environment while collecting dues that finance the national office's political efforts.

Another kind of benefit involves the appeal of an interest group's purpose. The best examples of such *purposive benefits* are those of religious interest groups. The Christian Right is made up of a number of interest groups that offer virtually no material benefits to their members, depending almost entirely on the religious identifications and affirmations of their members. Many religion-based interest groups have arisen throughout American history, such as those that drove abolition and prohibition.

The second component shared by all groups is that every one must build a financial structure capable of sustaining an organization and funding the group's activities. Most interest groups rely on annual membership dues and voluntary contributions from sympathizers. Many also sell some ancillary services, such as insurance and vacation tours, to members.

informational benefits Special newsletters, periodicals, training programs, conferences, and other information provided to members of groups to entice others to join.

material benefits Special goods, services, or money provided to members of groups to entice others to join.

social benefits Selective benefits of a group membership that emphasize friendship, networking, and consciousness-raising.

purposive benefits Selective benefits of group membership that emphasize the purpose and accomplishments of the group.

---

[6]Betsy Wagner and David Bowermaster, "B.S. Economics," *Washington Monthly* (November 1992), pp. 19–22.

Third, every group must have a leadership and decision-making structure. For some groups, this structure is very simple. For others, it can be quite elaborate and involve hundreds of local chapters that are melded into a national apparatus.

Last, most groups include an agency that actually carries out the group's tasks. This may be a research organization, a public relations office, or a lobbying office in Washington or a state capital.

The "Free Rider" Problem

Whether organizations need individuals to volunteer or merely to write checks, all must recruit and retain members. Yet many groups find this difficult, even with regards to those who agree strongly with the group's goals. The reason is because, as economist Mancur Olson explains, the benefits of a group's success are often broadly available and cannot be denied to nonmembers.[7] Such benefits can be called *collective goods.* This term is usually associated with certain government benefits, but it can also be applied to beneficial outcomes of interest-group activity.

Following Olson's theory, suppose a number of private property owners live near a mosquito-infested swamp. Each owner wants this swamp cleared. But if one or a few of the owners were to clear the swamp alone, their actions would benefit all the other owners as well, without any effort on the part of those other owners. Each of the inactive owners would be a *free rider* on the efforts of the ones who cleared the swamp. Thus, there is a disincentive for any of the owners to undertake the job alone.

Since the number of concerned owners is small in this particular case, they might eventually be able to organize themselves to share the costs as well as enjoy the benefits of clearing the swamp. But suppose the numbers of interested people are increased. Suppose the common concern is not the neighborhood swamp but polluted air or groundwater involving thousands of residents in a region, or in fact millions of residents in a whole nation. National defense is the most obvious collective good whose benefits are shared by every resident, regardless of the taxes they pay or the support they provide. As the number of involved persons increases, or as the size of the group increases, the free rider phenomenon becomes more of a problem. Individuals do not have much incentive to become active members and supporters of a group that is already working more or less on their behalf. The group would no doubt be more influential if all concerned individuals were active members—if there were no free riders. But groups will not reduce their efforts just because free riders get the same benefits as dues-paying activists. In fact, groups may try even harder precisely because there are free riders, with the hope that the free riders will be encouraged to join in.

The Characteristics of Members

Membership in interest groups is not randomly distributed in the population. People with higher incomes, higher levels of education, and management or professional occupations are much more likely to become members of groups than those

collective goods Benefits, sought by groups, that are broadly available and cannot be denied to nonmembers.

free riders Those who enjoy the benefits of collective goods but did not participate in acquiring them.

---

[7]Mancur Olson, *The Logic of Collective Action* (Cambridge, Mass.: Harvard University Press, 1971).

who occupy lower rungs on the socioeconomic ladder.[8] Well-educated, upper-income business and professional people are more likely to have the time and the money, and to have acquired through the educational process the concerns and skills needed to play a role in a group or association. Moreover, for business and professional people, group membership may provide personal contacts and access to information that can help advance their careers. At the same time, of course, corporate entities—businesses and the like—usually have ample resources to form or participate in groups that seek to advance their causes.

The result is that interest-group politics in the United States tends to have a very pronounced upper-class bias. Certainly, there are many interest groups and political associations that have a working-class or lower-class membership—labor organizations or welfare-rights organizations, for example—but the great majority of interest groups and their members are drawn from the middle and upper-middle classes. In general, the "interests" served by interest groups are the interests of society's "haves." Even when interest groups take opposing positions on issues and policies, the conflicting positions they espouse usually reflect divisions among upper-income strata rather than conflicts between the upper and lower classes.

In general, to obtain adequate political representation, forces from the bottom rungs of the socioeconomic ladder must be organized on the massive scale associated with political parties. Parties can organize and mobilize the collective energies of large numbers of people who, as individuals, may have very limited resources. Interest groups, on the other hand, generally organize smaller numbers of the better-to-do. Thus, the relative importance of political parties and interest groups in American politics has far-ranging implications for the distribution of political power in the United States. As we saw in Chapter 11, political parties have declined in influence in recent years. Interest groups, on the other hand, as we shall see shortly, have become much more numerous, active, and influential.

Response to Changes in the Political Environment

If interest groups and our concerns about them were a new phenomenon, we would not have begun this section with James Madison. As long as there is government, as long as government makes policies that add value or impose costs, and as long as there is liberty to organize, interest groups will abound. And if government expands, so will interest groups. There was, for example, a spurt of growth in the national government during the 1880s and 1890s, arising largely from the first government efforts at economic intervention to fight large monopolies and regulate some aspects of interstate commerce. In the latter decade, a parallel spurt of growth occurred in national interest groups, including the imposing National Association of Manufacturers and numerous other trade associations. Many groups organized around specific agricultural commodities as well. This period also

---

[8]Kay Lehman Schlozman and John T. Tierney, *Organized Interests and American Democracy* (New York: Harper & Row, 1986), p. 60.

FIGURE 12.1 PAC Count, 1974–2008

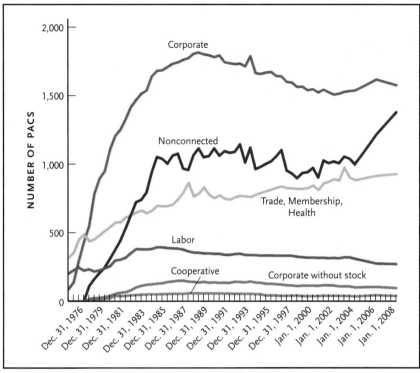

SOURCE: Federal Election Commission, "FEC Records Slight Increase in the Number of PACs," 17 January 2008 (www.fec.gov/press/press2008/20080117paccount.shtml).

marked the beginning of the expansion of trade unions as interest groups. Later, in the 1930s, interest groups with headquarters and representation in Washington began to grow significantly, concurrent with that decade's expansion of the national government.

Over the past forty years, there has been an enormous increase both in the number of interest groups seeking to play a role in the American political process and in the extent of their opportunity to influence that process. The total number of interest groups in the United States today is not known. There are certainly tens of thousands of groups at the national, state, and local levels. One indication of the proliferation of such groups' activity is the growth over time in the number of PACs attempting to influence U.S. elections. Nearly six times as many PACs operated in 2008 as in the 1970s (Figure 12.1). A *New York Times* report, for example, noted that during the 1970s, expanded federal regulation of the automobile, oil, gas, education, and health-care industries impelled each of these interests to increase substantially its efforts to influence the government's behavior. These efforts, in turn, had the effect of spurring the organization of other groups to augment or counter the activities of the first.[9] Similarly, federal social programs have occasionally sparked political organization and action on the part of clientele groups seeking to influence the distribution of benefits and, in turn, the organization of groups opposed to the programs or their cost. For example, federal programs and court decisions in such areas as abortion and school prayer were the stimuli for political action and organization by fundamentalist religious groups. These groups include the Christian Coalition of America, the Family Research Council, the Traditional Values Coalition, Focus on the Family, and Christian Voice. Struggles over such issues as abortion and gay marriage have helped these groups expand their membership roles and build a network of state and local chapters. As we have noted, religious conservatives played key roles in George W. Bush's presidential victories in both 2000 and 2004. In response, Bush launched his so-called faith-based initiative. Under the terms of this program, federal grants and contracts were given to religious organizations to provide social services to children, seniors, and others. By using so-called faith-based groups as federal contractors, Bush has sought to reward religious conservatives for their loyalty to the GOP and ensure that these groups have a continuing stake in Republican success.

Another factor accounting for the explosion of interest-group activity in recent years was the emergence of a new set of forces in American politics that can collectively be called the new politics movement, a movement made up of upper-middle-class professionals and intellectuals for whom the civil rights and antiwar movements were formative experiences, just as the Great Depression and World War II had been for their parents. The crusade against racial discrimination and the Vietnam War led these young men and women to see themselves as a political force in opposition to the public policies and politicians associated with the nation's postwar regime. In more recent years, the forces of new politics have focused their attention on such issues as environmental protection, women's rights, and nuclear disarmament.

Members of the new politics movement constructed or strengthened public interest groups such as Common Cause, the Sierra Club, the Environmental Defense Fund, Physicians for Social Responsibility, the National Organization for Women, and the various organizations formed by the consumer activist Ralph Nader. Through these groups, new politics forces were able to influence the media, Congress, and even the judiciary and enjoyed a remarkable degree of success during the late 1960s and early 1970s in securing the enactment of policies they favored. New politics activists also played a major role in securing the enactment of environmental, consumer, and occupational health and safety legislation.

Among the factors contributing to the rise and success of new politics forces was technology. In the 1970s and 1980s, computerized direct-mail campaigns allowed public interest groups to reach hundreds of thousands of potential sympathizers and contributors. Today the Internet and e-mail serve the same function. Electronic communication allows relatively small groups to efficiently identify and

---

[9]John Herbers, "Special Interests Gaining Power as Voter Disillusionment Grows," *New York Times,* 14 November 1978.

FIGURE 12.2 How Interest Groups Influence Congress

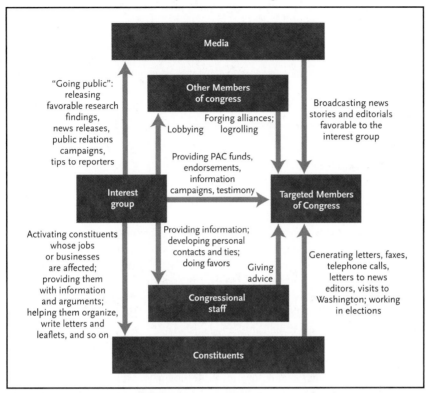

mobilize their adherents throughout the nation. Individuals with perspectives that might be in the minority everywhere can become conscious of one another and mobilize for national political action through the magic of electronic politics. For example, only a handful of Americans scattered across the nation might be intensely concerned with the protection of whales and other aquatic mammals. These individuals form an active and vocal community on the Internet, however. They communicate with one another, reach out to potential sympathizers, and bombard politicians with e-mail. In this way, the Internet can facilitate group formation and political action, overcoming the limitations of geography and numbers.

STRATEGIES FOR INFLUENCING POLICY

Interest groups work to improve the probability that they and their policy interests will be heard and treated favorably by all branches and levels of the government. The quest for political influence or power takes many forms. Insider strategies include access to key decision makers and using the courts. Outsider strategies include going public and using electoral politics. These strategies do not exhaust all the possibilities, but they paint a broad picture of ways that groups utilize their resources in the fierce competition for power (see Figure 12.2).

Many groups employ a mix of insider and outsider strategies. For example, environmental groups like the Sierra Club lobby members of Congress and key congressional staff members, participate in bureaucratic rule making by offering comments and suggestions to agencies on new environmental rules, and bring lawsuits under various environmental acts like the Endangered Species Act, which authorizes groups and citizens to come to court if they believe the act is being violated. At the same time, the Sierra Club attempts to influence public opinion through media campaigns and to influence electoral politics by supporting candidates whom they believe share their environmental views and opposing candidates whom they view as foes of environmentalism.

Direct Lobbying

Lobbying is an attempt by an individual or a group to influence the passage of legislation by exerting direct pressure on members of the legislature. The First Amendment to the Constitution provides for the right to "petition the Government for a redress of grievances." But as early as the 1870s, "lobbying" became the common term for petitioning—and it is an accurate one. Petitioning cannot take place on the floor of the House or Senate. Therefore, petitioners must confront members of Congress in the lobbies, giving rise to the term "lobbying."

The 1946 Federal Regulation of Lobbying Act defines a lobbyist as "any person who shall engage himself for pay or any consideration for the purpose of attempting to influence the passage or defeat of any legislation to the Congress of the United States." The Lobbying Disclosure Act requires all organizations employing lobbyists to register with Congress and to disclose whom they represent, whom they lobby, what they are lobbying for, and how much they are paid. More than 7,000 organizations, collectively employing many thousands of lobbyists, are currently registered.

Lobbying involves a great deal of activity on the part of someone speaking for an interest. Lobbyists badger and buttonhole legislators, administrators, and committee staff members with facts about pertinent issues and facts or claims about public support of them.[10] Lobbyists can serve a useful purpose in the legislative and administrative process by providing this kind of information. In 1978, during debate on a bill to expand the requirement for lobbying disclosures, Democratic Senators Edward Kennedy of Massachusetts and Dick Clark of Iowa joined with Republican Senator Robert Stafford of Vermont to issue the following statement: "Government without lobbying could not function. The flow of information to Congress and to every federal agency is a vital part of our democratic system."[11]

Lobbying Members of Congress Interest groups also have substantial influence in setting the legislative agenda and in helping craft the language of legislation (Figure 12.2). Today sophisticated lobbyists win influence by providing information about policies to busy members of Congress. As one lobbyist noted, "You can't get access

lobbying Strategy by which organized interests seek to influence the passage of legislation by exerting direct pressure on members of the legislature; this term is derived from having to wait in the lobbies just outside the floor of the legislature, where outsiders are not permitted.

---

[10]For discussions of lobbying, see Allan J. Cigler and Burdett A. Loomis, eds., *Interest Group Politics* (Washington, D.C.: Congressional Quarterly Press, 1983). See also Jeffrey M. Berry, *Lobbying for the People* (Princeton, N.J.: Princeton University Press, 1977).

[11]"The Swarming Lobbyists," *Time*, 7 August 1978, p. 15.

without knowledge. . . . I can go in to see John Dingell [chairman of the House Committee on Energy and Commerce], but if I have nothing to offer or nothing to say, he's not going to want to see me."[12] In recent years, interest groups have also begun to build broader coalitions and comprehensive campaigns around particular policy issues.[13] These coalitions do not rise from the grassroots but instead are put together by Washington lobbyists who launch comprehensive campaigns that combine simulated grassroots activity with information and campaign funding for members of Congress.

Some interest groups are able to place their lobbyists directly on congressional staffs. In 2007, several experienced lobbyists and Washington insiders were "borrowed" by the new Democratic leadership to help organize the business of the new Congress. For example, Dennis Fitzgibbons, a lobbyist for DaimlerChrysler, was hired as chief of staff of the House Energy and Commerce Committee. In his capacity as an auto lobbyist, Fitzgibbons attempted to block efforts to force automakers to make vehicles more fuel efficient or to manufacture vehicles that would use alternative fuels. In his new job, Fitzgibbons plays a powerful role on the panel that will make the legislative decisions about these issues.[14]

Not every interest group can embed stealth lobbyists in Congress. Many, however, do the next best thing: They hire the spouses and relatives of members of Congress or important staffers to lobby for them. One extensive study of the congressional appropriations process conducted in 2006 found thirty instances in which lobbyists related to members and senior staffers of the House and Senate appropriations committees sought money in the appropriation bills their family members helped to write. In twenty-two cases, relatives were able to get specific language inserted in bills that guaranteed money for their clients.[15]

Some interest groups have strong ties to the Democrats and others to the Republicans. Most interest groups, however, endeavor to maintain good relations with both political parties and are prepared to work with the party in power to achieve their legislative goals. When Republicans controlled Congress, trade associations and corporate interests hired Republican lobbyists and built close ties to the GOP leadership. In 2007, as Democrats returned to power, the same interest groups hired Democratic lobbyists and worked to build close ties to the new Democratic leadership. And when it came to campaign contributions, corporate interests cheerfully backed both sides, making sure to befriend the winners, whoever they might be.[16]

What happens to interests that do not engage in extensive lobbying? They often find themselves "Microsofted." In 1998, the software giant was facing antitrust

---

[12]Daniel Franklin, "Tommy Boggs and the Death of Health Care Reform," *Washington Monthly*, April 1995, p. 36.

[13]Marie Hojnacki, "Interest Groups' Decisions to Join Alliances or Work Alone," *American Journal of Political Science* 41 (1997) pp. 61–87; Kevin W. Hula, *Lobbying Together: Interest Group Coalitions in Legislative Politics* (Washington, DC: Georgetown University Press, 1999).

[14]Birnbaum, "In the Loop on K Street."

[15]Matt Kelley and Peter Eisler, "Relatives Have Inside Track in Lobbying for Tax Dollars," *USA Today*, 17 October 2006, p. 1. ○ ONLINE READING

[16]"Cash Flow: Congress Changes Hands—or Does It?" *Washington Post*, 7 January 2007, p. B2.

action from the Justice Department and had few friends in Congress. One member of the House, Representative Billy Tauzin (R-La.), told Microsoft chairman Bill Gates that without an extensive investment in lobbying, the corporation would continue to be "demonized." Gates responded by quadrupling Microsoft's lobbying expenditures and hiring a group of lobbyists with strong ties to Congress. The result was congressional pressure on the Justice Department, resulting in a settlement of the Microsoft suit on terms favorable to the company.

Providing access is only one of the many services lobbyists perform. Lobbyists often testify on behalf of their clients at congressional committee and agency hearings; lobbyists sometimes help their clients identify potential allies with whom to construct coalitions; lobbyists provide research and information to government officials; lobbyists often draft proposed legislation or regulations to be introduced by friendly lawmakers; lobbyists talk to reporters, place ads in newspapers, and organize letter-writing, e-mail, and telegram campaigns. Lobbyists also play an important role in fund-raising, helping to direct clients' contributions to members of Congress and presidential candidates.

Lobbying the President So many individuals and groups clamor for the president's time and attention that only the most skilled and well-connected members of the lobbying community can hope to influence presidential decisions. One Washington lobbyist who fills this bill is Tom Kuhn, president of the Edison Electric Institute, a lobbying organization representing the electric power industry. Kuhn is a friend and former college classmate of President George W. Bush. In 2000, Kuhn was among the leading "Pioneers"—individuals who raised at least $100,000 for the Bush election campaign. Later, the electric power companies represented by Kuhn gave nearly $20 million to congressional candidates in the 2001–2002 election cycle. Kuhn's close relationship with the president and his efforts on behalf of the president's election have given Kuhn enormous leverage with the White House. During the 2000 transition, candidates for a presidential nomination to head the EPA felt compelled to pay "courtesy calls" to Kuhn. Subsequently, Kuhn led a successful effort to delay and weaken proposed new EPA controls on electric-power-plant emissions of mercury, a toxic substance linked to neurological damage, especially in children.[17] This was a victory for the electric power industry that promised to save the industry hundreds of millions of dollars a year and illustrates the influence that can be brought to bear by a powerful lobbyist.

Lobbying the Executive Branch Even when an interest group is very successful at getting its bill passed by Congress and signed by the president, the prospect of full and faithful implementation of that law is not guaranteed. Often, a group and its allies do not pack up and go home as soon as the president turns their lobbied-for new

---

[17]"Edison Electric Institute Lobbying to Weaken Toxic Mercury Standards," http://tristatenews.com, 28 February 2003.

law over to the appropriate agency. On average, 40 percent of interest-group representatives regularly contact both legislative and executive branch organizations, while 13 percent contact only the legislature and 16 percent only the executive branch.[18]

In some respects, interest-group access to the executive branch is promoted by federal law. The Administrative Procedure Act, first enacted in 1946 and frequently amended in subsequent years, requires most federal agencies to provide notice and an opportunity for comment before implementing proposed new rules and regulations. So-called notice and comment rule-making is designed to allow interests an opportunity to make their views known and to participate in the implementation of federal legislation that affects them. In 1990, Congress enacted the Negotiated Rule-making Act to encourage administrative agencies to engage in direct and open negotiations with affected interests when developing new regulations. These two pieces of legislation—which have been strongly enforced by the federal courts—have played an important role in opening the bureaucratic process to interest-group influence. Today, few federal agencies would consider attempting to implement a new rule without consulting affected interests.[19]

Cultivating Access Exerting influence on Congress or government agencies by providing their members with information about issues, support, and even threats of retaliation requires easy and constant access to decision makers. One interesting example of why groups need to cultivate and maintain access is provided by the dairy farmers. Through the 1960s, dairy farmers were part of the powerful coalition of agricultural interests that had full access to Congress and the Department of Agriculture. During the 1960s, a series of disputes over commodities prices broke out between the dairy farmers and the producers of corn, grain, and other agricultural commodities. Dairy farmers, whose cows consume grain, prefer low commodities prices, whereas grain producers obviously prefer high prices. The commodities producers won the battle, and Congress raised commodities prices, in part at the expense of the dairy farmers. In the 1970s, the dairy farmers left the agriculture coalition, set up their own lobby and political action groups, and became heavily involved in public relations campaigns and both congressional and presidential elections. Thus the dairy farmers lost their traditional access and had to pursue an "outsider" strategy. Indeed, the political fortunes of the dairy operations were badly hurt when they were accused of making illegal contributions to President Richard Nixon's reelection campaign in 1972.

Cultivating access usually requires considerable time and effort, and a successful long-term strategy for gaining access may entail the sacrifice of short-run influence. For example, many of the most important organized interests in agriculture devote far more time and resources to cultivating the staff and trustees of state agriculture schools and county agents back home than to buttonholing members of Congress or bureaucrats in Washington.

---

[18]John P. Heinz et al., *The Hollow Core: Private Interests in National Policy Making* (Cambridge, Mass.: Harvard University Press, 1993).

[19]For an excellent discussion of the political origins of the Administrative Procedure Act, see Martin Shapiro, "APA: Past, Present, Future," 72 *Virginia Law Review* 377 (March 1986), pp. 447–92.

Regulations on Lobbying As a result of the constant access to important decision makers that lobbyists seek out and require, stricter guidelines regulating the actions of lobbyists have been adopted in the last decade. For example, as of 1993, businesses may no longer deduct from their taxes the cost of lobbying. Trade associations must report to members the proportion of their dues that goes to lobbying, and that proportion may not be reported as a business expense. The most important attempt to limit the influence of lobbyists was the 1995 Lobbying Disclosure Act, which significantly broadened the definition of people and organizations that must register as lobbyists. According to the filings under this act, there were almost 11,500 lobbyists working the halls of Congress in 2006.

In 1996, Congress passed legislation limiting gifts from a single source to $50 and no more than $100 annually. It also banned the practice of honoraria, which had been used by special interests to supplement congressional salaries. But Congress did not limit the travel of representatives, senators, their spouses, or congressional staff members. Interest groups can pay for congressional travel as long as a trip is related to legislative business and is disclosed on congressional reports within thirty days. On these trips, meals and entertainment expenses are not limited to $50 per event and $100 annually. The rules of Congress allow its members to travel on corporate jets as long as they pay an amount equal to first-class airfare.

In 2007, congressional Democrats secured the enactment of a package of ethics rules designed to fulfill their 2006 campaign promise to bring an end to lobbying abuses. The new rules prohibited lobbyists from paying for most meals, trips, parties, and gifts for members of Congress. Lobbyists were also required to disclose the amounts and sources of small campaign contributions they collected from clients and "bundled" into large contributions. And interest groups were required to disclose the funds they used to rally voters to support or oppose legislative proposals. As soon as these new rules were enacted, lobbyists and politicians hurried to find ways to cirumvent them, and it remains to be seen whether these reforms will have any major impact.

Using the Courts

Interest groups sometimes turn to the courts to augment other avenues of access. They can use the courts to affect public policy in at least three ways: (1) by bringing suit directly on behalf of the group itself, (2) by financing suits brought by individuals, or (3) by filing a companion brief as *amicus curiae* (literally "friend of the court") to an existing court case.

Among the most significant modern illustrations of the use of the courts as a strategy for political influence are those that accompanied the "sexual revolution" of the 1960s and the emergence of the movement for women's rights. Beginning in the mid-sixties, a series of cases was brought into the federal courts in an effort to force definition of a right to privacy in sexual matters. The case began with a challenge to state restrictions on obtaining contraceptives for nonmedical purposes, a challenge that was effectively made in *Griswold v. Connecticut,* where the Supreme Court held that states could neither prohibit the dissemination of information about nor prohibit the actual use of contraceptives by married couples. That case was soon followed by *Eisenstadt v. Baird,* in which the Court held that the states could not prohibit the use of contraceptives by single persons any more than they could prohibit their use by married couples. One year later, the Court held, in the 1973 case of *Roe v. Wade,* that states could not impose an absolute ban on voluntary abortions. Each of these cases, as well as others, was part of the Court's enunciation of a constitutional doctrine of privacy.[20]

The 1973 abortion case sparked a controversy that brought conservatives to the fore on a national level. These conservative groups made extensive use of the courts to whittle away the scope of the privacy doctrine. They obtained rulings, for example, that prohibit the use of federal funds to pay for voluntary abortions. And in 1989, right-to-life groups used a strategy of litigation that significantly undermined the *Roe v. Wade* decision in the case of *Webster v. Reproductive Health Services* (see Chapter 4), which restored the right of states to place restrictions on abortion.[21]

Another extremely significant set of contemporary illustrations of the use of the courts as a strategy for political influence is found in the history of the NAACP. The most important of these court cases was, of course, *Brown v. Board of Education of Topeka,* in which the U.S. Supreme Court held that legal segregation of the schools was unconstitutional.[22]

Business groups are also frequent users of the courts because of the number of government programs applied to them. Litigation involving large businesses is most mountainous in such areas as taxation, antitrust, interstate transportation, patents, and product quality and standardization. Major corporations and their trade associations pay tremendous amounts of money each year in fees to the most prestigious Washington law firms. Some of this money is expended in gaining access. A great proportion of it, however, is used to keep the best and most experienced lawyers prepared to represent the corporations in court or before administrative agencies when necessary.

The forces of the new politics movement made significant use of the courts during the 1970s and 1980s, and judicial decisions were instrumental in advancing their goals. Facilitated by changes in the rules governing access to the courts (these rules of standing were discussed in Chapter 8), the new politics agenda was clearly visible in court decisions handed down in several key policy areas. In the environmental policy area, new politics groups were able to force federal agencies to pay attention to environmental issues, even when the agency was not directly involved in activities related to environmental quality.

Mobilizing Public Opinion

Going public is a strategy that attempts to mobilize the widest and most favorable climate of opinion. Many groups consider it imperative to maintain this climate at all times, even when they have no issue to fight about. An increased use of this kind

---

[20]*Griswold v. Connecticut,* 381 U.S. 479 (1965); Eisenstadt v. Baird, 405 U.S. 438 (1972); Roe v. Wade, 410 U.S. 133 (1973).

[21]*Webster v. Reproductive Health Services,* 109 S. Ct. 3040 (1989).

[22]*Brown v. Board of Education of Topeka,* 347 U.S. 483 (1954).

going public A strategy that attempts to mobilize the widest and most favorable climate of opinion.

of strategy is usually associated with modern advertising. As early as the 1930s, political analysts were distinguishing between the "old lobby" of direct group representation before Congress and the "new lobby" of public relations professionals addressing the public at large to reach Congress.[23]

One of the best-known ways of going public is the use of institutional advertising. A casual scanning of important mass circulation magazines and newspapers will provide numerous examples of expensive and well-designed ads by the major oil companies, automobile and steel companies, other large corporations, and trade associations. The ads show how much these organizations are doing for the country, for the protection of the environment, or for the defense of the American way of life. Their purpose is to create and maintain a strongly positive association between the organization and the community at large in the hope that these favorable feelings can be drawn on as needed for specific political campaigns later on.

Another form of going public is the ***grassroots lobbying*** campaign. In such a campaign, a lobby group mobilizes ordinary citizens to write to their representatives in support of the group's position. A grassroots campaign can cost anywhere from $40,000 to sway the votes of one or two crucial members of a committee or subcommittee, to millions of dollars to mount a national effort aimed at the Congress as a whole.

During the past several years, grassroots lobbying campaigns have played an important role in battles over presidential appointments. In 2005, President George W. Bush was presented with an opportunity to fill two Supreme Court vacancies occasioned by the death of Chief Justice William Rehnquist and the retirement of Justice Sandra Day O'Connor. Immediately, liberal and conservative advocacy groups mobilized their members for battle. In particular, pro-choice and pro-life groups saw the two Supreme Court appointments as a decisive point in the long-standing national struggle over abortion. Pro-choice groups feared that Bush would appoint justices hostile to abortion rights while pro-life groups feared that he would not. As each side urged its members to pressure the Congress, hundreds of thousands of calls, letters, telegrams, and e-mails flooded Capitol Hill. These campaigns had a major impact on the appointment process, forcing President Bush to withdraw the name of one nominee, Harriet Miers, and very nearly derailing a second Bush nominee, Judge Samuel Alito.

Grassroots lobbying has become more prevalent in Washington over the last couple of decades because the adoption of congressional rules limiting gifts to members has made traditional lobbying more difficult. This circumstance makes all the more compelling the question of whether grassroots campaigning has reached an intolerable extreme. One case in particular may have tipped it over: in 1992, ten giant companies in the financial services, manufacturing, and high-tech industries began a grassroots campaign and spent millions of dollars over the next three years to influence a decision in Congress to limit the ability of investors to sue for fraud. Retaining an expensive consulting firm, these corporations paid for

grassroots lobbying
A lobbying campaign in which a group mobilizes its membership to contact government officials in support of the group's position.

---

[23]E. Pendleton Herring, *Group Representation before Congress* (New York: McGraw-Hill, 1936).

the use of specialized computer software to persuade Congress that there was "an outpouring of popular support for the proposal." Thousands of letters from individuals flooded Capitol Hill. Many of those letters were written and sent by people who sincerely believed that investor lawsuits are often frivolous and should be curtailed. But much of the mail was phony, generated by the Washington-based campaign consultants; the letters came from people who had no strong feelings or even no opinion at all about the issue. More and more people, including leading members of Congress, are becoming quite skeptical of such methods, charging that these are not genuine grassroots campaigns but instead represent "Astroturf lobbying" (a play on the name of an artificial grass used on many sports fields). Such "Astroturf" campaigns have increased in frequency in recent years as members of Congress grow more skeptical of Washington lobbyists and far more concerned about demonstrations of support for a particular issue by their constituents. But after the firms mentioned above spent millions of dollars and generated thousands of letters to members of Congress, they came to the somber conclusion that "it's more effective to have 100 letters from your district where constituents took the time to write and understand the issue," because "Congress is sophisticated enough to know the difference."[24]

Using Electoral Politics

In addition to attempting to influence members of Congress and other government officials, interest groups also seek to use the electoral process to elect the right legislators in the first place and to ensure that those who are elected will owe them a debt of gratitude for their support. To put matters into perspective, groups invest far more resources in lobbying than in electoral politics. Nevertheless, financial support and campaign activism can be important tools for organized interests.

Political Action Committees   By far the most common electoral strategy employed by interest groups is that of giving financial support to the parties or to particular candidates. But such support can easily cross the threshold into outright bribery. Therefore, Congress has occasionally made an effort to regulate this strategy. A recent effort was the Federal Election Campaign Act of 1971 (amended in 1974), which we discussed in Chapter 10. This act limits campaign contributions and requires that each candidate or campaign committee itemize the full name and address, occupation, and principal business of each person who contributes more than $100. These provisions have been effective up to a point, considering the rather large number of embarrassments, indictments, resignations, and criminal convictions in the aftermath of the Watergate scandal.

The Watergate scandal itself was triggered by the illegal entry of Republican workers into the office of the Democratic National Committee in the Watergate apartment building. But an investigation quickly revealed numerous violations of campaign finance laws, involving millions of dollars in unregistered cash from

---

[24]Jane Fritsch, "The Grass Roots, Just a Free Phone Call Away," *New York Times*, 23 June 1995, pp. A1, A22.

Lobbying

Influencing the passage or defeat of legislation.

Three types of lobbyists:

Amateur—loyal members of a group seeking passage of legislation that is currently under scrutiny.

Paid—often lawyers or professionals without a personal interest in the legislation who are not lobbyists full time.

Staff—employed by a specific interest group full-time for the express purpose of influencing or drafting legislation.

Access

Development of close ties to decision makers on Capitol Hill and bureaucratic agencies.

Litigation

Taking action through the courts, usually in one of three ways:

Filing suit against a specific government agency or program.

Financing suits brought against the government by individuals.

Filing companion briefs as *amicus curiae* (friend of the court) to existing court cases.

Going Public

Especially via advertising; also through boycotts, strikes, rallies, marches, and sit-ins, generating positive news coverage.

Electoral Politics

Giving financial support to a particular party or candidate.

Congress passed the Federal Election Campaign Act of 1971 to try to regulate this practice by limiting the amount of funding interest groups can contribute to campaigns.

corporate executives to President Nixon's reelection committee. Many of these revelations were made by the famous Ervin committee, whose official name was the Senate Select Committee to Investigate the 1972 Presidential Campaign Activities.

Reaction to Watergate produced further legislation on campaign finance in 1974 and 1976, but the effect has been to restrict individual rather than interest group campaign activity. Individuals may now contribute no more than $2,100 to any candidate for federal office in any primary or general election. A ***political action committee (PAC)***, however, can contribute $2,300, provided it contributes to at least five different federal candidates each year. Beyond this, the laws permit corporations, unions, and other interest groups to form PACs and to pay the costs of soliciting funds from private citizens for the PACs.

Electoral spending by interest groups has been increasing steadily despite the flurry of reform following Watergate. The number of PACs has also increased significantly, as we saw earlier in this chapter (see Figure 12.1). Although the reform legislation of the early and mid-1970s attempted to reduce the influence of special interests over elections, the effect has been almost the exact opposite. Opportunities for legally influencing campaigns with large donations are now widespread.

political action committee (PAC) A private group that raises and distributes funds for use in election campaigns.

Given the enormous costs of television commercials, polls, computers, and other elements of the new political technology, most politicians are eager to receive PAC contributions and are at least willing to give a friendly hearing to the needs and interests of contributors. Most politicians probably will not simply sell their services to the interests that fund their campaigns, but there is some evidence that interest groups' campaign contributions do influence the overall pattern of political behavior in Congress and in the state legislatures.

Indeed, PACs and campaign contributions provide organized interests with such a useful tool for gaining access to the political process that calls to abolish PACs have been quite frequent among political reformers. Concern about PACs grew through the 1980s and 1990s, creating a constant drumbeat for reform of federal election laws. Proposals were introduced in Congress on many occasions, perhaps the most celebrated being the McCain-Feingold bill, which became the Bipartisan Campaign Reform Act (BCRA) of 2002. When originally proposed in 1996, McCain-Feingold was aimed at reducing or eliminating PACs. But when campaign finance reform was adopted in 2002, it did not restrict PACs in any significant way. Rather, it eliminated unrestricted *soft money* donations to the national political parties (see Chapter 10). One consequence of this reform, as we saw in Chapters 10 and 11, was the creation of a host of new organizations known as 527 committees. These are often directed by former party officials but nominally unaffiliated with the two parties. This change probably will continue strengthening interest groups and weakening parties. For a fuller discussion of spending rules, see Chapter 10.

Campaign Activism   Financial support is not the only way in which organized groups seek influence through electoral politics. Sometimes activism can be even more important than campaign contributions.

In 2008, a number of advocacy groups supporting the Democratic party made a concerted effort to register and mobilize millions of new voters, who they hoped would support Democratic candidates. Organized labor, of course, targeted union households. Civil rights groups worked to register African Americans. And a number of groups, including MoveOn.org, labored to reach young people via the Internet. Their presumption was that young voters would disproportionately favor the Democrats.

Republicans, for their part, worked with church groups and such advocates of conservative causes as the National Rifle Association and the National Federation of Independent Business to register and mobilize voters likely to support the GOP. Ultimately, the Democrats were more successful than their Republican counterparts. Young people and African Americans came to the polls in larger-than-usual numbers to help hand the Democratic party and Barack Obama a solid victory.

The Initiative   Another political tactic sometimes used by interest groups is sponsorship of ballot initiatives at the state level. The initiative, a device adopted by a number of states around 1900, allows laws proposed by citizens to be placed on the general election ballot and submitted directly to the state's voters. This procedure bypasses the state legislature and governor. The initiative was originally promoted

soft money Money contributed directly to political parties for voter registration and organization.

by late-nineteenth-century Populists as a mechanism that would allow the people to govern directly. Populists saw the initiative as an antidote to interest group influence in the legislative process.

Ironically, many studies have suggested that most initiative campaigns today are actually sponsored by interest groups seeking to circumvent legislative opposition to their goals. In recent years, for example, initiative campaigns have been sponsored by the insurance industry, trial lawyers' associations, and tobacco companies.[25] The role of interest groups in initiative campaigns should come as no surprise since such campaigns can cost millions of dollars.

ARE INTEREST GROUPS EFFECTIVE?

Do interest groups have an impact on government and policy? The short answer is yes, certainly they do. One of the best academic studies of the impact of lobbying was conducted in 2001 by John M. De Figueiredo of MIT and Brian Silverman of the University of Toronto.[26] Figueiredo and Silverman focused on a particular form of lobbying: efforts by lobbyists for colleges and universities to obtain "earmarks," special, often disguised, congressional appropriations for their institutions. Millions of dollars in earmarks are written into law every year.

The authors discovered that lobbying had an impact. The more money schools spent on lobbying activities, the larger the total quantity of earmarked funds they received. The extent of lobbying's impact, however, varied with institutional factors. Schools whose state's senator served on the Senate Appropriations Committee received $18 to $29 in earmarks for every dollar spent on lobbying. Schools located in congressional districts whose representative served on the House Appropriations Committee received between $49 and $55 for every dollar spent on lobbying. Schools lacking such representation, however, averaged only about $1.09 for every dollar spent on lobbying—hardly worth the effort.

These results suggest, as is so often the case, that institutions and politics are profoundly related. Schools without access to members of Congress in a position to help them cannot gain much from lobbying. Schools with such access still need to lobby to take advantage of the potential that representation on the Senate and House Appropriations committees can give them. But, if they do so, the potential return from lobbying is substantial.

Do Interest Groups Foster or Impede Democracy?

We would like to think that policies are products of legislators' concepts of the public interest. Yet the truth of the matter is that few programs and policies ever reach the public agenda without the vigorous support of important national interest groups. In the realm of economic policy, social policy, international trade policy, and even such

---

[25]Elisabeth R. Gerber, *The Populist Paradox* (Princeton, N.J.: Princeton University Press, 1999).

[26]John M. P. de Figueiredo and Brian S. Silverman, "Academic Earmarks and the Returns to Lobbying" (May 2002). Harvard Law and Economics Discussion Paper no. 370; MIT Sloan Working Paper no. 4245-02.

seemingly interest-free areas as criminal justice policy—where, in fact, private prison corporations lobby for longer sentences for law breakers—interest-group activity is a central feature. Of course, before we throw up our hands in dismay, we should remember that the untidy process and sometimes undesirable outcomes of interest-group politics are virtually inherent aspects of democratic politics.

James Madison wrote that "liberty is to faction what air is to fire."[27] By this he meant that the organization and proliferation of interests were inevitable in a free society. To seek to place limits on the organization of interests, in Madison's view, would be to limit liberty itself. Madison believed that interests should be permitted to regulate themselves by competing with one another. So long as competition among interests was free, open, and vigorous, there would be some balance of power among them and none would be able to dominate the political or governmental process.

There is considerable competition among organized groups in the United States. For example, pro-choice and anti-abortion forces continue to be locked in a bitter struggle. Nevertheless, interest-group politics is not as free of bias as Madisonian theory might suggest. Though the weak and poor do occasionally organize to assert their rights, interest-group politics is generally a form of political competition in which the wealthy and powerful are best able to engage.

Moreover, though groups sometimes organize to promote broad public concerns, interest groups more often represent relatively narrow, selfish interests. Small, self-interested groups can be organized much more easily than large and more diffuse collectives. For one thing, the members of a relatively small group—say, bankers or hunting enthusiasts—are usually able to recognize their shared interests and the need to pursue focused goals in the political arena. Members of large and more diffuse groups—say, consumers or potential victims of firearms—often find it difficult to recognize their shared interests or the need to engage in collective action to achieve them.[28] This is why causes presented as public interests by their proponents often turn out, on examination, to be private interests wrapped in a public mantle.

The responsiveness of government agencies to interest groups is a challenge to democracy. Groups seem to have a greater impact than voters upon the government's policies and programs. Yet, before we decide that we should do away with interest groups, we should think carefully: if there were no organized interests, would the government pay more attention to ordinary voters, or would the government simply pay no attention to anyone? In his great work *Democracy in America*, Alexis de Tocqueville argued that the proliferation of groups promoted democracy by encouraging governmental responsiveness. Does group politics foster democracy or impede democracy? It does both.

Thus, we have a dilemma to which there is no ideal answer. To regulate interest-group politics is, as Madison warned, to limit freedom and to expand governmental

---

[27] Rossiter, ed., *The Federalist Papers*, No. 10, p. 78.

[28] Mancur Olson, Jr., *The Logic of Collective Action* (Cambridge, Mass.: Harvard University Press, 1971).

Interest Groups and Representation

As noted in the chapter, Americans have been attuned to the dangers of organized interests since the earliest days of the republic. James Madison, in *Federalist* 10, notes the concern of "our most considerate and virtuous citizens" regarding factions, a "dangerous vice" of "popular governments."[1] Yet Madison also writes that the "causes of faction are ... sown in the nature of man" due to our tendency to form different opinions and passions under conditions of political liberty.[2] Thus the problem of faction, or what we might term the dangers of interest groups, is a part of democratic politics. Madison proposed a two-pronged solution that included (1) representation and (2) extending the "sphere" of interests and factions by having a larger society. In this chapter, we have looked at the theory of pluralism (which corresponds to the second part of Madison's solution): this is the idea that the number and diversity of interests serves both to moderate the influence of any particular group and to make political moderation more likely. How, though, might *representation* serve to check the influence of interest groups?

On one level, we might expect that the presence and power of interest groups would hinder representation. Let us take the U.S. Congress as our example. If we view the task of the House and the Senate to be the expression of the interests of their constituents, we can see why interest groups may pose a problem. While interest groups lend financial support to candidates as part of their effort to influence them, critics of these contributions argue that interest groups distort the legislative process and that "special interest money is drowning out representation."[3] The latter criticism focuses on the concern that because members of Congress generally rely on contributions to fund their reelection campaigns, they may serve the interests of their backers rather than their constituents.

PAC type	Contributions to Candidates (in millions)		
	1999–00	2001–02	2003–04
Total	259.8	282.0	310.5
Corporate	91.5	99.6	115.6
Labor	51.6	53.9	52.1
Trade/membership/health	71.8	46.3	83.2
Nonconnected	37.3	75.1	52.5
Cooperative	2.4	2.7	2.9
Corporation without stock	5.3	4.4	4.2

[1] James Madison, *Federalist* 10, in *The Federalist Papers*, ed. Clinton Rossiter (New York: Penguin, 1961), 77.
[2] *Ibid.* 78–79.
[3] Richard Bolling, "Money in Politics," *Annals of the American Academy of Political and Social Science*, Vol. 486 (July 1986): 76–85, 80.

Yet Madison suggested that representation can "refine and enlarge the public views" in part because these views pass through a select body. Members of Congress face a particular dilemma. While Senators and Representatives "may wish to develop expert-informed legislation," their constituents are rarely experts on policy intricacies.[4] In committee hearings, some members of Congress engage in detailed policy discussion, while others "routinely engage in unscientific anecdotal discourse aimed at constituents."[5] Research by Kevin Esterling suggests that interest groups contribute more heavily to members of Congress who have "a higher analytical capacity to work on policies" because these groups want to be sure that the information they provide receives a more attentive and expert audience.

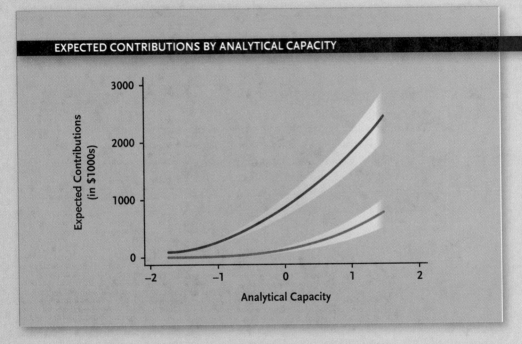

EXPECTED CONTRIBUTIONS BY ANALYTICAL CAPACITY

From this perspective, interest groups do not distort policy, but actually foster political behavior that leads to better policies. Keeping this in mind, we may note that Madison argued that representation helps to prevent the evils of faction not by ensuring that elected officials listen to and serve only their constituents, but rather because of the qualities—"wisdom ... patriotism and love of justice"—of those to whom government is delegated.[6]

[4] Kevin M. Esterling, "Buying Expertise: Campaign Contributions and Attention to Policy Analysis in Congressional Committees," *The American Political Science Review*, Vol. 101 (February 2007): 93–109, 93.
[5] *Ibid.* 93.
[6] Madison, *Federalist* 10, 82.

power. Not to regulate interest-group politics, on the other hand, may be to ignore justice. Those who believe that there are simple solutions to the problems of political life would do well to ponder this problem.

CHAPTER REVIEW

Efforts by organized groups to influence government and policy are becoming an increasingly important part of American politics. The expansion of government over the past several decades has fueled an expansion of interest-group activity. In recent years upper-middle-class Americans have organized public interest groups to vie with more specialized interests. All groups use a number of strategies to gain power.

Lobbying is the act of petitioning legislators. Lobbyists—individuals who receive some form of compensation for lobbying—are required to register in the House and the Senate. In spite of an undeserved reputation for corruption, they serve a useful function, providing members of Congress with a vital flow of information.

Access is participation in government. Groups with access have less need for lobbying. Most groups build up access through great effort. They work for years to get their members into positions of influence on congressional committees.

Litigation sometimes serves interest groups when other strategies fail. Groups may bring suit on their own behalf, finance suits brought by individuals, or file *amicus curiae* briefs.

Going public is an effort to mobilize the widest and most favorable climate of opinion. Advertising is a common technique in this strategy.

Groups engage in electoral politics either by embracing one of the major parties, usually through financial support, or through a nonpartisan strategy. Interest groups' campaign contributions now seem to be flowing into the coffers of candidates at a faster rate than ever before.

FOR FURTHER READING

Ainsworth, Scott. *Analyzing Interest Groups.* New York: Norton, 2002.

Alexander, Robert, ed. *The Classics of Interest Group Behavior.* New York: Wadsworth, 2005.

Birnbaum, Jeffrey H. *The Money Men.* New York: Crown, 2000.

Cigler, Allan J., and Burdett A. Loomis, eds. *Interest Group Politics.* 7th ed. Washington, D.C.: Congressional Quarterly Press, 2006.

ONLINE READING ○ Esterling, Kevin. *The Political Economy of Expertise.* Ann Arbor: University of Michigan Press, 2004.

ONLINE READING ○ Kollman, Kenneth W. *Outside Lobbying: Public Opinion and Interest Group Strategies.* Princeton, N.J.: Princeton University Press, 1998.

Lowi, Theodore J. *The End of Liberalism: The Second Republic of the United States.* 2nd ed. New York: Norton, 1979.

ONLINE READING ○ Moe, Terry M. *The Organization of Interests: Incentives and the Internal Dynamics of Political Interest Groups.* Chicago: University of Chicago Press, 1980.

Nownes, Anthony. *Total Lobbying: What Lobbyists Want and How They Try to Get It.* New York: Cambridge University Press, 2006.

Olson, Mancur, Jr. *The Logic of Collective Action: Public Goods and the Theory of Groups.* 1965. Reprinted with new preface and appendix. Cambridge, Mass.: Harvard University Press, 1965.

Rosenthal, Alan. *The Third House: Lobbyists and Lobbying in the States.* Washington, D.C.: Congressional Quarterly Press, 2001.

Rozell, Mark, Clyde Wilcox, and David Madland. *Interest Groups in American Campaigns.* Washington, D.C.: Congressional Quarterly Press, 2005.

Sheingate, Adam. *The Rise of the Agricultural Welfare State: Institutions and Interest Group Power in the United States, France, and Japan.* Princeton, N.J.: Princeton University Press, 2003.

Truman, David B. *The Governmental Process: Political Interests and Public Opinion.* New York: Knopf, 1951.

○ ONLINE READING

Introduction to Public Policy

HOW DOES PUBLIC POLICY WORK?

Public policy is an officially expressed intention backed by a sanction, and that sanction can be a reward or a punishment. Thus public policy may be a law, a rule, a statute, an edict, a regulation, or an order. Its purpose is to provide incentives, whether carrot-like rewards or stick-like punishments, to induce people to change what they are currently doing and do something else, or to do more or less of what they are currently doing.

As we said in Chapter 1 and emphasized elsewhere, governments do what they do in part because of the concerns, ambitions, and purposes of politicians and other government officials and the institutional contexts in which these concerns, ambitions, and purposes get played out. Since the policy-making process affords many opportunities to change the purposes of government, politicians and officials constantly take advantage of their capacities as agenda setters. But policy change re-

---

● Core of the Analysis

● Governments are essential to the creation and maintenance of a capitalist economy and a national market.

● The Social Security Act of 1935 distinguished between two kinds of welfare policies: contributory programs, generally called "social security," to which people must pay in order to receive benefits; and noncontributory programs, also called "welfare" or "public assistance," for which eligibility is determined by means testing.

● Governments establish order by using three techniques of control: promotional, regulatory, and redistributive policies.

● Promotional techniques bestow benefits, regulatory techniques directly control individual conduct, and redistributive techniques manipulate the entire economy.

quires success at every step of the rather lengthy and intricate policy-making process. The institutional arrangements of a government create hurdles that a proposed change in policy must clear. This often means that change is nearly impossible. Because change is difficult, policies—once put in place—possess a degree of durability. This durability, in turn, provides a semblance of order and predictability in an otherwise uncertain world.

Governments adopt many policies to pursue many goals. In contrast, there are very few types of sanctions to provide government with the means of fulfilling those purposes. We call these sanctions "techniques of control" to indicate the coercive aspect of policy. But we will first look at the substantive goals and uses of economic and social policies.

ECONOMIC AND SOCIAL POLICIES

Until 1929, most Americans believed that the government had little role to play in managing the economy or in helping those at the bottom of the economic ladder. The world was guided by Adam Smith's theory that the economy, if left to its own devices, would produce full employment and maximum production. This traditional view of the relationship between government and the economy crumbled in 1929 before the stark reality of the Great Depression of 1929–33. Some misfortune befell nearly everyone. Around 20 percent of the workforce became unemployed, and few of these individuals had any monetary resources or the old family farm to fall back on. Banks failed, wiping out the savings of millions who had been prudent enough or fortunate enough to have any. Thousands of businesses failed, throwing middle-class Americans onto the bread lines alongside unemployed laborers and dispossessed farmers. The Great Depression had finally proven to Americans that imperfections in the economic system could exist.

Demands mounted for the federal government to take action. In Congress, some Democrats proposed that the federal government finance public works to aid the economy and put people back to work. Other members of Congress introduced legislation to provide federal grants to the states to assist them in their relief efforts.

When President Franklin D. Roosevelt took office in 1933, he energetically threw the federal government into the business of fighting the Depression. He proposed a variety of temporary measures to provide federal relief and work programs. Most of the programs he proposed were to be financed by the federal government but administered by the states. In addition to these temporary measures, Roosevelt presided over the creation of several important federal programs designed to provide future economic security for Americans. Since that time, the government has been instrumental in ensuring that the economy will never again collapse as it did during the Depression.

For example, in September and October 2008, the nation's financial crisis led the federal government to bail out a number of major banks and financial institutions in order to ward off an economic collapse. The government injected billions of dollars into America's threatened financial institutions, forced several major banks to merge or sell themselves to their competitors, and took ownership positions in a large number of financial institutions. This unprecedented government

public policy A law, rule, statute, or edict that expresses the government's goals and provides for rewards and punishments to promote their attainment.

intervention restored a measure of investor confidence and prevented the economy from grinding to a halt. It also reflected the widely shared expectation that the federal government would act to address so grave an economic problem.

Goals of Economic Policy

The 2008 financial-industry bailout package revealed the many purposes that drive government involvement in the economy. First and foremost is the goal of ensuring a healthy economy. As they debated the legislation, many members of Congress pointed to the fact that allowing big Wall Street financial institutions to fail would likely hurt the entire economy. Government also routinely intervenes in the economy to protect the welfare of its citizens and promote the public good. Many politicians and activists argued that the 2008 financial rescue package should include provisions to help homeowners who were affected by the related mortgage crisis. Another objective of economic policy is to promote business development. In the years prior to 2008, many policymakers felt that deregulation and less government involvement were the best way to help businesses prosper. However, in the congressional hearings surrounding the ongoing crisis, even some former proponents of deregulation conceded that the government should have done more to regulate the risky practices that ultimately brought down several big financial companies. Former chairman of the Federal Reserve Alan Greenspan, long an advocate of deregulation of the financial industry, admitted that "Those of us who have looked to the self-interest of lending institutions to protect shareholders' equity, myself included, are in a state of shocked disbelief."[1]

Government involvement in the economy is now routine and widespread, touching practically every aspect of economic life. Nonetheless, specific decisions about governmental activity in the economy often provoke heated controversy over who benefits from it (and who does not). The 2008 financial bailout package was no exception. Many Democrats objected that it did not do enough to help ordinary Americans who risked losing their homes. Other politicians and activists insisted that the package should impose strict limits on the compensation of executives at companies that received government assistance. They were concerned that many of these executives were still being rewarded handsomely, despite their risky decisions that had brought about the crisis. On the Republican side, some conservative members of Congress argued that the financial institutions had brought this on themselves and should be allowed to fail and that the greater government intervention was not the answer. Congress considered (and largely rejected) these claims and, in the interest of taking action quickly to avert a crisis, passed the plan.

Governments are neither aloof nor separate from the economy but are inextricably bound up in its activities. Governments provide a structure and a framework—standards, rules, laws—as well as substantive support in the form of subsidies, regulations, and taxes, all of which allow the economy to operate. Through politics,

---

[1]Edmund L. Andrews, "Greenspan Concedes Error on Regulation," *New York Times,* 23 October 2008, p. B1.

however, governments and their agents create winners and losers. The winners may think of government's policies as benign; the losers do not.

Three major goals have guided government involvement in the economy since the early years of our nation's history: promoting public order and private property, promoting business development, and maintaining a stable and strong economy. Over time, the federal government has taken on greater responsibility for meeting each of these goals. The Great Depression of the 1930s marked a decisive turning point. As Washington created new agencies and new measures to monitor the nation's economic health, it transformed public expectations of the federal role in the economy. The federal government assumed primary responsibility for achieving established goals, and it faced heightened expectations of its ability to reach those goals.

Promoting Public Order and Private Property A system of law and order is necessary for a healthy market economy. Participants need to be able to assume that the people with whom they are dealing will be bound by a set of predictable laws. Under the American federalist system, there is no national police force, no national criminal law, no national common law, no national property laws. However, the national government does have a few policies directly concerned with public order, most of which are mandated by the Constitution itself. These include laws against counterfeiting, using the mails to defraud, and crossing state lines to avoid arrest for a violation of state laws. A few other offenses against public order have simply been presumed to be interstate crimes against which federal statutes have been enacted, mainly in the twentieth century. Important examples include kidnapping, dealing narcotics, and political subversion. But virtually all of the multitudes of other policies dealing with public order and the foundations of the economy are left to the states and their local governments.

In the wake of the terrorist attacks of September 11, the federal role in public order increased. President George W. Bush, in one of his first acts in response to the attacks, announced the creation of a new cabinet-level agency, the Office of Homeland Defense, which became the Department of Homeland Security. Its mission is to coordinate the federal government's role in the preservation of public order.

Another unique feature of the American approach to public order is the emphasis placed on private property. Private property is valued in most of the cultures of the world but not as centrally as in the United States, where it is embodied in the Constitution. Seizing private property for a public use, or ***expropriation***, is widely used in the United States, especially in land-use regulation. Almost all public works, from highways to parks to government office buildings, involve the forceful taking of some private property to assemble sufficient land and the correct distribution of land for the necessary construction. The vast interstate highway program required expropriation of thousands of narrow strips of private land. We generally call the power to expropriate ***eminent domain,*** and the eminent domain power is recognized as inherent in any government. The Fifth Amendment of the U.S. Constitution surrounds this expropriation power with important safeguards against abuse, so that government agencies in the United States are not permitted to use that

expropriation Confiscation of property with or without compensation.

eminent domain The right of government to take private property for public use, with reasonable compensation awarded for the property.

power except through a strict due process, and they must offer "fair market value" for the land sought.[2]

Many policies positively encourage property ownership on the theory that property owners are better citizens and, therefore, more respectful of public order. One of the most important national policies is the part of the tax code that permits homeowners to deduct from their taxes interest paid on mortgage loans. In addition, three large federal agencies—the Federal Housing Administration (FHA), the Farmers Home Administration, and the Veterans Benefits Administration (VBA)—encourage homeownership by making mortgage loans available at interest rates below the market rate. The Farm Credit Administration operates the extensive Farm Credit System, whose primary function is to make long-term and short-term loans to improve farm and rural real estate.

Promoting Business Development

During the nineteenth century, the national government was almost exclusively a promoter of markets. National roads and canals were built to tie states and regions together. National tariff policies promoted domestic markets by restricting imported goods; a tax on an import raised its price and weakened its ability to compete with similar domestic products. The national government also heavily subsidized the railroad. Until the 1840s, railroads were thought to be of limited commercial value. But between 1850 and 1872, Congress granted over 100 million acres of public domain land to railroad interests, and state and local governments pitched in an estimated $280 million in cash and credit. Before the end of the century, 35,000 miles of track existed—almost half the world's total.

Railroads were not the only clients of federal support aimed at fostering the expansion of private markets. Many sectors of agriculture also received federal subsidies during the nineteenth century. Agriculture remains highly subsidized. In 2001, an environmental group caused a stir by putting the exact amounts of subsidies received by individual farmers on a widely publicized Web site.[3] The top recipient of government aid in Texas, for example, received $1.3 million in 2001. President Bush continued the tradition of generous agricultural subsidies, approving a 2002 law that increased federal payments to farmers by 80 percent.

In the twentieth century, traditional promotional techniques were expanded, and some new ones were invented. For example, a great proportion of the promotional activities of the national government are now done indirectly through *categorical grants-in-aid* (see Chapter 3). The national government offers grants to states on the condition that the state (or local) government undertake a particular activity. Thus to use motor transportation to improve national markets, a national highway system of 900,000 miles was built during the 1930s, based on a formula whereby the national government would pay 50 percent of the cost if the state would

categorical grants-in-aid Grants by Congress to states and localities given with the condition that expenditures be limited to a problem or group specified by the national government.

---

[2]For an evaluation of the politics of eminent domain, see Theodore J. Lowi, Benjamin Ginsberg, et al., *Poliscide: Big Government, Big Science, Lilliputian Politics*, 2nd ed. (Lanham, Md.: University Press of America, 1990), p. 235 and passim, esp. chapters 11 and 12, by Julia Vitullo-Martin and Thomas Vitullo-Martin.

[3]Farm Subsidy Database: A Project of Environmental Working Group (www.ewg.org/farm).

provide the other 50 percent. And then for over twenty years, beginning in the late 1950s, the federal government constructed over 45,000 miles of interstate highways. This project was brought about through a program whereby the national government agreed to pay 90 percent of the construction costs on the condition that each state provide for 10 percent of the costs of any portion of a highway built within its boundaries.[4] More recently, the federal government has been involved in the subsidization of urban mass transit, airport construction and modernization, and port improvements—a combination of promotional and security concerns at work.

The government also fosters business development by regulating competition. Federal economic regulation aims to protect the public from potential abuses by concentrated economic power in two ways. First, the federal government can establish conditions that govern the operation of big businesses to ensure fair competition. For example, it can require business to make available to the public information about its activities and its account books. Second, the federal government can force a large business to break up into smaller companies if it finds that the business has established a monopoly. This is called *antitrust policy.* In addition to economic regulation, the federal government engages in social regulation. Social regulation imposes conditions on businesses to protect workers, the environment, and consumers.

The modern epoch of comprehensive national regulation began in the 1930s. However, the extent to which government should regulate businesses is controversial. In the late 1970s, many economists began to argue that excessive regulation was hurting the economy. Congress and the president responded with a wave of *deregulation.* Economic conservatives are in principle opposed to virtually any sort of government intervention in the economy.[5] As President Reagan once put it, they see government not as part of the solution, but as part of the problem. They adamantly oppose intervention by techniques of promoting commerce and are even more opposed to intervention through techniques of regulation. They believe that markets would be bigger and healthier if not regulated at all.

President George W. Bush's support of deregulation contributed to the trend away from government intervention. Substantial deregulation in the telecommunications industry and in agriculture, and relaxation of regulatory activity in civil rights, pollution control, and protection of endangered species and natural resources, seemed to support the expectation that the antiregulation spirit will stay alive a while longer.

Maintaining a Stable and Strong Economy

A stable and strong economy is the basic goal of all economic policy. What makes reaching this goal so difficult is that the key elements of a strong economy— economic growth, full employment, and low inflation—often appear to conflict with

---

[4]A congressional act of 1956 officially designated the interstate highways the National System of Interstate and Defense Highways. It was indirectly a major part of President Eisenhower's defense program. But it was just as obviously a pork-barrel policy as any rivers and harbors legislation.

[5]Actually, this point of view is better understood as nineteenth-century liberalism, or free-market liberalism, following the theories of Adam Smith. However, after the New Deal appropriated "liberal" for their pro-government point of view, the Republican antigovernment wing got tagged with the conservative label. With Reagan, the conservative label took on more popular connotations, while "liberal" became stigmatized as the "L-word."

antitrust policy Government regulation of large businesses that have established monopolies.

deregulation A policy of reducing or eliminating regulatory restraints in the conduct of individuals or private institutions.

one another. Economic policy must manage the trade-offs among these goals. This is a complicated task because there is much disagreement about whether pursuing one of these economic goals really does mean sacrificing the others. Let us now turn to the actual policies designed to accomplish economic stability and growth.

Monetary Policies   *Monetary policies* manipulate the growth of the entire economy by controlling the availability of money to banks.

But banks did not become the core of the American economic system without intense political controversy. The Federalist majority in Congress, led by Alexander Hamilton, did in fact establish a Bank of the United States in 1791, but it was vigorously opposed by the agrarian interests, led by Thomas Jefferson, based on the fear that the interests of urban, industrial capitalism would dominate such a bank. The Bank of the United States was finally terminated during the administration of Andrew Jackson, but the fear of a central, *public* bank still existed eight decades later, when Congress in 1913 established an institution—the **Federal Reserve System**—to integrate private banks into a single system. The Federal Reserve System did not become a central bank in the European tradition but rather is composed of twelve Federal Reserve banks, each located in a major commercial city. The Federal Reserve banks are not ordinary banks; they are banker's banks: they make loans to other banks, clear checks, and supply the economy with currency and coins. They also play a regulatory role in relation to the member banks. Every national bank must be a member of the Federal Reserve System; each must follow national banking rules and must purchase stock in the Federal Reserve System (which helps make the system self-financing). State banks and savings and loan associations may also join if they accept the national rules. At the top of the system is the Federal Reserve Board (the Fed), made up of seven members appointed by the president (with Senate confirmation) for fourteen-year terms. The chairman of the Fed is selected by the president from among the seven members of the board for a four-year term. In all other concerns, however, the Fed is an independent agency inasmuch as its members cannot be removed during their terms except "for cause," and the president's executive power does not extend to them or their policies.

The major advantage of belonging to the federal system is that each member bank can borrow money from the Fed, using as collateral the notes on loans already made. This privilege enables them to expand their loan operations continually, as long as there is demand for new loans. The ability of a member bank to borrow money from the Fed is a profoundly important monetary policy. The Fed charges interest, called a *discount rate,* on its loans to member banks.

If the Fed significantly decreases the discount rate—that is, the interest it charges member banks when they apply for credit—that can be a good shot in the arm for a sagging economy. Manipulating interest rates is the Fed's most powerful tool. During 2001, the Fed cut interest rates eleven times to combat the combined effects of recession and the terrorist attacks. If the Fed adopts a policy of higher discount rates, it will serve as a brake on the economy if the economy is expanding too fast, because the higher rate pushes up the interest rates charged by leading private banks to their customers. In 2004 and 2005, the Fed reversed course and raised interest rates to keep inflation in check. In 2006 and 2007, the Fed held rates steady.

monetary policies (techniques) Efforts to regulate the economy through manipulation of the supply of money and credit. America's most powerful institution in the area of monetary policy is the Federal Reserve Board.

Federal Reserve System Consisting of twelve Federal Reserve Banks, an agency that facilitates exchanges of cash, checks, and credit; it regulates member banks; and it uses monetary policies to fight inflation and deflation.

discount rate The interest rate charged by the Federal Reserve when commercial banks borrow in order to expand their lending operations; an effective tool of monetary policy.

FIGURE 13.1 The Federal Government Dollar, Fiscal Year 2005 Estimates

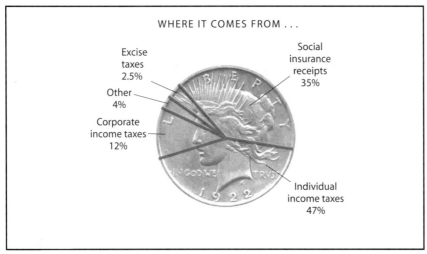

WHERE IT COMES FROM . . .

Excise taxes 2.5%

Social insurance receipts 35%

Other 4%

Corporate income taxes 12%

Individual income taxes 47%

SOURCE: Office of Management and Budget, *Budget of the U.S. Government, Fiscal Year 2005* (Washington, D.C.: Government Printing Office, 2006), pp. 32, 117.

Other monetary policies implemented by the Fed include increasing or decreasing the **reserve requirement,** which sets the proportion of deposited money that a bank must keep "on demand" as it makes all the rest of its deposits available for new loans. A third important technique used by the Fed is **open-market operations**—the buying and selling of Treasury securities to absorb excess dollars or to release more dollars into the economy. Finally, a fourth power is derived from one of the important services rendered by the Federal Reserve System, which is the opportunity for member banks to borrow from one another. This exchange is called the federal funds market, and the interest rate charged by one bank to another, the **federal funds rate,** can be manipulated just like the discount rate, to expand or contract credit.

The federal government also provides insurance to foster credit and encourage private capital investment. The Federal Deposit Insurance Corporation (FDIC) protects bank deposits up to $100,000. Another important promoter of investment is the federal insurance of home mortgages provided by the Department of Housing and Urban Development.

Fiscal Policies *Fiscal policies* include the government's taxing and spending powers. Personal and corporate income taxes, which raise most government revenues, are the most prominent examples. Although the direct purpose of an income tax is to raise revenue, each tax has a different impact on the economy, and the government can plan for that impact (Figure 13.1). For example, although the main reason for a significant increase in the Social Security tax (which is an income tax) under President Carter was to keep Social Security solvent, a big reason for it in the mind of many legislators was that it would reduce inflation by shrinking the amount of money people had in their hands to buy more goods and services.

reserve requirement The amount of liquid assets and ready cash that the Federal Reserve requires banks to hold to meet depositors' demands for their money.

open-market operations The buying and selling of government securities to help finance government operations and to loosen or tighten the total amount of credit circulating in the economy.

federal funds rate The interest rate on loans between banks that the Federal Reserve Board influences by affecting the supply of money available.

fiscal policies (techniques) The government's use of taxing, monetary, and spending powers to manipulate the economy.

A tax is called ***progressive*** if the rate of taxation goes up with each higher income bracket. The decision to make the income tax progressive was one of the most important policy choices Congress made. A tax is called ***regressive*** if people in lower income brackets pay a higher proportion of their income in taxes than people in higher income brackets. For example, a sales tax is deemed regressive because everybody pays at the same rate, so that the proportion of total income paid in taxes goes down as the total income goes up (assuming, as is generally the case, that as total income goes up, the amount spent on taxable purchases increases at a lower rate).

In 2001, the newly elected Republican administration pursued a program of massive tax cuts. This followed several years of vigorous economic growth under Clinton, which had produced large revenue surpluses (which the proposed tax cuts would diminish). The Bush administration's policy increased the income threshold for paying taxes, thus relieving some of the poorest taxpayers of any tax obligations at all. But the bulk of the reduction was enjoyed by wealthier taxpayers. The Republicans thus were able to reward their natural electoral constituency and demonstrate their ideological commitment to a smaller role for government. However, a subsequent economic recession, combined with the huge outlays required by September 11 and the wars in Afghanistan and Iraq, turned tax cuts aimed at reducing the surplus into tax cuts that produced record deficits. On top of all this, the tax cuts made more problematic the requirements of the Social Security program in light of retiring baby boomers. Many experts concluded that the Bush tax cuts were fiscally reckless.

Government Spending   The federal government's power to spend is one of the most important tools of economic policy. Decisions about how much to spend affect the overall health of the economy. They also affect aspects of American life, from the distribution of income through the availability of different modes of transportation to the level of education in society. It is not surprising that the fight for control over spending is one of the most contentious in Washington, as interest groups and politicians strive to determine the priorities and appropriate levels. Decisions about spending are made as part of the annual budget process. During the 1990s, when the federal ***budget deficit*** became a major political issue and parties were deeply split on spending, the budget process became the focal point of the entire policy-making process. Even though the budget deficit disappeared in the late 1990s, the budget continued to dominate the attention of policy makers. With the deficit on the rise again since September 11, budget politics are sure to remain on the national agenda.

The president and Congress have each created institutions to assert control over the budget process. The OMB, in the Executive Office of the President, is responsible for preparing the president's budget. This budget contains the president's spending priorities and the estimated costs of the president's policy proposals. It is viewed as the starting point for the annual debate over the budget. When different parties control the presidency and Congress, the president's budget may have little influence on the budget that is ultimately adopted. Members of the president's own party may also have different priorities.

Congress has its own budget institutions. It created the Congressional Budget Office in 1974 so that it could have reliable information about the costs and economic impact of the policies it considers. At the same time, Congress set up a

progressive/regressive taxation Taxation that hits the upper income brackets more heavily (progressive) or the lower income brackets more heavily (regressive).

budget deficit The amount by which government spending exceeds government revenue in a fiscal year.

FIGURE 13.2 Uncontrollables as a Percentage of the Total Federal Budget

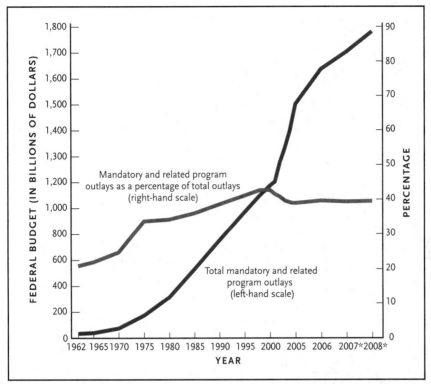

SOURCE: Office of Management and Budget, *Budget of the U.S. Government, Fiscal Year 2007: Historical Tables* (Washington, D.C.: Government Printing Office, 2006), tables 8.1, 8.3, pp. 137, 139.

*Data for 2007 and 2008 are estimates.

budget process designed to establish spending priorities and consider individual expenditures in light of the entire budget. A key element of the process is the annual budget resolution, which designates broad targets for spending. By estimating the costs of policy proposals, Congress hoped to control spending and reduce deficits. When the congressional budget process proved unable to hold down deficits in the 1980s, Congress instituted stricter measures to control spending, including "spending caps" that limit spending on some types of programs.

A very large and growing proportion of the annual federal budget takes the form of **mandatory spending**, expenditures that are, in the words of the OMB, "relatively uncontrollable." Interest payments on the national debt, for example, are determined by the size of the national debt. Legislation has mandated payment rates for such programs as retirement under Social Security, retirement for federal employees, unemployment assistance, Medicare, and farm price supports (Figure 13.2). These payments increase with the cost of living; they increase as the average age of the population goes up; they increase as national and world agricultural

mandatory spending
Federal spending that is made up of "uncontrollables."

The Income Gap

Examined carefully, data often raise more questions than they answer. When viewing a table or figure, especially in the context of policy debates, it is usually prudent to make a list of the questions raised by the data presented rather than simply accepting the interpretation offered by the analyst presenting the data. Take, for example, the so-called income gap that has become a major issue in contemporary American politics. As indicated by the table below, in the last several years the difference or "gap" between the share of America's income going to the richest and poorest segments of the population has been increasing. Many Democrats blame Republican tax cuts for making the rich richer and the poor poorer and assert that major changes in tax policy are needed to restore a measure of equality to American society.

▼

The Proportion of Money Income Going to Each Fifth of the Population

Family Income Bracket	1929 (%)	1934 (%)	1944 (%)	1950 (%)	1960 (%)	1970 (%)	1980 (%)	1990 (%)	2002 (%)
Lowest fifth	5.4	5.9	4.9	4.5	4.8	4.1	4.3	3.9	3.5
Second fifth	10.1	11.5	10.9	12.0	12.2	10.8	10.3	9.6	8.8
Third fifth	14.4	15.5	16.2	17.4	17.8	17.4	16.9	15.9	14.8
Fourth fifth	18.8	20.4	22.2	23.5	24.0	24.5	24.9	24.0	23.3
Highest fifth	51.3	49.7	45.8	42.6	41.3	43.3	43.7	46.6	49.7
Gap between lowest and highest fifths	45.9	43.8	40.9	38.1	36.5	39.2	39.4	42.7	46.2

Source: Data for 1929–50, Allan Rosenbaum, "State Government, Political Power, and Public Policy: The Case of Illinois" (Ph.D. diss., University of Chicago, 1974), chaps. 10–11, used by permission; for 1960–2002, U.S. Bureau of the Census, *Income in the United States: 2002*, Current Population Reports, series P60 (Washington, D.C.: Government Printing Office, 2003).

Note: Figures are not strictly comparable because of difference in calculating procedures.

These data may indicate an emergent social problem in the United States, but at least two questions must be answered before we can draw any meaningful conclusions from them and before we can make policy recommendations. First, the data deal with differences among income groups but they do not show the absolute income of any group. It is possible that all income groups are better off today than they were in prior years. If everyone is better off, perhaps we do not want to change our tax policies, even if they tend to increase income inequality. This possibility is at least partially borne out by census data: Between 1980 and 2004, the average incomes of every income group increased—though the incomes of the wealthiest Americans increased more sharply than those of any others.

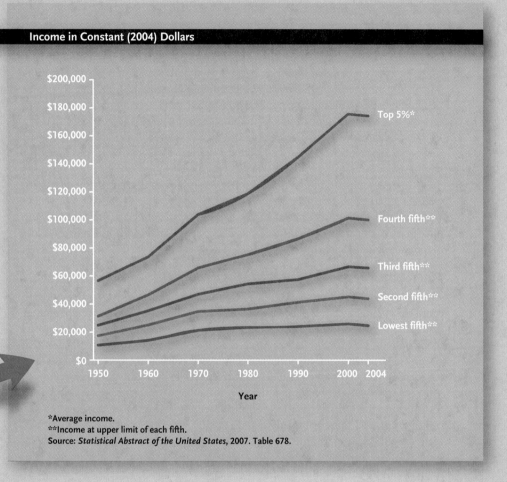

Income in Constant (2004) Dollars

- Top 5%*
- Fourth fifth**
- Third fifth**
- Second fifth**
- Lowest fifth**

Year

*Average income.
**Income at upper limit of each fifth.
Source: *Statistical Abstract of the United States*, 2007. Table 678.

A second consideration is that the data showing a growing income gap deal with aggregates, not individuals. We cannot know from the data presented whether families are generally locked into a particular income quartile or are likely to move from year to year. If the latter, then the apparent increase in inequality shown in the first table is at least mitigated by social mobility. In recent years, for example, the percentage of black families in the lowest income group has decreased more sharply than the percentage of white families in that group. At the same time, the percentage of black families in the highest income group has increased more substantially than their white counterparts, suggesting that there is social mobility across the income groups.[1] Thus, in considering the income gap, we may want to consider whether policies designed to reduce inequality might interfere with social mobility.

[1]*Statistical Abstract of the United States*, 2007. Table 676.

surpluses go up. In 1970, 38.6 percent of the total federal budget was made up of these *uncontrollables;* in 1975, 52.5 percent fell into that category; and by 2001, around 64.7 percent was in the uncontrollable category. This means that the national government now has very little ***discretionary spending*** with which to counteract fluctuations in the business cycle.

This has a profound political implication. With mandatory or relatively uncontrollable spending on the rise, there is less scope for the exercise of discretion. If a budget has to be cut and categories of mandatory spending are taken off the table, then the cuts will fall disproportionately on what remains. With the pain of cutting "available" programs, the prospects for distributing the cuts in a manner acceptable to all interested parties grow dim. Thus the politics will be more intense and dirty; groups will be more highly mobilized and energized—they will be at one another's throats; Congress and the president will be eyeball to eyeball as they seek to protect their different constituencies; and political partisans will not be in the mood for compromise.[6]

Government spending as a fiscal policy works fairly well when deliberate deficit spending is used to stop a recession and speed up the recovery period. But it does not work very well in fighting inflation because elected politicians are politically unable to make the drastic expenditure cuts necessary to balance the budget, much less to produce a budgetary surplus.

The Welfare System as Fiscal and Social Policy

Government involvement in the relief of poverty and dependency was insignificant until the twentieth century because of Americans' antipathy to government and because of their confidence that all of the deserving poor could be cared for by private efforts alone. This traditional approach crumbled in 1929 in the wake of the Great Depression, when some misfortune befell nearly everyone. Americans finally confronted the fact that poverty and dependency could be the result of imperfections of the economic system itself, rather than a result of individual irresponsibility. Americans held to their distinction between the deserving and undeserving poor but significantly altered these standards regarding who was deserving and who was not. And once the idea of an imperfect system was established, a large-scale public approach became practical not only to alleviate poverty but also to redistribute wealth and to manipulate economy activity through fiscal policy.

The architects of the original Social Security system in the 1930s were probably well aware that a large welfare system can be good *fiscal* policy. When the economy is declining and more people are losing their jobs or are retiring early, welfare pay-

uncontrollables
Budgetary items that are beyond the control of budgetary committees and can be controlled only by substantive legislative action in Congress. Some uncontrollables, such as the interest on the debt, are beyond the power of Congress because the terms of payments are set in contracts.

discretionary spending Federal spending on programs that are controlled through the regular budget process.

---

[6]Of course, it should be underscored that "relatively uncontrollable" is itself a policy decision taken by the president and Congress. It is not carved in granite; it can be undone. To undo some things, like not making a promised payment on the national debt, would have horrible consequences in credit markets. A modest across-the-board reduction in outlays for hospital assistance under Medicare, on the other hand, while painful (literally and figuratively), might nevertheless be accommodated (with hospitals and patients sharing the burden in various ways—for example, by deferring elective procedures or delaying a salary increase). That is, things that are alleged to be off the table can be put right back on the table.

TABLE 13.1 Public Welfare Programs

	Year Enacted	Federal Outlays in 2006 (in billions of dollars)	Federal Outlays (2007 estimate in billions of dollars)	Federal Outlays (2008 estimate in billions of dollars)
Contributory				
Old-Age and Survivors Insurance; Disability Insurance (Social Security)	1935	457.7	482.1	503.0
Medicare	1965	375.6	430.3	454.0
Unemployment compensation	1935	31.8	32.6	34.9
Noncontributory				
Medicaid	1965	180.6	191.8	201.9
Food Stamps	1964	30.0	35.6	39.0
Supplemental Security Income	1974	34.3	33.4	38.9
National School Lunch Program (listed as Child Nutrition and Special Milk Programs)	1946	12.4	13.6	13.8
Temporary Assistance for Needy Families (TANF, listed as Family Support Payments to States)	1996	20.8	21.8	21.4

SOURCE: Office of Management and Budget, *Budget of the U.S. Government, Fiscal Year 2008, Historical Tables* (Washington, D.C.: Government Printing Office, 2007), table 11.3, pp. 205–229.

ments go up automatically, thus maintaining consumer demand and making the "downside" of the business cycle shorter and shallower. Conversely, during periods of full employment or high levels of government spending, when inflationary pressures can mount, welfare taxes take an extra bite out of consumer dollars, tending to dampen inflation, flattening the "upside" of the economy.

However, the authors of Social Security were more aware of the *social* policy significance of the welfare system. They recognized that a large proportion of the unemployment, dependency, and misery of the 1930s was due to the imperfections of a large, industrial society and occurred through no fault of the victims of these imperfections. They also recognized that opportunities to achieve security, let alone prosperity, were unevenly distributed in our society. This helps explain how the original Social Security laws came to be called—both by supporters and by critics—"the welfare state." The 1935 Social Security Act provided for two separate categories of *welfare—contributory* and *noncontributory.* Table 13.1 outlines the key programs in each of these categories.

Social Security   *Contributory programs* are financed by taxation in a way that can be called "forced savings." These programs are what most people have in mind when they refer to Social Security or social insurance. Under the original old-age insurance program, the employer and the employee were each required to pay equal amounts, which in 1937 were set at 1 percent of the first $3,000 of wages, to be deducted from the paycheck of each employee and matched by the same amount from the employer. This percentage has increased over the years; the total contribution is now 7.65 percent subdivided as follows: 6.20 percent on the first $90,000 of income for the Social Security benefits and an additional 1.45 percent on all earnings for Medicare.[7]

Social Security is a rather conservative approach to welfare. In effect, the Social Security (FICA) tax is a message that people cannot be trusted to save voluntarily in order to take care of their own needs. But in another sense, it is quite radical. Social Security is not real insurance; workers' contributions do not accumulate in a personal account like an annuity. Consequently, contributors do not receive benefits in proportion to their own contributions, and this means that there is a redistribution of wealth. In brief, contributory Social Security mildly redistributes wealth from higher- to lower-income people, and it quite significantly redistributes wealth from young to old people and from younger workers to older retirees.

Reforming Social Security   Since its creation in 1935, the Social Security system has provided retirement, survivor, and disability benefits to millions of Americans. Up until now, the system has run "in the black"—that is, it has collected more money than it has given out. In 2004, almost 48 million Americans received a total of $506 billion in Social Security benefits, given to 40 million retirees, dependents, and survivors of deceased workers, and to 8 million disabled workers. Even today, more than half of all American workers do not have a private pension plan; they will have to rely solely on Social Security for their retirement. If there were no Social Security, half of all senior citizens would be living below the poverty line. Thus, Social Security guarantees a measure of equality.

Nearly all wage earners and self-employed individuals pay into Social Security. Yet many fear that the system cannot sustain itself. When the baby boomer generation—a relatively large percentage of Americans, born between 1946 and 1964—reaches retirement age, their large numbers and longer life expectancies may place too great a demand on the system, forcing today's young people to pay ever more into a system that may be bankrupt by the time they retire.

Those who argue for a major change in Social Security point out that Social Security benefits are not drawn from an interest-bearing account; rather, they are paid for from taxes collected from current workers. Therefore, current workers carry the primary financial burden for the system. When baby boomers retire, their political and economic clout will be so great that they will be able to push aside any effort to limit benefits or relieve the financial burden on a much smaller number of younger

contributory programs Social programs financed in whole or in part by taxation or other mandatory contributions by their present or future recipients. The most important example is Social Security, which is financed by a payroll tax.

Social Security A contributory welfare program into which working Americans contribute a percentage of their wages, and from which they receive cash benefits after retirement.

---

[7]The figures cited are for 2005. Although on paper the employer is taxed, this is all part of "forced savings," because in reality the employer's contribution is nothing more than a mandatory wage supplement that the employee never sees or touches before it goes into the trust fund held exclusively for the contributory programs.

wage earners. For Social Security to continue, it may have to borrow, or draw money from the federal Treasury, leaving younger generations with a staggering debt. If no changes are made in the current system, the Social Security Trust Fund (the account where surplus monies are held) will, according to projections, experience a shortfall beginning in 2042.

Contrary to popular impressions, Social Security benefits are not a simple repayment, plus interest, of money contributed by workers. The average retiree receives back the equivalent of all the money he or she contributed over a lifetime of work, plus interest, in the space of four to eight years. Most retirees receive far more than they put in. Why should today's student-age population provide subsidies to retirees who do not need the extra income?

In 2004, the debate about Social Security's future had heated up when Federal Reserve Chairman Alan Greenspan warned Congress that growing federal deficits would require Social Security and Medicare benefits to be reduced in the future. The large generation of baby boomers expected to retire by the end of 2010, combined with federal deficits, would put too much pressure on the program. Greenspan recommended that the retirement age for Social Security benefits be raised above 67 and that adjustments for inflation be slowed. In an election year, few politicians, including the president, wanted to be associated with remarks that could be interpreted as undermining Social Security.

President George W. Bush came to office supporting Social Security reforms, including the creation of private retirement accounts. Given the politically volatile character of debates about Social Security, President Bush waited until his second term to propose changes in the program. Bush advocated a reform plan that offered workers the choice of contributing a portion of the payroll tax to an individual account. The worker's traditional benefits would be reduced by the amount diverted to the individual account. According to Bush's vision for an "ownership society," individual plans would create a better system because they would allow workers to accumulate assets and build wealth, wealth that could be passed on to their children.

Supporters of the current Social Security system contend that the system's financial troubles are exaggerated. They dispute arguments, such as Greenspan's, that deficits require cuts in Social Security. They point out that Social Security taxes were raised in 1983—on the recommendation of a commission that Greenspan himself chaired—so that the program would be prepared to serve the aging baby boomer generation. Instead of saving that money, however, the federal government cut taxes on the wealthy and used Social Security taxes to finance the deficit. Advocates of the current system believe that many of Social Security's troubles could be solved by raising income taxes on the wealthy and eliminating the cap on payroll taxes. In 2005, only the first $90,000 of income was subject to the payroll tax. If this cap were lifted, these critics argue, the resulting revenues would cover more than 75 percent of the expected shortfall in the Social Security Trust Fund.

Supporters of the current system are also deeply skeptical about the benefits of individual accounts. They charge the president with presenting a rosy scenario that overestimates likely gains through the stock market. When more realistic assumptions are adopted and the costs of the private accounts are considered, they argue, individual accounts do not provide higher benefits than the current system. Moreover, these critics note that the reforms would still not solve the budget crisis that Social Security will face.[8]

Finally, supporters of the present system emphasize that Social Security is not just a retirement account; it is a social insurance program that provides "income protection to workers and their families if the wage earner retires, becomes disabled or dies."[9] Because it provides this social insurance protection, supporters argue, Social Security's returns should not be compared to those of a private retirement account.

In 1972, Congress decided to end the grind of biennial legislation by establishing *indexing*, whereby benefits paid out under contributory programs would be modified annually by *cost of living adjustments (COLAs)* based on changes in the Consumer Price Index, so that benefits would increase automatically as the cost of living rose. But, of course, Social Security taxes (contributions) also increased after almost every benefit increase. This made Social Security, in the words of one observer, "a politically ideal program. It bridged partisan conflict by providing liberal benefits under conservative financial auspices."[10]

Medicare   The biggest single expansion in contributory programs since 1935 was the establishment in 1965 of *Medicare,* which provides substantial medical services to elderly persons who are already eligible to receive old-age, survivors', and disability insurance under the original Social Security system. Medicare provides hospital insurance but allows beneficiaries to choose whether or not to participate in a government-assisted insurance program to cover doctors' fees. A major role is guaranteed to the private health-care industry by essentially limiting Medicare to a financing system. Program recipients purchase all their health services in the free market. The government's involvement is primarily payment for these services. As a result, there is little government control over the quality of the services provided and the fees that health-care providers charge.

Like Social Security, Medicare is not means tested. The benefits are available to all former workers and their spouses over the age of sixty-five—over 40 million people today—whether they are poor or not. Spending on Medicare has proved difficult to control in recent years, in part because of the growing numbers of people eligible for the programs but also because of rising health-care costs. Health-care expenditures, especially the cost of prescription drugs, have risen much more sharply than inflation in recent years.

Between the 1970s and the 1990s, there was mounting concern among policy makers about the rising costs of Medicare, and cost containment was a constant theme. The start of the Medicare prescription-drug benefit debate in the mid-1990s,

---

indexing Periodic adjustments of welfare payments, wages, or taxes, tied to the cost of living.

Medicare National health insurance for the elderly and for the disabled.

[8]*Goldberg v. Kelly,* 397 U.S. 254 (1970).

[9]See U.S. House of Representatives, Committee on Ways and Means, *Where Your Money Goes: The 1994–95 Green Book* (Washington, D.C.: Brassey's, 1994), pp. 325, 802.

[10]Edward J. Harpham, "Fiscal Crisis and the Politics of Social Security Reform," in *The Attack on the Welfare State,* ed. Anthony Champagne and Edward Harpham (Prospect Heights, Ill.: Waveland Press, 1984), p. 13.

stemming from the exorbitant medication costs being borne by people with Medicare, coupled with worries about the impending retirement of the baby-boom generation, led to the birth of a full-fledged movement to "overhaul" Medicare. Proponents of this effort propagated the idea that the Medicare program needed to be "saved," claiming Medicare was out-of-date and on the brink of bankruptcy.

In 2003, Congress enacted a major reform of the Medicare program, which has provided health care to seniors since 1964. Most notably, Congress added a prescription drug benefit to the package of health benefits for the elderly. The high cost of prescription drugs is an issue of growing concern to millions of older Americans.

Public Assistance Programs   Programs to which beneficiaries do not have to contribute—**noncontributory programs**—are also known as public assistance programs, or, derisively, as welfare. Until 1996, the most important noncontributory program was *Aid to Families with Dependent Children (AFDC,* originally called Aid to Dependent Children, or ADC), which was founded in 1935 by the original Social Security Act. In 1996, Congress abolished AFDC and replaced it with the *Temporary Assistance to Needy Families (TANF)* block grant. Eligibility for public assistance is determined by *means testing,* a procedure that requires applicants to show a financial need for assistance. Between 1935 and 1965, the government created programs to provide housing assistance, school lunches, and food stamps to other needy Americans.

As with contributory programs, the noncontributory public assistance programs also made their most significant advances in the 1960s and 1970s. The largest single category of expansion was the establishment in 1965 of *Medicaid,* a program that provides extended medical services to all low-income persons who have already established eligibility through means testing under AFDC or TANF. Noncontributory programs underwent another major transformation in the 1970s in the level of benefits they provide. Besides being means tested, noncontributory programs are federal rather than national; grants-in-aid are provided by the national government to the states as incentives to establish the programs (see Chapter 3). Thus, from the beginning there were considerable disparities in benefits from state to state. The national government sought to rectify the disparities in levels of old-age benefits in 1974 by creating the *Supplemental Security Income (SSI)* program to augment benefits for the aged, the blind, and the disabled. SSI provides uniform minimum benefits across the entire nation and includes mandatory COLAs. States are allowed to be more generous if they wish, but no state is permitted to provide benefits below the minimum level set by the national government. As a result, twenty-five states increased their own SSI benefits to the mandated level.

The new TANF program is also administered by the states and, like the old-age benefits just discussed, benefit levels vary widely from state to state (see Figure 13.3). For example, although the median national "standard of need" for a family of three was $1306 per month (55 percent of the poverty-line income) in 2004, the states' monthly TANF benefits varied from $170 in Mississippi to $923 in Alaska.[11]

---

[11]Ways and Means Committee Print, WMCP: 108–6, *2003 Green Book,* from U.S. GPO Online via GPO Access at waysandmeans.house.gov/media/pdf/greenbook2003/section7.pdf.

noncontributory programs Social programs that provide assistance to people based on demonstrated need rather than any contribution they have made.

Aid to Families with Dependent Children (AFDC) Federal funds, administered by the states, for children living with persons or relatives who fall below state standards of need. Abolished in 1996 and replaced with TANF.

Temporary Assistance to Needy Families (TANF) A policy by which states are given block grants by the federal government in order to create their own programs for public assistance.

means testing Procedure by which potential beneficiaries of a public assistance program establish their eligibility by demonstrating a genuine need for the assistance.

Medicaid A federally financed, state-operated program providing medical services to low-income people.

Supplemental Security Income (SSI) A program providing a minimum monthly income to people who pass a "means test" and who are sixty-five or older, blind, or disabled. Financed from general revenues rather than from Social Security contributions.

FIGURE 13.3 Variations in State Spending on TANF Benefits

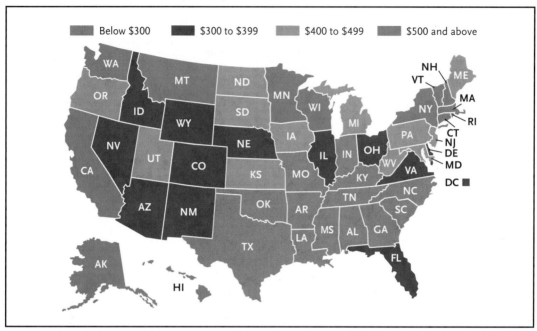

Below $300 $300 to $399 $400 to $499 $500 and above

SOURCE: U.S. House of Representatives, Ways and Means Committee, *2003 Green Book* (waysandmeans.house.gov/media/pdf/greenbook2003/section7.pdf).

The number of people receiving AFDC benefits expanded in the 1970s, in part because new welfare programs had been established in the mid-1960s: Medicaid (discussed earlier) and *Food Stamps,* which are coupons that can be exchanged for food at most grocery stores. These programs provide what are called *in-kind benefits*—noncash goods and services that would otherwise have to be paid for in cash by the beneficiary. In addition to simply adding on the cost of medical services and food to the level of benefits given to AFDC recipients, the possibility of receiving Medicaid benefits provided an incentive for poor Americans to establish their eligibility for AFDC, which would also establish their eligibility to receive Medicaid. At the same time, the government significantly expanded its publicity efforts to encourage the dependent unemployed to establish their eligibility for these various programs.

Another more complex reason for the growth of AFDC in the 1970s was that it became more difficult for the government to terminate people's AFDC benefits for lack of eligibility. In the 1970 case of *Goldberg v. Kelly,* the Supreme Court held that the financial benefits of AFDC could not be revoked without due process—that is, a hearing at which evidence is presented, and so on.[12] This ruling inaugurated the concept of the *entitlement,* a class of government benefits with a status similar to that of property (which, according to the Fourteenth Amendment, cannot be taken from people "without due process of law"). *Goldberg v. Kelly* did not provide that the

Food Stamps
Coupons that can be exchanged for food at most grocery stores; the largest in-kind benefits program.

in-kind benefits
Goods and services provided to needy individuals and families by the federal government.

entitlement Eligibility for benefits by virtue of a category of benefits defined by legislation.

ONLINE READING ○ [12]*Goldberg v. Kelly,* 397 U.S. 254 (1970).

beneficiary had a "right" to government benefits; it provided that once a person's eligibility for AFDC was established, and as long as the program was still in effect, that person could not be denied benefits without due process. The decision left open the possibility that Congress could terminate the program and its benefits by passing a piece of legislation. If the welfare benefit were truly a property right, Congress would have no authority to deny it by a mere majority vote.

Thus the establishment of in-kind benefit programs and the legal obstacles involved in terminating benefits contributed to the growth of the welfare state. But it is important to note that real federal spending on AFDC itself did not rise after the mid-1970s. Unlike Social Security, AFDC was not indexed to inflation; without cost of living adjustments, the value of AFDC benefits fell by more than one-third. Moreover, the largest noncontributory welfare program, Medicaid (as shown by Table 13.1), actually devotes less than one third of its expenditures to poor families; the rest goes to the disabled and the elderly in nursing homes.[13] Together, these programs have significantly increased the security of the poor and the vulnerable and must be included in a genuine assessment of the redistributive influence and the cost of the welfare system today.

Welfare Reform   During the 1992 presidential campaign, Bill Clinton promised to "end welfare as we know it," but not until the approach of the 1996 presidential campaign was the Personal Responsibility and Work Opportunity Act (PRA) signed into law.

The new law replaced the sixty-one-year-old program of AFDC and its education/work training program, known as JOBS, with block grants to the states over a five-year period for Temporary Assistance to Needy Families (TANF). The Act not only imposed the five-year time limit on the TANF benefits but also required work after two years of benefits. It also required community service after two months of benefits, unless the state administrators agree to an exemption of the rule. Many additional requirements for eligibility were spelled out in the law. And the states are under severe obligation to impose all these requirements on the threat of losing their TANF federal grants.

---

[13]See U.S. House of Representatives, Committee on Ways and Means, *Where Your Money Goes: The 1994–95 Green Book* (Washington, D.C.: Brassey's, 1994) pp. 325, 802.

Since this new welfare law was enacted, the number of families receiving assistance has dropped by 58 percent.[14] Some observers take this as a sign that welfare reform is working; indeed, former welfare recipients have been more successful at finding and keeping jobs than many critics of the new law predicted.

Other additional evidence suggests more caution in declaring welfare reform a success. Early studies show that welfare recipients are not paid enough to pull their families out of poverty and that child care and transportation continue to cause many problems for people seeking to leave welfare.[15] Moreover, one big question remains unanswered: What will happen to former welfare recipients and other low-income workers when there is an economic downturn and fewer jobs are available? Welfare reform was implemented in a time of record low unemployment levels; when employers are less desperate for workers, welfare recipients are more likely to have difficulty finding jobs. These concerns suggest that the 1996 law may not mark the end of welfare reform but may be a prelude to a round of future reforms.

IMPLEMENTING PUBLIC POLICIES: THE TECHNIQUES OF CONTROL

Up to this point, our introduction to public policy has focused on the substance and goals of policies, particularly economic policies. But underlying each substantive policy issue and each policy goal are means and methods for satisfying the substantive demands and for implementing the goals. These are called *techniques of control*. Techniques of control are to policy makers roughly what tools are to a carpenter. There are a limited number of techniques; there is a logic or an orderliness to each of them; and there is an accumulation of experience that helps us know if a certain technique is likely to work. There is no unanimous agreement on technique, just as carpenters will disagree about the best tool for a task. But we offer here a workable elementary handbook of techniques that will be useful for analyzing all policies.

The In Brief Box on page 407 lists important techniques of control available to policy makers. They are grouped into three categories—promotional, regulatory, and redistributive techniques. In this section, the specifics of each will be discussed and explained. Each category of policy is associated with a different kind of politics. In other words, since these techniques are different ways of using government, each type is likely to develop a distinctive pattern of power.

Promotional Techniques

Promotional techniques are the carrots of public policy. Their purpose is to encourage people to do something they might not otherwise do, or to get people to do more of what they are already doing. Sometimes the purpose is merely to compensate people for something done in the past. As the In Brief Box demonstrates, promo-

promotional technique A technique of control that encourages people to do something they might not otherwise do, or to continue an action or behavior. Three types of promotional techniques are subsidies, contracts, and licenses.

---

[14]Ways and Means Committee Print, WMCP: 105–7, *1998 Green Book*, from U.S. GPO Online via GPO Access at www.access.gpo.gov/congress/wm001.html (accessed June 1998).

[15]See National Conference of State Legislatures, "Tracking Recipients after They Leave Welfare," at www.ncsl.org/statefed/welfare/followup.htm (accessed June 1998).

Types of Techniques	Techniques	Definitions and Examples
Promotional techniques	Subsidies and grants of cash, land, etc.	"Patronage" is the promotion of private activity through what recipients consider "benefits" (example: in the nineteenth century the government encouraged westward settlement by granting land to those who went West)
	Contracting	Agreements with individuals or firms in the "private sector" to purchase goods or services
	Licensing	Unconditional permission to do something that is otherwise illegal (franchise, permit)
Regulatory techniques	Criminal penalties	Heavy fines or imprisonment; loss of citizenship
	Civil penalties	Less onerous fines, probation, exposure, restitution
	Administrative regulation	Setting interest rates, maintaining standards of health, investigating and publicizing wrongdoing
	Subsidies, contracting, and licensing	Regulatory techniques when certain conditions are attached (example: the government refuses to award a contract to firms that show no evidence of affirmative action in hiring)
	Regulatory taxation	Taxes that keep consumption or production down (liquor, gas, cigarette taxes)
	Expropriation	"Eminent domain"—the power to take private property for public use
Redistributive techniques	Fiscal use of taxes	Altering the distribution of money by changing taxes or tax rules
	Fiscal use of budgeting	Deficit spending to pump money into the economy when it needs a boost; creating a budget surplus through taxes to discourage consumption in inflationary times
	Fiscal use of credit and interest (monetary techniques)	Changing interest rates to affect both demand for money and consumption. When rates are low it is easy to borrow and thus invest and consume

tional techniques can be classified into at least three separate types—subsidies, contracts, and licenses.

Subsidies *Subsidies* are simply government grants of cash, goods, services, or land. Although subsidies are often denounced as "giveaways," they have played a fundamental role in the history of government in the United States. As we discussed in Chapter 3, subsidies were the dominant form of public policy of the national government throughout the nineteenth century. They continue to be an

subsidies Government grants of cash or other valuable commodities, such as land, to individuals or organizations; used to promote activities desired by the government, to reward political support, or to buy off political opposition.

important category of public policy at all levels of government. The first planning document ever written for the national government, Alexander Hamilton's *Report on Manufactures,* was based almost entirely on Hamilton's assumption that American industry could be encouraged by federal subsidies and that these were not only desirable but constitutional.

The thrust of Hamilton's plan was not lost on later policy makers. Subsidies in the form of land grants were given to farmers and to railroad companies to encourage western settlement. Substantial cash subsidies have traditionally been given to commercial shipbuilders to help build the commercial fleet and to guarantee the use of the ships as military personnel carriers in time of war.

Subsidies have always been a technique favored by politicians because subsidies can be treated as "benefits" that can be doled out in response to many demands that might otherwise produce profound conflict. Subsidies can, in other words, be used to buy off the opposition.

So widespread is the use of the subsidy technique in government that it takes encyclopedias to keep track of them all. Indeed, for a number of years, one company published an annual *Encyclopedia of U.S. Government Benefits,* a thousand-page guide to benefits

> for every American—from all walks of life . . . [R]ight now, there are thousands of other American Taxpayers who are missing out on valuable Government Services, simply because they do not know about them. . . . Start your own business. . . . Take an extra vacation. . . . Here are all the opportunities your tax dollars have made possible.[16]

Another secret of the popularity of subsidies is that those who receive the benefits do not perceive the controls inherent in them. In the first place, most of the resources available for subsidies come from taxation. (In the nineteenth century, there was a lot of public land to distribute, but that is no longer the case.) Second, the effect of any subsidy has to be measured in terms of what people *would be doing* if the subsidy had not been available. For example, many thousands of people settled in lands west of the Mississippi only because land subsidies were available. Hundreds of research laboratories exist in universities and corporations only because certain types of research subsidies from the government are available. And finally, once subsidies exist, the threat of their removal becomes a very significant technique of control.

Contracting   Like any corporation, a government agency must purchase goods and services by contract. The law requires open bidding for a substantial proportion of these contracts because government contracts are extremely valuable to businesses in the private sector and because the opportunities for abuse are great. But contracting is more than a method of buying goods and services. Contracting is also an important technique of policy because government agencies are often authorized to

---

[16]Roy A. Grisham and Paul McConaughty, eds., *Encyclopedia of U.S. Government Benefits* (Union City, N.J.: William H. Wise, 1972). The quote is taken from the dust jacket. A comparable guide published by the *New York Times* is called *Federal Aid for Cities and Towns* (New York: Quadranble Books, 1972). It contains 1,312 pages of federal government benefits that cities and towns, rather than individuals, can apply for.

use their ***contracting power*** as a means of encouraging corporations to improve themselves, as a means of helping to build up whole sectors of the economy, and as a means of encouraging certain desirable goals or behavior, such as equal employment opportunity.

For example, the infant airline industry of the 1930s was nurtured by the national government's lucrative contracts to carry airmail. A more recent example is the use of contracting to encourage industries, universities, and others to engage in research and development.

The power of contracting was of great significance for administrations like those of Reagan and Bush because of their commitment to "privatization." When a presidential administration wants to turn over as much government as possible to the private sector, it may seek to terminate a government program and leave the activity to private companies to pick up. That would be true privatization. But in most instances, true privatization is neither sought nor achieved. Instead, the government program is transferred to a private company to provide the service *under a contract with the government,* paid for by the government, and supervised by a government agency. In this case, privatization is only a euphemism. Government by contract has been around for a long time and has always been seen by business as a major source of economic opportunity.

Licensing A ***license*** is a privilege granted by a government to do something that it otherwise considers to be illegal. For example, state laws make practicing medicine or driving a taxi illegal without a license. The states then create a board of doctors and a "hack bureau" to grant licenses for the practice of medicine or for the operation of a cab to all persons who have met the particular qualifications specified in the statute or by the agency.

Like subsidies and contracting, licensing has two sides. One is the giveaway side, making the license a desirable object of patronage. The other side of licensing is the control or regulatory side.

Regulatory Techniques If promotional techniques are the carrots of public policy, ***regulatory techniques*** are the sticks. Regulation comes in several forms, but every regulatory technique shares a common trait—direct government control of conduct. The conduct—such as drunk driving or false advertising—may be regulated because people feel it is harmful or threatens to be. Or the conduct—such as prostitution, gambling, or drinking—may be regulated because people think it's just plain immoral, whether it's harming anybody or not. Because there are many forms of regulation, we subdivide them here: (1) police regulation, through civil and criminal penalties, (2) administration regulation, and (3) regulatory taxation.

Police Regulation "Police regulation" is not a technical term, but we use it for this category because these techniques come closest to the traditional exercise of ***police power.*** After a person's arrest and conviction, these techniques are administered by courts and, where necessary, penal institutions. They are regulatory techniques.

Civil penalties usually refer to fines or some other form of material restitution (such as public service) as a sanction for violating civil laws or such common law

contracting power The power of government to set conditions on companies seeking to sell goods or services to government agencies.

license Permission to engage in some activity that is otherwise illegal, such as hunting or practicing medicine.

regulatory techniques Techniques that government uses to control the conduct of the people.

police power Power reserved to the state to regulate the health, safety, and morals of its citizens.

principles as negligence. Civil penalties can range from a $5 fine for a parking violation to a heavier penalty for late payment of income taxes to the much more onerous penalties for violating antitrust laws against unfair competition or environmental protection laws against pollution. *Criminal penalties* usually refer to imprisonment but can also involve heavy fines and the loss of certain civil rights and liberties, such as the right to vote or the freedom of speech.

Administrative Regulation Police regulation addresses conduct considered immoral. In order to eliminate such conduct, strict laws have been passed and severe sanctions enacted. But what about conduct that is not considered morally wrong but has harmful consequences? There is, for example, nothing morally wrong with radio or television broadcasting. But broadcasting on a particular frequency or channel is regulated by government because there would be virtual chaos if everybody could broadcast on any frequency at any time.

This kind of conduct is thought of less as *policed* conduct and more as *regulated* conduct. When conduct is said to be regulated, the purpose is rarely to eliminate the conduct but rather to influence it toward more appropriate channels, toward more appropriate locations, or toward certain qualified types of persons, all for the purpose of minimizing injuries or inconveniences. This type of regulated conduct is sometimes called **administrative regulation** because the controls are given over to administrative agencies rather than to the police. Each regulatory agency in the executive branch has extensive powers to keep a sector of the economy under surveillance and also has powers to make rules dealing with the behavior of individual companies and people. But these administrative agencies have fewer powers of punishment than the police and the courts have, and the administrative agencies generally rely on the courts to issue orders enforcing the rules and decisions made by the agencies.

Sometimes a government will adopt administrative regulation if an economic activity is considered so important that it is not to be entrusted to competition among several companies in the private sector. This is the rationale for the regulation of local or regional power companies. A single company, traditionally called a "utility," is given an exclusive license (or franchise) to offer these services, but since the one company is made a legal monopoly and is protected from competition by other companies, the government gives an administrative agency the power to regulate the quality of the services rendered, the rates charged for those services, and the margin of profit that the company is permitted to make.

At other times, administrative regulation is the chosen technique because the legislature decides that the economy needs protection from itself—that is, it may set up a regulatory agency to protect companies from destructive or predatory competition, on the assumption that economic competition is not always its own solution. This is the rationale behind the Federal Trade Commission, which has the responsibility of watching over such practices as price discrimination or pooling agreements between companies when their purpose is to eliminate competitors.

Subsidies, licensing, and contracting are listed twice in the In Brief Box on page 407 because although these techniques can be used strictly as promotional policies, they can also be used as techniques of administrative regulation. It all depends on

administrative regulation Rules made by regulatory agencies and commissions.

whether the law sets serious conditions on eligibility for the subsidy, license, or contract. To put it another way, the threat of losing a valuable subsidy, license, or contract can be used by the government as a sanction to improve compliance with the goals of regulation. For example, the threat of removal of the subsidies called "federal aid to education" has had a very significant influence on the willingness of schools to cooperate in the desegregation of their student bodies and faculties. For another example, social welfare subsidies (benefits) can be lowered to encourage or force people to take low-paying jobs, or they can be increased to placate people when they engage in political protest.[17]

Like subsidies and licensing, government contracting can be an entirely different kind of technique of control when the contract or its denial is used as a reward or punishment to gain obedience in a regulatory program. For example, Presidents Kennedy and Johnson initiated the widespread use of executive orders, administered by the Office of Federal Contract Compliance in the Department of Labor, to prohibit racial discrimination by firms receiving government contracts.[18] The value of these contracts to many private corporations was so great that they were quite willing to alter if not eliminate racial discrimination in employment practices if that was the only way to qualify to bid for government contracts. Today it is common to see on employment advertisements the statement "We are an equal opportunity employer."

Regulatory Taxation   Taxation is generally understood to be a fiscal technique, and it will be discussed as such below. But in many instances, the primary purpose of the tax is not to raise revenue but to discourage or eliminate an activity altogether by making it too expensive for most people. For example, since the end of Prohibition, although there has been no penalty for the production or sale of alcoholic beverages, the alcohol industry has not been free from regulation. First, all alcoholic beverages have to be licensed, allowing only those companies that are "bonded" to put their product on the market. Federal and state taxes on alcohol are also made disproportionately high, on the theory that, in addition to the revenue gained, less alcohol will be consumed.

We may be seeing a great deal more regulation by taxation in the future for at least the following reasons. First, it is a kind of hidden regulation, acceptable to people who in principle are against regulation. Second, it permits a certain amount of choice. For example, a heavy tax on gasoline or on smokestack and chemical industries (called an "effluent tax") will encourage drivers and these companies to regulate their own activities by permitting them to decide how much pollution they can afford. Third, advocates of regulatory taxation believe it to be more efficient than other forms of regulation, requiring less bureaucracy and less supervision.

---

[17]For an evaluation of the policy of withholding subsidies to carry out desegregation laws, see Gary Orfield, *Must We Bus?* (Washington, D.C.: Brookings Institution, 1978). For an evaluation of the use of subsidies to encourage work or to calm political unrest, see Frances Fox Piven and Richard Cloward, *Regulating the Poor: The Functions of Public Welfare* (New York: Random House, 1971).

[18]For an evaluation of Kennedy's use of this kind of executive power, see Carl M. Brauer, *John F. Kennedy and the Second Reconstruction* (New York: Columbia University Press, 1977), especially Chapter 3.

Expropriation Expropriation—seizing private property for a public use—is a widely used technique of control in the United States, especially in land-use regulation. Almost all public works, from highways to parks to government office buildings, involve the forceful taking of some private property in order to assemble sufficient land and the correct distribution of land for the necessary construction. The vast Interstate Highway Program required expropriation of thousands of narrow strips of private land. "Urban redevelopment" projects often require city governments to use the powers of seizure in the service of private developers, who actually build the urban projects on land that would be far too expensive if purchased on the open market. Private utilities that supply electricity and gas to individual subscribers are given powers to take private property whenever a new facility or a right-of-way is needed.

We generally call the power to expropriate eminent domain.[19] The Fifth Amendment of the U.S. Constitution surrounds this expropriation power with important safeguards against abuse, so that government agencies in the United States are not permitted to use that power except through a strict due process, and they must offer "fair market value" for the land sought. Another form of expropriation is forcing individuals to work for a public purpose—for example, drafting people for service in the armed forces.

Redistributive Techniques

Redistributive techniques are usually of two types—fiscal and monetary—but they have a common purpose: to control people by manipulating the entire economy rather than by regulating people directly. As observed earlier, regulatory techniques focus on individual conduct. The regulatory rule may be written to apply to the whole economy: "Walking on the grass is not permitted," or "Membership in a union may not be used to deny employment, nor may a worker be fired for promoting union membership." Nevertheless, the regulation focuses on individual strollers or individual employers who might walk on the grass or discriminate against a trade union member. In contrast, techniques are redistributive if they seek to control conduct more indirectly by altering the conditions of conduct or manipulating the environment of conduct.

Fiscal Techniques Fiscal techniques of control are the government's taxing and spending powers. Personal and corporate income taxes, which raise most government revenues, are the most prominent examples. While the direct purpose of taxes is to raise revenue, each type of tax has a different impact on the economy, and government can plan for that impact. For example, although the main reason given for increasing the Social Security tax (which is an income tax) under President Carter was to keep Social Security solvent, a big reason for it in the minds of many legislators was that it would reduce inflation by shrinking the amount of money people could spend on goods and services.

---

[19]For an evaluation of the politics of eminent domain, see Theodore Lowi, Benjamin Ginsberg, et al., *Poliscide* (New York: Macmillan, 1976 and 1990), especially Chapters 11 and 12, written by Julia and Thomas Vitullo-Martin.

Likewise, President Clinton's commitment in his 1992 campaign to a "middle-class tax cut" was motivated by the goal of encouraging economic growth through increased consumption. Soon after the election, upon learning that the deficit was far larger than had earlier been reported, he had to break his promise of such a tax cut. Nevertheless, the idea of a middle-class tax cut is still an example of a fiscal policy aimed at increased consumption, because of the theory that people in middle-income brackets will tend to spend a high proportion of unexpected earnings or windfalls, rather than saving or investing them.[20]

Monetary Techniques   Monetary techniques also seek to influence conduct by manipulating the entire economy through the supply or availability of money. The Federal Reserve Board (the Fed) can adopt what is called a "hard money policy" by increasing the interest rate it charges member banks (called the discount rate). Another monetary policy is one of increasing or decreasing the reserve requirement, which sets the actual proportion of deposited money that a bank must keep "on demand" as it makes all the rest of the deposits available as new loans. A third important technique used by the Fed is open-market operations—the buying and selling of Treasury securities to absorb excess dollars or to release more dollars into the economy.

Spending Power as Fiscal Policy   Perhaps the most important redistributive technique of all is the most familiar one—the *"spending power"*—which is a combination of subsidies and contracts. These techniques can be used for policy goals far beyond the goods and services bought and the individual conduct regulated.

One of the most important examples of the national government's use of purchasing power as a fiscal or redistributive technique is found in another of the everyday activities of the Federal Reserve Board. As mentioned above, the Fed goes into the "open market" to buy and sell government bonds in order to increase or decrease the amount of money in circulation. By doing so, the Fed can raise or lower the prices paid for goods and the interest rate paid on loans.

CHAPTER REVIEW

Madison set the tone for this chapter in *The Federalist*, No. 51, in three sentences of prose that have more the character of poetry:

> Justice is the end of government.
>   It is the end of civil society.
>   It ever has been and ever will be
>   pursued
>   Until it be obtained,
>   Or until liberty be lost in the pursuit.

---

[20]For a fascinating behind-the-scenes look at how and why President Clinton abandoned his campaign commitment to tax cuts and economic stimulus, and instead accepted the fiscal conservatism advocated by the Federal Reserve and its chair, Alan Greenspan, see Bob Woodward, *The Agenda: Inside the Clinton White House* (New York: Simon & Schuster, 1994).

spending power A combination of subsidies and contracts that the government can use to redistribute income.

Our economic system is the most productive ever developed, but it is not perfect—and many policies have been adopted over the years to deal with its imperfections. Policy is the purposive and deliberate aspect of government in action. But if a policy is to come anywhere near obtaining its stated goal (clean air, stable prices, equal employment opportunity), it must be backed up by some kind of sanction—the ability to reward or punish—coupled with some ability to administer or implement those sanctions. These "techniques of control" were presented in three categories—promotional techniques, regulatory techniques, and redistributive techniques. These techniques are found in the multitude of actual policies adopted by legislatures and implemented by administrative agencies. Good policy analysis consists largely of identifying the techniques of control and choosing the policies that seek to manipulate "the economy as a system."

Promotional techniques are thought to be the carrots of public policy. Government subsidies, government contracts, and licensing are examples of incentives available to government to get people to do things they might not otherwise do, or to do more of what they are already doing. The first part of this chapter examined how promotional techniques are used to promote and maintain the national market economy.

Regulatory techniques seek to control conduct by imposing restrictions and obligations directly on individuals. Although many people complain about regulatory policies, the purpose of most such policies is to benefit the economy by imposing restrictions on companies thought to be engaging in activities harmful to the economy. For example, antitrust policies are intended to benefit economic competition by restricting monopolistic practices. Less popular regulatory policies seek to protect the consumer even if the regulation is an intervention in the economy that reduces competition or efficiency. Laws requiring companies to reduce air and water pollution, laws keeping new drugs off the market, and laws requiring the full labeling of the contents of foods and drugs are examples of such regulatory policies.

Redistributive techniques fall into two groups: fiscal and monetary policies. The government uses redistributive techniques to influence the entire economy, largely in a capitalistic direction. Currency, banks, and credit are heavily shaped by national monetary policies. Taxation, the most important fiscal policy, exists for far more than raising revenue. Taxation is a redistributive policy, which can be either progressive (with higher taxes for upper than for lower incomes) or regressive (applying one rate to all and therefore taking a higher percentage tax from the lowest brackets). Various exemptions, deductions, and investment credits are written into taxes to encourage desired behavior, such as more investment or more saving versus more consumption.

The capitalist system is the most productive type of economy on earth, but it is not perfect. Poverty amidst plenty continues. Many policies have emerged to deal with these imperfections. A part of this chapter discussed the welfare state and gave an account of how Americans came to recognize extremes of poverty and dependency and how Congress then attempted to reduce these extremes with policies that moderately redistribute resources.

Welfare state policies are subdivided into several categories. First there are the contributory programs. Virtually all employed persons are required to contribute a portion of their wages into welfare trust funds, and later on, when they retire or are disabled, they have a right, or entitlement, to draw on those contributions. Another category of welfare is composed of noncontributory programs, also called public assistance. These programs provide benefits for people who can demonstrate need by passing a means test. Assistance from contributory and noncontributory programs can involve either cash benefits or in-kind benefits.

FOR FURTHER READING

Barth, James, Gerard Caprio, and Ross Levine. *Rethinking Bank Regulation*. New York: Cambridge University Press, 2005.

Beland, Daniel. *Social Security: History and Politics from the New Deal to the Privatization Debate*. Lawrence: University Press of Kansas, 2007.   ○ ONLINE READING

Ehrenreich, Barbara. *Nickel and Dimed: On (Not) Getting By in America*. New York: Holt, 2001.

Epsing-Andersen, Gosta. *Why We Need a New Welfare State*. New York: Oxford University Press, 2002.

Farrier, Jasmine. *Passing the Buck: Congress, the Budget, and Deficits*. Lexington: University Press of Kentucky, 2004.   ○ ONLINE READING

Gilbert, Neil. *Transformation of the Welfare State*. New York: Oxford University Press, 2004.

Hacker, Jacob. *The Divided Welfare State: The Battle over Public and Private Social Benefits in the United States*. New York: Cambridge University Press, 2002.   ○ ONLINE READING

Ingham, Geoffrey. *The Nature of Money*. New York: Polity, 2004.

Keith, Robert, and Allen Schick. *The Federal Budget Process*. New York: Nova, 2003.

Meyers, Annette. *Evolution of United States Budgeting*. New York: Praeger, 2002.

Murray, Charles. *In Our Hands: A Plan to Remake the Welfare State*. Washington, D.C.: American Enterprise Institute Press, 2006.   ○ ONLINE READING

Sachs, Jeffrey. *The End of Poverty: Economic Possibilities for Our Time*. New York: Penguin, 2006.

Shipler, David. *The Working Poor*. New York: Vintage, 2005.

Skocpol, Theda. *The Missing Middle: Working Families and the Future of American Social Policy*. New York: Norton, 2000.   ○ ONLINE READING

Stern, Gary, and Ron Feldman. *Too Big to Fail: The Hazards of Bank Bailouts*. Washington, D.C.: Brookings Institution, 2004.

Stiglitz, Joseph. *Making Globalization Work*. New York: Norton, 2006.   ○ ONLINE READING

Trattner, Walter. *From Poor Law to Welfare State*. 6th ed. New York: Free Press, 1998.

Weir, Margaret, ed. *The Social Divide: Political Parties and the Future of Activist Government*. Washington, D.C.: Brookings Institution, 1998.

Wells, Donald. *The Federal Reserve System*. Jefferson, N.C.: McFarland, 2004.

Wilson, Graham. *Business and Politics*. Washington, D.C.: Congressional Quarterly Press, 2003.

Foreign Policy and Democracy

HOW DOES FOREIGN POLICY WORK?

At first glance, the basic contours of the foreign-policy arena seem similar to those of America's other policy domains. The nation's chief foreign-policy makers are the president, Congress, and the bureaucracy. Just as in the cases of economic and social policy, battles over foreign policy often erupt between and within these institutions as competing politicians and a variety of organized groups and rival political forces pursue their own version of the national interest or their own more narrow purposes, which they seek to present as the national interest. In many instances, the outcome of these battles among competing forces depends on the rela-

---

● Core of the Analysis

● All foreign policies must be made and implemented in the name of the president.

● Certain values—fear of centralized power and of foreign entanglements—have traditionally shaped American foreign policy; today these values find expression in the intermingling of domestic and foreign policy institutions and the tendency toward unilateralism.

● American foreign policy is carried out through certain instruments, including diplomacy, the United Nations, the international monetary structure, economic aid, collective security, and military deterrence.

● In the conduct of foreign policy, nations can play one of several roles: the Napoleonic role, the Holy Alliance role, the balance-of-power role, and the economic expansionist role.

● The United States plays different roles in foreign affairs, depending on what it seeks to achieve in a particular situation; the Holy Alliance role seems to be the most typical American role in the post–cold war era.

tive power of the institutions they control. Institutions affect foreign as well as domestic policy outcomes. In the foreign-policy arena, the institutional powers of the presidency give presidents and their allies an advantage over political forces based in Congress, although Congress is not without institutional resources of its own through which to influence the conduct of foreign policy. Moreover, like domestic-policy matters, foreign-policy issues often figure prominently in public debate and national election campaigns as competing forces seek to mobilize popular support for their positions or at least to castigate the opposition for the putative shortcomings of its policies.

Despite these similarities, the foreign- and domestic-policy arenas differ in at least three important ways. The first is history. History always matters, but history and historical memory play a larger role in the foreign-policy realm than in most areas of domestic policy. Foreign policy, as we shall see, is guided by historical events, experiences, and commitments. Debates over foreign policy tend to be strongly affected by competing historical perceptions. For example, those who argue in favor of confronting Iran, North Korea, and other potentially hostile powers often refer to the disastrous consequences of pre–World War II efforts by Britain and France to "appease" Nazi Germany. On the other hand, those who favor withdrawing American forces from Iraq cite the parallels to America's failed efforts in Vietnam. Each group's view of the present is strongly shaped by its understanding of the past.

Second, in the foreign-policy arena, questions of the national interest figure more prominently than in most domestic-policy debates. To be sure, advocates of competing social and economic policies argue that their preferred programs promote the interests of the nation as a whole. Yet such pronouncements are usually taken with a grain of salt, and we are usually prepared to forgive advocates whose preferred economic or social policies turn out to serve discrete constituencies rather than the entire nation. In the realm of foreign policy, though, the public interest looms larger. In a world where entities ranging from rival nation-states to shadowy terrorist goups present genuine threats to the security of the entire nation, advocates of particular foreign policies are more likely than their domestic counterparts to be asked to demonstrate that the policies they espouse serve broad national interests. In the realm of foreign policy, unlike, say, the arena of health-care reform, advocates can and do accuse one another of threatening the nation's security and demonstrating outright disloyalty.

Finally, the foreign-policy arena is affected by America's historic wariness of foreign commitments and the difficulties of making and justifying what are often cold, harsh, calculating foreign-policy decisions in a democratic context. Ever since George Washington, in his Farewell Address, warned the American people "to have . . . as little political connection as possible" to foreign nations and to "steer clear of permanent alliances," Americans have been distrustful of foreign policy. Despite this distrust, the United States has been forced to pursue its national interests in the world, even when this has meant fighting a war. As a result of its foreign entanglements, the United States emerged as a world power, but not without maintaining some misgivings about foreign policy.

Who Makes and Shapes Foreign Policy?

The President   The terrorist attacks of September 11, 2001, accentuated the president's role and place in foreign policy immensely. Congress's first action after the attacks was to approve virtually unanimously in both the House and Senate an authorization for the president to use "all necessary and appropriate force," coupled with a $40 billion emergency appropriation bill for home defense and reconstruction. Significant as this was, however, it only emphasized what was already true—that the president is our head of state and the epicenter of foreign policy (see Table 14.1). Although many foreign policy decisions can be made without the president's approval, these decisions must be made and implemented in the name of the president. This is not simply a matter of American preference. It is in the nature of international relations that all foreign policies must come from the president as head of state.

The Bureaucracy   The major foreign policy players in the bureaucracy are the secretaries of the departments of state, defense, and the treasury; the Joint Chiefs of Staff (JCOS), especially the chair of the JCOS; and the director of the Central Intelligence Agency (CIA). A separate unit in the bureaucracy comprising these people and a few others is the National Security Council (NSC), whose main purpose is to iron out the differences among the key players and to integrate their positions in order to confirm or reinforce a decision the president wants to make in foreign policy or military policy. The secretary of commerce has also become an increasingly important foreign-policy maker, with the rise and spread of economic globalization.

To this group another has been added: the Department of Homeland Security. The department has four main divisions: Border and Transportation Security; Emergency Preparedness and Response; Chemical, Biological, Radiological, and Nuclear Countermeasures; and Information Analysis and Infrastructure Protection.

Coordinating the diverse missions of a single agency is a challenge; coordinating the efforts of multiple agencies is especially problematic. The National Security Council and now the Department of Homeland Security attempt to keep the various players on the same page. But will these agencies—each with their own authority, interests, and priorities—follow the same protocol?

In addition to top cabinet-level officials, key lower-level staff members have policy-making influence as strong as that of the cabinet secretaries—some may occasionally exceed cabinet influence. These include the two or three specialized national security advisors in the White House, the staff of the NSC (headed by the national security advisor), and a few other career bureaucrats in the departments of state and defense whose influence varies according to their specialty and to the foreign policy issue at hand.

Congress   In foreign policy, Congress has to be subdivided into three parts. The first part is the Senate. For most of American history, the Senate was the only important congressional foreign policy player because of its constitutional role in reviewing and approving treaties. The treaty power is still the primary entrée of the Senate into foreign-policy making. But since World War II and the continual involvement of the United States in international security and foreign aid, Congress as a whole

TABLE 14.1 Presidential and Congressional Powers and Roles in Foreign Policy

Power	Constitutional Provision		Informal Roles	
	President	Congress	President	Congress
War power	Acts as commander in chief	Declares war, provides for the "common defense"	Makes preemptive military commitments, threatens war, makes secret agreements	Refuses to appropriate funds, investigates and exposes, threatens to impeach
Treaty power	Negotiates treaties	Ratifies treaties (by two-thirds vote in Senate)	Makes executive agreements	Issues resolutions condemning the refusal to appropriate funds
Appointment power	Selects and nominates ambassadors	Approves appointment of ambassadors (by majority vote in Senate)	Makes recess appointments	Issues resolutions condemning appointments, rejects later appointments
Foreign commerce power	Negotiates treaties	Regulates foreign commerce	Makes executive agreements, requests foreign aid	Cuts or reduces aid
Recognition power	Receives ambassadors	Has no explicit powers	Makes friendly visits, conducts negotiations	Makes symbolic visits, issues resolutions

has become a major foreign-policy maker because most modern foreign policies require financing, which requires approval from both the House of Representatives and the Senate. Congress has also become increasingly involved in foreign-policy making because of the increasing use by the president of *executive agreements* to conduct foreign policy. Executive agreements have the force of treaties but do not require prior approval by the Senate. They can, however, be revoked by action of both chambers of Congress.

The third congressional player is the foreign-policy and military policy committees: in the Senate these are the Foreign Relations Committee and the Armed Services Committee; in the House, these are the International Affairs Committee and the Armed Services Committee. Usually, a few members of these committees who have spent years specializing in foreign affairs become trusted members of the foreign-policy establishment and are actually makers rather than mere shapers of

executive agreement
Agreement between the president and another country, which has the force of a treaty but does not require the Senate's "advice and consent."

foreign policy. In fact, several members of Congress have left to become key foreign affairs cabinet members.[1]

Interest Groups   Far and away the most important category of nonofficial player is the interest group—that is, the interest groups to whom one or more foreign-policy issues are of long-standing and vital relevance. The type of interest group with the reputation for the most influence is the economic interest group. Yet the heft of the myths about their influence far outweighs the reality. The influence of organized economic interest groups in foreign policy varies enormously from issue to issue and year to year. Most of these groups are "single-issue" groups and are therefore most active when their particular issue is on the agenda. On many of the broader and more sustained policy issues, such as the North American Free Trade Agreement (NAFTA) or the general question of American involvement in international trade, the larger interest groups find it difficult to maintain tight enough control of their many members to speak with a single voice. The most systematic study of international trade policies and their interest groups concluded that the leaders of these large, economic interest groups spend more time maintaining consensus among their members than lobbying Congress or pressuring major players in the executive branch.[2] The economic interest groups more successful in influencing foreign policy are the narrower, single-issue groups such as the tobacco industry, which over the years has successfully kept American foreign policy from putting heavy restrictions on international trade in and advertising of tobacco products. Likewise, computer hardware and software industries have successfully hardened the American attitude toward Chinese piracy of intellectual property rights.

Another type of interest group with a well-founded reputation for influence in foreign policy is made up of people with strong attachments and identifications to their country of origin. The interest group with the reputation for greatest influence is Jewish Americans, some of whom maintain family and emotional ties to Israel that may make them particularly concerned with U.S. policies toward Israel. Similarly, some Americans of Irish heritage, despite having resided in the United States for two, three, or four generations, still maintain a vigilance about American policies toward Ireland and Northern Ireland. Many other ethnic and national interest groups wield similar influence over American foreign policy.

A third type of interest group, one with a reputation that has been growing in the past two decades, is the human rights interest group. Such groups are made up of people who, instead of having self-serving economic or ethnic interests in foreign policy, are genuinely concerned for the welfare and treatment of people throughout the world—particularly those who suffer under harsh political regimes. A relatively small but often quite influential example is Amnesty International, whose exposés of human rights abuses have altered the practices of many regimes around the

---

[1]For example, under President Clinton, Senator Lloyd Bentsen and Representative Les Aspin left Congress to become the secretaries of the treasury and defense, respectively.

[2]Raymond A. Bauer, Ithiel de Sola Pool, and Lewis Anthony Dexter, *American Business and Public Policy: The Politics of Foreign Trade*, 2nd ed. (Chicago: Aldine-Atherton, 1972).

Makers

the president

the bureaucracy (secretaries of state, defense, and the treasury; the Joint Chiefs of Staff, and the director of the Central Intelligence Agency)

Congress (Senate approves treaties; both chambers vote on financing; foreign-policy and military policy committees in each chamber)

Shapers

interest groups (economic, cultural/ethnic groups, human rights groups, environmental groups)

the media

world. In recent years, the Christian Right has also been a vocal advocate for the human rights of Christians who are persecuted in other parts of the world, most notably in China, for their religious beliefs. For example, the Christian Coalition joined groups like Amnesty International in lobbying Congress to cut trade with countries that permit attacks against religious believers.

A related type of group with a fast-growing influence is the ecological or environmental group, sometimes called the "greens." Groups of this nature often depend more on demonstrations than on the usual forms and strategies of influence in Washington—lobbying and using electoral politics, for example. Demonstrations in strategically located areas can have significant influence on American foreign policy. Recent important examples were the demonstrations against the World Trade Organization (WTO) and its authority to impose limits and restrictions on sovereign nations, even in the United States, such as the 1999 protests in Seattle, Washington, and the 2005 protest in Hong Kong.

The Media The most important element of the policy influence of the media is the speed and scale with which the media can spread political communications. In that factor alone, the media's influence is growing—more news reaches more people faster, and people's reaction times are therefore shorter than ever before. When we combine this ability to communicate faster with the "feedback" medium of public opinion polling, it becomes clear how the media have become so influential—they enable the American people to reach the president and the other official makers of foreign policy.[3]

---

[3]For further discussion of the vulnerability of modern presidents to the people through the media, see Theodore Lowi, *The Personal President: Power Invested, Promise Unfulfilled* (Ithaca, N.Y.: Cornell University Press, 1985); Jeffrey K. Tulis, *The Rhetorical Presidency* (Princeton, N.J.: Princeton University Press, 1987); Samuel Kernell, *Going Public: New Strategies of Presidential Leadership* (Washington, D.C.: Congressional Quarterly Press, 1986); Richard Rose, *The Postmodern President: The White House Meets the World* (Chatham, N.J.: Chatham House, 1988); and George C. Edwards, *The Public Presidency: The Pursuit of Popular Support* (New York: St. Martin's, 1983).

Putting It Together

What can we say about who really makes American foreign policy? First, except for the president, the influence of players and shapers varies from case to case—this is a good reason to look with some care at each example of foreign policy in this chapter. Second, since the one constant influence is the centrality of the president in foreign-policy making, it is best to evaluate other actors and factors as they interact with the president.[4] Third, the reason influence varies from case to case is that each case arises under different conditions and with vastly different constraints: for issues that arise and are resolved quickly, the opportunity for influence is limited. Fourth, foreign-policy experts will usually disagree about the level of influence any player or type of player has on policy making.

But just to get started, let's make a few tentative generalizations and then put them to the test with the substance and experience reported in the remainder of this chapter. First, when an important foreign-policy decision has to be made under conditions of crisis—where "time is of the essence"—the influence of the presidency is at its strongest. Second, under those time constraints, access to the decision-making process is limited almost exclusively to the narrowest definition of the "foreign-policy establishment." The arena for participation is tiny; any discussion at all is limited to the officially and constitutionally designated players. To put this another way, in a crisis, the foreign-policy establishment works as it is supposed to.[5] As time becomes less restricted, even when the decision to be made is of great importance, the arena of participation expands to include more government players and more nonofficial, informal players—the most concerned interest groups and the most important journalists. In other words, the arena becomes more pluralistic, and therefore less distinguishable from the politics of domestic policy making. Third, because there are so many other countries with power and interests on any given issue, there are severe limits on the choices the United States can make. As one author concludes, in foreign affairs, "policy takes precedence over politics."[6] Thus, even though foreign-policy making in noncrisis situations may more closely resemble the pluralistic politics of domestic policy making, foreign-policy making is still a narrower arena with few participants.

THE VALUES OF AMERICAN FOREIGN POLICY

When President Washington was preparing to leave office in 1796, he crafted with great care, and with the help of Alexander Hamilton and James Madison, a farewell

---

ONLINE READING

[4]A very good brief outline of the centrality of the president in foreign policy will be found in Paul E. Peterson, "The President's Dominance in Foreign Policy Making," *Political Science Quarterly* 109, no. 2 (Summer 1994), pp. 215, 234.

[5]One confirmation of this will be found in Theodore Lowi, *The End of Liberalism*, 2nd ed. (New York: Norton, 1979), pp. 127–30; another will be found in Stephen Krasner, "Are Bureaucracies Important?" *Foreign Policy* 7 (Summer 1972), pp. 159–79. However, it should be added that Krasner was writing his article in disagreement with Graham T. Allison, "Conceptual Models and the Cuban Missile Crisis," *American Political Science Review* 63, no. 3 (September 1969), pp. 689–718.

[6]Peterson, "The President's Dominance in Foreign Policy Making," p. 232.

address that is one of the most memorable documents in American history. In it, one of Washington's greater concerns was to warn the nation against foreign influence:

> History and experience prove that foreign influence is one of the most baneful foes of republican government. . . . The great rule of conduct for us in regard to foreign nations is, in extending our commercial relations to have with them as little political connection as possible. So far as we have already formed engagements let them be fulfilled with perfect good faith. Here let us stop. . . . There can be no greater error than to expect or calculate upon real favors from nation to nation. . . . Trust to temporary alliances for extraordinary emergencies, [but in all other instances] steer clear of permanent alliances with any portion of the foreign world. . . . Such an attachment of a small or weak toward a great and powerful nation dooms the former to be the satellite of the latter.[7]

With the exception of a few leaders such as Thomas Jefferson and Thomas Paine, who were eager to take sides with the French against all others, Washington was probably expressing sentiments shared by most Americans. In fact, during most of the nineteenth century, American foreign policy was to a large extent no foreign policy. But Americans were never isolationist, if isolationism means the refusal to have any associations with the outside world. Americans were eager for trade and for treaties and contracts facilitating trade. Americans were also expansionists, but their vision of expansionism was limited to the North American continent.

Three familiar historical factors help explain why Washington's sentiments became the tradition and the source of American foreign-policy values. The first was the deep antistatist ideology shared by most Americans in the nineteenth century and into the twentieth century. Although we witness widespread antistatism today, in the form of calls for tax cuts, deregulation, privatization, and other efforts to "get the government off our backs," such sentiments were far more intense in the past, when many Americans opposed foreign entanglements, a professional military, and secret diplomacy. The second factor was federalism. The third was the position of the United States in the world as a ***client state*** (a state that has the capacity to carry out its own foreign policy most of the time but still depends on the interests of one or more of the major powers). Most nineteenth-century Americans recognized that if the United States became entangled in foreign affairs, national power would naturally grow at the expense of the states, and so would the presidency at the expense of Congress. Why? Because foreign policy meant having a professional diplomatic corps, professional armed forces with a general staff—and secrets. This meant professionalism, elitism, and remoteness from citizens. Being a client state gave Americans the luxury of being able to keep its foreign policy to a minimum. Moreover,

client state A nation-state dependent upon a more powerful nation-state but still with enough power and resources to conduct its own foreign policy up to a point.

---

[7]A full version of the text of the farewell address, along with a discussion of the contribution to it made by Hamilton and Madison, will be found in Daniel J. Boorstin, ed., *An American Primer* (Chicago: University of Chicago Press, 1966), vol. 1, pp. 192–210. This editing is by Richard B. Morris.

maintaining American sovereignty was in the interest of the European powers, because it prevented any one of them from gaining an advantage over the others in the Western Hemisphere.

Legacies of the Traditional System

Two identifiable legacies flowed from the long tradition based on antistatism, federalism, and client status. One is the intermingling of domestic and foreign policy institutions. The second is unilateralism—America's willingness to go it alone. Each of these reveals a great deal about the values behind today's conduct of foreign policy.

Intermingling of Domestic and Foreign Policy   Because the major European powers once policed the world, American political leaders could treat foreign policy as a mere extension of domestic policy. The *tariff* is the best example. A tax on one category of imported goods as a favor to interests in one section of the country would directly cause friction elsewhere in the country. But the demands of those adversely affected could be met without directly compromising the original tariff, by adding a tariff to still other goods that would placate those who were complaining about the original tariff. In this manner, Congress was continually adding and adjusting tariffs on more and more classes of commodities.

An important aspect of the treatment of foreign affairs as an extension of domestic policy was amateurism. Unlike many other countries, Americans refused to develop a tradition of a separate foreign service composed of professional people who spent much of their adult lives in foreign countries, learning foreign languages, absorbing foreign cultures, and developing a sympathy for foreign points of view. Instead, Americans have tended to be highly suspicious of any American diplomat or entrepreneur who spoke sympathetically of any such foreign viewpoints.[8] No systematic progress was made to create a professional diplomatic corps until after the passage of the Foreign Service Act of 1946.

Unilateralism   Unilateralism, not isolationism, was the American posture toward the world until the middle of the twentieth century. Isolationism means to try to cut off contacts with the outside, to be a self-sufficient fortress. America was never isolationist; it preferred *unilateralism,* or "going it alone." Americans have always been more likely to rally around the president in support of direct action rather than sustained, diplomatic involvement.

The Great Leap to World Power

The traditional era of U.S. foreign policy came to an end with World War I for several important reasons. First, the "balance of power" system[9] that had kept the

tariff A tax placed on imported goods.

unilateralism A foreign policy that seeks to avoid international alliances, entanglements, and permanent commitments in favor of independence, neutrality, and freedom of action.

---

[8]E. E. Schattschneider, *Politics, Pressures, and the Tariff* (Englewood Cliffs, N.J.: Prentice-Hall, 1935).

[9]"Balance of power" was the primary foreign policy role played by the major European powers during the nineteenth century, and it is a role available to the United States in contemporary foreign affairs, a role occasionally adopted but not on a world scale. This is the third of the four roles identified and discussed later in this chapter.

major European powers from world war for a hundred years had collapsed.[10] In fact, the great powers themselves had collapsed internally. The most devastating of all wars up to that time had ruined their economies, their empires, and, in most cases, their political systems. Second, the United States was no longer a client state but in fact one of the great powers. Third, as we saw in earlier chapters, the United States was soon to shed its traditional domestic system of federalism with its national government of almost pure promotional policy. Thus, virtually all the conditions that contributed to the traditional system of American foreign policy had disappeared. Yet there was no discernible change in America's approach to foreign policy in the period between World War I and World War II. After World War I, as one foreign-policy analyst put it, "the United States withdrew once more into its insularity. Since America was unwilling to use its power, that power, for purposes of foreign policy, did not really exist."[11]

The great leap in foreign policy was finally made thirty years after conditions demanded it and only after another world war. Following World War II, pressure for a new tradition came into direct conflict with the old. The new tradition required foreign entanglements; the old tradition feared them deeply. The new tradition required diplomacy; the old distrusted it. The new tradition required acceptance of antagonistic political systems; the old embraced democracy and was aloof from all else.

The values of the new tradition were all apparent during the ***cold war.*** Instead of unilateralism, the United States pursued ***multilateralism,*** entering into treaties with other nations to achieve its foreign policy goals. The most notable of these treaties is the one that formed the ***North Atlantic Treaty Organization (NATO)*** in 1949, which allied the United States, Canada, and most of Western Europe. With its NATO allies, the United States practiced a two-pronged policy in dealing with its rival, the Soviet Union: ***containment*** and ***deterrence.*** Fearing that the Soviet Union was bent on world domination, the United States fought wars in Korea and Vietnam to "contain" Soviet power. And in order to deter a direct attack against itself or its NATO allies, the United States developed a multibillion-dollar nuclear arsenal capable of destroying the Soviet Union many times over.

An arms race between the United States and the Soviet Union was extremely difficult if not impossible to resist because there was no way for either side to know when they had enough deterrent power to continue preventing aggression by the other side. The cold war ended abruptly in 1989 after the Soviet Union had spent itself into oblivion and allowed its empire to collapse. Many observers called the end of the cold war a victory for democracy. But more important, it was a victory for capitalism over communism, a vindication of the free market as the best way to produce the greatest wealth of nations. Furthering capitalism has long been one of the values guiding American foreign policy and this might be more true at the beginning of the twenty-first century than at any time before.

---

[10] The best analysis of what he calls the "100 years' peace" will be found in Karl Polanyi, *The Great Transformation* (New York: Rinehart, 1944; Beacon paperback ed., 1957), pp. 5ff.

[11] John G. Stoessinger, *Crusaders and Pragmatists: Movers of Modern American Foreign Policy* (New York: Norton, 1985), pp. 21, 34.

cold war The period of struggle between the United States and the former Soviet Union between the late 1940s and 1990.

multilateralism A foreign policy that seeks to encourage the involvement of several nation-states in coordinated action, usually in relation to a common adversary, with terms and conditions usually specified in a multicountry treaty, such as NATO.

North Atlantic Treaty Organization (NATO) A treaty organization comprising the United States, Canada, and most of Western Europe, formed in 1948 to counter the perceived threat from the Soviet Union.

containment The policy used by the United States during the cold war to restrict the expansion of communism and limit the influence of the Soviet Union.

deterrence The development and maintenance of military strength as a means of discouraging attack.

THE INSTRUMENTS OF MODERN AMERICAN FOREIGN POLICY

Any nation-state has at hand certain instruments, or tools, to use in implementing its foreign policy. Any instrument is neutral, capable of serving many goals. There have been many instruments of American foreign policy, and we can deal here only with those instruments we deem to be most important in the modern epoch: diplomacy, the United Nations, the international monetary structure, economic aid, collective security, and military deterrence. Each of these instruments will be evaluated in this section for its utility in the conduct of American foreign policy, and each will be assessed in light of the history and development of American values.

Diplomacy

We begin this treatment of instruments with diplomacy because it is the instrument to which all other instruments should be subordinated, although they seldom are. ***Diplomacy*** is the representation of a government to other foreign governments. Its purpose is to promote national values or interests by peaceful means. According to Hans Morgenthau, "a diplomacy that ends in war has failed in its primary objective."[12]

The first effort to create a modern diplomatic service in the United States was made through the Rogers Act of 1924, which established the initial framework for a professional foreign-service staff. But it took World War II and the Foreign Service Act of 1946 to forge the foreign service into a fully professional diplomatic corps.

Diplomacy, by its very nature, is overshadowed by spectacular international events, dramatic initiatives, and meetings among heads of state or their direct personal representatives. The traditional American distrust of diplomacy continues today, albeit in weaker form. Impatience with or downright distrust of diplomacy has been built not only into all the other instruments of foreign policy but also into the modern presidential system itself.[13] So much personal responsibility has been heaped upon the presidency that it is difficult for presidents to entrust any of their authority or responsibility in foreign policy to professional diplomats in the state department and other bureaucracies. And the American practice of appointing political friends and campaign donors to major ambassadorial positions does not inspire trust.

Distrust of diplomacy has also produced a tendency among all recent presidents to turn frequently to military and civilian personnel outside the state department to take on a special diplomatic role as direct personal representatives of the president. As discouraging as it is to those who have dedicated their careers to foreign service to have political hacks appointed over their heads, it is probably even more discouraging when they are displaced from a foreign-policy issue as soon as relations with the country they are posted in begin to heat up. When a special personal representative is sent abroad to represent the president, that envoy holds a status higher than that of the local ambassador, and the embassy becomes the envoy's

---

diplomacy The representation of a government to other foreign governments.

[12]Hans Morgenthau, *Politics among Nations*, 2nd ed. (New York: Knopf, 1956), p. 505.

[13]See Lowi, *The Personal President*, pp. 167–69.

temporary residence and base of operation. Despite the impressive professionalization of the American foreign service—with advanced training, competitive exams, language requirements, and career commitment—this practice of displacing career ambassadors with political appointees and special personal presidential representatives continues.

For instance, when President Clinton in 1998 sought to boost the peace process in Northern Ireland, he called on former senator George Mitchell. Mitchell received almost unanimous praise for his skill and patience in chairing the Northern Ireland peace talks. The caliber of his work in Northern Ireland led to Senator Mitchell's becoming involved in another of the world's apparently unsolvable conflicts, that between the Israelis and the Palestinians.

Despite the United States' track record of distrusting diplomacy, immediately following September 11, 2001, questions arose about how the United States could go after terrorist networks without the active cooperation of dozens of governments. Getting access to terrorists in various countries, plus assembling and keeping together the worldwide alliance of governments necessary to fight terrorism was a diplomatic, not a military, chore. In calls to more than eighty nations, then-Secretary of State Colin Powell helped to extract dozens of pledges that would have been more difficult to get months later, when worldwide sympathy for America would have waned. In short, global unity and success fighting terrorism required constant diplomatic efforts on the part of Powell and the State Department, as well as other leading players including President Bush himself. Diplomacy began losing its promise by the summer of 2002, with the increasing strength of the Bush doctrine, which asserted a national right and determination to engage in preemptive attacks when and where our vital interests are at stake. This meant that Powell's diplomatic approach to multilateral containment of terrorism was losing out to a more military-driven approach, led by Vice President Cheney, Secretary of Defense Rumsfeld, a host of highly committed deputy and assistant secretaries of defense, and the influential national security adviser, Condoleezza Rice, who would replace Powell as secretary of state after the 2004 election. The Bush doctrine contributed to the decision by many allied powers to resist entering an alliance against Iraq that would, in their opinion, almost certainly end in "preemptive war."

The significance of diplomacy and its vulnerability to domestic politics may be better appreciated as we consider the other instruments. Diplomacy was an instrument more or less imposed on Americans as the prevailing method of dealing among nation-states in the nineteenth century. The other instruments to be identified and assessed are instruments that Americans self-consciously crafted for themselves to take care of their chosen place in world affairs in the second half of the twentieth century. They are, therefore, more reflective of American culture and values than is diplomacy.

The United Nations

The utility of the **United Nations (UN)** to the United States as an instrument of foreign policy can too easily be underestimated. During the first decade or more after its founding in 1945, the United Nations was a direct servant of American interests. The most spectacular example of the use of the United Nations as an instrument of

United Nations (UN)
The organization of nations founded in 1945, mainly to serve as a channel for negotiation and a means of settling international disputes peaceably. It has had frequent successes in providing a forum for negotiation and on some occasions a means of preventing international conflicts from spreading. On a number of occasions, the UN has been a convenient cover for U.S. foreign-policy goals.

American foreign policy was the official UN authorization and sponsorship of intervention in Korea with an international "peacekeeping force" in 1950. Thanks to the Soviet boycott of the United Nations at that time, which deprived the U.S.S.R. of its ability to use its veto in the Security Council of the UN, the United States was able to conduct the Korean War under the auspices of the United Nations.

As the cold war intensified with the Bay of Pigs, the Cuban Missile Crisis, and then the Vietnam War, the UN became more of a domestic political issue. For example, in 1960, over 60 percent of the American public, when polled, were of the opinion that the UN was "doing a good job." By 1970, this positive support had dropped to just over 30 percent. And although positive opinion was climbing for a while in the 1990s, negative opinion (that the UN was doing a poor job) had climbed from a low of 10 percent in 1960 to highs of 50 percent in the '70s and '80s, fluctuating around the 40-plus percent level in the '90s. The main factor behind those variations in public opinion support was probably the involvement of U.S. armed forces in peace*keeping* missions and (especially) peace *enforcing* missions, including instances where our troops were under foreign command. This does not sit well with many Americans or their representatives in Congress, even though U.S. troops have served under foreign command in World War I, World War II, and some earlier cold war involvements. These were some of the reasons for Congress's decision in 1993 to refuse to pay our UN dues until the UN "met certain conditions." The precise amount of our UN debt is in dispute, but most estimates put it close to $1.5 billion in 1999—making us, according to the *New York Times,* the world's "biggest deadbeat."[14]

In 1999, Congress authorized payment of $926 million of its acknowledged debt to the UN in three installments, whenever the Secretary of State determines that the UN has met various conditions, including reform of UN management and reduction of our annual dues. In addition to the $926 million, Congress agreed to forgive $107 million the UN allegedly owes the United States. Regular U.S. dues for the UN organization budget, which had been 40 percent in 1946 (the first full year of operation), were reduced in 2001 from 25 percent to 22 percent. U.S. dues for peacekeeping were reduced from over 30 percent to 25 percent.[15]

The United Nations gained a new lease on life in the post–cold war era, first with its performance in the 1991 Gulf War. Although President Bush's immediate reaction to Iraq's invasion of Kuwait was unilateral, he quickly turned to the UN for sponsorship. The UN General Assembly immediately adopted resolutions condemning the invasion and approving the full blockade of Iraq. Once the blockade was seen as having failed to achieve the unconditional withdrawal demanded by the UN, the General Assembly adopted further resolutions authorizing the twenty-nine-nation coalition to use force if, by January 15, 1991, the resolutions were not ob-

---

[14] This paragraph owes a great deal to Bruce Jentleson, *American Foreign Policy—The Dynamics of Choice in the 21st Century* (New York: Norton, 2000), pp. 237–45.

[15] In 1997, the next five biggest dues payers were Japan (16.0%), Germany (9.0%), France (6.7%), the United Kingdom (5.6%), and the Russian Federation (4.4%). These figures are neither up-to-date nor precise, but they do give an accurate impression of the relative contribution made to the financing of the United Nations and its various commissions, committees, and diplomatic peacekeeping activities.

served. The Gulf War victory was a genuine UN victory. The cost of the operation was estimated at $61.6 billion. First authorized by Congress, actual U.S. outlays were offset by pledges from the other participants—the largest shares coming from Saudi Arabia ($15.6 billion), Kuwait ($16 billion), Japan ($10 billion), and Germany ($6.5 billion). The final U.S. costs were estimated at a maximum of $8 billion.[16]

Whether or not the UN is able to maintain its central position in future border and trade disputes, demands for self-determination, and other provocations to war depend entirely upon the character of each dispute. The Gulf War was a special case because it was a clear instance of invasion of one country by another that also threatened the control of oil, which is of vital interest to the industrial countries of the world. But in the case of the former Yugoslavia, although the Bosnian conflict violated the world's conscience, it did not threaten vital national interests outside the country's region.

When Yugoslavia's communist regime collapsed in the early 1990s, the country broke apart into historically ethnically distinct regions. In one of these, Bosnia, a fierce war broke out among Muslims, Croatians, and Serbians. From the outset, all outside parties urged peace, and United Nations troops were deployed to create "safe havens" in several Bosnian cities and towns. But faced with resistance from NATO allies and from Russia, and with the unwillingness of the American people to risk the lives of U.S. soldiers over an issue not vital to U.S. interests, President Clinton gave up his stern warnings and accepted the outcome: the international community's failure to prevent Serbs from waging a war of aggression and genocide.

Not until November 1995, after still another year of frustration and with UN peacekeeping troops in increasingly serious danger from both sides in the Yugoslav civil war, was President Clinton able to achieve a ceasefire and a peace agreement in Dayton, Ohio, among the heads of the warring factions. (UN peacekeepers and aid workers were again present in Kosovo immediately following the pullout of hostile Serbian troops in 1999.) Despite the difficulty of restoring peace, the UN and its peacekeeping troops did an extraordinary job in the former Yugoslavia, dealing both with the intransigence of the warring parties and with the disagreement among the European powers about how to deal with a vicious and destructive civil war in their own neighborhood.

The 2001 terrorist attacks also implicated the United Nations. Less than three weeks after September 11, the UN Security Council unanimously (15–0) approved a U.S.-sponsored resolution requiring all countries to deny safe haven to anyone financing or committing a terrorist act. The resolution criminalized the financing of terrorist activity and extended its coverage beyond countries to individuals and "entities" within countries. The United Nations also created a committee of the Security Council members to monitor implementation of the resolution, which included the freezing of all monetary assets available to terrorists and the passage of tougher laws to detain suspected terrorists as well as to share information regarding terrorism.

---

[16] There was, in fact, an angry dispute over a "surplus" of at least $2.2 billion, on the basis of which Japan and others demanded a rebate. *Report of the Secretary of Defense to the President and Congress* (Washington, D.C.: Government Printing Office, 1992), p. 26.

Moreover, although this resolution stresses economic rather than military means, it does not prohibit "use of force," which the UN Charter allows as long as force is used for self-defense and not for "armed reprisals" after the fact.

The UN Security Council was central in the debate over the United States' potential invasion of Iraq during the fall of 2002. At first, President Bush was reluctant to seek UN approval because he believed that he already had enough UN authority based on past Security Council resolutions that Saddam Hussein had so egregiously disregarded. But growing opposition to unilateral U.S. action against Iraq on the part of several Security Council members produced second thoughts and led Bush to appear at the United Nations and request a renewed and more authoritative, unconditional resolution. In response to this renewed U.S. cooperativeness, the Security Council unanimously adopted a resolution, calling on Iraq's president Saddam Hussein to disarm and to allow weapons inspectors into Iraq.

Following authorization for weapons inspections, the Bush administration in early 2003 pressured the UN Security Council to support military action in Iraq, but met resistance from France, Russia, Germany, and others. Knowing they faced a veto by France and possibly Russia, the Bush administration ultimately decided to go to war without another UN Security Council vote. These recent UN interventions show the promise and the limits of the United Nations in the post–cold war era. Although the United States can no longer control UN decisions, as it could in the United Nations' early days, the UN continues to function as a useful instrument of American foreign policy.[17]

The International Monetary Structure

Fear of a repeat of the economic devastation that followed World War I brought the United States together with its allies (except the U.S.S.R.) to Bretton Woods, New Hampshire, in 1944 to create a new international economic structure for the postwar world. The result was two institutions: the International Bank for Reconstruction and Development (commonly called the World Bank) and the International Monetary Fund.

The World Bank was set up to finance long-term capital. Leading nations took on the obligation of contributing funds to enable the World Bank to make loans to capital-hungry countries. (The U.S. quota has been about one third of the total.)

The *International Monetary Fund (IMF)* was set up to provide for the short-term flow of money. After the war, the dollar, instead of gold, was the chief means by which the currencies of one country would be "changed into" currencies of another country for purposes of making international transactions. To permit debtor countries with no international balances to make purchases and investments, the IMF was set up to lend dollars or other appropriate currencies to needy member countries to help them overcome temporary trade deficits. For many years after World

International Monetary Fund (IMF) An institution established in 1944 at Bretton Woods, New Hampshire, to provide loans to needy member countries and to facilitate international monetary exchange.

[17]Not all American policy makers agree that the UN is a worthy instrument of American foreign policy. The UN is on the verge of bankruptcy. For a review, see Barbara Crossette, "U.N., Facing Bankruptcy, Plans to Cut Payroll by Ten Percent," *New York Times*, February 6, 1996, p. A3.

War II, the IMF, along with U.S. foreign aid, in effect constituted the only international medium of exchange.

The IMF, with $93 billion, has more money to lend poor countries than the United States, Europe, or Japan (the three leading IMF shareholders) do individually and it makes its policy decisions in ways that are generally consonant with the interests of the leading shareholders.[18] Not surprisingly, the IMF immediately became involved in the crises following September 11. Within two weeks it had approved a $135 million loan to economically troubled Pakistan, a strategic player in the war against the Taliban government of Afghanistan because of its location. Turkey, with its proximity to relevant areas in the Middle East, was also put back in the IMF pipeline.[19]

Economic Aid

Commitment to rebuilding war-torn countries came as early as commitment to the basic postwar international monetary structure. This is the way President Franklin Roosevelt put the case in a press conference in November 1942, less than one year after the United States entered World War II:

> Sure, we are going to rehabilitate [other nations after the war]. Why? . . . Not only from the humanitarian point of view . . . but from the viewpoint of our own pocketbooks, and our safety from future war.[20]

The particular form and timing for enacting American foreign aid was heavily influenced by Great Britain's sudden decision in 1947 that it would no longer be able to maintain its commitments to Greece and Turkey (full proof that America would now have to *have* clients rather than *be* one). Within three weeks of that announcement, President Truman recommended a $400 million direct aid program for Greece and Turkey, and by mid-May of 1947, Congress approved it. Since President Truman had placed the Greece-Turkey action within the larger context of a commitment to help rebuild and defend all countries the world over, wherever the leadership wished to develop democratic systems or to ward off communism, the Greek-Turkish aid was followed quickly by the historically unprecedented program that came to be known as the Marshall Plan, named in honor of Secretary of State (and former five-star general) George C. Marshall.[21]

---

[18]James Dao and Patrick E. Tyler, "U.S. Says Military Strikes Are Just a Part of Big Plan," *The Alliance,* 27 September 2001; and Joseph Kahn, "A Nation Challenged: Global Dollars," *New York Times,* 20 September 2001.

[19]Turkey was desperate for help to extricate its economy from its worst recession since 1945. The Afghanistan crisis was going to hurt Turkey all the more, and its strategic location helped its case with the IMF. *New York Times,* 6 October 2001, p. A7.

[20]Quoted in John Lewis Gaddis, *The United States and the Origins of the Cold War* (New York: Columbia University Press, 1972), p. 21.

[21]The best account of the decision and its purposes will be found in Joseph Jones, *The Fifteen Weeks* (New York: Viking, 1955).

The *Marshall Plan*—officially known as the European Recovery Plan (ERP)—was essential for the rebuilding of war-torn Europe. By 1952, the United States had spent over $34 billion for the relief, reconstruction, and economic recovery of Western Europe. The emphasis was shifted in 1951, with passage of the Mutual Security Act, to building up European military capacity. Of the $48 billion appropriated between 1952 and 1961, over half went for military assistance, the rest for continuing economic aid. Over those years, the geographic emphasis of U.S. aid also shifted toward South Korea, Taiwan, the Philippines, Vietnam, Iran, Greece, and Turkey—that is, toward the rim of communism. In the 1960s, the emphasis shifted once again, toward what became known as the Third World. From 1962 to 1975, over $100 billion was sent, mainly to Latin America for economic assistance. Other countries of Africa and Asia were also brought in.[22]

Many critics have argued that foreign aid is really aid for political and economic elites, not for the people. Although this is to a large extent true, it needs to be understood in a broader context. If a country's leaders oppose distributing food or any other form of assistance to its people, there is little the United States, or any aid organization, can do, short of terminating the assistance. Goods have to be exchanged across national borders before they can reach the people who need them. Needy people would probably be worse off if the United States cut off aid altogether. The lines of international communication must be kept open. That is why diplomacy exists, and foreign aid can facilitate diplomacy, just as diplomacy is needed to help get foreign aid where it is most needed.

Another important criticism of U.S. foreign aid policy is that it has not been tied closely enough to U.S. diplomacy. The original Marshall Plan was set up as an independent program outside the state department and had its own separate missions in each participating country. Essentially, "ERP became a Second State Department."[23] This did not change until the program was reorganized as the Agency for International Development (AID) in the early 1960s. Meanwhile, the defense department has always had principal jurisdiction over that substantial proportion of economic aid that goes to military assistance. The department of agriculture administers the commodity aid programs, such as Food for Peace. Each department has in effect been able to conduct its own foreign policy, leaving many foreign diplomats to ask, "Who's in charge here?"

That brings us back to the history of U.S. efforts to balance traditional values with the modern needs of world leadership. Economic assistance is an instrument of American foreign policy, but it has been less effective than it might have been because of the inability of American politics to overcome its traditional opposition to foreign entanglements and build a unified foreign policy—something that the older nation-states would call a foreign ministry. The United States has undoubtedly made progress, but those outside its borders still often wonder who is in charge.

Marshall Plan The U.S. European Recovery Plan, in which over $34 billion was spent for relief, reconstruction, and economic recovery of Western Europe after World War II.

---

[22]Robert A. Pastor, *Congress and the Politics of U.S. Foreign Economic Policy* (Berkeley: University of California Press, 1980), pp. 256–80.

[23]Quoted in Lowi, *The End of Liberalism*, 2nd ed., p. 162.

Collective Security

In 1947, most Americans hoped that the United States could meet its world obligations through the United Nations and economic structures alone. But most foreign-policy makers recognized this as a vain hope even as they were permitting and encouraging Americans to believe it. They had anticipated the need for military entanglements at the time of drafting the original UN charter by insisting upon language that recognized the right of all nations to provide for their mutual defense independently of the United Nations. And almost immediately after enactment of the Marshall Plan, the White House and a parade of state and defense department officials followed up with an urgent request to the Senate to ratify mutual defense alliances and to Congress to finance them.

At first quite reluctant to approve treaties providing for national security alliances, the Senate ultimately agreed with the executive branch. The first collective security agreement was the Rio Treaty (ratified by the Senate in September 1947), which created the Organization of American States (OAS). This was the model treaty, anticipating all succeeding collective security treaties by providing that an armed attack against any of its members "shall be considered as an attack against all the American States," including the United States. A more significant break with U.S. tradition against peacetime entanglements came with the North Atlantic Treaty (signed in April 1949), which created the North Atlantic Treaty Organization (NATO). ANZUS, a treaty tying Australia and New Zealand to the United States, was signed in September 1951. Three years later, the Southeast Asia Treaty created the Southeast Asia Treaty Organization (SEATO).

In addition to these multilateral treaties, the United States entered into a number of bilateral treaties—treaties between two countries. As one author has observed, the United States has been a *producer* of security while most of its allies have been *consumers* of security.[24] Figure 14.1 demonstrates that the United States has constantly devoted a greater percentage of its gross domestic product (GDP) to defense than have its NATO allies and Japan.

This pattern has continued in the post–cold war era, and its best illustration is in the Persian Gulf War, where the United States provided the initiative, the leadership, and most of the armed forces, even though its allies were obliged to reimburse over 90 percent of the cost.

It is difficult to evaluate collective security and its treaties, because the purpose of collective security as an instrument of foreign policy is prevention, and success of this kind has to be measured according to what did *not* happen. The critics have argued that U.S. collective security treaties posed a threat of encirclement to the Soviet Union, forcing it to produce its own collective security, particularly the Warsaw Pact.[25] Nevertheless, no one can deny the counterargument that the world has enjoyed more than forty-five years without world war.

---

[24]George Quester, *The Continuing Problem of International Politics* (Hinsdale, Ill.: Dryden Press, 1974), p. 229.

[25]The Warsaw Pact was signed in 1955 by the Soviet Union, the German Democratic Republic (East Germany), Poland, Hungary, Czechoslovakia, Romania, Bulgaria, and Albania. Albania later dropped out. The Warsaw Pact was terminated in 1991.

FIGURE 14.1 Defense Spending as a Percentage of Gross Domestic Product

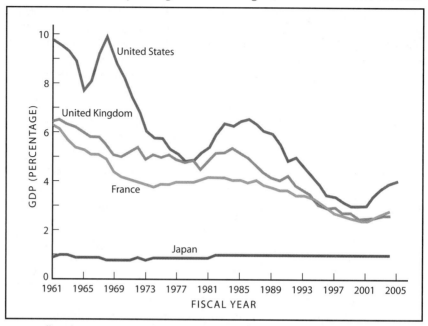

SOURCE: Office of Management and Budget, *Budget of the U.S. Government, Fiscal Year 2006, Historical Tables* (Washington, D.C.: Government Printing Office, 2005), p. 128; Stockholm International Peace Research Institute, *SIPRI Yearbook 2003* (New York: Oxford University Press, 2003), p. 303.

Although the Soviet Union has collapsed, Russia has emerged from a period of confusion and consolidation signaling its determination to play once again an active role in regional and world politics. The challenge for the United States and NATO in coming years will be how to broaden membership in the alliance to include the nations of Eastern Europe and some of the former Soviet republics without antagonizing Russia, which might see such an expansion of NATO as a new era of encirclement.

In 1998 the expansion of NATO took its first steps, extending membership to Poland, Hungary, and the Czech Republic. Most of Washington embraced this expansion as the true and fitting end of the cold war, and the U.S. Senate echoed this support with a resounding 80 to 19 vote to induct these three former Soviet satellites into NATO. The expansion was also welcomed among European member nations, who quickly approved the move, which was hailed as the final closing of the book on Yalta, the 1945 treaty that divided Europe into Western and Soviet spheres of influence after the defeat of Germany. But some strong voices did not support NATO expansion. George Kennan, architect of the United States' containment policy, predicted that NATO expansion was "the beginning of a new Cold War . . . a tragic mistake. . . . Our differences in the Cold War were with the Soviet Communist regime. And now we are turning our backs on the very people [Russia's current leaders] who mounted the greatest bloodless revolution in history to remove that Soviet Regime."[26]

NATO's ability to assist in implementing the uncertain peace in the former Yugoslavia was a genuine test of the viability of NATO, and collective security in general, now that the cold war is over. Efforts to halt the "ethnic cleansing" in Kosovo by the Serbs included months of a relentless bombing campaign, and while NATO prevailed, Kosovo's future seemed uncertain.

The September 11 attack on the United States was the first time in its fifty-plus year history that Article 5 of the North Atlantic Treaty had to be invoked; it provides that an attack on one country is an attack on all the member countries. The global coalition initially forged after September 11 numbered over 170 countries. Not all joined the war effort in Afghanistan, but most if not all provided some form of support for some aspect of the war on terrorism, such as economic sanctions and intelligence. The war in Iraq, however, put the "coalition of the willing" to a test. The Bush administration was determined not to make its decision to go to war subject to the UN or NATO or any other international organization. The breadth of the United States' coalition was deemed secondary to its being nonconstraining. As a result, other than the British government, no major power supported the United States' actions.

NATO and the other mutual security organizations throughout the world are likely to survive. But these organizations are going to be less like military alliances and more like economic associations to advance technology, reduce trade barriers, and protect the world environment or diplomatic associations to fight terrorism. Another form of collective security may well have emerged from the 1991 Persian Gulf War, with nations forming temporary coalitions under UN sponsorship to check a particularly aggressive nation.

Military Deterrence

For the first century and a half of its existence as an independent republic, the United States held strongly to a "Minuteman" theory of defense: Maintain a small corps of professional officers, a few flagships, and a small contingent of marines; leave the rest of defense to the state militias. In case of war, mobilize as quickly as possible, taking advantage of the country's immense size and its separation from Europe to gain time to mobilize.

The United States applied this policy as recently as the post–World War I years and was beginning to apply it after World War II, until the new policy of preparedness won out. The cycle of demobilization-remobilization was broken, and in its place the United States adopted a new policy of constant mobilization and preparedness: deterrence, or the development and maintenance of military strength as a means of discouraging attack. After World War II, military deterrence against the

---

[26]Quoted in Thomas Friedman, "NATO Expansion Starting New Cold War?" *Times-Picayune*, 5 May 1998, p. B5. See also *Baltimore Sun*, 2 May 1998, p. 12A.

Soviet Union became the fundamental American foreign policy objective, requiring a vast commitment of national resources. With preparedness as the goal, peacetime defense expenditures grew steadily over the course of the cold war.

The end of the cold war raised public expectations for a "peace dividend" at last, after nearly a decade of the largest peacetime defense budget increases in U.S. history. Many defense experts, liberal and conservative, feared what they called a budget "free-fall," not only because deterrence was still needed but also because severe and abrupt cuts could endanger private industry in many friendly foreign countries as well as in the United States.

The Persian Gulf War brought both points dramatically into focus. First, the Iraqi invasion of Kuwait revealed the size, strength, and advanced modern technological base not only of the Iraqi armed forces but of other countries—Arab and non-Arab—including their capability, then or soon, to make atomic weapons and other weapons of massive destructive power. Moreover, the demand for advanced weaponry was intensifying. The decisive victory of the United States and its allies in the Gulf War, far from discouraging the international arms trade, gave it fresh impetus. Following the Gulf War victory, *Newsweek* reported that "industry reps quickly realized that foreign customers would now be beating a path to their doors, seeking to buy the winning weaponry." The Soviet Union at one time led the list of major world arms sellers, and Russia and several other republics of the former Soviet Union have continued to make international arms sales, particularly since now there are "no ideological limitations" in the competition for customers.[27] The United States now leads the list of military weapons exporters, followed by Russia, France, Great Britain, and China. Thus, some shrinkage of defense expenditure has been desirable, but Democrats and Republicans alike agree that this reduction must be guided by the continuing need to maintain U.S. and allied credibility as a deterrent to post–cold war arms races.

As to the second point, domestic pressures join international demands to fuel post–cold war defense spending. Each cut in military production and each closing of a military base or plant translates into a significant loss of jobs. Moreover, the conversion of defense industries to domestic uses is not a problem faced by the United States alone.

While we no longer have a conventional arms race toward some kind of balance—as was the case during the cold war when it was called Mutual Assured Destruction (MAD)—there is greater awareness, post–September 11, that one small nuclear, biological, or chemical device delivered in a suitcase, a shipping carton, or a suicide bomber's waistband might be sufficient to bring a powerful nation-state to its knees. Here is deterrence put to its ultimate test.

Indeed, it's this new political reality that served as the impetus for the **Bush doctrine** of preemptive use of force. Preemption means striking first based on credible evidence that the adversary is likely to attack you. Deterrence is based on striking back, on the logic that the threat of second-strike capacity will stop an adversary from striking first. Although deterrence held up well during the cold war, the nature

Bush doctrine Foreign policy based on the idea that the United States should take preemptive action against threats to its national security.

---

[27]"Arms for Sale," *Newsweek*, 8 April 1991, pp. 22–27.

Napoleonic role—A country feels that in order to safeguard its form of government (i.e., democracy), it must ensure (by force if necessary) that other countries adopt the same form of government.

Holy Alliance role—Using every political instrument available to keep existing governments in power, whatever form those governments may take; keeping peace is more important than promoting one particular form of government.

Balance-of-power role—Major powers play off each other so that no one power or combination of powers can impose conditions on others.

Economic expansionist role—Being primarily concerned with what other countries have to buy or to sell and with their dependability in honoring contracts, regardless of their form of government.

of the enemy and of the threat has changed in the war on terrorism, requiring, at least according to the Bush doctrine, a different kind of response. Preemption might not be used often, but proponents argue that it needs to be an option if deterrence fails. The war in Iraq was the first major application of the Bush doctrine. Some allegations were made of Iraqi connections to Al Qaeda, but the main contention was that if Saddam Hussein was not disarmed of his weapons of mass destruction, and if he was not removed from power, the threat he posed to the U.S. would escalate from potential to actual. Before and during the war in Iraq, debate over whether Iraq actually possessed weapons of mass destruction has continued. In addition to questioning the basis of war, critics also questioned the strategy of the Bush doctrine. Preemptive force requires careful planning for enemy countermoves and other contingencies, including the enemy's own possible decision to act "pre-preemptively" and strike first. These critics further added that if the United States can take preemptive action in the name of its own security, what will stop other countries from doing so? These are all legitimate criticisms that will continue to be debated. And two other questions will persist: Did the Bush doctrine make the world a safer place? Is there a substitute for war?

ROLES NATIONS PLAY

Although each president has hundreds of small foreign fires to fight and can choose whichever instruments of policy best fit each particular situation, the primary foreign-policy problem any president faces is choosing an overall role for the country in foreign affairs. Roles help us to define a situation in order to control the element of surprise in international relations. Surprise is in fact the most dangerous aspect of international relations, especially in a world made smaller and more fragile by advances in and the proliferation of military technology.

Choosing a Role

The problem of choosing a role can be understood by identifying a limited number of roles played by nation-states in the past. Four such roles will be drawn from history—the Napoleonic, the Holy Alliance, the balance-of-power, and the economic expansionist roles. Although the definitions given here will be exaggerations of the real world, they do capture in broad outline the basic choices available.

The Napoleonic Role   The ***Napoleonic role*** takes its name from the role played by postrevolutionary France under Napoleon. The French at that time felt not only that their new democratic system of government was the best on earth but also that France would not be safe until democracy was adopted universally. If this meant intervention in the internal affairs of France's neighbors, and if that meant warlike reactions, then so be it. President Woodrow Wilson expressed a similar viewpoint when he supported the U.S. declaration of war in 1917 with his argument that "the world must be made safe for democracy." Obviously such a position can be adopted by any powerful nation as a rationalization for intervening at its convenience in the internal affairs of another country. But it can also be sincerely espoused, and in the United States it has from time to time enjoyed broad popular consensus. The United States played the Napoleonic role recently in ousting Philippine dictator Ferdinand Marcos (February 1986), Panamanian leader Manuel Noriega (December 1989), the Sandinista government of Nicaragua (February 1990), the military rulers of Haiti (September 1994), and Iraqi dictator Saddam Hussein (April 2003).

The Holy Alliance Role   The concept of the ***Holy Alliance role*** emerged out of the defeat of Napoleon and the agreement by the leaders of Great Britain, Russia, Austria, and Prussia to preserve the social order against *all* revolution, including democratic revolution, at whatever cost. (Post–Napoleonic France also joined it.) The Holy Alliance made use of every kind of political instrument available—including political suppression, espionage, sabotage, and outright military intervention—to keep existing governments in power. The Holy Alliance role is comparable to the Napoleonic role in that each operates on the assumption that intervention in the internal affairs of other countries is justified for the maintenance of peace. But Napoleonic intervention is motivated by fear of dictatorship, and it can accept and even encourage revolution. In contrast, Holy Alliance intervention is antagonistic to any form of political change, even when this means supporting an existing dictatorship.[28] Because the Holy Alliance role became more important after the cold war ended, illustrations of this role will be given later in the chapter.

The Balance-of-Power Role   The ***balance-of-power role*** is basically an effort by the major powers to play off each other so that no great power or combination of great and lesser powers can impose conditions on others. The most relevant example of the use of this strategy is found in the nineteenth century, especially the latter half. The feature of the balance-of-power role that is most distinct from the two previously identified roles is that this role accepts the political system of each country, asking no questions except whether the country will join an alliance and will use its

---

Napoleonic role
Strategy pursued by a powerful nation to prevent aggressive actions against itself by improving the internal state of affairs of a particular country, even if this means encouraging revolution in that country.

Holy Alliance role A strategy pursued by a superpower to prevent any change in the existing distribution of power among nation-states, even if this requires intervention into the internal affairs of another country in order to keep a ruler from being overthrown.

balance-of-power role
The strategy whereby many countries form alliances with one or more other countries in order to counterbalance the behavior of other, usually more powerful, nation-states.

[28]For a thorough and instructive exposition of the original Holy Alliance Pattern, see Paul M. Kennedy, *The Rise and Fall of the Great Powers: Economic Change and Military Conflict from 1500 to 2000* (New York: Random House, 1987), pp. 159–60. And for a comparison of the Holy Alliance role with the balance-of-power role, to be discussed next, see Polanyi, *The Great Transformation*, pp. 5–11 and 259–62.

resources to ensure that each country will respect the borders and interests of all the others.[29]

The Economic Expansionist Role   The **economic expansionist role,** also called the capitalist role, shares with the balance-of-power role the attitude that the political system or ideology of a country is irrelevant; the only question is whether a country has anything to buy or sell and whether its entrepreneurs, corporations, and government agencies will honor their contracts. Governments and their armies are occasionally drawn into economic expansionist relationships in order to establish, reopen, or expand trade relationships, and to keep the lines of commerce open. But the role is political, too. The point can be made that the economic expansionist role was the role consistently played by the United States in Latin and Central America, until the cold war (perhaps in the 1960s and beyond) pushed us toward the Holy Alliance role with most of those countries.

Economic expansion does not happen spontaneously, however. In the past, economic expansion owed a great deal to military backing, because contracts do not enforce themselves, trade deficits are not paid automatically, and new regimes do not always honor the commitments made by regimes they replace. The only way to expand economic relationships is through diplomacy.

The Choice of Roles for America Today

These four roles should not be literally translated into models that heads of state or foreign-policy establishments consciously adopt. They are the names of patterns of policy conduct that have prevailed during certain important points in history. These labels were actually used by key participants during those points in history or by historians to capture and evaluate the patterns of conduct. In our time, they remain useful descriptions of patterns that enable us to compare an important pattern of conduct today with real moments in the past. The sequence of these roles in post–World War II history is not precisely the same as the sequence in historical time. They do, however, capture the highlights of our own epoch, and the comparisons do give us a better basis for evaluation.

A new alliance with a new purpose was struck in response to the terrorist attacks of September 11, 2001. Such a great-power alliance for international order has not been seen since the mid-nineteenth century, when the threat came from middle-class revolutionaries rather than religious fanatics. But even though the enemies are different, the goals and strategies are about the same. All countries in the West are vulnerable because Al Qaeda and its associated groups are opposed to the West. All capitalist and developing countries are susceptible because terrorism is intensely anti-capitalist. And all moderate Arab regimes are vulnerable because they are seen by Al Qaeda as traitors and as collaborators with the West. All of these vulnerable nation-states need one another to deprive terrorists of the turf they need for safe havens, headquarters, training, and communication, not to mention financing. Even though the war against the Taliban regime was conducted almost entirely by the United States, there was no hope for a sustained campaign without

economic expansionist role The strategy often pursued by capitalist countries to adopt foreign policies that will maximize the success of domestic corporations in their dealings with other countries.

---

[29]Felix Gilbert et al., *The Norton History of Modern Europe* (New York: Norton, 1971), pp. 1222–24.

The Democratic Peace and Foreign Policy

In 1795, the philosopher Immanuel Kant proposed the idea that representative governments were far less likely than other types of regimes to initiate wars. Hence, if representative governments replaced monarchies and other autocracies throughout the world, the result would be "perpetual peace." Today, Kant's idea is called democratic peace theory and has considerable support among scholars, commentators, and government officials.

Immanuel Kant

This idea has significant implications for foreign policy. For example, the Bush administration argued that transforming Iraq into a democracy would help to promote peace in the Middle East. And many policy makers believe that by helping China develop a more open and responsive government, the United States can increase the likelihood of peace with that nation.

Proponents of democratic peace theory assert that democracies seldom, if ever, fight one another. Many argue that democracies are usually reluctant to attack non-democracies, as well. The core logic of democratic peace theory is that ordinary citizens bear the burdens of war and are usually not eager to send their children to fight unless it is absolutely necessary. Thus, to the extent that governments answer to ordinary citizens, they will be constrained from going to war. Critics of the theory point out that even in democracies, wars are often initially popular, though citizens may eventually become disenchanted with the bloodshed. Many scholars have attempted to collect data on the involvement of democracies in wars.

The table on the following page is a fairly comprehensive list of military conflicts involving democratic regimes. Whether these data support or call into question democratic peace theory depends on how the information is assessed. Relatively few conflicts have pitted one democracy against another. Yet, on many occasions, democracies have launched attacks against other nations. Does this mean that if all the world's regimes were democracies there would be no more wars, or could there be other factors at work? For example, the contemporary democracies might be members of the same trade and military alliances and these alliances, rather than their democratic constitutions, could keep them at peace with one another.

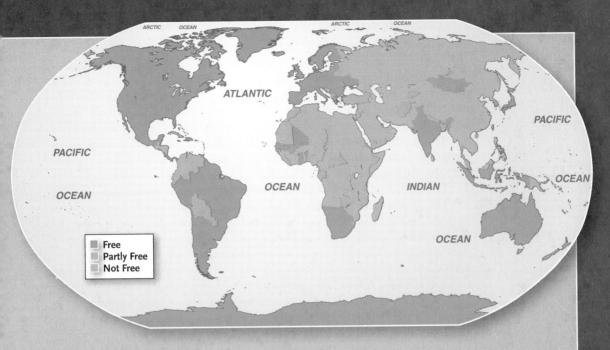

Free
Partly Free
Not Free

Freedom House ranks 89 countries in the worlds as "free" electoral democracies and 58 countries as "partly free" electoral democracies*, yet many of these countries have been involved in wars at some point since adopting democratic regimes.

MILITARY CONFLICTS INVOLVING DEMOCRATIC REGIMES

American Revolutionary War	1775–1783	World War II	1939–1945
War of 1812	1812–1815	Continuation War	1941–1944
Mexican-American War	1846–1848	Indo-Pakistani War of 1947	1947–1948
Sonderbund War	1847	1948 Arab-Israeli War	1947–1949
French Second Republic vs. Roman Republic (19th century)	1849	Cod Wars	1958–1976
		Operation Power Pack	1965
Ecuadorian-Colombian War	1863	Six-Day War	1967
War of the Pacific	1879–1884	Turkish invasion of Cyprus	1974
First Boer War	1880–1881	Paquisha War	1981
Spanish-American War	1898	Yugoslav Wars	1991–1999
Philippine-American War	1899–1913	Cenepa War	1995
Second Boer War	1899–1902	Eritrean-Ethiopian War	1998–2000
World War I	1914–1918	Kargil War	1999
Irish War of Independence	1919–1921	2006 Lebanon War	2006
Polish-Lithuanian War	1920		

*Source: Freedom House, Map of Freedom in the World, 2007 Edition, (www.freedomhouse.org).

the substantial cooperation and participation of many other countries. Pakistan was most vital, and its participation came at the risk of undermining its own regime. Russia and several other former Soviet republics on the northern border of Afghanistan were vital as well. The NATO nations were contractually an important part of the alliance, if only because the NATO charter was built on a solemn promise that an attack on any member was tantamount to an attack on all members.

Yet once the Afghan phase of the war on world terrorism began quieting down, the United States confronted a new challenge: the resurgence of Iraq and the possibility—which turned out to be unfounded—that the weapons of mass destruction that Saddam had once possessed would be used against the United States or one of its allies. President Bush's response, the Bush doctrine, was a significant departure from the Holy Alliance model and a move toward a Napoleonic role. The tenets of the doctrine allowed the United States to (1) take preemptive action against a hostile state without waiting for an attack on us, (2) eliminate permanently the threat of WMDs, (3) eliminate the regime itself, and (4) remain as an occupying power in Iraq long enough to rebuild the country into a modern democratic state.

Although the Holy Alliance role continues to be the principal role among the four historically and conventionally defined roles, it is not the only one that America plays, and more to the point, it is never played exactly the same way in every case. Even in Afghanistan, the alliance to defeat the Taliban and contain terrorism was accompanied by a genuine, albeit secondary version of the Napoleonic role. The Bush administration seemed determined not to "hit and run," as the United States had done when it fought with the Taliban against the Russians in the early 1980s. American policy is strongly committed to both rebuilding the Afghan economy along capitalist lines and moving the Afghan regime toward some form of democratization. But in the short run at least, the United States quickly settled for an imposed national leader presiding over a domestic coalition of mutually distrustful warlords, with only the barest hint of any kind of democratic process. That is the underlying Holy Alliance at work. Moreover, the Bush administration is just as committed as its predecessors to a balance-of-power role in the perennial Middle East hot spot, the Israel-Palestine conflict. The United States has succeeded in keeping the neighboring Arab countries from forming their own anti-Israel (and therefore anti–United States) alliance. (Keeping antagonistic alliances from forming is an essential feature of the balance-of-power role: Like spokes on a wheel, each country is kept dependent on the United States at the hub while separated from one another.) But the use of terrorism by the Palestinians has prevented the United States from playing the balance-of-power role of "honest broker."

No foreign-policy role—however the roles are categorized—can ever relieve the United States of the need for sustained diplomacy. In fact, diplomacy has become all the more important because despotic regimes eventually fail and, in their failure, create instability. Since September 11, it has also become clear that failing regimes can become the breeding grounds for world terrorism. This is not to argue that war is never justifiable or that peace can always be achieved through discussions among professional diplomats. It is only to argue that there are limits to any role a country chooses to play and that failure will come faster and will be more serious if the choice of the role is not made with patience, deliberation, rationality, and, most important, a knowledge of and sensitivity to history.

CHAPTER REVIEW

This chapter began by raising some dilemmas about forming foreign policy in a democracy like the United States. Skepticism about foreign entanglements and the secrecy surrounding many foreign-policy issues form the basis of these dilemmas. Although we cannot provide solutions to the foreign-policy issues that the United States faces, we can provide a well-balanced analysis of the problems of foreign policy.

The first section of this chapter looked at the players in foreign policy: the makers and the shapers. The influence of institutions and groups historically has varied from case to case, with the important exception of the president. Since the president is central to all foreign policy, it is best to assess how other actors interact with the president. In most instances, this interaction involves only the narrowest element of the foreign policy establishment. The American people have an opportunity to influence foreign policy, but primarily through Congress or interest groups.

The next section, on values, traced the history of American values that had a particular relevance to American perspectives on the outside world. We found that the American fear of a big government applied to foreign as well as domestic governmental powers. The founders and the active public of the founding period all recognized that foreign policy was special, that the national government had special powers in its dealings with foreigners, and that presidential supremacy was justified in the conduct of foreign affairs. The only way to avoid the big national government and presidential supremacy was to avoid the foreign entanglements that made foreign policy, diplomacy, secrecy, and presidential discretion necessary. Americans held on to their "antistatist" tradition until World War II, long after world conditions cried out for American involvement. And even as it became involved in world affairs, the United States held on tightly to the legacies of one hundred fifty years of tradition: the intermingling of domestic- and foreign-policy institutions, and unilateralism, the tendency to "go it alone" when confronted with foreign conflicts.

We then looked at the instruments—that is, the tools—of American foreign policy. These are the basic statutes and the institutions by which foreign policy has been conducted since World War II: diplomacy, the United Nations, the international monetary structure, economic aid, collective security, and military deterrence. Although Republicans and Democrats look at the world somewhat differently, and although each president has tried to impose a distinctive flavor on foreign policy, they have all made use of these basic instruments, and that has given foreign policies a certain continuity. When Congress created these instruments after World War II, the old tradition was still so strong that it moved Congress to try to create instruments that would do their international work with a minimum of diplomacy—a minimum of human involvement. This is what we called power without diplomacy.

The next section concentrated on the role or roles the president and Congress have sought to play in the world. To help simplify the tremendous variety of tactics and strategies that foreign-policy leaders can select, we narrowed the field down to four categories of roles nations play, suggesting that there is a certain amount of consistency and stability in the conduct of a nation-state in its dealings with other nation-states. These were labeled according to actual roles that diplomatic historians have identified in the history of major Western nation-states: the Napoleonic, Holy Alliance, balance-of-power, and economic expansionist roles. We also attempted to identify and assess the role of the United States in the post–cold war era, essentially the Holy Alliance role. But whatever its advantages may be, the Holy Alliance approach will never allow the United States to conduct foreign policy without diplomacy. America is tied inextricably to the perils and ambiguities of international relationships, and diplomacy is still the monarch of all available instruments of foreign policy.

FOR FURTHER READING

Bacevich, Andrew. *The New American Militarism: How Americans Are Seduced by War.* New York: Oxford University Press, 2006.

Berman, Paul. *Terror and Liberalism.* New York: Norton, 2004.

ONLINE READING Daalder, Ivo H., and James M. Lindsay. *America Unbound—The Bush Revolution in Foreign Policy.* Washington, D.C.: Brookings Institution Press, 2003.

Fisk, Robert. *The Great War for Civilisation: The Conquest of the Middle East.* New York: Knopf, 2005.

Gaddis, John L. *The Cold War: A New History.* New York: Penguin, 2005.

Hook, Stephen, and John Spanier. *American Foreign Policy since World War II.* Washington, D.C.: Congressional Quarterly Press, 2006.

Jentleson, Bruce. *American Foreign Policy—The Dynamics of Choice in the Twenty-First Century.* 3rd ed. New York: Norton, 2006.

Johnson, Chalmers. *The Sorrows of Empire.* New York: Holt, 2004.

Kagan, Robert. *Dangerous Nation.* New York: Knopf, 2006.

Kennan, George F. *Around the Cragged Hill: A Personal and Political Philosophy.* New York: Norton, 1993.

ONLINE READING Mandelbaum, Michael. *The Case for Goliath: How America Acts as the World's Government in the Twenty-First Century.* Washington, D.C.: Public Affairs Press, 2005.

Mann, James. *Rise of the Vulcans.* New York: Penguin, 2004.

Reid, T. R. *The United States of Europe—The New Superpower and the End of American Supremacy.* New York: Penguin, 2004.

U.S. Congress. *Report of the Congressional Committees Investigating the Iran-Contra Affair.* Washington, D.C.: Government Printing Office, 1987.

ONLINE READING Yoo, John. *The Powers of War and Peace.* Chicago: University of Chicago Press, 2005.

Appendix

The Declaration of Independence

In Congress, July 4, 1776

**The Unanimous Declaration of the
Thirteen United States of America**

Jefferson

When in the course of human events, it becomes necessary for one people to dissolve the political bands which have connected them with another, and to assume among the Powers of the earth, the separate and equal station to which the Laws of Nature and of Nature's God entitle them, a decent respect to the opinions of mankind requires that they should declare the causes which impel them to the separation.

We hold these truths to be self-evident, that all men are created equal, that they are endowed by their Creator with certain unalienable rights, that among these are Life, Liberty, and the pursuit of Happiness. That to secure these rights, Governments are instituted among Men, deriving their just powers from the consent of the governed. That whenever any Form of Government becomes destructive of these ends, it is the Right of the People to alter or to abolish it, and to institute new Government, laying its foundation on such principles and organizing its powers in such form, as to them shall seem most likely to effect their Safety and Happiness. Prudence, indeed, will dictate that Governments long established should not be changed for light and transient causes; and accordingly all experience hath shown, that mankind are more disposed to suffer, while evils are sufferable, than to right themselves by abolishing the forms to which they are accustomed. But when a long train of abuses and usurpations, pursuing invariably the same Object evinces a design to reduce them under absolute Despotism, it is their right, it is their duty, to throw off such Government, and to provide new Guards for their future security.—Such has been the patient sufferance of these Colonies; and such is now the necessity which constrains them to alter their former Systems of Government. The history of the present King of Great Britain is a history of repeated injuries and usurpations, all having in direct object the establishment of an absolute Tyranny over these States. To prove this, let Facts be submitted to a candid world.

He has refused his Assent to Laws, the most wholesome and necessary for the public good.

He has forbidden his Governors to pass Laws of immediate and pressing importance, unless suspended in their operation till his Assent should be obtained; and when so suspended, he has utterly neglected to attend to them.

He has refused to pass other Laws for the accommodation of large districts of people, unless those people would relinquish the right of Representation in the Legislature, a right inestimable to them and formidable to tyrants only.

He has called together legislative bodies at places unusual, uncomfortable, and distant from the depository of their public Records, for the sole purpose of fatiguing them into compliance with his measures.

He has dissolved Representative Houses repeatedly, for opposing with manly firmness his invasions on the rights of the people.

He has refused for a long time, after such dissolutions, to cause others to be elected; whereby the Legislative powers, incapable of Annihilation, have returned to the People at large for their exercise; the State remaining in the mean time exposed to all dangers of invasion from without, and convulsions within.

He has endeavored to prevent the population of these States; for that purpose obstructing the Laws of Naturalization of Foreigners; refusing to pass others to encourage their migrations hither, and raising the conditions of new Appropriations of Lands.

He has obstructed the Administration of Justice, by refusing his Assent to Laws for establishing Judiciary powers.

He has made Judges dependent on his Will alone, for the tenure of their offices, and the amount and payment of their salaries.

He has erected a multitude of New Offices, and sent hither swarms of Officers to harass our People, and eat out their substance.

He has kept among us, in times of peace, Standing Armies without the Consent of our legislature.

He has affected to render the Military independent of and superior to the Civil Power.

He has combined with others to subject us to a jurisdiction foreign to our constitution, and unacknowledged by our laws; giving his Assent to their Acts of pretended Legislation:

For quartering large bodies of armed troops among us:

For protecting them, by a mock Trial, from Punishment for any Murders which they should commit on the Inhabitants of these States:

For cutting off our Trade with all parts of the world:

For imposing taxes on us without our Consent:

For depriving us in many cases, of the benefits of Trial by jury:

For transporting us beyond Seas to be tried for pretended offences:

For abolishing the free System of English Laws in a neighboring Province, establishing therein an Arbitrary government, and enlarging its Boundaries so as to render it at once an example and fit instrument for introducing the same absolute rule into these Colonies:

For taking away our Charters, abolishing our most valuable Laws, and altering fundamentally the Forms of our Governments:

For suspending our own Legislatures, and declaring themselves invested with Power to legislate for us in all cases whatsoever.

He has abdicated Government here, by declaring us out of his Protection and waging War against us.

He has plundered our seas, ravaged our Coasts, burnt our towns, and destroyed the lives of our people.

He is at this time transporting large armies of foreign mercenaries to compleat the works of death, desolation, and tyranny, already begun with circumstances of Cruelty & perfidy scarcely paralleled in the most barbarous ages, and totally unworthy the Head of a civilized nation.

He has constrained our fellow Citizens taken Captive on the high Seas to bear Arms against their Country, to become the executioners of their friends and Brethren, or to fall themselves by their Hands.

He has excited domestic insurrections amongst us, and has endeavored to bring on the inhabitants of our frontiers, the merciless Indian Savages, whose known rule of warfare, is an undistinguished destruction of all ages, sexes, and conditions.

In every stage of these Oppressions We have Petitioned for Redress in the most humble terms: Our repeated Petitions have been answered only by repeated injury. A Prince, whose character is thus marked by every act which may define a Tyrant, is unfit to be the ruler of a free people.

Nor have We been wanting in attention to our British brethren. We have warned them from time to time of attempts by their legislature to extend an unwarrantable jurisdiction over us. We have reminded them of the circumstances of our emigration and settlement here. We have appealed to their native justice and magnanimity, and we have conjured them by the ties of our common kindred to disavow these usurpations, which would inevitably interrupt our connections and correspondence. They too must have been deaf to the voice of justice and of consanguinity. We must, therefore, acquiesce in the necessity, which denounces our Separation, and hold them, as we hold the rest of mankind, Enemies in War, in Peace Friends.

WE, THEREFORE, the Representatives of the UNITED STATES OF AMERICA, in General Congress, Assembled, appealing to the Supreme Judge of the world for the rectitude of our intentions, do, in the Name, and by Authority of the good People of these Colonies, solemnly publish and declare, That these United Colonies are, and of Right ought to be FREE AND INDEPENDENT STATES; that they are Absolved from all Allegiance to the British Crown, and that all political connection between them and the State of Great Britain, is and ought to be totally dissolved; and that as Free and Independent States, they have full Power to levy War, conclude Peace, contract Alliances, establish Commerce, and to do all other Acts and Things which Independent States may of right do. And for the support of this Declaration, with a firm reliance on the Protection of Divine Providence, we mutually pledge to each other our Lives, our Fortunes, and our sacred Honor.

The foregoing Declaration was, by order of Congress, engrossed, and signed by the following members:

John Hancock

NEW HAMPSHIRE
Josiah Bartlett
William Whipple
Matthew Thornton

MASSACHUSETTS BAY
Samuel Adams
John Adams
Robert Treat Paine
Elbridge Gerry

RHODE ISLAND
Stephen Hopkins
William Ellery

CONNECTICUT
Roger Sherman
Samuel Huntington
William Williams
Oliver Wolcott

DELAWARE
Caesar Rodney
George Read
Thomas M'Kean

MARYLAND
Samuel Chase
William Paca
Thomas Stone
Charles Carroll,
* of Carrollton*

VIRGINIA
George Wyth
Richard Henry Lee
Thomas Jefferson
Benjamin Harrison
Thomas Nelson, Jr.
Francis Lightfoot Lee
Carter Braxton

NEW YORK
William Floyd
Philip Livingston
Francis Lewis
Lewis Morris

NEW JERSEY
Richard Stockton
John Witherspoon
Francis Hopkinson
John Hart
Abraham Clark

PENNSYLVANIA
Robert Morris
Benjamin Rush
Benjamin Franklin
John Morton
George Clymer
James Smith
George Taylor
James Wilson
George Ross

NORTH CAROLINA
William Hooper
Joseph Hewes
John Penn

SOUTH CAROLINA
Edward Rutledge
Thomas Heyward, Jr.
Thomas Lynch, Jr.
Arthur Middleton

GEORGIA
Button Gwinnett
Lyman Hall
George Walton

Resolved, That copies of the Declaration be sent to the several assemblies, conventions, and committees, or councils of safety, and to the several commanding officers of the continental troops; that it be proclaimed in each of the United States, at the head of the army.

The Constitution of the United States of America

Annotated with references to the Federalist Papers

Federalist Paper
Number ★ Author

[PREAMBLE]

We the People of the United States, in Order to form a more perfect Union, establish Justice, insure domestic Tranquility, provide for the common defence, promote the general Welfare, and secure the Blessings of Liberty to ourselves and our Posterity, do ordain and establish this Constitution for the United States of America.

84 ★ (Hamilton)

Article I

Section 1

[LEGISLATIVE POWERS]

All legislative Powers herein granted shall be vested in a Congress of the United States, which shall consist of a Senate and House of Representatives.

10, 45 ★ (Madison)

Section 2

[HOUSE OF REPRESENTATIVES, HOW CONSTITUTED, POWER OF IMPEACHMENT]

The House of Representatives shall be composed of Members chosen every second Year by the People of the several States, and the Electors in each State shall have the Qualifications requisite for Electors of the most numerous Branch of the State Legislature.

39 ★ (Madison)
45 ★ (Madison)
52–53, 57 ★ (Madison)
52 ★ (Madison)
60 ★ (Hamilton)

No Person shall be a Representative who shall not have attained to the Age of twenty-five Years, and been seven Years a Citizen of the United States, and who shall not, when elected, be an inhabitant of that State in which he shall be chosen.

Representatives and *direct Taxes*[1] shall be apportioned among the several States which may be included within this Union, according to their respective Numbers, *which shall be determined by adding to the whole Number of free Persons, including those bound to Service for a Term of Years,* and excluding Indians not taxed, *three-fifths of all other Persons.*[2] The actual Enumeration shall be made within three Years after the

54 ★ (Madison)

54 ★ (Madison)
58 ★ (Madison)

---

[1]Modified by Sixteenth Amendment.
[2]Modified by Fourteenth Amendment.

first Meeting of the Congress of the United States, and within every subsequent Term of ten Years, in such Manner as they shall by Law direct. The Number of Representatives shall not exceed one for every thirty Thousand, but each State shall have at Least one Representative; *and until such enumeration shall be made, the State of New Hampshire shall be entitled to chuse three, Massachusetts eight, Rhode-Island and Providence Plantations one, Connecticut five, New-York six, New Jersey four, Pennsylvania eight, Delaware one, Maryland six, Virginia ten, North Carolina five, South Carolina five, and Georgia three.*[3]

When vacancies happen in the Representation from any State, the Executive Authority thereof shall issue Writs of Election to fill such Vacancies.

The House of Representatives shall chuse their Speaker and other Officers; and shall have the sole Power of Impeachment.

Section 3
[THE SENATE, HOW CONSTITUTED, IMPEACHMENT TRIALS]

The Senate of the United States shall be composed of two Senators from each State, *chosen by the Legislature thereof,*[4] for six Years; and each Senator shall have one Vote.

Immediately after they shall be assembled in Consequence of the first Election, they shall be divided as equally as may be into three Classes. The Seats of the Senators of the first Class shall be vacated at the Expiration of the second Year, of the second Class at the Expiration of the fourth Year, and of the third Class at the Expiration of the sixth Year, so that one third may be chosen every second Year: *and if vacancies happen by Resignation, or otherwise, during the Recess of the Legislature of any State, the Executive thereof may make temporary Appointments until the next Meeting of the Legislature, which shall then fill such Vacancies.*[5]

No person shall be a Senator who shall not have attained to the Age of thirty Years, and been nine Years a Citizen of the United States, and who shall not, when elected, be an Inhabitant of that State for which he shall be chosen.

The Vice-President of the United States shall be President of the Senate, but shall have no Vote, unless they be equally divided.

The Senate shall chuse their other Officers, and also a President pro tempore, in the Absence of the Vice-President, or when he shall exercise the Office of President of the United States.

The Senate shall have the sole Power to try all Impeachments. When sitting for that Purpose, they shall be on Oath or Affirmation. When the President of the United States is tried, the Chief Justice shall preside: And no Person shall be convicted without the Concurrence of two-thirds of the Members present.

Judgment in Cases of Impeachment shall not extend further than to removal from Office, and disqualification to hold and enjoy any Office of honor, Trust or Profit under the United States: but the Party convicted shall nevertheless be liable and subject to Indictment, Trial, Judgment and Punishment, according to Law.

---

[3]Temporary provision.
[4]Modified by Seventeenth Amendment.
[5]Modified by Seventeenth Amendment.

55–56 ★ (Madison)

79 ★ (Hamilton)

39, 45 ★ (Madison)
60 ★ (Hamilton)
62–63 ★ (Madison)
59 ★ (Hamilton)

68 ★ (Hamilton)

62 ★ (Hamilton)

39 ★ (Madison)
65–67, 79 ★ (Hamilton)
65 ★ (Hamilton)

84 ★ (Hamilton)

Section 4
[ELECTION OF SENATORS AND REPRESENTATIVES]

The Times, Places and Manner of holding Elections for Senators and Representatives, shall be prescribed in each State by the Legislature thereof; but the Congress may at any time by Law make or alter such Regulations, except as to the Places of chusing Senators.

The Congress shall assemble at least once in every Year, and such Meeting shall be on the first Monday in December, unless they shall by Law appoint a different Day.[6]

59–61 ★ (Hamilton)

Section 5
[QUORUM, JOURNALS, MEETINGS, ADJOURNMENTS]

Each House shall be the Judge of the Elections, Returns and Qualifications of its own Members, and a Majority of each shall constitute a Quorum to do Business; but a smaller Number may adjourn from day to day, and may be authorized to compel the Attendance of absent Members, in such Manner, and under the Penalties as each House may provide.

Each House may determine the Rules of its Proceedings, punish its Members for disorderly Behavior, and, with the Concurrence of two-thirds, expel a Member.

Each House shall keep a Journal of its Proceedings, and from time to time publish the same, excepting such Parts as may in their Judgment require Secrecy; and the Yeas and Nays of the Members of either House on any questions shall, at the Desire of one-fifth of the present, be entered on the Journal.

Neither House, during the Session of Congress, shall, without the Consent of the other, adjourn for more than three days, nor to any other Place than that in which the two Houses shall be sitting.

Section 6
[COMPENSATION, PRIVILEGES, DISABILITIES]

The Senators and Representatives shall receive a Compensation for their Services, to be ascertained by Law, and paid out of the Treasury of the United States. They shall in all Cases, except Treason, Felony and Breach of the Peace, be privileged from Arrest during their Attendance at the Session of their respective Houses, and in going to and returning from the same; and for any Speech or Debate in either House, they shall not be questioned in any other Place.

No Senator or Representative shall, during the time for which he was elected, be appointed to any civil Office under the authority of the United States, which shall have been created, or the Emoluments whereof shall have been encreased during such time; and no Person holding any Office under the United States, shall be a Member of either House during his Continuance in Office.

55 ★ (Madison)
76 ★ (Hamilton)

Section 7
[PROCEDURE IN PASSING BILLS AND RESOLUTIONS]

All Bills for raising Revenue shall originate in the House of Representatives; but the Senate may propose or concur with Amendments as on other Bills.

66 ★ (Hamilton)

---

[6]Modified by Twentieth Amendment.

69, 73 ★ (Hamilton)

Every Bill which shall have passed the House of Representatives and the Senate, shall, before it become a Law, be presented to the President of the United States; if he approve he shall sign it, but if not he shall return it, with his Objections to that House in which it shall have originated, who shall enter the Objections at large on their Journal, and proceed to reconsider it. If after such Reconsideration two-thirds of that House shall agree to pass the Bill, it shall be sent, together with the Objections, to the other House, by which it shall likewise be reconsidered, and if approved by two-thirds of that House it shall become a Law. But in all such Cases the Votes of both Houses shall be determined by Yeas and Nays, and the Names of the Persons voting for and against the Bill shall be entered on the Journal of each House respectively. If any Bill shall not be returned by the President within ten Days (Sundays excepted) after it shall have been presented to him, the Same shall be a Law, in like Manner as if he had signed it, unless the Congress by their Adjournment prevent its Return, in which Case it shall not be a Law.

69, 73 ★ (Hamilton)

Every Order, Resolution, or Vote to which the Concurrence of the Senate and House of Representatives may be necessary (except on a question of Adjournment) shall be presented to the President of the United States; and before the Same shall take Effect, shall be approved by him, or being disapproved by him, shall be repassed by two-thirds of the Senate and House of Representatives, according to the Rules and Limitations prescribed in the Case of a Bill.

Section 8
[POWERS OF CONGRESS]

The Congress shall have Power

30–36 ★ (Hamilton)
41 ★ (Madison)
56 ★ (Madison)
42, 45, 56 ★ (Madison)

To lay and collect Taxes, Duties, Imposts and Excises, to pay the Debts and provide for the common Defence and general Welfare of the United States; but all Duties, Imposts and excises shall be uniform throughout the United States;

To borrow Money on the Credit of the United States;

To regulate Commerce with foreign Nations, and among the several States, and with the Indian Tribes;

32 ★ (Hamilton)

To establish an uniform Rule of Naturalization, and uniform Laws on the subject of Bankruptcies throughout the United States;

42 ★ (Madison)

To coin Money, regulate the Value thereof, and of foreign Coin, and fix the Standard of Weights and Measures;

42 ★ (Madison)

To provide for the Punishment of counterfeiting the Securities and current Coin of the United States;

42 ★ (Madison)

To establish Post Offices and post Roads;

43 ★ (Madison)

To promote the Progress of Science and useful Arts, by securing for limited Times to Authors and Inventors the exclusive Right to their respective Writings and Discoveries;

81 ★ (Hamilton)
42 ★ (Madison)

To constitute Tribunals inferior to the supreme Court;

To define and Punish Piracies and Felonies committed on the high Seas, and Offences against the Law of Nations;

41 ★ (Madison)

To declare War, grant Letters of Marque and Reprisal, and make Rules concerning Captures on Land and Water;

To raise and support Armies, but no Appropriation of Money to that Use shall be for a longer Term than two Years; 23, 24, 26 ★ (Hamilton)

To provide and maintain a Navy; 41 ★ (Madison)

To make Rules for the Government and Regulation of the land and naval forces;

To provide for calling for the Militia to execute the Laws of the Union, suppress Insurrections and repel Invasions; 29 ★ (Hamilton)

To provide for organizing, arming, and disciplining, the Militia, and for governing such Part of them as may be employed in the Service of the United States, reserving to the States respectively, the Appointment of the Officers, and the Authority of training the Militia according to the discipline prescribed by Congress; 29 ★ (Hamilton) / 56 ★ (Madison) / 32 ★ (Hamilton)

To exercise exclusive Legislation in all Cases whatsoever, over such District (not exceeding ten Miles square) as may, by Cession of particular States, and the Acceptance of Congress, become the Seat of the Government of the United States, and to exercise like Authority over all Places purchased by the Consent of the Legislature of the State in which the Same shall be, for the Erection of Forts, Magazines, Arsenals, dock-Yards, and other needful Buildings;—And 43 ★ (Madison) / 43 ★ (Madison) / 29, 33 ★ (Hamilton)

To make all Laws which shall be necessary and proper for carrying into Execution the foregoing Powers, and all other Powers vested by this Constitution in the Government of the United States, or in any Department or Officer thereof. 44 ★ (Madison)

Section 9

[SOME RESTRICTIONS ON FEDERAL POWER]

The Migration or Importation of such Persons as any of the States now existing shall think proper to admit, shall not be prohibited by the Congress prior to the Year one thousand eight hundred and eight, but a Tax or Duty may be imposed on such Importation, not exceeding ten dollars for each Person.[7] 42 ★ (Madison)

The privilege of the Writ of *Habeas Corpus* shall not be suspended, unless when in Cases of Rebellion or Invasion the public Safety may require it. 83, 84 ★ (Hamilton)

No Bill of Attainder or ex post facto Law shall be passed. 84 ★ (Hamilton)

No Capitation, or other direct, Tax shall be laid, unless in Proportion to the Census or Enumeration herein before directed to be taken.[8]

No Tax or Duty shall be laid on Articles exported from any State.

No Preference shall be given by any Regulation of Commerce or Revenue to the Ports of one State over those of another; nor shall vessels bound to, or from, one State, be obliged to enter, clear, or pay Duties in another. 32 ★ (Hamilton)

No Money shall be drawn from the Treasury, but in Consequence of Appropriations made by Law; and a regular Statement and Account of the Receipts and Expenditures of all public Money shall be published from time to time.

No Title of Nobility shall be granted by the United States: And no Person holding any Office of Profit or Trust under them, shall, without the Consent of the Congress, accept of any present, Emolument, Office or Title, of any kind whatever, from any King, Prince, or foreign State. 39 ★ (Madison) / 84 ★ (Hamilton)

---

[7]Temporary provision.
[8]Modified by Sixteenth Amendment.

Section 10
[RESTRICTIONS UPON POWERS OF STATES]

33 ★ (Hamilton)
44 ★ (Madison)

No State shall enter into any Treaty, Alliance, or Confederation; grant Letters of Marque and Reprisal; coin Money; emit Bills of Credit; make any Thing but gold and silver Coin a Tender in Payment of Debts; pass any Bill of Attainder, ex post facto Law, or Law impairing the Obligation of Contracts, or grant any Title of Nobility.

32 ★ (Hamilton)
44 ★ (Madison)

No State shall, without the Consent of the Congress, lay any Imposts or Duties on Imports or Exports, except what may be absolutely necessary for executing its inspection Laws: and the net Produce of all Duties and Imposts, laid by any State on Imports or Exports, shall be for the Use of the Treasury of the United States; and all such Laws shall be subject to the Revision and Control of the Congress.

No State shall, without the Consent of Congress, lay any Duty of Tonnage, keep Troops, or Ships of War in time of Peace, enter into any Agreement or Compact with another State, or with a foreign Power, or engage in War, unless actually invaded, or in such imminent Danger as will not admit of Delay.

ARTICLE II

Section 1
[EXECUTIVE POWER, ELECTION, QUALIFICATIONS OF THE PRESIDENT]

39 ★ (Madison)
70, 71, 84 ★ (Hamilton)
69, 71 ★ (Hamilton)
39, 45 ★ (Madison)
68, 77 ★ (Hamilton)

The executive Power shall be vested in a President of the United States of America. *He shall hold his Office during the Term of four years and, together with the Vice-President, chosen for the same Term, be elected, as follows:*[9]

Each State shall appoint, in such Manner as the Legislature thereof may direct, a Number of Electors, equal to the whole Number of Senators and Representatives to which the State may be entitled in the Congress: but no Senator or Representative, or Person holding an Office of Trust or Profit under the United States, shall be appointed an Elector.

66 ★ (Hamilton)

The electors shall meet in their respective States, and vote by ballot for two Persons, of whom one at least shall not be an Inhabitant of the same State with themselves. And they shall make a List of all the Persons voted for, and of the Number of Votes for each; which List they shall sign and certify, and transmit sealed to the Seat of the Government of the United States, directed to the President of the Senate. The President of the Senate shall, in the Presence of the Senate and House of Representatives, open all the Certificates, and the Votes shall then be counted. The Person having the greatest Number of Votes shall be the President, if such Number be a Majority of the whole Number of Electors appointed; and if there be more than one who have such Majority and have an equal Number of Votes, then the House of Representatives shall immediately chuse by Ballot one of them for President; and if no person have a Majority, then from the five highest on the List the said House shall in like Manner chuse the President. But in chusing the President, the Votes shall be taken by States, the Representation from each State having one Vote; A quorum for this Purpose shall consist of a Member or Members from two-thirds of the States, and a Majority of all the States shall be necessary to a Choice. In every Case, after the Choice of the President, the person having the greatest Number of Votes of the Electors shall be the

---

[9]Number of terms limited to two by Twenty-second Amendment.

Vice-President. But if there should remain two or more who have equal vote, the Senate shall chuse from them by Ballot the Vice-President.[10]

The Congress may determine the Time of chusing the Electors, and the Day on which they shall give their Votes; which Day shall be the same throughout the United States.

64 ★ (Jay)

No Person except a natural born Citizen, or a Citizen of the United States, at the time of the Adoption of this Constitution, shall be eligible to the Office of President; neither shall any Person be eligible to that Office who shall not have attained to the Age of thirty-five Years, and been fourteen Years a Resident within the United States.

In Case of the Removal of the President from Office, or his Death, Resignation, or Inability to discharge the Powers and Duties of the said Office, the same shall devolve on the Vice-President, and the Congress may by Law provide for the Case of Removal, Death, Resignation, or Inability, both of the President and Vice-President, declaring what Officer shall then act as President, and such Officer shall act accordingly, until the Disability be removed, or a President shall be elected.

The President shall, at stated Times, receive for his Services, a Compensation, which shall neither be encreased nor diminished during the Period for which he shall have been elected, and he shall not receive within that Period any other Emolument from the United States, or any of them.

73, 79 ★ (Hamilton)

Before he enter on the Execution of his Office, he shall take the following Oath or Affirmation:—"I do solemnly swear (or affirm) that I will faithfully execute the Office of President of the United States, and will to the best of my Ability, preserve, protect and defend the Constitution of the United States."

Section 2
[POWERS OF THE PRESIDENT]

The President shall be Commander in Chief of the Army and Navy of the United States, and of the Militia of the several States, when called into the actual Service of the United States; he may require the Opinion, in writing, of the principal Officer in each of the executive Departments, upon any Subject relating to the Duties of their respective Offices, and he shall have Power to grant Reprieves and Pardons for Offences against the United States, except in Cases of Impeachment.

69, 74 ★ (Hamilton)

74 ★ (Hamilton)

69 ★ (Hamilton)

74 ★ (Hamilton)

42 ★ (Madison)

He shall have Power, by and with the Advice and Consent of the Senate, to make Treaties, provided two-thirds of the Senators present concur; and he shall nominate, and by and with the Advice and Consent of the Senate, shall appoint Ambassadors, other public Ministers and Consuls, Judges of the Supreme Court, and all other Officers of the United States, whose Appointments are not herein otherwise provided for, and which shall be established by Law: but the Congress may by Law vest the Appointment of such inferior Officers, as they think proper, in the President alone, in the Courts of Law, or in the Heads of Departments.

64 ★ (Jay)

66 ★ (Hamilton)

42 ★ (Madison)

66, 69, 76, 77 ★ (Hamilton)

The President shall have Power to fill up all Vacancies that may happen during the Recess of the Senate, by granting Commissions which shall expire at the End of their next Session.

67, 76 ★ (Hamilton)

---

[10]Modified by Twelfth and Twentieth Amendments.

Section 3

[POWERS AND DUTIES OF THE PRESIDENT]

77 ★ (Hamilton)
69, 77 ★ (Hamilton)
77 ★ (Hamilton)
69, 77 ★ (Hamilton)
42 ★ (Madison)
69, 77 ★ (Hamilton)
78 ★ (Hamilton)

He shall from time to time give to the Congress Information of the State of the Union, and recommend to their Consideration such Measures as he shall judge necessary and expedient; he may, on extraordinary Occasions, convene both Houses, or either of them, and in Case of Disagreement between them, with Respect to the Time of Adjournment, he may adjourn them to such Time as he shall think proper; he shall receive Ambassadors and other public Ministers; he shall take Care that the Laws be faithfully executed, and shall Commission all the Officers of the United States.

Section 4

[IMPEACHMENT]

39 ★ (Madison)
69 ★ (Hamilton)

The President, Vice-President and all civil Officers of the United States shall be removed from Office on Impeachment for, and Conviction of, Treason, Bribery, or other high Crimes and Misdemeanors.

Article III

Section 1

[JUDICIAL POWER, TENURE OF OFFICE]

81, 82 ★ (Hamilton)
65 ★ (Hamilton)
78, 79 ★ (Hamilton)

The judicial Power of the United States, shall be vested in one supreme Court, and in such inferior Courts as the Congress may from time to time ordain and establish. The Judges, both of the supreme and inferior Courts, shall hold their Offices during good Behavior, and shall, at stated Times, receive for their Services, a Compensation, which shall not be diminished during their Continuance in Office.

Section 2

[JURISDICTION]

80 ★ (Hamilton)

The judicial Power shall extend to all Cases, in Law and Equity, arising under this Constitution, the Laws of the United States, and Treaties made, or which shall be made, under their Authority;—to all Cases affecting Ambassadors, other public Ministers and Consuls;—to all Cases of admiralty and maritime Jurisdiction;—to Controversies to which the United States shall be a party;—to Controversies between two or more States;—*between a State and Citizens of another State;*—between Citizens of different States,—between Citizens of the same State claiming Lands under Grants of different States, *and between a State,* or the Citizens thereof, *and foreign States, Citizens or Subjects.*[11]

81 ★ (Hamilton)

In all Cases affecting Ambassadors, other public Ministers and Consuls, and those in which a State shall be Party, the supreme Court shall have original Jurisdiction. In all the other Cases before mentioned, the supreme Court shall have appellate Jurisdiction, both as to Law and Fact, with such Exceptions, and under such Regulations as Congress shall make.

83, 84 ★ (Hamilton)

The Trial of all Crimes, except in Cases of Impeachment, shall be by Jury; and such Trial shall be held in the State where the said Crimes shall have been commit-

---

[11]Modified by Eleventh Amendment.

ted; but when not committed within any State, the Trial shall be at such Place or Places as the Congress may by Law have directed.

Section 3

[TREASON, PROOF, AND PUNISHMENT]

Treason against the United States, shall consist only in levying War against them, or in adhering to their Enemies, giving them Aid and Comfort. No Person shall be convicted of Treason unless on the Testimony of two Witnesses to the same overt Act, or on Confession in open Court.

43 ★ (Madison)
84 ★ (Hamilton)

The Congress shall have Power to declare the Punishment of Treason, but no Attainder of Treason shall work Corruption of Blood, or Forfeiture except during the Life of the Person attained.

43 ★ (Madison)
84 ★ (Hamilton)

ARTICLE IV

Section 1

[FAITH AND CREDIT AMONG STATES]

Full Faith and Credit shall be given in each State to the public Acts, Records, and judicial Proceedings of every other State. And the Congress may by general Laws prescribe the Manner in which such Acts, Records and Proceedings shall be proved, and the Effect thereof.

42 ★ (Madison)

Section 2

[PRIVILEGES AND IMMUNITIES, FUGITIVES]

The Citizens of each State shall be entitled to all Privileges and Immunities of Citizens in the several States.

80 ★ (Hamilton)

A person charged in any State with Treason, Felony or other Crime, who shall flee from Justice, and be found in another State, shall on Demand of the executive Authority of the State from which he fled, be delivered up to be removed to the State having Jurisdiction of the Crime.

No person held to Service or Labour in one State, under the Laws thereof, escaping into another, shall, in Consequence of any Law or Regulation therein, be discharged from such Service or Labour, but shall be delivered up on Claim of the Party to whom such Service or Labour may be due.[12]

Section 3

[ADMISSION OF NEW STATES]

New States may be admitted by the Congress into this Union; but no new State shall be formed or erected within the Jurisdiction of any other State; nor any State be formed by the Junction of two or more States, or Parts of States, without the Consent of the Legislatures of the States concerned as well as of the Congress.

43 ★ (Madison)

The Congress shall have Power to dispose of and make all needful Rules and Regulations respecting the Territory or other Property belonging to the United States; and nothing in this Constitution shall be so construed as to Prejudice any Claims of the United States, or of any particular State.

43 ★ (Madison)

---

[12]Repealed by the Thirteenth Amendment.

Section 4

[GUARANTEE OF REPUBLICAN GOVERNMENT]

39, 43 ★ (Madison)

The United States shall guarantee to every State in this Union a Republican Form of Government, and shall protect each of them against Invasion; and on Application of the Legislature, or of the Executive (when the Legislature cannot be convened) against domestic Violence.

ARTICLE V

[AMENDMENT OF THE CONSTITUTION]

39, 43 ★ (Madison)

85 ★ (Hamilton)

The Congress, whenever two-thirds of both Houses shall deem it necessary, shall propose Amendments to this Constitution, or, on the Application of the Legislatures of two-thirds of the several States, shall call a Convention for proposing Amendments, which, in either Case, shall be valid to all Intents and Purposes, as Part of this Constitution, when ratified by the Legislatures of three-fourths of the several States, or by Conventions in three-fourths thereof, as the one or the other Mode of Ratification may be proposed by the Congress; *Provided that no Amendment which may be made prior to the Year One thousand eight hundred and eight shall in any Manner affect the first and fourth Clauses in the Ninth Section of the first Article;*[13] and that no

43 ★ (Madison)

State, without its Consent, shall be deprived of its equal Suffrage in the Senate.

ARTICLE VI

[DEBTS, SUPREMACY, OATH]

43 ★ (Madison)

All Debts contracted and Engagements entered into, before the Adoption of this Constitution, shall be as valid against the United States under this Constitution, as under the Confederation.

27, 33 ★ (Hamilton)

39, 44

This Constitution, and the Laws of the United States which shall be made in Pursuance thereof; and all Treaties made, or which shall be made, under the Authority of the United States, shall be the supreme Law of the Land; and the Judges in every State shall be bound thereby, any Thing in the Constitution or Laws of any State to the Contrary notwithstanding.

27 ★ (Hamilton)

44

The Senators and Representatives before mentioned, and the Members of the several State Legislatures, and all executive and judicial Officers, both of the United States and of the several States, shall be bound by Oath or Affirmation, to support this Constitution; but no religious Test shall be required as a Qualification to any Office or public Trust under the United States.

ARTICLE VII

[RATIFICATION AND ESTABLISHMENT]

39, 40, 43 ★ (Madison)

The Ratification of the Conventions of nine States, shall be sufficient for the Establishment of this Constitution between the States so ratifying the Same.[14]

---

[13]Temporary provision.
[14]The Constitution was submitted on September 17, 1787, by the Constitutional Convention, was ratified by the conventions of several states at various dates up to May 29, 1790, and became effective on March 4, 1789.

Done in Convention by the Unanimous Consent of the States present the Seventeenth Day of September in the Year of our Lord one thousand seven hundred and Eighty seven and of the Independence of the United States of America the Twelfth. *In Witness* whereof We have hereunto subscribed our Names,

G:º WASHINGTON—
Presidt, and Deputy from Virginia

New Hampshire	JOHN LANGDON	Delaware	GEO READ
	NICHOLAS GILMAN		GUNNING BEDFOR JUN
Massachusetts	NATHANIEL GORHAM		JOHN DICKINSON
	RUFUS KING		RICHARD BASSETT
			JACO: BROOM
Connecticut	WM SAML JOHNSON	Maryland	JAMES MCHENRY
	ROGER SHERMAN		DAN OF ST. THOS.
New York	ALEXANDER HAMILTON		JENIFER
New Jersey	WIL: LIVINGSTON		DANL CARROLL
	DAVID BREARLY	Virginia	JOHN BLAIR—
	WM PATERSON		JAMES MADISON JR.
	JONA: DAYTON	North Carolina	WM BLOUNT
Pennsylvania	B FRANKLIN		RICHD DOBBS SPAIGHT
	THOMAS MIFFLIN		HU WILLIAMSON
	ROBT MORRIS	South Carolina	J. RUTLEDGE
	GEO. CLYMER		CHARLES COTESWORTH
	THOS. FITZSIMONS		PINCKNEY
	JARED INGERSOLL		PIERCE BUTLER
	JAMES WILSON	Georgia	WILLIAM FEW
	GOUV MORRIS		ABR BALDWIN

Amendments to the Constitution

Proposed by Congress and Ratified by the Legislatures of the Several States, Pursuant to Article V of the Original Constitution

Amendments I–X, known as the Bill of Rights, were proposed by Congress on September 25, 1789, and ratified on December 15, 1791. *The Federalist Papers* comments, mainly in opposition to a Bill of Rights, can be found in number 84 (Hamilton).

AMENDMENT I
[FREEDOM OF RELIGION, OF SPEECH, AND OF THE PRESS]

Congress shall make no law respecting an establishment of religion, or prohibiting the free exercise thereof; or abridging the freedom of speech, or of the press; or the right of the people peaceably to assemble, and to petition the Government for a redress of grievances.

AMENDMENT II
[RIGHT TO KEEP AND BEAR ARMS]

A well regulated Militia, being necessary to the security of a free State, the right of the people to keep and bear Arms, shall not be infringed.

AMENDMENT III
[QUARTERING OF SOLDIERS]

No Soldier shall, in time of peace be quartered in any house, without the consent of the Owner, nor in time of war, but in a manner to be prescribed by law.

AMENDMENT IV
[SECURITY FROM UNWARRANTABLE SEARCH AND SEIZURE]

The right of the people to be secure in their persons, houses, papers, and effects, against unreasonable searches and seizures, shall not be violated, and no Warrants shall issue, but upon probable cause, supported by Oath or affirmation, and particularly describing the place to be searched, and the persons or things to be seized.

Amendment V

No person shall be held to answer for a capital, or otherwise infamous crime, unless on a presentment or indictment of a Grand Jury, except in cases arising in the land or naval forces, or in the Militia, when in actual service in time of War or in public danger; nor shall any person be subject for the same offence to be twice put in jeopardy of life or limb; nor shall be compelled in any Criminal Case to be a witness against himself, nor be deprived of life, liberty, or property, without due process of law; nor shall private property be taken for public use, without just compensation.

Amendment VI
[RIGHT TO SPEEDY TRIAL, WITNESSES, ETC.]

In all criminal prosecutions, the accused shall enjoy the right to a speedy and public trial, by an impartial jury of the State and district wherein the crime shall have been committed, which district shall have been previously ascertained by law, and to be informed of the nature and cause of the accusation; to be confronted with the witnesses against him; to have compulsory process for obtaining Witnesses in his favor, and to have the Assistance of Counsel for his defence.

Amendment VII
[TRIAL BY JURY IN CIVIL CASES]

In suits at common law, where the value in controversy shall exceed twenty dollars, the right of trial by jury shall be preserved, and no fact tried by a jury shall be otherwise re-examined in any Court of the United States, than according to the rules of the common law.

Amendment VIII
[BAILS, FINES, PUNISHMENTS]

Excessive bail shall not be required, nor excessive fines imposed, nor cruel and unusual punishments inflicted.

Amendment IX
[RESERVATION OF RIGHTS OF PEOPLE]

The enumeration in the Constitution, of certain rights, shall not be construed to deny or disparage others retained by the people.

Amendment X
[POWERS RESERVED TO STATES OR PEOPLE]

The powers not delegated to the United States by the Constitution, nor prohibited by it to the States, are reserved to the States respectively, or to the people.

Amendment XI
[Proposed by Congress on March 4, 1794; declared ratified on January 8, 1798.]
[RESTRICTION OF JUDICIAL POWER]

The Judicial power of the United States shall not be construed to extend to any suit in law or equity, commenced or prosecuted against one of the United States by Citizens of another State, or by Citizens or Subjects of any Foreign State.

Amendment XII

[Proposed by Congress on December 9, 1803; declared ratified on September 25, 1804.]
[ELECTION OF PRESIDENT AND VICE-PRESIDENT]

The Electors shall meet in their respective states, and vote by ballot for President and Vice-President, one of whom, at least, shall not be an inhabitant of the same state with themselves; they shall name in their ballots the person voted for as President, and in distinct ballots the person voted for as Vice-President, and they shall make distinct lists of all persons voted for as President, and of all persons voted for as Vice-President, and of the number of votes for each, which lists they shall sign and certify, and transmit sealed to the seat of the government of the United States, directed to the President of the Senate;—The President of the Senate shall, in presence of the Senate and House of Representatives, open all the certificates and the votes shall then be counted;—The person having the greatest number of votes for President, shall be the President, if such number be a majority of the whole number of Electors appointed; and if no person have such majority, then from the persons having the highest numbers not exceeding three on the list of those voted for as President, the House of Representatives shall choose immediately, by ballot, the President. But in choosing the President, the votes shall be taken by states, the representation from each state having one vote; a quorum for this purpose shall consist of a member or members from two-thirds of the states, and a majority of all states shall be necessary to a choice. And if the House of Representatives shall not choose a President whenever the right of choice shall devolve upon them, before the fourth day of March next following, then the Vice-President, shall act as President, as in the case of the death or other constitutional disability of the President. The person having the greatest number of votes as Vice-President, shall be the Vice-President, if such a number be a majority of the whole number of Electors appointed, and if no person have a majority, then from the two highest numbers on the list, the Senate shall choose the Vice-President; a quorum for the purpose shall consist of two-thirds of the whole number of Senators, and a majority of the whole number shall be necessary to a choice. But no person constitutionally ineligible to the office of President shall be eligible to that of Vice-President of the United States.

Amendment XIII

[Proposed by Congress on January 31, 1865; declared ratified on December 18, 1865.]

Section 1
[ABOLITION OF SLAVERY]

Neither slavery nor involuntary servitude, except as a punishment for crime whereof the party shall have been duly convicted, shall exist within the United States, or any place subject to their jurisdiction.

Section 2
[POWER TO ENFORCE THIS ARTICLE]

Congress shall have power to enforce this article by appropriate legislation.

AMENDMENT XIV

[Proposed by Congress on June 13, 1866; declared ratified on July 28, 1868.]

Section 1

[CITIZENSHIP RIGHTS NOT TO BE ABRIDGED BY STATES]

All persons born or naturalized in the United States, and subject to the jurisdiction thereof, are citizens of the United States and of the State wherein they reside. No state shall make or enforce any law which shall abridge the privileges or immunities of citizens of the United States; nor shall any State deprive any person of life, liberty, or property, without due process of law; nor deny to any person within its jurisdiction the equal protection of the laws.

Section 2

[APPORTIONMENT OF REPRESENTATIVES IN CONGRESS]

Representatives shall be apportioned among the several States according to their respective numbers, counting the whole number of persons in each State, excluding Indians not taxed. But when the right to vote at any election for the choice of electors for President and Vice-President of the United States, Representatives in Congress, the Executive and Judicial officers of a State, or the members of the Legislature thereof, is denied to any of the male inhabitants of such State, being twenty-one years of age, and citizens of the United States, or in any way abridged, except for participation in rebellion, or other crime, the basis of representation therein shall be reduced in the proportion which the number of such male citizens shall bear to the whole number of male citizens twenty-one years of age in such State.

Section 3

[PERSONS DISQUALIFIED FROM HOLDING OFFICE]

No person shall be a Senator or Representative in Congress, or elector of President and Vice-President, or hold any office, civil or military, under the United States, or under any State, who, having previously taken an oath, as a member of Congress, or as an officer of the United States, or as a member of any State legislature, or as an executive or judicial officer of any State, to support the Constitution of the United States, shall have engaged in insurrection or rebellion against the same, or given aid or comfort to the enemies thereof. But Congress may by a vote of two-thirds of each House, remove such disability.

Section 4

[WHAT PUBLIC DEBTS ARE VALID]

The validity of the public debt of the United States, authorized by law, including debts incurred for payment of pensions and bounties for services in suppressing insurrection or rebellion, shall not be questioned. But neither the United States nor any State shall assume or pay any debt or obligation incurred in aid of insurrection or rebellion against the United States, or any claim for the loss or emancipation of any slave; but all such debts, obligations and claims shall be held illegal and void.

Section 5
[POWER TO ENFORCE THIS ARTICLE]

The Congress shall have power to enforce, by appropriate legislation, the provisions of this article.

AMENDMENT XV

[Proposed by Congress on February 26, 1869; declared ratified on March 30, 1870.]

Section 1
[NEGRO SUFFRAGE]

The right of citizens of the United States to vote shall not be denied or abridged by the United States or by any State on account of race, color, or previous condition of servitude.

Section 2
[POWER TO ENFORCE THIS ARTICLE]

The Congress shall have power to enforce this article by appropriate legislation.

AMENDMENT XVI

[Proposed by Congress on July 12, 1909; declared ratified on February 25, 1913.]
[AUTHORIZING INCOME TAXES]

The Congress shall have power to lay and collect taxes on incomes, from whatever source derived, without apportionment among the several States, and without regard to any census or enumeration.

AMENDMENT XVII

[Proposed by Congress on May 13, 1912; declared ratified on May 31, 1913.]
[POPULAR ELECTION OF SENATORS]

The Senate of the United States shall be composed of two Senators from each State, elected by the people thereof, for six years; and each Senator shall have one vote. The electors in each State shall have the qualifications requisite for electors of the most numerous branch of the State Legislature.

When vacancies happen in the representation of any State in the Senate, the executive authority of such State shall issue writs of election to fill such vacancies: Provided, That the Legislature of any State may empower the executive thereof to make temporary appointment until the people fill the vacancies by election as the Legislature may direct.

This amendment shall not be so construed as to affect the election or term of any Senator chosen before it becomes valid as part of the Constitution.

AMENDMENT XVIII

[Proposed by Congress December 18, 1917; declared ratified on January 29, 1919.]

Section 1
[NATIONAL LIQUOR PROHIBITION]

After one year from the ratification of this article the manufacture, sale, or transportation of intoxicating liquors within, the importation thereof into, or the exportation thereof from the United States and all territory subject to the jurisdiction thereof for beverage purposes is hereby prohibited.

Section 2
[POWER TO ENFORCE THIS ARTICLE]

The Congress and the several states shall have concurrent power to enforce this article by appropriate legislation.

Section 3
[RATIFICATION WITHIN SEVEN YEARS]

This article shall be inoperative unless it shall have been ratified as an amendment to the Constitution by the legislatures of the several states, as provided in the Constitution, within seven years from the date of the submission hereof to the states by the Congress.15

AMENDMENT XIX
[Proposed by Congress on June 4, 1919; declared ratified on August 26, 1920.]
[WOMAN SUFFRAGE]

The right of the citizens of the United States to vote shall not be denied or abridged by the United States or by any state on account of sex.

Congress shall have power to enforce this article by appropriate legislation.

AMENDMENT XX
[Proposed by Congress on March 2, 1932; declared ratified on February 6, 1933.]

Section 1
[TERMS OF OFFICE]

The terms of the President and Vice-President shall end at noon on the 20th day of January, and the terms of the Senators and Representatives at noon on the 3rd day of January, of the years in which such terms would have ended if this article had not been ratified; and the terms of their successors shall then begin.

Section 2
[TIME OF CONVENING CONGRESS]

The Congress shall assemble at least once in every year, and such meeting shall begin at noon on the 3rd day of January, unless they shall by law appoint a different day.

Section 3
[DEATH OF PRESIDENT-ELECT]

If, at the time fixed for the beginning of the term of the President, the President-elect shall have died, the Vice-President-elect shall become President. If a President shall not have been chosen before the time fixed for the beginning of his term, or if

---

15Repealed by the Twenty-first Amendment.

the President-elect shall have failed to qualify, then the Vice-President-elect shall act as President until a President shall have qualified; and the Congress may by law provide for the case wherein neither a President-elect nor a Vice-President-elect shall have qualified, declaring who shall then act as President, or the manner in which one who is to act shall be selected, and such person shall act accordingly until a President or Vice President shall have qualified.

Section 4
[ELECTION OF THE PRESIDENT]

The Congress may by law provide for the case of the death of any of the persons from whom the House of Representatives may choose a President whenever the right of choice shall have devolved upon them, and for the case of the death of any of the persons from whom the Senate may choose a Vice-President whenever the right of choice shall have devolved upon them.

Section 5
[AMENDMENT TAKES EFFECT]

Sections 1 and 2 shall take effect on the 15th day of October following ratification of this article.

Section 6
[RATIFICATION WITHIN SEVEN YEARS]

This article shall be inoperative unless it shall have been ratified as an amendment to the Constitution by the legislatures of three-fourths of the several States within seven years from the date of its submission.

AMENDMENT XXI

[Proposed by Congress on February 20, 1933; declared ratified on December 5, 1933.]

Section 1
[NATIONAL LIQUOR PROHIBITION REPEALED]

The eighteenth article of amendment to the Constitution of the United States is hereby repealed.

Section 2
[TRANSPORTATION OF LIQUOR INTO "DRY" STATES]

The transportation or importation into any State, Territory, or Possession of the United States for delivery or use therein of intoxicating liquors, in violation of the laws thereof, is hereby prohibited.

Section 3
[RATIFICATION WITHIN SEVEN YEARS]

This article shall be inoperative unless it shall have been ratified as an amendment to the Constitution by conventions in the several States, as provided in the Constitution, within seven years from the date of the submission hereof to the States by the Congress.

AMENDMENT XXII

[Proposed by Congress on March 21, 1947; declared ratified on February 26, 1951.]

Section 1

[TENURE OF PRESIDENT LIMITED]

No person shall be elected to the office of President more than twice, and no person who has held the office of President or acted as President for more than two years of a term to which some other person was elected President shall be elected to the Office of the President more than once. But this Article shall not apply to any person holding the office of President when this Article was proposed by the Congress, and shall not prevent any person who may be holding the office of President, or acting as President, during the term within which this Article becomes operative from holding the office of President or acting as President during the remainder of such term.

Section 2

[RATIFICATION WITHIN SEVEN YEARS]

This Article shall be inoperative unless it shall have been ratified as an amendment to the Constitution by the legislatures of three-fourths of the several states within seven years from the date of its submission to the States by the Congress.

AMENDMENT XXIII

[Proposed by Congress on June 21, 1960; declared ratified on March 29, 1961.]

Section 1

[ELECTORAL COLLEGE VOTES FOR THE DISTRICT OF COLUMBIA]

The District constituting the seat of Government of the United States shall appoint in such manner as the Congress may direct:

A number of electors of President and Vice-President equal to the whole number of Senators and Representatives in Congress to which the District would be entitled if it were a State, but in no event more than the least populous State; they shall be in addition to those appointed by the States, but they shall be considered, for the purposes of the election of President and Vice-President, to be electors appointed by a State; and they shall meet in the District and perform such duties as provided by the twelfth article of amendment.

Section 2

[POWER TO ENFORCE THIS ARTICLE]

The Congress shall have power to enforce this article by appropriate legislation.

AMENDMENT XXIV

[Proposed by Congress on August 27, 1963; declared ratified on January 23, 1964.]

Section 1

[ANTI-POLL TAX]

The right of citizens of the United States to vote in any primary or other election for President or Vice-President, for electors for President or Vice-President, or for

Senator or Representative of Congress, shall not be denied or abridged by the United States or any State by reasons of failure to pay any poll tax or other tax.

Section 2

[POWER TO ENFORCE THIS ARTICLE]

The Congress shall have power to enforce this article by appropriate legislation.

AMENDMENT XXV

[Proposed by Congress on July 7, 1965; declared ratified on February 10, 1967.]

Section 1

[VICE-PRESIDENT TO BECOME PRESIDENT]

In case of the removal of the President from office or his death or resignation, the Vice-President shall become President.

Section 2

[CHOICE OF A NEW VICE-PRESIDENT]

Whenever there is a vacancy in the office of the Vice-President, the President shall nominate a Vice-President who shall take the office upon confirmation by a majority vote of both houses of Congress.

Section 3

[PRESIDENT MAY DECLARE OWN DISABILITY]

Whenever the President transmits to the President pro tempore of the Senate and the Speaker of the House of Representatives his written declaration that he is unable to discharge the powers and duties of his office, and until he transmits to them a written declaration to the contrary, such powers and duties shall be discharged by the Vice-President as Acting President.

Section 4

[ALTERNATE PROCEDURES TO DECLARE AND TO END PRESIDENTIAL DISABILITY]

Whenever the Vice-President and a majority of either the principal officers of the executive departments, or of such other body as Congress may by law provide, transmit to the President pro tempore of the Senate and the Speaker of the House of Representatives their written declaration that the President is unable to discharge the powers and duties of his office, the Vice-President shall immediately assume the powers and duties of the office as Acting President.

Thereafter, when the President transmits to the President pro tempore of the Senate and the Speaker of the House of Representatives his written declaration that no inability exists, he shall resume the powers and duties of his office unless the Vice-President and a majority of either the principal officers of the executive departments, or of such other body as Congress may by law provide, transmit within four days to the President pro tempore of the Senate and the Speaker of the House of Representatives their written declaration that the President is unable to discharge the powers and duties of his office. Thereupon Congress shall decide the issue, assembling within 48 hours for that purpose if not in session. If the Congress, within 21 days after receipt of the latter written declaration, or, if Congress is not in session, within 21 days after Congress is required to assemble, determines by two-thirds vote of both houses that the President is unable to discharge the powers and duties of his office, the Vice-President shall continue to discharge the same as Acting President; otherwise, the President shall resume the powers and duties of his office.

AMENDMENT XXVI

[Proposed by Congress on March 23, 1971; declared ratified on June 30, 1971.]

Section 1
[EIGHTEEN-YEAR-OLD VOTE]

The right of citizens of the United States, who are eighteen years of age or older, to vote shall not be denied or abridged by the United States or by any State on account of age.

Section 2
[POWER TO ENFORCE THIS ARTICLE]

The Congress shall have power to enforce this article by appropriate legislation.

AMENDMENT XXVII

[Proposed by Congress on September 25, 1789; ratified on May 7, 1992.]

No law varying the compensation for the services of the Senators and Representatives shall take effect until an election of Representatives shall have intervened.

The Federalist Papers

No. 10: Madison

Among the numerous advantages promised by a well-constructed Union, none deserves to be more accurately developed than its tendency to break and control the violence of faction. The friend of popular governments never finds himself so much alarmed for their character and fate as when he contemplates their propensity to this dangerous vice. He will not fail, therefore, to set a due value on any plan which, without violating the principles to which he is attached, provides a proper cure for it. The instability, injustice, and confusion introduced into the public councils have, in truth, been the mortal diseases under which popular governments have everywhere perished, as they continue to be the favorite and fruitful topics from which the adversaries to liberty derive their most specious declamations. The valuable improvements made by the American constitutions on the popular models, both ancient and modern, cannot certainly be too much admired; but it would be an unwarrantable partiality to contend that they have as effectually obviated the danger on this side, as was wished and expected. Complaints are everywhere heard from our most considerate and virtuous citizens, equally the friends of public and private faith and of public and personal liberty, that our governments are too unstable, that the public good is disregarded in the conflicts of rival parties, and that measures are too often decided, not according to the rules of justice and the rights of the minor party, but by the superior force of an interested and overbearing majority. However anxiously we may wish that these complaints had no foundation, the evidence of known facts will not permit us to deny that they are in some degree true. It will be found, indeed, on a candid review of our situation, that some of the distresses under which we labor have been erroneously charged on the operation of our governments; but it will be found, at the same time, that other causes will not alone account for many of our heaviest misfortunes; and, particularly, for that prevailing and increasing distrust of public engagements and alarm for private rights which are echoed from one end of the continent to the other. These must be chiefly, if not wholly, effects of the unsteadiness and injustice with which a factious spirit has tainted our public administration.

By a faction I understand a number of citizens, whether amounting to a majority or minority of the whole, who are united and actuated by some common impulse of passion, or of interest, adverse to the rights of other citizens, or to the permanent and aggregate interests of the community.

There are two methods of curing the mischiefs of faction: the one, by removing its causes; the other, by controlling its effects.

There are again two methods of removing the causes of faction: the one, by destroying the liberty which is essential to its existence; the other, by giving to every citizen the same opinions, the same passions, and the same interests.

It could never be more truly said than of the first remedy that it was worse than the disease. Liberty is to faction what air is to fire, an aliment without which it instantly expires. But it could not be a less folly to abolish liberty, which is essential to political life, because it nourishes faction than it would be to wish the annihilation of air, which is essential to animal life, because it imparts to fire its destructive agency.

The second expedient is as impracticable as the first would be unwise. As long as the reason of man continues fallible, and he is at liberty to exercise it, different opinions will be formed. As long as the connection subsists between his reason and his self-love, his opinions and his passions will have a reciprocal influence on each other; and the former will be objects to which the latter will attach themselves. The diversity in the faculties of men, from which the rights of property originate, is not less an insuperable obstacle to a uniformity of interests. The protection of these faculties is the first object of government. From the protection of different and unequal faculties of acquiring property, the possession of different degrees and kinds of property immediately results; and from the influence of these on the sentiments and views of the respective proprietors ensues a division of the society into different interests and parties.

The latent causes of faction are thus sown in the nature of man; and we see them everywhere brought into different degrees of activity, according to the different circumstances of civil society. A zeal for different opinions concerning religion, concerning government, and many other points, as well of speculation as of practice; an attachment to different leaders ambitiously contending for pre-eminence and power; or to persons of other descriptions whose fortunes have been interesting to the human passions, have, in turn, divided mankind into parties, inflamed them with mutual animosity, and rendered them much more disposed to vex and oppress each other than to co-operate for their common good. So strong is this propensity of mankind to fall into mutual animosities that where no substantial occasion presents itself the most frivolous and fanciful distinctions have been sufficient to kindle their unfriendly passions and excite their most violent conflicts. But the most common and durable source of factions has been the various and unequal distribution of property. Those who hold and those who are without property have ever formed distinct interests in society. Those who are creditors, and those who are debtors, fall under a like discrimination. A landed interest, a manufacturing interest, a mercantile interest, a moneyed interest, with many lesser interests, grow up of necessity in civilized nations, and divide them into different classes, actuated by different sentiments and views. The regulation of these various and interfering interests forms the principal task of modern legislation and involves the spirit of party and faction in the necessary and ordinary operations of government.

No man is allowed to be judge in his own cause, because his interest would certainly bias his judgment and, not improbably, corrupt his integrity. With equal, nay with greater reason, a body of men are unfit to be both judges and parties at the same time; yet what are many of the most important acts of legislation but so many judicial determinations, not indeed concerning the rights of single persons, but concerning the rights of large bodies of citizens? And what are the different classes of legislators but advocates and parties to the causes which they determine? Is a law proposed concerning private debts? It is a question to which the creditors are parties on one side and the debtors on the other. Justice ought to hold the balance between them. Yet the parties are, and must be, themselves the judges; and the most numerous party, or in other words, the most powerful faction must be expected to prevail. Shall domestic manufacturers be encouraged, and in what degree, by restrictions on foreign manufacturers? are questions which would be differently decided by the landed and the manufacturing classes, and probably by neither with a sole regard to justice and the public good. The apportionment of taxes on the various descriptions of property is an act which seems to require the most exact impartiality; yet there is, perhaps, no legislative act in which greater opportunity and temptation are given to a predominant party to trample on the rules of justice. Every shilling with which they overburden the inferior number is a shilling saved to their own pockets.

It is in vain to say that enlightened statesmen will be able to adjust these clashing interests and render them all subservient to the public good. Enlightened statesmen will not always be at the helm. Nor, in many cases, can such an adjustment be made at all without taking into view indirect and remote considerations, which will rarely prevail over the immediate interest which one party may find in disregarding the rights of another or the good of the whole.

The inference to which we are brought is that the *causes* of faction cannot be removed and that relief is only to be sought in the means of controlling its *effects*.

If a faction consists of less than a majority, relief is supplied by the republican principle, which enables the majority to defeat its sinister views by regular vote. It may clog the administration, it may convulse the society; but it will be unable to execute and mask its violence under the forms of the Constitution. When a majority is included in a faction, the form of popular government, on the other hand, enables it to sacrifice to its ruling passion or interest both the public good and the rights of other citizens. To secure the public good and private rights against the danger of such a faction, and at the same time to preserve the spirit and the form of popular government, is then the great object to which our inquiries are directed. Let me add that it is the great desideratum by which alone this form of government can be rescued from the opprobrium under which it has so long labored and be recommended to the esteem and adoption of mankind.

By what means is this object attainable? Evidently by one of two only. Either the existence of the same passion or interest in a majority at the same time must be prevented, or the majority, having such coexistent passion or interest, must be rendered, by their number and local situation, unable to concert and carry into effect schemes of oppression. If the impulse and the opportunity be suffered to coincide, we well know that neither moral nor religious motives can be relied on as an adequate control. They are not found to be such on the injustice and violence of individuals, and lose their efficacy in proportion to the number combined together, that is, in proportion as their efficacy becomes needful.

From this view of the subject it may be concluded that a pure democracy, by which I mean a society consisting of a small number of citizens, who assemble and administer the government in person, can admit of no cure for the mischiefs of faction. A common passion or interest will, in almost every case, be felt by a majority of the whole; a communication and concert results from the form of government itself; and there is nothing to check the inducements to sacrifice the weaker party or an obnoxious individual. Hence it is that such democracies have ever been spectacles of turbulence and contention; have ever been found incompatible with personal security or the rights of property; and have in general been as short in their lives as they have been violent in their deaths. Theoretic politicians, who have patronized this species of government, have erroneously supposed that by reducing mankind to a perfect equality in their political rights, they would at the same time be perfectly equalized and assimilated in their possessions, their opinions, and their passions.

A republic, by which I mean a government in which the scheme of representation takes place, opens a different prospect and promises the cure for which we are seeking. Let us examine the points in which it varies from pure democracy, and we shall comprehend both the nature of the cure and the efficacy which it must derive from the Union.

The two great points of difference between a democracy and a republic are: first, the delegation of the government, in the latter, to a small number of citizens elected by the rest; secondly, the greater number of citizens and greater sphere of country over which the latter may be extended.

The effect of the first difference is, on the one hand, to refine and enlarge the public views by passing them through the medium of a chosen body of citizens, whose wisdom may best discern the true interest of their country and whose patriotism and love of justice will be least likely to sacrifice it to temporary or partial considerations. Under such a regulation it may well happen that the public voice, pronounced by the representatives of the people, will be more consonant to the public good than if pronounced by the people themselves, convened for the purpose. On the other hand, the effect may be inverted. Men of factious tempers, of local prejudices, or of sinister designs, may, by intrigue, by corruption, or by other means, first obtain the suffrages, and then betray the interests of the people. The question resulting is, whether small or extensive republics are most favorable to the election of proper guardians of the public weal; and it is clearly decided in favor of the latter by two obvious considerations.

In the first place it is to be remarked that however small the republic may be the representatives must be raised to a certain number in order to guard against the cabals of a few; and that however large it may be they must be limited to a certain number in order to guard against the confusion of a multitude. Hence, the number of representatives in the two cases not being in proportion to that of the constituents, and being proportionally greatest in the small republic, it follows that if the proportion of fit characters be not less in the large than in the small republic, the former will present a greater option, and consequently a greater probability of a fit choice.

In the next place, as each representative will be chosen by a greater number of citizens in the large than in the small republic, it will be more difficult for unworthy candidates to practise with success the vicious arts by which elections are too often carried; and the suffrages of the people being more free, will be more likely to center on men who possess the most attractive merit and the most diffusive and established characters.

It must be confessed that in this, as in most other cases, there is a mean, on both sides of which inconveniencies will be found to lie. By enlarging too much the number of electors, you render the representative too little acquainted with all their local circumstances and lesser interests; as by reducing it too much, you render him unduly attached to these, and too little fit to comprehend and pursue great and national objects. The federal Constitution forms a happy combination in this respect; the great and aggregate interests being referred to the national, the local and particular to the State legislatures.

The other point of difference is the greater number of citizens and extent of territory which may be brought within the compass of republican than of democratic government; and it is this circumstance principally which renders factious combinations less to be dreaded in the former than in the latter. The smaller the society, the fewer probably will be the distinct parties and interests composing it; the fewer the distinct parties and interests, the more frequently will a majority be found of the same party; and the smaller the number of individuals composing a majority, and the smaller the compass within which they are placed, the more easily will they concert and execute their plans of oppression. Extend the sphere and you take in a greater variety of parties and interests; you make it less probable that a majority of the whole will have a common motive to invade the rights of other citizens; or if such a common motive exists, it will be more difficult for all who feel it to discover their own strength and to act in unison with each other. Besides other impediments, it may be remarked that, where there is a consciousness of unjust or dishonorable purposes, communication is always checked by distrust in proportion to the number whose concurrence is necessary.

Hence, it clearly appears that the same advantage which a republic has over a democracy in controlling the effects of faction is enjoyed by a large over a small republic—is enjoyed by the Union over the States composing it. Does this advantage consist in the substitution of representatives whose enlightened views and virtuous sentiments render them superior to local prejudices and to schemes of injustice? It will not be denied that the representation of the Union will be most likely to possess these requisite endowments. Does it consist in the greater security afforded by a greater variety of parties, against the event of any one party being able to outnumber and oppress the rest? In an equal degree does the increased variety of parties comprised within the Union increase this security? Does it, in fine, consist in the greater obstacles opposed to the concert and accomplishment of the secret wishes of an unjust and interested majority? Here again the extent of the Union gives it the most palpable advantage.

The influence of factious leaders may kindle a flame within their particular States but will be unable to spread a general conflagration through the other States. A religious sect may degenerate into a political faction in a part of the Confederacy;

but the variety of sects dispersed over the entire face of it must secure the national councils against any danger from that source. A rage for paper money, for an abolition of debts, for an equal division of property, or for any other improper or wicked project, will be less apt to pervade the whole body of the Union than a particular member of it, in the same proportion as such a malady is more likely to taint a particular county or district than an entire State.

In the extent and proper structure of the Union, therefore, we behold a republican remedy for the diseases most incident to republican government. And according to the degree of pleasure and pride we feel in being republicans ought to be our zeal in cherishing the spirit and supporting the character of federalist.

PUBLIUS

No. 51: Madison

To what expedient, then, shall we finally resort, for maintaining in practice the necessary partition of power among the several departments as laid down in the Constitution? The only answer that can be given is that as all these exterior provisions are found to be inadequate the defect must be supplied, by so contriving the interior structure of the government as that its several constituent parts may, by their mutual relations, be the means of keeping each other in their proper places. Without presuming to undertake a full development of this important idea I will hazard a few general observations which may perhaps place it in a clearer light, and enable us to form a more correct judgment of the principles and structure of the government planned by the convention.

In order to lay a due foundation for that separate and distinct exercise of the different powers of government, which to a certain extent is admitted on all hands to be essential to the preservation of liberty, it is evident that each department should have a will of its own; and consequently should be so constituted that the members of each should have as little agency as possible in the appointment of the members of the others. Were this principle rigorously adhered to, it would require that all the appointments for the supreme executive, legislative, and judiciary magistracies should be drawn from the same fountain of authority, the people, through channels having no communication whatever with one another. Perhaps such a plan of constructing the several departments would be less difficult in practice than it may in contemplation appear. Some difficulties, however, and some additional expense would attend the execution of it. Some deviations, therefore, from the principle must be admitted. In the constitution of the judiciary department in particular, it might be inexpedient to insist rigorously on the principle: first, because peculiar qualifications being essential in the members, the primary consideration ought to be to select that mode of choice which best secures these qualifications; second, because the permanent tenure by which the appointments are held in that department must soon destroy all sense of dependence on the authority conferring them.

It is equally evident that the members of each department should be as little dependent as possible on those of the others for the emoluments annexed to their offices. Were the executive magistrate, or the judges, not independent of the legislature in this particular, their independence in every other would be merely nominal.

But the great security against a gradual concentration of the several powers in the same department consists in giving to those who administer each department the necessary constitutional means and personal motives to resist encroachments of the others. The provision for defense must in this, as in all other cases, be made commensurate to the danger of attack. Ambition must be made to counteract ambition. The interest of the man must be connected with the constitutional rights of the place. It may be a reflection on human nature that such devices should be necessary to control the abuses of government. But what is government itself but the greatest of all reflections on human nature? If men were angels, no government would be necessary. If angels were to govern men, neither external nor internal controls on government would be necessary. In framing a government which is to be administered by men over men, the great difficulty lies in this: you must first enable the government to control the governed; and in the next place oblige it to control itself. A dependence on the people is, no doubt, the primary control on the government; but experience has taught mankind the necessity of auxiliary precautions.

This policy of supplying, by opposite and rival interests, the defect of better motives, might be traced through the whole system of human affairs, private as well as public. We see it particularly displayed in all the subordinate distributions of power, where the constant aim is to divide and arrange the several offices in such a manner as that each may be a check on the other—that the private interest of every individual may be a sentinel over the public rights. These inventions of prudence cannot be less requisite in the distribution of the supreme powers of the State.

But it is not possible to give to each department an equal power of self-defense. In republican government, the legislative authority necessarily predominates. The remedy for this inconveniency is to divide the legislature into different branches; and to render them, by different modes of election and different principles of action, as little connected with each other as the nature of their common functions and their common dependence on the society will admit. It may even be necessary to guard against dangerous encroachments by still further precautions. As the weight of the legislative authority requires that it should be thus divided, the weakness of the executive may require, on the other hand, that it should be fortified. An absolute negative on the legislature appears, at first view, to be the natural defense with which the executive magistrate should be armed. But perhaps it would be neither altogether safe nor alone sufficient. On ordinary occasions it might not be exerted with the requisite firmness, and on extraordinary occasions it might be perfidiously abused. May not this defect of an absolute negative be supplied by some qualified connection between this weaker branch of the stronger department, by which the latter may be led to support the constitutional rights of the former, without being too much detached from the rights of its own department?

If the principles on which these observations are founded be just, as I persuade myself they are, and they be applied as a criterion to the several State constitutions, and to the federal Constitution, it will be found that if the latter does not perfectly correspond with them, the former are infinitely less able to bear such a test.

There are, moreover, two considerations particularly applicable to the federal system of America, which place that system in a very interesting point of view.

First. In a single republic, all the power surrendered by the people is submitted to the administration of a single government; and the usurpations are guarded against by a division of the government into distinct and separate departments. In the compound republic of America, the power surrendered by the people is first divided between two distinct governments, and then the portion allotted to each sub-divided among distinct and separate departments. Hence a double security arises to the rights of the people. The different governments will control each other, at the same time that each will be controlled by itself.

Second. It is of great importance in a republic not only to guard the society against the oppression of its rulers, but to guard one part of the society against the injustice of the other part. Different interests necessarily exist in different classes of citizens. If a majority be united by a common interest, the rights of the minority will be inse-cure. There are but two methods of providing against this evil: the one by creating a will in the community independent of the majority—that is, of the society itself; the other, by comprehending in the society so many separate descriptions of citizens as will render an unjust combination of a majority of the whole very improbable, if not impracticable. The first method prevails in all governments possessing an heredi-tary or self-appointed authority. This, at best, is but a precarious security; because a power independent of the society may as well espouse the unjust views of the major as the rightful interests of the minor party, and may possibly be turned against both parties. The second method will be exemplified in the federal republic of the United States. Whilst all authority in it will be derived from and dependent on the society, the society itself will be broken into so many parts, interests and classes of citizens, that the rights of individuals, or of the minority, will be in little danger from inter-ested combinations of the majority. In a free government the security for civil rights must be the same as that for religious rights. It consists in the one case in the mul-tiplicity of interests, and in the other in the multiplicity of sects. The degree of secu-rity in both cases will depend on the number of interests and sects; and this may be presumed to depend on the extent of country and number of people comprehended under the same government. This view of the subject must particularly recommend a proper federal system to all the sincere and considerate friends of republican gov-ernment, since it shows that in exact proportion as the territory of the Union may be formed into more circumscribed Confederacies, or States, oppressive combina-tions of a majority will be facilitated; the best security, under the republican forms, for the rights of every class of citizen, will be diminished; and consequently the sta-bility and independence of some member of the government, the only other securi-ty, must be proportionally increased. Justice is the end of government. It is the end of civil society. It ever has been and ever will be pursued until it be obtained, or until liberty be lost in the pursuit. In a society under the forms of which the stronger fac-tion can readily unite and oppress the weaker, anarchy may as truly be said to reign as in a state of nature, where the weaker individual is not secured against the vio-lence of the stronger; and as, in the latter state, even the stronger individuals are prompted, by the uncertainty of their condition, to submit to a government which may protect the weak as well as themselves; so, in the former state, will the more powerful factions or parties be gradually induced, by a like motive, to wish for a government which will protect all parties, the weaker as well as the more powerful. It can be little doubted that if the State of Rhode Island was separated from the Confederacy and left to itself, the insecurity of rights under the popular form of government within such narrow limits would be displayed by such reiterated oppressions of factious majorities that some power altogether independent of the people would soon be called for by the voice of the very factions whose misrule had proved the necessity of it. In the extended republic of the United States, and among the great variety of interests, parties, and sects which it embraces, a coalition of a majority of the whole society could seldom take place on any other principles than those of justice and the general good; whilst there being thus less danger to a minor from the will of a major party, there must be less pretext, also, to provide for the security of the former, by introducing into the government a will not dependent on the latter, or, in other words, a will independent of the society itself. It is no less certain than it is important, notwithstanding the contrary opinions which have been entertained, that the larger the society, provided it lie within a practicable sphere, the more duly capable it will be of self-government. And happily for the *republican cause,* the practicable sphere may be carried to a very great extent by a judicious modification and mixture of the *federal principle.*

PUBLIUS

Glossary

administrative legislation   Rules made by **regulatory agencies** and commissions.

administrative regulation   Rules made by **regulatory agencies** and commissions.

affirmative action   A policy or program designed to redress historic injustices against specified groups by actively promoting equal access to educational and employment opportunities.

agencies of socialization   Social institutions, including families and schools, that help to shape individuals' basic political **beliefs** and **values**.

agency representation   The type of representation by which representatives are held accountable to their constituents if they fail to represent them properly.

agenda setting   The power of the media to bring public attention to particular issues and problems.

Aid to Families with Dependent Children (AFDC)   Federal funds, administered by the states, for children living with persons or relatives who fall below state standards of need. Abolished in 1996 and replaced with **Temporary Assistance to Needy Families (TANF)**.

amicus curiae   Literally, "friend of the court"; individuals or groups who are not parties to a lawsuit but seek to assist the court in reaching a decision by presenting an additional **briefs.**

Antifederalists   Those who favored strong state governments and a weak national government and who were opponents of the constitution proposed at the American Constitutional Convention of 1787.

antitrust policy   **Government** regulation of large businesses that have established **monopolies.**

appropriations   The amounts of money approved by Congress in statutes (bills) that each unit or agency of government can spend.

Articles of Confederation   America's first written constitution. Adopted by the Continental Congress in 1777, the Articles of Confederation and Perpetual Union was the formal basis for America's national **government** until 1789, when it was supplanted by the Constitution.

attitude (or opinion)   A specific preference on a particular issue.

Australian ballot   An electoral format that presents the names of all the candidates for any given office on the same ballot. Introduced at the turn of the twentieth century, the Australian ballot replaced the partisan ballot and facilitated split-ticket voting.

authoritarian government   A system of rule in which the **government** recognizes no formal limits but may nevertheless be restrained by the power of other social institutions.

autocracy   A form of **government** in which a single individual—a monarch or dictator—rules.

balance-of-power role   The strategy whereby many countries form alliances with one or more other countries in order to counterbalance the behavior of other, more powerful, nation-states.

bandwagon effect   A situation wherein reports of voter or delegate opinion can influence the actual outcome of an election or a nominating convention.

bicameralism   Division of a legislative assembly into two houses, chambers, or branches.

Bill of Rights   The first ten amendments to the U.S. Constitution, ratified in 1791. They ensure certain rights and liberties to the people.

block grants   Federal grants-in-aid that allow states considerable discretion in how the funds should be spent.

brief   A written document in which attorneys explain why a court should rule in favor of their client.

budget deficit   The amount by which **government** spending exceeds government revenue in a fiscal year.

bureaucracy   The complex structure of offices, tasks, rules, and principles of organization that are employed by all large-scale institutions to coordinate the work of their personnel.

bureaucratic drift   The oft-observed phenomenon of bureaucratic implementation that produces policy more to the liking of the **bureaucracy** than to the original intention of the legislation that created it, but without triggering a political reaction from elected officials.

Bush doctrine   Foreign policy based on the idea that the United States should take preemptive action against threats to its national security.

cabinet   The secretaries, or chief administrators, of the major departments of the federal **government**. Cabinet secretaries are appointed by the president with the consent of the Senate.

casework   An effort by members of Congress to gain the trust and support of constituents by providing personal service. One important type of casework consists of helping constituents obtain favorable treatment from the federal **bureaucracy.**

categorical grants-in-aid   Grants by Congress to states and localities given with the condition that expenditures be limited to a problem or group specified by the national government.

caucus (political)   A normally closed meeting of a political or legislative group to select candidates, plan strategy, or make decisions regarding legislative matters.

checks and balances Mechanisms through which each branch of **government** is able to participate in and influence the activities of the other branches.

chief justice Justice on the **Supreme Court** who presides over the Court's public sessions.

civil law A system of jurisprudence, including private law and governmental actions, to settle disputes that do not involve criminal penalties.

civil liberties Areas of personal freedom with which governments are constrained from interfering.

civil rights Legal or moral claims that citizens are entitled to make upon the **government** to protect them from the illegal actions of other citizens and government agencies.

clientele agencies Departments or bureaus of **government** whose mission is to promote, serve, or represent a particular interest.

client state A nation-state dependent upon a more powerful nation-state but still with enough power and resources to conduct its own foreign policy up to a point.

closed primary A primary election in which voters can participate in the nomination of candidates, but only of the party in which they are enrolled for a period of time prior to primary day. Contrast with **open primary.**

closed rule Provision by the House Rules Committee limiting or prohibiting the introduction of amendments during debate.

cloture Rule allowing a majority, two thirds, or three fifths of the members in a legislative body to set a time limit on debate over a given bill.

coercion Forcing a person to do something by threats or pressure.

cold war The period of struggle between the United States and the former Soviet Union between the late 1940s and 1990.

collective goods Benefits, sought by groups, that are broadly available and cannot be denied to nonmembers.

commander in chief The position of the president as commander of the national military and the state national guard units (when they are called into service).

commerce clause Article I, Section 8, of the Constitution, which delegates to Congress the power "to regulate Commerce with foreign Nations, and among the several States, and with the Indian Tribes. . . ." The Supreme Court interpreted this clause in favor of national power over the economy.

concurrent powers Authority possessed by *both* state and national **governments**, such as the power to levy taxes.

conference committee A joint committee created to work out a compromise on House and Senate versions of a piece of legislation.

conscription An aspect of **coercion** whereby the **government** requires certain involuntary services of citizens, such as compulsory military service, known as "the draft."

conservative Today this term refers to one who generally supports the social and economic status quo and is suspicious of efforts to introduce new political formulae and economic arrangements. Conservatives believe that a large and powerful **government** poses a threat to citizens' freedom.

constituency   Members of the district from which an official is elected.

constitutional government   A system of rule in which formal and effective limits are placed on the powers of the **government.**

containment   The policy used by the United States during the cold war to restrict the expansion of communism and limit the influence of the Soviet Union.

contracting power   The power of **government** to set conditions on companies seeking to sell goods or services to government agencies.

contributory programs   Social programs financed in whole or in part by taxation or other mandatory contributions by their present or future recipients. The most important example is **Social Security,** which is financed by a payroll tax.

cooperative federalism   A type of **federalism** existing since the New Deal era, in which **grants-in-aid** have been used strategically to encourage states and localities (without commanding them) to pursue nationally defined goals. Also known as intergovernmental cooperation.

court of appeals   A court that hears the appeals of trial court decisions.

criminal law   The branch of law that deals with disputes or actions involving criminal penalties (as opposed to **civil law**). It regulates the conduct of individuals, defines crimes, and provides punishment for criminal acts.

***de facto* segregation**   Racial segregation that is not a direct result of law or **government** policy but is, instead, a reflection of residential patterns, income distributions, or other social factors.

defendant   The individual or organization against whom a complaint is brought in criminal or civil cases.

***de jure* segregation**   Racial segregation that is a direct result of law or official policy.

delegate   A representative who votes according to the preferences of his or her **constituency.**

delegated powers   Constitutional powers that are assigned to one governmental agency but are exercised by another agency with the express permission of the first.

democracy   A system of rule that permits citizens to play a significant part in the governmental process, usually through the election of key public officials.

deregulation   A policy of reducing or eliminating regulatory restraints in the conduct of individuals or private institutions.

deterrence   The development and maintenance of military strength as a means of discouraging attack.

devolution   A policy to remove a program from one level of government by delegating it or passing it down to a lower level of government, such as from the national government to the states.

diplomacy   The representation of a government to other foreign governments.

discount rate   The interest rate charged by the **Federal Reserve** when commercial banks borrow in order to expand their lending operations; an effective tool of monetary policy.

discretionary spending   Federal spending on programs that are controlled through the regular budget process.

dissenting opinion Decision written by a justice in the minority in a particular case, in which the justice wishes to express his or her reasoning in the case.

distributive tendency The tendency of Congress to spread the benefits of a bill over a wide range of members' districts.

divided government The condition in American **government** in which one party controls the presidency while the opposing party controls one or both houses of Congress.

dual federalism The system of **government** that prevailed in the United States from 1789 to 1937 in which most fundamental governmental powers were shared between the federal and state governments. Compare with **cooperative federalism.**

due process To proceed according to law and with adequate protection for individual rights.

economic-expansionist role The strategy often pursued by capitalist countries to adopt foreign policies that will maximize the success of domestic corporations in their dealings with other countries.

electoral college The presidential electors from each state who meet in their respective state capitals after the popular election to cast ballots for president and vice president.

electoral realignment The point in history when a new party supplants the ruling party, becoming in turn the dominant political force. In the United States, this has tended to occur roughly every thirty years.

eminent domain The right of the **government** to take private property for public use, with reasonable compensation rewarded for the property.

entitlement Eligibility for benefits by virtue of a category of benefits defined by legislation.

equality of opportunity A universally shared American ideal that all people should have the freedom to use whatever talents and wealth they have to reach their fullest potential.

equal protection clause A clause in the Fourteenth Amendment that requires that states provide citizens "equal protection of the laws." This clause has served as the basis for the **civil rights** of African Americans, women, and other groups.

equal time rule The requirement that broadcasters provide candidates for the same political office an equal opportunity to communicate their messages to the public.

establishment clause The First Amendment clause that says, "Congress shall make no law respecting an establishment of religion." This law means that a wall of separation exists between church and state.

exclusionary rule The ability of the court to exclude evidence obtained in violation of the Fourth Amendment.

executive agreement Agreement between the president and another country, which has the force of a treaty but does not require the Senate's "advice and consent."

executive order A rule or regulation issued by the president that has the effect and formal status of legislation.

executive privilege The claim that confidential communications between a president and close advisers should not be revealed without the consent of the president.

expressed power   The notion that the Constitution grants to the federal government only those powers specifically named in its text. E.g. Those powers granted to Congress under Article 1, Section 8 of the Constitution, or specific powers granted to the president under Article II, Sections 2 and 3 of the Constitution.

expropriation   Confiscation of property with or without compensation.

fairness doctrine   An FCC requirement that broadcasters who air programs on controversial issues provide time for opposing views.

federal funds rate   The interest rate on loans between banks that the Federal Reserve Board influences by affecting the supply of money available.

federalism   System of **government** in which power is divided by a constitution between a central government and regional governments.

Federalists   Those who favored a strong national government and supported the constitution proposed at the American Constitutional Convention of 1787.

Federal Reserve System (Fed)   Consisting of twelve Federal Reserve Banks, an agency that facilitates exchanges of cash, checks, and credit; it regulates member banks; and it uses monetary policies to fight inflation and deflation.

fighting words   Speech that directly incites damaging conduct.

filibuster   A tactic used by members of the Senate to prevent action on legislation they oppose by continuously holding the floor and speaking until the majority backs down. Once given the floor, senators have unlimited time to speak, and it requires a vote of three fifths of the Senate to end a filibuster.

fiscal policies   The government's use of taxing, monetary, and spending powers to manipulate the economy.

527 committees   Nonprofit independent groups that receive and disburse funds to influence the nomination, election, or defeat of candidates. Named after Section 527 of the Internal Revenue Code, which defines and provides tax-exempt status for nonprofit advocacy groups.

Food Stamps   Coupons that can be exchanged for food at most grocery stores; the largest **in-kind benefits** program.

formula grants   **Grants-in-aid** in which a formula is used to determine the amount of federal funds a state or local **government** will receive.

framing   The power of the media to influence how events and issues are interpreted.

free riders   Those who enjoy the benefits of **collective goods** but did not participate in acquiring them. See also **public good.**

full faith and credit clause   Article IV, Section I, of the Constitution provides that each state must accord the same respect to the laws and judicial decisions of other states that it accords to its own.

gender gap   A distinctive pattern of voting behavior reflecting the differences in views between women and men.

gerrymandering   Apportionment of voters in districts in such a way as to give unfair advantage to one political party.

going public   A strategy that attempts to mobilize the widest and most favorable climate of opinion.

government   Institutions and procedures through which a territory and its people are ruled.

grand jury   A jury that determines whether sufficient evidence is available to justify a trial. Grand juries do not rule on the accused's guilt or innocence.

grants-in-aid   A general term for funds given by Congress to state and local **governments**. See also **categorical grants-in-aid.**

grassroots lobbying   A lobbying campaign in which a group mobilizes its membership to contact government officials in support of the group's position.

Great Compromise   Agreement reached at the Constitutional Convention of 1787 that gave each state an equal number of senators regardless of its population, but linked representation in the House of Representatives to population.

habeas corpus   A court order demanding that an individual in custody be brought into court and shown the cause for detention. *Habeas corpus* is guaranteed by the Constitution and can only be suspended only in cases of rebellion or invasion.

Holy Alliance role   A strategy pursued by a superpower to prevent any change in the existing distribution of power among nation-states, even if this requires intervention into the internal affairs of another country in order to keep a ruler from being overthrown.

home rule   Power delegated by the state to a local unit of **government** to manage its own affairs.

illusion of salience   Impression conveyed by polls that something is important to the public when actually it is not.

impeachment   To charge a governmental official (president or otherwise) with "Treason, Bribery, or other high Crimes and Misdemeanors" and bring him or her before Congress to determine guilt.

implementation   The efforts of departments and agencies to translate laws into specific bureaucratic routines.

implied powers   Powers derived from the **necessary and proper clause** of Article I, Section 8, of the Constitution. Such powers are not specifically **expressed** but are implied through the expansive interpretation of **delegated powers.**

incumbency   Holding a political office for which one is running.

indexing   Periodic adjustments of welfare payments, wages, or taxes, tied to the cost of living.

informational benefits   Special newsletters, periodicals, training programs, conferences, and other information provided to members of groups to entice others to join.

inherent powers   Powers claimed by a president that are not expressed in the Constitution but are inferred from it.

initiative   The process that allows citizens to propose new laws and submit them for approval by the state's voters.

in-kind benefits   Goods and services provided to needy individuals and families by the federal **government**. The largest in-kind federal welfare program is **Food Stamps.**

institutions   The rules and procedures that guide political behavior.

interest group   A group of people organized around a shared belief or mutual concern who try to influence the government to make policies promoting their belief or concern.

intermediate scrutiny   The test used by the Supreme Court in gender discrimination cases. Intermediate scrutiny places the burden of proof partially on the government and partially on the challengers to show that the law in question is constitutional.

International Monetary Fund (IMF)   An institution established in 1944 at Bretton Woods, New Hampshire, to provide loans to needy member countries and to facilitate international monetary exchange.

issue advocacy   Independent spending by individuals or **interest groups** on a campaign issue but not directly tied to a particular candidate.

judicial activism   Proclivity of a court to select cases because of their importance to society rather than adhere to strict legal standards of jurisdiction.

judicial restraint   Judicial deference to the views of legislatures and adherence to strict jurisdictional standards.

judicial review   Power of the courts to declare actions of the legislative and executive branches invalid or unconstitutional. The **Supreme Court** asserted this power in *Marbury v. Madison* (1803).

jurisdiction   The authority of a court to consider a case initially. Distinguished from appellate jurisdiction, which is the authority to hear appeals from a lower court's decision.

legislative initiative   The president's inherent power to bring a legislative agenda before Congress.

legislative supremacy   The preeminence of Congress among the three branches of government, as established by the Constitution.

***Lemon* test**   Rule articulated in *Lemon v. Kurtzman* according to which governmental action in respect to religion is permissible if it is secular in purpose, does not lead to "excessive entanglement" with religion, and neither promotes nor inhibits the practice of religion.

libel   A written statement made in "reckless disregard of the truth" and considered damaging to a victim because it is "malicious, scandalous, and defamatory."

liberal   A liberal today generally supports political and social reform; extensive governmental intervention in the economy; the expansion of federal social services; more vigorous efforts on behalf of the poor, minorities, and women; and greater concern for consumers and the environment.

license   Permission to engage in some activity that is otherwise illegal, such as hunting or practicing medicine.

line-item veto   Power that allows a governor (or the president) to strike out specific provisions (lines) of bills that the legislature passes. Without a line-item veto, the governor (or president) must accept or reject an entire bill. The line-item veto is no longer in effect for the president.

lobbying   Strategy by which organized interests seek to influence the passage of legislation by exerting direct pressure on members of the legislature; this term is derived from having to wait in the lobbies just outside the floor of the legislature, where outsiders are not permitted.

logrolling   A legislative practice wherein reciprocal agreements are made between legislators, usually in voting for or against a bill. In contrast to bargaining, parties to logrolling have nothing in common but their desire to exchange support.

majority leader   The elected leader of the party holding a majority of the seats in the House of Representatives or the Senate. In the House, the majority leader is subordinate in the party hierarchy to the Speaker.

majority party   The party that holds the majority of legislative seats in either the House or the Senate.

majority system   Type of electoral system in which, to win a seat in the parliament or other representative body, a candidate must receive a majority of all the votes cast in the relevant district.

mandatory spending   Federal spending that is made up of **"uncontrollables."**

Marshall Plan   The U.S. European Recovery Plan, in which over $34 billion was spent for relief, reconstruction, and economic recovery of Western Europe after World War II.

material benefits   Special goods, services, or money provided to members of groups to entice others to join.

means testing   Procedure by which potential beneficiaries of a public assistance program establish their eligibility by demonstrating a genuine need for the assistance.

measurement error   Failure to identify the true distribution of opinion within a population because of errors such as ambiguous or poorly worded questions.

Medicaid   A federally financed state-operated program providing medical services to low-income people.

Medicare   National health insurance for the elderly and the disabled.

minority leader   The elected leader of the party holding less than a majority of the seats in the House or Senate.

Miranda rule   Principles developed by the **Supreme Court** in *Miranda v. Arizona* (1966) requiring those under arrest be informed of their legal rights, including right to counsel, prior to police interrogation.

monetary policies   Efforts to regulate the economy through manipulation of the supply of money and credit. America's most powerful institution in the area of monetary policy is the Federal Reserve Board.

mootness   A criterion used by courts to screen cases that no longer require resolution.

Motor Voter bill   A legislative act passed in 1993 that requires all states to allow voters to register by mail when they renew their drivers' licenses and provides for the placement of voter registration forms in motor vehicle, public assistance, and military recruitment offices.

multilateralism   A foreign policy that seeks to encourage the involvement of several nation-states in coordinated action, usually in relation to a common adversary, with terms and conditions usually specified in a multicountry treaty, such as NATO.

multiple-member district   An electorate that selects all candidates at large from the whole district; each voter is given the number of votes equivalent to the number of seats to be filled.

Napoleonic role   Strategy pursued by a powerful nation to prevent aggressive actions against itself by improving the internal state of affairs of a particular country, even if this means encouraging revolution in that country.

National Security Council (NSC)   A presidential foreign policy advisory council composed of the president; the vice president; the secretaries of state, defense, and the treasury; the attorney general; and other officials invited by the president. The NSC has a staff of foreign policy specialists.

nation-state   A political entity consisting of a people with some common cultural experience (nation), who also share a common political authority (state), recognized by other sovereignties (nation-states).

necessary and proper clause   Article I, Section 8, of the Constitution, which enumerates the powers of Congress and provides Congress with the authority to make all laws "necessary and proper" to carry them out; also referred to as the "elastic clause."

New Jersey Plan   A framework for the Constitution, introduced by William Paterson, which called for equal representation in the national legislature regardless of a state's population.

nomination   The process through which political parties select their candidate for election to public office.

noncontributory programs   Social programs that provide assistance to people based on demonstrated need rather than any contribution they have made. Also known as *public assistance programs.*

North Atlantic Treaty Organization (NATO)   A treaty organization comprising the United States, Canada, and most of Western Europe, formed in 1948 to counter the perceived threat from the Soviet Union.

oligarchy   A form of **government** in which a small group—landowners, military officers, or wealthy merchants—controls most of the governing decisions.

open-market operations   The buying and selling of **government** securities to help finance government operations and to loosen or tighten the total amount of credit circulating in the economy.

open primary   A primary election in which the voter can wait until the day of the primary to choose which party to enroll in to select candidates for the general election. Contrast with **closed primary.**

open rule   Provision by the House Rules Committee that permits floor debate and the addition of amendments to a bill.

opinion   The written explanation of the **Supreme Court**'s decision in a particular case.

oral argument   Oral presentations to a court made by attorneys for both sides in a dispute.

oversight   The effort by Congress, through hearings, investigations, and other techniques, to exercise control over the activities of executive agencies.

party caucus (party conference)   A normally closed meeting of a political or legislative group to select candidates, plan strategy, or make decisions regarding legislative matters.

party vote   A **roll-call vote** in the House or Senate in which at least 50 percent of the members of one party take a particular position and are opposed by at least 50 percent of the members of the other party. Party votes are rare today although they were fairly common in the nineteenth century.

patronage   The resources available to higher officials, usually opportunities to make partisan appointments to offices and to confer grants, licenses, or special favors to supporters.

permanent campaign   Description of presidential politics in which all presidential actions are taken with reelection in mind.

plaintiff   The individual or organization who brings a complaint in court.

plea bargains   Negotiated agreements in criminal cases in which a **defendant** agrees to plead guilty in return for the state's agreement to reduce the severity of the criminal charge the defendant is facing.

pluralism   The theory that all interests are and should be free to compete for influence in the **government.** The outcome of this competition is balance and compromise.

plurality system   Type of electoral system in which, to win a seat in the parliament or other representative body, a candidate need only receive the most votes in an election, not necessarily a majority of votes cast.

pocket veto   A presidential veto of legislation wherein the president takes no formal action on a bill. If Congress adjourns within ten days of passing a bill, and the president does not sign it, the bill is considered to be vetoed.

police power   Power reserved to the state to regulate the health, safety, and morals of its citizens.

political action committee (PAC)   A private group that raises and distributes funds for use in election campaigns.

political caucus   A normally closed meeting of a political or legislative group to select candidates, plan strategy, or make decisions regarding legislative matters.

political ideology   A cohesive set of beliefs that form a general philosophy about the role of **government.**

political parties   Organized groups that attempt to influence the government by electing their members to important government offices.

political socialization   The induction of individuals into the political culture; learning the underlying **beliefs** and **values** upon which the political system is based.

politics   The conflicts and struggles over the leadership, structure, and policies of government.

poll tax   A state-imposed tax on voters as a prerequisite for registration. Poll taxes were rendered unconstitutional in national elections by the Twenty-fourth Amendment, and in state elections by the Supreme Court in 1966.

pork-barrel legislation   Appropriations made by legislative bodies for local projects that are often not needed but are created so that local representatives can win reelection their home district.

power   Influence over a government's leadership, organization, or policies.

precedents   Prior cases whose principles are used by judges as the bases for their decisions in present cases.

priming   When media coverage affects public perception and evaluation of political leaders and candidates.

principal-agent relationship   The relationship between a principal and his or her agent; this relationship may be affected by the fact that each is motivated by their own self-interest.

prior restraint   An effort by a government agency to block the publication of material it deems libelous or harmful in some other way; censorship. In the United States, the courts forbid prior restraint except under the most extraordinary circumstances.

privatization   Removing all or part of a program from the public sector to the private sector.

privileges and immunities clause   Provision from Article IV, Section 2, of the Constitution that a state cannot discriminate against someone from another state or give its own residents special privileges.

probability sampling   A method used by pollsters to select a representative sample in which every individual in the population has an equal probability of being selected as a respondent.

progressive taxation   Taxation that hits the upper income brackets more heavily.

project grants   Grant programs in which state and local **governments** submit proposals to federal agencies and for which funding is provided on a competitive basis.

promotional technique   A technique of control that encourages people to do something they might not otherwise do, or to continue an action or behavior. Three types of promotional techniques are **subsidies**, contracts, and **licenses.**

proportional representation   A multiple-member district system that awards seats based on the percentage of the vote won by each candidate. By contrast, the "winner-take-all" system of elections awards the seat to the one candidate who wins the most votes.

prospective voting   Voting based on the imagined future performance of a candidate.

public good   A good that (1) may be enjoyed by anyone if it is provided and (2) may not be denied to anyone once it has been provided. See also **free riding.**

public law   Cases in private law, **civil law,** or **criminal law** in which one party to the dispute argues that a license is unfair, a law is inequitable or unconstitutional, or an agency has acted unfairly, violated a procedure, or gone beyond its jurisdiction.

public opinion   Citizens' attitudes about political issues, personalities, institutions, and events.

public opinion polls   Scientific instruments for measuring public opinion.

public policy   A law, rule, statute, or edict that expresses the **government**'s goals and provides for rewards and punishments to promote their attainment.

purposive benefits   Selective **benefits** of group membership that emphasize the purpose and accomplishments of the group.

push polling   A polling technique in which the questions are designed to shape the respondent's opinion.

random digit dialing   Polls in which respondents are selected at random from a list of ten-digit telephone numbers, with every effort made to avoid bias in the construction of the sample.

recall   Procedure to allow voters an opportunity to remove state officials from office before their terms expire.

referendum   The practice of referring a measure proposed by a legislature to the vote of the electorate for approval or rejection.

regressive taxation   Taxation that hits the lower income brackets more heavily.

regulated federalism   A form of **federalism** in which Congress imposes legislation on the states and localities requiring them to meet national standards.

regulatory agencies   Departments, bureaus, or independent agencies whose primary mission is to impose limits, restrictions, or other obligations on the conduct of individuals or companies in the private sector.

regulatory techniques   Techniques the government uses to control the conduct of people.

representative democracy   A system of government that provides the populace with the opportunity to make the government responsive to its views through the selection of representatives who, in turn, play a significant role in governmental decision making.

reserve requirement   The amount of liquid assets and ready cash that the **Federal Reserve** requires banks to hold to meet depositors' demands for their money.

responsible party government   A set of principles that idealizes a strong role for parties in defining their stance on issues, mobilizing voters, and fulfilling their campaign promises once in office.

retrospective voting   Voting based on the past performance of a candidate.

right to privacy   The right to be let alone, which has been interpreted by the Supreme Court to entail free access to birth control and abortions.

right of rebuttal   An FCC regulation giving individuals the right to have the opportunity to respond to personal attacks made on a radio or TV broadcast.

roll-call vote   A vote in which each legislator's yes or no vote is recorded as the clerk calls the names of the members alphabetically.

salient interests   Attitudes and views that are especially important to the individual holding them.

sample   A small group selected by researchers to represent the most important characteristics of an entire population.

sampling error   A polling error that arises on account of the small size of the sample.

selection bias   Polling error that arises when the sample is not representative of the population being studied, which creates errors in overrepresenting or underrepresenting some opinions

senatorial courtesy   The practice whereby the president, before formally nominating a person for a federal judgeship, will seek approval of the nomination from the senators who represent the candidate's own state.

seniority   Priority or status ranking given to an individual on the basis of length of continuous service in a committee in Congress.

"separate but equal" rule   Doctrine that public accommodations could be segregated by race but still be equal.

separation of powers   The division of governmental power among several institutions that must cooperate in decision making.

single-member district   An electorate that is allowed to elect only one representative from each district; the normal method of representation in the United States.

slander   An oral statement made in "reckless disregard of the truth" and considered damaging to a victim because it is "malicious, scandalous, and defamatory."

social benefits   Selective benefits of a group membership that emphasize friendship, networking, and consciousness-raising.

Social Security   A **contributory** welfare **program** into which working Americans contribute a percentage of their wages and from which they receive cash benefits after retirement.

soft money   Money contributed directly to political parties for voter registration and organization.

solicitor general   The top government lawyer in all cases before the appellate courts where the government is a party.

Speaker of the House   The chief presiding officer of the House of Representatives. The Speaker is elected at the beginning of every Congress on a straight **party vote.** The Speaker is the most important party and House leader and can influence the legislative agenda, the fate of individual pieces of legislation, and members' positions within the House.

speech plus   Speech accompanied by activities such as sit-ins, picketing, and demonstrations. Protection of this form of speech under the First Amendment is conditional, and restrictions imposed by state or local authorities are acceptable if properly balanced by considerations of public order.

spending power   A combination of **subsidies** and contracts that the government can use to redistribute income.

standing   The right of an individual or organization to initiate a court case.

standing committee   A permanent committee with the power to propose and write legislation that covers a particular subject such as finance or appropriations.

stare decisis   Literally "let the decision stand." A previous decision by a court applies as a precedent in similar cases until that decision is overruled.

state sovereign immunity   Legal doctrine that holds that states cannot be sued for violating an act of Congress.

states' rights   The principle that states should oppose increasing authority of the national **government.** This view was most popular before the Civil War.

strict scrutiny   Higher standard of judicial protection for speech cases and other civil liberties and civil rights cases, in which the burden of proof shifts from the complainant to the government.

subsidies   Government grants of cash or other valuable commodities, such as land, to individuals or organizations; used to promote activities desired by the **government**, reward political support, or buy off political opposition.

Supplemental Security Income (SSI)   A program providing a minimum monthly income to people who pass a **"means test"** and who are sixty-five or older, blind, or disabled. Financed from general revenues rather than **Social Security** contributions.

supremacy clause   Article VI of the Constitution, which states that all laws passed by the national **government** and all treaties are the supreme laws of the land and superior to all laws adopted by any state or any subdivision.

supreme court   The highest court in a particular state or in the United States. This court primarily serves an appellate function.

tariff   A tax placed on imported goods.

Temporary Assistance to Needy Families (TANF)   A policy by which states are given **block grants** by the federal government in order to create their own programs for public assistance. *See* **Aid to Families with Dependent Children (AFDC)**.

third parties   Parties that organize to compete against the two major American political parties.

Three-fifths Compromise   Agreement reached at the Constitutional Convention of 1787 stipulating that for purposes of the apportionment of congressional seats, every slave would be counted as three-fifths of a person.

trial court   The first court to hear a criminal or civil case.

trustee   A representative who votes based on what he or she thinks is best for his or her **constituency**.

uncontrollables   Budgetary items that are beyond the control of budgetary committees and can be controlled only by substantive legislative action in Congress. Some uncontrollables such as interest on the debt, are beyond the power of Congress because the terms of payments are set in contracts.

unfunded mandates   Regulations or conditions for receiving grants that impose costs on state and local governments for which they are not reimbursed by the federal government.

Uniform Commercial Code   A set of standards for contract law, recognized by all states, that greatly reduces interstate differences in the practice of contract law.

unilateralism   A foreign policy that seeks to avoid international alliances, entanglements, and permanent commitments in favor of independence, neutrality, and freedom of action.

United Nations (UN)   The organization of nations founded in 1945, mainly to serve as a channel for negotiation and a means of settling international disputes peaceably. It has had frequent successes in providing a forum for negotiation and on some occasions a means of preventing international conflicts from spreading. On a number of occasions, the UN has been a convenient cover for U.S. foreign-policy goals.

values (or beliefs)   Basic principles that shape a person's opinions about political issues and events.

veto   The president's constitutional power to turn down acts of Congress. A presidential veto may be overridden by a two-thirds vote of each house of Congress.

Virginia Plan   A framework for the Constitution, introduced by Edmund Randolph, which called for representation in the national legislature based upon the population of each state.

War Powers Resolution   A resolution of Congress that the president can send troops into action only by authorization of Congress or if American troops are already under attack or serious threat.

whip system   Primarily a communications network in each house of Congress, whips take polls of the membership in order to learn their intentions on specific legislative issues and to assist the **majority** and **minority leaders** in various tasks.

writ of *certiorari*   A decision of at least four of the nine Supreme Court justices to review a decision of a lower court; from the Latin "to make more certain."

Index

American Indian Movement (AIM), 104
American Medical Association, 363
American National Election Studies (ANES), 348
American Political Science Association (APSA), 356
American Revolution, 18, 20, 22
Americans Coming Together, 352
Americans with Disabilities Act (1990), 105–6
America Votes, 335
amicus curiae, 235
Amnesty International, 420–21
Amtrak, 192
Anderson, John, 321, 345
Animal and Plant Health and Inspection Service (APHIS), 195
Annapolis Convention, 46
Anti-Federalists, 32, 33, *33,* 41, 47
antistatism, 423, 424, 443
antitrust policy, 391
ANZUS Treaty, 433
APHIS (Animal and Plant Health and Inspection Service), 195
appropriations, 143–44, 371
APSA (American Political Science Association), 356
Arizona, 125, 317
Armey, Dick, 127, 128
Articles of Confederation, 19, 22, 29, 33, 40, 46
    adoption of, 43
    flaws of, 23
    versus Constitution, *30*
Asian Americans, 101, 102–3
Asian Law Caucus, 103
Astroturf lobbying, 377
attitudes, 251–52
Australia ballot, 304

Baker, James, 172
Bakke, Allan, 108
Bakke case, 108, 110, 111
"balance of power" system, 424–25, 438–39, 444
bandwagon effect, 286
Bank of the United States, 392
banks, 392–93
    Federal Reserve, 196, 392–93
    see also World Bank
Banks, Dennis, 104
Barron v. Baltimore, 74–78, 112
Bartels, Larry, 268
Barton, Joe, 285
Bay of Pigs invasion, 428
BBC, 275
BCRA (Bipartisan Campaign Reform Act, 2002), 239, 319, 321, 379
Belgium, elections in, 292
beliefs, 251–52
"benign" gerrymandering, 298
Benton v. Maryland, 79

bicameralism, 25, 120–21
Bickel, Alexander, 104
Biden, Joe, 172, 314, 316
Bill of Rights, 9, 25, 31–32, 34, 37, *37,* 42, 47, 72–73, 76–78, 80–90, 112
    nationalization of, 112
    state v. national, 74–78
    see also specific amendments
bills, 133, *134,* 135–36
    see also specific bills
Bipartisan Campaign Reform Act (BCRA) (2002), 83, 239, 319, 321, 379
Blackmun, Harry, 242
blacks, *see* African Americans
Blair, Tony, 249
block grants, 59
blogs, 275
BoB (Bureau of the Budget), 181
Bokat, Stephen, 106
Border and Transportation Security, 418
Bosnia, 155, 429
Boston Tea Party, 18
bourgeoisie, 11, 12
Bowers v. Hardwick, 88, 106
Bradley, Bill, 341
Brady Handgun Violence Prevention Act (1993), 61, 286
Brandenburg, Charles, 82
Bretton Woods, N.H., 430
Breyer, Stephen, 224, 239
broadcast media, 272–73, 275–76
Brookings Institution, 69, 364
Brown, Linda, 92
Brown, Oliver, 92
Brown University, 100
Brown v. Board of Education, 78–79, 92, 113, 375
Buchanan, James, 180
Buchanan, Pat, 263
Buckley v. Valeo, 83, 320
Budget and Accounting Act, 200
Budget and Impoundment Control Act (1974), 181–82
budget deficits, 396
bureaucracy, 46, 184–90
    budget-maximizing theory and, 197–98
    Congress and, 188–89, 200–203
    control of, 197–203
    credibility of, 188
    efficiency of, 188, 211–13
    of executive branch, 190–96
    possible reduction of, 203–11
    principle-agent problem and, 198–99
bureaucratic drift, 199, 203
Bureau of Indian Affairs, 105
Bureau of the Budget (BoB), 181
Burger, Warren, 99, 101
Burr, Aaron, 303
Bush, George H. W., 59, 110, 163, 310
    Cheney as secretary of defense for, 172
    judicial appointees of, 223–24, 238–39, 245

NSC staff of, 170
Panama invasion ordered by, 155
public appearances of, 175
as vice president, 172
Weinberger pardoned by, 157
Bush, George W., 70, 157, 159, 163, 175, 178, 276, 337, 342, 368
ads for, 320
approval ratings, 175–76, 249–50, *250*
cabinet of, 170
Cheney as vice president of, 172
as compassionate conservative, 263
Congress and, 149, 152, 161
congressional party squabbling and, 138–39
Democratic oversight of, 144
deregulation supported by, 391
drug company funding of, 359
election of, 178, 303
executive orders of, 179
executive privilege claimed by, 228–29
federalism of, 60
government power used by, 161, 162
hurricanes and, 156
immigration laws and, 104
Internet as campaign tool of, 352
Iraq War and, 70, 121, 152, 155, 161, 181, 249–51, 265, 272, 338, 430
judicial appointees of, 223–24
Kerry's debates with, 315
Kuhn as friend of, 372
Libby's sentence commuted by, 157
management strategy of, 200
media portrayal of, 177, 272–73, 275, 277, 280
Miers nomination and, 224, 376
national protection and, 154
partisan loyalty and, 307
policies of, 337
public appearances of, 175, 272–73
public opinion and, 269–70
reelection of, 250, 312–16, 332
Republican leaders' meeting with, 173
same-sex marriage and, 49
Social Security reforms supported by, 401
tax cuts of, 139, 268–69, 394
2000 campaign funds of, 321
2000 election and, 215, 246, 316
2004 campaign of, 304, 309, 321
2004 election and, 8, 264, 292, 334, 397
War on Terror of, 70, 90, 152, 161, 177, 229, 262, 338, 442
White House staff of, 170, 171
Bush, Jeb, 351
Bush (G.H.W.) administration, contracting and, 409
Bush doctrine, 436–37, 442
business, 4

cabinet, 170, 190, 199
California:

illegal alien referendum in, 306
Proposition 209 in, 287–88
recall election in, 306
same sex marriage and, 49
California Civil Rights Initiative, 111
Cameron, Charles M., 164
campaign finance, 318–24
campaign finance reform, 321–24
canals, 390
Cannon, "Uncle" Joe, 181
Carter, Jimmy, 163, 393
draft evaders pardoned by, 157
presidential batting average of, 174
Social Security tax and, 412
Case Act (1972), 145
case work, 123
categorical grants-in-aid, 54–55, 390
caucuses, 132–33, 148, 352
CBO (Congressional Budget Office), 58–59, 132
CBS Evening News, 274
CBS News, 269, 275
CBS poll, 249–50
Central Intelligence Agency (CIA), 154, 192, 418
Chamber of Commerce, 270
checks and balances, 15, 25, 31, 40–41, 46, 63, 65, 66–67, 70, 158, 163
Chemical, Biological, Radiological, and Nuclear Countermeasures, 418
Cheney, Dick, 157, 170, 172, 229, 316, 427
Chicago, University of, National Opinion Research Center, 283
Children's Internet Protection Act, 84
China, 420, 421, 436
Chinese Exclusion Act, 102, 103
Chinese immigrants, 102–3
Christian coalition, 421
Christian Coalition of America, 368
Christian Right, 364, 421
    see also religious Right
Christian Voice, 368
CIA (Central Intelligence Agency), 154, 192, 418
Cicero, 8
Citadel, 100
Citizens for the American Way, 235
City of Boerne v. Flores, 61–62, 81
civil law, 216, *217*
civil liberties, 40
    Brown v. Board of Education, 78–79
    definition of, 72, 112
    nationalization of, 76–78
    right to privacy as, 79–80
civil penalties, 409–10
civil rights, 58, 90–113, *98,* 238, 239, 260
    Brown v. Board of Education, 79
    controversies regarding, 73
    definition of, 73, 112
    Fourteenth Amendment and, 90–91
Civil Rights Act (1875), 90

Civil Rights Act (1964), 69, 93
   Title VII, 97, 100–101, 178
Civil Rights Commission, 93
Civil War, 75, 154, 260
Clark, Dick, 370
class action suit, 245
Clay, Henry, 303
Clear Channel Communications, 276
Cleveland, Grover, 303
clientele agency, 192–93
client state, U.S. as, 423
Clinton, Bill, 40, 159, 163, 178, 189, 310, 394
   affirmative action and, 109, 110
   Bosnia and, 429
   budget negotiations of, 138, 278
   campaigns of, 175, 309
   Congress and, 149
   "Don't ask, don't tell" policy of, 106
   executive privilege claimed by, 228–29
   Gore as vice president of, 172
   health care plan of, 137
   impeachment of, 145
   judicial nominees of, 223, 224
   line-item veto used by, 159
   military base closings proposed by, 194–95
   as moderate Democrat, 266
   "momentum" of, 278
   Motor Voter bill signed by, 295
   as "new Democrat," 336–37
   new federalism and, 59
   Northern Ireland and, 427
   NPR and, 200, 212
   polls taken by, 347
   popularity loss of, 340
   scandals of, 68, 158, 274, 277, 317
   tax cut promise of, 412
   welfare reform of, 405–6
Clinton, George, 33
Clinton, Hillary Rodham, 278, 312, 314, 341
Clinton administration, public relations
   efforts of, 269
closed primary, 334
closed rule, 133
cloture, 135, 149
CNN, 249, 272, 274
Coast Guard, 156
coercion, 48
   liberty and, 14–15
coinage, 47
COLAs (cost of living adjustments), 403
Cold War, 425, 436
collective-action principle, 267
collective goods, 365
Colorado, 317
   attempted redistricting in, 302
commander in chief, 154–55
commerce, 53–54
   in Constitution, 47
   state power and, 43
Commerce and Labor Department, U.S., 193
commerce clause, 51

Commerce Department, U.S., 156
committee assignments, 141
committee system, 128–32, 133
Common Cause, 271, 363, 368
common law, 230
Communications Decency Act (CDA), 84
Compromise of 1850, 341
Concerned Senators for the Arts, 133
concurrent powers, 48
Conference Board, 310
conference committee, 135
Congress, U.S., 47, 85, 102, 153, *201*, 208
   agenda control in, 130–31
   airline industry aided by, 387–88
   under Articles of Confederation, 19, 22
   budget and, 171, 200, 394–95, 398
   bureaucracy and, 188–89, 198–99,
      200–203, 212–13
   caucus system in, 132–33
   Cheney in, 172
   Clinton's proposed military base closings
      and, 194–95
   Committee on Committees in, 129, 338
   committee system in, 128–32, 133, 147–48
   in Connecticut Plan, 24
   constitutional amendments and, 36
   Contract with America and, 58
   delegated powers and, 153, 177–78
   districts and, 125–26
   economic policy and, 167
   effectiveness of, 146–48
   electoral system in, 121–26
   electoral votes and, 303
   equal rights amendment and, 98–99
   Fed created by, 196
   federal judicial system and, 220
   First Amendment and, 37, 83
   foreign policy and, 118, 416–17, 418–20
   grassroots campaigns and, 376–77
   Great Depression and, 387
   immigration laws and, 103, 104
   impeachment and, 145–46
   incumbency and, 122–25, *124*
   influences on, 136–43
   interest groups and, 361, *369*, 370, 372–74,
      382–83
   Iraq War and, 70, 121, 181
   judicial review and, 215, 225–27
   lobbying of, 370–72
   loss of power by, 168
   monetary policies of, 392
   mutual defense alliances financed by,
      433
   Nixon, 158
   organization of, 126–33, 146–48
   oversight and, 143–44, 202–3, 204–5
   party organization in, 121, 331
   party system and, 148, 337–38
   political struggles in, 4
   presidential batting average and, 174
   presidential nomination by, 166

presidential power and, 151–52, 161–64, 173, 177, 178–79
railroads and, 390
representation in, 118–26, *119*
as representative organization, 180
separation of powers and, 67
Social Security and, 401, 402
staff system in, 132, 148
Supreme Court size decided by, 222
Supreme Court's relationship with, 242–43, 244
Supreme Court's review of, 239
telecommunications legislation and, 84–85, 276
treaties and, 144
2004 election and, 159, 312
2006 election and, 360
U.N. and, 428
vetoes and, 159–61, 162–63
war powers of, 155
Congressional Black Caucus, 133
Congressional Budget Office (CBO), 58–59, 132, 394
Congressional Caucus for Women's Issues, 133
Congressional Government (Wilson), 165
congressional redistricting, 300–301
Congressional Research Service, 132
Connecticut:
    Constitution ratified by, 33
    Virginia Plan opposition of, 24
Connecticut Compromise, 24
consent approach, 291
Conservative Party, 345
conservatives, conservatism, 251, 262–66, 287, 288
    "Contract with America" and, 40
    as Democratic base, 337
    Tenth Amendment and, 61
constituency, 118–20, 136–37
Constitution, U.S., 17, *27*, 29, 31, 43, 104, 287, 361
    amendments to, 29, 33–40, *35, 38, 39*, 49, 126, 242; *see also* constitutional amendments
    Article I, 20–21, *21*, 26, 31, 37, 38, 43, 50, 51, 52, 53, 79, 117–18, 159, 165
    Article II, 27, 31, 43, 144, 152, 154, 157, 159
    Article III, 28, 31, 37, 43, 220, 231
    Article IV, 29, 43, 48, 50, 155
    Articles of Confederation versus, *30*
    Article V, 29, 33, 35, 43
    Article VI, 29, 43, 47, 227
    Article VII, 29, 43
    congressional term lengths in, 120
    constitutional review by, 217–18
    contradictions in, 14
    courts' interpretation of, 221
    Democratic Party and, 340
    direct elections in, 302
    economic and political forces and, 18

enduring strength of, 17
equality and, 90, 260
Equal Rights Amendment and, 98–99
executive branch in, 27–28, 153–55, 179–81
federalism in, 47–51
federal jurisdiction and, 220, 221
House of Representatives in, 120–21
judicial branch in, 28, 222, 227, 231–32
legislative branch in, 26–27, 118, 156
legislative supremacy in, 70
liberalism vs. republicanism in, 20–21
national government restrained by, 68
new states and, 29
presidential power and, 161
public order policies in, *389*
ratification of, 33
right to privacy and, 88
Senate in, 143
slavery in, 24
supremacy clause, 29, 227
treaties in, 143
viability of, 40–43
vice presidency in, 171–72
war powers in, 155, 181
see also Bill of Rights
constitutional amendments:
    First, 9, 37, 74, *78*, 80–85, 112–13, 233, 276, 370
    Second, 37, 74
    Third, 37, 88
    Fourth, 37, 79, 86, 87, 88
    Fifth, 37, 73, 74, 76, 79, 86, 87, 88, 218, *389*, 412
    Sixth, 37, 86, 87
    Seventh, 37
    Eighth, 37, 86, 87–88
    Ninth, 89
    Tenth, 47, 60–61
    Eleventh, 38, 61–62
    Twelfth, 303
    Thirteenth, 35, 38, 40, 90
    Fourteenth, 35, 38, 73, 75–78, 79, 86–87, 89, 90–91, 92, 112, 113, 404
    Fifteenth, 35, 90
    Sixteenth, 38, 40
    Seventeenth, 26, 63
    Eighteenth, 34, 36, 40
    Twenty-first, 34, 36
    Twenty-seventh, 38
Constitutional Convention, 17, 33, 40, 46
constitutional government, 11
Consumer Confidence Index, 310, *311*
containment, 425
Continental Congress, First, 19
Continental Congress, Second, 19
contract cases, 216
Contract with America, 40, 58
conventions, national, 352–53
    see also Democratic National Conventions
Coolidge, Calvin, 180

Disney, 363
distributive tendency, 147
District Court, U.S., 215, 246
District of Columbia v. Heller, 85
divided government, 64, 70, 343
division of labor, 187
DNC (Democratic National Committee), 352, 353, 377
DOE, *see* Energy Department, U.S.
Dole, Bob, 61, 340
DOT, *see* Transportation Department, U.S.
double jeopardy, 79, 87
Douglas, Stephen, 88, 281
Dred Scott case, 64
Drudge, Matt, 274
dual federalism, 50
due process of law, 72, 73, 76, 219

earmarks, 380
East Europe, 13
East India Company, 18
economic aid, 431–32
economic crisis of 2008, 185, 309, 387–88
economic expansionist role, 439, 444
economics, economy, 387–98
    Congress and, 167
    Constitution and, 18
    elections and, 310, *311*
    executive branch and, 167
    gap between blacks and whites in, 95
    goals of policy in, 388–90
    maintaining a stable and strong, 391–98
    public order and private property and, 389–90
    see also taxes
Edison Electric Institute, 372
education, 94, 255–57, 260, *261*
Education Act, Title IX of, 99–100
Education Department, U.S., 100, 193
Edwards, John, 172, 315
EEOC (Equal Employment Opportunity Commission), 98, 105
Eighteenth Amendment, 34, 36, 40
Eighth Amendment, 37, 86, 87–88
Eisenhower, Dwight D., 93, 156, 163, 341
    presidential batting average of, 174
Eisenstadt v. Baird, 375
elastic clause, 26–27
election, campaign finance in, 318–24
Election Day, 326, 327, 335
elections, 15, 172, 290–329, 333
    of 1800, 303
    of 1824, 303
    of 1828, 340, 342
    of 1858, 341
    of 1860, 341
    of 1876, 303
    of 1888, 303
    of 1896, 342
    of 1936, 282, 341
    of 1948, 346

of 1968, 345, 346
of 1992, 310, 340, 344, 345
of 1994, 143, 340
of 1996, 340, 342, 344
of 1998, 128, 351
of 2000, 215, 246, 274–75, 301, 303, 340–41, 346, 351
of 2004, 8, 264, 285, 292, 301, 304, 311, 312–16, 321, 323–24, 332, 337, 341, 342, 346, 352, 397
of 2006, 249–50, 251, 272, 309, 332–33, 337, 360
of 2008, 70, 128, 137, 172, 293, 295, 304, 309, 312–18, 341–42, 345, 352
campaign finance reform and, 321–24
complexity of, 4
congressional redistricting and, 300–301
criteria for victory in, 296–97
economy and, 310, *310*
electoral composition and, 292–96
frequency of, 304
funding for, 318–24
issues, 308–9
midterm, 326
nominations for, 333–34
partisan loyalty in, 307–8
primary, 333–34
registration for, 293–95
regulating involvement in, 291–96
turnout of, 292–94, *293,* 296
voters' decisions in, 307–12
see also voting rights
electoral college, 153, 302–4, 312, 326
electoral influence, 305
electoral realignment, 342–44, *343*
electoral system, 121–26
Eleventh Amendment, 38, 61–62
Emanuel, Rahm, 316, 317, 333
Emergency Preparedness and Response, 418
Emergency Price Control Act (1942), 228
EMILY's List, 122, 324
eminent domain, 87, 389, 412
employment, discrimination in, 97
Encyclopedia of U.S. Government Benefits, 408
Endangered Species Act, 370
Energy Department, U.S., 156, 193
England, 170
Enron, 202, 321
entitlement, 404
Environmental Defense Fund, 368
environmental protection, 58, 319, 368
Environmental Protection Agency (EPA), 198, 199, 372
EOP (Executive Office of the President), 170, 171, 175, 177, 181
EPA (Environmental Protection Agency), 198, 199, 372
Equal Employment Opportunity Commission (EEOC), 98, 105
equality, in Constitution, 42
equality of opportunity, 252

equal protection clause, 73, 90
Equal Rights Amendment (ERA), 36
equal time rule, 276
ERP (European Recovery Plan), 432
Ervin committee, 378
Espy, Mike, 298
Establishment Clause, 80–81, 238
Esterling, Kevin, 383
European Recovery Plan (ERP), 432
exclusionary rule, 79, 86
executive agreements, 144–45, 157, 419
executive branch, *201*
  congressional oversight and, 202, 204–5
  in Constitution, 27–28, 153–55, 179–81
  economy and, 167
  lobbying of, 372–73
  organization of, 190–96
  see also presidency
executive decree, 179
Executive Office of the President (EOP), 170,
  171, 175, 177, 181, 394
Executive Order No. 11246, 178
executive orders, 164, 173, 177, 178–79, *179*
executive privilege, 68, 158
expressed powers, 26, 47, 153
expropriation, 189–90, 412

fairness doctrine, 276
Family Research Council, 368
Farm Credit Administration, 390
farmers, 4, 18
Farmers Home Administration, 390
Faubus, Orval, 93, 156
FBI (Federal Bureau of Investigation), 155,
  192, 194
FCC (Federal Communications Commission),
  275–76
FDA (Food and Drug Administration), 69, 195
FDIC (Federal Deposit Insurance
  Corporation), 393
FEC (Federal Election Commission), 192, 318,
  319
federal appellate courts, 221–22
Federal Bureau of Investigation (FBI), 155,
  192, 194
Federal Communications Commission (FCC),
  275–76
Federal Deposit Insurance Corporation
  (FDIC), 393
Federal Election Campaign Act (1971), 319,
  377
Federal Election Commission (FEC), 192, 318,
  319
Federal Elections Campaign Act (1972), 320
Federal Emergency Management Agency
  (FEMA), 156
federal fund rates, 393
Federal Housing Administration (FHA), 390
federalism, 31, 32–33, 40, 45–54, *52, 56*, 66,
  68–70, 166
  in Constitution, 47–51

cooperative, 54–58
dual, 50
foreign policy and, 423
grants-in-aid, 54–58
layer cake v. marble cake, 56–57
legacies of, 424
new, 59–60
regulated, 57–59
Supreme Court and, 60–63, 79
Federalist Papers, 33, 34, 291, 302
  No. 10, 382
  No. 51, 66, 165, 413
  No. 78, 241
Federalist Party, 303, 338, 342, 392
Federalists, 32–33, *33*, 47
federal jurisdiction, 220–24
Federal Occupation Safety and Health, 59
Federal Register, 189
Federal Regulation of Lobbying Act, 370
Federal Reserve banks, 196, 392
Federal Reserve Board, 196, 392–93, 413
  discount rate and, 392, 413
  open market operations of, 393, 413
  reserve requirement and, 393, 413
Federal Reserve System, 196, 392–93
federal service, 203, 206–7
Federal Trade Commission (FTC), 85, 192,
  195, 410
federal trial courts, 221
FEMA (Federal Emergency Management
  Agency), 156
FHA (Federal Housing Administration),
  390
Fifteenth Amendment, 35, 90
Fifth Amendment, 37, 73, 74, 76, 79, 86, 87,
  88, 218, 389, 412
fighting words, 85
filibuster, 135, 149
fire-alarm oversight, 205
First Amendment, 9, 37, 74, *78*, 80–85,
  112–13, 233, 276, 370
  establishment clause of, 80–81
  freedom of religion and, 80–81
  freedom of speech and press and, 82–85
First Hundred Days, 166
fiscal policies, 393–94
Fisher, Louis, 85, 181, 182
Fitzgibbons, Dennis, 371
527 committees, 319, 323–24, 325, 379
Florida, 125, 305
  in 2000 election, 274–75
  in 2004 election, 215, 304, 314, 315
Focus on the Family, 368
FOIA (Freedom of Information Act) (1966),
  189
Food and Drug Administration (FDA), 69, 195
Food for Peace, 432
Food Safety and Inspection Service, 192
food stamps, 404
Ford, Gerald, 157, 163, 302
  presidential batting average of, 174

King Caucus, 166
Know-Nothings, 341
Korean War, 155, 425, 428
Korematsu v. United States, 111
Kosovo, 262, 429, 435
Kuhn, Tom, 372
Kuwait, 272, 428–29, 436

Labor Department, U.S., 195, 411
labor unions, 4, 259, 270, 315, 320, 336, 340, 346, 378
Lambda Legal Defense and Education Fund, 106
Landon, Alfred M., 282, 341
La Raza Unida party, 102
Lasswell, Harold, 10
Latin America, 337, 432, 439
Latinos, 101, 103, 255–57, 317, 337
Lawrence v. Texas, 88–89, 107
Law v. Nichols, 103, 105
League of United Latin American Citizens (LULAC), 102
League of Women Voters, 335
Ledbetter v. Good Year Tire and Rubber Co., 97
Lee, Richard Henry, 33
legislative branch, 4, 190
    in Constitution, 26
    from 1800–1933, 165–66
legislative initiative, 161–64
legislative service organizations (LSOs), 132–33
legislative supremacy, 64, 165
Lemon test, 81
Lewinsky, Monica, 145, 274, 317
Libby, Lewis "Scooter," 157
libel, 84, 276–77
Liberal Party, 345
liberals, liberalism, 251, 262–66, 287, 288
    civil rights movement and, 40
    classical, 20–21
    as Democratic base, 336
libertarians, 263
liberty:
    coercion and, 14–15
    Constitution and, 42–43
    limitations of, 42–43
    see also specific freedoms
Lieberman, Joseph, 341
Lincoln, Abraham, 151
    Douglas's debates with, 281
    election of, 341, 342
    executive orders of, 151, 154
    as strong president, 165, 180
line-item veto, 159, 182
Line-Item Veto Act (1996), 68
Lippmann, Walter, 329
Literary Digest poll (1936), 282
Little Rock, Ark., 93, 156
Livingston, Robert, 19
Livingston, Robert (Congressman), 127

lobbies, lobbying, 370–73
    of Congress, 360, 370–72
    of executive branch, 372–73
    going public strategy of, 375–77
    grassroots, 376–77
    of president, 372
    see also interest groups
Lobbying Disclosure Act (1995), 370, 374
Locke, John, 8, 20
logrolling, 142
Lott, Trent, 275
Louisiana:
    affirmative action in, 109
    same-sex marriage banned in, 107
LSOs (legislative service organizations), 132–33

McCain, John, 172, 304, 307, 312, 313, 316, 317, 321, 332, 351
McCain-Feingold Act (2002), *see* Bipartisan Campaign Reform Act (BCRA) (2002)
McCarthy, Joseph, 279
McConnell v. Federal Election Commission, 83, 239
McCubbins, Mathew, 130, 202–3, 205
McCulloch V. Maryland, 51–53
Mack v. United States, 61
MAD (Mutual Assured Destruction), 436
Madison, James, 24, 33, 165, 197, 291, 304, 413
    on class conflict, 259
    on constitutional amendments, 34
    on factions, 42, 381, 382, 383
    on legislative branch, 165
    on liberty, 42, 381
    on pluralism, 361–62, 366
    on separation of powers, 63, 66–67, 163
    Washington's farewell address and, 422
    see also Marbury v. Madison
Maine, electoral college in, 302
majority leader, 127
majority party, 337
majority rule, instability of, 15
majority system, 296–97
mandates, 68
mandatory spending, 395–98
Mann, Thomas, 204
Mapp v. Ohio, 79
Marbury, William, 226
Marbury v. Madison, 64, 226, 247
Marcos, Ferdinand, 438
markets, 390
marriage, same-sex, 48–49, 257, 287, 368
Marshall, John, 52, 53, 64, 74, 226
Marshall Plan, 431–32
martial law, 151
Maryland:
    Constitution ratified by, 33
    slavery in, 24
Massachusetts, 304
    Constitution ratified by, 33

Poland, 434
police-patrol oversight, 205
police power, 48, 409–10
policy entrepreneurs, 337
policy-making powers, 168
political action committees (PAC), 83, 106,
    122, 128, 137–38, 319, 324, 325, 359, 361,
    367, 377–79
political ideology, 251, 266
political knowledge, 266–69
political opinions, formation of, 266–71
political parties, 331–57
    candidate recruitment by, 332–33
    and Congress, 148, 337–38
    evolution of, 339
    functions of, 332–38
    interest groups v., 366
    nomination for, 333–34
    organization of, 352–55, 353
    policy entrepreneurs of, 337
    technology used by, 347–52
    third parties and, 344–47
political socialization, 254–62
politics:
    classic political thought vs. social contract
        theory in, 8–9
    complexity of, 4–5
    definition of, 10
    government's influence on, 10–11
Politics (Aristotle), 8
polling, 347
polls, 280–87, 288, 311–12
    design of, 283
    measurement error of, 283
    probability sampling in, 281
    push polling and, 283–85
    random digital dialing in, 282
    sample size of, 282–83
    sampling and margin of error in, 282–83
    selection bias in, 282
poll tax, 292
popular sovereignty, 14, 15
Populist movement, 251, 380
Populists, 344
pork barrel, 123, 194–95
pornography and obscenity, 84–85
Postal Service, U.S., 192
poverty programs, 58
Powell, Colin, 427
Powell, Lewis, 111
PRA (Personal Responsibility and Work
    Opportunity Reconciliation Act), 59, 196,
    405
precedents, legal, 216–17
prescription drug plan, 360
presidency, 148, 165, 169, 392
    administrative capabilities of, 177–79
    bills and, 136
    budget and, 394, 398
    congressional influence of, 142
    in Constitution, 153–55

contemporary bases of power in, 173–77
1800–1933, 165–66
elections and, 302
expressed powers of, 154–64
foreign policy and, 416–17
formal resources of power by, 168–77
"going public" in, 173–77
legislative initiative and, 161–64
lobbying of, 372
management capacity and, 199–200
post–New Deal power gain by, 168, 180–82
and Supreme Court judges, 28
Supreme Court's relationship with, 243
vetoes used in, 160–61
war time power of, 151–52, 161
see also executive branch
Presidential Election Campaign Fund, 320
presidential power, 168
President's Committee on Administrative
    Management, 199
primary elections, 333–34
priming, 277–78
principle-agent problem, 198–99
print media, 274, 275–76
Printz v. United States, 61
prior restraint, 83–84, 276
privatization, 210–11, 409
privileges and immunities clause, 50
probability sampling, 281
procedural liberties, 73
Progressive Era, 347
Progressive Party, 346
Progressive reformers, 293–94, 344, 345
Prohibition, 36, 40, 43, 412
project grants, 55–56
proportional representation, 297
Proposition 22, 49
Proposition 187, 103–4
Proposition 209, 111–12, 287–88
prospective voting, 309
Public Affairs Council, 270
public assistance programs, 403–5
    noncontributory, 403
public interest groups, 362–64
public law, 217–18, 217
public opinion, 176–77, 251, 266–71
    origins of, 252–56
    political ideology and, 262–66
    political socialization and, 254–62
    polls of, 280–86
public policy, 386–415
    contracts and, 408–9, 410, 411, 414
    control techniques of, 406–12, 407, 411
    fiscal techniques and, 412–13
    licensing and, 409, 410, 411, 414
    monetary techniques and, 413
    promotional techniques of, 406–12, 407
    redistributive techniques of, 407, 412–13, 414
    regulatory techniques of, 407, 409, 411
    spending power of, 413
    subsidies and, 407–8, 410, 411, 414

Rule 10, 233
rulemaking, 189
Rumsfeld, Donald, 170, 427
Russia, 429, 430, 434–35, 436, 442
    see also Soviet Union

St. Louis Globe-Democrat, 279
salient interests, 285
same-sex marriage, 48–49, 257, 287, 368
sample, 281
Sandinistas, 438
San Francisco, Calif., same-sex marriage in,
    107
San Francisco Superior Court, 49
Saudi Arabia, 429
Scalia, Antonin, 223, 224, 236, 239
school prayer amendment, 36
Schumer, Charles, 316, 317, 333
Schwartz, Thomas, 202–3, 205
Schwarzenegger, Arnold, 273–74, 306
search and seizures, 86
SEATO (Southeast Asia Treaty Organization),
    433
Seattle, Wash., WTO protest in, 421
secession, 75
Second Amendment, 37, 74, 85–86
Securities and Exchange Commission,
    202
segregation, 90–97, 238, 239, 244, 253, 375
selection bias, 282
"Selling of the Pentagon, The" (documentary),
    269
Seminoles, 61
Senate, U.S.:
    agenda control in, 130
    Appropriations Committee of, 127, 128,
        371, 380
    Armed Services Committee of, 419
    bicameralism, 120–21
    cabinet approved by, 170
    campaign committees of, 354
    campaign costs in, 333
    checks and balances and, 63
    committees of, 128–29
    compromises in, 121
    in Connecticut Plan, 24
    in Constitution, 26
    constitutional amendments and, 35, 36,
        83
    Democrat control of, 340
    elections and, 38, 122, 302
    ergonomics regulations and, 324
    executive appointments approved by, 158
    Finance Committee of, 190
    floor debate in, 133–35
    foreign policy and, 418–20
    Foreign Relations Committee of, 280,
        419
    impeachment and, 145
    incumbency in, 123, 124, *124*
    interest groups and, 142, 382

    Judiciary Committee of, 223, 224
    mutual defense alliances ratified by, 433
    organization of, 120–21, 126–27
    oversight and, 143–44, 200–203, 204
    partisanship in, 121, 135
    party leadership in, 126–28, 138, 149
    party unity in, 138
    presidential veto and, 136
    principle-agent problem and, 198–99
    September 11 and, 418
    special powers of, 144–45
    Supreme Court judges and, 28, 222–23
    terms of, 26
    treaties and, 118, 144
    2004 election to, 312
    2006 election to, 309, 316, 317
    veto overridden by, 159
    vice president and, 172
Senate majority leader, 133, 141
Senate Select Committee to Investigate the
    1972 Presidential Campaign Activities,
    378
senatorial courtesy, 222
seniority, 132
"separate but equal" rule, 91
separation of powers, 31, *32*, 45–46, 63, 68,
    70, 173
September 11, 2001, terrorist attacks of, 3, 15,
    69, 89, 156, 175, 265, 313, 315, 394
    airline bailout for, 387–88
    alliance created by, 439, 442
    bureaucracy and, 184–85
    Bush's reaction to, 277, 338, 389
    congressional party squabbling and,
        139
    diplomacy and, 427
    foreign policy and, 418
    NATO and, 435
    possible impact of, 260
    presidential power after, 152, 161
    UN and, 429–30
Serbia, 155, 435
Seventeenth Amendment, 26, 63
Seventh Amendment, 37
sexual harassment, 100–101
sexual revolution, 374
Sharpton, Al, 341
Shaw v. Reno, 298
Shays, Christopher, 144
Shays, Daniel, 23
Shays's Rebellion, 23
Shelley v. Kraemer, 91
Shell Oil, 363
Sherman, Roger, 19
shopkeepers, 18
Sierra Club, 271, 319, 368, 370
Silverman, Brian, 380
Simpson, O. J., 255
single-member-district, 346
Sioux, 104
SixPAC, 319

war, declaration of, 47
  see also specific wars
War Department, U.S., 194
Wards Cove v. Atonio, 108–9
War on Terror, 89–90, 152, 161, 177, 229, 262, 312–13, 338, 442
  see also Afghanistan; Iraq War
War Powers Resolution (1973), 155, 181
Warren, Earl, 222, 239
Warsaw Pact (1955), 433
Washington, George, 17
  farewell address of, 417, 422–23
Washington, George (*cont.*)
  Genêt received by, 157
  House request refused by, 158
  parties deplored by, 338
Washington Post, 274, 277, 280
Watergate scandal, 83, 158, 204, 277, 377–78
weapons of mass destruction (WMDs), 280, 313, 437, 442
Webster v. Reproductive Health Services, 375
Weinberger, Caspar, 157
welfare, 195, 196, 398–99, *399*, 414–15
  in polls, 285
  reform plan of 1996, 405–6
  see also Personal Responsibility and Work Opportunity Reconciliation Act
welfare reform, 210
Whig party, 341, 342, 343–44, 345
whip system, 141

White House Communications Office, 175, 177
White House staff, 170–71, 177
whites, 255, *256*
  Iraq War and, 250
  racial equality and, 94–95
Wide Awake (magazine), 232
Wilson, Pete, 112
Wilson, Woodrow, 165, 173, 200, 279, 438
Wisconsin, 210, 317
WMDs (weapons of mass destruction), 280, 313, 437, 442
women, interest groups of, 364
  see also gender discrimination; gender gap; League of Women Voters; Violence Against Women Act (1994)
Women's Equity Action League (WEAL), 98
World Bank, 430
World Trade Organization (WTO), 421
World War I, 6
World War II, 6, 151, 260, 368, 417, 428, 443
Wounded Knee, S.Dak., 104
writ of *certiorari*, 233, 247
WTO (World Trade Organization), 421

Youngstown Sheet & Tube Company v. Sawyer, 178
Yugoslavia, 429